Fourth Edition

Research Decisions

Quantitative and

Qualitative

Perspectives

Ted Palys

Chris Atchison
Simon Fraser University

THOMSON

NELSON

Australia   Canada   Mexico   Singapore   Spain   United Kingdom   United States

THOMSON

NELSON

Research Decisions: Quantitative and
Qualitative Perspectives, Fourth Edition

by Ted Palys and Chris Atchison

**Associate Vice President,
Editorial Director:**
Evelyn Veitch

**Editor-in-Chief,
Higher Education:**
Anne Williams

Executive Editor:
Cara Yarzab

Senior Marketing Manager:
Lenore Taylor

Developmental Editor:
Glenn Herbert

Permissions Coordinator:
Wendy Clark

Copy Editor:
Lisa Berland

Proofreader:
Liba Berry

Indexer:
Dennis A. Mills

Manufacturing Coordinator:
Loretta Lee

Design Director:
Ken Phipps

Interior Design:
Katherine Strain

Cover Design:
Johanna Liburd

Cover Image:
Cesar Lucas Abreu/The Image
Bank/Getty Images

Compositor:
Carol Magee

Printer:
Thomson West

**Library and Archives Canada
Cataloguing in Publication Data**

Palys, T. S. (Theodore Stephen)
 Research decisions: quantitative
and qualitative perspectives/
Ted Palys, Chris Atchison.—4th ed.

Includes index.
Includes bibliographical references
and index.

ISBN-13: 978-0-17-610295-1
ISBN-10: 0-17-610295-7

 1. Social sciences—Research—
Textbooks. I. Atchison, Chris,
1971– II. Title.

H62.P34 2007   300.72
C2007-900384-2

Research Decisions

For Anne-Marie and Jodi

BRIEF CONTENTS

CONTENTS

PREFACE

The year 2007 marks 20 years since the very first draft was written of the book that would become *Research Decisions: Quantitative and Qualitative Perspectives*. In an area as fundamental as methods you would think little would change in that time, but in fact the amount of change that has occurred in those two decades is downright astonishing.

Some of the change has occurred because the constitution of the academy has changed dramatically during that time—broader inclusion has brought new perspectives that have encouraged reflection regarding the imprint that particular approaches and epistemologies leave when they are engaged in the task of generating understanding.

Also, practitioners of qualitative and quantitative approaches, who were easy to characterize as people from different planets a mere 20 years ago, are no longer so distant. Reflecting this, *Research Decisions* is no longer the only textbook on the block to see that there is something to be gained by understanding and employing both, and more and more researchers are now adopting the multi-method mixed-model approach that comprised an almost heretical suggestion when it appeared in the first edition of *Research Decisions* in the late 1980s and early 1990s.

Other changes have occurred in the world of methods as well. Two of particular interest are (1) the greater centralization of power over and commercialization of the research enterprise that has been orchestrated by the federal government in conjunction with university administrations; and (2) the incredible array of technological advances that have occurred as part of the digital revolution.

Just as the world and methods are changing, so, too is *Research Decisions*. And not surprisingly, the ways that *Research Decisions* is changing reflects those factors identified above. On behalf of the two of us, let me give you a brief tour of the new *Research Decisions* and the changes time hath wrought.

NEW TO THIS EDITION

Welcome, Chris

First on the list is to introduce you to my new co-author, Chris Atchison. I first met Chris when he was an MA student at Simon Fraser University, before he went off to the University of Toronto to do a PhD, and it was clear even in those early days that he was an exceptional individual. There are many talented young scholars in Canada and the rest of the planet, but none with whom I ever even considered sharing my baby, this book—which began as a labour of love in the late 1980s—until Chris. In my view he is among the best of the new cohort of scholars now making their way through the academy—he is proficient in both qualitative and quantitative methods, understands technology and sees the vast potential these have for the research enterprise, and can make his way through bureaucracies without losing himself to them. I am honoured that he responded positively to my invitation to join me for *Research Decisions* IV.

Chris's presence is evident in small ways throughout the book, but his biggest contributions for this edition have been in the way that he has brought *Research Decisions* up to speed when it comes to the impact of developing technologies on the research process. While many are now proficient in new technologies and take their presence as a given—students now appear in classes with their laptops, do text messaging on their cell phones, download tunes for their MP3 players, and pay for their purchases using a bank card rather than cash—Chris brings the insights of both participant and observer, has a real vision about the possibilities and pitfalls that emerging technologies have for methods, and despite (or perhaps because of) his relative youth, is already one of Canada's pioneers in the realm of computer-assisted research possibilities, and especially web-based survey research. His MA thesis in 1998 was based on data that arose from what may well have been the first large-scale web-based survey done in the country. I am thrilled that he brought those skills, interest, and vision to this book.

Chris's expertise in these areas helps maintain *Research Decisions*' status as a cutting-edge text that both reflects and sets the pace for trends in contemporary research. We do this in a way that also continues the book's historic emphasis on both epistemology and sociology of science, which we articulate here in relation to developing technologies. Chapter 3, for example, now includes discussion of the unique ethical issues that accompany web-based research. In Chapter 4, we consider sampling issues that arise in relation especially to web-based research, about which we have seen much confusion and misinformation in the literature. Advantages, disadvantages, and procedural considerations in relation to a wide array of computer-assisted research are considered in Chapter 6. And all of this culminates in the Epilogue (Chapter 14) with reflection about what all this means in relation to research, society, and the academy, and what we believe we should be looking at for the next several years during the life of this book.

If I were asked to offer reasons why *Research Decisions* has enjoyed the success it has, high on my list would be the authenticity it conveys—while abstract principles are discussed, part of what makes *Research Decisions* "real" is that from one cover to another, when students read about surveys, or interviews, or focus groups, or observational strategies, or whatever, it is obvious we have been there, have struggled with the issues ourselves, and are now

telling authentic stories to share the lessons we have learned. It is that sort of experience that Chris brings—not only in relation to the "standard" array of qualitative and quantitative methods (although that in itself is still all too rare)—but especially in relation to web-based surveys and other computer-assisted research. In that regard, he is simply the best there is, or at least that I've ever come across, and, again, I'm honoured that he has joined me for this new edition of what is now "our" book.

CHANGES

After an updated Chapter 1 that introduces and discusses qualitative and quantitative approaches and the book's interest in both epistemology and sociology of science, the first big change readers of earlier editions will notice is that what previously were three separate chapters—dealing with sources of research ideas, making connections between theory and data, and deciding on our research objectives—have been re-organized as parts of a singular discussion called "Getting Started."

This is followed by two chapters that appeared in previous editions and that have been revised extensively. The chapter on ethics incorporates developments in that domain that have occurred since *Research Decisions* III was published (in 2003), including the belated but welcome recognition by those who are part of the Tri-Council Policy Statement (TCPS) "family" that there is indeed a problem and that the TCPS requires change to be more relevant to diverse models of research beyond the experimental clinical trial (SSHWC 2004). Overall, however, we continue to believe that the costs of instituting the TCPS, to the social sciences and humanities, at least, have to this point outweighed the ethical gains for research participants, which appear to be nil. The next chapter on sampling now includes a discussion of sampling issues that arise in relation to computer-assisted social research (CASR).

A new element in *Research Decisions* IV is a chapter dealing with preparation of a research proposal (Chapter 5). We have placed it at the point in the course where we envision students will be receiving assignments after gathering enough information to begin thinking about a proposal, but where there still is much to be worked out about how to translate those aspirations into concrete questions and procedures.

With greater emphasis on the ability to seek funding, coupled with more onerous process requirements prior to getting approval to do one's work, proposal writing has become a requisite skill, and we are aware of more and more courses that require students to write a proposal as their term project. Our chapter outlines design elements would-be researchers must address that speak to the concerns of those who evaluate such proposals—including their research methods professors!

We offer our chapter on proposal writing in the spirit of thinking about one's research objectives and how to accomplish them, which is in keeping with the book's message that it is the objectives and questions that come first, because these then lead the consideration of how exactly one can achieve the objectives and answer the questions. While we laud the emphasis on proposal writing and agree it deserves attention in the book, our main concern is the extent to which we see how, in some quarters, the emphasis on proposal writing has been at the expense of actually doing research. Although many faculty do this by choice, we know of some institutions where student projects became impossible when burdensome requirements for ethics review meant student projects—most of which are anything but contentious and can easily be maintained within a reasonable zone via project specifications—could no longer be completed within a semester. We continue to believe there is no better way to learn about research—and the difference between idyllic proposals where everything happens perfectly and the real world where Murphy's law can prevail—than by doing some, and there is no reason why ethics review of student research cannot be delegated to course instructors in the social sciences, as is also done in many institutions across the country.

PEDAGOGICAL FEATURES

This edition of *Research Decisions* continues to include numerous pedagogical features to help professors, teaching assistants, and students work through and benefit from the material contained in the book:

- Each chapter ends with a "Summing Up and Looking Ahead" section that reviews the chapter's main themes and sets the stage for succeeding chapters.
- Sets of *study questions* are included at the end of each chapter. These can serve as a source of examination questions and help students focus their studying (either individually or as part of a study group). Included also are questions posing problems that would be useful to discuss in a class, lab, or tutorial group, and/or that could be a basis for student essays and term projects.
- A *glossary* appears at the end of the book, listing many of the technical terms and phrases that are inevitably involved in learning about methods. All glossed terms appear in bold type in the text.
- Liberal use of *citation* provides numerous literature sources for professors and more advanced students who wish to examine the issues discussed in this book in more detail.
- A series of *appendices* provides supplementary information that negates the need for other sources, particularly with respect to tests of significance.

Beyond the book itself, further material is available through the publisher to assist professors, students, and other readers:

- An *Instructor's Manual* offers teaching suggestions, sample examination questions, and a series of assignments and exercises designed to put the principles discussed in the book into practice.
- Sample examination questions are also available in a *Computerized Test Bank* that can be downloaded from diskette for examination construction.

Finally, we are also accessible via the Internet. You can e-mail me at palys@sfu.ca or visit my webpage at www.sfu.ca/~palys/, and/or email Chris at atch@shaw.ca and see his website at www.academic-freedom.ca. Both websites contain links that might be of interest to professors and students.

PERSONAL NOTES

As was the case with the three previous editions of this book, we are indebted to many for their collegiality and feedback along the way. At the top of the list are two fine colleagues and friends—John Lowman and Bob Menzies—who understand how much we appreciate their trenchant criticism and the unconditional affection in which it is always wrapped. They are a large part of what makes going to work worthwhile.

Others also have been helpful. We thank five reviewers—Greg Cann, Bill Glackman, Helga Hallgrimsdottir, Stefan Groschl, and Katherine Watson—for their suggestions about how *Research Decisions III* could be improved upon, which we have heeded. Many colleagues have read or heard different subsets of the material in different venues at different times and the book has benefited from their comments; these include Howard Becker, Louise Kidder, Michael Jackson, Michael McDonald, Julian Roberts, Patrick O'Neill, Will van den Hoonaard, Richard Ericson, Charles Singer, Robert Gordon, Kevin Haggerty, Mark Israel, and the late Donald T. Campbell. Their input and encouragement are appreciated.

At Thomson Nelson, numerous individuals have played a role in making the book what it is, and we have been blessed with a group of incredibly effective and capable people. Tony Luengo served as acquisitions editor for this edition, coordinated reviewer feedback, and took us to the point of agreeing among ourselves what the new edition of the book would look like. Glen Herbert, developmental editor, must have enjoyed the process so much for *Research Decisions* III that he came back again for this edition, and we appreciate that he did.

The efforts of copy editor Lisa Berland also were much appreciated; it was a pleasure working with someone who became involved with the material and made some great suggestions that improved the book.

Mostly, however, we thank the faculty who continue to use *Research Decisions* in universities and colleges across the country, and to the students whose questions and feedback help us speak to them. In the end it is only because of all of you that we get to deal with the challenge and the great fun of figuring out how to make the newest *Research Decisions* even better than the last. Our hope, of course, is that you enjoy this book as much as Chris and I enjoyed collaborating on it.

Ted Palys
Vancouver, BC
19 June 2006

I was first exposed to *Research Decisions* in 1991 as a student in a university transfer program in community college. At the time I, like many other students in the social sciences, was enrolled in one of several required methodology and data analysis courses. Also, like many of my fellow classmates, I recall not being particularly thrilled about having to take what everybody "knew" was a boring methods class. Moreover, I was not very happy to have to engage with what I was sure would be yet another long-winded academic text that spoke about issues that were a thousand miles away from my own life and experiences and that presented one more list of "facts" for me to memorize so that I could jump through another academic hoop in the seemingly endless circus of undergraduate life. Imagine my utter amazement when I found that all of my preconceived notions about social research and the intellectual traditions that underlie it were not only completely misguided but, dare I say, wrong!

As I forged ahead in my undergraduate studies, I kept finding myself coming back to *Research Decisions* and drawing upon the straightforward and accessible explanations of abstract topics such as epistemology and ontology and more concrete applications such as the theory and mathematics underlying chi-square and *t*-tests. Ted's presentation style spoke to me in a way that authors of many other books had not and it provided the catalyst for me to develop my own ways of understanding and presenting information in the many papers, assignments, and research projects that I was required to complete in classes that I took in sociology, anthropology, psychology, and criminology. The book that I was at first so reluctant to shell out my hard-earned money for was one that ended up opening my eyes and mind to techniques for critically observing and making sense of the social world that have helped me to achieve personal and professional accomplishments that many people around me proclaimed were "not realistic for someone like me." To this end the value of *Research Decisions* for me is, and always has been, found in Ted's ability to challenge readers to think outside the box, to challenge our preconceptions, to critically interrogate relations of knowledge/power, to strive for more complete understandings and to demand better

of ourselves and the social institutions that impinge on our lives.

Over the past ten years I have had the opportunity to get to know Ted first as a teacher, then as a colleague, and now as a friend and business partner. When he first approached me with the idea of collaborating on the next stage of growth of his "baby," I was both extremely honoured and overcome by anxiety. For Ted to even contemplate bringing me on board told me that he believed that my insights and experiences could actually bring something new and important to a book that already offered so much to students in a wide range of social science disciplines. By the same token I knew that I didn't want to do anything to stunt the growth of something that he had worked so long and hard to raise. In the end I hope that our collaboration on this next generation of *Research Decisions* will continue to build on the strong critical tradition that Ted started 20 years ago and that you enjoy the direction that we have taken it.

Chris Atchison
Vancouver, BC
3 July 2006

CHAPTER 1

PERSPECTIVES ON RESEARCH

Sociology, psychology, criminology, business administration, political science, communications, and the rest of the social sciences each have a designated academic "turf." But this book deals with something these disciplines have in common—a belief in the desirability of trying to understand human action through systematic study and analysis.

There are many reasons one might want to do so, the most basic of which is to address our curiosity about ourselves in all aspects of society. Indeed, there is no more basic human process than (a) being curious about something we want to understand or a question we want to answer, (b) identifying and gathering the information we need, (c) making sense of the information, and (d) forming some tentative conclusions on the basis of it. These are processes that certainly are not unique to academic research or researchers—physicians follow them when they try to figure out what the source of your complaints might be; courts do so when they try to ascertain guilt or innocence; mechanics do so when they try to figure out why your car won't work; journalists do it when they write stories and engage in analysis about events in the news; and all of us do it when we try to make sense of the world around us. We may not call the processes we follow "research methods," or take the time to articulate to ourselves the rules of inference we follow, but people and events engage our curiosity, and we try to understand. Our aspiration in this book is to consider some of the diverse ways researchers in the social and health sciences try to understand the world in a self-conscious and rigorous way.

RESEARCH AS ENGAGEMENT

In *The Passenger,* a film directed by Michelangelo Antonioni, a journalist visits a remote desert village to make a documentary about one of the peoples indigenous to the area. He is surprised to meet someone who, after travelling extensively in the industrialized world, returned to become a respected Elder in the village of his birth. The journalist asks how this man's view of his people changed after being exposed to life beyond the dunes. After some reflection, the Elder replies, "Mr. Locke ... There are perfectly satisfactory answers to all your questions ... But I don't think you understand how little you can learn from them.... Your questions are much more revealing about *your*self than my answers would be about me." The scene ends when the Elder turns the camera around so that it looks toward the journalist asking the questions.

When, for whatever reason, a phenomenon catches a social scientist's interest, the social scientist must decide how to approach and investigate that phenomenon. Researchable questions can be posed in myriad ways. In this book, we argue that research methods *can* provide us with at least tentative "facts" or "answers" to the questions we pose, but we also maintain that "knowledge" is not an entity, like gold, that merely awaits our discovery of it. The relation between researcher and researched is more complex than that: the questions we ask and the way we ask them reveal a considerable amount about us and necessarily constrain the answers that we can find. As Morgan (1983a) states, it is important to acknowledge that science is basically a process of interaction, or better still, of *engagement*. Scientists engage a subject of study by interacting with it through means of a particular frame of reference, and what is observed and discovered in the object (i.e., its objectivity) is as much a product of this interaction and the protocol and technique through which it is operationalized as it is of the object itself. Moreover, since it is possible to engage an object of study in different ways—just as we might engage an apple by looking at it, feeling it, or eating it—we can see that the same object is capable of yielding many different forms of knowledge. This leads us to see knowledge as a potentiality resting in an object of investigation, and to see science as being concerned with the realization of potentialities—of possible knowledges. (13)

The view that the research process involves *engaging* a subject or phenomenon of interest has a fundamentally important set of implications associated with it. In particular, it suggests that *what* we find— the "truths" we unearth about the world—is only partly related to how the world *is,* but also is related to *where* we look and *how* we choose to examine what we find there. Acknowledging these implications leads us to consider the varying perspectives that researchers bring to the research process.

We say *perspectives* (plural) because the first thing to understand about the research enterprise is just how diverse it is. Indeed, its diversity is one of its greatest strengths. When many different people enjoy the academic freedom to engage many different issues from a wide variety of perspectives, a vibrant research process is the result, with society its major benefactor (e.g., Horn 1999).

Of course, there are other points on which most researchers also would agree. For example, most would agree that science is a community whose boundaries extend across both space and time: Aristotle and Plato (who lived and died on the other side of the planet about 2000 years ago) are as much our academic colleagues as are the faculty members whose offices neighbour ours. Researchers also

believe that "knowledge," however each of us might define it, should be treated seriously, developed systematically, and aired in a public forum where criticism and reflection are encouraged and valued.

But beyond these principles there are few things on which all scientists agree, and the variation among perspectives can be immense. This seems appropriate given what is perceived to be at stake— ultimately no less than truth itself.

Not surprisingly, over millennia, much time has been devoted to considering such fundamental questions about truth and knowledge as whether "facts" exist; how we can recognize one if we see one; and how to distinguish "legitimate" data and "reasonable" interpretations from their opposites. If you're serious about becoming a researcher, you owe it to yourself and to your colleagues not only to enroll in research courses where these issues are discussed, but also to take courses in such disciplines as history and philosophy, where the nuances of those issues are considered more fully than we can do here.

QUANTITATIVE AND QUALITATIVE RESEARCH

This chapter embodies more modest goals—to begin to talk about the varied methods and perspectives of the social sciences by introducing you to and then interweaving two research traditions or perspectives: **qualitative approaches** and **quantitative approaches.**

When we **dichotomize** all research into only two traditions, we are simultaneously on solid ground and shaky ground. There's abundant evidence to suggest that dividing research and researchers into these two categories describes a state of affairs that really exists in the world. Practically any social science department in any university, and certainly any discipline as a whole, will contain people whose research falls within one of these two perspectives. And although such persons sometimes coexist quite happily, and more and more researchers over the years have come to embrace combinations of both perspectives (as we advocate in this text), they sometimes can inhabit two virtually separate worlds where they speak with those in their own group more often than with those in the other, read and publish in different journals, and attend different conferences, congregating only with people who share their epistemological assumptions.

Nor did we make up these terms: members of each camp actually use the term "qualitative" or "quantitative" to describe their data, or the approach underlying how the data were gathered, when they write books and journal articles. But the knowledge that qualitative and quantitative researchers have about each other—at least as revealed in **polemical** articles—can be very simplistic and stereotypical. Members of each group can be extremely self-righteous, believing that their perspective is the only "rational" choice any truly thinking person would make. Of course, by implication, this means that anyone who makes the opposite choice cannot be a very thoughtful person at all. Kidder and Fine (1987) capture the spirit well with their tongue-in-cheek description of how quantitative researchers perceive themselves as seekers of "numerical precision," characterizing qualitative researchers as "navel-gazers." In contrast, qualitative researchers refer to their data as "rich in detail," writing off quantitative researchers as "number crunchers." Both "betray not only a preference for one but also a distrust of the other" (57).

But our distinction between qualitative and quantitative perspectives is not simply descriptive. In abstracting the concepts *qualitative* and *quantitative* to explain what appear to be consistent patterns in what we observe, we are also being *inferential.* And that's where we're admittedly on less solid ground because the boundary between qualitative and quantitative can be a hard one to demarcate clearly. It's a bit like dividing people according to whether they're "short" or "tall": it may be a useful distinction to make when picking players for the basketball team, but any dividing line between the two groups is bound to be arbitrary and hard to justify beyond the specific circumstances in which it's used. Despite many clear differences between the two research camps, there are also areas of significant overlap, and researchers who are allegedly from one side often incorporate features from the other.[1]

But dichotomies *can* be useful pedagogical devices, and because we think that's the case here, we'll use this one to give you the flavour of each tradition. We'll first discuss the dichotomy in abstract terms and then show how one dispute that appeared in the literature can be understood in qualitative–quantitative terms. Keep in mind, though, that in distinguishing between qualitative and quantitative research and researchers, we're actually much more interested in forging links of communication between the two than in driving them further apart.

Quantitative Approaches

A NATURAL SCIENCE MODEL

Although quantitative approaches have a long philosophical lineage, their contemporary forms are often traced to the mid- to late 19th century. Individuals such as Auguste Comte (in sociology and social psychology) and Wilhelm Wundt (in psychology) noted the tremendous theoretical and technological advances in the natural sciences and believed that natural science methods could be of service to the social sciences as well. The metaphors they used to describe the challenge to social scientists were replete with natural science imagery. For Comte, "societies and groups [were] organisms—analogous to biological or physical organisms—that exist and behave in accordance with objective and external laws" (Faulconer & Williams 1985: 1181). For Wundt, physics and chemistry were the models to which social scientists should aspire; he viewed psychology's task as one of uncovering the "atoms of consciousness" (Adair 1973).

A POSITIVIST EPISTEMOLOGY

Comte, Wundt, and others embraced an empirical tradition known as **positivism.** Bhaskar (1986) notes that

the term "positivism" was first used systematically by Saint-Simon. It was adopted by his erstwhile secretary Auguste Comte, to express the ideas that the world consists of phenomena which are real, useful, certain, precise, organic, and relative and that knowledge consists in and only in the description of the coexistence and succession of such phenomena. (225)

Many have treated "positivism" and "quantitative approaches" as virtually synonymous (e.g., see Blumer 1969; Denzin 1978; Schwartz & Jacobs 1979). Although equating these terms may have been understandable in the 19th century, it's no longer accurate to do so. Being a positivist typically implies a quantitative approach, but engaging in quantitative research no longer means you are necessarily a positivist. Those who have avoided quantification because they are dissatisfied with positivism are simply practising guilt by association, and an imperfect association at that.

A REALIST PERSPECTIVE

The attribute most strongly associated with positivism is its **realist perspective.** Filstead (1979) notes that "at the heart of the distinction between the quantitative and qualitative paradigms lies the classic argument in philosophy between the schools of realism and idealism" (34). Most vigorously applied in the context of positivism, realism implies adhering to the notion that there is a reality out there that awaits our discovery. Positivists aim to uncover *the* facts and to understand the laws or principles that account for those facts. Positivists maintain that we need only think of the "right" theoretical concepts and develop techniques that are sufficiently precise to measure and test them.

The positivist reliance on a natural science model and a realist perspective influences the types of theoretical concepts and data considered legitimate for inclusion in any science of human behaviour. References to Charles Darwin's evolutionary theory were frequent among turn-of-the-20th-century positivists. John B. Watson (e.g., 1913), for example, was clearly impressed by Darwin's work and its impact on the biological sciences. A prime reason for this advance, said Watson, was that Darwin resisted the temptation to treat the human species as a spe-

cial entity; instead, he treated humans as just another organism, subject to the same scientific principles as any other. Regarding psychology's love affair with **metaphysical** notions like "consciousness," Watson asserted that

it is granted that the behaviour of animals can be investigated without appeal to consciousness ... The position is taken here that the behaviour of man and the behaviour of animals must be considered on the same plane; as being equally essential to a general understanding of behaviour. [The social sciences] can dispense with consciousness. (176)

The ideal theory would be both simple and comprehensive, involving concepts that are adaptable to any specific situation, in the same way that the theoretical concept of "gravity" or "gravitational forces" can be used to explain the big (e.g., the movement of the galaxies), the small (e.g., why and how electrons revolve around an atom), and the mundane (e.g., why you need to wear suspenders when your trousers are too big). The ideal theory would also limit itself to expressing relationships among variables and to expressing them precisely, preferably in mathematical terms, rather like Einstein's simple but provocative statement that $E = mc^2$.

OBSERVABLE CAUSES AND EFFECTS

This mechanistic purity also was sought with respect to the variables that were to be included in any analysis. The world was seen to be made up of causes and effects (or outcomes) like billiard balls being knocked around a table. We see the causes (e.g., the white cue ball hits a red ball), observe the effects (e.g., the red ball moves and bounces into a pocket), and can develop principles to describe that action (e.g., the angle of incidence equals the angle of reflection, as any physicist or pool player knows) without worrying about what is going on "inside" either ball.

Similarly, early positivists felt that organisms can be treated as "black boxes": any invisible processes that might go on inside (such as thinking in humans) are deemed irrelevant; all that *really* counts is what goes in (the causes) and what comes out (the effects or outcomes). Only those causes external to individuals were deemed "legitimate" to scrutinize, largely because such forces and processes are most amenable to observation and measurement. We can't see people's thoughts or motives, but we can see what people *do*. Classic positivists argued that only external, observable forces can be considered "real" and that only such "real" variables are worth considering in the "science" of human behaviour.

In sociology, for example, positivism was originally epitomized by Emile Durkheim. Like Watson, Durkheim argued for a knowledge that was based on objective, observable causes and effects. For him, this implied getting outside the individual:

> We must, therefore, consider social phenomena in themselves as distinct from the consciously formed representations of them in the mind; we must study them objectively as external things, for it is this character that they present to us. (Durkheim 1968 [1938]: 252)

Natural science perspectives on "objectivity" were also adapted to the quantitative cause. Dealing with "reality," while a necessary step, was not in itself seen as sufficient to ensure scientific progress. Clearly, we would also have to avoid tainting our measurement of reality with subjectivity. Demonstrating the reliability and validity of one's techniques was thus also paramount, since such demonstrations provide assurance that the constructs being considered are more than just the fuzzy and self-serving creations of an isolated investigator.

OBJECTIVITY THROUGH SOCIAL DISTANCE

Positivists suggest that the route to objectivity requires investigators to *depersonalize* the research situation, like the proverbial Martian who naively investigates these strange beings called humans (see Lofland, Snow, Anderson, & Lofland 2006). "Good" data are dispassionate data, far removed from their source. The closer one comes to dealing with people on a one-to-one basis, the more dangerous the situation becomes, since one might be tempted to resort to metaphysical concepts such as thoughts, perceptions, attitudes, and values.

Indeed, many quantitatively oriented research textbooks suggest that the worst event that can befall anyone who engages in field research is for him or her to "go native" or **overidentify**[2] with those being studied. This is said to occur when researchers become so attuned and sensitive to the culture or group they're investigating that they take on the perspective of the group's members, leaving their supposedly more appropriate detached, analytical perspective behind. Hagan (1989) makes the common argument that the appropriate role for researchers is studied neutrality; one should neither love nor hate the group one studies, and one should always maintain some social distance. He explains that a problem commonly experienced in fieldwork is

> the *tendency of observers to overidentify with groups.* There are examples in the literature of an anthropologist who married a cannibal chief and of other individuals who, without being aware of it, have taken on the mannerisms of the groups they have studied. "Going native" is a situation in which the researcher identifies with and becomes a member of the study group, and in the process abandons his or her role as an objective researcher. (156–57; italics in original)

Hagan also quotes a case in which one social scientist chastised another for "romanticising criminals" and losing his sense of objectivity:

> We ought to restrain impulses, including benign impulses, that prevent us from seeing the world realistically. Just as anthropologists cannot be trusted (intellectually) when they "go native" to the extent that they glorify rather than study their preliterate societies, so a criminologist who has gone native cannot be trusted to tell us what criminals are like. (Toby 1986 [1938]: 2, quoted in Hagan 1989: 157)[3]

NOMOTHETIC ANALYSIS

The ideal of detachment is also consistent with the quantitative preference for **aggregated data,** which compile responses from many persons so that general trends or patterns across people are made visible, a process called **nomothetic analysis,** as opposed to **idiographic analysis,**[4] which is oriented toward the case study. This approach assumes that, across many responses, all "exceptions to the rule," whether in a positive or negative direction, will cancel one another out in any group as a whole, making the group "average" the purist statement of how someone in a given situation "typically" or "normally" behaves.

THE INDEPENDENT (CAUSAL) VARIABLES: SOCIAL FACTS

The belief in the desirability of aggregation can also be seen in the quantitative attachment to **social facts,** influential aspects of social life that individuals do not create and that continue to operate no matter how we feel about them. Durkheim (e.g., 1968 [1938]) argued that social facts, the most appropriate causal factors for social scientists to investigate, exert their influence coercively, particularly when we try to resist:

> A social fact is to be recognized by the power of external coercion which it exercises or is capable of exercising over individuals, and the presence of this power may be recognized in its turn either by the existence of some specific sanction or by the resistance offered against every individual effort that tends to violate it. (1968 [1938]: 250)

Social facts were seen as desirable research foci because they represented an external reality that was thought to influence us and exist entirely independently of our opinions of it:

> The most important characteristic of a thing is the impossibility of its modification by a simple effort of the will ... Social facts have this characteristic. Far from being a product of the will, they determine it from without; they are like molds in which our actions are inevitably shaped. (Durkheim 1968 [1938]: 253)

Thus, for Durkheim, the important social facts of life, and hence the appropriate causal variables to study, were social practices and institutions such as education, religion, the law, and the economic system.[5] We clearly did not cause them; they existed before we did. They influence us all, although the nature of the effect may vary. And even had we not been born, they would still exist and still influence whoever happened to be here. For example, if you were born in Canada, you were born into a capitalist economic system; Canada would still be capitalist even if you had not been born here. That system is a social fact of your life; it has affected you in ways that differ from the effects of being born in, say, a socialist or communist country.

THE DEPENDENT (OUTCOME) VARIABLES: AGGREGATED RATE DATA

To measure the effects of social facts, Durkheim recommended relying on official **rate data** (e.g., birth rates, divorce rates, suicide rates, crime rates). Such data deal with matters relevant to and affected by "social facts," are outside the influence of researchers or of the individuals the data described, and describe "reality." In addition, they make it easier to compare two areas or to compare an area with itself over time.

> Since each of these [rate] figures contains all the individual cases indiscriminately, the individual circumstances which may have had a share in the production of the phenomenon are neutralized and, consequently, do not contribute to its determination. The average, then, expresses a certain state of the group mind. (Durkheim 1968 [1938]: 249)

A DEDUCTIVE APPROACH

For classic positivists, prediction demonstrates understanding: if you truly understand a phenomenon (e.g., hurricanes, depression, birth rates), you should be able to predict its occurrence. Not surprisingly, therefore, quantitative researchers prefer the **hypothetico-deductive method** (known more simply as deduction, or the deductive method), which involves making predictions and assessing their success in an ongoing process of theory development.

Chapter 2 discusses this approach in detail; here we need only note that it involves beginning with a theory; deducing a hypothesis (prediction) from the theory; gathering data to test the prediction (and hence also the theory that gave rise to it); and then either looking for another situation in which to test the theory (if the prediction is borne out) or discarding or revising the theory (if the prediction proves inaccurate). In the ideal situation, the effects of certain variables can be assessed with all other influences held constant, making the **true experiment** the deductivist's method of choice (see Chapter 9).

Qualitative Approaches

The choices that characterize qualitative approaches have traditionally been the opposite of those made by quantitative researchers on every dimension discussed above. Although qualitative researchers' opinions about quantitative science vary considerably (from respectful tolerance to complete rejection), Schutz (1970) is neither extreme nor atypical.

Schutz disagrees with behaviourists' and other positivists' choice to investigate a mechanistic world from the aloof stance of the knowledgeable social scientist, but his disagreement isn't based on a belief that such a science would necessarily give "wrong" information. Rather, he feels that in the long run, such an approach would inevitably fall short of a comprehensive understanding of human action. And it is important, Schutz asserts, to adopt a method for the right reasons: *not* because that method is easier, *not* because we associate it with some prestigious field of inquiry, and *not* because it's expedient to adopt it in the short term, but because, over the long haul, it's the right thing to do:

> The basic postulate of the methodology of social science, therefore, must be the following: choose the scheme of reference adequate to the problem you are interested in, consider its limits and possibilities, make its terms compatible and consis-

tent with one another, and having once accepted it, stick to it! (Schutz 1970: 270)

A HUMAN-CENTRED APPROACH

Qualitative researchers assert that "adequacy" in the social sciences begins with acceptance of a more human-centred methodology, since social scientists, in trying to understand *human* behaviour, face challenges fundamentally different from those faced by the natural scientist:

> The world of nature, as explored by the natural scientist, does not "mean" anything to the molecules, atoms and electrons therein. The observational field of the social scientist, however, ... has a specific meaning and relevance structure for the human beings living, acting, and thinking therein. By a series of common-sense constructs they have pre-selected and pre-interpreted this world which they experience as the reality of their daily lives. It is these thought objects of theirs which determine their behaviour by motivating it. (Schutz 1970: 272–73)

Schutz thus believes that social science ought to view humans as thinking, motivated actors, while acknowledging that, as both social scientists and humans, social scientists are part of the very entity we seek to understand. The philosophy that expresses this view is known as **phenomenologism.**

PHENOMENOLOGISM

Phenomenologists maintain that any effort to understand human behaviour must take into account that humans are cognitive beings who actively perceive and make sense of the world around them, have the capacity to abstract from their experience, ascribe meaning to their behaviour and the world around them, and are affected by those meanings. W. I. Thomas (1928) stated that "perceptions are real because they are real in their consequences"; that is, in many situations the influence of "reality" (if indeed such a thing exists independently of our experience of it) pales in comparison to the influence of our *perceptions* of the situation—indeed, those perceptions *define* our "reality."

Suppose that next week you were expected to give a class presentation on some topic related to research methods. In "reality," such a situation is a fairly trivial event; among the "big" things that will happen in your life, it probably won't even rank in the top 500. Your career, your future happiness, and your ultimate impact on the human race are unlikely to be significantly affected by your performance on that one day.

Yet if you're like most students, you won't treat it as trivial. You'll do the appropriate preparation at the library or through the Internet; you'll read your presentation a dozen times before the actual day you present, making last-minute changes and trying to learn it by heart; you may not sleep well the night before you present; and you'll probably come to class on "the big day" feeling at least a little nervous. Can we, as social scientists, adequately understand your behaviour without recourse to the way you perceive this situation and the meaning you ascribe to it?

To take another example, many Canadians these days seem deeply concerned about violent crime. Julian Roberts of the University of Ottawa reported that concern about violent crime had increased significantly during the preceding five years (e.g., see Mitchell 1994b), an increase that in turn is related to our collective belief that the rate of violent crime in Canada escalated significantly over that same period. In response to these concerns, citizens and their elected representatives frequently call for more punitive sentencing, more caution in the granting of parole, and "special measures" that would give courts greater leeway to incarcerate particularly nasty people and habitual offenders for a long, long time. Yet Roberts also documented the "reality" that, at least as measured by the rates reported by Statistics Canada, violent crime in Canada didn't increase at all during that period. This tendency continues today—Stephen Harper's Conservative party argued during the 2006 election campaign for tougher measures against criminals to appease Canadians' concerns about crime, and were joined in some of their proposals by the Liberals and New Democrats,

notwithstanding that the facts according to Statistics Canada are that crime rates are steadily going down, not up. Which is more important in accounting for Canadians' behaviour regarding violent crime: the "reality" of the situation or people's perceptions of it?

Phenomenologists feel that positivists, in their zeal to mimic the natural sciences, did an injustice to the very humans they wanted to understand. Qualitative researchers therefore argue that any science of human behaviour is destined to be trivial and/or incomplete unless it takes people's perceptions into account. Any approach that defines itself as phenomenological makes understanding human perceptions its major research focus: if perceptions are real in their consequences, and if they are a major determinant of what we do, then clearly we must understand them and their origins.

This approach obviously clashes with the positivist emphasis on observables: suddenly we must "get inside people's heads" and understand how they perceive their world. Yet this transition may be less revolutionary than it might at first appear. Even many positivists have come to accept that at least some aspects of phenomenological approaches have some merit and that strategies that ignore our ability to think, imagine, and so on are destined to come up short. Perhaps as a result, contemporary positivism (often known as **postpositivism** or *neopositivism*) is far less dogmatic about excluding "unobservables"— attitudes, values, beliefs, perceptions, and motives— from the research vocabulary.[6]

Although such changes have altered what more positivistically inclined researchers do—it's now acceptable to talk to people, ask them about their beliefs and experiences, and consider "cognitive processes" and their associations with behaviour— fundamental differences between qualitative and quantitative researchers remain. While quantitative researchers may now talk to their research participants, the belief that one must still retain an aloof, socially distant stance remains; "overidentification" is still seen as a problem, and the ideal of the researcher as a detached analyst is still sought and praised. We may talk to "subjects," but we can't trust what they say. Their job is simply to provide us with raw data for analysis; deciding what their verbal utterances mean is still *our* job.

The difference is subtle but important. For qualitative researchers, the choice comes down to whether it's better to ask people what *they* think is important, and incorporate their answers into our efforts to make sense of their behaviour, or to ask only what *we* think is important, and then try to infer what they must have been thinking in order to give such answers. But surely it is better to ask respondents directly for their own reasons than for us to try to invent them (see also Becker [1996] and Blumer [1969] on this point).

NUMBERS CREATE DISTANCE

The shift to phenomenologism affected many other aspects of theory and method. For example, a central aim of positivism was to establish functional relations among explanatory concepts, expressed, ideally, in mathematical (quantitative) form. Many phenomenologists believe that imposing a quantitative measurement just removes researchers further from directly understanding human experience. Instead of trying to come to grips with the anger and powerlessness a woman feels when assaulted, for example, the requirements of quantification leave us either merely counting the frequency of such occurrences (with all the attendant technical problems of how to count "correctly") or asking women to describe their experience on a series of ten-point rating scales. Phenomenologists, in contrast, argue that the closer we can come to such experiences, say, by listening to women explain, in their own words, the nature of their experiences, the better.

UNDERSTANDING EQUALS *VERSTEHEN*

Once the variables of analysis are quantified, positivists argue that the language of mathematics makes our statements far more precise. "Explanation" in the positivist sense involves investigating which "big" variables (e.g., social facts) most significantly affect human existence. Being able to identify these factors and to predict their occurrence and magnitude becomes the acid test of understanding. The rationale is that if you can successfully predict the

values a variable will take on, you must understand the phenomenon in question; conversely, if you understand a phenomenon, you should be able to predict its occurrence with some degree of consistency.

Qualitative researchers reject the idea that a statistical criterion can ever define explanation or understanding. Instead, they embrace Max Weber's concept of *Verstehen*, which involves the more intimate and empathic understanding of human action in terms of its **interpretive** meaning to the subject. While quantitative researchers sought general principles of behaviour, Weber argued that, in themselves, such principles couldn't account for action in context:

> An "objective" analysis of cultural events, which proceeds according to the thesis that the ideal of science is the reduction of empirical reality to "laws," is meaningless ... The knowledge of social laws is not knowledge of social reality but is rather one of the various aids used by our minds for attaining this end ... Knowledge of *cultural* events is inconceivable except on a basis of the *significance* which the concrete constellations of reality have for us in *individual* concrete situations. (Weber 1968a [1949]: 91)

Weber didn't completely dismiss quantitative research or the theories associated with it; he just felt that one had to go beyond blanket assertions to account for action in context. He wasn't averse to quantification in principle, but he *was* cautious about how useful it might be for articulating subjective meaning:

> Causal explanation depends on being able to determine that there is a probability, which in the rare ideal case can be numerically stated, but is always in some sense calculable, that a given observable event (overt or subjective) will be followed or accompanied by another event ... [Nonetheless], statistical uniformities constitute understandable types of action in the sense of this discussion, and thus constitute "sociological

generalizations," only when they can be regarded as manifestations of the understandable subjective meaning of a course of social action. (Weber 1968b [1947]: 30–31)

VALIDITY REQUIRES INTIMACY

Qualitative researchers believe that understanding people's perceptions requires getting close to "research participants" or "informants" or "collaborators." You must spend time with them, get to know them, feel close to them, be able to empathize with their concerns, perhaps even be one of them, if you hope to *truly* understand. This approach directly contradicts the quantitative view that "objective" understanding requires aloof detachment, lest the researcher "lose perspective."

Some qualitative researchers believe that one can never understand a group of which one is not a part—that male researchers can never truly understand what it means to be a woman, for example, or that non-Aboriginal researchers can never know what it means to "grow up Indian," or that someone who has never spent time in prison will never completely understand what it means to do time.[7]

AN INDUCTIVE CASE STUDY APPROACH

Associated with the view that closeness is desirable is the idea that researchers should *listen* to their informants, aiming to understand categories and theoretical dimensions from the perspective of their informants' experience and to incorporate those understandings into their analysis, rather than relying exclusively on predefined measures and theoretical categories imposed from the "outside." Accordingly, qualitative researchers emphasize **inductive approaches** (where observation in the field *precedes* the generating of theoretical concepts; see Chapter 2) and **case study analysis.** Instead of beginning with theory and assuming that there's *one* theory that will eventually account for everything, the qualitative approach typically involves beginning with individual case studies in context, trying to understand each situation on its own terms, and leaving open, for the moment, the question of

whether generalizable theoretical concepts can ever eventually be drawn together in anything resembling a grand theory. For qualitative researchers, theory isn't something you start with; it's something you build.

CONSTRUCTIONISM

We saw earlier that classic positivists embraced a philosophical perspective known as *realism*. Phenomenologists, in emphasizing the role of human perception in understanding human behaviour, adopt a contrasting perspective known as **constructionism.** As described by Schwandt (1994),

> constructivists are deeply committed to the … view that what we take to be objective knowledge and truth is [actually] the result of perspective. Knowledge and truth are created, not discovered by mind. They emphasize the pluralistic and plastic character of reality—pluralistic in the sense that reality is expressible in a variety of symbol and language systems; plastic in the sense that reality is stretched and shaped to fit purposeful acts of intentional human agents. They endorse the claim that, "contrary to commonsense, there is no unique 'real world' that preexists and is independent of human mental activity and human symbolic language." (125; the last sentence quotes Bruner 1986: 95)

Suppose we were interested in the phenomenon of "cheating," known in some universities as "academic dishonesty." A realist approach to studying cheating would affirm that there are behaviours we consensually recognize as "cheating" and that some people are more or less likely to cheat than others. Given these two assertions, our attention might turn to trying to measure either "frequency of cheating" or how likely a given person or group of persons is to cheat; investigating why some people are more likely to cheat than others; or why some situations result in more or less cheating than others.

A constructionist looking at cheating probably wouldn't deny the usefulness of any of these approaches. But he or she also would encourage us to take a step back and look at "cheating" as a socially produced construct. "Cheating" per se doesn't exist in the world in any "real" sense; instead, our using the word says as much about those of us who are *identifying* the "cheating" as it does about the people *doing* it. A comprehensive analysis of cheating requires us to ask other kinds of questions: Why do we consider "cheating" something worth asking about? Why do we consider some behaviours "cheating" (e.g., looking over another person's shoulder to see what answers he or she puts down in an exam) but not others (e.g., studying together)? We might also want to interview people who have been identified as cheaters about how they perceived their actions: Did *they* consider it "cheating" or did they call it something else? How did they come to engage in that behaviour?

The realist, then, takes the existence of certain behaviour categories as a given, believing that there are such things as "cheating," "aggression," and "crime," along with such supposedly "apparent" givens as "birth," "death," "taxes," and "murder." Constructionists, on the other hand, are at least as interested in why these categories interest us, whom or where we decide to sample in order to investigate the phenomenon firsthand, where the boundaries of the phenomenon are, what meanings the terms have for us, and how those boundaries and meanings change over time. To be a constructionist is not to deny that certain phenomena exist, but just to insist that their existence cannot be completely understood unless one understands why, how, and to whom they are applied. This perspective, which falls clearly within the phenomenological traditions exemplified by Weber and Schutz, has several implications.

For one thing, many of the research results we take at face value and perceive as enduring may be little more than transient relationships that reflect the prevailing social order. While realists may be content to try to assess *the* effects of race, poverty, being gay, or taking illicit drugs, constructionists argue that we can understand such matters only if we also understand something about how they're construed and about the context in which they occur.

Bronfenbrenner (1977), for example, argues that much of the research that purports to evaluate the "effects" of particular familial arrangements (e.g., single-parent families, children of divorce, daycare use) on developmental outcomes (e.g., school achievement, involvement in crime) is, in itself, meaningless. From a constructionist perspective, there's no *inherent* or "real" effect to being a child of divorce or attending daycare that's true across all time and space. We can understand the effects of divorce only if we understand the context in which divorce occurs and people's perceptions of it. If children of divorce are indeed more likely to become involved in juvenile delinquency, this pattern may simply reflect the social stigma often associated with divorce or the social conditions that typically prevail upon separation (e.g., where mothers often end up with both the children and the more economically disadvantaged situation). Similarly, studies that show daycare to be associated with positive effects on later school performance may reflect the lack of universal daycare; most children who go to daycare are from professional and better-educated families and, hence, are more advantaged and likely to succeed anyway. In sum, the "effects" of daycare or divorce are associated less with the statuses themselves than with the social context in which they exist.

For another thing, this approach argues that the world's structures are in no sense given, nor is our observation of them in any sense dispassionate or conceptually free. How can we observe anything without having implicit categories—a product of language, which in turn is a product of culture—with which to begin our observation? And if we already possess those categories, how can we argue that the theoretical categories we derive are inherently real? Perhaps our observations say as much about us (the observers) and about the social context in which we operate as about the behaviour we observe.

One example of research guided by a constructionist perspective (that incorporates both qualitative and quantitative data) is by Menzies and his colleagues on constructions of mental illness (e.g., see Menzies 1999; Menzies & Chunn 1999; Menzies &

Palys 2006). A focus of Menzies's research is the manner in which labels of mental illness follow prevailing social and cultural conceptions of "appropriate" behaviour. Making mental illness itself—how it evolved as a construct, who employed it, how it was employed and on whom—an object of inquiry encourages us to take a step back and consider the ways that we define and control socially marginalized behaviour.

Menzies's work reveals that decision-making processes in the adjudication of sanity say at least as much about the social beliefs and constraints of the decision-makers as they do about the behaviour of those being assessed. Gergen (1985) reports that

> similar kinds of critiques have been launched against the taken-for-granted character of suicide, ... beliefs, ... schizophrenia, ... altruism, ... psychological disorder, ... childhood, ... domestic violence, ... menopause, ... and situational causes ... In each case, the objective criteria for identifying such "behaviours," "events," or "entities" are shown to be either highly circumscribed by culture, history, or social context or altogether nonexistent. (267)[8]

As a third and perhaps broader example, consider the variety of meanings that some social institutions have for different peoples. A realist perspective on matters of "criminal justice," for example, would take "the criminal justice system" and the existing *Criminal Code* as givens, starting any analysis with the view that "criminals" are those who violate the *Code* and that the extent to which "crime" and "criminality" exist in a society is best reflected by such data as the official crime rates reported annually by Statistics Canada.[9]

Such an approach may be fine for those who subscribe to mainstream conceptions of justice and the underlying values they represent, but many argue that "the law" and those it deems "criminal" are best seen as socially constructed entities. Critical theorists note how the criminal law (and even the very division between criminal and civil law) and its agencies appear to systematically benefit the upper classes

more than the lower ones, men more than women, and those with Western European/colonialist roots more than other (e.g., indigenous) peoples (e.g., see Faith 1993; Jackson 1992; Lowman & Palys 1991; Monture-Okanee & Turpel 1992).

According to these views, the *Criminal Code* and crime statistics are anything but neutral descriptions of criminal behaviour and its frequency of occurrence. Instead, crime statistics embody just one of many possible conceptions of justice and can't be understood outside the context that makes them meaningful.

EMPHASIZING PROCESS

A distinct difference in emphasis also follows from either seeing the important elements of the world as essentially stable and awaiting discovery (the realist view) or seeing the world as something that is actively constructed, deconstructed, and reconstructed on an ongoing basis (the constructionist view). According to those who hold the latter view, our constructions of the world—and hence the world itself—are open to change.

As we've seen, positivist/quantitative researchers tend to emphasize the measurement of *outcomes* in their research. This is consistent with the positivist division of the world into causes and effects and with the view that there are real, monolithic forces that rule our lives. But constructionists consider the world a more ephemeral, transient place whose dynamics are more directly contingent on the meanings and understandings we use to negotiate our world. Accordingly, qualitative approaches are also characterized by greater attention to *processes,* particularly the processes by which constructions arise and, by implication, the processes by which constructions can be changed.

COMPARING RESEARCH PERSPECTIVES

Thus far, we've seen that numerous differences have traditionally characterized the approaches of qualitative and quantitative researchers. Table 1.1 compares these differences more explicitly, at least as they've been associated with each approach historically.

Table 1.1
Comparing Qualitative and Quantitative Approaches

Qualitative Approach	Quantitative Approach
Human-centred approach: people's ability to think and abstract requires special consideration	Natural science model: humans are just another organism
Phenomenological	Positivist
Constructionist	Realist
No variables ruled out; internal, perceptual variables expressly considered	Emphasis on observable variables that are external to the individual; social facts
Direct, qualitative verbal reports are preferred; quantifying responses is a step removed from people's words and perceptions	Quantitative measures are preferred for their precision and amenability to mathematical analysis
Emphasis on processes: perceptions and their meanings and how these emerge and change	Emphasis on causes and effects: what goes in and how it comes out; inputs, outcomes
Valid data come from closeness and extended contact with research participants	Objectivity is achieved through social distance and a detached, analytical stance
The criterion for understanding is *Verstehen:* understanding behaviour in context in terms meaningful to the actor	The criteria for understanding are the ability to predict and statistically significant associations between variables
Preference for idiographic, case study analysis	Preference for nomothetic analysis aggregated over many cases
Preference for an inductive approach: starting with observation and allowing grounded theory to emerge	Preference for a deductive approach: starting with theory and creating situations in which to test hypotheses

Each element in the table has been discussed in the preceding pages, so you should now be able to define and explain them and understand why and how each is characteristic of one or the other of the two perspectives discussed in this chapter and throughout this book. But be aware, too, that the quantitative–qualitative dichotomy is more than an abstract set of principles that philosophers of science debate over afternoon tea; these approaches still affect how people do research and are fundamental to understanding any research you read. To see the quantitative–qualitative distinction in action, we will look at a dispute in the literature, a dispute that can best be explained by the different (quantitative versus qualitative) perspectives that two sets of authors bring to the table.

A DISPUTE IN THE LITERATURE: WHAT ARE THE EFFECTS OF IMPRISONMENT?

Bonta and Gendreau on Prison Life

In 1990, James Bonta and Paul Gendreau published an article entitled "Reexamining the Cruel and Unusual Punishment of Prison Life," in which they "critically examined ... the evidence pertaining to the effects of imprisonment" (347).

Scholarly articles always begin with a statement by the authors of why they thought it important to do the research and write the article, why they felt a journal should publish it, and why they think you'll be better informed after reading it. Bonta and

Gendreau (1990) justify their research by stating that (a) because prisons are here to stay, at least for the foreseeable future, it's important to know what happens when we send someone there; (b) many people believe, and much of the existing literature states, that prisons—in and of themselves, but also because of overcrowding and such practices as solitary confinement—are despicable places that only damage those who are sent there; but (c) many others argue that there are few if any deleterious effects associated with going to prison. With an important topic, and an apparent division of opinion about the "real" effects, the stage is set for the authors to review the literature, outlining for us what social scientists currently know about the effects of imprisonment.[10]

With respect to the qualitative–quantitative distinction, the first pages of Bonta and Gendreau (1990) simply ooze identity clues. First, they distinguish "common" knowledge—what "everybody knows" to be true—from the scientist's "careful," "critical" evaluations, clearly affirming their allegiance with the latter: their task is to identify the real "cold, hard facts" about the effects of imprisonment. Here, the authors show several things about their own beliefs: they think that there are "real" effects associated with imprisonment and that these effects can be identified and assessed; that what people "think" they know is secondary to the "truth" or "objective reality" of the situation; and that social scientists, armed with scientific knowledge and procedures, are in the best position to push back the frontiers of ignorance.

But not just any social scientist will do. The authors designate their favoured way of knowing when they go on to attribute the more damning evidence about prisons to authors who appear more interested in "polemics" than "facts." They refer pejoratively to "investigative journalists" and "academics who write text books" as those most guilty of these leanings. Such dilettantes are contrasted with scientists, whose "careful empirical evaluations" have failed to find that prison is an overwhelmingly negative experience. Clearly, Bonta and Gendreau believe that more "careful empirical evaluations" are required, since only these can objectively and definitively tell us the "truth" about the prison experience.

But what exactly does a "careful empirical evaluation" look like? The authors convey their opinion on that matter when they begin to separate wheat from chaff prior to their review of the literature: Step 1 is to distinguish "good" from "poor" studies. Having separated the studies this way, one can ignore the "poor" research, since surely only "good" research should be considered. Okay. But what exactly constitutes "good" research, and what sorts of "poor" research are not worth considering? The authors spell out their preferences very quickly:

> This review focusses on quantitative studies about effects of imprisonment. Qualitative or phenomenological studies are not included. To be included in the review, a study was required to employ objective measures of the variables of interest and to evaluate the relationship between them by means of statistical tests. (Bonta & Gendreau 1990: 349)

"Worthy" research, in their eyes, assesses the effects of imprisonment using standardized measures that are either physiological, psychological, or behavioural. For example, in their review of the literature on the effects of prison overcrowding, effects associated with crowding were typically assessed using such measures as changes in systolic blood pressure over time; paper-and-pencil measures (e.g., structured questionnaires) that assessed perceived overcrowding; and institutional records of behavioural misconduct.

Their findings on overcrowding are fairly typical of the various domains considered. By way of general summary, the authors note that, despite some evidence that prison crowding may produce changes in blood pressure and in self-reported reports of discomfort, "we cannot conclude that high population density is always associated with aggressive behaviour" (353). Their data show, instead, that "it depends": whether overcrowding results in negative effects depends on other considerations, such as the types of inmates being housed, an institution's managerial policies, and whether the crowded conditions are chronic or temporary.

In other areas, the authors find no evidence that prison has a deleterious effect on inmates' health. In fact, it may "have the fortuitous benefit of isolating the offender from a highly risky lifestyle in the community" (357). Regarding the effects of long-term incarceration, the authors scrutinize various studies in which scores from psychological tests (e.g., the MMPI)[11] are compared among groups of inmates who have served varying lengths of time in prison, concluding that "there is little to support the conclusion that long-term imprisonment necessarily has detrimental effects" (359).

Even when considering the effects of solitary confinement, the authors rely on the experimental literature regarding sensory deprivation to conclude that no negative effects appear to be inherently associated with solitary. Instead, "the real culprit may not necessarily be ... solitary *per se* but the manner in which the inmates have been treated" (361).

The final conclusions offered by Bonta and Gendreau (1990) are accompanied by a plea that we be guided by the rationality and objectivity of the science they espouse:

> When it comes to scholarly inquiry in the field of criminal justice, a pernicious tendency has been to invoke rhetoric over reality and affirm ideology over respect for empirical evidence ... [But], if we are to make progress in understanding what it is our prisons do to inmates, then we must respect the available evidence ... The facts are that long-term imprisonment and specific conditions of confinement such as solitary, under limiting and humane conditions, fail to show any sort of profound detrimental effects. (364)

Clearly, Bonta and Gendreau view science as an activity in which one gathers objective, neutral, non-ideological knowledge. Scientists are in the fact business, and the facts, say these authors, are that prison—even under crowded conditions or when solitary confinement is used—is not an inherently negative or psychologically damaging experience.

Roberts and Jackson Take Exception

A reaction to Bonta and Gendreau was swift in coming. Julian Roberts and Michael Jackson (1991) begin their critical response by referring to the earlier article's "startling conclusions" that "long-term imprisonment and specific conditions of confinement such as solitary, under limiting and humane conditions, fail to show any sort of profound detrimental effects" (Roberts & Jackson 1991: 557; Bonta & Gendreau 1990: 364) and that "many prisons may actually be conducive to good health" (Roberts & Jackson: 557; Bonta & Gendreau: 357). They go on to state that their study of the question—which encompasses both research and sworn testimonies from witnesses—does not support Bonta and Gendreau's "upbeat" conclusions. They're unwilling to reject the view that incarceration is ultimately harmful to prisoners, particularly when the only evidence to the contrary has come from the type of research practised by Bonta and Gendreau.

Further inspection of Roberts and Jackson (1991) reveals that their dispute is not over whether the effects of imprisonment *can* or *should* be assessed, but over *how* they have typically been assessed. Like Bonta and Gendreau, Roberts and Jackson apparently accept that there is a "reality" to prison life and that social science data can be used to shed light on the problem. But according to the latter authors, the view of Bonta and Gendreau ignores the phenomenology of the prison experience and the meaning such a sanction has in Western society. Roberts and Jackson continue:

> This is not to say that the effects of imprisonment are impervious to scientific investigation, but simply that the experience of incarceration might not be adequately captured by the usual social science dependent variables. Can the effects of an experience such as living on death row really be captured by psychiatric interviews or the MMPI? (Roberts & Jackson 1991: 557–58)

Thus, say Roberts and Jackson (1991), the weakness of Bonta and Gendreau (1990) is not that they seek empirical evidence, but that they are myopic and misguided in the evidence they consider. For example, Roberts and Jackson suggest that Bonta and Gendreau ignore the *meaning* that the experience of incarceration has in society and for individuals. A prison sentence isn't simply a punishment that's more severe than a slap on the wrist; it's a socially constructed response that affects a web of relationships, denies the incarcerated person many aspects of life that most people take for granted (e.g., liberty, raising a family, taking your dog for a walk, planning a holiday), is socially stigmatizing, and involves profound psychological experiences that most people never have to consider. Indeed, a central difference between the two sets of authors is that what Bonta and Gendreau (1990) label "outside the bounds of ... interest" is exactly what Roberts and Jackson (1991) feel should be the *heart* of the research.

After noting that one implication of Bonta and Gendreau's conclusions is that the state may actually be doing inmates a favour by locking them away for extended periods, Roberts and Jackson cite a Supreme Court decision to release a man, Mr. Steele, who had been held in prison for 37 years on an indeterminate sentence, on the grounds that the time he spent in prison constituted "cruel and unusual punishment." They note that had Bonta and Gendreau's "objective indices of negative effects of imprisonment" been used, the man might well have been considered "better off" for having spent nearly four decades in prison. In contrast, the Supreme Court recognized it as a travesty. As Roberts and Jackson (1991) explain, it is only through an examination of the life experiences of prisoners like Mr. Steele that the full negative impact of lengthy imprisonment can be understood. Over the 37 years Mr. Steele has been isolated from his peers, life has gone on without him. Men and women in the free community have enjoyed children and grandchildren and now greet retirement with the fruits of their life achievements. Mr. Steele, in contrast, must begin his life anew, at a very advanced age, with nothing and no one.

For Roberts and Jackson, therefore, Bonta and Gendreau's bowing before the altar of objectivity

may have left them with reams of quantitative data, but this apparent precision masks a critical problem: they completely miss the point. Understanding the impacts of imprisonment, for Roberts and Jackson, implies understanding what it *means* to be imprisoned and thus requires some understanding of the experience from the perspective of those imprisoned.

> Bonta and Gendreau would argue that this is to confuse rhetoric with science. We would argue that their approach substitutes a spurious objectivity for the human dimension of punishment as it is experienced by prisoners. (Roberts & Jackson 1991: 558–59)

SHIPS PASSING IN THE NIGHT

Both Bonta and Gendreau (1990) and Roberts and Jackson (1991) set out their arguments at greater length than we review here, but our summary should suffice to show the basis of their debate. At times, the interaction seems quite venomous; both sides express their views with considerable indignation. Roberts and Jackson, for example, assert at various times that Bonta and Gendreau "seriously overstate what their kind of empirical research can tell us" (560) and that

> by defining empirical research in such a way as to exclude studies such as those cited here, Bonta and Gendreau reduce the horizon of empirical research relevant to the evaluation of solitary confinement to studies that are, in effect, quite irrelevant to the real-life experience of prisoners. (560–61)

Bonta and Gendreau, in responding to these criticisms (Gendreau & Bonta 1991), were equally acrimonious:

> [Roberts and Jackson (1991)] have resorted to "knowledge destruction" arguments in order to dismiss the empirical evidence we presented on the effects of prison life ... Positivism is scorned and phenomenology embraced. Knowledge is political, partial, relative, socially constructed, and accepted according to its personal value.

Many of Roberts and Jackson's comments, unfortunately, typify the above. Witness their recourse to knowledge generated from "centuries of human experience," which they can tap into while we apparently cannot given that we are bound by the strictures of rational empiricism and its methodological requirements. (563)

Qualitative versus Quantitative?

With one of us (Ted) having known one author from each of the two sets (Gendreau and Jackson) reasonably well, and having more recently come to know a third (Roberts), it is very clear that all these people are sane, rational, highly intelligent, compassionate human beings who are productive and well-respected scholars. All also no doubt hope their work will help make the world better and more humane. How could such intelligent, reasonable people, who aspire to such noble accomplishments, who believe in the value of research, and who address exactly the same topic, be so scathing in debate?

As we hope you'll appreciate from reading this chapter and from the points we've drawn from their papers, Bonta, Gendreau, Roberts, and Jackson may all be members of the social science community, but the two sets of authors, at least where these two articles are concerned, might as well be from different planets.

Each set of researchers believes that they understand the phenomenon of imprisonment while the others don't, and that the others will *never* understand if they keep doing "research" the way they do now. At the core of these views are fundamental differences between the two groups of researchers regarding the "correct" way to do research, what sorts of evidence count as "knowledge," and even what sorts of information are useful to know. The differences that separate the two groups can be clustered together under the terms "quantitative" and "qualitative," exemplified here by Bonta and Gendreau (1990) and Roberts and Jackson (1991), respectively.

Look again at Table 1.1. Can you see how Bonta and Gendreau exemplify many elements from the quantitative side? They're self-proclaimed positivists who accept the realist belief that there are facts in the world that can be discovered; they prefer quantitative data that can be analyzed statistically; view the world in terms of causes and effects, believe that scientists can and should analyze the world from a neutral and objective vantage point; prefer aggregate data by which one can make global comparisons between groups of people (e.g., comparing inmates to non-inmates or comparing inmates who have been in prison for varying lengths of time); and distrust qualitative data, which they seem loath even to consider worthy of the title "data." Note, for example, how Bonta and Gendreau (1990) completely omit qualitative studies from their analysis. In their response to Roberts and Jackson (1991), Gendreau and Bonta (1991) talk of "human experience" and "the strictures of rational empiricism and its methodological requirements" as opposites. One is data; the other is not.

In contrast, Roberts and Jackson (1991) exemplify many elements from Table 1.1's qualitative side. They advocate a phenomenological perspective where "getting close" to inmates and understanding their view is a virtue, not a vice; accept that going to prison involves real effects but believe that understanding those effects requires knowing the *meaning* such an experience has in and for people's lives; analyze their data but do not require those data to be amenable to statistical analysis in order to be considered informative; show appreciation for case study analysis as a way to understand general trends and identify broader issues; and distrust quantitative data that do not reflect the understandings of inmates. According to these criteria, quantitative studies like those revered by Bonta and Gendreau are seen as little more than number-crunching exercises that might occasionally achieve the status of "interesting" or "helpful" but that are more often misleading and dangerous.

As Bonta and Gendreau (1990) and Roberts and Jackson (1991) thus illustrate, the qualitative–quantitative distinction this book addresses is not simply an abstraction. Differences on that dimension produce different research practices, from the types of questions asked and the way data are gathered to how the whole relationship between research and knowledge, and between researchers and those being researched, is conceived.

Oppositions and Complementarities

One word Bonta and Gendreau (1990) use to describe qualitative research is "polemical." The root of that word helps make sense of it: "pole," as in "polar extremes" or opposites. The earliest uses of "polemic" actually date to the mid-1600s, when it referred to arguments that were contrary to religious teachings, that is, disputatious argument seen as controversial because it reflected an entirely different pole of thought, involving fundamentally different premises. For example, an atheist's contention that God doesn't exist runs completely contrary to religious belief and, hence, would be considered disputatious or "polemical" by a religious person.

But in the past 200 years, the term has come to be used more broadly: it now refers to any disputatious argument or controversy in which someone makes an argument completely opposed to accepted beliefs. Someone trying to play "devil's advocate," then, might be considered to be making a polemical argument or engaging in polemics. In the qualitative–quantitative realm, since quantitative traditions have been the dominant ones so far, quantitative researchers often label qualitative researchers and their work "polemical"; the term is typically meant to have pejorative and demeaning connotations, since it implies that someone is adopting a position so outlandish that it couldn't possibly be true and so out to lunch that it scarcely deserves consideration.

But there's another way of looking at "poles," a more figurative use of the term that construes poles either as *opposites* or as *complementary parts* of the same whole. In the debate between Bonta and Gendreau (1990) and Roberts and Jackson (1991), each side seems to take an oppositional stance, arguing over which approach is "correct" and apparently assuming that only one side can claim that distinction. It might be more productive to see the two not as a set of mutually exclusive either/or options but as opposite sides of

the same coin: despite their differences, each perspective might have valid contributions to make to understanding some broader whole. Perhaps the opposite of a great truth is not a great falsity, but yet another great truth (e.g., see McGuire 1973).

Many would argue that commonalities do exist between qualitative and quantitative research and researchers. Certainly neither group would have a problem with the assertions that scientists are a community of scholars who systematically inquire into phenomena of interest and who believe that the products of such efforts should be made available in public forums for scrutiny by one's peers. Becker (1996) takes this idea one step further, suggesting that the similarities between the two types of research are even more significant than the differences since both groups are in search of the same thing: an understanding of how society works. Some differences in approach do exist: some social scientists are interested in the overall picture, in "the form of laws about whole classes of phenomena," whereas others are interested in the individual lines that make up the picture, in "how those general statements worked out in this case" (53).

Although Becker acknowledges some fundamental differences between qualitative and quantitative inquiry, he emphasizes the complementarity of the two approaches:

> The two styles also imply one another. Every analysis of a case rests, explicitly or implicitly, on some general laws, and every general law supposes that the investigation of particular cases would show that law at work. Despite the differing emphases, it all ends up with the same sort of understanding, doesn't it? (54)

Becker leaves us with a great question, and answering it is partly what the rest of this book aims to do. Our answer will be partly yes and partly no. Qualitative and quantitative study remain two distinct approaches to understanding and knowledge. Members of the two camps often don't even know how to talk to one another: they differ in the language they use to talk about research, the places they look in and find interesting, the questions they ask, the criteria by which they judge whether a piece of research is "done well," and even whether they consider certain work to be "research" at all. But one shouldn't be carried away by those differences. As Becker (1996) suggests,

> practitioners of qualitative and quantitative methods may seem to have different philosophies of science, but they really just work in different situations and ask different questions. The politics of social science can seduce us into magnifying the differences. But it needn't, and shouldn't. (65)

This book emphasizes that qualitative and quantitative researchers *are* pursuing similar overall objectives and may well have much to learn from and contribute to each other.

For example, although Bonta and Gendreau (1990) offer a fairly broad data set from more than a dozen different studies, we agree with Roberts and Jackson (1991) that the indicators Bonta and Gendreau use are incomplete: they don't incorporate the perspective of inmates. Indeed, we find it highly problematic that Bonta and Gendreau could feel they'd done a comprehensive job of understanding "the impacts of imprisonment" without taking those views into account. This does *not* mean that Bonta and Gendreau should now feel obliged to fall into what they perceive as the abyss of phenomenology. As quantitative researchers whose professional nutrition requires aggregated data and who revel in such criteria as statistically demonstrated reliability and validity of measurement, they'd probably prefer professional exile to engaging in the touchy-feely process of conducting open-ended interviews and recording oral histories. But they needn't do so in order to engage in a more comprehensive analysis. One can be informed by qualitative analysis without being required to subscribe to it.

Bonta and Gendreau could easily extend their indicators to include the sorts of dimensions pointed to by Roberts and Jackson, such as postrelease adjustment or social isolation, without abandoning

their quantitative approach. It's quite possible to create what they refer to as "objective" measures of those phenomena, as we'll see in Chapters 6, 7, and 8, and as their own article shows in using self-report data (e.g., about the impacts of crowding).

Incorporating those dimensions might require more extended follow-up than Bonta and Gendreau thus far have been prepared or able to exercise, but saying "that's not my department" turns a blind eye to the very milieu in which a whole set of the "effects of imprisonment" is most likely to be observed, that is, after release. Ignoring those factors without acknowledging the limitations of their data makes Bonta and Gendreau seem to be apologists for a social institution that would benefit from critique and reflection, showing that they are as "ideological" as the critics they accuse. In sum, Bonta and Gendreau and other quantitative researchers have every right, and considerable justification, to continue doing research in the manner they do. But they'd do even better research if they considered input from their qualitative colleagues about variables that might be addressed in a more comprehensive quantitative analysis.

Qualitative advocates like Roberts and Jackson are equally justified in continuing to explore the benefits of qualitative inquiry. But their research, too, would gain much if they heeded their quantitative colleagues. Qualitative inquiry's openness and flexibility make it ideally suited for in-depth case study analysis. After such studies, we may want to ask, "But how widespread is this problem?" or "Who (collectively or individually) is most likely to experience that situation?"—questions that quantitative research is particularly well suited to address. When quantitative researchers find that the nature of an effect "depends" on other personal or social variables, qualitative researchers might do well to use such results to help place their case study and its analysis in perspective.

If both groups of researchers viewed the others as collaborators rather than opponents, each engaging and shedding light on social phenomena in their own way, and showed tolerance for those who make other choices, all social sciences would benefit.

Nor is picking one approach and being "informed" by the other the only possible resolution. More and more researchers now acknowledge the benefits of incorporating both types of data into any piece of research (e.g., see Lowman & Fraser 1995; Menzies 1989; Palys, Boyanowsky, & Dutton 1984), thereby more fully exploiting the strengths and overcoming the limitations of each. This emerging perspective on understanding has come to be known as mixed methods research. While this perspective originated in the disciplines of psychology and sociology through the work of Campbell and Fiske (1959) and Denzin (1978) it has only recently become more widely acknowledged with the growing popularity of health and evaluation research (Tashakkori & Teddlie 2003). Today mixed methods designs are a common feature in both the social and behavioural sciences. The challenge that mixed methods advocates appear to have taken quite seriously is trying to explain *all* the data in a theoretically meaningful way, rather than simply ignoring some of them because of some quasi-religious empirical allegiance.

Polemics, Ideology, and Other Dirty Words

Of course, there are matters on which we suspect that the authors of the papers considered here will never agree. Gendreau,[12] for example, now retired from the University of New Brunswick, spent many years before that as an administrator/psychologist in Ontario's corrections system and has written extensively on evaluating therapeutic effectiveness. His paper with Bonta expresses the view that prisons, as part of the contemporary landscape, should be made as humane and effective as possible. Although the paper has the overall theme that prisons, crowding, and solitary confinement per se are not negative in their effects (at least within the confines of what was measured), it does *not* say that these variables are all non-problematic. The authors carefully note that the effects are not *necessarily* negative, but depend instead on a host of other variables, which prison administrators and therapeutic agents might do well to consider. Such a conclusion doesn't question the legitimacy of prisons or how

they're used; instead, it accepts prisons and offers suggestions for making them more helpful, or at least less negative, to those who are sent there. Gendreau and Bonta (1991) conclude with an invitation to "join with us in the prisons and generate the necessary data that will benefit offenders' lives" (564).

Jackson, in contrast, has been a long-term advocate of prisoners' rights and an outspoken critic of the prison as an overused response to crime. A practising lawyer, he has spent many days as an advocate in parole hearings and has argued cases (e.g., the Steele case discussed earlier) in the Supreme Court of Canada. Although he might acknowledge that evaluating the effects of imprisonment could be useful, depending on how such an analysis is conducted, he'd probably also assert that there are limits to what such analyses can reveal (even if they incorporate the views of prisoners), since not all the relevant questions are empirical.

For example, if one believes that prisons are inhumane because of their very structure, evaluating the effects of prison may be rather like trying to evaluate the effects of slavery. One can imagine an advocate of slavery in the pre–Civil War South doing a study like Bonta and Gendreau's and concluding that, because the data show that some slave owners are nice people who treat their slaves well, so that their chattel show no deleterious increases in blood pressure or decrements in psychological performance variables, the problem lies not in slavery as such but in how slaves are treated. Whether slavery is a reasonable institution or not is not an empirical issue but a reflection of a society's moral values.

There is indeed, then, an ideological component to the sort of research in which one engages. The choices you make, as revealed by the questions you ask, what you see as "interesting" to know, and what data you see as "relevant" to the task—and, conversely, by the questions you do *not* ask, what you do *not* find "interesting," and what you do *not* believe is "relevant"—will say a lot about you with respect to the non-empirical value issues that underlie any kind of social science or natural science research.[13]

Thus, we agree with Gendreau and Bonta (1991) when they refer to Roberts and Jackson's (1991) critique as "ideological," but we'd add that the same can be said of their own. Both pieces of research have implications for the future: both not only describe what is, but also have varying capacities to reinforce—or change—the structures that give rise to the phenomenon of interest. Bonta and Gendreau's (1990) research is clearly based on the assumption that the prison is okay, and their recommendations operate within that framework; Roberts and Jackson (1990) operate from the opposite assumption, that the prison is of limited appropriateness and is seriously overused, and hence are particularly critical of research that justifies the institution partly by denying the validity of all the data that Roberts and Jackson consider most important.

Bonta and Gendreau were not alone in accusing their critics of being ideological. Interestingly, it's typically those who operate within existing structures who believe their work is *not* ideological—they believe themselves to be "neutral" and "objective"—while those who are critical of those structures are considered "ideological." This brings us to another theme that will underlie this book: the links between power and knowledge, and the implications of that view for science and knowledge.

THE SOCIOLOGY OF SCIENCE

The last 20 or 30 years have been a period of considerable transition in the social sciences, fuelled largely by two concurrent trends: growing awareness of and dissatisfaction with the limits of positivist approaches; and the democratization of science and growth of other perspectives.

Dissatisfaction with Positivism

Although critics of positivist approaches have been around for many years, during the 1960s and 1970s a significant shift took place: positivists themselves began to express doubts about some of the most fundamental aspects of their approach. Manicas and Secord (1983), for example, cite *Psychology: A Study of a Science* (Koch 1959–63), a monumental six-volume work in which

one eminent psychologist after another, after many years—or even a lifetime of research—admitted to strong doubts about where they had been and what they had been achieved, and some suggested that our most basic assumptions about the nature of psychology as a science and a method had to be questioned. (399)

Not all positivists were so forthcoming, but the reflection and reconsideration were widespread enough that a "crisis of confidence" was acknowledged (e.g., see Elms 1975). A flurry of conferences, books, and articles tried to identify and address the perceived inadequacies (e.g., see Israel & Tajfel 1972; Palys 1978; Strickland, Aboud, & Gergen 1976). Although some have yet to acknowledge any limitations to positivist science (e.g., recall Bonta and Gendreau's positions cited earlier in this chapter), considerable transformation has occurred. A full understanding of methods in contemporary social science requires some sense of what that transformation—which is still very much in process—has entailed.

Kuhn's (1970) *Structure of Scientific Revolutions* (originally published in 1962) put the philosophy of science on the map for many researchers. Kuhn was particularly influential in describing the *social* aspects of science and affirming that to understand scientific knowledge, one must understand the social processes by which, and the social context in which, that knowledge is produced. Kuhn (1970) also introduced the word "paradigm" to the methodological vocabulary, sensitizing us to the idea that scientists' theories embody a worldview, and that observation, the cornerstone of scientific practice, is "theory-laden" rather than "theory-neutral" (as the positivists had maintained).[14] But, note Manicas and Secord (1983), this created something of a problem: "If there is no theory-neutral data base (foundationism) … what are the criteria of truth?" (401)

Now that's a *very* good question: *Is* there any single set of rules that we can declare to be *the* criteria for truth? Kuhn's 1970 book was an important departure from previous works in that it was less concerned with discussing how science *should* be or *ought* to be done and more concerned with describing how it *was* being done. Becker (1996) addresses this point when he distinguishes between philosophical and empirical disciplines and, correspondingly, between "epistemology" and the "sociology of science":

> Epistemology has been a … negative discipline, mostly devoted to saying what you shouldn't do if you want your activity to merit the title of science, and to keeping unworthy pretenders from successfully appropriating it. The sociology of science, the empirical descendant of epistemology, gives up trying to decide what should and shouldn't count as science, and tells what people who claim to be doing science do, how the term is fought over, and what people who win the right to use it can get away with. (54–55)

Research Decisions deals with both epistemology *and* the sociology of science. As we've already indicated, there has been and continues to be considerable diversity among researchers about the appropriateness of different perspectives on research. Our aim is not to identify the one true method or the one true perspective, but to encourage us to revel in the strength that arises from the continuing existence of theoretical and perspectival diversity.

The Democratization of Science

A significant element in the transformations we've been referring to has involved the membership of the academy. Until roughly the late 1950s and the early 1960s, university faculties were dominated by white males who traced their intellectual heritage to the ancient Greeks, and whose institutional structures began with the earliest universities in Italy, France, Poland, and England. The university was also an institution where existing reward structures (e.g., the big-money grants, which in turn affected who could publish the most and be promoted the fastest) pretty much revolved around status quo interests. But the protests that engulfed North American and Western European universities in the late 1960s and

early 1970s reflected a desire for change that was to influence universities and, hence, science.

Although much of the university-based protest in those years centred on U.S. involvement in the Vietnam War, protesters also questioned the universities' apparent complicity in that war (and others), charging that educational institutions served the interests of existing power structures (including the "military–industrial complex") to the disadvantage of other interests. The gaps in the wall of knowledge were not random, suggesting that knowledge developed in ways governed by more than simply the curiosity of independent researchers. Why did we know so much more about the effects of extended isolation (as used in prison and during torture) than about the causes and effects of poverty? Why were Native Studies courses always taught by non-Aboriginal anthropologists? Why were there no programs or even courses in such areas as African-American Studies or Women's Studies?

Blacks (through the civil rights and Black Power movements), Aboriginal peoples (through the American Indian movement), and women (through the feminist movement) argued that they deserved the same rights and opportunities available to white males and that their voices deserved to be heard. Nor were the universities monolithic: a growing conscientiousness within the institutions themselves led many faculty members and administrators to ask similar questions. The 1960s and 1970s thus saw the start of unprecedented democratization in the universities.

Those years also marked a constructionist boom in the social sciences. Before that, university faculties were relatively homogeneous. It was easy to know what "the standards" were and what "objectivity" meant: those who occupied the seats of power set the standards. But with growing heterogeneity, the consensus model (which positivist approaches pretty much take as a starting point) that had dominated the social sciences suddenly came in for intense scrutiny. Women, Blacks, Aboriginal peoples, and Third World academics did not see their experience being addressed or their worldviews considered in what passed for "scientific understanding." Allegedly "neutral" and "objective" science was now seen to be anything but. "Social facts" were now seen to be anything but. "Knowledge" came to be seen as constrained by the perspective of the research that had generated it. The constructed nature of science and knowledge became obvious when many new participants made clear that they would construct truth another way. Reality became negotiable.

Constructionism's Implications for Science

The implications of constructionist views of science are so far-reaching that it's beyond the scope of this book to consider them all. But let us say a bit about Michel Foucault, a provocative author who considered these implications.

Two aspects of Foucault's conceptual contributions are of interest to us here.[15] First, in the realm of day-to-day methods, Foucault posed probing challenges concerning the way we "manufacture" our understandings, and the non-neutral role of certain "standards" and general human tendencies in constraining what comes to be viewed as "knowledge." Second, Foucault commented on science as a social institution, noting that the way we investigate phenomena can either serve or challenge existing power structures.

Power–Knowledge

Fascinated by the concepts of knowledge and power in isolation, Foucault was also interested in how the two are related. He eventually came to speak always of **power–knowledge,** a term that reflects his belief that the two are inherently and intricately linked, with each embedded in the other. At one level, this view implies that those who have knowledge have power, while those who have power control the ability to gather and disseminate knowledge. But stopping at that level leads only to the conclusion that equality (and perhaps social justice) is reaffirmed when information is shared (see Pepinsky 1987), an important point, but there's more to this dual concept than that.

You may think of knowledge as the stuff you find in the library, read at your desk, or generate through research. But recognizing knowledge as a social product suggests that it also stands as a monument to those who produced it. Having power influences the choice of what is *important* or *relevant* to know and where *funding* priorities should lie, and allows one to define the terms in and through which knowledge will be constructed. Knowing *about* something or someone increases your power in that domain. Foucault therefore aimed to scrutinize the ways in which power is both exercised and exorcised, and encouraged us to do the same.

Foucault hoped to make us more aware of the ways in which knowledge has been and is produced, particularly with respect to the relations of power embedded in it. Here, we'll consider these issues in two ways. We'll look first at how social arrangements and patterns of social influence may shape, constrain, or encourage the types of research that go on in a society. Then we'll examine how the choices each of us makes, as an individual, can empower or oppress those we try to understand.

SOCIAL ARRANGEMENTS AND SOCIAL INFLUENCE
The question of "external influences" may seem easy to write off as a non-issue with respect to universities, which have traditionally guaranteed academic freedom. In theory, at least, university researchers can investigate whatever they want, whenever they want, however they want, as long as they don't violate the ethical standards of their discipline. But such a blithe dismissal ignores many realities of doing research: any kind of research requires funds for phones, fax machines, computers, photocopying, and possibly assistants, not to mention for attending conferences to share and discuss the results. There are also reward structures within all universities: certain capabilities—the ability to acquire grants or contracts, to provide a resource base that allows graduate students to do thesis-related research, and to show that one's work has acquired a national or international reputation—are vital for anyone hoping to get tenure, a promotion, and salary increases. Because of this pressure to

perform, researchers feel an associated pressure to frame their work in ways that fit available funding guidelines. Thus research is influenced in the sense that it often goes where the money is.

Universities themselves are subject to many of the same pressures, particularly in contemporary Canada, where fiscal concerns have provided federal and provincial governments with the justification for huge cutbacks in educational and research funding. Accompanying this has been an exhortation to universities and university researchers to seek "partnerships" with the private sector to make up for the evaporating pool of funding.

Among the first to see the advantages of a bourgeoning university–industry liaison were multinational pharmaceutical companies. For example, by the mid-1990s the University of British Columbia had entered into a deal with Merck Frosst, an international drug conglomerate: the university received $15 million and a new building for the pharmacy department in return for "first rights" to any patentable drugs developed at UBC.

Although one can understand how UBC researchers and students might be thrilled with a new building, a boom in funding, and state-of-the-art facilities, a host of perplexing issues arise. Has Merck Frosst essentially bought itself a university laboratory for a relatively small sum? Has the university committed itself to the drug development business? How will the agreement affect more basic research, the kind that doesn't always produce immediate financial gain? And can UBC still be considered "independent" when it comes to doing research, such as when UBC researchers conduct clinical trials to assess the effects of a drug in which their patron, Merck Frosst, has a vested interest?

Much of the credibility that has always been associated with university research arose from its relative independence from external influence. This was facilitated by the academy's zealous safeguarding of the principle of academic freedom and the provision (particularly in Canada) of "no strings attached" research funding by governments through major operating grants to universities, as well as through the major federal granting councils such as SSHRC

(the Social Sciences and Humanities Research Council). What would happen now if, in order to maintain the funding base and infrastructure that is required to do research, universities became "partners" with corporate interests whose commitment to curiosity and knowledge was tied to the desire to increase its bottom line for its shareholders? Some researchers warned of the negative possibilities this clash of cultures would produce:

> There are benefits to be gained through this courtship [between universities and business]. Nonetheless, I sincerely hope that the relationship remains platonic, since I would argue that science, and ultimately all of us, would be ill-served by a marriage. The inherent conflicts are several. Science flourishes through the open exchange of information; business covets secrecy in order to retain a competitive edge. In science, knowledge is a public resource; in business, one attempts to secure proprietary rights to knowledge through patents. Science seeks long-term goals and believes these are best served through freedom of inquiry; business seeks more immediate payoffs, emphasizing focussed objectives and centralized control in the interests of efficiency. Thus, although we have much to offer one another, I would prefer that we just remain friends. (Palys 1988: 157)

The mere existence of such relationships is not the problem—there are many people in every university whose curiosity and interests match those in the corporate community. The problem is how attendant decreases in funding alternatives may constrain those whose research interests lie somewhere else.

In the long run, a diversified strategy that includes tolerance for and appreciation of academe's curiosity-guided (and often esoteric) pursuit of knowledge will bring greater rewards than a myopic strategy in which business attempts to re-create the universities in its own image. (Palys 1988: 158)

SOCIAL RESPONSIBILITY Foucault's ideas encourage us to consider our role as producers of contemporary knowledge. This book outlines some of the logic, assumptions, and procedures involved in various methods current in the social sciences. None is "best." Each has its own advantages and disadvantages, slicing up reality with its own particular edge.

But the edge can slice in many ways; science isn't a dispassionate observer operating in a vacuum. Although the university community may revel in the institution's social role as the location of "state-of-the-art" insights and activity and as a place where esoteric pursuits produce profound but often not immediate payoffs, the research we do affects the way people understand things and influences the world. Stated bluntly, knowledge is *used*. Although most of us won't have the impact of Michel Foucault or Albert Einstein, the ripples of our research are felt nonetheless.

> Foucault [makes] explicit the view that knowledge and power are inherently related. A most depressing aspect of Foucault's work is the synonymy or similarity he sees between "knowledge" and "surveillance"—in that darker sense, knowledge is a tool which serves the interests of those who wield power, by allowing them to exert control over language, and understandings, and people … Foucault's analysis was primarily a study of power, in which he identifies the knowledge factory, which includes the universities, as one of the arenas in which power is manifest … Indeed, in his more substantive works … he shows us as much. As researchers and hence knowledge producers, we are reminded to always consider whose interests we serve when we design a piece of research, since we serve some no matter what we do. (Palys 1993: 3)

Most research occurs in some local agency, corporation, institution, or lab and involves a relationship with the people who inhabit those sites. One of the questions addressed frequently in this book involves whose constructions and understandings we incorporate into our analyses, since those choices will influence whose voices are heard in our conclusions and recommendations.

The title *Research Decisions* embodies the view that learning about research methodology is not simply a matter of learning how to make a questionnaire or develop an observational protocol. It means being able to see alternatives, choose among them, and appreciate that what you do will reveal something about you as well as about the phenomena you investigate. View your work as a piece of history, a nudge in the direction that "progress" will take in influencing what people might think. Cast your empirical vote for a liberating epistemology that, in encouraging tolerance and diversity, brings a wide range of voices to the table.

The Foundations of Knowledge Reconsidered

In some ways, these are tense times in academe. Yet we hope you'll join us in feeling that this is also an incredibly exciting time to be learning about research methods. As people go on doing research and making their unique contributions to knowledge, much of the discussion *about* research revolves around power and around who, if anyone, has the moral and academic authority to determine the criteria for truth. Some people wish these questions would disappear. And to some degree they do: it's "business as usual" whenever researchers stay in their own enclaves, talking only to like-minded people in an orgy of mutual reaffirmation.

But when researchers are willing to hear what's happening on the other side of the fence, issues of epistemology come to the fore. Becker (1996) likens the process to any encounter between two cultures, with each scholarly community having its own territory and its own criteria for acceptable research behaviour. Each is safe in its own community, where social scientists feel comfortable following the standards set by colleagues who share their epistemological position. But problems can arise when two or more communities come together, and questions arise about which community's criteria—whose language and what standards—will be used to determine the quality of research.

The interaction can be mutually respectful or asymmetric. Certainly the latter has more often been the case in the social sciences historically, where positivists have dominated the academy and required conformity to their standards in assessments of academic quality. But, as Becker (1996) describes it, the use of positivist criteria as an academic yardstick is more a statement of power than of logic. Rather like the stereotypical American tourist who goes to Jakarta and is incensed when few people can speak English, having one epistemological group impose its standards on another is little more than the academic equivalent of cultural imperialism.

But much has changed in the academy. The democratization of the university has broadened the array of voices discussing how research is done, the relations between researcher and researched, and the understandings research embodies. And yet, at the same time, a growing tendency to a more "corporate" approach has seen the rise of more centralized decision-making structures in the university, which opens the door to competition between disciplines, research approaches, and visions of the university, and for dominant approaches to set the rules in their own image. These issues arise throughout this book, but without resolution, since all remain contentious. Whether this dialogue results in the triumph of one perspective, the emergence of some consensus built on multi-perspectival input, or a science that accepts the complexity of a multi-cultural, multi-perspectival, multi-epistemological reality remains to be seen. With process at least as important as product, the point to be noted is simply that the dialogue has been engaged. There's a long way to go before there is full joint ownership of the house, but at least the guest list is longer and there are more seats at the table. That shift alone is a heartening sign.

SUMMING UP AND LOOKING AHEAD

This chapter introduces the qualitative–quantitative dichotomy that underlies this book. If you haven't taken a course in research methods before, you might feel slightly overwhelmed by now. But fear not; these themes will crop up on several occasions

in the rest of the book, giving you lots of chances to review and understand them. From your first reading, you need only understand that social scientists generally adopt one of two approaches and that each approach investigates human social life in very different ways.

Quantitative researchers embrace a perspective known as positivism, borrowing from the natural sciences a realist epistemology or way of knowing, and arguing that human beings can be scrutinized in the manner of any living organism because they are subject to and shaped by the same laws of nature. This viewpoint prefers observable variables—concrete expressions of variables that meet predefined standards of reliability and validity. Quantitative researchers favour social facts—mega-variables whose monolithic impact is felt by all of us—as independent variables, measuring their effects through rate data, where aggregate tendencies are believed to give true indications of social effects unaffected by the idiosyncrasies of any single case. Emphasis is placed on being aloof and dispassionate in the interests of "objective" analysis. The hypothetico-deductive method is the foundation of this tradition: researchers specify a theory, deduce a hypothesis, and then gather data to test the hypothesis and, hence, also the theory. The trick, says the positivist, is to be inventive in our theorizing, to look for general principles or laws that guide and shape human action. "Good" theory is thought to be simple, to be capable of being expressed in precise mathematical form, and to accurately reflect the relationship between causes and outcomes.

Qualitative researchers argue that people's perceptions should be the focus of analysis: "Perceptions are real because they are real in their consequences" (Thomas 1928). We must understand those perceptions if we want to understand human behaviour: what people *think* about the world influences how they *act* in it. Acknowledging that people *construct* reality implies that there are actually many "realities" and possible realities that exist, and that we negotiate on an ongoing basis. "Understanding" or *Verstehen* involves being able to explain unique behaviour in context, after investigating the ways in which reality is constructed and negotiated. One must get close to the people one studies in order to understand them. "Good" theory is not imposed; rather, it emerges from direct observation and contact with people in context.

This notion of "multiple realities" or "negotiating reality" may sound strange or obvious to you. But every day's news reports present evidence of its accuracy. At a meeting involving the First Ministers (of Canada and the provinces) and the National Chief of the Assembly of First Nations, for example, each brings a very different set of "understandings" to the table regarding Canada's history, what today's "problems" are, and how a satisfactory future would look. Overtly, they may be negotiating policy, but they spend much of their time sharing, critiquing, sometimes denying, and certainly trying to persuade others of what "reality" is and how the future should be encountered.

We hope this chapter has begun to show you the role social science can play in such "reality negotiation." At one level, social science research can shed light on certain issues by gathering data on any "factual" matters involved in some of these debates. *Are* women typically paid less than men for similar work? *Are* Aboriginal peoples over-represented in prisons? *Can* psychiatrists predict future dangerous behaviour any better than chance or better than their secretaries can? As the rest of this book shows, providing answers to such questions may be less simple than initially appears. Still, there *are* data that bear on these issues, and we've designed this book to help you understand the research decisions that must be made along the way to designing research that effectively gathers and analyzes those data.

There is yet another level in which these issues reside, a level this chapter introduces. When we recognize science itself as a human activity and knowledge as a social and cultural product that inevitably embodies certain "understandings" of the world and the way it operates, we may begin to see how science has been used to justify oppression. Ted has observed exactly that in one of his research areas: histories of relations between European nation-states and indigenous nations in North America

and elsewhere. Many injustices and travesties perpetrated on indigenous peoples in the 19th century (the residues of which are still being felt today) were clearly fuelled by Darwin's scientific theories. Colonizing nations defined themselves as culturally more "evolved" than those they colonized. They used the science of the day to justify horrendous behaviour that "civilized" people could engage in only by rationalizing that they were dealing with "inferior" or "subhuman" species. That they could perpetrate such injustices with such a sense of mission, self-righteousness, and even zeal underscores the power of "understandings" and "knowledge" to both shape and justify behaviour.

"Science" has similarly been used to justify the goals of the Nazis and their treatment of Jews during the Holocaust; the subjugation of women by men, at least in patriarchal cultures; and the "legitimacy" of the kidnapping and enslavement of Blacks from Africa. Fortunately, science has also been used to expose inequity and rectify imbalances. "Now" is the history of the future, and among the concepts we hope you'll glean from this book is the idea that you must consciously decide what role you'll play. Publishing a piece of research puts you in the archives of history; make sure you and your descendants will be proud of your small place.

Finally, this chapter outlines some of the debates that occur within science, where, like everywhere else, reality is always being negotiated. The public interchange between Bonta and Gendreau (1990) and Roberts and Jackson (1991) illustrates how quantitative and qualitative researchers bring different perspectives to understanding the same phenomenon.

Science is changing, as it has been doing for hundreds, if not thousands, of years, and so are its products (knowledge). Many quantitative researchers now incorporate qualitative elements into their research strategies, and many qualitative researchers now realize that numbers aren't inherently sinful. As science slowly democratizes, with progressively greater representation from women, Aboriginal peoples, Third World academics, and others, new voices are heard, and the effects of arguing with data, in a public forum, become evident. This book is offered in a spirit of tolerance and rapprochement: by understanding the differences between competing perspectives, we can also, we believe, come to understand what we share and how we can benefit from one another's experiences.

STUDY QUESTIONS

1. Morgan (1983a) uses the concept of *engagement* to describe what we do in research. What does he mean by that term, and what implications does it hold for the way we conceive of knowledge?
2. Consider the dimensions of difference between the qualitative and quantitative approaches shown in Table 1.1; explain in your own words what each dimension entails.
3. Outline the differences between realism and constructionism as ways of perceiving the world. Give an example of how a person's perspective on this issue might be evident in research.
4. Outline the difference between positivism and phenomenologism.
5. Why do orthodox positivists argue that humans can and should be studied in the same manner one might use to understand the structure and behaviour of pigeons and plants?
6. What are "social facts," and what role do they play in positivist inquiry?
7. Compare and contrast the approaches that might be taken by a realist and a constructionist if each set out to study the effects associated with being a child of divorce.
8. In your school's library, locate complete versions of Bonta and Gendreau (1990), Roberts and Jackson (1991), and Gendreau and Bonta (1991). Review the original research and both sets of authors' complete arguments, considering the extent to which they illustrate the dimensions listed in Table 1.1. Are any aspects of their positions not listed in that table?

9. Why does Michel Foucault treat power and knowledge as power–knowledge, a single construct?
10. What does it mean to say that a piece of research is "ideological"? Is *all* research "ideological"?
11. How does Becker (1996) distinguish between *epistemology* and the *sociology of science?* What difference does this distinction make in how one looks at research?
12. Set up a discussion group or debate about how closely universities and businesses should be related, how closely universities and governments should be related, or simply how autonomous or dependent universities should be in relation to other interests in society.

NOTES

1. The issue is whether the qualitative–quantitative dichotomy is "real" or "constructed." A "real" dichotomy might be something like male versus female or whether a certain Quebecker voted yes or no in the most recent sovereignty referendum. In both cases, a person falls into one category or the other, period. In contrast, a "constructed" dichotomy is created for convenience. Categorizing people as tall versus short represents a reasonable distinction to make, since some people are clearly tall and others are clearly short. Such a distinction may even be useful if you're trying to understand someone's likelihood of becoming a jockey, a ballet dancer, or a model. But people actually exist on a continuum of height, with no clear boundary between tall and short; most people would be hard to classify as either one or the other.
2. The term "go native" has a longer history, having originally appeared in anthropology, where it referred to the way anthropologists who study indigenous peoples sometimes—after extensive contact with those peoples—

leave their "more appropriate" scientific values behind and take on the perspective of those they're studying. This term's implicit **othering** of indigenous peoples is considered offensive by many, so we use "overidentify" to communicate the same idea.

3. This quote is particularly telling. Its realist tone suggests that there is *a* (i.e., one) truth and that such truths are the exclusive domain of social scientists, who shouldn't be "misled" by what their subjects think about themselves. To that extent it is elitist, an apparent example of empirical imperialism. Further, describing indigenous cultures as "preliterate" betrays the author's subscription to the 19th-century view that all societies should be measured by the extent to which they incorporate European ideals. Both ideas are associated with classic positivist thought; the statement's 1986 date suggests that we're not as removed from such antiquated views as some have suggested or hoped.

4. *Idiographic* analysis refers to analysis within the individual case, while *nomothetic* analysis involves analyzing aggregate units. A clinical case study would be an example of idiographic analysis. While the analysis might interest those involved, some might want to know whether the processes observed are relevant or generalizable beyond the individual case. In contrast, a study that looks at the relationship between two variables (e.g., a personality attribute and some social behaviour) across a sample of persons is an example of nomothetic analysis. Most social science research, being nomothetic, leaves open a different question: Can aggregate trends help us understand individual cases? Historically, most researchers have adopted one strategy or the other. Few have attempted to bridge the two levels of analysis; for examples of some who have tried, see Kelly (1955) and Palys and Little (1983).

5. Readers in sociology will no doubt recognize these variables as some of the favourites of soci-

ologists, particularly demographers, namely, variables like race, class, education, and income.

6. The exact source of this shift isn't really clear to us; it may rest at least partly on the growing realization, after a century of positivist purity, that it's very difficult to explain the behaviour of humans using only those terms that could also be used to describe the behaviour of cats and tree toads. What's more, those the early positivists most wanted to emulate—physicists and other "real" scientists—have begun resorting to many concepts (e.g., quarks and black holes) that aren't directly observable but are merely inferred to help explain phenomena that would otherwise be impossible, given the current state of our understanding.

7. Our view of this controversy is that while having had certain life experiences may give researchers special insights, and while we should all be aware of the limitations imposed by our experience, there should be no predefined limits on what topics are "appropriate" for any given person to study.

8. The deletions here represent citations to numerous articles and books that report research in the respective areas noted. Because these citations are secondary to our point and make the quote harder to read, we've edited them out. Readers are invited to pursue the original source for references in areas that interest them.

9. We say "best reflected" here because even realists acknowledge that crime rate data imperfectly represent the amount of crime that exists. For realists, though, such data's imperfections represent a primarily technological challenge. To create "better" data, realists maintain, we need only enhance the reliability and validity of data collection procedures, as well as find some way of better estimating that "dark figure" of crime (i.e., how much crime goes unreported and hence never shows up in criminal justice statistics). In contrast, those

with a more constructionist bent question the very notions of "crime" and "criminality," arguing that the issue is less *how* to count than *what* is being counted. See Brantingham (1991), Brantingham and Brantingham (1984), Lowman and Palys (1991), and Chapter 8 of this text for further consideration of these issues.

10. You might find this an instructive lesson for how to write your own papers: first show that an issue is contentious, setting up your paper as an effort to resolve the dispute. Such a format helps make your paper interesting from a social science point of view.

11. The Minnesota Multiphasic Personality Inventory, or MMPI, is an "objective" psychometric test that requires the person being tested to respond "true" or "false" to 555 standardized statements. Responses are then scored by comparing a person's pattern of responses to norms generated from testing thousands of other participants.

12. We will refer mostly to Gendreau and Jackson in this section, since they're the two we know best, Ted having known them personally and being more familiar with their other writings.

We intend no slight to either Bonta or Roberts.

13. We include the natural sciences intentionally here; too many people seem ready to believe that such matters are relevant only to the social sciences. Physicists certainly believed this to be the case until they watched the fruits of their labour being used to blow up Hiroshima and Nagasaki and influence global politics ever since; so did biologists until their interest in genetics came to be associated with racist manipulation, and chemists until their research began to be used for purposes of warfare (e.g., see Lewontin 1991).

14. Later scientific case studies reaffirmed the point. Anthropologist Stephen Jay Gould (e.g., 1978; 1981), for example, shows how indices of measurement reflect and reaffirm broader cultural assumptions and hierarchies of power, while similar arguments have been made in psychology (e.g., see McReynolds 1975) and sociology (e.g., see Giddens 1979).

15. Detailed examinations of Foucault can be found in, for example, Burchell, Gordon, and Miller (1991); Cousins and Hussain (1984); Eribon (1991); Gordon (1980); and Gutting (1989).

CHAPTER 2

GETTING STARTED

The fact that you're reading this book suggests that you have some interest in the social sciences. You may even have articulated more specific interests for yourself, for example, studying juvenile delinquency, organizational dynamics, the socialization process, or prejudice and racism. Still, as you'll learn in this text, that's only the beginning. Doing research involves translating those general interests into specific researchable questions and then designing concrete research procedures that address those questions so that you can ultimately go out and conduct research of your own. Indeed, one of the first truisms you learn about research is that it is not an activity you can do in the abstract—"doing research" ultimately involves gathering very specific information from specific samples of people or files or other objects in particular places at a particular time.

Unless you are an experienced researcher who already has a research program underway, in most cases putting together a proposal will involve an **iterative** process in which you start with a broader and more amorphous topic and set of interests, which you then take through successive iterations of getting more and more specific until you reach a final proposal that constitutes your departure point for actually undertaking the research. Our objective in this and the next two chapters is to take you from the point of having a vague idea of a topic on which you might like to do research, to the point of being able to outline a general proposal for a plan of action to start addressing the even more specific design and procedural issues that we discuss in the chapters following that. In the current chapter, we will (a) outline where research ideas come from, (b) consider how the different research objectives you might have

will influence your research design, (c) discuss the importance of connecting with the literature, and (d) give a first glimpse at some of the options you have for operationalizing variables of interest to you.

SOURCES OF RESEARCH IDEAS

Three Models of Science

In logic, a distinction has traditionally been made between two different processes of reasoning: **deductive** and **inductive** processes. *Deductive* logic involves reasoning from the general to the particular; that is, one begins with broad theoretical generalizations and tests their ability to deal with specific instances of phenomena. This approach involves (1) developing theories about a phenomenon, (2) expressing hypotheses (predictions) based on these theories, (3) creating or observing instances of the phenomenon to see whether things happen as the theory predicts they should, and then (4) looking for new situations in which to test or expand the theory if it succeeds, or revising the theory or even abandoning it entirely if its predictions are not supported. As you know from Chapter 1, the deductive model of science has been preferred by quantitative researchers.

In contrast, *inductive* reasoning begins with specifics and uses these to generate general principles. You *start* by observing, in other words, and then move from observation to theory rather than the other way around. This tends to be the approach of choice for qualitative researchers, who believe that theory should not be imposed from above but, rather, should emerge from or be grounded in the context of everyday life (e.g., see Glaser & Strauss 1967; Strauss & Corbin 1997).

Although at one time there was scathing debate between practitioners of the respective approaches (e.g., see McKinlay & Potter 1987) as to which was "right" or truly worthy of the title "science," more recently there has been recognition of their inherent complementarity. One of the first to make that point was Wallace (1971), who asserted that inductive and deductive approaches are not in either/or opposition, but rather are better seen as opposite sides of the same coin. *Wallace's wheel* (see Figure 2.1) shows an essentially circular (or iterative), and hence infinite, process that encompasses *both* deductive *and* inductive methods.

Wallace's (1971) "wheel of science" offers an important representation of the scientific process. It acknowledges the different leanings of individual researchers, but also shows their commonalities. Whether they emphasize deduction or induction, all scientists are involved in an ongoing dialectic relationship involving both *theory* and *data*, that is, processes that involve the formulation of abstract principles *and* the requirement that one's speculations and theories be subjected to some form of empirical test or validation.

The elegance of Wallace's wheel is that it shows very simply how the question "Which comes first?"

Figure 2.1

Wallace's "Wheel of Science"

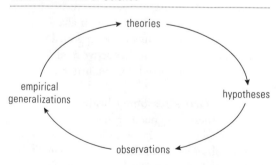

Source: W. Wallace (1971), *The Logic of Science in Sociology* (Hawthorne, NY: Aldine Atherton). Reprinted with permission.

is actually quite trivial; deciding where to "start counting" in an ongoing process is relatively arbitrary. Can we ever start with "pure theory," completely devoid of any informal knowledge gained from our earlier observation and experience? Probably not. Can we ever start with "pure data," completely devoid of any prior theoretical organization related to our own naive or "commonsensical" beliefs (as human beings) about how the world works? Probably not.

Deductive Sources of Research Ideas

Returning now to the question of where research ideas come from, the deductive–inductive distinction suggests a number of alternatives.

THEORY AS A SOURCE OF RESEARCH IDEAS

From the deductive orientation, we see the important role that **theory** can play in guiding and generating research. A theory is essentially a set of *concepts* and a delineation of their *interrelationships* that, taken together, purport to explain a phenomenon or set of phenomena. One function of theory is to help make sense of the world or of a particular class of phenomena. In doing so, theories also guide research, which makes them both powerful and constraining.

Perhaps an example will help here. Suppose we're interested in explaining why some people suddenly become "criminals." An infinite number of variables could potentially "explain" criminality—everything from people's shoe sizes to their nutrition to their family background, their hormonal levels, and/or their social context.

A theorist takes a particular subset of these variables and tries to offer a convincing explanation of why and how they combine to generate "criminality." These speculations, made public, give theorists and others a research direction to pursue by offering propositions that can be tested. Lombroso (1911), for example, theorized that some people are, in essence, "born criminals" who differ in systematic physiological ways from non-criminals.[1] Once articulated, Lombroso's theory led him and others to test the notions implied by the theory or its variants. Once created, the theory itself helps direct research (through its implications). Not surprisingly, in Lombroso's case this involved taking all sorts of measurements of the bodies of imprisoned criminals and others in order to identify those physiological characteristics that might distinguish the two.

But theories have a downside as well insofar as they impose a virtual set of blinders on how you view the world. Because Lombroso's theory focused on physiological differences between criminals and noncriminals, he spent all his time measuring criminals and completely ignored such phenomena as social factors that might cause some behaviours to be called "criminal" while others are not, or labelling processes and environmental factors that other theorists have seized upon to try to explain "criminality."

As this suggests, an important dimension on which theories vary is in their prospective *comprehensiveness*. Lombroso's theory was narrow, since it focused "only" on criminality and remained at a physiological level of explanation. In contrast, Eysenck's (e.g., 1953) theory of personality is often given as an example of a "broad" or "general" theory, since it attempted to offer an integrated explanation of everything from physiological differences through individual and social behaviour to cultural differences.

In sum, "good" theories are useful devices because they help coordinate research by *providing a research focus* and by *implying hypotheses* that can be tested empirically. Their weakness is that they may blind you to other variables or other perspectives that are beyond the scope of the theory.

APPLYING THEORY TO SITUATIONS

Many research ideas emerge from theory. If a theory states that some set of events *should* go together, you can test the theory by thinking of a specific situation in which the theory should be able to predict or account for what occurs. For example, a once-popular attitude theory known as dissonance theory (see Festinger 1957) suggested that people will feel differently about things after they have committed themselves to a course of action than before. Knox and Inkster (1968) decided to test that theoretical proposition at their local racetrack. They approached two groups of bettors—some who were in the lineup waiting to place their bets, and others who had just finished placing their bets. Sure enough, those who were asked *after* they had placed their bet how confident they felt about their wager expressed significantly greater certainty about whether their horse would win than those who had not yet made it to the betting window, even though the difference between the two situations was less than a minute.

EXTENDING OR LIMITING A THEORY'S COVERAGE

Another procedure for generating research ideas is to try to *extend the coverage* of an existing theory. One person might have posited a theory that explains a certain social dynamic within business organizations. You'd be making a significant contribution by showing that the same theoretical principles also apply to family dynamics. Conversely, you'd also be making a contribution if you were to *point out limitations* to the applicability of existing theories. Theories of aggression, for example, have typically been developed to account for aggression toward minority groups and/or sources of frustration. But do these theories also account for violent behaviour toward intimates, such as child abuse by parents or wife assault by husbands?

OFFERING ALTERNATIVE EXPLANATIONS

Yet another source of research ideas involves trying to formulate *alternative explanations* for a given phenomenon. Early criminological theories (e.g., Lombroso 1911) saw those who went through the justice system as "criminals" and tried to ascertain the ways in which "criminals" differed from the rest of us. But later theorists (e.g., see Rubington & Weinberg 1968) demonstrated that many, if not most, of us have indulged in "criminal" behaviour at various points in our lives. This finding shifted the major focus of interest from what we do to the process by which a person or action is labelled "criminal"; that is, what are the social processes by which deviant labels are conferred, and what do such processes imply for future criminality? D. G. Wagner (1984) refers to this process of theory development as *variation* and offers numerous other examples of theorists building on one another's work by offering competing explanatory mechanisms for similar phenomena.

All the above suggestions reaffirm the statement that one role of theory in science is to generate research possibilities; if a theory doesn't suggest research possibilities, it's not a very good theory. Perhaps even more importantly, in order to be considered "scientific," a theory must be capable of being disproved. If there are no data that can possibly lead us to say, "Oh, I guess we were wrong," then we are not talking about theory or science, but about faith.

Note also that theories are an integral starting point for the deductive approach to science. But what about inductive approaches? How might research ideas be derived using them? Inductivists place no less emphasis on theory than deductivists, but they disagree over whether theory should *guide* or *emerge from* the research process. Recall that, for deductivists, one *begins* with theory, and then "good" theory suggests or implies what to research. In contrast, inductivists argue that such theory is unlikely to be profound and may represent little more than a premature imposition of theoretical blinders that says more about the theoretician than about the phenomenon under consideration. They suggest that ideas and theories should emerge from interacting with and observing the phenomenon itself. Listed below are some ways in which this might occur.

INDUCTIVE SOURCES OF RESEARCH IDEAS

Starting from Where You Are

From within qualitative perspectives, the inductive (grounded) approach to data gathering and theorizing is encouraged, and "intimate knowledge" of the phenomenon under consideration is not considered a sin. Accordingly, while quantitative researchers might be worried if you are "too close" to a phenomenon of interest because of the propensity to "over-identify" and the concern that you might be unable to remain "appropriately" detached and analytical, qualitative researchers recognize that those who have undergone particular life experiences may bring special insights to their research because of having experienced a phenomenon from the "inside."

Lofland and colleagues (2006), for example, suggest that one way to begin research is to "start from where you are"; that is, to begin with your own life situation and the concerns and issues that arise therefrom. Dozens of examples could be cited of researchers who did exactly that:

> For example, Gary Alan Fine's *Gifted Tongues* (2001), a study of high school debate and adolescent culture, was connected to his son Todd's distinguished career as a high school debater. In a similar vein, John Irwin's interest in *The Felon* (1970), in *Prisons in Turmoil* (1980), and in *The Jail* (1985) was intimately related to his own felony conviction at the age of 21 and the five years he spent in a California state prison. And Mary Romero's study of domestic workers (*Maid in the U.S.A.* 1992) may be said to have had its origins in the fact that as a teenager she had worked as a domestic, as had her mother, sister, relatives, and neighbors. (10)

Several advantages accrue from starting from where you are. The assets you bring to such a project include: (1) an interest in the research topic, because of its meaningfulness to you, that will help sustain you through the persistence of effort required to actually complete a piece of research; (2) insights into those aspects of the phenomenon with which you are familiar; and probably (3) knowledge of at least some others who are in the same position as you, which may help provide access to needed research sites and to an initial sample of people you can approach regarding their experiences.

At the same time, there are also some potential potholes in this road that need to be avoided. Making part of your life a research site may, depending on the nature of the research, be an overwhelmingly emotional experience. A student in one of our classes, for example, started a project on incest survivors because of her own experiences in that domain. Ultimately, it became clear that she hadn't yet really come to grips with the experience herself, and interviewing others brought back too much of the pain she'd experienced in her own life. The project was put on hold until the timing was right for her.

Starting from where you are also can be problematic because of role conflicts that can emerge from making part of your life a research site. Suppose you're employed as a nurse, for example, and want to do a study regarding doctor–nurse relationships. Information derived from interviews with doctors and nurses in the ward where you work might be problematic when and if your role as a researcher is pitted against your ongoing role as nurse. For example, as a researcher you may end up asking questions related to your research that you otherwise might not ask of your colleagues, leading you to hear about things you otherwise might not hear. Some of this information may involve conflicting standards—for example, as a researcher you are normally expected to keep the source of everything you hear confidential; as a nurse, there may be reporting requirements associated with your role in which you are supposed to report certain categories of behaviour to your union, hospital officials, or supervisor. Even if you *are* able to compartmentalize your role for the duration of the study—something you are ethically obliged to do to ensure your primary interests are those of the research participants—once the study is completed, you go back to your former role. But you now have information you might not otherwise have obtained about certain people, information you can't simply "forget."

A third potential problem can arise from being so embedded in a situation that you are unable to rise above it. The trick in starting from where you are is to use the insights to be gained from your own experience, but then to activate the "sociological imagination" (as C. W. Mills [1959] termed it) and be able to see yourself as one instance of many, thereby helping to contextualize your own experience. This is sometimes easier said than done: as Marshall McLuhan is reputed to have said, "The last person to

ask how the water is is a fish" (see Hagan 1989: 157). It's sometimes very difficult to see what's "interesting" about our lives, in the social science sense, when we are too wrapped up in experiencing them.

OBSERVATION AS A SOURCE OF IDEAS

As one might expect, research ideas within the inductive framework emerge through observation coupled with the natural curiosity of the social scientist who inevitably asks Why? or How? You might begin with a particular phenomenon that interests you (e.g., unemployment, criminality, depression, people buying membership in fitness centres, the surge of interest in "designer" dogs) and then try to suggest and test out factors that might influence it. Where does it come from? Who does it? Is there more of it in the summer than the winter? Are the patterns the same or different in Canada and Australia?

It was observation of this sort coupled with asking Why? that led Emile Durkheim to formulate his classic work (1951) on suicide. He began by observing that countries differ in their predominant religious affiliation, and that they also tend to differ in their suicide rates. This observed covariation ultimately led him to formulate his ideas that suicide is affected by both social regulation (norms) and social integration and group solidarity.

Although more modest in aspiration, the first piece of formal research Ted ever conducted was generated via a similar process. He was walking down a street and saw a movie marquee advertising a somewhat racy (for the time) Swedish movie entitled *I Am Curious Yellow*. But instead of the usual notations one sees on marquees, in which some obscure critic is quoted as saying that the film is "one of the year's ten best," this marquee said only that the movie had been "banned in Alberta." It made Ted wonder about movie classification and censorship, particularly whether the mere act of banning a movie or classifying it might (ironically) *enhance* interest. Thanks to an encouraging professor, Bob Altemeyer, the result was a field experiment (Palys 1971) in which he advertised a movie called *Prostitution in Denmark* in almost exactly the same way to various groups of people. Each group was given the same general description of the film. The only difference between the groups came near the end of the advertisement, when some of them were told that the film had been rated "G" (General, i.e., persons of any age admitted) by the Provincial Film Classification Board, but told others that it had been rated "Adult" (i.e., one must be an adult or accompanied by one) or "Restricted Adult" (i.e., only those over 18 admitted).[2]

INTENSIVE CASE STUDIES AND EXPERIENCE SURVEYS

Systematic observation in the context of *intensive case studies* is another useful source of research ideas, still within the inductive framework. Many of Jean Piaget's theories on child development emerged from observing his own children, for example, while many of Sigmund Freud's came from his discussions with clients. Similarly, if you're new to an area of research, an *oral history* or broader *experience survey* may suggest research ideas. If you want to study prejudice and discrimination toward minority groups, for example, you could talk to a Japanese person who lived in the internment camps in British Columbia or California during World War II, a Jew who lived in Germany at the same time, to Muslim women in North America who choose to wear the hijab, or a Maori in New Zealand. Be careful, though, not to let this process steer you away from a review of the relevant literature. Also don't assume that the first person you talk to is necessarily representative of his or her group. When doing this sort of exploratory research, talk to and observe as diverse an array of people and situations as possible.

Research Itself as Heuristic Process

RESEARCH ITSELF AS A HEURISTIC PROCESS

Other Research as a Source of Ideas

A third general category of sources of research ideas is the actual process of doing and reading about research. Researchers often conclude their papers with *suggestions for further research*. Why not take them up on it?

REPLICATION

Replication of prior research also can serve a useful function. Although most professional journals aren't interested in publishing a straight replication for its own sake, situations may arise where the replication provides interesting information. For example, many older studies that looked at sex differences might be interesting to replicate now that sex roles in our society have supposedly undergone a major transition over the last few decades. Similarly, American or European studies might be replicated by a Canadian if one had reason to posit that a comparison with the Canadian social context might yield different results.

WHEN NEW TECHNOLOGIES OPEN DOORS

A special occasion arises when new technologies open doors that previously were closed and thereby provide new opportunities for replicating earlier research with newly accessible samples, or moving into areas that were previously inaccessible. The Internet and the wide array of computer technologies that surround it is an example of exactly that as these technologies have brought together communities of persons, particularly through blogs, podcasts, newsgroups, instant messaging, and chat groups, who otherwise would be very difficult to locate in any significant numbers. Chris does research involving the sex trade, for example; in this field much research has been done on sex trade workers, but very little had been done regarding their clients because of difficulties in locating and contacting them. With the opportunities afforded by the Internet, however (e.g., see Atchison 1999; see also Chapter 6), Chris ended up conducting one of the first large-scale studies of sex worker clients when more than 500 clients responded to his solicitations to participate in an anonymous Internet-based survey of persons who had paid for sex (see Atchison 1998; Atchison, Lowman, and Fraser 1998). As new technology develops and becomes more integrated into our daily lives there is no end to the new research possibilities that will arise for members of the social science community to pursue.

CHALLENGING PRIOR RESEARCH

One might also generate new research by *challenging prior research*. Sherif (1935), for example, performed a number of studies that showed most people would conform to the judgments of others. Solomon Asch (1958) didn't dispute Sherif's results, but speculated that Sherif had overestimated the degree to which we conform to others because of his use of highly ambiguous stimuli. Positing that less ambiguity would lead to less conformity, he went on to demonstrate that this was indeed the case.

CLARIFYING UNDERLYING PROCESSES

Clarifying underlying processes is another useful research contribution. Many treatment variables or therapeutic interventions are actually packages of variables, and you may want to determine *which* aspects of the variable actually produced the effect. One researcher might find, for example, that a particular group-therapy program led to some positive social outcome for the participants. But what specifically about the program led to that success? Was it the individualized attention? The opportunity to practise new skills? A change in self-concept? The presence of social support? An overall finding that a new therapy is effective could be followed by research that attempts to analyze the processes involved in an ongoing process of program development.

Other Sources of Research Ideas

RESOLVING CONFLICTING RESULTS

Occasionally the literature contains conflicting results, and you may want to do research that attempts to *resolve the conflict*. In the early years of racial desegregation following World War II, for example, researchers and policy-makers in the United States began wondering whether extensive contact between races would lead members of those races (Blacks and whites, in this instance) to have more positive, or more negative, attitudes about each

other. Some studies found that attitudes became more positive with greater interracial contact, while others found that they became more negative. A famous set of studies by Deutsch and Collins (1951) tried to resolve these conflicting findings by investigating and delineating the conditions under which attitudes would become more positive and those under which they would become more negative.

ANALOGY

Research may also be generated on the basis of *analogy* to other domains. William McGuire (1973), for example, took the immunization model from biology and tried to apply it to the realm of attitude change. In biology, organisms are immunized against various diseases by giving them vaccines that actually contain weak strains of the disease. McGuire found that people who were first "immunized" by hearing samples of arguments that might be used against their own position were much less likely to change their attitudes than were those who had not been "immunized" when both were exposed to arguments in opposition to their own opinion.

SURPRISES: ANOMALY AND SERENDIPITY

The terms *anomaly* and *serendipity* refer to research that begins or is redirected because an unexpected and surprising state of affairs arises. **Anomalies** are situations that should *not* exist according to the theory that's guiding the research. An anomaly is "a fact that doesn't fit" and hence requires explanation for the deviation.

Kuhn (1970) argues that anomaly is a significant contributor to scientific discovery, although a state of affairs must first be *recognized* as an anomaly before the real process of discovery begins. He provides several examples of anomaly in the natural sciences, but also notes a number of instances where the same state of affairs clearly existed prior to someone's "discovery" of the anomaly. Yet the anomalous situation had been ignored, rationalized away, or otherwise not appreciated by the earlier researchers.

Similar to anomaly is **serendipity.** While anomaly refers to unearthing disconfirming evidence in the process of an ongoing inquiry, serendipity refers to unexpected findings that are virtually stumbled upon while looking for something else (e.g., the prospector who digs for gold and strikes oil). Once again, Kuhn (1970) notes that recognition of the event precedes "discovery" and that the history of science is replete with examples of individuals who ignored outcomes or considered them a mistake instead of taking the inferential leap required for discovery. The theme is reaffirmed in Barber and Fox's (1958) "case of the floppy-eared rabbits," where the authors compare two researchers who witnessed the same serendipitous phenomenon: one realizes the event's significance, while the other does not.

In sum, new research directions occasionally emerge in the process of doing research when puzzling anomalies and surprising outcomes occur. It helps to be in the right place when they occur and to be open enough to recognize their significance. A comprehensive understanding of the relevant literature makes both more likely. But there are still other sources of research ideas as well.

THE SUPPLIED PROBLEM

Many studies come about because someone *gives* you a problem. Such is particularly the case in applied settings, where myriad questions require systematic, empirical answers: Is our program effective? How can we better meet our objectives? What will happen if we change our intake criteria? How can we decide who has the best chance to benefit from our program?

For example, some years ago, Ted was approached by the federal Department of Communications about doing a behavioural and attitudinal evaluation of the computer terminals that had been installed in some city police patrol vehicles. The state-of-the-art system gave patrol officers access to various data banks through a computer terminal affixed to their car's dashboard. Studies of the system to that point had been dominated by the engineers who had designed it and had been limited to assessing its technological attributes. But were patrol officers actually using the system as effectively as the system designers had hoped? How did officers feel about the system

now that they had had a chance to use it? Had any unanticipated issues arisen? Ted was interested in these questions and had others of his own about the implications of computer technologies for decision making, for police–community relations, and for citizens' privacy issues, since the new system gave patrol officers access to information without any need to justify their search. The result was an intensive analysis that addressed all these issues (see Palys, Boyanowsky, & Dutton 1983, 1984).

CULTURAL FOLKLORE, THE COMMON WISDOM, AND "COMMON SENSE"

Much of what we feel we "know" is based on traditional, speculative, or polemical belief that has never been verified empirically. A valuable role of research is to help refute or confirm our beliefs about social "facts," assuming we believe that truth is a priority and that important social decisions should be based on evidence rather than on speculation or stereotyping.

One study on pornography was of this type. Social debate and discussion in Canada regarding pornography reached an apex during the period in which the federally appointed Special (Fraser) Committee on Pornography and Prostitution was preparing its report (1985). Reports in the media, as well as many of those submitted and/or presented to the committee, affirmed lobbyists' belief in the pervasiveness and easy availability of horrific video material that glorifies sexual violence and encourages misogynist attitudes. The committee wondered, Is it really so? The resulting study (Palys 1984, 1986) not only provided systematic evidence bearing on this question but also helped to address important theoretical and methodological issues (e.g., see W. A. Fisher 1986; Palys & Lowman 1984) in research on the relationship between exposure to erotic and sexually violent materials and aggression, particularly by males toward females (see also Palys 1994).

Other examples appear regularly in the press. Immigration policies, for example, have often been the subject of heated debate. Some politicians have even pointed to isolated examples of immigrants getting in trouble, and wondered aloud whether

Canada can really "afford" as many immigrants as it takes, given all the social costs and problems allegedly associated with them (e.g., see M. Campbell 1994: A1). A Statistics Canada study entitled *Canada's Changing Immigrant Population* examined census data, addressed that very issue, and concluded that such fears were unfounded:

> Amid widespread fears that Canada's immigration system lets in criminals and layabouts, Statistics Canada has published a study showing immigrants are more hard-working, better educated, and more stable than people born here. (Mitchell 1994b: A1)

Clearly, therefore, research has a significant role to play in going beyond stereotype. Gathering data and thereby providing systematic evidence about what "everyone knows" to be true—and often isn't—is an important role for research that attempts to facilitate the development of social policy and/or simply sets out to better inform us about ourselves.

RESEARCH OBJECTIVES

With a general topic in mind, a second issue to consider that will influence your design is the objectives you have in mind for your research. The relationship between research objectives and research design can be recognized easily by considering first what we mean by "research design."

"Research Design" Defined

One more quantitatively oriented text suggests that "a research design is the arrangement of conditions for collection and analysis of data in a manner that aims to combine relevance to the research purpose with economy in procedure" (Selltiz, Wrightsman, & Cook 1976: 90). From a more qualitative perspective, Denzin and Lincoln (1994; see also 2000) state that

> a research design describes a flexible set of guidelines that connects theoretical paradigms to strategies of inquiry and methods for collecting empirical material. A research design situates

researchers in the empirical world and connects them to specific sites, persons, groups, institutions, and bodies of relevant interpretive material, including documents and archives. A research design also specifies how the investigator will address the two critical issues of representation and legitimation. (14)

Denzin and Lincoln's allusion to the "critical issues" of **representation** and **legitimation** refers to the epistemologies, or ways of knowing, we discussed earlier—the philosophy of science we bring to our project. Their definition of research design subsumes that offered by Selltiz and colleagues by reminding us about the challenge involved in preparing a strategy of inquiry that effectively and elegantly addresses the research question at hand but also effectively gives a voice to our research participants (*representation,* i.e., how and by what authority we'll represent our participants through our data and interpretations) and the criteria by which we feel we can proclaim authority for our data (*legitimation*).[3]

Both definitions—the first from a more quantitative source, the second from a more qualitative one—assert that research design involves stating a game plan through which one can gather information that addresses one's research purpose in a simple, elegant, and systematic way. Like any game plan, research designs embody and reflect everything from very general considerations, such as your priorities and objectives, to very specific decisions regarding who, what, when, where, and how.

One Typology of Research Objectives

Any distinctions between research objectives are bound to be arbitrary, and the divisions between them frequently ambiguous; not every textbook draws the boundaries in exactly the same way. But one must begin somewhere, and we would cite five that one often sees in the literature:

1. *Exploratory* research (sometimes called *formulative* research) aims to gain familiarity with or to achieve new insights into a phenomenon,

often in order to formulate a more precise research question or to develop hypotheses.

2. *Descriptive* research aims to accurately portray the characteristics of a particular individual, situation, group, sample, or population, and/or to describe processes that operate within a particular milieu.

3. *Relational* research (sometimes called *correlational* research) aims to determine how two or more variables are related within a given sample or population.

4. *Explanatory* research aims to investigate causal relationships or other patterned conduct that is thought to characterize social processes.

5. *Transformative* research sets out to incorporate research in an ongoing process of personal or social development/change. Typically this research involves a more collaborative relationship between researcher and participants in which the two jointly define research priorities and longer-term personal or group objectives.

Let's briefly examine each of these.

EXPLORATORY OR FORMULATIVE RESEARCH

Suppose you're going on a trip to Montreal, that you've never been to Montreal before, and that you want to somehow feel that you "know" Montreal by the time your visit ends. This visit will inevitably provide only a first glimpse of the city, but you want to get at least a feel for what is important to know about the place and what you might do next time you visit to get to know it better.

There are at least two ways to proceed. You might begin by visiting a Montreal tourist bureau and collecting brochures. If you do, you'll probably have an enjoyable visit and may come away with lots of slides to show and stories to tell the folks at home. But do you *really* know Montreal? You may have come to appreciate that part of Montreal that the tourist bureau defines as "of interest," but you'll never know whether you "really" understand the place unless you also have some appreciation for what you missed.[4]

You might decide instead that you want to discover Montreal on your own. Perhaps you'd start by

hopping on a tour bus to look at some of the sights. Then you might go for a walk through Old Montreal or Westmount, looking at the architecture and talking to some of the people you meet in the parks or *brasseries*. Or you might rent a car and drive until you get lost, and then try finding your way back to some central location again. If you do this for a week or two until your trip is over, will you understand Montreal? You will certainly have a broader overview of the city than those who chose to follow the tourist bureau's guidance. You might now have a better understanding of what's *not* in those tourist brochures, allowing you to decide for yourself whether and in what sense the brochures represent Montreal. But you will also have spent more time pursuing dead ends and visiting places that weren't particularly interesting; the payoff is that you may also have found some experiential gems that are *not* in the travel brochures and, through your interactions with Montrealers, may have developed more of a sense of how *they* view their city. And over the long term, at least it will be you (rather than the authors of the travel brochures) who decides what is or isn't interesting to pursue in greater detail next time around.

You face similar choices as a social scientist. Recall the dichotomy between deductive and inductive approaches. Like the traveller who prepares for a trip by going to the tourist bureau and spends the first night reading brochures, deductive researchers believe that the place to start is with a good map. Why waste time going to places that aren't particularly interesting when someone else (the literature) has already done a lot of the legwork, describing the elements of the local geography and culture (the variables) that are of greatest interest in explaining (theorizing about) the phenomenon at hand? The "good map" comes in the form of a theory, and the inventory of "where to go" (i.e., of variables to investigate) is defined by the theorist.

Of course, this analogy is a generous one for deductive researchers, since tourist bureaus are generally quite good at identifying a range of alternatives that appeal to most travellers. The more extreme example would place us in some totally unfamiliar situation where the knowledge was thin and the reliability of maps was unknown. Yet the true deductivist would still argue for using a map, since it would at least serve to systematize our inquiry. The truth would ultimately reveal itself as we tested our preliminary map by interaction with the new environment. Gradually, we'd correct the map until it adequately represented the reality it proposed to describe.

The inductive researcher advances a different view. Is a map of all the washrooms in Montreal an "adequate" description of Montreal? If such a map had been the first one advanced to the deductivist, he or she would have gone through and systematically tested the location of all the washrooms and thereby come up with a "true" map. But who cares (except in the occasional biologically compelling moment)? A map can be accurate but trivial. The inductivist prefers to risk wasting time on some dead ends and false starts for the benefit of reaching his or her own conclusions about what is important to include on the map in the first place. The emphasis is on creating a map that is not only accurate but also interesting. Even better would be to construct the map in collaboration with some Montrealers, so that the ultimate product reflects *their* perceptions and love of their city as much as it does yours. The risk of inductive travel is that the investigator may wander aimlessly forever. The potential benefit is that he or she will emerge from the process with a more complete understanding of the phenomenon and its context, and having made some friends in the process.

As the travel example suggests, "exploratory research" means quite different things to inductive and deductive researchers. Deductivists are less concerned about doing preliminary exploration to isolate important variables, to define the important research questions, and to determine the important sites for further research. For them, *theory* defines what the important variables are, tells you what the important questions are, and points to appropriate sites for subsequent research. Remember that deductive research is theory *guided*: theory helps focus research by suggesting what we should look for and where such information can be gathered. The role of exploratory research among deductivists thus tends to be limited

to "pilot" studies, in which investigators test research instruments, ensure the feasibility of planned procedures, and check for the sensitivity of measures.

For inductivists, however, exploratory research is an integral and focal part of the research process. Since inductive research is theory *generating,* initial exploration is a virtual requirement as a base from which theory might emerge. Inductive researchers begin by assuming their naiveté about the phenomenon of interest and use the exploratory phase to acquire new insights, particularly through the perceptions of those who inhabit the research site. Exploratory research provides a heuristic benefit: by familiarizing the researcher with the phenomenon, such research helps identify important variables and questions of interest. But how do you do it?

First, the researcher must avoid foreclosing prematurely on what is "interesting" about the situation, remaining open to various perspectives. *Flexibility* and *breadth of coverage* are thus both paramount. While you might talk with people who are familiar with or otherwise part of the phenomenon of interest, and while you might even prepare a few questions ahead of time, you'd undoubtedly keep these questions open-ended and be prepared to follow the conversations wherever they might lead. Similarly, in observing a phenomenon, you would likely *not* bring along a predetermined observational coding scheme. Instead, you'd spend your preliminary time just watching events, keeping notes on whatever strikes you as interesting or significant or puzzling. Later you could review your notes, trying to identify research questions to pursue more comprehensively and systematically during your next visit.

Exploratory researchers tend to be less interested than deductivists in obtaining a large "representative" sample of persons or situations; instead, they favour a more *strategic* sampling of insightful informants or revealing situations. The ideal informant is someone who is either very *familiar with* or very *new* to a situation. For example, to understand social dynamics within corporate settings, it might be useful to talk both to individuals who have many years of business experience and to those who are just "learning the ropes."

Although all too frequently bypassed, exploratory or formulative research plays a very important role in the research process. Besides being a good source of research ideas, exploratory research helps ensure that when you *do* formulate more systematic research questions and research designs, they'll be meaningful, both to you (because of your understanding of the context in which those questions are being asked) and to your informants (because of their participation in the process).

Exploratory research has historically played a minor role in published research because the deductive mode has dominated traditional science; when theory defines what is important to scrutinize, the role of "exploratory" research is limited to a bit of pilot research that pretests existing research instruments. In contrast, the inductive mode emphasizes the generation of **grounded theory,** that is, theory that *emerges from* research; hence exploratory research is a major focus, and part of one's focus is to identify key variables/concepts/processes that will most fruitfully provide insights into a phenomenon, as well as to identify those persons and data sources that can most facilitate that process. (For a great example and one of the few where a researcher talks candidly about this initial period of fumbling around, see Becker 1993.)

To put it another way, for deductivists, "real" research involves testing the hypotheses implied by theory; exploratory research is a mere "warm-up" before you get to the "important" part. But for inductivists, exploration *is* the first important part, since the exploratory phase helps researchers begin to understand the points of view of actors in the setting, identify worthy research questions, articulate and operationalize variables of interest, and lay the foundation out of which theory can emerge.

DESCRIPTIVE RESEARCH

Exploration offers an important start to the research process because it involves direct interaction with the phenomenon of interest. But once the researcher has gained a preliminary understanding and identified variables/concepts that appear important to explanation, a more systematic description of the phenomenon and the context in which it occurs is called for. How often does the phenomenon or its variants occur? Who is involved? How are the variables that were identified as important distributed in the population? What are the processes by which it is produced?

For example, suppose we're interested in understanding university students' attitudes about militarism. Exploratory discussions with students may have helped flesh out our understanding of those attitudes, leading us to believe that variation in the respondent's sex, political attitudes, direct or indirect knowledge of war, religious background, experience with other cultures, and beliefs about violence as a conflict-resolving mechanism all appear to be associated with variation in support for militarism. We also may have found that attitudes about militarism appear to be associated with other social beliefs, for example, whether people believe toy guns are appropriate gifts for young children, and whether they support international organizations such as the United Nations. Our next task is to try to describe how all these variables are distributed in our population of interest (i.e., university students).

Since the goal in descriptive research is to adequately *represent* the phenomenon of interest as it occurs in the population of interest, *accuracy* is important. Our emphasis should be on minimizing bias, maximizing the **representativeness** and/or thoroughness of our sample (and hence of our results), and ensuring that our measures are reliable and valid. More quantitatively oriented researchers will want to establish the **reliability** and **validity** of their measures through psychometric testing; more qualitatively oriented researchers will address reliability and validity by looking for multiple data sources (**triangulation**) and identifying key informants or collaborators.

RELATIONAL RESEARCH

A third research objective, and one that flows immediately from description, involves determining how two or more variables are related to one another. Rather than merely describing university students' views about militarism and the distribution of the other potentially "relevant" variables one by one, relational research involves looking systematically at relationships among those variables (e.g., systematically testing whether and how sex, beliefs about violence as a conflict-resolving mechanism, and attitudes about militarism are related to one another).

In the quantitative realm, there will still be an emphasis on demonstrating that one's measures are *reliable* and *valid/authentic* (as was the case with descriptive objectives), but obtaining a representative sample is frequently lower in priority—the key issue here will normally be one of simply finding samples that vary considerably on variables of interest.[5]

Relational research (sometimes called *correlational research,* at least within the quantitative realm) is often seen as a first step toward explaining phenomena, since theoretical interests or views often lead you to be curious about the relationship between two particular variables in the first place. (For example, why does it "make sense" to you to look at the relationship between a respondent's sex and his or her attitudes about pornography but *not* at the connection between swimming ability and views on abortion?) Relational evidence is generally seen as *relevant to* and *necessary for* explaining and understanding phenomena of interest. But by itself, it isn't enough: two phenomena or events may be related for many reasons other than some integral, causal connection, which are no less interesting but equally in need of being addressed empirically.

Don't give too much of a quantitative spin to this term; it would be a mistake to think of "relational" research only in terms of computing correlation coefficients. In the more qualitative realm, "relational" research involves more in the way of searching for regular patterns and identifying the source of those regularities.

EXPLANATORY RESEARCH

A fourth research purpose is to attempt to *explain* phenomena by isolating causal relationships or other consistent patterns among variables. Having done all the appropriate groundwork, explanatory research requires the researcher to become very focused in his

or her research questions, engage in some preliminary hypothesizing and hypothesis testing, and probably use highly structured methods designed (or adapted) specifically for the task at hand.

Of the four research objectives cited thus far, explanation is often touted as the most closely linked to the very purpose of "science." Some social scientists even define the research enterprise in those terms, that is, being "scientific" involves "a commitment to establish causal laws that enable us to predict and explain specific phenomena" (e.g., Labovitz & Hagedorn 1981). But isolating causal laws or sequences is very difficult, partly because of the very notion of "cause." Some philosophers (e.g., Hume) argue that causes don't even exist in any "real" sense, that is, that the notion of "cause" is merely a convenient fiction we humans have created and found useful to impose on our perceptions of events. But even if we *do* decide to believe in and hence seek "causes" in our research, we find considerable disagreement among philosophers of science on what "causes" are and how we can ascertain them (see Cook and Campbell [1979] and Shadish et al. [2001] for excellent integrative discussions concerning various conceptions of causality). Many researchers also feel considerable discomfort in talking about "cause," a word associated with the mechanistic, natural science conception of social science that many of them would prefer to avoid.

A detailed discussion of "cause" is beyond the scope of this text. But the brand of empiricism offered here *does* see the notion of cause as useful. People in general, and social scientists in particular, often speak in causal terms. Even when the term "cause" itself doesn't appear, our language is rife with terms that suggest one or more variables being systematically associated with or otherwise affecting one or more other variables (e.g., *produces, generates, leads to, influences, impacts upon, gives us, emerges from*). We take these to be the sorts of relations referred to by authors like Denzin and Lincoln (1994) when they consciously avoid the word "cause" and replace it with "patterned conduct and social processes" (6). We include the word "cause" here because many social scientists and other people talk in those terms, and one of this book's goals is to be inclusive rather than exclusive. But the conception of cause we entertain is not mechanistic or deterministic, and it's equally compatible with both qualitative and quantitative approaches.

TRANSFORMATIVE AND EMANCIPATORY RESEARCH

It is perhaps little more than a truism that one research objective common to most researchers is a desire to change, or at least improve, the world. There are, of course, major differences among researchers in this regard: some believe that all will be better with some minor reform or technical improvements, while others aspire to a new social order; many fall somewhere between these two extremes. Those who take a more constructionist bent are perhaps more likely to differentiate "what is" from "what might be." Whatever their hopes, researchers' values and sense of social justice often influence both the topics they choose to investigate and the way they design their research.

These issues come up throughout this text, since one of its central themes is the social responsibility of the researcher and the research community, and the implications of the choices we make when we undertake a piece of research. So we won't dwell on them at length here, but the topics you choose to investigate, the way you investigate them, and the nature of the relations between researcher and participants should mirror the values you'd like to see incorporated into the world.

Hamilton (1994) summarizes some of the themes that he believes are manifest in qualitative research traditions (although not exclusive to them):

> At least three propositions seem to have been adopted by this movement. First, late twentieth century democracies should empower all citizens, not just privileged elites. Second, liberal social practice can never be morally or politically disinterested. And third, the managerial separation of conception (research) from execution (practice) is psychologically, socially, and economically inefficient. (67)

As Hamilton's second point reminds us, *all* research is directly or indirectly "political": in either mirroring or questioning the "understandings" held within the dominant social order, research either echoes or has the potential of criticizing the status quo. From this follows his third point: we cannot remain aloof from the implications of our work; if we take our work seriously and hope that others will, too, we must not ignore the possible effects of putting our ideas into practice. With his first point, Hamilton casts his vote—for a democratic, inclusive order in which no position or set of understandings is more privileged than any other.

Other researchers have reiterated these "social justice" themes, arguing that they should be incorporated directly into our work. Fine (1994), for example, discusses how researchers have treated the subjects of their investigations as an "Other," lamenting the imperialist research and understandings that have resulted from this perceived separation. She argues that part of the researcher's role is to enhance possibilities of social justice by intentionally trying to "disrupt Othering and provoke a sense of possibility" (79).

Kincheloe and McLaren (1994) take up this notion of a "discourse of possibility," arguing that "more emancipatory forms of research" could help foster "a more egalitarian and democratic social order" (139); the word "empowerment" turns up repeatedly in their essay. Later in the same article, they approvingly cite Lather's (1991) notion of **catalytic validity,** which suggests that researchers should evaluate their work by considering the extent to which it empowers people by enhancing their "self-understanding" and shows them possibilities of transformation: "the degree to which research moves those it studies to understand the world and the way it is shaped in order for them to transform it" (152).

These bold pronouncements and strong recommendations echo what Aboriginal peoples have told us for many years: that you must "Walk your talk" (Lee Thomas, personal communication); that is, what you do must reflect what you say and believe. The way you design your research should reflect the sort of social order you wish to promote. This might take the form of emphasizing analytic techniques more than manipulative ones when trying to draw inferences about process (Palys 1989; see also Chapter 11). Or, as some feminist researchers have reminded us, the fundamental act of empowerment involves ensuring that research participants' voices are heard at all stages of the research process, from framing the research question to collaborating in gathering, analyzing, interpreting, and presenting data (e.g., see Fine 1994; Fonow & Cook 1991; Olesen 1994; Reinharz 1992).

Table 2.1 summarizes these five research objectives and some of their implications for research design.

CONNECTING WITH THE LITERATURE

After you choose a topic and have some general sense of your objectives, making a connection with the lit-erature is a useful next step. Your initial review of the relevant literature will sometimes be cursory and sometimes quite exhaustive, but you do owe it to yourself and to your colleagues (via the literature) to have a look at what's been done in your area of interest. By familiarizing yourself with the literature, you can see the problems and successes experienced by others in the area; you can find out how others have approached a particular research question, what has been done in the area, and where gaps still remain.

Take a Broad View of Your Topic

One of the biggest mistakes novice researchers make is that, when they examine "the literature" on a topic, they construe the topic too narrowly and too con-cretely. Suppose, for example, that you're interested in understanding the decisions made by customs officials at border crossings. How do they decide whether to

Table 2.1
Summary of Various Research Purposes, Objectives, and Strategies

Research Purpose	Objective	Strategies/Comment
Exploratory or formulative	To achieve new insights, formulate research questions	Requires flexibility and breadth of coverage; use of atypical samples; open-ended techniques;
Descriptive	To adequately describe some person, situation, or group	Accuracy is paramount; measures must be reliable and valid; sampling must be representative
Relational	To discover how two or more variables are related to one another	Measures must be valid and reliable; may or may not be representative
Explanatory	To derive causal assertions, allow causal inference	Measures must be reliable and valid; sampling may or may not be an issue; emphasis on eliminating rival plausible explanations; research very focused and precise
Transformative	To use the research process as a springboard to bring about change, empowerment for an individual or social group	A collaborative approach in which researcher and participants jointly identify research priorities and objectives; often a longer-term commitment that will involve a program of research

wave someone through without further scrutiny or pass the person on to their colleagues for more detailed questioning and examination? What makes customs officers suspicious about some people but not others? What makes them decide to look through a person's suitcases, take a person into an interrogation room, or search or even dismantle someone's car?

If you begin your literature search by looking for studies that deal with that specific situation—customs agent decision making with respect to the identification of individuals who warrant further scrutiny—you'll find very few articles beyond an interesting master's thesis by Miriam Currey (1993). Many people would mistakenly leave off searching there, saying, "Gee, I guess there's nothing on this topic, so I'll just have to start off on my own."

But stopping there is quite inconsistent with the spirit of doing research. Any piece of research involves constantly working back and forth between theory and data, that is, between the abstract and the concrete. Seen in this manner, a researcher would rarely be interested in the decision making of customs officers per se. If that's as far as our interest goes, we might as well look at when people choose to mow their lawns or why some people prefer chocolate and others vanilla when they buy ice cream. The question to be asked is, What makes the decision making of customs officers more "interesting" (from a research perspective) than one's choice of ice cream?

A researcher would more typically choose to look at people like customs officers, and to scrutinize the decisions they make, because of the "larger" processes represented within that group of people or their decisions. Thus, "the literature" that one would seek out would comprise not only any studies that had looked at customs officers (since the results of such studies might help us understand more about who these people are, how they are trained, how their job is defined, how they perceive their job and their role, and so on) but also any literature that might be relevant because it addresses those "larger" processes that interest us.

For example, customs officers are government employees whose job involves aspects of social con-

trol. They are the first Canadians that a border crosser meets, and their job involves keeping apparently nasty people or other perceived undesirables (e.g., people who are escaping prosecution; people who are trying to bypass "normal" immigration channels) out of the country; keeping nasty things (e.g., weapons, unsafe products) out of the country; and ensuring that the *Customs Act*'s requirements are met (e.g., that people who bring goods into the country pay the legislated duties and fees). In the process of executing their jobs, customs officials have an incredible amount of power: you must answer any question they ask, they can seize your car or other belongings, and they can subject you to processes that most of us consider invasive and undesirable (e.g., interrogation, strip searches). But if they interrogated and searched every would-be border crosser, there would soon be lineups from the Canada–U.S. boundary down to Mexico, and many exasperated people would be calling for their heads. Instead, they're given discretion and are expected to use that discretion wisely. Perhaps only one in ten persons is asked more than a few simple questions (e.g., Where do you live? How long have you been away? Do you have any goods to declare?), and only a small sample is subjected to more detailed searches of their persons or belongings.

The social processes involved in making such judgments include decision making, control, and discretion. Customs officials must make judgments about the personality and character of each person who tries to cross the border. Accordingly, "relevant" literatures that a researcher might look at before engaging in a study with customs officers might include (a) the various literatures on how people make decisions in an atmosphere of uncertainty (since, after the person leaves without being checked, we can never know for sure whether he or she did indeed smuggle something into the country or import a dangerous weapon); (b) the "impression formation" literature, which deals with some of the factors people take into account when "sizing up" another person; these might include studies that look at both "lay people" and "professionals" (e.g., social workers, clinical psychologists); and (c) the "discretion" literature, which looks at the use of discretion by agents of social control (e.g., police officers, judges, parole boards, psychiatrists).

You might think of other areas that could be relevant to the study of customs officers and their decisions (e.g., whether and how stereotyping and racist or classist attitudes enter into the decision-making process or a study of interview techniques). But the above discussion should suffice to show that "the relevant literature" for such a study includes far more than just whatever research deals with that specific decision by that specific group. Belonging to the community of scholars who engage in research means always looking for ways to benefit from the work of others, whether for positive reasons (e.g., to incorporate methods they've used or to include factors shown to be important) or negative ones (e.g., to avoid repeating mistakes and pursuing dead ends). And as this text argues, your search for "relevant" literature should cast a necessarily wide net.

Real and Virtual Libraries

There are two main sources here. One is the library—the heart of every university. If you are uncertain about what to do once you get to the library, ask your librarian about tours of or brochures describing the library. Books, journals, and other materials are *not* filed randomly, and a working knowledge of what's available, where things are, and how to find them is invaluable. Knowing the general area in the library that contains material related to your topic of interest provides splendid opportunities for browsing.

Investigating the library and the literature has become both easier and more complex with the proliferation of personal computers, particularly within industrialized societies, and corresponding development of that vast online computer network known as the **Internet** (which includes the World Wide Web). With a computing account, which many universities provide to undergraduate and graduate students for free or a nominal charge, and a modem or home cable connection, the world is your library.

The two of us, for example, can check the holdings at our own university, all three local universities, and the city library system by subject, by author, or by title. We can just as easily check the holdings in the libraries of other universities, government departments, and institutions like the United Nations, on every continent. World Wide Web browsers such as Internet Explorer, Netscape, Safari, and Mozilla Firefox, and amazingly powerful search engines such as Google allow you to check the entire Internet for information about any subject, with return messages indicating what information various universities, government departments, institutes, and other agencies have on whatever subject you've searched for. At the same time, you have to remember that anyone can host a web page and make their views and analyses available to the world, i.e., there is no "peer review" or quality control on the Internet, so it becomes more and more critical that you evaluate the quality and perspective of what you read.

The Internet also allows us to get access to information more quickly than ever before. For example, recently Ted and a colleague were engaged in debate with their university regarding the ethics of research confidentiality. They were just in the process of finalizing a submission when an article appeared in *The Globe and Mail* about a highly relevant case that had been decided in a United States Court of Appeal the previous day. Ted immediately went to the court's website and was able to download a copy of the decision. An hour later they were incorporating relevant quotes from the decision into their submission. Years ago this would have meant waiting for a hard copy of the decision to be made available and be mailed—which would often take weeks—or to wait for its appearance in legal publications of court decisions—which might take months.

Another wonderful aspect of the World Wide Web is the extent to which it has maintained its character as a place where you can get all sorts of information for free. The Court of Appeal decision noted above, for example, cost nothing but the paper to print it on. And, as many others do, the two of us maintain personal web pages (Ted's is at http://www.sfu.ca/~palys/

while Chris hosts "Academic Freedom" at http://www.academic-freedom.ca) where we have links to other sites of interest and post papers we've written that aren't otherwise available (e.g., conference presentations, submissions to courts and/or commissions of inquiry) so that they get far better distribution than would have been possible before the Internet.

Having accumulated some background knowledge about your topic, your next step is to translate your interests into specific research questions.

IDENTIFYING A RESEARCHABLE QUESTION

Although your search of the literature involves a broadening of vision, your next task involves reining it in again to start translating what will still be a relatively amorphous research idea into a more concrete and specific research project. Researchers generally begin by formulating a *question* that helps guide and provide a focus for their research. As with research ideas, these questions can emerge from a number of different sources. Sometimes it is theory that provides us with a research question; other times it arises from our own observations and interests; on other occasions someone will give us a research question they would like us to answer; on still other occasions the identification of a research question is something that will emerge out of a more collaborative interchange between a researcher and some individual, group, or agency. However they arise, the big trick here is to ensure that our research question is indeed researchable. Some examples of researchable questions include

1. Why do people buy lottery tickets?
2. Have sexually explicit videos become more violent in recent years?
3. Have legislative changes regarding prostitution affected the street trade?
4. What are the effects of long-term incarceration?
5. What understandings and assumptions have guided this nation and its colonial predeces-

sors in their policies regarding the rights of Aboriginal peoples?
6. Are immigration "quota" systems effective in providing opportunities for and in changing stereotypical attitudes about visible minorities?
7. Through what verbal and nonverbal means is occupational status preserved and displayed in business organizations?

Each of these questions is reasonably focused and implies some real-world situation that we can look at to ascertain an answer. The first one is probably the vaguest ("why" questions tend to be the toughest), but even here, we might start off by tracking down some people who buy lottery tickets and asking them why they do so, or propose a theory that predicts which individuals or groups will be more or less likely to buy them.[6] We might proceed by comparing those who buy lottery tickets with those who never do, or those who buy frequently with those who buy less often, or those who buy lottery tickets with those who engage in other forms of gambling (e.g., racetrack betting, bingo, playing the stock market). The information obtained may not provide the ultimate answer to our question, but there *is* real-world information that can help inform the answers we do derive. This process of "posing a researchable question" may seem straightforward, but it's actually related to one of the most common mistakes people make when they undertake a piece of research.

The difficulty arises when a would-be researcher chooses a question that is not actually *researchable,* that is, no empirical answer can be derived. Consider the following questions: Is capitalism or communism the better economic system? Is democracy the best political system? What teaching style is best? How should we respond to terrorism? These are *not* empirical questions; they're questions of value and philosophy. Answers to such questions cannot be "discovered" without specific criteria by which to identify the "right" answer. Similarly, questions like "Are quota systems fair?" or "Is rehabilitation or punishment the most appropriate objective for sentencing?" or "What should we do about pornography?" are legal, philosophical, and political questions, but *not* researchable questions with strictly empirical answers.

Research *can* be done in such areas, but these questions aren't researchable in their present form. Look at them again. In each case, the questions are asking you to make value judgments, using words like "appropriate," "better," "too much," "effective," and "should." Although value judgments may well be of interest to us, researching such questions would require us to specify the criteria that will be used in making those judgments. Specifying criteria *does not* make answering such questions any less of a political, moral, or philosophical process, since the very choice of criteria embodies these dimensions, but it *does* require us to make that aspect of the process more explicit and, hence, more amenable to scrutiny by ourselves and others.

How can we turn a non-researchable question into a researchable question? Take the non-researchable question What should we do about pornography? This question is problematic for several reasons. It suggests that there *is* some inherently "right" thing to do. Obviously, what we should do will involve some basic value considerations concerning what limits, if any, and under what conditions, if any, we feel society has the right to impose on otherwise free patterns of producing and consuming written and pictorial material.

For the sake of argument, let's adopt the classic civil libertarian position espoused by John Stuart Mill (1956): no society should impose restrictions on its citizenry unless allowing the activity to continue would impose greater social harm than the harm that would be realized by curtailing individual freedoms in that realm. Now we have the beginnings of a research question, since we have a criterion—demonstrated harm—that we can address. We might turn our non-researchable question into a researchable question by asking, "Is there evidence to suggest that allowing people to expose themselves to pornography causes social harm?"

We still need to define "harm" more specifically, perhaps as "encouraging aggression," "encouraging negative attitudes," or "causing reductions in self-esteem." For example, we can ask, Does exposing individuals to pornography lead them to be more aggressive toward women? Does it encourage dehumanizing and negative attitudes toward women? Do males and/or females experience reductions in self-esteem after being exposed to pornography? There's still a long way to go before we actually begin to investigate these questions (e.g., What do we mean by "pornography"? How might we measure exposure? Aggression? Dehumanizing attitudes?), but at least we're off to a good start. We've identified a researchable question, that is, a question for which there *is* information in the world that we can look at and for which tentative answers *can* be unearthed.

The above suggestions aren't, of course, the *only* way we could turn "What should we do about pornography?" into a researchable question. Instead of pursuing the assessment-of-harm option implied by Mill, we might adopt the position that social policy in the pornography realm should be guided by community standards of (in)tolerance. The relevant data would thus involve assessing that standard, and our researchable question might become "What forms of pornographic material, if any, does the general public feel can be tolerated, and which, if any, does it feel cannot be tolerated?"

Although the above examples are policy oriented, not all research questions need be of this type. The research question may be rooted in curiosity and may be little more than "What is the relationship between variable *A* and variable *B*?" or "How do relations of power operate within situation *C*?" Both of these questions imply a real-world focus for the research, although further decisions remain to be articulated and resolved. For example, if our question concerns the relationship between personal awareness (variable *A*) and success (variable *B*), we'll still need to define these variables further, consider the context or situation in which we will scrutinize them, and be prepared to articulate what these choices say about us and the culture in which we operate (e.g., what do we mean by "success"?).

Similarly, if the social dynamics of some ecological niche (e.g., the business world) interest us, we must still decide where in that niche to focus (e.g., multinational versus domestic corporations; business in relation to other businesses or other elements of the social environment; on the front lines, or in the boardroom) and what dimension(s) of that niche interest us (e.g., power relations, socialization, interaction patterns, image management processes).

But the central points here should be clear: (1) although any type of question may have researchable aspects, the approaches considered in this book require that a question be expressed in researchable terms; and (2) researchable questions are specific, limited in scope, related to some empirical reality (i.e., there must be some sort of evidence that can be consulted) and should have specific evaluation criteria, so that you can tell whether you are getting closer to an answer. These criteria emerge from social negotiation and debate and will undoubtedly reveal something of the researcher's personal leanings. Any researcher's decisions about "relevant" criteria will necessarily preclude some options in preference for others and, hence, reflect particular values and assumptions about what's "important" to scrutinize.

One recurring problem is researchers' failure to acknowledge the values implicitly embedded in their choice of variables to investigate. The researcher who evaluates organizational interventions on the basis of changes in productivity alone, for example, is effectively adopting a utilitarian status quo approach that implicitly accepts productivity as the only important indicator of a "successful" intervention. Other researchers might evaluate the same interventions by looking at changes in group cohesiveness, worker safety, or job satisfaction. Each approach makes an implicit value statement about what's "important" to observe. As this suggests, the choices you make say something about you and your perception of "the problem." Such implicit statements are inevitable; your obligation is to make "what you say" the result of a conscious decision whose rationale can be articulated. Ideally, you'll consult broadly with "relevant" stakeholders in the setting and design a study whose results will "speak" to their interests, perspectives, and concerns.[7]

FORMULATING HYPOTHESES

Once you've identified a researchable question, the next steps are frequently to "operationalize" the key constructs involved and, some would argue, to articulate your theoretical conceptions by formulating a **hypothesis.** Advocates of hypothesis-oriented (deductive) inquiry adamantly maintain that this stage represents a crucial transition in the research process, since the researcher must begin to be extremely specific about what he or she will assess. Talarico (1980) writes that "while general questions may prompt a researcher to turn to a particular subject, and while vague ideas may incite curiosity, no research can properly be labelled scientific without the specific statement of a relationship for testing and scrutiny" (149).

Expressing a hypothesis involves making a specific statement about a state of affairs in the world that is open to empirical test. Your hypothesis may be seen as your speculative answer to the research question you're posing. In the context of deductive (theory-guided) inquiry, the hypothesis states what one's guiding theory says *should* happen in a particular situation.

Each hypothesis will mention at least two variables and will state how those variables might be related. Here are a few examples:

1. The more strongly that people agree that one should love one's neighbour "because it is God's word," the more racist their attitudes will be regarding visible minorities.
2. A communicator's perceived credibility will affect the extent to which an audience is persuaded by his or her arguments.
3. Work groups that are run on a democratic basis will have higher worker morale and group cohesiveness than those run autocratically.
4. Educational techniques that emphasize student–teacher interaction will result in higher rates of learning than unidirectional lecture techniques.

Each of these hypotheses asserts a state of affairs amenable to empirical test. The first one is based on the well-established finding (e.g., see Altemeyer 1981) that more conservative and fundamentalist religious affiliations are associated with less tolerance and greater hostility toward outgroups. Although everyone may agree that we should "love [our] neighbour," saying that the *reason* we should do so is because it is the "word of God" (as opposed to, say, being a good idea) would be a reasonable way to assess religious fundamentalism. We *can* find a group of individuals and ask them to what extent they agree with that statement, and we *can* use any of a dozen measures that have been developed to assess those same people's attitudes toward visible minorities. By correlating the results of those two measures together across a sample of people, we can see whether the two variables are related (i.e., whether racism increases with greater religious fundamentalism) the way the hypothesis predicts.

In sum, a hypothesis is a testable statement. Any research project will involve recognizing, structuring, or creating a situation in which you can gather information to discover whether the evidence supports or refutes your assertion about the relationship(s) among two or more variables.

As noted earlier, researchers from the deductive tradition have been the most adamant about the virtues of hypothesis-oriented inquiry. Kerlinger (1973), for example, has asserted that "it can almost be said that the hypothesis is the most powerful tool man has invented to achieve dependable knowledge" (25). Why? Three reasons are cited.

The Strengths of Hypotheses

HYPOTHESES AS INSTRUMENTS OF THEORY

Scientific epistemology necessarily affirms that dependable knowledge requires an ongoing interaction between theory and data. Although authors like Kerlinger sometimes assert emphatically that theory is *the* aim of science, theory is actually judged by its ability to account for data. Hypotheses are thus crucial to scientific inquiry, since they provide a link between theory and data. A theory specifies relationships among constructs in the abstract; the

hypothesis applies the theory to a concrete situation, bringing the theory into contact with the real world so that its viability can be assessed.

HYPOTHESES IMPLY A TEST

Since a hypothesis represents a concrete specification of a testable state of affairs, the deductive tradition affirms that one can proceed to gather relevant evidence to establish the truth or falsity of the proposition. This tradition asserts that the true nature of reality can be made to reveal itself unambiguously through empirical inquiry; that is, we can create or observe a situation in which the truth or falsity of a hypothesis (and hence of the theory that gave rise to it) can be assessed (e.g., Stinchcombe 1968).

Others have more reserved views of how much can be accomplished. Popper (1959) argues that, although disconfirming evidence allows us to *falsify* our hypotheses (and hence our theories), *confirmatory* evidence (i.e., results consistent with our prediction) can "provide support for" but *not* "prove" their veracity. There are two reasons for this. First, a supportive datum is only a single victory in a theoretically infinite series of challenges that can be made to the theory; "proof" would require showing that a theory is correct in *all* situations in which it might be used to predict. In contrast, a pattern of disconfirmation is more quickly set. In other words, it takes a long time to get to the Hall of Fame, but not long at all to be banished to the minor leagues. Second, as Cook and Campbell (1979) have explained, although a given datum may be consistent with a theory, the theory that gave rise to the prediction may not be the *only* theory that can account for the results. Other theories may turn out to be broader in coverage than the theory at hand and, hence, more preferred in the long run.

There is also the inevitable question of reality. The whole notion of "testing" a hypothesis suggests that there *is* some objective reality that exists independent of our opinions of it. The notion of testing a hypothesis against "the facts" obviously requires the existence of facts. Such testing is no problem for positivists like Kerlinger, who argue that the facts ultimately speak for themselves; reality is what it is, and research will tell us whether we are correct or incorrect.

In contrast, subjectivist or constructivist positions argue that we can never observe reality itself, but only our constructions of it. Reality may reveal itself, but only through the means we provide for it to do so. Kuhn (1970) and others have argued that, because our observations are necessarily theory-laden, and because scientists themselves are human beings who are part of a social/communal activity, we must acknowledge that our criteria for truth are ultimately socially constructed rather than completely empirical (e.g., see also Wagner 1984). Indeed, an extreme subjectivist view espoused by orthodox phenomenologists and some ethnomethodologists suggests that we should virtually ignore "reality" altogether and focus entirely on the processes by which we generate constructions of it (e.g., see Gergen 1985).

An intermediate position, summarized by Cook and Campbell (1979) and Manicas and Secord (1983), has been labelled *fallibilist realism* or *critical realism*. This perspective acknowledges that we deal with reality not directly, but only through our constructions of it. Yet it maintains that the task of science is to construct theories that aim to represent the world. In constructing these theories, we *can* be "wrong." But if it's possible for us to be wrong, then there must be a reality that exists independent of our analysis of it (see Bhaskar 1986).

Thus, although our constructions *are* social and historical products (i.e., knowledge at any given time is "produced" by a community of scientists and flavoured by its historical context), it is *not* the case that "anything goes." We should indeed be able to develop rational criteria by which the adequacy, or at least the utility, of our formulations can be judged. And it is a reasonable endeavour to collect evidence through empirical inquiry; we need only remind ourselves that while "facts" may exist, their meaning and relative importance are negotiable. This is not particularly threatening if one views science as a dynamic rather than a static entity, that is, as an ongoing process, rather than an existing pile onto which more knowledge is heaped.

HYPOTHESES AVOID FOLIE À UN(E)

A most important quality of hypotheses is that they are public. "Stating your hypothesis" implies an attitude of self-disciplined honesty: you're putting your money where your mouth is. If you think you understand the dynamics underlying some social phenomenon, tell us *ahead of time* what will happen in any situation you choose. Articulate your theory. Explain what your theoretical constructs mean to you and how you'll observe them. We ask gamblers to indicate their bets *before* the dice are thrown, and we chastise pseudoscientific astrologers, whose predictions are so vague that they're always "right" no matter what happens. Surely the foundations of knowledge are valued more highly than mere money; surely the sciences are capable of more than the vague and self-serving accounts of mystics.

There are numerous fringe benefits to be gained by this attitude. It promotes the communal nature of science by allowing others to comment on one's efforts. The possibility of critique and review is afforded only by the public presentation of one's research logic. And if one views science as dynamic—as an ongoing process—then one should value components that enhance that process by fostering communication and debate.

Thus, for Kerlinger, "being public" and "expressing hypotheses" are synonymous, and the two together are an excellent way to generate dependable knowledge. As Kerlinger (1973) says, "the investigator who does not hypothesize a relation in advance ... does not give the facts a chance to prove or disprove anything ... As Darwin pointed out long ago, all observations have to be for or against some view if they are to be of any use" (21–22). In contrast, individuals who do not follow a hypothesis-testing mode of inquiry are seen as prescientific throwbacks who are prepared to capitalize on chance events and *post hoc* (after-the-fact) explanations.

The Other Side

DO HYPOTHESES ADEQUATELY REPRESENT THE RESEARCH PROCESS?

Inductive researchers have problems with Kerlinger's account. The biggest criticism is that it emphasizes a mythical "scientism" that courts triviality and phenomenological injustice if it's true and that seriously distorts the process of science if it's not true. You're about to do research in a new area: Is your hypothesis ready? If specifying a hypothesis is a prerequisite to engaging in research, then surely the one you come up with from your office armchair will be superficial and trite. If a hypothesis is generated in the absence of any interaction with the phenomenon in question, then surely it would be miraculous if it were insightful. The legwork must be done first.

Deductivists would counter that even though one's preliminary hypotheses might be trivial, coming face to face with reality would, over the long run (like a self-correcting feedback loop), encourage more elaborate and sophisticated revision. But that claim is more an expression of faith than a statement of fact. Once you're committed to the research focus and direction that a hypothesis requires, will further revision simply become mired in variations on the superficial preliminary theme, or will more substantial revision occur? Surely it would make greater sense to more fully explore the phenomenon *before* imposing hypothetical constructs from afar. Thus, while deductivists argue that "real" science starts with the specification of research questions and the delineation of hypotheses for empirical testing, inductivists argue that these things do not simply materialize, and hence the process of generating research questions and hypotheses should itself receive focus.

The implication is that the hypothesis-oriented accounts we see in journals actually represent a distortion of the research process. Silverman (1985) is not alone in suggesting that the specification of hypotheses, methods, and results may look squeaky clean and objective when documented in the journals but that published articles misrepresent the research process by relegating the preliminary skirmishes with research phenomena in the exploratory phase to "non-scientific" (or, at least, not-worth-writing-about) status.

Thus, while Kerlinger might suggest that one is not being forthright if one's speculations are not hung out for *a priori* scrutiny, inductivists would assert that Kerlinger chooses to ignore how his formulations actually emerged. By acknowledging formulative inquiry as an integral part of the empirical process, inductivists argue that they more adequately and honestly represent the process of science, do not prematurely foreclose on the identification of important research questions, and are in fact more public about the important conceptualization process that deductivists sweep under the rug. In contrast, deductivists would argue that exploratory research that is not explicitly hypothesis-driven is loose science, and hence is best considered a warm-up for "real" scientific activity.

IS PREDICTION THE PRIMARY CRITERION?

The hypothesis-oriented inquiry espoused by the deductivists sees "ability to predict" as the acid test of theory. If you can predict it, deductivists would say, then you must understand it; that is, explanation and prediction are symmetrical. Other philosophers of science (e.g., Manicas & Secord 1983) would agree with this point, but only for closed systems of the type created in a laboratory. Laboratory research is a powerful mode of inquiry because it creates conditions that allow the ***ceteris paribus*** assumption to operate.

Ceteris paribus is Latin for "all else being equal." In the laboratory, researchers literally create conditions that let them investigate the impact of variable *A* on variable *B* with all other variables held constant or otherwise equalized. Given this imposed closure, it makes sense that the researcher can predict effects.

When we move outside the laboratory, though, differences between positivists like Kerlinger (1973) and critical realists like Manicas and Secord (1983) become apparent. For positivists, predicting behaviour in the world requires little more than merely extrapolating from behaviour in the laboratory, although it *is* acknowledged that prediction in the world is a more complex task, because of the multiplicity of variables that operate freely there. Still, prediction is seen as possible; one just needs a larger prediction equation that either takes more variables (and their interactions) into account or more adequately identifies the most potent variables for scrutiny.

But for critical realists, the real world is a whole new ball game. Unlike the laboratory, the real world is an open system, where the *ceteris paribus* assumption that guides laboratory research no longer holds. The problem, as Manicas and Secord (1983) describe it, is that in the real world, *ceteris* is never *paribus*: all else is never equal. And because it's typically impossible to predict the particular status that "all other variables" will occupy (except in other closed systems), prediction in the real world becomes an impossible task. Manicas and Secord suggest that it is still reasonable to *explain* how a particular phenomenon was produced, although we may not have been able to *predict* its occurrence; that is, they argue that in open systems, prediction and explanation are *not* symmetrical—one can explain and understand without necessarily being able to predict. Furthermore, they and others (e.g., Cook & Campbell 1979) suggest that it's possible to offer this explanation in a compelling manner that would rise above the pejorative characterizations of positivists such as Kerlinger.

To Hypothesize or Not to Hypothesize?

As we've seen, the status of the hypothesis is not as clear-cut as the positivist accounts found in most research textbooks would imply. The arguments against always requiring explicit hypothesizing are very compelling, but there is value in the idea of making one's research logic public. The difficulty arises from two sources. First is a misplaced belief that "making public" and "hypothesis testing" are synonymous. Researchers do themselves and science a disservice when they do not formulate their procedures and explanations in a way that allows scrutiny by other scientists. Neither inductive nor deductive researchers would disagree with that point.

As for hypothesis testing per se, a formalized hypothesis may not be appropriate for every research inquiry. Whether it is will depend on such considerations as the work that has already been done in the area in question, your research objectives, and other aspects of your research perspective. This book aims to delineate a methodology that is compatible with both hypothesis-driven (i.e., deductive) and hypothesis-generating (i.e., inductive) modes of inquiry.

A second difficulty arises from the way a hypothesis is defined in more quantitative and experimental types of research (which involves specifying a hypothesis and parallel "null" hypotheses that can be tested statistically) as definitive. Alternatively, one can focus more on the process of *hypothesizing*— maybe "speculating" would be a better word—that permeates all forms of research. In that sense, hypotheses or speculations are the gas that propels and helps guide the empirical bus.

OPERATIONALIZING VARIABLES

Stating the variables of interest to you, whether as a formal hypothesis (X is related to Y) or as a research question (What is the relationship between X and Y?) is a big step forward, but it's still not enough. The next step involves becoming *even more specific* about what you mean by your key variables of interest and how you propose to measure and/or manipulate those variables. You must define exactly what operations you will perform and what procedures you'll follow to measure the phenomena of interest. Remember that science embraces theory *and* data; you must now decide how to articulate the link between the two. Normally, you will consider two types of definitions: a **nominal definition** and an **operational definition.**

Nominal or Constitutive Definitions

The nominal definition (sometimes called the constitutive definition) involves articulating what you mean by the concept under scrutiny. It's a bit like supplying a dictionary definition, although the nominal definition may be linked to one's theoretical stance. The nominal definition of "suicide," for example, might be "the intentional taking of one's own life." "Aggression" might be "the intentional hurting of another person by word and/or deed." A "reinforcer" is defined theoretically as anything that increases the probability that a particular response will be emitted again. A "crime" may be "any violation of the criminal law."

But nominal definitions aren't always so straightforward. Individuals with differing theoretical backgrounds, and even researchers and research participants, may mean very different things by a particular concept. The term "pornography" is illustrative. Although it has a lengthy tradition of referring only to material that is in some sense sexually explicit (e.g., see Wilson 1973; see also U.S. Commission on Obscenity & Pornography 1970), feminist writing in this area distinguishes between "pornography" and "erotica" (e.g., see R. Morgan 1980; Steinem 1980). "Pornography" refers specifically to materials that portray violent or otherwise power-imbalanced relations, and although it typically refers to such relations in the context of sexual activity, it's not necessarily limited to that domain. A lack of sensitivity to this different definitional base, as well as considerable self-righteousness among researchers in both theoretical camps about the supposedly inherent "correctness" of their respective definitions, has led to considerable superfluous conflict: individuals who argue about "pornography" can actually be talking about very different things.

As the preceding paragraphs suggest, variations among researchers in the constitutive definition of theoretical variables may reflect ideological, theoretical, or disciplinary differences among those researchers. We noted earlier, for example, that a crime might be defined as "any violation of the criminal law." Although this is obviously a reasonable and defensible definition, many would argue that such a choice reflects tacit agreement with status quo interests and should be replaced with a broader, narrower, or even totally different focus.

Because one's choice of constitutive definition affects how one goes about conceptualizing one's research strategy, Kuhn (1970) argues that our observations are not *theory-neutral* but *theory-laden*. Such variation among researchers is not unhealthy; what's important is that researchers articulate their definitions and be aware of the values inherent in those choices.

Operational Definitions

Following from the nominal definition is the operational definition, which is more closely linked to what we will *do*. The operational definition involves giving specific empirical meaning to a concept. We delineate the specific indicators or operations that are to be taken as representative of a concept. The trick here is to be specific about how you will derive, create, identify, or measure the indicator, and to choose one or more indicators that best approximate your nominal definition. The nominal definition articulated what you were after; the operational definition specifies how you propose to capture it.

INDICATORS

This process might still sound somewhat foreign to you, but it's analogous to processes we engage in every day. If you meet someone for the first time, the number of questions that person asks about you, the amount of eye contact he or she makes, and his or her tone of voice may be seen as indicators of how interested that person is in you. If the other person laughs at your jokes and the space between you begins to shrink, those may be taken as indicators that you like each other. Or if you hear two people calling each other "Sputtums" and "Bunky," you might see this as an indication that they are deliriously in love and/or have been watching too many 1950s Hollywood movies. In each case, you're observing concrete actions (e.g., two people holding hands) and, on the basis of your observation, inferring the existence of some underlying construct or variable (i.e., the two people like each other).

Of course, there *are* times when these indicators may be erroneous. A person may hold another's hand to restrain him or her rather than to demonstrate affection. Someone who asks a lot of questions about you may not be particularly interested in you, but may want to divert attention away from himself or herself. And people sometimes laugh at your jokes only out of politeness or to relieve tension, and the space between you may be shrinking only because the other person can't hear what you're saying. But despite such exceptions, these indicators are probably, in general, fairly accurate ones and, hence, overall, fairly useful, particularly when they are observed in combination.

At the same time, one can also envision bad or poor indicators of a concept. If we took "a person running" to be an indicator of "a crime having just been committed," we would likely be wrong more often than we were right and would probably get on the wrong side of many joggers, soccer players, and people in a hurry. Similarly, many people are so socially insensitive that when someone they are attracted to does anything short of telling them to "get lost," they perceive the other person as "coming on" to them or otherwise encouraging further interaction.

Much the same occurs in the social sciences, although the process varies depending on whether the researcher follows an inductive or a deductive approach. Deductive researchers begin with a variable of interest (e.g., liking) and then try to generate a list of indicators that can be used systematically to classify people on that dimension. The indicators might be behavioural (e.g., whether two people hold hands or how much eye contact they make with each other); archival (e.g., the content of letters the two people exchange); physiological (e.g., changes in galvanic skin response that occur for one person when a second enters the room); or self-report (e.g., answers to the question "Do you like that person?"). None of these indicators is *itself* "liking"—we never observe pure reality, only our constructions of it—but each can arguably be linked to our understanding of that construct. Demonstrating this linkage involves assessing the **epistemic relationship** between the theoretical variable and the particular indicator or measure we have chosen to represent it.

Inductive researchers are apt to see specifying operational definitions in advance, particularly in the exploratory phases of research, as imposing meaning on a situation prematurely. In inductive inquiry, rather than being externally *imposed by* a naive researcher, one's theoretical constructs and operationalizations of them should *emerge from* the process of exploratory inquiry; one must first take the time to understand the meaning that participants attach to different situations and behaviours.

Despite the differences between inductive and deductive researchers in the way they go about operationalizing variables, *both* sets of researchers *do* operationalize. This is little more than a truism: we ultimately cannot observe reality itself but must instead focus on its manifestations (e.g., behaviour, perceptions, products). Deductive researchers are more interested in specifying indicators ahead of time because for them part of the challenge of science is to develop constructs and operationalizations that are generalizable across different situations; the researcher is viewed as the privileged individual who "knows best" and can grasp the bigger picture that few others see. Inductive researchers are prepared for such generalizations to reveal themselves over time, but in the interim wish to ensure that they treat the particular situation at hand with some integrity, which means listening to the understandings that exist among those participating in the research.

But note that both sets of researchers try to link abstract theoretical constructs and particular empirical attributes that are indicators of those constructs. This textbook adopts a position that is not inconsistent with either mode of inquiry; the main requirement is that researchers articulate their constructs and operationalizations in a way that affords communication between researchers and is amenable to public scrutiny. This says little more than that "being empirical" requires a commitment to both theory (abstract explanatory concepts) and data (real-world evidence) and that researchers are obliged to articulate the links (i.e., the epistemic relationship) they make between the two.

OPERATIONS

Note that all the indicators discussed above involve deciding which real-world events we consider indicative of a particular theoretical construct. Kerlinger (1973) calls these *measured* operational definitions. At issue is how to capture the variable in some systematic fashion. But not all indicators are of that type.

Some researchers, particularly those involved in experimental research, prefer to create variables of theoretical interest,[8] in which case the way the variable is created operationally defines the variable. For example, in one classic study, Barker, Dembo, and Lewin (1943) set out to test the hypothesis that frustration leads to aggression. They created a situation in which the children who participated were frustrated by being placed in a room where attractive toys were clearly visible but could not be reached. In another classic study, Aronson and Mills (1959) investigated the relationship between severity of initiation and liking for a group. To create a "severe" initiation researchers had participants read sexually oriented passages aloud in the presence of others.

Both of these are examples of what are known as *experimental* operational definitions (e.g., see Kerlinger 1973). Manipulating a situation to create variables of interest is characteristic of experimental methods, and the operational definition of the construct is the set of experimental procedures used to create it. Thus, frustration was operationally defined by Barker and colleagues (1943) as the emotion a child feels when denied access to an attractive toy. A "severe initiation" was operationally defined by Aronson and Mills (1959) as the experience of university students asked to speak publicly about sexual matters in the course of demonstrating their eligibility for group membership.

Clearly, these two examples do not encompass "all" that frustration or a severe initiation involves, but the two studies *do* seem to create situations likely to produce the desired constructs. Further, note two benefits of this technique. First, creating the situation allows researchers to validate their operations by including other measures, often known as **manipulation checks,** in their procedures. Thus, if asking students to read sexual passages aloud really does embarrass them, and if volunteers for the experiment are asked to rate how embarrassed they feel, then we would expect the group of volunteers who read such passages to rate themselves as more embarrassed, on the average, than a comparable group of students who were not asked to read those passages.

Second, researchers are obliged to describe their operations in sufficient detail for others to replicate their procedures, thereby encouraging debate about the validity and/or limitations of those operations. For example, Gerard and Mathewson (1966) later argued that the students in Aronson and Mills's study may have been "turned on" by the sexually explicit passages and may therefore have rated the group discussion more positively because of the sexual glow they felt, rather than because of the extremity of their initiation.

Evaluating Operational Definitions

There's no reason to believe that researchers are blessed with inherently greater insight about people or human behaviour than anyone else, at least not insight that exists independently of the information they unearth by empirical methods. Developmental psychologists likely have as many "problem" children; marital counsellors likely have as many problem marriages and divorces; and clinical psychologists likely have as many personal problems, overall, as the rest of us. Similarly, social scientists are as likely to show the same lack of insight that sometimes characterizes us all in our non-professional lives: occasionally poor decision making, a difficulty in differentiating what we *wish* were true from what *is,* and a difficulty in empathizing with perspectives other than our own. If social scientists have *any* special insights, it is because they occasionally get lucky, as we all sometimes do, or because they are particularly creative, as we all sometimes are, or because they subject their insights to the rigours of empirical method before they espouse their beliefs.

Empirical method requires researchers to articulate the bases of their procedures and inferences. Intuitive revelation on the part of researchers—or anyone—is *not* the stuff of science. Accordingly, researchers are expected to present some sort of argument to show why that choice of indicators or operations was a good one. This procedure, referred to as assessing the epistemic relationship or as establishing the validity of your operations or indicators, is generally done in one or (preferably) more of three ways: citing tradition, rational argument, or empirical demonstration.

CITING TRADITION

As we've asserted before, science is a *communal* enterprise. Thus, establishing connections between you and other researchers—by noting the ways in which your conceptualizations and operationalizations are similar to and/or different from those of other researchers—is an important responsibility.

For example, laboratory researchers looking at aggression often use the Buss Shock Apparatus. Participants are told that they can use this apparatus to deliver one of five levels of electric shock to another participant (who is generally a confederate of the experimenter's and who never actually receives any shocks). The average level of shock delivered is taken as an index of the aggressiveness of the participant's behaviour (e.g., see Altemeyer 1981; Donnerstein & Berkowitz 1981). Similarly, in the field of interpersonal dynamics, a participant's tendency to engage in cooperative or competitive behaviour was typically assessed with the "prisoner's dilemma" (e.g., see Deutsch 1973).

On the one hand, there's good reason to encourage such practices. Using similar measures makes it easier to compare results between studies and can encourage the embellishment of knowledge systems across researchers. But such practices also encourage **mono-operationism** (also known as *mono-operation bias*) and **mono-method bias** (e.g., see Campbell 1969a; Cook & Campbell 1979), that is, respectively, an over-reliance on a particular measure of a construct and on a particular *way* of measuring it (e.g., by self-report questionnaire). By itself, "That's how others did it" isn't sufficient justification for considering a measure to be valid. One also would want to consider at least one, and preferably both, of the other two ways of assessing the epistemic relationship.

RATIONAL ARGUMENT

You also should be prepared to explain on a purely rational basis why you feel the indicator you choose is a reasonable one and, in particular, why you feel that it's better for your purposes than others you might have chosen. You might present such arguments through some open-ended narrative or use the schema offered in Table 2.2. Either way, the researcher must explain to others why a particular operationalization "makes sense" and must articulate the relationship between concept and indicator.

Table 2.2 uses the example of "aggression" to show some of the possibilities that exist whenever we use an operational definition to categorize an event. Across the top of the table we see the "real" situation according to what we mean by aggression—whether,

Table 2.2

The Four Possibilities Generated by the Cross-tabulation of the Situation as It "Really" Is and as Coded through the Operational Definition

| | | Is act "really" aggressive according to nominal definition? | |
		YES	NO
Is act categorized as "aggressive" according to operational definition?	YES	1 Correct categorization (true positive)	2 Erroneous categorization (false positive or Type I error)
	NO	3 Erroneous categorization (false negative or Type II error)	4 Correct categorization (true negative)

according to our *nominal* definition, the behaviour we're looking at is "really" aggressive. On the left-hand side of the table are the two possibilities we have open to us: if the indicator *is* present and/or some specified criterion *is* met, the act is labelled "aggressive"; if the indicator is *not* present and/or if some specified criterion is *not* met, we label the act "non-aggressive." The cross-tabulation of these two dimensions yields four possibilities.

We might do any of the following:

1. Label an act "aggressive" when it really *is* an aggressive act (cell 1; a correct categorization). This is also sometimes known as a *true positive,* since one is accurately saying "yes, it is."
2. Label an act "aggressive" when it's actually non-aggressive (cell 2; an error). This type of error is sometimes referred to as a *false positive,* since one is erroneously saying "yes, it is" when really it's not (i.e., it is falsely categorized as a positive); it is also sometimes referred to as a *Type I error.*
3. Label an act "non-aggressive" when it's actually an aggressive act (cell 3; an error). This type of error is sometimes called a *false negative,* since one is erroneously saying "no, it is not" when really it is; it is also sometimes referred to as a *Type II error.*
4. Label an act "non-aggressive" when it really is a non-aggressive act (cell 4; a correct categorization). This is sometimes referred to as a *true negative,* since one is accurately saying "no, it is not."

As an example, let's begin with the nominal definition of aggression as "any intentional effort to hurt through word or deed." Operationally, we might decide to count "any physical contact accompanied by loud vocalizations" as aggressive. You'll learn how to assess the epistemic relationship empirically later in this text (e.g., Chapter 6); here, we can rationally consider it via the alternatives expressed in Table 2.1.

First, it is clear that our operational definition may yield many *accurate* classifications. Someone who yells at and strikes another person with the intention of hurting is clearly aggressive according to our nominal definition, and that person will be accurately categorized that way according to our operational definition (i.e., a true positive; see cell 1). Similarly, many acts that do *not* involve striking and yelling (e.g., telling a joke, asking directions to the washroom, eating a canapé) will accurately be labelled non-aggressive (i.e., a true negative; see cell 4).

But prospective errors of classification might also be envisioned. Mock fighting and horseplay, for example, would not be aggressive acts according to our nominal definition (because of the absence of intent to hurt), but might well be classified as aggressive according to our operational definition if they were boisterous and engaged in physical contact (i.e., a false positive, or Type I error; see cell 2). A major source of error, however, would be false negatives, or Type II errors (see cell 3): many aggressive acts (e.g., insults, surreptitious aggression, intentional embarrassment or humiliation) would not be covered by the operational definition. Obviously, one indicator can be considered better than another indicator of the same concept to the extent that it yields more accurate classifications and fewer erroneous ones.

In sum, operational definitions represent an effort to articulate the connections between our conceptual variables (theory) and the procedures we use to capture them (data). We must identify not only the presence of some attribute or phenomenon, but also its absence.

The goal is to define one's concepts operationally in a way that allows systematic application of the definition, maximizing accurate classification and minimizing inaccurate classification. Empirically, the question of how well an operational definition mirrors real differences in the phenomenon under study is a question of assessing the epistemic relationship between concept and indicator. The more accurate the classification, the better the epistemic relationship.

Adequate operationalizations are often hard to generate; no indicator you choose will be perfect. As an example, recall that we nominally defined "suicide" as "the intentional taking of one's own life." An obvious operationalization of suicide would be the "suicide rate" or "deaths proclaimed to be suicides by a coroner or other legitimate authority." But do suicide statistics properly identify all those people who intentionally took their own lives? Probably not. There undoubtedly will be some people who took their own lives but managed to make it look like an accident. Similarly, some true accidents—and even some homicides—may be proclaimed suicides because of the circumstances surrounding the death. The greater the prospective loss if the judgment is "suicide," the more likely coroners might be to err on the side of caution before declaring the death a suicide.

Let's take another example. Suppose you want to evaluate whether students who receive a pep talk from the president of the university ultimately become better students than those who do not receive the talk. You would need some way to operationalize student "goodness." What would you propose?

We've asked that question of students in our classes, and they always offer numerous possibilities. Their suggestions have included (a) grade point average, (b) frequency of participation in class discussions, (c) quality of participation in class discussions, (d) involvement in extracurricular activities, (e) frequency of attendance, and (f) hours spent studying.

Each of these proposed operational definitions has strengths and weaknesses. Grade point averages are quantitative and easy to gather. But grades may not be comparable across courses, departments, and faculties, a situation that may pose a problem, depending on our research design. Frequency of participation in class discussions may be a good indicator, since one might argue that "better" students contribute more often than do "poorer" students. But the time investment required to gather those data would be significant. If we go ahead and do so anyway, can we just count the number of times a student says something? If so, should questions be treated the same as statements? Should confused, incoherent comments receive the same weight as clear, insightful ones? And if we want to assess the quality of the contribution, who is the appropriate judge?

EMPIRICAL DEMONSTRATION

The third way to evaluate the epistemic relationship between a theoretical construct and its operational

indicator is to assess it empirically. When it comes to manipulated independent variables, this assessment is most often done by manipulation checks.

In one classic study, Stanley Schachter (1959) wanted to examine the relationship between anxiety and affiliation; he needed to find a way to manipulate the anxiety level of participants. He decided to do this by telling participants, when they showed up for the study, that they would be receiving painful electric shocks as part of the procedures. That certainly sounds like the sort of thing that might induce anxiety, or perhaps fear, but Schachter went a step further: he asked students to rate (as part of a bigger questionnaire) how they felt at that time. And sure enough, participants who expected shocks rated themselves as significantly more anxious and expressed significantly greater reservations about participating in the study than did other participants.

That is not a particularly surprising finding, nor should it be. But it does increase our confidence that Schachter really did manipulate anxiety levels as he had intended. Once again, the question is, Did Schachter really manipulate the variable he *thought* he was manipulating?[9]

Manipulation checks are often easily included in many experimental procedures: participants in a "democratic" group structure should rate the group as more democratic and should believe themselves to have more opportunity for participation and influence than should participants in a group with an "autocratic" structure; participants exposed to an "educational" video should rate themselves as "more informed about the topic" than should another group not exposed to the video; and so forth.

For *measured* indicators, the situation becomes a bit more complex but is generally considered to be a two-stage process. The researcher first demonstrates the reliability of his or her operationalizing schema. Having shown the measure to be reliable, he or she would then demonstrate that it is also valid.

Reliability

"Reliability" is generally synonymous with consistency, whether of the same phenomenon over time or of judgments about the same phenomenon across different observers. Many constructs that interest social scientists are considered to be relatively stable. For example, attitudes, aptitudes, personality traits, personal values, cognitive styles, and organizational processes may change to some degree over time but are generally fairly consistent, particularly over shorter periods and in the absence of significant relevant life events.

To use a physical example, our height doesn't change much from week to week. If we have a good measure of height, it should thus show us to be about the same height from week to week. If we measure 1.8 metres (six feet) tall one week, but only 1.4 metres (four feet seven inches) the next, we might suspect that our measuring stick isn't a very good one.[10]

Now imagine that we administer a test of mechanical aptitude to a person one week, and it reveals her to be a prospective Thomas Alva Edison. We administer the same test to the same person one week later, and on this second occasion it reveals that she would probably have difficulty operating a light switch. If this occurred, we hope you would be more than a little surprised. Given that the attribute you're dealing with is a reasonably stable one, any legitimate measurement of that attribute *should* classify the person consistently over repeated measurements. In fact, researchers often test a measure of some attribute by administering it to the same group of persons on two successive occasions. This procedure, known as **test–retest reliability,** reveals whether classifications on the attribute are indeed consistently (i.e., reliably) produced.

A second reliability strategy is known as **interrater reliability.** If you've adequately specified what a particular construct means to you, other researchers should be able to read your explanation (or be trained in your procedures) and then proceed to make the same judgments you would. If they cannot, then you haven't explained it clearly enough. For example, in one study, Ted was interested in doing a content analysis of video pornography that involved scene-by-scene coding of videos according to their sexual, violent, and sexually violent content

(Palys 1986). Five different people were to code the videos, so it was clearly very important that they all did so consistently (i.e., reliably).

Ted first read the literature and wrote a coding manual that outlined what *he* understood sex, violence, and sexual violence to be and detailed how he felt they should be coded. After a period of preliminary training, but before actually going ahead with the study, he and his assistants sat down and coded the same set of about 100 scenes without communicating with one another. When they compared notes afterward, it turned out that they were generally quite consistent. But a number of problems also emerged that had not been anticipated when the original manual was prepared. So, it was back to the drawing board, where Ted clarified and elaborated on the initial coding scheme; what began as a 12-page manual soon grew to about 35 pages. But it was well worth it. When the five members of the team again sat down to independently code another set of about 100 scenes, they averaged between 80 percent and 90 percent exact agreement in their categorizations, which was sufficient to go ahead.

As a bonus, the coding manual exists as an archival document; any researcher can use the same coding scheme should they wish to replicate or extend that research. And the manual itself is also an elaborate specification of the links between the various theoretical constructs Ted was employing (e.g., sex, violence, sexual violence, aggression, power, consent) and the data his research team were gathering. Finally, the manual can serve as a departure point for researchers who wish to discuss the limitations of the method and to contribute further to the spirit of discovery by offering an alternative.

Validity

Although the demonstration of reliability is considered a prerequisite to validity, the two terms are *not* synonymous. Rather, they should be seen as two successive hurdles. If a measure fails the reliability hurdle, there's no use going any further, since in most cases it can't be valid.[11] If the measure *is* shown to be reliable, its validity remains an open question.

Consider a variable like shoe size. Shoe size is a relatively stable attribute, at least among adults, and we could develop a technique of measuring shoe size (as shoe manufacturers have) that would let us score individuals consistently (i.e., reliably) both over time (test–retest) and across observers (i.e., inter-rater). But shoe size is probably invalid as an indicator of intelligence or creativity.

Operationalizations are considered to be valid *for some purpose.* To demonstrate validity, you must therefore show that your particular operationalization accomplishes the purpose for which you intend to use it. The researcher's task is to pick a relevant criterion in which the construct is embodied and then show that the operationalization is indeed related to that criterion (**convergent validation**), but *not* related to other constructs you do not want to measure (**divergent validation**).

For example, if you develop an operationalization for a construct like "love" (as did Rubin 1973), people who proclaim themselves to be "in love" should score or be classified differently on your measure from persons who do not declare themselves to be "in love" (as Rubin in fact showed). You'd also want to show that it's loving itself you're assessing most directly, as opposed to either related but different constructs (e.g., liking, infatuation, respect) or clearly unrelated constructs (e.g., the tendency to respond to questions in a socially desirable manner).

If both the operationalization (e.g., Rubin's measure of "loving") and the independent criterion (e.g., self-reports of whether the persons were in love) are obtained at about the same time, then we speak of **concurrent validation.** In **predictive validation,** administering the operational measure and observing the criterion occur at different times. For example, a researcher who wishes to assess the predictive validity of a measure of "dangerousness" among convicted offenders would administer the measure, make decisions about dangerousness, and then follow up the sample over time to see who had indeed exhibited "dangerous" behaviour in accordance with prediction (e.g., see Menzies 1989; Menzies, Webster, & Sepejak 1985).

Assessments of validity will be dealt with in greater detail later in this book (Chapters 6 and 9). Here, we need only note that empirical requirements recall the legendary Missourian who says "Show me." Recall also that operationalizations are never considered valid in a general sense, but rather are demonstrably valid (or invalid) *for some purpose* and within demonstrated constraints. Thus, if a procedure is shown to be a valid predictor of success in graduate school, that's all it's good for. A measure that's been shown to differentiate between criterion groups may not be valid for categorizing individuals. And if the validation process involves criterion groups that are clearly different (e.g., a group of neo-Nazis is shown, as expected, to have more authoritarian attitudes than a group of civil libertarians), the measure's validity must still be considered tentative with respect to finer distinctions.

Caveats Regarding Operationism

As we saw earlier, the process of research in the social sciences involves a continuing interaction between theory and data. Theoretical constructs are important entities in this scheme, and the operational definitions we choose represent our pragmatic attempts to gather information about the world that bears on our theoretical conceptions. Listed below are a few final admonitions.

MONO-OPERATION BIAS
Rarely can a single operationalization of a construct fully capture the richness of a theoretical construct. We do a disservice both to our theoretical constructs and to the research process if we repeatedly deal with only a single operationalization of a particular variable of interest to us. This problem is referred to as *mono-operation bias.*

Similarly, since all methods of gathering information have their respective advantages and limitations, we run the risk of producing method-dependent results if we always use, say, self-reports or archival sources. This problem is referred to as *mono-method bias.*

Researchers should use multiple operationalizations and multiple methods whenever possible. If you get the same results even when the theoretical construct is operationally defined in three different ways, you can draw conclusions more confidently than if you've defined it in only one way. And if the results *differ* depending on which operationalization is used, the inconsistency is provocative. Multiple operationalizations may also help resolve previous inconsistencies in the literature, by showing the relationships that exist among the respective operationalizations.

DEFINITIONAL OPERATIONISM

A particularly despicable example of mono-operation bias has been termed **definitional operationism** (e.g., see Campbell 1969a; Cook & Campbell 1979). This process involves essentially imposing a definition by fiat and ignoring the theoretical issues inherent in that choice. Rather than discussing the theoretical construct "intelligence," for example, and attempting to deal with the considerable difficulties of generating measures of that construct, definitional operationists seize on a particular operational definition—an IQ test, for example—and consider it to be definitive of the construct. The result is a tautological and hence trivial statement: "The scores from the IQ test are my operational definition of intelligence. What is intelligence? It is what the IQ test measures."

Besides being obviously circular, this data-oriented approach must also be considered anti-scientific: it implies a contentment with manipulating numbers without considering the theoretical constructs that underlie them and, hence, deflects rather than encourages embellishment and revision. Operationalizations are a means to an end, *not* an end in themselves.

SHOOTING FISH IN A BARREL

A common image in the Canadian North is the *inukshuk*: a huge stone humanoid figure, constructed with sharply angled rocks, giving the impression of a child's stick figure in three dimen-

sions. The Inuit used these figures when they hunted caribou. Two of the stone figures would be built quite some distance apart, one on either side of the caribou herd, so that the two figures formed a gateway leading toward a river or lake. A bit closer to the river or lake, two more figures would be constructed, somewhat closer together. Another pair would be located closer still, both to each other and to the river.

A sufficient number of these pairs in sequence creates a sort of connect-the-dots funnel with its smaller opening at the river. The Inuit would then show themselves to the caribou, who would run into the funnel and, because of their fear of the humanoid figures, would gradually be funnelled into the river. Caribou are easily hunted when swimming through the water, and the Inuit merely waited to hunt them from their kayaks. Thus, instead of trying to chase the caribou across half the Arctic, the Inuit elegantly created a situation where the caribou, in essence, come to them.

Laboratory experimentalists use an analogous strategy. Recall the examples of operationalizing "aggression" and "quality of student" cited earlier; clearly, no one operationalization could ever completely capture all aspects of a given variable. One solution to this dilemma is to use multiple operationalizations of the construct under consideration, capturing it in a variety of forms. Of course, this tactic requires considerable initiative on the part of the investigator and can pose difficulties when looking for many things at the same time.

To reduce this complexity, experimentalists have been encouraged (e.g., see Aronson & Carlsmith 1968; Festinger 1953) to construct situations that limit the research participants' response choices, "shutting off" other avenues and ensuring that behaviour is channelled into the desired avenue of expression. Many experiments on aggression, for example, construct situations where communication between participants cannot take place except by means of a numerically graded shock generator (e.g., see Altemeyer 1981; Donnerstein & Berkowitz 1981; Milgram 1963).

Although situations created for this purpose are convenient to the investigator and ensure a quantified dependent measure that consistently captures any aggressive leanings, such experiments have been accused of engendering the very behaviour whose existence is at issue. In a review of the laboratory-based research on how viewing aggressive pornography affects behaviour, for example, Fisher (1986) notes that the broader applicability of this research is seriously thwarted by the lack of any *other* response alternatives.[12] Participants cannot discuss the matter, nor can they indicate displeasure in other ways. Consequently, while such research may be useful for addressing theoretical questions of interest, it's not necessarily applicable to field situations with markedly different social structures.

DON'T BE TRIVIAL

"Good" operational definitions are difficult to create, and sometimes it seems that the more interesting the concept, the more difficult it is to operationalize. Take that as a challenge rather than as an excuse for getting into trivial areas of research.

You are what you do. When designing research, make what you do a conscious reflection of who you are and of what you believe is important.

SUMMING UP AND LOOKING AHEAD

In this chapter we have outlined some of the issues that one must address even before beginning the research process. One of the first involves getting an idea of *what* to research. The inductive-deductive dichotomy was introduced not only to explain in more detail a concept introduced in Chapter 1 as one on which researchers' preferences often differ, but also to show the complementarity of the two perspectives in achieving general scientific goals and the role that each can play in generating research possibilities.

We then outlined a set of five research objectives and discussed the role they play in any particular study. In the process, we suggested first that each of the objectives is integral to the overall process of understanding. No objective is inherently superior to any other. The central issue is whether the approach we adopt is suitable, given what we want and need to accomplish. We also described how the research objective you have will have major implications for *how* you sample, *who* or *what* you sample, and how you *design* your research. No research design is "best" for every situation. A research design is evaluated by how well it allows you to meet your research objectives, and different types of designs will be more or less useful for different objectives. Procedures that are extremely useful in an exploratory setting might be completely inappropriate for explanatory research, and vice versa.

We then discussed the usefulness of connecting with the literature—both in the library and through Internet-based sources—and encouraged researchers to avoid conceptualizing their research too narrowly.

The next consideration involves researchers taking their concerns and phrasing them in the form of a "researchable question." Although our aim is to do research in the broad sense, getting it done ultimately means concretely addressing a specific, researchable question in a particular setting at a given time. Notwithstanding the fact that some research is done simply to *find out* what a good research question would be, *serious* research cannot begin until the researcher has a focused issue on which to concentrate his or her energies. Put bluntly, it's difficult to search for an answer if you don't know what the question is. Doing research involves engaging reality, partly on its terms and partly on ours.

Once particular variables have been isolated for analysis, a next step in some cases, but not all, will be to specify a hypothesis for test. Although there are often good reasons for asserting a hypothesis, particularly when engaging in the deductive process of theory testing, there are at least as many situations where the researcher and the phenomenon under investigation would be ill served by engaging in such hypothetico-deductive inquiry. This is particularly so with respect to exploratory or formulative research, where priority is placed on ensuring that the research question(s) being posed and any hypotheses being expressed have meaning within the context being investigated.

Whether one engages in specific hypothesis testing or not, another issue that must be addressed concerns the links between one's theoretical variables and the actual measures or indicators that are taken as representative of those concepts in any given piece of research. The literature can be useful in identifying these operationalizations, or they emerge at the site from observation, collaborative strategizing, or the development of valid and reliable instruments. The issue here is one of considering and assessing the epistemic relationship that exists between one's theoretical (conceptual) variables and those concrete indicators that are used in one's research.

The notion of operationalization reflects science's dual commitment to theory *and* data. Deductivists and inductivists may argue about whether one should begin with the theoretical constructs and operationalize them or with exploratory observations from which grounded theoretical constructs can emerge. Qualitative and quantitative researchers may argue over whether variables of interest are most adequately described verbally or according to some numerical scale. But all researchers believe in an interplay between theory and data. And part of the turf that invariably comes with this dual commitment is the issue of how to move back and forth between these two levels of interest. The operational definition is little more than the procedural articulation of a variable of theoretical interest. *All* researchers operationalize, since all are committed to an ongoing dialectic involving both theory and data, and hence must at some point be explicit about the particular data in which their theoretical concepts live.

The question to be posed of *every* theoretical assertion is, What's the evidence for that? And operationalization addresses the links between theory and data. Constitutive (or nominal) definitions and operational definitions, respectively, draw attention to the theoretical and procedural worlds in which social scientists operate. Part of doing research involves being sufficiently detailed and vigilant about one's theoretical constructs and procedures that the links between these two levels can be articulated and examined.

Taken together, the issues described in this chapter offer a conceptual framework for approaching any given piece of research—you find a topic, determine your objectives, connect with the literature, and start thinking about how you will operationalize your terms (where the literature will again offer you some help). For some researchers theory will provide the questions and much of the design can be done from your desk; for other researchers, and particularly those in the field, the whole process may be a more collaborative one that emerges from interaction at the research site. How it happens will differ, but it will happen.

We're almost ready to start talking about gathering data. But before we do so, Chapters 3 through 5 will guide you over a crucial bridge between thinking about research and actually going out and doing it. In Chapters 3 and 4 we review two further foundations: the ethical principles that guide social scientists' efforts, and sampling considerations when deciding on whom or what to focus. At that point we will have enough of the big picture of our research to identify our interests and outline a general strategy of inquiry for addressing them; Chapter 5 describes the elements we need to have considered and will need to explain in a proposal.

STUDY QUESTIONS

1. Practitioners of the *inductive* and *deductive* approaches to science were perceived for many years as being in conflict with one another. Differentiate between these two models of science, and indicate how Wallace (1971), through his *wheel of science,* tries to resolve the conflict between them.

2. What role do *theories* play in empirical research, and in what sense are they both *uplifting* and *constraining*?

3. What do practitioners of the inductive and deductive approaches agree on and disagree on with respect to the role of theory?

4. From the deductive perspective, one begins with a theory, generates hypotheses that are implied by the theory, and then gathers data to

test the hypothesis (and hence the theory). If the data do *not* support the hypothesis, we say that the theory has been refuted or disproved. If the data are consistent with the theory, we can say that the theory has been "supported," but we do *not* say that it has been "proved." Why?

5. Look at the definitions of "research design" offered by Selltiz, Wrightsman, and Cook (1976) and Denzin and Lincoln (1994), and explain in your own words what each says. On what elements do the two sets of authors agree, and where do you sense differences between them?

6. Explain the concepts of *legitimation* and *representation*.

7. Pick a research setting of interest to you (e.g., a courtroom, a restaurant, a video arcade) and indicate the different ways you might approach that setting depending on whether your research objectives are *exploratory, descriptive, relational,* or *explanatory.*

8. Explain the roles relegated to exploratory research in inductive and deductive approaches and why they differ.

9. Why is it impossible to identify one or two "best" methods for all social science research?

10. In what sense are a researcher's values and attitudes reflected in that person's research? How might a researcher who values democracy and egalitarianism ensure that these values are manifest in his or her research?

11. Social scientists argue that you should always begin your research by *reviewing the literature* in the relevant area. What benefits are gained by doing so?

12. "Should the use of marijuana be decriminalized?" is a good question, but is it a *researchable* question? If so, explain why; if not, indicate why not and how you might change it into one.

13. Should you feel obliged to specify a formal hypothesis when doing research? What, in your own words, are the strongest arguments for both sides? Are positions on the induc-

tive–deductive issue related to positions on the hypothesis issue?

14. Because of budget cuts to the universities and the consequent limitations on resources, your department has decided to impose a quota system: only a limited number of students will be allowed to major in the program and to take senior-level (third- and fourth-year) courses. Feeling that access, if it must be limited, should be limited to the "better" students, the department is looking for ways to operationalize "student quality." Suggest an appropriate *nominal definition* of "student quality," indicate at least two ways in which you might operationally define that variable, and evaluate the epistemic relationship of each.

15. How do *nominal* and *operational* definitions relate to *hypotheses*?

16. On what three bases might one justify the choice of any given operationalization or indicator?

17. At the library, locate two recent empirical articles, one each from two of your areas of interest. What concepts are being scrutinized in each study? How are they operationalized? Evaluate the *epistemic relationships* created. What values are implicit in the authors' choice of variables and operationalizations? On what basis (or bases) do the authors justify their choice of operationalization?

18. Compare and contrast *measured* and *experimental* operational definitions.

19. What is *definitional operationism*, and why is it problematic?

20. Do both inductive and deductive researchers engage in operationalization when they do research? In what ways do they differ in how they do research?

NOTES

1. Recall here the statements made in Chapter 1 about knowledge as a social product and about the social responsibility of researchers. At the turn of the 20th century, Lombroso's theory fit

very well into the social Darwinism that was prevalent at the time, helping to reaffirm the alleged "inferiority" of nonwhite races (see Gould [1981] and Lewontin [1991] for an excellent analysis of the racism inherent in many such physiognomic schemes).

2. When the day of the movie showing finally arrived, Ted found that although all members of the audience had heard exactly the same film description, only 4 of the attendees were from groups that had been told that the film had received a "general" rating. About 40 attendees were from groups who had been told about the film's "adult" rating, and more than 100 had heard the "restricted adult" classification.

3. For example, a feminist theorist might engage in oral history interviews with women who worked in munitions factories during World War II. She engages in *representation* by deciding to quote the women at length. She *legitimizes* this by stating that women's words have been undervalued in research, so that including them in her article is an important effort to alleviate that error. As for the quotations themselves, she may also *legitimize* them by stating that the women were given the opportunity to read a draft of the article in order to voice any concerns over how they were quoted.

4. Of course, this begs consideration of the realist–constructionist issue of whether it's *ever* possible to "really" know Montreal, that is, whether there is a "real" truth about Montreal to be known. Realists would argue that there are "objective" truths about Montreal that we could discover: its history, demographics, and so on. Constructionists, on the other hand, would assert that while such information represents one way of "knowing" Montreal, there are many other, equally legitimate ways of knowing the city, for example, from the perspective of the anglophone and francophone, the taxi driver and the politician, young and old, and so on.

5. Actually, the sampling issue begins to get a bit complex here. Please bear with us as we skirt those complexities now, leaving them for later in the book (see Chapter 6); if you can't wait, see Cook and Campbell (1979) and/or Mook (1983). To give you only the bottom line here, the major requirement for relational research is not representativeness per se, but whether the sample has a reasonable degree of variability on all the variables (e.g., a mix of males and females, different militarist and non-militarist attitudes represented, etc.).

6. A favourite graffiti Ted saw painted on a wall a few years ago theorized that "A society that makes dreams impossible makes dreams big business."

7. We use the term "stakeholders" frequently in this text to mean people that you, as a researcher, recognize as having a legitimate stake in the outcome of your research. All stakeholders should have a chance to offer input at the design stage. Note, by the way, that although we refer to the stakeholders as "them," you, too, are a stakeholder in the research, since you, too, have constituencies to whom you must answer (e.g., yourself, colleagues, journal editors).

8. The reasons behind this preference are not important here but are detailed in Chapter 9.

9. Part of the reason for doing that assessment in the experimental setting is to ensure that one is able to interpret the experiment's results when it is concluded. For example, let's say that Schachter did the experiment and did not find the effect he hypothesized. Why might that have happened? One possibility would be that his hypothesis was wrong; that is, there is *no* relationship between anxiety and affiliation. But the second possibility would be that he never gave the result a *chance* to happen because his manipulation didn't effectively raise the anxiety level of his research participants; that is, it was not an adequate or fair test of the hypothesis. By including the manipulation check, Schachter not only shows us that

his manipulation was a valid one, he also precludes the rival plausible explanation (see Chapter 9) that any non-significant result was due to his never having really manipulated the variable he wanted in the first place.

10. The height example is an apt one in another way, since it is also the case that height may change significantly over some periods (e.g., between ages 2 and 12) but not others (e.g., between ages 30 and 40). In the former case, a "good" measure would *look* "unreliable" because the phenomenon itself (i.e., the child's height) is changing. In the latter case, however, we *would* expect the measure to be "reliable": measurements at the two points in time *should* be similar, and dissimilar measurements would lead us to be suspect about our ruler. The example should also sensitize you to the way in which knowledge from other areas (e.g., child development, anatomy) can be used to inform measurement concerns, as well as to the way "commonsensical" knowledge may underlie much of the measurement process. Note that this latter situation can be both a strength *and* a weakness.

11. Note, incidentally, that we are assuming here that the phenomenon with which one is dealing is in fact relatively stable, such that "reliability" (in the sense of consistency) should be expected. If one is dealing with a more dynamic phenomenon, however, a valid method *should* show change, which might *appear* as "unreliability." For example, if we look at the thermometer on the back porch on a hot August day and see that it shows 30° Celsius, and then look at it again on a cool September evening and see that it still shows 30° Celsius, we would be more likely to wonder whether the thermometer works than to extol its "reliability." In such cases, methods of reliability assessment that emphasize inter-rater reliability rather than test–retest reliability would be preferred, and a clear prospective research focus might be to explain the source of these variations. (See also note 10.)

12. These issues are revisited in Chapter 9, which discusses experimentation and considers in greater detail the experimental research that has investigated the links between exposure to pornography and violence against women.

CHAPTER 3

ETHICS IN SOCIAL RESEARCH

After some beginning lessons about "science" and "empiricism," followed by a discussion of the preliminary stages of conceptualizing research, we're almost ready to tackle the procedural aspects of gathering data. Our emphasis thus far has been on the *strategy* of investigation. But as Schatzman and Strauss (1973) remind us, the conscientious researcher "needs both strategy and morality. The first without the second is cruel; the second without the first is ineffectual" (146).

In talking about research ethics, there are two things we must distinguish: **research ethics** and the ***regulation* of research ethics.** "Research ethics" refers to principles that guide the way we interact with research participants and the commitment to safeguard their rights and interests.

The "regulation of ethics" refers to the way that "research ethics" are interpreted and adjudicated—that is, the bureaucratization and institutionalization of research ethics review. Focusing on the regulation of ethics brings us to the way certain bodies define and regulate "ethical action." These include (a) disciplinary associations (e.g., the Canadian Psychological Association, the American Sociological Association, the American Anthropological Association), which require researchers trained in and/or identifying with those disciplines to adhere to disciplinary norms and standards; (b) university ethics review committees, which are often mandated in university ethics policies to approve or reject on ethical grounds the research that those in the university propose; and (c) governmental entities, such as Canada's three federal granting agencies (the Canadian Institutes of Health Research, the Social Sciences and Humanities Research Council, and the

National Sciences and Engineering Research Council), which first produced the *Tri-Council Policy Statement: Ethical Conduct for Research Involving Humans* (Canadian Institutes of Health Research et al. 1998) that now governs all university researchers and others applying for granting council funds to adhere to its code of conduct.[1]

One fascinating thing about ethics is that few researchers disagree over what the major principles of research ethics are. However, they often disagree vehemently about what the principles mean and how they apply to the specific issues that arise in any given research project. In this chapter we will try to leave you with an appreciation of how and why that happens. First, we will examine major principles of ethics that appear in list after list of ethics principles; then we will look at trends in the regulation of ethics and issues that arose at the turn of the 21st century.

ETHICS PRINCIPLES

To Research or Not to Research

The choice that resides at the beginning of any research project that involves human research participants is whether to do the research at all. This "basic ethical dilemma" sees the researcher balancing two important and sometimes conflicting obligations: to science and to the participants. The first is a *scientific obligation* to *do* research in the *best* way we know how. Being a social scientist involves a commitment to the value of knowledge and understanding. Our social mandate is to understand all aspects of society not only as an end in itself, but also thereby to contribute to the development of rational social policy. Since much of our research involves human participants we also have a *humanistic obligation* to treat people with dignity and to safeguard their interests. When participants are volunteers who are participating only because we entered their lives and asked them to do so, our obligation only increases to ensure that no harm should come to them. That responsibility rises exponentially when the participants do not even know they are participating in a piece of research, as often occurs, for example, when we do observational research in public settings, in archives, or perhaps even after a person's death.

The problem is that the scientific and humanistic obligations frequently are at odds with each other. In some cases the comparison of the two interests makes it obvious which is the "right" choice. For example, beginning in 1932 the United States Public Health Service (USPHS) undertook the Tuskegee syphilis study, which ended up being a 40-year **longitudinal** study of the consequences of untreated syphilis. The USPHS did not infect anyone with syphilis; rather, it identified a group of men who had contracted the disease and, without their consent, decided it would be useful to observe systematically their deterioration over time. When the study began, there was no known treatment for the disease. However, even after a cure was identified, the researchers made sure that the men in their sample—all of whom were African-American—received no treatment, since doing so would have "spoiled" the study.

Even if we were to assume that the Tuskegee syphilis study may initially have had legitimate aspirations for furthering scientific understanding of syphilis in the 1930s when no cure yet existed,[2] there is absolutely nothing that could justify continuation of the study—and simply watching the men degenerate and die—after a cure had been developed. The scientific gains were minimal while the human cost was monolithic. To continue the study was no less than a denial of the dignity of the participants as human beings, as U.S. President Bill Clinton (1997) declared when he made a formal apology to the eight participants still alive in 1997 and the surviving families of the others.

The Tuskegee syphilis study is not the only biomedical horror to have been perpetrated in the name of science. There are the two Brooklyn physicians who injected live-cancer cells into their unsuspecting geriatric subjects; the CIA-sponsored LSD/brainwashing experiments conducted on psychiatric patients in Montreal during the 1960s; Canadian and U.S. pharmaceutical researchers who used convicts as test subjects in risky drug trials; and the government and church authorities who saw Aboriginal children attending residential schools being used as subjects in a variety of experiments without their or their parents' consent. The stories seem to go on and on (e.g., Berg 2007; Bronskill & Blanchfield 1998; Collins 1988; "Native Kids Used for Experiments" 2000). Nor are these simply examples from another time when there were different sensibilities in the world ("Vancouver Island Native Indians ..." 2000).

All too often, and particularly in the biomedical realm, overzealous researchers have mixed the "noble" motives of science with self-interest, an overblown sense of self-importance, and a dehumanization of their "subjects"—who all too commonly are members of socially vulnerable groups such as Jews, Blacks, Indigenous peoples, women, psychiatric patients, the poor, the drug addicted, the homeless, the elderly, and citizens of the Third World—and have forgotten about such fundamental ethical issues as consent and human rights. Clearly, in these cases, the research should never have been done in the first place; no gain in knowledge can justify the denial of human dignity that is involved when human beings are treated as no more than means to an end.

Research in the social sciences and humanities is not without risks—and some social science research can pose considerable risk, particularly in relation to maintaining confidentiality—but in the social sciences we do not kill people. The more typical situation arises with those studies that challenge us to consider where exactly we should draw the line between ethical and unethical. Stanley Milgram's obedience research (e.g., Milgram 1963, 1974) is often discussed in this regard. His research dealt with an important social behaviour: blind obedience to a presumably legitimate authority figure. However, to obtain his data Milgram deceived his participants by telling them his experiment was about the effects of punishment on learning, when "really" (from Milgram's perspective) it was about how obedient ordinary people would be when ordered to deliver what they believed were real and painful electric shocks to another innocent human being.

Many were surprised and disturbed that 65 percent of Milgram's participants were completely obedient to the end, even when every indication was that they had certainly hurt, and may even have killed, the other participant. Perhaps even more disturbing were their rationalizations for doing so, along the lines of "I was only following orders" and "It was not *my* responsibility to decide," which were chillingly reminiscent of the rationalizations of the Nazis charged and tried at Nuremberg following World War II, and of U.S. Lieutenant Calley after his murder of innocent civilians in Vietnam. The guilt and stress that participants felt during their participation was considerable. You get a feeling for what it must have been like for the participants when you read Milgram's (1963) original account of how "real" the situation was for the participants.[3] His general characterization of the atmosphere created is as follows:

> In a large number of cases the degree of tension reached extremes that are rarely seen in sociopsychological laboratory studies. Subjects were observed to sweat, tremble, stutter, bite their lips, groan, and dig their fingernails into their flesh. These were characteristic rather than exceptional responses to the experiment … Full-blown, uncontrollable seizures were observed for 3 subjects. On one occasion we observed a seizure so violently convulsive that it was necessary to call a halt to the experiment. (375)

Milgram presents evidence from the debriefings that always followed participation that his research subjects accepted the deceit. But *was* the infliction

of deception and stress he routinely induced warranted? Milgram argued that it was and received various awards for his research from such prestigious authorities as the American Association for the Advancement of Science; others (e.g., Baumrind 1964) believed what he had done was despicable and that his research would remain the albatross about our necks for many years to some.

The purpose of this section is not to turn you away from research dealing with sensitive topics. Trying to understand the negative aspects of human experience—aggression, blind conformity, prejudice and discrimination, depression—is a profoundly good and important thing to do, but however considerable the social value we attach to research and the pursuit of knowledge, we have to remember it is but one social good among many. The researcher must always be prepared to ask whether doing or continuing the research is "worth it" and, if the area of research is important, whether there is a more ethical way to proceed.

Conflict of Interest

Being "ethical" as a researcher means that you have an essentially fiduciary obligation to consider things from research participants' perspectives and to ensure participants' rights are safeguarded. In many cases the interests of researcher and participant coincide. Researchers become researchers for many different reasons, but two we frequently hear include the desire to understand something deeply and well for its own sake (whether as a general motive or to understand some specific domain) and to generate knowledge that will help produce some social good. Research participants are also typically altruistic; none of them gets any direct or large reward for participating. So in that sense, both researchers and participants often share the belief that something is important, and both hope their actions will produce knowledge that will benefit the greater good.

And of course there is some extent to which even self-interest encourages us to consider things from the perspective of our research participants: any research enterprise that exploits research participants for its own gain at their expense will not last very long. Depending on your approach, research participants are either important collaborators or an important resource; either way, we neglect the rights and interests of research participants at our peril.

However, it would be naive of us to assume that the interests of researchers and research participants always coincide. Occasions may arise when it is in the researcher's or the university's self-interest to gloss over the details in order to ensure a ready supply of research participants from whom one can gather information. And these days many university researchers are engaged in entrepreneurial interests in addition to their university "day job": consulting; creating standardized tests that are used in schools, hospitals, prisons, and other institutions; and other product development such as pharmaceuticals, software, and educational materials. Concern arises over the conflicts of interest these activities may bring to the underlying research, for example, where development of a particular product can result in considerable wealth being generated from patents, royalties, fees, and commissions, or where a favourable evaluation may result in an increase in share value. In these situations the university researcher is no longer an "independent" researcher who is simply following knowledge for its own sake with no stake in the outcome.

This conflict of interest is particularly problematic when the researcher is in a position of power relative to the research participant, and is especially worrisome in the case of captive audiences who depend on the researcher for other rewards. For example, it used to be that many psychology departments would require students—especially the hundreds or even thousands who take Introductory Psychology at some universities—to participate in research in return for partial course credit, in part because it gave students the experience of what it was like to be a research participant but also to keep up the supply of bodies required for faculty member and graduate student research. The practice still continues in many places, but there is now more effort made to ensure that students have reasonable options if they would prefer to decline the opportunity.

Of course, many of those studies entail little or no risk whatsoever; the major one is probably the possibility of dying of boredom. However, other "captive" situations are far more problematic, as the following incident reveals:

> We used prison inmates in a number of research projects and always asked for their consent. However, in retrospect, it seems to me that since I also sat on boards that made recommendations for parole and had other important influences on their prison lives, it might be questioned whether they really felt free to refuse in view of their high need in these areas. (APA 1973: 47)

Ethics problems arise when the power differential between researcher and participant is considerable. They are exacerbated when the prospective risk to participants or the possible cost to them if they refuse to participate is high, for example, where the researcher is also the teacher who hands out grades, the physician who is also responsible for treatment, or the prison authority who is also responsible for maintaining discipline or making recommendations for positive rewards like day passes or parole. From an ethical perspective, it is incumbent on the researcher to seek out independent advice on how best to deal with any appearance of conflict of interest—conflict that would be evident to any neutral third party looking at the situation. The most common ways of doing so are taking steps to alleviate the conflict—for example, by divesting oneself from one side or the other of the conflict, such as by divesting oneself of shares in the company, or getting an independent decision-maker involved who has no vested interest in the outcome and is not in any way dependent on or related to the researcher.

And while we have discussed these elements thus far as they pertain to the researcher, such issues are becoming more and more relevant for university administrations as well. The last two decades have seen diminished funding of universities by governments, along with the clear message that universities should pursue partnerships with private sector companies in order to generate revenues to replace that shortfall. However, academic institutions that seek to contribute to society's knowledge base and private sector corporations that seek to maximize profit and maintain their own market edge represent in many ways a clash of cultures (see Palys 1988). The end result is that universities now find themselves in the position of having institutional conflicts of interest that may have adverse effects on research participants. A recent Canadian example exemplifies the problem.

RUSSEL OGDEN AND SIMON FRASER UNIVERSITY
Russel Ogden was a criminology graduate student who, for his master's thesis, interviewed people who had assisted in the suicides and euthanasia of people with AIDS. This ground-breaking research illuminated a highly controversial practice to which no one other than the participants would normally ever be exposed. Knowing something about this niche of life—the circumstances of its occurrence and the perspectives of those who engage in it—provides important information that enriches the quality of public debate and our understanding of law in context. Such research is impossible without the assurances of confidentiality, privacy, and anonymity provided for by research ethics policies and the trust that participants have in researchers' and the university's adherence to those principles. Because the very freedom of research participants is at stake, the ethical burden on researchers who undertake such research is high.

All research undertaken at Canadian universities involving human participants requires ethics review, and Russel Ogden's was no exception. Regarding informed consent, Ogden proposed to tell participants there was no obligation for them to disclose identifying information, that there was a small chance he might be subpoenaed, and that he would protect anonymity in any event. Because this research could not be done without a meaningful assurance of confidentiality, Ogden made it clear to the SFU Ethics Committee that he would offer "absolute confidentiality" to his research participants. The committee approved his proposal.

Although few people were interested in the topic of Ogden's research when he was beginning it, it was national news by the time he was completing it

because of a woman named Sue Rodriguez. Ms. Rodriguez had a degenerative neurological condition commonly known as Lou Gehrig's disease, and, in anticipation of the day when she would be unable to act, she began petitioning the Parliament of Canada for legislation that would enable her to have an assisted suicide. Media outlets across the country—and a Senate committee established on the topic—looked for an expert in the area of assisted suicide. Russel Ogden was that person. Simon Fraser University bathed in the media spotlight, and the university's media relations department helped him manage the dozens of requests for interviews that were arriving. Ogden's research was a perfect example of the role that university research can fulfill by offering information about certain niches of life to those charged with developing social policy, such as Members of Parliament and senators.

All went well until the Vancouver coroner read an article about Ogden's thesis and decided that the information Ogden had gathered might be helpful to him in investigating a death that had come to his attention, the case of the Unknown Female. Who was she? How exactly had she died? Information contained in a newspaper article suggested to him that the death might have been an assisted suicide and that one or two of Ogden's research participants might have attended her death. He subpoenaed Ogden to give evidence at the inquest.

Ogden appeared and answered all the more general questions that the coroner asked him regarding assisted suicide among people with HIV/AIDS, but he refused to answer any questions that would have allowed for any of his research participants to be identified. He then became the first researcher in Canada ever to be threatened with a charge of contempt of court if he did not reveal confidential research information. Ogden claimed researcher–participant privilege and again refused.

A trial dealing with the claim of privilege ensued. The circumstances had never arisen in Canada for such a claim to be tested, and it was a historic opportunity for the university to come to Ogden's aid to defend academic freedom and assert researcher–participant privilege. Instead, the university administration dropped him like a hot potato. Ogden defended his research participants nonetheless, arguing that his research was done in accordance with the highest ethical standards of his discipline and could not be done without a guarantee of confidentiality, which he was now honour-bound to uphold. The coroner agreed and "release[d] him from any stain or suggestion of contempt" (*Inquest of Unknown Female* 1994: 10).

The struggle to have the university recognize the error of its decision not to defend Ogden would go on for several years, with the university lambasted along the way by a Provincial Court judge and an independent committee established by then-President Jack Blaney to review the university's decision making in the case. The case in Provincial Court arose when Ogden sued the university for breach of contract. He argued that he was required to do original research as part of the requirements for his MA degree, that he did so in a manner that followed SFU's research policies and the highest ethical standards of his discipline, and hence that there was an implicit contract obliging the university to support him in court when the guarantee of confidentiality he made—which the university research ethics committee had approved—was challenged.

There were several respects in which this case was noteworthy, not the least of which was that it allowed Ogden to subpoena then-President John Stubbs as well as Bruce Clayman (a physicist who at that time simultaneously occupied the roles of Dean of Graduate Studies, Vice-President of Research, and Chair of the University Ethics Committee) and require them to explain the basis of their decision to refuse to support Ogden's principled defence of his participants, research confidentiality, and academic freedom. It turned out their decision had nothing to do with ethics; their primary concerns were liability considerations and "image." In the end, Judge Steinberg sided with the university as a matter of contract law—it was up to the university to decide which cases it would litigate and which it would not—but with Ogden on the moral issues that permeated the case:

The vague statements of personal support as expressed by the president of the University, Dr. Stubbs, and the dean of Graduate Studies, Dr. Clayman, sound hollow and timid when compared with the opportunity they had as leaders of the University, to promote the demonstrated value of academic freedom and academic privilege as evidenced in this case. To set aside this opportunity because of fear that if they were to financially support Ogden by paying his legal fees in this context, some people might misapprehend that they were in favour of euthanasia, demonstrates a surprising lack of courage. (*Russel Ogden* v. *Simon Fraser University* 1998: 68)

An independent review of the university's decision making conducted by SFU professors Nick Blomley (geography) and Steven Davis (philosophy) followed and was consistent with the tenor of Judge Steinberg's decision. Blomley and Davis concluded that the university administration had erred in its decision and should (1) send a letter of apology to Ogden; (2) reimburse Ogden for his legal fees; and (3) guarantee that, in future, any graduate student whose academic freedom was challenged by a third party in the way that Ogden's was would receive legal help. Then-President Blaney accepted all three recommendations (see also Lowman & Palys 2000).

Informed Consent

Another core ethical principle is that of **informed consent,** the idea that it is important for researchers to get consent from people before involving them in research, and that their consent, when and if they give it, should be based on honest and complete information regarding what their participation will involve.

This process will involve an oral or, in some instances, a written agreement with participants that ensures fairness by letting them know from the outset, as well as we can, what their participation will involve, what the costs will be to them, what benefits they or others will actually or potentially receive in return, what risks they may run by being involved in the research, and any other factors that a reasonable person would want to know before deciding whether to participate. The researcher should be both clear and realistic about what is being offered, making neither grandiose claims about the prospective utility of the research nor any promises that he or she is not prepared to keep.

In some types of research, the participants might never even know that they were a part of a study, for example, in covert participant-observation research such as Lofland and Lejeune's (1960) study at Alcoholics Anonymous in which researchers actually joined a group and surreptitiously kept notes of the group's activities and dynamics. Perhaps the most famous study of this type was Laud Humphreys's (1970) *Tearoom Trade,* in which Humphreys played the role of a "watch queen" in order to observe intimate homosexual encounters in public washrooms.

Even when the investigator *does* set out to secure informed consent, it is sometimes easier said than done. Myriad prospective difficulties present themselves. One was noted earlier, that a fundamental attribute of research is that investigators typically do not know for certain what will happen; otherwise, why would they be doing the research? In such a case, fully informed consent is obviously a problem, and the best the investigator can do is to present a "best estimate" of the range of possible effects.

A second difficulty, noted by Reynolds (1982), is that there may be reason to believe that telling participants about the study's objectives may influence the very phenomenon one is trying to observe. For example, in one study commissioned by a federal government committee looking into issues regarding pornography and prostitution (Palys 1986), Ted was interested in ascertaining the social (and particularly the sexual, aggressive, and sexually violent) content of video pornography available in neighbourhood video establishments. Should he have approached video outlet proprietors and told them that he was (in part) interested in determining whether videos involving sexual violence were as pervasive as the media suggested?

He felt that if proprietors did indeed have an array of sexually violent material, and if they came to realize that their offerings were under systematic scrutiny, they might delete some of their more questionable videos for the duration of the study. Ted also reasoned that, in this instance, the videos were "public" materials and that this was a straight economic exchange in which his only obligations were to pay the required fee and return the tapes in good condition. That he took the tape home to systematically code its content was his choice. At the same time, because these proprietors did not know of the study, Ted felt obliged to ensure confidentiality and thus never referred to any particular establishment by name. A record of the establishments was in a file of which only he knew the location; all lists were destroyed after the study was completed.

Pragmatic problems also may arise in securing informed consent. The information to be conveyed might be too technical or esoteric for prospective participants to appreciate fully, or some attribute of them might virtually preclude the assurance of communication (e.g., in the study of young children or some psychiatric patients; APA 1973). The investigator should nonetheless attempt to communicate those aspects of the study that might reasonably affect willingness to participate and, in the latter case, would normally contact guardians or other advocates of the prospective participant(s).

Finally, securing informed consent is sometimes impossible or highly impractical. When coding archival records or photographs of crowds, for example, it may not be possible to identify or contact all the people involved. Lack of identification may not be a problem since it implies anonymity, although one would also want to ensure that subsequent accounts avoided inadvertently providing identifying information through other clues (e.g., personal characteristics, place of work). When people can be identified but not contacted, precautions should normally be taken to ensure confidentiality, although in some instances (e.g., public events such as football games or most courtroom proceedings), it is unlikely anyone will feel his or her privacy has been violated.

DECEPTION

The above discussion regarding informed consent suggests that, generally speaking, openness and honesty are two highly desired characteristics of the researcher–participant relationship. It also suggests that there are exceptions, for example, when doing research in public settings or with public figures. Another exception deserves special note because of the unique controversy that has arisen where some researchers have argued tenaciously for their right to deceive. Experimental psychologists have been the major defenders of this practice (e.g., Dion 1998; Latham 1999), which is controversial because it violates the principle of informed consent and replaces it with a misdirected consent.

Methodological lore in experimental psychology has it (e.g., see Festinger & Katz 1953) that deception is required in order to ensure the "true" (i.e., experimenter-defined) purpose of the research is not transparent, so that the behaviour of research subjects is not influenced by what they think you want to hear or see them do. Notwithstanding a series of publications from members of the discipline that chastised experimental psychologists for such pervasive use of deception (e.g., Kelman, 1967; Ring 1967; Stricker 1967) and/or tried to offer alternatives (e.g., Mixon 1972; Palys 1978), psychologists have clung to deception as a justifiable practice in the face of threats to it from other ethics regulators (e.g., Dion 1998).

These days deception is allowed only in situations where a third party has had an opportunity to review whether (1) the problem is of considerable importance and cannot be addressed in any other way, (2) there is sufficient reason to believe that participants will not be particularly perturbed when they are told of the deception afterward, (3) participants are allowed to withdraw their data afterward if they object to the deception, (4) the researcher takes full responsibility for detecting and removing any harmful aftereffects of the deception, and/or (5) input on the acceptability of procedures is sought from individuals similar to the population to be studied (e.g., when university students are to be solicited, one would hope that a student representative would be among those scrutinizing the proposal).

Confidentiality

People have a right to keep information about themselves private or to share it only with those whom they trust to safeguard it. When we approach people and ask them to divulge information about themselves, and especially when that information could cause them embarrassment or harm if it were to be released, it is incumbent on researchers to take every precaution to ensure that confidentiality is respected. In order to provide that protection, however, it is important to consider where the threat to confidentiality might come from and, hence, what we are protecting ourselves and our participants against.

By far the most pervasive threats to confidentiality are those that come from people in the milieu we are researching. These are what you might call relatively "low-grade" threats because they disappear most times with a simple "no," but they occur frequently and must be safeguarded against. They arise most commonly when multiple people are being interviewed in one setting—a given organization, community, or family, for example. Some of them will inevitably be curious about what another research participant said. It may be quite well-meaning: a concerned parent might ask for hints about what his or her uncommunicative son or daughter divulged to the researcher about illicit drug use or something as apparently innocuous as what they said about their career plans. Or it may be more maliciously motivated: a respondent might give the impression that he or she is an "insider" on some issue and look for confirmation from you that another person divulged a particular opinion, allegiance, or point of view as a way of justifying a vendetta or other campaign of action against the person.

Researchers must be very careful not to say anything to any one person that another person told them. This may sound very simple, but guarding against it requires considerable vigilance. The problem arises because we want to appear competent, intelligent, and "in the know" so that people will respect us as interviewers and feel confident giving us information; but if we start sharing what others have told us, even if the information seems innocuous, we begin to tread on very dangerous ground because our typical status as "outsiders" to the setting makes us very unlikely to know enough about the internal dynamics of the setting to make good choices about what is safe to share and what is not. Things that to us seem innocent may have significant consequences within the setting we are researching. The best way to inspire confidence in research participants is to show them how vigilant you are in safeguarding the information that others give you; it tells them that you will show the same vigilance with their information and that they really can trust you. Conversely, if you are sloppy with others' confidences, why should they believe you will be careful with theirs?

Far less common are more formal efforts by third parties to acquire information from confidential research sources through legal means such as subpoenas. In the litigation-happy United States the literature contains a few dozen examples of legal threats to confidentiality that have arisen in the last 30 years out of what is no doubt hundreds of thousands of research projects that have been carried out in that time (see Cecil & Wetherington 1996 or Lowman & Palys 2001a for a sample of U.S. cases).

In the late 1960s and 1970s these cases most often involved legal authorities (police, grand juries, prosecutors) trying to acquire confidential research information from researchers in order to prosecute the research participant or someone known to the research participant for violations of law. Thanks to the development in the U.S. of Confidentiality Certificates (for health research) and Privacy Certificates (for justice research), such threats have all but disappeared (see Lowman & Palys 2001a). In the 1980s and 1990s the more common scenario was for one group of people to be suing a multinational pharmaceutical, tobacco, oil, or computer company, citing an independent researcher's work in their statement of claim and the company then subpoenaing the researcher in order to try to enlist or discredit him

or her as part of its legal defence. In Canada, there has only ever been one case of a researcher being subpoenaed—the case of Russel Ogden described earlier—and asked to divulge information that would identify particular participants.

As this suggests, the likelihood of you or any other researcher being subpoenaed, particularly in Canada, where litigation happens less frequently and where grand juries (the biggest source of subpoenas in the United States in criminal cases) do not exist, is about equal to the likelihood of you being hit by a bolt of lightning on your birthday—theoretically possible but unlikely. Nonetheless, since your ethical obligation is to protect your research participants and because in general it is so easy to build some degree of protection into your research, you should do so. There are two primary ways to maximize such protection to participants: procedurally and through law.

PROCEDURAL PROTECTIONS AND CARE

The easiest way to protect the confidentiality of respondents is simply never to obtain or record participants' names in the first place, that is, to safeguard their confidentiality by providing them with anonymity from the moment you begin gathering data. There are many kinds of research—particularly more quantitative kinds of research such as surveys and questionnaires—where this is the easiest rule to follow.

In situations where you must obtain people's names, either because you need them ahead of time in order to know whom to approach or because the circumstances of the situation lead you to obtain that information, you should **anonymize** your records at the first opportunity. Sometimes you may need to keep some form of identifier that allows you to distinguish between respondents; in that situation use **pseudonyms,** that is, invented names that are used continuously through your notes so that you can keep together all the quotations from the person you'll call "Kim" and be able to differentiate "Kim" from "Pat." Should your notes ever inadvertently fall into the wrong hands, no one but you will know who "Kim" and "Pat" "really" are.

In the event you are generating more quantified and structured data that are maintained in digital files, your options are simply to delete any identifying information from the file as soon as is practical or, better yet, to keep identifying information in a separate file, preferably in a different order than exists in the "content" file, but linkable through some designator included in each file that only you know about.[4] In some cases—and the more sensitive the data the more you are advised to do this—researchers save their data in files using encryption programs such as PGP (Pretty Good Privacy) or AxCrypt, which gives as good an assurance as one can get that no one else will be able to make use of the data to identify particular respondents.[5] Other strategies for anonymizing, encrypting, and hiding computerized data are given in Boruch and Cecil (1979); although the specific technologies they describe are in many cases obsolete, the conceptual guidelines they provide for devising anonymizing strategies are as relevant today as they were at the time that book was written.

Although high-tech, computer-based approaches can create a challenge to third parties who might be interested in your data, another defence is offered by going precisely in the opposite direction, that is, the low-tech solution of using a notebook of sorts (especially for non-quantitative field note data), which can be hidden more easily than your computer's hard drive. The thing to do here is to seek and pursue approaches that are appropriate for the kinds of data you are compiling. The more sensitive the data, the greater the harm that can come to participants if the data were to be revealed, and the more interested third parties are likely to be in your data, the greater the level of protection you should seek.

LEGAL MECHANISMS FOR MAXIMIZING CONFIDENTIALITY

In Canada, the only research participants whose information enjoys statutory protection are those who participate in research conducted by Statistics Canada. The *Statistics Act* gives Statistics Canada employees a privilege to ensure that identifiable information unearthed by research by one portion of government (Statistics Canada) cannot be used by any other branch of government or in any other court or other proceedings in a manner that would violate the confidence of any individual respondent. Researchers in Canada who are not employees or "deemed employees" of Statistics Canada[6] are not so fortunate; they do not have the *guaranteed* privilege that exists via the *Statistics Act*, but in the end may be no less protected because of the possibility for recognition of privilege through the common law (Palys & Lowman 2000).

To say that some relationship is "privileged" means that persons in that relationship are exempt from the normal requirement that all of us have to testify when asked to do so in a court of law when and if information discussed in the context of that relationship becomes of interest to the court. Because privileges can interfere with the court's search for truth—evidence that might otherwise be useful to a court adjudication is not available—privileges are very rarely granted. However, it is recognized that certain socially valued relationships simply could not exist without the confidence that what is said in the context of that relationship will remain confidential. Some of these are recognized in statute; any others have to be claimed in court via common law.

In Canada and the United States, making a claim via common law means designing one's research in anticipation of the **Wigmore criteria** or **Wigmore test,** a set of four criteria that the Supreme Court of Canada has stated it will use to adjudicate whether a privilege should be recognized given the circumstances in the case at hand (Palys & Lowman 2000), and that has also been recognized as appropriate for this purpose by the U.S. Supreme Court (Palys & Lowman 2002). The criteria specify that

(1) The communications must originate in a *confidence* that they will not be disclosed;

(2) This element of *confidentiality must be essential* to the full and satisfactory maintenance of the relation between the parties;

(3) The *relation* must be one which in the opinion of the community ought to be sedulously *fostered;* and

(4) The *injury* that would inure to the relation by the disclosure of the communications must be *greater than the benefit* thereby gained for the correct disposal of litigation. (Wigmore 1905: 3185; italics in original)

A successful claim of privilege by the Wigmore test requires evidence that speaks to all four requirements (e.g., Crabb 1996; Daisley 1994; Jackson & MacCrimmon 1999; O'Neil 1996; *R. v. Gruenke* 1991; Traynor 1996; Wiggins & McKenna 1996). That is exactly what Russel Ogden did when he was subpoenaed by the coroner, and his research stands as a legacy for researchers dealing with sensitive topics on how to do it right (see especially Jackson & MacCrimmon 1999; Palys & Lowman 2000, 2002).

DESIGNING RESEARCH TO ASSERT RESEARCH–PARTICIPANT PRIVILEGE

ESTABLISHING A SHARED UNDERSTANDING OF CONFIDENCE

The first criterion tells us that a prerequisite for claiming privilege is that the two or more people involved in the relation must have a shared understanding that their communication was, in fact, confidential. As Wigmore (1905: 3233) wrote, "The moment confidence ceases, privilege ceases." In practical terms, this means researchers should ensure there is a clear "expectation of confidentiality" that is shared by researcher and participant and that the research record includes evidence that speaks to that understanding.

In the few U.S. cases where things have gone badly for researchers (e.g., see Lowman & Palys 2001a; Palys & Lowman 2002), it is noteworthy that none had evidence regarding this first element. For example, neither Mario Brajuha[7] (Brajuha & Hallowell 1986) nor Richard Scarce[8] (Scarce 1994) had clearly established that their interactions were part of a researcher–participant relationship; neither had completed a formal research proposal, and, consequently, neither had subjected his proposed research to ethics review. No record existed of the pledge they had made to participants, nor was there any formal indication or approval that showed they were engaged in an activity that was university-approved and being executed in accordance with the canons of their discipline. Nor had either of the two kept records of their and the participants' understanding regarding confidentiality in field notes. Brajuha, for example, could say only that he had guaranteed confidentiality to some but not all participants and could not recall to whom he had guaranteed confidentiality and to whom he had not (Brajuha & Hallowell 1986; O'Neil 1996).

In cases where a researcher–participant privilege was recognized, the opposite held true. For example, when the Vancouver coroner subpoenaed Russel Ogden (see *Inquest of Unknown Female* 1994; Lowman & Palys 2000) and asked him to identify research participants who may have witnessed the death, Ogden presented evidence showing that he had completed a proposal and undergone a research ethics review, and he produced copies of the pledge of confidentiality he had made to prospective participants. This established that Ogden was indeed engaged in "research," that appropriate officials at the university believed his plan reflected the highest ethical standards of his discipline, and that he and his participants shared the understanding that their interactions were completely confidential. Although no legal authority in Canada had ever subpoenaed a researcher and asked him or her to reveal confidential information, Ogden and his supervisor correctly anticipated that if anyone were to challenge the confidentiality of their information it would be the coroner. Ogden's pledge meant he would refuse to divulge identifying information even if threatened with contempt of court.

A matter of no small importance with respect to Ogden's pledge was that it was unequivocal. Anything less runs the risk of being treated as a "waiver of privilege" by the courts. For example, in *Atlantic Sugar* v. *United States* (1980), corporate respondents to an International Trade Commission questionnaire were told that the information they provided would not be disclosed "except as required by law." A U.S. Customs Court later used this exception to justify its order of disclosure of research information from researchers, saying they were the law and "required" the information. The lesson here is that researchers should (1) be prepared to discuss confidentiality issues with participants; (2) make that discussion part of the research record; (3) be clear on what they are prepared to guarantee; (4) guarantee it; and (5) live up to that guarantee.

ESTABLISHING THAT THE CONFIDENCE IS ESSENTIAL Because claims of research–participant privilege are decided on a case-by-case basis, general claims about the importance of confidentiality to research are not enough. Researchers also should be ready to demonstrate that confidentiality was crucial to their research in particular (Daisley 1994; Jackson & MacCrimmon 1999; Palys & Lowman 2000, 2002). Traynor (1996) suggests that consideration of the necessity of confidentiality should be given in research proposals, thereby showing that confidentiality was part of a considered plan and neither capricious nor rote. For example, Ogden's research proposal explained why he believed it would be impossible to gather reliable and valid data and to meet the ethical standards of his discipline unless he offered complete confidentiality to participants.

Claims that confidentiality was "essential" can be weakened by behaviour that is inconsistent with such claims. For example, in one case, the courts seemed skeptical about the researcher's claim of privilege when it became known that he and the research participant who was the prime suspect in the case were friends outside the research context. Was the researcher truly claiming privilege because of the research relationship? Or was he using it out of convenience and his allegiance to a friend? The claim of privilege was undermined further when it became evident the researcher's wife was at a key meeting where a confession may have been made, when the wife had not been shown in evidence to be part of the research team (*In re Grand Jury Proceedings: James Richard Scarce* 1993; O'Neil 1996; Scarce 1994, 1999).

In contrast, Russel Ogden only strengthened his claim for privilege by asking participants directly—

and recording their answers—how important the provision of confidentiality was to their participation. All participants who had witnessed or participated in an assisted suicide or euthanasia stated that anonymity was vital to their participation. They would divulge information to Ogden *only* if he promised to maintain their anonymity. The coroner found this evidence persuasive, noting that the information he sought would never have existed in the first place had it not been for Ogden's guarantee, which he was now obliged ethically to live by (*Inquest of Unknown Female* 1994).

ESTABLISHING THAT THE COMMUNITY VALUES THE RELATIONSHIP The third criterion asks whether the relationship under scrutiny is so socially valued that "the community" believes it should be protected. Various "communities" can be considered here, such as the research community; the community of which participants in the research at hand are members; those who engage in policy formulation and implementation and who value independent research that contributes to that task; and the broader citizenry, who benefit from the knowledge created through research. Much of this information would come from expert testimony when and if the researcher is subpoenaed. However, there is also evidence that can be gathered and material that should be retained as one goes through the process of preparing for and executing the research.

For example, any research that has satisfied peer review, secured funding, and/or undergone ethics review must clearly be valued by the research community. Court decisions, too, have noted the high value that society places on academic research (e.g., *Dow Chemical* v. *Allen* 1982; *In re: Michael A. Cusumano and David B. Yoffie* 1998; *Richards of Rockford* v. *Pacific Gas and Electric Co.* 1976).

A BALANCING OF INTERESTS Any well-designed social science research on a sensitive topic that anticipates the evidentiary requirements of the Wigmore test should satisfy the first three criteria easily. The fourth criterion sees the court balance the social values upheld in the researcher–participant relationship against the costs that would be incurred by withholding relevant evidence in the case at hand. In Ogden's case, this came down to Ogden's need to maintain his ethical pledge to participants and the impact a disclosure would have on the research enterprise if Ogden complied versus the coroner's need for the evidence to make an accurate determination of the Unknown Female's identity and cause of death in the inquest at hand.

But note the asymmetry here: until a "class" privilege is recognized, researchers have to make their decisions ahead of time and can only hope they are correct in their speculation of the range of circumstances that might arise, while the courts make their decisions after the fact on the basis of the concrete facts that are presented to them. The U.S. Supreme Court recognized this paradox in a recent case involving therapist–client privilege (*Jaffee v. Redmond* 1996):

> We part company with the Court of Appeals on a separate point. We reject the balancing component of the privilege implemented by that court and a small number of States. Making the promise of confidentiality contingent upon a trial judge's later evaluation of the relative importance of the patient's interest in privacy and the evidentiary need for disclosure would eviscerate the effectiveness of the privilege. As we explained in *Upjohn,* if the purpose of the privilege is to be served, the participants in the confidential conversation "must be able to predict with some degree of certainty whether particular discussions will be protected. An uncertain privilege, or one which purports to be certain but results in widely varying applications by the courts, is little better than no privilege at all."

Researchers face exactly this dilemma. Natural justice requires that law be known in advance; with case-by-case analysis all we know in advance is that the law will be made after the fact. However, researchers must make their decisions ahead of time. One would hope that Canada's ethics powers (see below) will seek to rectify this problem in the

manner that it has been done with Statistics Canada's research participants via the *Statistics Act* and in the United States for some kinds of research through Confidentiality Certificates and Privacy Certificates, but as of this writing there has been no visible movement on this issue.

In the interim, the question we need to ask ourselves for any piece of research we do is whether we believe the rights of our participants and the knowledge we are gaining outweigh any other foreseeable concerns or interests that might arise in the research. If the answer to that question is yes, then one proper ethical course is to give an unqualified pledge of confidentiality, and, having made that decision and the promise that goes with it, we are ethically obliged to keep it. If the answer is no, then we believe the proper course of action is to not do the research because you would have to limit confidentiality, and that would be placing research participants at risk— albeit a very small risk because no researcher has ever been ordered to divulge confidential research information to a Canadian court—for your benefit.

If we look to the United States, where there have been more cases and where in at least three instances researchers *have* been ordered to divulge information that would violate particular research participants' confidentiality,[9] a search of the literature that describes the subpoenaing of researchers has yet to reveal a case where we believe violating a research confidence would have been the ethical thing to do. Accordingly, we will continue to ask ourselves the balancing question before we engage in any piece of research and, where the answer is yes, will continue to offer an unqualified guarantee of confidentiality to the participants in our research.

OTHER CONFIDENTIALITY CONSIDERATIONS

A debate that John Lowman and Ted Palys became embroiled in at SFU involved the right of a researcher to make an unqualified pledge of confidentiality and to abide by that pledge (e.g., Lowman & Palys 2000). They take that stance for a variety of reasons. One is that the ethical standards of their discipline—criminology—expects them to make and maintain that pledge, in part because of a unique aspect of the discipline of criminology, which is that it involves the study of law and legal mechanisms. This aspect almost by definition takes one to the grey area between legal and illegal where one finds how the law operates and is given life on a day-to-day basis. Criminology as a discipline would not be possible unless researchers were prepared to take a nonjudgmental approach to many of the people they study, and the same is true of many other disciplines. How can epidemiologists understand the spread of disease if persons having them are unwilling to talk to researchers because they will be reported if they admit exposure? How can political scientists understand the development of political attitudes and social policies if members of oppositional groups see the researcher as a prospective agent of the state? If we believe that studying these difficult and controversial areas is a prerequisite to the positive, rational, and humane development of law and policy, ensuring research participant confidentiality is safeguarded so that they do not pay a price for their altruism and our benefit is a fundamental ethical requirement.

This stance is reflected in the draft Code of Ethics of the American Society of Criminology, which states,

> Confidential information provided by research participants must be treated as such by criminologists, even when this information enjoys no legal protection or privilege and legal force is applied. (2001: 30)

Other disciplines say much the same thing. For example:

> Informants have a right to remain anonymous. This right should be respected both where it has been promised explicitly and where no clear understanding to the contrary has been reached. These strictures apply to the collection of data by means of cameras, tape recorders, and other data-gathering devices, as well as to data collected in face-to-face interviews or in participant observa-

tion. (American Anthropological Association *Statement on Ethics* 1986, principle 1c)

> [S]cholars also have a professional duty not to divulge the identity of confidential sources of information or data developed in the course of research, whether to governmental or non-governmental officials or bodies, even though in the present state of American law they run the risk of suffering an applicable penalty. (American Political Science Association *Guide to Professional Ethics in Political Science* 1998)

> Sociologists have an obligation to ensure that confidential information is protected. They do so to ensure the integrity of research and the open communication with research participants and to protect sensitive information obtained in research, teaching, practice, and service. When gathering confidential information, sociologists should take into account the long-term uses of the information, including its potential placement in public archives or the examination of the information by other researchers or practitioners.

> Confidential information provided by research participants, students, employees, clients, or others is treated as such by sociologists even if there is no legal protection or privilege to do so. Sociologists have an obligation to protect confidential information and not allow information gained in confidence from being used in ways that would unfairly compromise research participants, students, employees, clients, or others. (American Sociological Association [ASA] *Code of Ethics* 1999)

However, all these codes also enjoin researchers to understand the law as it relates to their work, to consider possible limitations to confidentiality that may arise from either legal or ethical considerations, to make an ethical choice about how these will or will not affect their work, and to be honest and forthcoming to research participants about these choices.

People who choose to limit confidentiality have the obligation to tell prospective participants about these limits because in many cases these will affect the willingness of participants to take part in the research. Also, limiting confidentiality is unethical when it involves no more than the researcher downloading risk to the research participant, as well as the responsibility of deciding what is or is not legally appropriate to say. This would make research participation an unfair and exploitative exchange: the researcher takes no risk but gets all the gains in information and whatever else accrues from it (royalties, patents, publications); the volunteer research participant takes all the risks and, if trouble should ever arise, is greeted by a researcher who says, "Gee, that's too bad, but I told you that might happen."

Limiting confidentiality does not limit one's ethical obligations. First and foremost is the ethical obligation to ensure research participants know the researcher's commitment to confidentiality is limited, but to do so without causing them to waive any rights they may have, for example, those that can be asserted under the Wigmore criteria. In part, this may involve being crystal clear about what unique set of circumstances might lead to disclosure—so that the courts cannot see the limitation as a general waiver of privilege—and do everything possible otherwise to ensure that the research participant is protected.

For example, in one Canadian case involving a claim of therapist–client privilege, where both therapist and client considered the fact that a court might subpoena the therapy records (*M. [A.] v. Ryan* [1997] 1 S.C.R. 157), the therapist promised to do "everything possible" to defend the confidentiality of the records. She then put this into practice by being vigilant in the way records were maintained so that nothing appeared in the records that would cause the patient harm if it were disclosed in court, not including some information in records in the first place when therapist and client agreed that some information was best not recorded, and living up to the promise by defending the privilege all the way to the Supreme Court of Canada.

If there is a more difficult issue to consider, it is the one that deals with the possible scenario whereby a researcher learns of some dastardly harm that will befall some innocent third party. In this case, a researcher might wish to consider violating confidentiality not because of some legal imposition or fear but for ethical reasons. The key thing to consider here is whether or not such revelations of prospective harm are anticipated (e.g., Palys & Lowman 2000). If they are not anticipated, then it makes little sense to refer to them in informed consent statements. For example, it would be a tad absurd to start off interviews with parents by saying something like, "These interviews about your children's teachers are completely confidential unless you tell me that you are going to kill one of them." We assume the best of our interviewees unless there is reason to assume otherwise, and a pledge of confidentiality about their views of teachers is exactly that, a pledge about their provision of that information. Any plot to kill the principal would be beyond the realm of the research, and the researcher would have to figure out some ethical way to prevent that harm without denying the rights of the participant he or she is still obliged to protect.

The decision making becomes a bit more dicey in situations where we might well *anticipate* getting information involving harm to third parties. For example, in the literature on prisons there is a debate on the effects of solitary confinement on prisoners. One set of researchers has argued that there is really no problematic effect to solitary confinement per se, while another group of researchers has argued that the effects of solitary confinement can be very debilitating, and in particular may lead prisoners to become more violent to themselves (i.e., suicidal, self-mutilating) and/or others (i.e., assaultive).

If we wanted to do research in which we checked what exactly happened to prisoners who were placed in solitary confinement, it seems unlikely that prisoners would tell us about these tendencies if they knew we would inform authorities as soon as they told us. Imagine you are a prisoner placed in solitary confinement, whereupon a researcher comes up to you and says, "I really want to find out the effects of solitary confinement. I would particularly like to hear whether you have any intention to harm yourself or others. However, I should warn you that if you tell me, I'll be obliged to tell prison authorities."

If you were a prisoner who was planning on doing harm to yourself or someone else, would you tell the researcher about those desires, knowing that the researcher would then go and tell prison authorities? We suspect not. And yet that is exactly what Ivan Zinger and his colleagues (Zinger 1999; Zinger, Wichmann, & Andrews 2001) did in research conducted in three of Canada's maximum security prisons concerning the effects of solitary confinement on prisoners. In the end, he found that prisoners in solitary confinement were no more likely than inmates in the general prison population to report a desire to harm themselves or others and, because of that, sided with researchers who had argued that there are no terrible effects to solitary confinement. Surprise, surprise. Given that Zinger was at that time an employee of Corrections Canada and that this result reaffirms the appropriateness of Corrections Canada policies—"Problems with the use of solitary confinement? What problems?"—we can only see the limitation of confidentiality in this case as an exercise in self-interest (see Lowman & Palys 2001b; Palys & Lowman 2001).

To the extent that other researchers follow Zinger's lead and routinely limit confidentiality, one can envision a huge credibility gap arising in situations where self-interest leads a variety of authorities to want to find nothing, that is, to do research "with eyes wide shut." Imagine wanting to study police interrogations in order to determine whether and how frequently they violate the rights of accused, and limiting confidentiality by telling officers that any violations will be reported to superiors. Or imagine studying the ways that forestry and mining companies circumvent environmental regulations and telling employees that anything they tell you might be subject to subpoena. We can imagine the headlines now: "Police Always Follow Procedure, Says Study." "Study Finds Resource Companies Always Respect Environmental Regulations." How convenient.

We don't mean to minimize the difficulties and ethical torment that can characterize such situations, but remember again that there are two things we need to consider whenever we undertake a piece of research. One is what it takes to ensure that the data we end up with are valid and reliable—the scientific obligation. If we end up with data whose validity is questionable, then we have wasted everyone's time and placed people at risk for nothing. Indeed, that is our biggest concern with Zinger's research regarding the effects of solitary confinement; however important the question he addressed and however thoughtful other elements of his research design may have been, his decision to limit confidentiality made whatever information he gathered useless. So why do it in the first place?

The second part of the equation involves the humane considerations that we have for our research participants and those around us. And on that score we have to consider whether hearing about some things and gaining some kinds of knowledge are worth it. Zinger began his research by noting that 19 prisoners died in custody in Canadian prisons from suicide or homicide in the year preceding his research. To what extent did solitary confinement contribute to that number? Could more humane policies or procedures or the simple banishment of forced solitary confinement reduce that number? Do we want to know or don't we? By limiting confidentiality, Zinger will never know. Is the long-term benefit of potentially saving 19 lives per year worth going into this research with an unqualified guarantee of confidentiality? In our view, that is exactly the question that has to be answered. Because the validity of the data depends on the guarantee of confidentiality, the choice is between deciding that the benefits are worth it and doing the research with full confidentiality or deciding that it is not and withdrawing from the research. This does not prevent the researcher from taking actions designed to try to avoid the harm that would otherwise result, but he or she must do so in a way that respects the rights of the informant as well.

If we have not already succeeded in doing so, we hope our discussion of these special circumstances has helped convince you that ethics issues are not easily resolved, that the ones that face you in real life cannot be dismissed by applying simplistic ethical formulas, and that what characterizes most interesting and provocative research is the need for detailed case-by-case ethical consideration of how ethics issues can play out in the given context you want to investigate. The less experience you have, and the greater the humane costs that are potentially involved in executing a piece of research, the more detailed your consideration should be, and the more obliged you are to seek the advice and counsel of trusted colleagues with experience in that area before you make the final decisions for which you are accountable.

A Shared Responsibility

A final principle that deserves mention here is that everyone who is involved in research—from the principal investigator who designs and coordinates the research, to research assistants who gather data, to secretarial help who transcribe interviews, to the network administrator who transfers and stores the data—shares the ethical responsibility to ensure that the rights and interests of research participants are protected. This principle also implies that each of those persons must respect the obligations of the other members of the research team to engage in ethical practice.

We emphasize this principle because most of those reading this book will be doing so as part of a course in research methods and, as novice researchers, are more likely in the imminent future to be research assistants rather than principal investigators. People who are not experienced in research (and even some who are) might be tempted to displace responsibility for ethical matters onto the principal investigator. They may feel uncomfortable about some aspect of the research procedures but fail to draw attention to it because they believe that the principal investigator must know better, or that it is not their role to attend to such matters, or because they fear reprisals. And it *is* true that the principal investigator has a more major role to play since he or she designs the study. Nonetheless, *everyone*

involved in a research project is responsible for ensuring that ethical procedures are followed.

Thus, if you are a research assistant and feel that some aspect of these ethical principles is not adequately addressed, then it would be your *obligation* to bring this matter to the attention of the principal investigator and to pursue the issue until you feel satisfied. In some instances, you might find that your concerns will have been anticipated by the principal investigator, in which case you will feel better once you have received an explanation. In other instances, the chief researcher may not have anticipated something that you noticed, in which case he or she should be pleased at your sense of responsibility in speaking up. Everyone gains in a situation where all individuals act ethically and show mutual respect. However, if you continue to be dissatisfied with the explanation you receive or with the ameliorative action that is taken, then there are other people to approach, such as your department chairperson, the head of your university's Research Ethics Board, or an ethics committee that is part of the researcher's disciplinary association.

BALANCING AND COMBINING ETHICAL PRINCIPLES

Although not exhaustive, the list above describes some of the major principles that characterize ethical research. You have now been introduced to some of the debates and issues that have arisen in their implementation. The role of the researcher is to treat research participants with care. A general rule we always try to apply is to ask what standard we would expect a researcher to follow if the participant was our mother, son, or a close friend.

And of course there are many issues we haven't gone into in this relatively introductory treatise: situations that arise in particular research contexts that pose unique dilemmas and have been the subject of considerable debate. However, we hope you understand how difficult ethics issues can be to resolve. If "being ethical" involved no more than following a bunch of principles in relatively predictable scenarios, then everything would be easy. We're all intelligent people; we all want to be ethical; we all have a sense of right and wrong. However, problems arise for at least four main reasons, all of which suggest that it's not as easy as it looks.

First is that the very nature of research involves some degree of unpredictability. If we know exactly what is going to happen, there is no need to do the research. The implication is that, instead of relatively *certain* costs and benefits, we are often weighing our best *guesses* of costs and benefits.

Second is that the environment in which we operate is to some degree uncertain, particularly when it comes to the intersection of our research activities and the rights of our research participants with other activities and the rights of other people in society. This is particularly true where issues of ethics intersect with issues of law. We want to be ethical, and of course we want to be legal. But what do we do when one of those rare occasions arises when "being legal" points in one direction and "being ethical" points in another? Of course we should make every effort to make the two coincide, but in that final instant, if the two are at odds, do you believe it is more important to be ethical or legal?

A third source of difficulty is that ethical principles themselves do not exist in isolation. All of them operate in any given situation and sometimes they conflict. "Being ethical" thus involves not simply following a set of rules but trying to find a way to resolve competing demands, balancing and trading off different "goods," and making decisions based on the perspective and best interests of our research participants.

An implication of the above is the fourth difficulty, that there are rarely any clear-cut "right" and "wrong" ethical answers. Add to this the fact that researchers and participants are individual human beings who differ from one another, have different belief systems, and value ethical principles differently—because of the value systems they bring to the research—and part of the "problem" is to recognize that there are potentially different ways to deal with situations, more than one of which can be ethically "correct."

Indeed, far too much time is spent by would-be ethicists arguing about what the "right answers" are, as if these were things that could be determined absolutely once and for all, when (arguably) the more important issue is whether the *process* of ethics consideration engaged in by the researcher has adequately taken into account the perspective of participants and the specifics of the case as they are known. At bottom is the question of whether the research can survive mechanisms of accountability that revere two core principles: whether we adequately consider and protect the rights of the research participant, whose dignity we value and without whose participation the research enterprise would not exist, and whether it is respectful of the academic freedom of the researcher, which is a cornerstone of the research enterprise and without which the social value of research would be undermined.

Beyond some reading that discusses ethics issues and some of the more contentious debates that have raged in the social sciences on these issues, your ethics education will come in large part from a front-line involvement with research where you meet real people and, we hope, take the time to know your research participants as people. And notwithstanding the general principles that books like this espouse, ethics considerations always come down to case-by-case considerations that involve a unique mix of the people who are your participants, the specific issue you are researching, your own perspective and interests, the norms and standards of your discipline, the social and legal context in which you are operating, and on and on. There are few simple answers, and you owe it to yourselves and your participants to give these matters deep consideration.

Regardless of how ethical we set out to be, and no matter how strong our allegiance to research participants, the concern that we should have about each of us as researchers is that, as ethics decision makers, we are always subject to a certain degree of conflict of interest. This arises from the simple fact that most researchers do *not* embark on careers and engage in research on matters that they think are trivial. People research the areas they do because they believe that it is the most important thing they can be doing right now and that an understanding of the topic under consideration is crucial to developing rational social policy, developing a cure for some disease, developing a technique that will help solve illiteracy, bring peace on earth, or whatever.

But recall that the very basic and first question of whether to do the research in the first place involves a weighing of the costs to participants against the benefits that might accrue from the research. A conflict of interest arises because any over-inflated sense of our own importance and the worth of our research may work to the disadvantage of research participants. It is in part for this reason that, from at least the late 1960s, universities have required researchers to engage in a process of ethics review. That is a positive development to the extent it ensures a third party who presumably has no conflict of interest of his or her own is mandated to ensure that each researcher who wishes to commence a research project has given adequate consideration to the rights and interests of the research participants.

However positive that development, the introduction of a new entity to the ethics consideration process—the third party who articulates standards and/or makes judgments about the adequacy of the ethics consideration engaged in by the researcher—introduces a whole new dynamic to the process of ethics consideration and a whole new set of questions: Who is this third party? How and by what authority is he or she constituted? What powers does this person have? How have the powers been implemented? What conflicts of interest are there? And so on. This starts to take us from our more narrow consideration of principles of ethics to matters in the sociology of science, considerations of ethics regulation. It is to an understanding of that that we now turn.

REGULATING ETHICS

Early Formulations

We have already mentioned some of the biomedical disasters that raised concerns about the ethics of research involving human participants, such as the Tuskegee syphilis study and several other examples. But perhaps the most grotesque example of experimentation for the glory of a hateful state came from the Nazis, who engaged in medical research on the Jews they had incarcerated in concentration camps. As the postwar Nuremberg trials revealed, the Nazis' "experiments" included such procedures as severing and exchanging limbs between live people, made all the more torturous by a lack of anesthetic. Or, with clipboards and observational protocols in hand, the researchers would place their captives in ice baths to see how long it took them to die from hypothermia.

If there was a positive development from this experience, it was that the Nuremberg trials resulted in development of the "Nuremberg Code," which was the first contemporary statement of research ethics that offered guidelines for conducting research involving human participants. That code subsequently "became the foundation of the Declaration of Helsinki, adopted by the World Health Organization in 1964 and revised in 1975. It was also the basis for the 'Ethical Guidelines for Clinical Investigation' adopted by the American Medical Association in 1966" (Berg 2007: 55).

In the social sciences, the development of ethics guidelines had two sources. One that is often cited relates to the completion of contentious research as the enervating factor. Most often cited are studies such as Milgram's laboratory-based obedience research (Milgram 1963, 1974); the Stanford prison simulation (Haney, Banks, & Zimbardo 1973); Laud Humphreys's field research on brief sexual encounters among gays described in *Tearoom Trade* (Humphreys 1970); the Wichita jury study in which social scientists "bugged" a jury room in order to gain "uncontaminated" information about jury deliberations (e.g., see Punch 1994); "Project Camelot," in which the CIA sponsored research designed to understand how to destabilize foreign governments (Horowitz 1967); and student researchers who posed as alcoholics to study members of Alcoholics Anonymous without their knowledge or consent (Lofland & Lejeune 1960). All of these studies were highly controversial, each attracting detractors and supporters.

And although we can't discount the ire and calls for regulation these studies generated, it has to be noted that discussion regarding the development of codes of ethics within the research disciplines predates all of that contentious research. Thus, those commonly noted studies could not have been a "cause" of a discussion that began before them, although they may have helped give direction to the discussion that was ongoing and become part of a rationale for regulation as it unfolded.

Indeed, if we go back to the literatures that developed when the research disciplines were debating the question of whether to go ahead and develop codes of research ethics, we see reasons advanced *other than* a need to control the excesses of some researchers. In his 1959 presidential address to the American Sociological Association, Talcott Parsons noted the burgeoning interest among sociologists in applied issues and, believing these would create new conflicts of interest, suggested that "perhaps a working code of relationships particularly needs to be worked out" (Parsons 1959: 558).

Sociology did not jump at the opportunity to develop a code of ethics, however. Most of the 1960s were spent debating whether or not developing a disciplinary code of ethics was desirable. Some members of the American Sociological Association argued that the task was not worth pursuing, and that "ethics regulation" was best left in the hands of individual researchers who would remain accountable for their actions (e.g., Becker 1964; Freidson 1964; Roth 1969). Their worry was that the creation of an external standard—to the extent it took the locus of ethical decision making away from researchers and handed it to bureaucrats who might or might not understand the research process—would mark the beginning of the end of academic freedom both for individual researchers and the academic research enterprise as a whole.

Others argued the opposite: far from *impeding* academic freedom, codes of ethics would help *preserve* it by serving as a buffer against third-party intervention into the research process (Schuler 1967). For example, when and if a government were to point to this or that isolated example of an ethics

violation and propose seizing control of the research-regulating apparatus that most codes of ethics represent, researchers could point to their disciplinary code and say, "Thanks, but no thanks; we are already regulating ourselves."

Similarly, when threats to the research enterprise arise—as they did in the United States in the late 1960s and early 1970s when various legal authorities tried to force researchers to disclose confidential research information for law enforcement purposes (see Lowman & Palys 2001a)—some believed a written code of ethics would help researchers defend against such attacks in court. Confidentiality provisions in the code, for example, could be used to show that research confidentiality in any challenged study was provided as part of a considered research ethic whose maintenance was as important to the research enterprise and to maintaining the researcher–participant relationship as it was to other relationships where confidentiality had been acknowledged by government and/or the courts as an integral component of maintaining a socially valued relation (e.g., the lawyer–client, husband–wife, and priest–penitent relationships).

Researchers' desire to "be ethical" was never at issue; rather, the question was whether, in the long run, the formalization of codes of ethics would actually help or hinder researchers, research participants, and society as a whole. In the early 1960s, the answer was no: ASA's membership rejected the idea of a disciplinary code of ethics. A decade later, the answer was yes, and ASA joined other disciplines in developing a formalized code of research ethics.[10]

To explain this change of policy, it is important to recognize that the first sets of social science research ethics codes were being produced in the United States in a very particular social and legal context. These were years of huge intergenerational conflict surrounding the Vietnam War. What had been "core" social values were being questioned, as evidenced by the contemporary resurgence of the Women's Liberation Movement, Black Power, and Red Power. Unrest at the universities was associated with new questioning of that institution's role as the location *par excellence* for critical questioning of what and who we are. And it was also a time when the U.S. government, particularly during Richard Nixon's presidency, was showing that it was prepared to do everything in its power to suppress threats to the status quo.

The literatures of the time, and especially the literatures in sociology and anthropology, were particularly concerned with the threats to academic freedom and disciplinary integrity that were arising from federal government intervention in research practices. Project Camelot showed that the U.S. government, in particular the CIA, was quite prepared to adopt "researcher" identities and exploit researcher contacts in developing nations in order to further "national security" interests by fomenting revolution and internal discord where that suited U.S. objectives (Horowitz 1967).

At the same time, legal authorities during the Nixon years, including grand juries, governmental commissions of inquiry, and legal agencies such as the FBI, were beginning to issue subpoenas to researchers in the hope that legal pressure could be brought to bear that would see them testifying about their "inside" knowledge in order to further law enforcement interests (Lowman & Palys 2001a). In sum, while researchers at the beginning of the 1960s may have preferred to take their chances based on a clear societal tradition of respect for the research enterprise, by the end of the decade the thought of creating buffers against external threats offered a welcome respite.

An accompanying development in the universities was the advent of university ethics review committees whose job was to ensure that researchers had considered their discipline's standards in the design of their research. Although some concern was expressed that if codes of ethics were the death sentence for academic freedom, ethics reviews committees would be the executioners (e.g., Roth 1969), it appears these concerns were overstated, at least at that time.

The Locus of Responsibility Lies with the Researcher

If there is one monumental change that has happened in the ethics area over the last three decades it is the substantial shift in how ethics are regulated. In the 1970s, researchers were seen as an accountable group of individuals who were responsible for ensuring that no harm came to their participants. The first discipline-generated "codes" of ethics were just coming into existence at that time, as were the first university research ethics review committees.

The idea that anyone but the researcher was driving the ethics bus was laughable. How could one possibly predict all the things that could possibly happen during a research project (especially when one does research in the first place to find out what is going on)? Who but the researcher would have the knowledge and experience *in situ* to make responsible ethical decisions as issues arose? How could academic freedom survive any other way? Research ethics review boards in that era took their job as one of ensuring that researchers had considered and applied the standards of their disciplines and that the interests of research subjects had a central role in that determination.

These issues seemed self-evident when the initial social science codes were formulated. The American Psychological Association's statement of principles (APA 1973) reminded us there are few inherently right or wrong answers; one is always weighing advantages and disadvantages. In the end, the APA recognized that each researcher must choose his or her own resolution to ethical questions. Their ethics "guidelines" were exactly that: advice for researchers to *consider* when designing their research. That they did not carry the force of "commandments" or "rules" was affirmed explicitly by noting that the choice of whether and how to do any given piece of research should reside with the "considered judgment" of the "individual social scientist." Investigators were obliged to take "personal responsibility" for ensuring that ethical issues were considered, and the principles were offered as an ideal to which they should aspire. But the choice of what to do belonged ultimately to the researcher, whose job would be to consider how those principles played out in the specifics of the context at hand.

The American Anthropological Association (AAA; 1971) made a similar assumption, apparently in part because it felt that the array of specific circumstances that would face any researcher was simply impossible to predict, such that any ethics code designed to cover every possible happenstance would have to be the size of a *Criminal Code*. Further, the AAA code revealed particular concern with external interference in the research process and in the rights of researchers:

> The best interests of scientific research are not served by the imposition of external restrictions. [For example,] the review procedures instituted for foreign area research contracts by the Federal Affairs Research Council of the Department of State (following a Presidential Directive of July, 1965) offer a dangerous potential for censorship of research. (AAA 1971: 3)

It hardly would be consistent for the AAA to decry the interference of others, only to reserve that role for itself. Instead, the AAA seemed to see its code as serving more of an educational and sensitizing role:

> To err is human, to forgive humane. This statement of principles of professional responsibility is not designed to punish, but to provide guidelines which can minimize the occasions upon which there is a need to forgive. (AAA 1971: 4)

The American Sociological Association (ASA) seemed to have chosen a more interventionist tack while also paying heed to academic freedom. Thus, on the one hand it affirmed the value of free inquiry:

> We affirm the autonomy of sociological inquiry. The sociologist must be responsive, first and foremost, to the truth of his investigation ... The fate

of sociology as a science is dependent upon the fate of free inquiry in an open society. (ASA 1968: 318)

On the other hand, the ASA's longer-term goal seems to have involved developing a more normative set of expectations:

> In the situation which sociology presently faces, one in which there is a lack of consensus among sociologists about not only the substance of, but even the need for, a code of ethics, we must start with a constitution, not a statute book, a set of general premises and principles, not the set of specific norms toward which we hope slowly to move. For the moment, sociology rests content with a statement of ethical principles that is nearly as general as the Mosaic Tablets. But it recognizes the need to move on, as soon as possible, to more specific normative expressions of these general ethical principles. In recognizing this need to move on, sociology considers its eventual, more specific code an homology to the Common Law. The specific code for sociology, like the specific code for all professional associations, should be built up as the Common Law has been built up, on the slow accumulation and testing of case law. (ASA 1968: 317)

The question for sociologists, therefore, was one of finding the appropriate balance of freedom and constraint. Nonetheless, the impression is that even in 1968 the ASA saw itself as the determining authority: principle 12 asserted that when the application of the principles was unclear, "the sociologist should seek the *judgment* of the relevant agency or committee designated by the ASA" (ASA 1968: 318; emphasis added).

Centralizing Authority

Three decades later, much on the ethics landscape has changed. Canadian associations that once simply adopted the codes of their U.S.–based counterparts have developed codes of their own (e.g., Canadian Sociology and Anthropology Association 1994;

Canadian Psychological Association 1991, 2000; Sinclair et al. 1987). The new codes offer nothing original in their inventories of principles but differ significantly insofar as both the Canadian and U.S. associations (1) have (all but one) embraced a more centralized decision-making structure that assumes/ gives the discipline/agency regulatory authority, and (2) have emphasized the creation of one-size-fits-all mega-codes that transcend boundaries within and between disciplines. Accompanying these changes (all of which have been made in the name of ethics) has been a bureaucratization of the ethics regulation process that, in the view of at least one well-placed observer (McDonald 2001), has made "getting ethics approval" rather than "engaging in ethics consideration" the focus of researchers' considerations.

The disciplines themselves have attempted to remove boundaries between professional roles within disciplines. The American Psychological Association, for example, decided in 1997 to stop formulating unique sets of ethical principles for particular roles or settings (e.g., one set directed to researchers, another developed for therapists) and, instead, to generate one overarching set of principles to cover the whole range of roles that psychologists occupy. This obviously made for a lengthier list of principles (15 pages as opposed to 1) and a new order of complexity. A similar approach—essentially a photocopied code with few discipline-specific adaptations—was followed by the ASA (1997). Both disciplines moved in the direction of greater centralized control—issuing "standards" instead of "guidelines" and placing the respective associations instead of the researcher as the final arbiters of ethical practice. In contrast, the most recent revision of the Canadian Psychological Association *Code of Ethics* (2000) continues to assert a role for conscience, noting in section IV-17, for example, that,

> In adhering to the Principle of Responsibility to Society, psychologists would:
>
> Familiarize themselves with the laws and regulations of the societies in which they work, especially those that are related to their activities as

psychologists, and abide by them. If those laws or regulations seriously conflict with the ethical principles contained herein, psychologists would do whatever they could to uphold the ethical principles. If upholding the ethical principles could result in serious personal consequences (e.g., jail or physical harm), decision for final action would be considered a matter of personal conscience.

The American Anthropological Association (1996) is unique because it is the only discipline to have avoided rather than embraced a centralization of authority. In considering its objectives in creating a code, the commission concluded there are two purposes served by such codes:

> A professional code of ethics should be a useful educational document, laying out rules and ideals as to what is expected of persons in the field to which the code applies. A code of ethics can also be the basis for adjudicating claims of unethical behaviour. The current [i.e., 1967, 1971] AAA *Statements on Ethics* are intended to serve both purposes. (1996: 3)

For its newest code, however, the commission has accepted the first purpose but rejected the second on the grounds that it is doubtful the AAA would be able to construct and administer an adjudication process that could be both "fair and legally defensible." The result is a draft document that emphasizes educating/sensitizing researchers about ethical issues and offers guidelines for the resolution of ethical dilemmas. In the words of the AAA (1996):

> Anthropological research, teaching, and application, like any human actions, pose choices for which anthropological researchers, teachers, or individuals applying anthropological techniques and knowledge individually and collectively bear ethical responsibility. Since anthropological researchers, teachers, and practitioners are members of a variety of groups and subject to a variety of ethical codes, choices must sometimes be made

not only between the varied obligations presented in the code, but also between those of this code and those incurred in other statuses or roles. This statement does not dictate choice or propose sanctions. Rather, it is designed to promote discussion and provide general guidelines for ethically responsible decisions. (Sec. VI)

It is also noteworthy that the AAA code is the only code of ethics that not only acknowledges the rights and responsibilities of researchers to make their own ethical choices, but also includes a skeptical note about itself and other codes as well:

> Anthropological researchers, teachers, and practitioners must be sensitive to and continually assess all appropriate ethical claims on their work. When conflicts or special situations exist, violations of this or any other applicable code of ethics might be justified. (AAA 1996: Sec. II)

Government Intervention

The idea of centralizing ethics regulation and placing government in a watchdog/overseer role seems to have originated in the U.S. Department of Health and Human Services with the establishment of the Office for Protection from Research Risk, which more recently became the Office for Human Research Protections (see their website at http://www.hhs.gov/ohrp). Canada's formal entry into the ethics regulation business came in the mid-1990s with the development of the *Tri-Council Policy Statement* on ethics in research regarding human participants, which all universities that wish to continue receiving funding from the federal granting agencies are required to follow (see CIHR et al. 1998).

The "Tri-Council" portion of the title refers to Canada's three major granting councils: the Social Sciences and Humanities Research Council (SSHRC), the National Sciences and Engineering Research Council (NSERC), and the Medical Research Council (MRC; now known as CIHR, the Canadian Institutes of Health Research). These three

agencies were given the mandate to create an ethics policy that would apply to all research done in Canada, or outside of Canada by Canadians, involving human participants. Although the process was launched in 1994, the first time most members of the Canadian research community heard about it was in 1996, when a first draft code was released for comment.

It is clear that much of the concern that gave rise to the Tri-Council Policy Statement (TCPS) issued in relation to biomedical research and the conflicts of interest that were beginning to arise in an era when money-hungry university administrations were being asked to engage in ethics review of proposals by private benefactors with very deep pockets. In particular, the prospect of big money from pharmaceutical windfalls, genome patents, and the like (large grants to the faculty; large overhead for the university) gave rise to concern about the extent to which universities and university researchers caught up in an entrepreneurial spirit had perhaps forgotten their allegiances and responsibilities to society in general and to their research subjects in particular. In this regard, Michael McDonald, Director of the University of British Columbia Centre for Applied Ethics and a member of the Tri-Council Working Group that created the 1996 and 1997 drafts of what eventually became the *Tri-Council Policy Statement* (CIHR et al. 1998), offered the following reflections:

> In constructing the *Code,* our concern was to address central features of Canadian research involving humans, including:
>
> ♦ Increasing private sector dollars pouring particularly into medical research, much of this in the private sector
>
> ♦ Attendant pressures on REBs [Research Ethics Boards] to issue quick and favourable verdicts on research proposals (McDonald 1998)

Another objective of the federal government presumably was to generate a code of ethics relevant to all researchers in Canada who engage in research with human participants, thereby further expediting its own science policy, which emphasizes university–private sector partnerships, multidisciplinary collaboration, and multi-site trials. Instead of a patchwork of ethics decision making across various institutions using various codes, the interest was in creating a harmonized ethics code that emphasized common ethical principles and to which all researchers in all disciplines in all institutional contexts could be held accountable. Clearly this approach represents a significant departure from the discipline-driven, localized process of ethics review, which has been replaced with a more centralized process using a "one-size-fits-all" model to which, presumably, all researchers can subscribe.

Unfortunately, there was little effort to accommodate the diversity of methodologies and perspectives that characterize the social sciences and humanities. The "one size" that was supposed to fit all reflected a biomedical, experimentalist, quantitative model, with little attention or concern over how these principles would translate into other epistemologies and approaches (e.g., see Palys 1996a). Not surprisingly, there has been little or no complaint from quantitative, experimentalist researchers who "see themselves" in the regulations and find categories and approaches that make sense to them. Others, especially more qualitatively oriented researchers who engage in field research that takes a more collaborative and inductive approach, have expressed grave concern (e.g., see Haggerty 2004; van den Hoonaard 2002). The Social Sciences and Humanities Research Ethics Special Working Committee (SSHWC), a committee established to assess how implementation of the TCPS was affecting the social sciences and humanities and to advise on future developments in the TCPS, consulted with Canada's social science and humanities research communities and found there was good reason for this concern. They concluded that,

> If there is a fundamental problem we can identify, it is that the granting agencies' desire to create a regulatory structure to deal with the stereotypical clinical trial has resulted in a document and set of

structures that assume different modes of research involving different relationships and different concerns than most social science and humanities researchers seek and encounter. Stated simply, the TCPS does not "speak" to their experience, leaving REBs that may lack appropriate breadth of expertise free to impose default assumptions that threaten free inquiry for no ethical gain. The further one's research gets from the paradigmatic/positivist/experimentalist assumptions and understandings that permeate the TCPS, the more ill fitting the TCPS's application becomes. As this implies, although the deleterious effects of the TCPS have been felt across the social sciences and humanities, it is the more collaborative, inductive, field- and text-based research traditions that have been the most adversely affected. (2004: 10)

These problems with the TCPS and the regulatory system it invokes are not unique to Canada. The centralization of authority in government and federal agencies that the Canadian system involves parallels those taking place in other countries. Not surprisingly, the problems identified by SSHWC in Canada are echoed by researchers from the United States (e.g., see Adler and Adler 2002; Christians 2000), Australia (e.g., Israel 2004a, 2004b), and Great Britain (e.g., Pearce 2002), all of which have similar systems in place. The concerns expressed are several.

HAS THE TCPS MADE A DIFFERENCE?

There's no doubt that the creation and implementation of the TCPS has had a significant impact on the academic research culture in Canada. Every university in the country is now subject to its provisions, and many universities, like our own, have created new ethics policies in order to ensure that their ethics review committees have been created and will operate in a manner that is consistent with the TCPS's principles. Many hospitals and other types of medical facilities that engage in research with human participants also follow the TCPS, and many structures have been established in response to what can only be described as Canada's Big Bang in the bureaucratization and regulation of ethics. The result has been the development of national advisory councils, the proliferation of ethics review boards and in particular private research ethics boards that will undertake review for a fee, a new formality in the way that ethics review is conducted, and the "legalization" of research contracts with many prospective participant groups.

ARE RESEARCH PARTICIPANTS BETTER PROTECTED?

John Mueller of the University of Calgary has been one of Canada's most vocal critics regarding the need to take an empirical approach to be able to evaluate whether the expensive and extensive imposition of a new ethics bureaucracy and ethics review process actually makes research participants any safer. In one tongue-in-cheek paper (see Mueller 2003) he describes the origins of the federal Rogue Elephant Board (REB), which was created when an Ottawa bureaucrat realized the extensive damage that could be done to universities and the students who attend them if they were to be attacked by a stampede of wild elephants. The bureaucrat designs a plan that calls for universities to develop appropriate policies and create, staff, and fund Rambunctious Elephant Brigades (REBs) to ensure all are protected. One university builds a picket fence around the campus and ensures that there is a staff of paid and volunteer sentinels at the fence all the time to ensure everyone approaching the campus fills out forms showing they have been made aware of the prospective dangers. He continues,

> Although this scheme was initially criticized by Professor Pita on the grounds that such a modest structure could not keep out rogue criminal elephants, he and other critics were soundly rebuked for their lack of sensitivity with regard to the need to "do something" to assure the safety of the campus and community.
>
> The REB now proudly notes that the fence has been in place for a year, and there have been

NO ELEPHANTS ON CAMPUS in all that time—the system is working! The hour-long wait to enter campus each morning must just be accepted as the price we pay for the safety of all.

Although made in a humorous way, his point is a serious one. First, he wonders where the evidence is for there having been any harms arising from social science and humanities research in the first place, as he can find none other than the same three or four studies—Milgram (1963), Humphreys (1970), Project Camelot (Horowitz 1967), the 1953 Wichita Jury Study (cited in Barnes 1977), the Stanford prison simulation (Zimbardo 1972)—that every research methods text (including this one) seems to cite. Is that it? If that is true, then in contrast to the biomedical domain where several people seem to die every year from participating in clinical trials, the holus-bolus imposition of a monolithic bureaucracy on the social sciences to save us all from a non-problem whose success is affirmed by no more than the non-occurrence of anything becomes highly questionable.

This is not to say that ethical dilemmas do not exist in the social sciences, or that harms are not possible, but rather that earlier less bureaucratic and interventionist approaches may already have been up to the task. Second, even if we assume that there are and were such harms occurring, why is there no evidence being gathered about the occurrence of harms to show whether any new policy that purports to deal with them is in fact successful at doing so? This leads Mueller (2003) to question whether what is at stake is concern about research participants, or liability management and control: "Rules (policies) have been established, and adherence to these rules has become more important than the substance or principles behind the rules, much less the research. Thus we have an 'agenda of control' rather than an 'agenda of inquiry.'"

One way that the main bodies in the TCPS's new regulatory regime can show that their allegiance is to research participants and the pursuit of knowledge rather than control and liability management is to ensure that institutional conflicts of interest—on the part of both the federal government and its granting agencies that fund, as well as the universities that do, the research.

INSTITUTIONAL CONFLICTS OF INTEREST

The Russel Ogden case and its outcomes showed how universities can undermine the rights of participants by impeding certain research practices that researchers traditionally have engaged in to maintain the interests of their research participants and preserve the integrity of the research enterprise. Ogden's only desire was to act ethically, and he showed tremendous courage and principle in putting his career and livelihood on the line in order to protect those who took part in his research even when his university faltered. Protecting the rights of his research participants required a university commitment to fight for those rights in court, which competed with the university's interest in minimizing liability and managing its image in the face of those who might interpret its battle for research participant rights as "challenging law" or taking a stand with respect to euthanasia and assisted suicide (see Lowman & Palys 2000).

The TCPS presumably avoids that administrative conflict of interest by requiring those who are involved in ethics administration and the protection of research participants to be independent of the university administration:

> The REB must act independently from the parent organization. Therefore, institutions must respect the autonomy of the REB and ensure that the REB has the appropriate financial and administrative independence to fulfill its primary duties. Situations may arise where the parent organization has a strong interest in seeing a project approved before all ethical questions are resolved. As the body mandated to maintain high ethical standards, however, the public trust and integrity of the research process require that the REB maintain an arms-length relationship with the parent organization and avoid and manage real or apparent conflicts of interest. (4.2)

Are the granting councils vigilant about ensuring that independence is maintained? Universities across the country routinely locate their Directors of Research Ethics and Offices of Research Ethics within the jurisdiction of their Vice-President of Research.

When we look to other places in the ethics bureaucracy—such as the Interagency Advisory Panel on Research Ethics (PRE), whose role includes interpreting the TCPS and advising the presidents of the granting councils regarding future development of the TCPS, membership is mixed. At last glance, the 12-member panel comprised about half researchers and half administrators. An ironic development came when SFU's former Vice-President of Research—the same individual who played a central role in the Ogden debacle—was appointed Chair of the PRE by the presidents of the granting councils. While Judge Steinberg of the B.C. Provincial Court had labelled Dr. Clayman's actions in defence of Ogden, his research participants, and academic freedom "hollow and timid" and showing a "surprising lack of courage," the presidents of the granting councils stated in their appointment letter that "they were impressed by Dr. Clayman's outstanding commitment to research ethics in Canada to date and felt that his leadership will be instrumental in serving their common goal to promote high ethical standards in human research" (see Government of Canada 2005).

And of course we can look at the granting councils themselves and the conflict of interest they must manage as part of the government of Canada. As part of government, they have a vested interest in the rule of law that gives them status, credibility, and power, and in appeasing the Parliament to whom they owe their existence. Their role as funders of research gives them the opportunity, if they choose to exercise it, to establish priorities and give direction. Are the granting agencies willing to reaffirm the need for research on topics and in ways that may question what government does and how it does it, including questioning the very policies and legal order to which the granting councils owe their existence? We have seen the granting councils take an aggressive stance on issues that challenge the integrity of the research enterprise when it comes to their own viability and ability to fund research. Will they show that same aggressiveness now when, as stewards of the TCPS and the high ethical standards it presumably stands for, the integrity of the research enterprise and the welfare of research subjects/participants is concerned, just as the disciplines have done when the standards espoused in their ethics codes have been challenged, for example, when research confidentiality has been challenged via a prosecutor's subpoena?

The record in this regard is mixed. On the one hand, the TCPS acknowledges that ethical and legal approaches "may lead to different conclusions," and the granting councils have formally acknowledged that although one should make every effort to be both ethical and legal, in the final instant researchers must make a choice of conscience for which they are accountable. However, their record in doing something about this gap is less than stellar. They have never intervened even when directly requested to do so, for example, when Russel Ogden was subpoenaed in Canada a second time, and have done nothing thus far to lobby for statute-based protections for research participants who share information that could be harmful to them if disclosed (see Palys and Lowman in 2006).

Similar conflicts of interest exist in the United States with the federal Office for Human Research Protections (OHRP) that is housed within the U.S. Department of Health and Human Services. Research in the United States is ultimately governed by what is called the "Common Rule," which outlines ethical obligations in any research that is funded by government. It is thus less extensive than the TCPS in its claimed jurisdiction, but because of being based in statute has far more teeth—a whole university's research program can be and has been shut down in an instant when deviations from the requirements of the Common Rule are unearthed.

One of the requirements of the Common Rule involves research participant confidentiality, as is the case with the TCPS, and, as we mentioned, the United States has shown considerable leadership in

the development of statute-based protections (in the form of Confidentiality Certificates and Privacy Certificates). All of this changed following 9/11, however, when territorial security began to trump all other considerations and the U.S. government adopted HR3162, "*An Act to deter and punish terrorist acts in the United States and around the world, to enhance law enforcement investigatory tools, and for other purposes,*" otherwise known as the "*Uniting and Strengthening America by Providing Appropriate Tools Required to Intercept and Obstruct Terrorism Act,*" or more simply, as the *USA Patriot Act* (2001).

Of particular concern for researchers in the *USA Patriot Act* is section 215, which gives the FBI authority to obtain "any tangible things (including books, records, papers, documents, and other items) for an investigation to protect against international terrorism or clandestine intelligence activities." Once an order is obtained, it cannot be challenged, and any person or institution that discloses information about someone cannot inform the person that there has been a demand for information or a disclosure. In essence, it gives the FBI powers to gather information involving "terrorism" or "clandestine intelligence activities" that relate to "national defence" and "national security." These are sweeping powers and one doesn't have to be a professor of criminology to know that legal authorities can be very creative in using legal mechanisms to deal with people they find troublesome, and there is a lengthy history in both Canada and the United States of legal authorities having difficulty making distinctions in what are supposed to be free and democratic societies between criminal subversion and legitimate activism and dissent. Even within the last year in British Columbia we have seen the RCMP calling indigenous activist groups such as the former West Coast Warrior Society "terrorists" in an aggressive initiative designed to curb their activity. In any event, the implications of the *USA Patriot Act* for research confidentiality is a significant enough threat that various university research ethics boards in Canada no longer believe data stored in the United States meet the same standard of confidentiality they once did, and researchers are being dissuaded from using survey companies such as Survey Monkey that are U.S.–based and/or have U.S.–based servers when the information being gathered is at all sensitive.

How surprising, therefore, that when one goes to the Office of Human Research Protections (OHRP) website and does a search for "Patriot Act," nothing comes up! Not one word about this threat to research confidentiality from the federal agency whose primary purpose is to be concerned about keeping research participants from harm? Ted sent a query to OHRP asking whether they were concerned at all about the implications of the *USA Patriot Act* for research participants, and if so, what they have done to encourage alteration of or amendment to the act to protect participants in research. The reply he received stated, "The questions you raise are interesting however to date the issue of protecting human subjects participating in research in the setting of the Patriot Act have not been raised." Problems? What problems?

These situations highlight a difficulty that arises when federal agencies seize control over a country's research apparatus, which is that they operate at least at the level of policy on the basis of blind faith that law is just and fair, that the state operates in nothing but benevolent and hospitable ways, and that research participants have nothing to fear from the state because it is researchers they must be protected from. Our experience is quite the opposite, however. Some of the biggest threats to research confidentiality—probably the singular most important ethical principle in relation to research participants in the social sciences—in Canada, the United States, Australia, and Great Britain (e.g., see Israel 2004; Lowman & Palys 2000), for example, have arisen from the state in the form of prosecutors and, in the United States, from the FBI and grand juries. And the very reason we have Bills of Rights and Charters of Rights and Freedoms is to protect us from the state. Law may be mostly just and mostly fair and mostly something that we should maintain faith in, but both criminology and history tell us that it is constructed by some people to control others, and that it seeks justice and fairness but sometimes falls short in profoundly tragic ways. Government as a

matter of policy has a difficult time admitting that, but at some level must do so if it is truly to encourage the highest ethical standards that it purports to espouse. The alternative is to adopt the lower ethical standard of "meeting legal requirements," and transform "research ethics" into nothing more than a *caveat emptor* ethic that is based solely on informed consent—"We'll tell you what might happen, and you decide whether you'd like to take part. If the worst happens, don't say we didn't tell you." That is not research ethics; that is liability management.

DIVERSITY OF INTERESTS TO BE REPRESENTED

Many articles in the TCPS affirm the need to ensure that diverse interests and perspectives are represented in the ethics review process. For example, in its initial overview entitled "Context of an Ethics Framework," the TCPS reminds REBs that,

> For meaningful and effective application, the foregoing ethical principles must operate neither in the abstract, nor in isolation from one another. Ethical principles are sometimes criticized as being applied in formulaic ways. To avoid this, they should be applied in the context of the nature of the research and of the ethical norms and practices of the relevant research discipline. (Section G).

In order to ensure this sort of sensitivity to diversity, Article 1.3 requires the following with respect to REB membership:

> The REB shall consist of at least five members, including both men and women, of whom:
> (a) at least two members have broad expertise in the methods or in the areas of research that are covered by the REB;
> (b) at least one member is knowledgeable in ethics;
> (c) for biomedical research, at least one member is knowledgeable in the relevant law; this is advisable but not mandatory for other areas of research; and

(d) at least one member has no affiliation with the institution, but is recruited from the community served by the institution.

Two issues arise here: community membership and epistemological diversity.

COMMUNITY MEMBERSHIP A notable feature of the TCPS is its requirement that at least one member be "recruited from the community served by the institution." On this point, the TCPS (MRC et al. 1998) explains:

> The community member requirement of Article 1.3(d) is essential to help broaden the perspective and value base of the REB beyond the institution, and thus advances dialogue with, and accountability to, local communities. (1.4)

"Accountability" is a popular buzzword these days, but it is interesting to consider its possible meanings here. There are at least two, one of which is quite heartening, the other more problematic.

The heartening one is the greater diversity that having a community member brings to REBs and the role that community members can play in bringing the "subject-centered perspective" the TCPS requires (i.7) to the dialogue. For example, in much biomedical research, community members can be seen as the embodiment of the "reasonable person" that judges often talk about, that is, as in "informed consent statements should be written in a way that a 'reasonable person'—an average rational and reasonably intelligent community member—can understand them, and agree that all 'relevant' information has been included." As "lay" representatives of subject populations, community members thus can be a valuable sounding board for REBs. And to that extent, virtually any community member will do. As a non-academic who likely has a respect for the research enterprise but a limited understanding of research design issues, the person is ideally placed to give feedback as to whether a researcher's proposed solicitation process is too pushy, contains too much jargon, and whether it contains the sort of information someone would want to know in order to make an informed decision about participating.

Of course, any sample of $N = 1$ community member can become problematic to the extent that no one person, unless duly elected, can legitimately claim to be "representative" of any community. The limitations of what any single individual can offer must be recognized, along with the sorts of biases that are inevitable in the selection process. For example, at Simon Fraser University, the two community members on an 11-person committee are a businessperson and a video producer, that is, middle-class folks like all the other members of the committee. Will these people have anything unique to add about research regarding more marginalized members of the community? More importantly, will any members of the most vulnerable populations who become participants in research—the homeless, prison inmates, sex trade workers—ever become members of REBs? Not likely. It will be interesting, therefore, to see just what steps REBs will take to ensure participant perspectives are included.

EPISTEMOLOGICAL DIVERSITY AND ACADEMIC FREEDOM Censorship and the denial of academic freedom come not only from outside the university but also from within its corridors, where interfaculty and intrafaculty and interdisciplinary and intradisciplinary rivalries and differences in perspective are reflected in squabbles about what is most important to do (and hence most deserving of the university's inevitably limited resources) and the "right" way to do those things:

> Academic freedom ... depends crucially on the autonomy and integrity of the disciplines. For it is the departments, and the disciplines to which they belong, that constitute the spaces in which rival scholarly and pedagogical positions are negotiated. Academic freedom not only protects sociology professors from the interference of trustees and public officials in the exercise of their jobs as

teachers and scholars; it protects them from physics professors as well. It mandates that decisions about what counts as good work in sociology shall be made by sociologists. (Menaud 1996: 17)

"Ethics" committees by definition carry a banner of moral authority, and the biggest worry about them is that the people on them will start to see debates and disagreements that are really reflections of epistemological, perspectival, and even ideological differences as somehow grounded in ethics and not those other domains. Indeed, giving a limited number of members on a university ethics committee the ability to reject or approve the research of their colleagues will be problematic to the extent that members confuse those two domains.

Will the *Policy Statement* ensure such violations of academic freedom will not occur? We wish the answer were yes, but it seems not to be so. In one recent case, a graduate student sought ethics approval for her master's thesis proposal, which involved interviewing sex trade workers working in off-street venues. Access to this sample came through her supervisor, John Lowman, who is known internationally for his work in the area and is highly respected by sex trade workers who have participated in his research; by members of the parliamentary committees who have sought his advice when considering how to formulate better laws and policies in relation to sex workers; and by the media who frequently seek him out for commentary on legal policy issues and events in relation to the sex trades. Given the vulnerability of people in these trades—mostly women—to violence, and the number of missing persons reports and deaths of street prostitutes that have been identified in Vancouver and other cities across the country, there is clearly an urgency and importance to doing such research. Furthermore, the risks to sex trade workers for participating would appear minimal—thousands of sex trade workers have been interviewed in studies over decades without one sex trade worker anywhere that we know of having been "harmed" by the expe-

rience. The director of the Office of Research Ethics at SFU considered the graduate student's proposal "minimal risk" and approved it.

Approvals by the director, however, are contingent on subsequent ratification by the REB, and when the REB got hold of it, everything changed. The proposal was immediately classified "more than minimal risk," and eventually rejected because of the committee's assertion that the benefits of the research were not worth the risks. The number of ways this review violated SFU's ethics policy and the TCPS were quite incredible. First to be violated were the TCPS's conflict of interest provisions. The REB of the time included as one of its community members a civic politician who had argued both vehemently and publicly (e.g., on radio interview shows) with Lowman regarding the City of Vancouver's policies regarding street prostitution. Notwithstanding the obvious conflict of interest when it came to evaluating Lowman's supervisee's proposal, she did not withdraw from the discussion, nor, apparently, did the chair insist upon it.

As we quoted above, the TCPS also requires at least two members of the committee to have appropriate research experience to be able to make a reasonable evaluation of a project, but no members of the committee who evaluated the proposal that day had any experience with field research—only one committee member had any such experience and he did not attend that day. There were two psychologists on the committee at that time; no other social science department was represented. Indeed, there were more people on the committee at the time from the Department of Molecular Biology and Biochemistry than from Criminology, Sociology, Anthropology, Political Science, Women's Studies, Geography, and Communications combined! The committee also did not let their lack of expertise stop them from violating another aspect of both SFU's ethics policy and the TCPS—the requirement that all "greater than minimal risk" proposals should be reviewed by persons qualified to do so in a process both policies outline. The SFU REB went ahead and did their own review anyway.

The policy violations continued when the committee gave no "detailed reasons" for their decision as both policies require when there is a rejection of a proposal, which in turn created the ironic situation where the REB were declaring the research "greater than minimal risk" but refusing to identify what that risk might be, thereby making it impossible for the student to meet the ethical criterion of appropriately informing her prospective research participants about what risks that participation in the project might entail!

In the end it took eight months (!) and the intervention of the SFU Faculty Association to straighten this out, at which time the project was approved as a "minimal risk" project as it had been by the Director of Research Ethics at the outset; the Vice-President of Research investigated the procedures followed and found that the REB had indeed violated the SFU ethics policy in the way they dealt with that proposal; and the graduate student was awarded two semesters of free tuition in "recognition of delays to [her] research program caused by the actions of the Research Ethics Board." Notwithstanding all their violations of policy, the SFU administration has done nothing to hold the REB and its chair accountable, and the chair has never apologized to the graduate student and her supervisor for the huge amount of time the REB cost both parties.

What is missing in the TCPS is an effective mechanism for holding REBs accountable; the amount of power they hold is enormous, and appropriate checks and balances to their authority that would allow reasonably speedy resolution to blatant policy violations such as those perpetrated by the SFU REB are absent. A similar case example involving Lowman and Palys in days prior to implementation of the TCPS was described in an earlier edition of this book (see Palys 2003). The example described above reaffirms that while advent of the TCPS has had a huge impact on the ability of social science researchers to do minimal risk research it has done nothing to quell excess displays of committee power. Even if vindication is forthcoming over the longer term, for field researchers it can be a pyrrhic

victory as field-based research is not something that can be scheduled and re-scheduled at whim. The research that Lowman and Palys had proposed, for example, was never done because the research opportunity was no longer there after the 18 months it took to resolve the debate.

Is there any rescue in sight? At this writing, unfortunately not. One of the federal committees whose mandate includes addressing procedural issues in the TCPS has put forth a proposal that calls for even greater discretion for REBs and offers no counterbalance—accountability mechanisms—to ensure that discretion is not abused (see Subgroup on Procedural Issues for the TCPS [ProGroup] 2005).

SQUARE PEGS, ROUND HOLES

One thing that characterizes ethical decision making is recognition of the complexity and values that go into that process. Ethics considerations are complex because they are not simply choices between right and wrong. They are more likely "mostly right and a little bit wrong this way" versus "another way of being right but also a little bit wrong the other way." Centralizing the process of ethics regulation requires the creation of a monolithic bureaucracy to deal with the hundreds or thousands of projects that are proposed in any given year in any given university.

While every individual who proposes research may be able to give his or her proposal detailed consideration, and while relatively decentralized committees may still be able to give fairly detailed consideration to their reviews of those decisions, a more centralized process must find some way to deal with hundreds of proposals quickly. What we see different universities doing is reducing the "ethics review" process and changing it into an "ethics approval" process based on checklists, gatekeepers, and the formulaic application of certain principles that make sense to the small range of perspectives represented on the committee.

The creation of these mechanisms is not in itself problematic if one is dealing with a limited array of research that can be dealt with by centralized committees or individuals with specialized expertise, using a document written from a limited perspective in terms of the range of research that was considered during its design. The TCPS is for the most part exactly such a document: the bulk of those who designed it, and the bulk of those who have become charged with implementing it, are people whose experience and expertise involve a particular model of research. The research best captured by the TCPS's principles is biomedical, but the mechanism fits well with any sort of structured, repetitive, experimentally based procedure that involves a powerful researcher and vulnerable participant who do not have much, if any, relationship beyond the time the procedure is administered to them; even then, the procedure is likely administered by an assistant one has never seen before and is unlikely to see again.

To its credit, the TCPS does acknowledge some of its own limitations, acknowledging that it "does not offer definitive answers" (CIHR et al. 1998: i.3) on controversial questions and that it focuses only on matters "that transcend disciplinary boundaries" (i.2). Similarly, when it comes to the review process itself, the TCPS reminds REBs that

> the effective working of ethics review—across the range of disciplines conducting research involving human subjects—requires a reasonable flexibility in the implementation of common principles. The Policy therefore seeks to avoid imposing one disciplinary perspective on others, while expressing the shared principles and wisdom of researchers in diverse fields. It is designed to help both researchers and REBs, as a matter of sound ethical reasoning, to scrutinize the contexts and accommodate the needs of specialized research disciplines. (i.2)

Whether the ethics regulatory infrastructure that is formed to implement the TCPS lives up to this sensitivity is another matter. Although the horror stories we presented above involve people and situations with whom/which we are directly familiar, similar experiences exist across the country (e.g., see SSHWC 2004). Our biggest concern is for the future of qualitative research, which can be uniquely disadvantaged by a centralized process of ethics

review that sees people with no experience making decisions guided by assumptions that may hold well in their own research but that create havoc in the qualitative domain (see Shea 2000).

For example, the review process as it is now constructed requires researchers to submit a proposal that outlines one's procedures, what the participant's role will be, and how the researcher will inform the participant about these matters to ensure informed consent. This is no problem when one takes a deductive approach where the researcher defines the question on the basis of theory, where the procedure involves administering a standardized procedure to each and every participant, and where the possible responses by the participant are confined to a limited set of alternatives that the researcher gives them. If there are any "surprises," they occur within a very narrowly constructed range.

In the qualitative domain, the unpredictability of where more inductive and field-based research will go is not only part of the thrill of doing such research, it is also part of an epistemology that eschews presupposition and values emergent and collaboratively driven research designs. What we have seen at SFU—and what the SSHWC (2004) observed happening in other universities across the country—is that, far from valuing the thrill that a more qualitative approach offers the researcher because of its open-endedness at the inception of the project, some REBs see threat. Heaven knows what can happen! The process of ethics review becomes a process of questions along the lines of "What if *this* were to happen? And what if *that* were to happen?" with each successive question more outlandish than the last. For example, Ted was asked many times during the limited confidentiality debates at SFU what he would do if one of his research participants said that he or she was going to kill someone. And while he has developed an answer to it because of having been forced to consider that scenario, the fact is that in 25 years or more of research involving people in several countries, and including everyone from ordinary citizens to prisoners to police officers to judges to sports figures to parents to indigenous leaders and on and on, no one has ever confessed to him that he or she planned to kill someone. And even though he teaches in a school of criminology, where his colleagues do research with a varied assortment of street people and offenders who have been convicted of everything from prostitution to murder, as far as he knows not one of them has been warned about an impending murder either.

It is not unimportant to consider such scenarios, and we are not trying to say they never occur, but to base policy on extreme events that rarely if ever occur, or exist only in theory, seems ludicrous and guided by nothing better than a liability management that operates out of fear. Field research operates within a different set of parameters and requires a different approach to ethics review, one that takes into account the emergent quality of research, the often long-term familiarity that exists between researcher and participants, the fact that one does not have to make a one-shot set of decisions that one is then bound to forever, and the significant role that open-ended participant observation and ethnographic research have played and should continue to play across several disciplines. As one spends more time in the research setting, gets to know people better, gains a better understanding of what range of activities occurs and what people are prepared to talk about, and establishes a certain comfort level (or finds it absent), one has the time and luxury of renewing and renegotiating arrangements.

Qualitative and field-based research often (but not necessarily) also involves more of an "underdog" perspective. Such research that aims to uncover the dynamics of a niche of life that has been stigmatized or seen as deviant is often qualitative in nature, although not all qualitative research aspires to that particular objective. Becker's (1963) research with marijuana smokers, for example, or Humphreys's (1970) research with homosexuals,[11] Lowman's (e.g., see Lowman, Atchison, & Fraser 1997) research with sex trade workers, Ogden's (1994) research with euthanasia among persons with HIV/AIDS, and Duneier's (1999) research with sidewalk entrepreneurs represent a tiny sample of studies whose aim was to take us beyond stereotype and inform us about a niche of life most of us never encounter.

Doing such research requires the ability to take a nonjudgmental approach where one's highest priority is to understand what makes that niche of life tick. And such research participant groups, no matter how "deviant" we perceive them to be or how marginalized they are, have the same entitlements to rights as all other research participants. Members of research ethics boards who do not have experience with or interest in marginalized groups must take extra steps to ensure that the perspectives of these participants are considered and an imposition of their own views avoided.

And finally, the kind of research envisioned by the TCPS is largely research done by researchers who are used to operating in environments that are highly legalistic and involve a more bureaucratic model of how research is done, complete with forms, signatures, and records of protocols administered, such as is typical in hospitals and other sites of biomedical study. In contrast, much qualitative research, and especially much research involving stigmatized populations, involves people who distrust bureaucracies, are prepared to participate and do so willingly only because of their trust in the researcher, and do not want any records kept on their participation because the records themselves may violate their confidentiality, and they don't trust anyone beyond the researcher to maintain them properly. They most certainly would not trust a governmental body, and many—particularly after SFU's initial response to the Russel Ogden case, for example—would not trust the university that the researcher is associated with either.

It is to the credit of the stewards of the TCPS—the presidents of the three granting councils—that they formed a committee in 2003 called the Social Sciences and Humanities Research Ethics Special Working Committee (SSHWC)[12] to advise the Interagency Advisory Panel on Research Ethics (PRE) on how the TCPS might evolve to better reflect the diversity of research perspectives and approaches that exist in the social sciences, humanities, and performing arts, and particularly to accommodate the very different epistemologies inherent in qualitative approaches. Their preliminary report that identified the problems, *Giving Voice to the Spectrum* (2004), was well received by researchers in Canada and internationally, and the committee—first under Chair Will van den Hoonaard (a sociologist) and now Patrick O'Neill (a more field-based community psychologist) is now in the process of formulating its recommendations. Time will tell how these proposals will fare in a bureaucratic context in which the epistemological approaches and perspectives they seek to protect are a small minority, but succeed they must if the overall diversity and health of the research enterprise, and thereby of the quality of discussion and debate in the country about important social issues of the day, is to flourish.

SUMMING UP AND LOOKING AHEAD

In this chapter we have attempted to convey some of the many complexities that must be faced whenever one does research with human participants. Some arguments border on the polemical, but ethical guidelines must be considered not only in terms of the potential good they encourage, but also of the potential abuses they allow. If there is a central point to this chapter, it is to think about the relations you allow to exist between researcher and researched.

Research participants are a crucial resource to social science disciplines that attempt to understand human action, and, particularly when we are in a position of power over participants, we must live up to our obligation to maintain their dignity and treat them with care. In this regard, several major ethics principles that transcend disciplinary boundaries were introduced. These include the balancing of scientific and human considerations that influence whether we engage the research in the first place, issues of conflict of interest, the principles of informed consent and the maintenance of confidentiality, and the idea that ethics responsibility is an undertaking and obligation shared by all members of a research team.

A separate focus of the chapter involved examination of the regulation of ethics by third parties: disciplines, universities, granting agencies, and the federal government. It was argued there has been a trend toward more extensive and more centralized ethics regulation over time. Although general support was expressed for the idea of ethics review because of the opportunity this allows for an independent look at the proposed research by a third party, concerns arise to the extent these third parties are themselves involved in conflicts of interest that lead them to advance views and interests that can be at odds with the rights and interests of research participants and the ethical obligations and academic freedom interests of researchers.

Special heed was taken of the *Tri-Council Policy Statement* (TCPS) on ethics for research involving human participants that now governs all research done in universities across Canada. Some possible strengths of this intervention have been noted, as well as possible deleterious effects on research participant rights and the academic freedom of researchers. Particularly worrisome is the negative effect of the biomedically and experiment-driven research mentality that frames the TCPS on other research perspectives, particularly on more qualitative field-based research traditions. Readers of this book are encouraged to keep themselves informed on these matters as the TCPS continues to be implemented and Canada's ethics bureaucracy grows.

STUDY QUESTIONS

1. According to the chapter, what is the "basic ethical dilemma"? Why is it a dilemma?
2. What does each of the following concepts mean, and how can you ensure that they are implemented in your research: informed consent, confidentiality, anonymity.
3. Look up a recent issue of a journal in your area of study, pick an article that interests you, and evaluate it in terms of the ethical principles outlined in this chapter.
4. Seek out the ethical guidelines of the discipline or career for which you are studying. Are the principles discussed in this chapter included among the guidelines of your discipline? What new issues arise that are not dealt with here?

5. At this stage of your academic career, you are more likely to find yourselves in the role of research assistants rather than principal investigators. This means that the ethical dilemmas we discussed, and which the ethical principles addressed, will not be relevant to you for some time because ethics are the responsibility of senior researchers. Discuss that statement.

6. What is the difference between anonymity and confidentiality? What procedures can you follow to ensure confidentiality? What legal mechanisms exist for the protection of the confidentiality of research participants?

7. What are the Wigmore criteria, and why is it beneficial to know them? Give some concrete suggestions on how you can integrate your knowledge of the Wigmore criteria into your research.

8. A federal government department approaches you to do research for them that is in your area of research interest. What would you like to know in order to decide whether to do the project? Indicate some of the contractual and other ethical issues that should be addressed.

9. Describe some of the ways ethics regulation has changed over the last 30 years.

10. Go to your university's website and read the university's ethics policy. What does your university do to ensure there is no administrative conflict of interest?

11. Who are the members of your REB? Do they represent the full range of research done at your institution? Are there committee representatives for both qualitative and quantitative research traditions?

12. Discuss the question of the rights of researchers in relation to the rights of participants, and generate your own criteria for how conflicting interests might be resolved (a) when the researcher is in a position of power over participants and (b) when the researcher is dependent on an agency and/or participants for continued funding and access.

13. This chapter has argued that, while researchers should make every effort to be both "ethical"

and "legal," situations might arise where those two are placed in conflict, that is, you must choose between acting ethically but in violation of a particular law (e.g., you can live up to your ethical obligation to protect the rights of your research participants only by defying a court order to disclose confidential research information) or to act legally but in violation of an ethical obligation (e.g., follow a court order to disclose confidential research information even though this brings harm to your participant). Put yourself in these situations. Which do you believe is more important?

14. You are undertaking a study in a psychiatric clinic for which you have signed an agreement guaranteeing confidentiality to the caregivers you are observing. You soon begin to notice cases where patients are apparently being denied their rights to refuse treatment, and you see two instances of what you perceive as physical abuse. Revealing this information to another authority would be a violation of the confidentiality you guaranteed. What would you do in this situation?

15. The TCPS requires research ethics boards to have at least one "community member" on the board. In what way might the presence of such persons be beneficial for researchers and research participants? In what ways might it be detrimental? Who is/are the community member(s) at your institution?

NOTES

1. Interestingly, federal government researchers have no similar requirement.

2. Even this assumption is tenuous, since there is nothing in the facts of this research that would have precluded the researchers ensuring that the men who participated in the study were made aware of the risks and consented freely.

3. Milgram continued doing research along these lines for many years and eventually published

a book (Milgram 1974) summarizing his contributions. Since our interest here is not in his substantive findings but in the ethical issues involved in doing such research, we find it most informative to use his earliest reports. These were written with the enthusiasm of someone who felt he had overcome the reputed artificiality of laboratory settings to discover something important and before controversy broke out.

4. You should understand that simply deleting a file from your computer does not actually remove it from your hard drive; it simply removes it from view. Deleted files can often be recovered from drives up to five years after they have been deleted using file recovery software or hardware.

5. AxCrypt is available as "freeware," which means that the software is available for free to anyone wishing to use it for non-commercial purposes (but it can also be bought in for-profit situations). While PGP was originally distributed as "freeware" by the Michigan Institute of Technology (MIT), it is now only available commercially through the PGP web site (http://www.pgp.com) or directly from the program creator Philip Zimmermann (http://www.philzimmermann.com). At the time of this writing AxCrypt can be downloaded for free Sourceforge.net (http://sourceforge.net).

6. Section 6 is entitled "Oath of Office." It asserts that "The Chief Statistician and every person employed or deemed to be employed pursuant to this Act shall, before entering on his duties, take and subscribe the following oath or solemn affirmation: 'I, ..., do solemnly swear (*or* affirm) that I will faithfully and honestly fulfil my duties as an employee of Statistics Canada in conformity with the requirements of the *Statistics Act*, and of all rules and instructions thereunder and that I will not without due authority in that behalf disclose or make known any matter or thing that comes to my knowledge by reason of my employment.'"

7. Brajuha was a graduate student doing participant observation at a restaurant where he worked as a waiter while doing an MA thesis on the sociology of the American restaurant. One day the restaurant burned to the ground under mysterious circumstances, perhaps arson. When the grand jury looking into the matter heard that a researcher was on site and had been maintaining field notes, the grand jury subpoenaed the field notes in the hope they might contain clues on the cause and perpetrator of the fire. Brajuha claimed privilege and refused to share his field notes with the grand jury. In the end, his claim for privilege was not accepted—the Court of Appeal said that while a privilege *might* exist, Brajuha had failed to make the case—but he was allowed to anonymize his field notes before submitting them.

8. Richard Scarce was a graduate student doing research with members of the Animal Liberation Front (ALF), a radical animal rights group that occasionally engaged in "direct action." When Scarce and his family went on vacation one year, a member of the ALF took care of his house. On returning from the trip, Scarce discovered that the university's animal care facility had been vandalized extensively and that the ALF member who had house-sat for him was the prime suspect. The grand jury looking into the matter subpoenaed Scarce. Scarce became only the second researcher ever to be jailed (for 159 days) for contempt of court.

9. Two of these cases involved subpoenas from grand juries; grand juries do not exist in Canada. The third case was the Atlantic Sugar case cited above, where the researchers limited confidentiality, and the court treated the limitation as a waiver of privilege.

10. The United States–based associations were first off the mark here. Although there are parallel Canadian associations, these initially were content to follow the codes of their U.S. counterparts. In psychology, for example, it would

be two decades before the Canadian Psychological Association developed its own made-in-Canada code (see Sinclair et al. 1987).

11. We include this research here because, at the time, the homosexual acts that Humphreys was researching were illegal. A major contribution of his research was to show that the people in his research were not horned devils but relatively normally people living relatively normal lives.

12. It should be noted that Ted is a member of the SSHWC and, as such, played a role in writing the reports that are cited here.

CHAPTER 4

SAMPLING

The next several chapters will describe ways of gathering data and discuss some of the concerns and procedures to be addressed in constructing an attitude scale, an interview or a questionnaire, an observational strategy, and so forth. But first, how do we decide *from whom* (or *what*) these data will be gathered? In other words, how do we identify a sample of people (or objects) that can best help us achieve our research objectives?

Sampling permeates *all* aspects of the research process. To do research, we inevitably sample from among all the possible questions we could ask, all the behaviours (or other attributes) we could observe, and all the people or situations we could approach. Our choice of methods is a sample of all the methods we could use, our analysis of the data is a sample of all the analyses we could perform, and the pattern of findings we choose to focus on in our final report is a sample of all the possible patterns we might have identified.

Earlier chapters discussed our choices (sampling) of perspectives, approaches, and ethics, and should be reconsidered in that light. The rest of this book considers some of the many methods from which we can sample when designing any given piece of research. This chapter addresses how we sample people (or objects) for inclusion in a study. What constitutes an "adequate" sample depends very much on one's research objectives, on one's understanding of the phenomenon under scrutiny, and on practical constraints.

SAMPLING ATTRIBUTES OF PEOPLE

All social science research is devoted in some way or another to understanding phenomena of interest.

We may wish to understand people, but we do so by understanding how people make decisions; how their attitudes develop and manifest themselves in action; how people differ from one another; why some people become, or at least come to be called, psychopathic; how societies define and exert control over activity that's "criminal"; and so on. We come to understand people by describing and trying to explain who they are, what they do, how they do it, what they believe, and the precursors, products, and context of their actions. We don't describe "people"; we describe "attributes of people." This distinction may sound trivial, but it's quite important.

Focusing on People

By saying that we want to describe "people," we adopt a research focus that necessarily begins with deciding which people to assess and how to acquire such a sample. The question of *what* to assess becomes a secondary research decision. Such a focus also suggests that studies are deficient unless participants are formally representative of the larger group or unit about which we hope to generalize. But that's not necessarily so.

Focusing on Attributes

If we acknowledge that our quest to understand people involves an attempt to assess people's *attributes,* our attention turns to the attributes as a focus of study. The attributes we choose to assess are *not* a given but a primary focus for research decisions: *Which* attributes? and *Why?* Moreover, it becomes clear that the definition of an "adequate" sample in any given instance depends on the nature of and our understanding of the attributes we are examining.

Homogeneity versus Heterogeneity

An important dimension to introduce at this point is homogeneity/heterogeneity. **Homogeneity** refers to a similarity among all units or elements being studied. Although it's possible to have units that are completely homogeneous in at least one aspect (e.g., all patients in the maternity ward of your local hospital are women and, hence, homogeneous with respect to sex), homogeneity is most often considered in more relative terms (e.g., judges in the court system are more homogeneous than the general population).

The opposite of homogeneity is **heterogeneity.** This refers to the degree of diversity in your **population** of interest with respect to whatever attribute(s) you choose to focus on. Again, the term is most commonly used in a relative sense: you might, for example, say that, at least with respect to such attributes as sex and ethnicity, the athletes who compete at the Olympics are more heterogeneous than the athletes who compete in the National Hockey League.

The homogeneity or heterogeneity of the population you're interested in, with respect to the attributes that most interest you, will affect the way you sample. If you plan to study a situation where the sample is completely *homo*geneous with respect to the attribute of interest, issues of "sampling" are unimportant; any sample will do. The blood in your body is homogeneous, for example, so the laboratory technician who wants to assess your blood needs to draw only one sample from your finger instead of poking holes all over your body. Similarly, the physical anthropologist who wants to determine a fossil's age needs to take only one piece for analysis, since the fossil is equally old in all its parts. In contrast, to accurately describe a *hetero*geneous entity, we must sample more than one element, and we must choose a sample carefully to ensure, for example, that any resulting description is representative.

Thus, the homogeneity or heterogeneity of the attributes we're assessing in the unit on which we're focusing (e.g., people, groups, attitudes, situations, products) affects our choice of an "adequate" sampling method or procedure in important ways. But the matter can get even more complex, since we can't always say whether a given unit is homogeneous or heterogeneous with respect to the attributes we wish to assess.

For example, consider cars. We could argue that cars are very heterogeneous. They come in blue, green, and grey; they're made by Chrysler, Nissan, and BMW; they come in convertibles, hardtops, and sedans. Even all red 2005 Chevrolet sedans are different since they have been driven differently, maintained differently, and outfitted uniquely by their respective owners. Yet we could also argue that cars are very homogeneous. They all have seats, steering wheels, tires, and batteries, and all need fuel to run. Neither homogeneity nor heterogeneity is thus a property of "cars" per se; each reflects the attributes of interest to us.

Similarly, we can argue that people are all unique or that we are all essentially the same. As Denzin and Lincoln (1994) point out,

> every instance of a case or process bears the stamp of the general class of phenomena it belongs to. However, any given instance is likely to be particular and unique. Thus, for example, any given classroom is like all classrooms, but no two classrooms are the same. (201)

In the same manner, some aspects of humanity are shared by all people (e.g., universals such as the use of language), some aspects are shared by clusters of people (e.g., a set of cultural understandings), and some aspects are unique to each individual (e.g., his or her particular life experiences). To paraphrase Krech, Crutchfield, and Ballachey (1962), there are ways in which each of us is like *all* other people, like *some* other people, and like *no* other people.

Thus, how we go about soliciting participants for research depends partly on the attributes we wish to assess and partly on our approach to research. If we want to describe attributes on which people (or other objects of assessment) vary, we must sample carefully to ensure that the overall picture we end up with is representative. If we want to describe attributes that are invariant—distributed equally across people or groups of people—any sample will do.

As this suggests, our approach to sampling will also reflect the way we perceive the research mission. Psychologists, for example, have often been chastised—not only by outsiders, but also by psychologists—for their notorious reliance on "unrepresentative" samples. Schultz (1969) and Carlson (1975) deplore the fact that 80 percent of the published articles in psychology have used introductory psychology students (usually male) as research participants. We have no doubt that introductory psychology students are *not* representative in many ways of the general population to which we might wish to generalize. But *does it matter?* Our response would be "It depends."

The above argument suggests that when social scientists are interested in *variability* among people (the expressed goal of those in "individual difference" or "personality" psychology), they do themselves a disservice by relying on the atypical introductory psychology student population. But when social scientists are interested in unearthing general principles that are *invariant* across humanity (the expressed goal of some "experimental" psychologists), anyone, including the atypical introductory psychology student, will do.

We can see the logic of this matter in the extreme by looking back to B. F. Skinner (e.g., 1953), whose goal was to unearth basic principles of learning that were invariant not only across all persons, but also across all organisms. According to Skinner, any learning process, any behaviour, is at some level produced by the same set of rules or principles; that is, the way we form our attitudes about minority groups or the way we learn how to do research is fundamentally no different from the way a pigeon in a Skinner box or a rat in a maze learns to perform a particular behaviour in order to acquire a bit of food.

Given that such processes were believed to be invariant across organisms and that the research mission was to *find* processes that were invariant across organisms, it *didn't matter,* from a sampling perspective, whether Skinner and his followers studied rats, pigeons, introductory psychology students, or IBM executives. Indeed, given their perception of the research mission, Skinnerians would have been silly to try to acquire "representative" samples of people. You can spend thousands of hours and many thousands of dollars acquiring such a sample. Pigeons, in contrast, can be ordered from your local supplier, always show up for their appointments, and probably aren't very worried about what you might think about them if they fail to perform adequately. We may wish to argue with Skinnerians for a variety of *other* reasons, but their views on sampling were entirely consistent with their view of psychology's empirical mission.

In short, the sampling issue isn't as straightforward as it might appear. Nor have you heard the complete story. Just two more points for now: first, the examples offered so far have assumed that the distribution of attributes in the population (i.e., with respect to their homogeneity or heterogeneity) is known. But what if it isn't? In that instance, a sampling strategy that assumes heterogeneity is clearly safer.

Second, in choosing Skinner as an example of a strange but logical sampling strategy, we chose a representative of the deductive model of science. Recall (from Chapter 2) that the deductive model *begins* with theory and then tests, refines, extends, and determines the bounds of that theory. So Skinner did *not* begin by trying to *find out* whether learning is the same across all organisms but rather *assumed* that it is and proceeded logically based on that assumption. Such research does not *test* but *affirms* one's assumptions: Skinner's experiments demonstrated the "truth" of his theory partly because his experiments took for granted that the theory's underlying assumptions were true.

Our socialization instills some "commonsense" notions about phenomena that influence our sampling. For example, where would you look for a sample if you were interested in studying heroin use? Most people in our society see heroin as a despicable drug associated with junkies, other criminal involvement, and a generally sleazy lifestyle. To study "real-world" heroin use therefore suggests spending time on society's margins, as many researchers have done. Their findings have reaffirmed an understanding of heroin's devastating and addictive effects on those who place themselves in its path.

But more recent research in other social contexts suggests that those earlier efforts were limited in what they *could* find because of the boundaries to analysis imposed by our preconceptions of the phenomenon. The legalization of heroin use in hospitals as pain relief for terminally ill patients, along with the return to the United States of thousands of soldiers who were regular users of heroin during the Vietnam War, focused attention on "non-deviant" consumers of the drug. Surprisingly, some qualities that many considered virtually inherent to the drug, such as its addictive properties, were not seen among hospitalized populations or among the vast majority of Vietnam veterans (e.g., see Boyd 1991). To some extent, then, the "effects" we observe may be the result of realities created by our policies rather than of the drug itself. Once again, a procedural research decision implicitly reaffirms and supports a particular social arrangement.

Similar concerns are echoed by Michel Foucault, who is perhaps best known for the power–knowledge themes that run through his books (e.g., 1970, 1972; see also Gordon 1980 and Chapter 1 of this text). Foucault argues that knowledge serves not only an *information* function, but also a *surveillance* one. Knowledge, he maintains, could theoretically be developed in myriad different directions; the directions it actually takes reflect existing understandings and power structures. As Liazos (1972) indicates, it's no accident that we know far more about "nuts, sluts and preverts [sic]" than we know about those who occupy corporate boardrooms (see also Palys 1993). This, then, is the sampling issue in its broadest sense. The very sampling of objects and phenomena for scrutiny influences not only what that batch of facts we call "knowledge" looks like, but also the directions it might or can take.

Thus, some case *can* be made for the idea that much more research, particularly in areas where the distribution of attributes is not yet known, should be done with diverse, if not formally representative, samples of people. But how do we sample? And why?

Why Sample?

The main reason we sample is that it's frequently impossible, impractical, or just plain silly to assess *every* unit or object of interest to us. Suppose we want to predict how Canadians will vote in the next election. If we could somehow simultaneously ask every Canadian who's eligible to vote the relevant question, we could be fairly confident that our results would mirror the election's actual outcome. But a study of the 22 million or so eligible Canadian voters would take a long time and require incredible resources to complete. (Consider the many millions of dollars the Canadian government spends performing a complete census every ten years; consider also the several years it takes to compile, code, and summarize the census data.) Clearly this approach is impractical for most ordinary studies. Yet professional pollsters have made astonishingly accurate election predictions (within a percentage point or two) on the basis of national samples of only 2000 people. How do they do it?

Some special constraints exist in the voting example we've given you. First, the research objective of an election pollster is to be descriptive; that is, to describe *accurately* the attributes (voting preferences, in this case) of a well-defined population (i.e., Canadians who are eligible to vote). Second, the attribute under consideration (i.e., voting preference) is heterogeneously distributed (i.e., different people prefer different parties or candidates). Third, it's crucial that the pollster obtain a result that is formally *representative* of the larger group.

DECIDING WHOM TO SAMPLE

The question of whom or what to sample is intricately tied into the researcher's objectives and perspective. Most important here are the questions of what information you want to obtain and who has access to that information (Gorden 1980). For example, suppose your research question has to do with how we teach research methods courses at our university. If you want to know how our students feel about their experience, the "appropriate sample" will comprise students who have enrolled in our methods courses—and the bigger and more representative the sample the better.

If you want to compare the reactions of our students with the reactions of those who take methods courses from *other* professors, you'll need to sample students from other courses as well. Here, too, the more students the better, but your sampling of other courses will depend on the kinds of comparisons you want to make. If you simply want to compare our students' reactions to those of students taught by "other professors," you might simply sample methods courses taught by other professors. But if you want to compare the way students react to our teaching methods (which tend to be more Socratic) with the way they react to *other* teaching methods (e.g., a more traditional lecture style), your sampling of other courses and students must be more strategic: you'll want to ensure that other teaching styles of interest to you and other students taught by professors who favour those styles are represented.

But suppose your research question involves determining *why* Chris teaches his courses the way he does. *No* sample of students, no matter how large or how representative it might be, has access to that information. His students might *speculate* about why he teaches the way he does and might have *partial* information that he has shared with them at one time or another. But the best person to ask is Chris, a sample of one. In sum, "bigger" isn't *necessarily* better, nor is "formal representativeness" a *necessary* requirement. The issue is always what you're trying to accomplish and what sample best suits that task.

Procedurally, these issues boil down to two different sets of sampling techniques, known collectively as **probabilistic sampling** and **nonprobabilistic sampling.** The former techniques aim primarily to generate formally representative samples, while the latter either aim to generate strategi-

cally chosen samples or are used when probabilistic techniques aren't feasible.

PROBABILISTIC SAMPLING TECHNIQUES

A probabilistic technique is desirable when researchers' objectives are descriptive, the attribute being assessed is heterogeneously distributed, and the researcher requires a formally representative sample. Probability theory, on which these methods are based, has given rise to a language that we need to know in order to fully comprehend it.

Some Relevant Terminology

REPRESENTATIVENESS

Probabilistic techniques are the best ones to use if you want to obtain a representative sample of some target population. A sample is *representative* of some larger group when the distribution of relevant attributes in the sample mirrors the distribution of those attributes in the population. Thus, if our target population is 52 percent female, while 80 percent are right-handed, 23 percent prefer the Conservative party, and 13 percent own Toyotas, then a "representative" sample of 100 people drawn from the target population should contain approximately 52 females, 80 right-handed persons, 23 who say they prefer the Conservatives, and 13 Toyota owners. Probabilistic techniques minimize the difference between the sample and the population; that is, they minimize *sampling error.*

Units of Analysis or Sampling Elements

Any study involves a choice of *units of analysis* or *sampling elements,* that is, the units or elements about which information will be gathered. If we wish to find out how people in North Dakota feel about the state government's approach to education issues, for example, the individual person is our unit of analysis. If we wish to determine the attention given to environmental issues in *The Globe and Mail* by doing some form of newspaper content analysis, individual issues of or individual articles in that newspaper become our unit of analysis. If we wish to sample your attitudes about public-health issues, the individual attitude statement is our unit of analysis. Units of analysis or sampling elements aren't inherent or inevitable divisions among entities; they're defined by the researcher, depending on his or her research interests. Your unit of analysis might be the individual person, family units, larger groupings (e.g., university departments), or even whole countries; it is little more than a statement of what "things" you want to study.

THE UNIVERSE

A **universe** is a theoretical aggregation of all possible sampling elements. If our sampling element is the individual British citizen, our theoretical universe is "all citizens of Great Britain." If our unit of analysis is the newspaper, our universe is "all newspapers." The notion of "universe" is not especially practical, since one's universe is generally so amorphous and huge that it's impossible to define in detail. Its major role, instead, is to keep us attuned to two ideas: that there's often a broader realm to which we might ultimately wish to generalize our results and that we must consider the limitations of our empirical pursuits.

THE POPULATION

A more practical and perhaps less presumptuous term is *population*. Like "universe," "population" refers to an aggregation of sampling elements, but "population" delineates the exact boundaries that define our sample elements. While "all Ontarians" might be our universe of interest, we might define our population as "all people over 18 years of age who are Canadian citizens and resident in the province of Ontario on January 1, 2006." The term "population" is thus more precise than "universe" in delimiting who *specifically* makes up our study's *target group*. Defining our population can be seen as the beginning of our sampling procedures, since it requires us to specify, in no uncertain terms, who or what is "eligible" for participation in our research.

SAMPLING FRAME

The **sampling frame** is a complete list of all the sampling elements of the population we wish to study. If our population of interest is "all students enrolled on a full-time basis at the University of California at Davis as of February 1, 2007," our sampling frame is the list of all students who fit the description. If our population of interest is "all divorce cases adjudicated in Manitoba courts during 2005 in which child custody was contested," our sampling frame is a list of all such cases.

Although the sampling frame's list of all elements would *ideally* reflect our population exactly, it typically does *not*. Many lists are imperfect to begin with, and others quickly become obsolete. For example, if our population is "all persons eligible to vote in the province of Ontario" (i.e., persons who are 18 or older, Canadian citizens, and residents of the province), the voters list (the list of people who have been enumerated) might seem an obvious choice for a sampling frame. But some eligible people will not be enumerated, and some technically ineligible people may be included on the list. So even the voters list starts out as a good but imperfect list of eligible voters. And all lists also decay or become obsolete, some more quickly than others.

For example, some years ago, David Williams and Ted wanted to send a questionnaire they'd developed to a diverse sample of local residents (see Palys & Williams 1983). Since a provincial election had been held only two months before the study, they decided to use the voters list as their sampling frame. But about 8 percent of the letters came back stamped "deceased" or "moved." Even good lists can become obsolete quickly. Others (e.g., the phone directory) are obsolete even before they're published and delivered.

In many situations, no appropriate sampling frame exists, and constructing one would be impossible or impractical. A list of "all people in Chicago who were sexually abused during their adolescence," for example, is impossible to construct, as is a list of "all people in Halifax who are consumers of pornography." The same is true of lists of homosexuals, sex trade workers, corporate executives, and people who like lemon in their tea. For many groups (or other units of analysis), sampling must occur without a sampling frame.

Probability-Based Sampling Methods

SIMPLE RANDOM SAMPLING

Simple **random sampling** is theoretically the best way to identify a representative sample. It minimizes **sampling error** (deviation of the characteristics of the sample from the characteristics of the population) and allows us to calculate the degree of sampling error that probably exists. But such precision comes at a price. To perform simple random sampling, you *must* have a sampling frame in which every sampling element is listed once and only once.[1] Simple random sampling is then accomplished by merely choosing sample elements at random from the list. This can be done by putting all the names (or whatever) into a hat or drum and pulling them out at random, by numbering all elements in the sampling frame and then using a table of random numbers (see Appendix A) to guide your selection, or using a computer program to select randomly from the sampling frame.

Other procedures are possible but two criteria are essential for random selection: nothing but chance must govern the selection process, and every sampling element must have an equal probability of being selected. If these criteria are met, the resulting sample will be representative of the population included in the sampling frame, within some margin of error, known as "sampling error."

SAMPLING ERROR

"Sampling error" refers to the extent to which the sample's characteristics deviate from those of the population. There are two types of sampling error: *systematic error* and *random error*.

Systematic error occurs when aspects of your sampling procedure act in a consistent, systematic way to make some sampling elements more likely to be chosen for participation than others. If you're interested in the opinions of *all* the students at your university or college (i.e., the entire population of students enrolled that semester), but place ballot boxes for a referendum only in the buildings where arts classes are held, you've made voting easier for arts students than for science students. This situation introduces a systematic bias to the referendum, all but ensuring that arts students' opinions will be *over*represented while science students' opinions will be *under*represented. Similarly, when we survey city dwellers by using the city's list of homeowners as our sampling frame, we systematically bias the resulting sample to reflect the views of wealthier and possibly older people (i.e., those more likely to own homes) and systematically ignore younger and less wealthy people, as well as all renters, the transient, and the homeless.

A **random error** has no systematic biasing effect, but merely reflects the vagaries of chance variation. If we flip a coin 100 times, we may *expect* (theoretically) to see the coin fall heads up 50 times and tails up 50 times, but we wouldn't find it particularly unusual if the coin were to fall heads up 53 times and tails up 47 times. Such things happen, purely as a result of chance variation. You may hear such expressions of sampling error when poll results are reported during election campaigns.

When you use a random sampling method, the amount of sampling error you may incur depends on the size of your sample: the bigger the sample, the smaller the sampling error.[2] Suppose your city councillors are trying to decide whether to commission an up-and-coming local artist or a world-renowned artist from another city to create a new sculpture to place in front of City Hall. The council is at a stalemate, with three councillors voting for each alternative; instead of casting the deciding vote, the mayor suggests looking to the citizens for guidance. The council hires you to take the pulse of the city and to report back on what the people want.

Because you're able to acquire a sampling frame that lists all city residents, you're confident that you have a good handle on the population whose views you hope to represent. From this list, you randomly sample 10 people and find that 7 of them, or 70 percent, would prefer to give the job to the up-and-coming local artist. If your 10-person sample was indeed randomly chosen, you can expect (in theory) that these people are representative of your population of interest, within some margin of error. Chapter 12 looks at some of the mathematics associated with computing the sampling error. For now, we need only know that, with a sample size of 10, our estimate that 70 percent of the population would like to see the local artist get the commission must be qualified by stating that the "real" figure could be as low as 34 percent or as high as 94 percent (see Gray & Guppy 1994: 145). Why such a wide range? With a sample of only 10 people, it wouldn't be unusual, simply due to the capriciousness of chance, to get a "weird" result that would be unlikely to repeat itself twice in a row.

If you take such a result to the city councillors, they won't be impressed. Being "95 percent confident" that the "real" figure is somewhere between 34 percent and 94 percent (a range of 60 percentage points) isn't much better than saying that overall, people might agree or disagree with the decision. You might as well have flipped a coin. The council will send you back to the field to draw another sample.

The degree of sampling error you incur relates most strongly to the *absolute* sample size you draw rather than to the *proportional* sample size (see Warwick & Lininger 1975). Table 4.1 shows the relationship between sample size and the margin of error. Each case assumes that 70 percent of the sample indicates a certain preference (e.g., that the local artist should get the job). When we increase the sample size to 50 and find that 70 percent support the local artist, the "real" figure is now 95 percent likely to be between 55 percent and 83 percent (a range of 28 percent). A sample of 100 reduces the range to 19 percent. And increasing the sample size to 1000 reduces our confidence interval to a mere 6 percent: if 70 percent of that 1000-person sample supports the local artist, we can be 95 percent confident that the "real" figure is somewhere between 67 percent and 73 percent (i.e., 70 percent plus or minus 3 percent).

If we push for greater and greater accuracy, and hence require a larger and larger sample, we eventually face the need to acquire a huge sample, which would require equally huge resources to contact and interview. Indeed, we soon reach a point of diminishing returns, where whopping increases in sample size produce only very small gains in accuracy. Gray

Table 4.1

Margin of Error by Sample Size

If 70% of a sample agrees, then with	the population value might be			
a sample size of	as low as	as high as	Size of confidence interval (high–low)	
10	34%	94%	60%	(±30%)
50	55%	83%	28%	(±14%)
100	59%	78%	19%	(±9.5%)
250	64%	76%	12%	(±6%)
1000	67%	73%	6%	(±3%)

Source: Adapted from G. Gray and N. Guppy (1994), *Successful Surveys* (Toronto: Thomson Nelson), p. 145. Reprinted with permission of publisher.

and Guppy (1994) explain that "the rules of probability theory tell us that we reduce our margin of error by one half if we quadruple our sample size" (144). It follows that, to go beyond the figures shown in Table 4.1, we'd have to increase our sample size from 1000 to 4000 in order to reduce our 95 percent confidence interval to 3 percent (i.e., ± 1.5 percent), or to 16 000 to reach ± 0.75 percent, or to 64 000 to reach ± 0.375 percent, and so on.

At some point, such increases simply aren't worth the improved confidence they bring us. Each researcher must determine where that point is, considering such factors as the available resources, how precise the estimate needs to be given the importance and consequences of the decision involved, and how the available funds might otherwise be spent. The researcher must also keep in mind how accurate other elements of the process will be. It would be silly to spend many thousands of dollars to increase sampling accuracy from plus or minus 1.5 percent to 0.75 percent, for example, when small changes in the wording of a question or in the interviewer's demeanour can easily cause estimates to vary as much as 5 percent to 10 percent. Forgetting those other elements of the process produces nothing but a specious scientism and a spurious sense of precision that simply does not exist (see also Chapter 6).

Another matter to be considered is the extent to which the researcher wants to compare different subgroups of the population. For example, the city council might realize that emphasizing majority opinion sometimes merely opens the door to a "tyranny of the majority," whereby a dominant group consistently uses its majority position to trample over the concerns of others. The council might therefore want you to look at subgroups within the population, for example, ensuring that men and women are equally supportive of commissioning the local artist or that the opinions of Indigenous people and ethnic minorities are adequately considered. In that case, the question of sampling error changes slightly: because any subgroup will, by definition, be smaller than the overall sample, the degree of sampling error that exists within any of the subgroups will obviously be larger.

For example, public opinion polls published in newspapers are often based on a random sample of 2000 people from across the country. Such a sample can give a decent approximation of "how Canadians feel" about a social issue, given the question's wording and context, to within plus or minus about 2 percent, 19 times out of 20. The polls also often give breakdowns by province so that you can compare provinces. But with 10 provinces and an average of, say, 200 respondents per province, the provincial figures are accurate only to within about plus or minus 6 percent, 19 times out of 20. The central point here is this: given random sampling of a population, the larger the absolute size of the sample, the lower the expected sampling error you might incur.

SYSTEMATIC SAMPLE WITH RANDOM START

A type of random sample with a slight twist to it is the *systematic sample with random start*. Like simple random sampling, this technique also requires a sampling frame in which each element is numbered and appears only once. But instead of randomly sampling from the entire list each time, you begin at a *randomly determined starting point*, and then sample every *n*th element on the list.

To illustrate, assume you have a voters list with 10 000 names on it and wish to draw a representative sample of 500 people from that list. Your **sampling ratio,** in other words, is 1:20 (or 1 in 20). To do a systematic sample with random start, you would first randomly choose a number from 1 to 20. Suppose you throw a dart at your random number table, hitting the number 13. That's your random start: the first person you sample is number 13 on your voters list. The systematic part is dictated by your sampling ratio of 1:20; that is, you now systematically pick every 20th person on the list. Thus, given that you began with person number 13, the next one you sample will be number 33, then 53, then 73, then 93, and so on through the sampling frame, until you come to your 500th sample person, who would be number 9993 on the original list of 10 000 people.

While this technique is effective for acquiring a probabilistic sample from a sampling frame, it's not quite as good as the simple random sample. Recall that one of the criteria that make a selection completely *random* (and hence likely to be representative) is that every sampling element (and type of sampling element) must have an equal probability of being selected. If subject numbers are pulled from a random number table, then no matter how the list is organized, every number (and hence every person or element) has an equal probability of being selected. But in a systematic sample with random start, properties associated with the list itself may result in a biased sample. The most worrisome property is the cyclical nature of many lists, which causes a problem known as **periodicity.**

Suppose we want to generate a 1:12 sample of players in the National Hockey League (NHL). Each team sends us a list of its players, ordered by their jersey number. We add these lists to our master list in the order in which we receive them. Once the whole list is compiled, we randomly choose number 1 as our starting point and then select every 12th player thereafter, that is, the first on the list, then the 13th, 25th, 37th, and so on. This approach sounds reasonable, but it would get us in serious trouble. The problem stems from two facets of the NHL: each team is allowed 24 players on its roster and the lowest jersey number on a team is usually number 1, a number traditionally worn by goaltenders. Our sample would thus not be representative, since half the players sampled would be goaltenders, who actually comprise less than 10 percent of the players on each team.

The main problem with periodicity in systematic samples with random starts lies in recognizing when it's present. Once recognized, periodicity is fairly easily addressed. In the NHL example, we could avoid the problem by choosing a different interval (e.g., every 11th or 13th player instead of every 12th) or by first randomizing the elements in the list to destroy its cyclical nature.

STRATIFIED RANDOM SAMPLING

A third type of probabilistic sample is the *stratified random sample*. In this procedure, the researcher first divides the population into groupings (or *strata*) of interest and then samples randomly within each stratum. This technique is used when there is some meaningful *grouping variable* on which the investigator wishes to make comparisons and where the probabilities of group membership are known ahead of time.

Suppose a researcher wants to survey a representative sample of students who have declared a major in the Faculty of Arts at Dalhousie University. Suppose further that we know that 10 percent of Dalhousie's arts students are sociology majors, another 30 percent are psychology majors, 5 percent are English majors, and the remaining 30 percent are in the other arts disciplines. Just to keep the numbers easy, suppose there are 1000 students with declared majors in the Faculty of Arts. They are represented by the "population" drawing in the upper portion of Figure 4.1.

A researcher who's interested only in "polling students from the Faculty of Arts" could get a list of the 1000 students from the registrar's office (i.e., a sampling frame) and then draw a simple random sample or a systematic sample with random start. If properly done, the sample should contain, within the limits of sampling error, roughly 35 percent sociology majors, 30 percent psychology majors, and 5 percent English majors, while roughly 30 percent of the sampled students should have majors that don't fall into any of these categories and are therefore labelled "other."

But suppose our researcher wants to *compare* the responses of the four groups (sociology, psychology, English, and other) and hence doesn't want to rely on chance alone to produce the exact numbers of students that would be expected. Since, for example, 5 percent of the students are English majors, we would *expect* to find 10 English majors in a randomly drawn sample of 200 of these students. But the vagaries of chance might leave us with more or fewer than 10 English majors in the sample. If the researcher wishes to ensure that the sample is *exactly* representative of the population with respect to the grouping variable of interest, stratified random sampling is more appropriate than simple random sampling.

Figure 4.1
Proportional and Disproportional Stratified Random Sampling

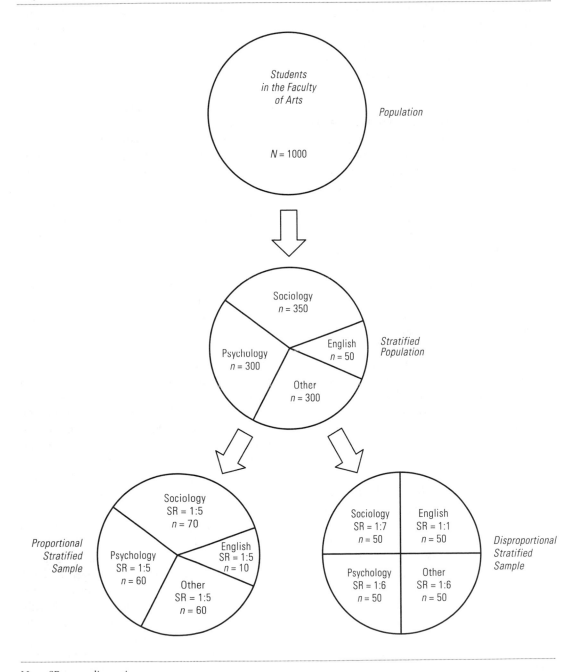

Note: SR = sampling ratio

The first step in this technique involves stratifying the population according to the grouping variable of interest, as shown in the section of Figure 4.1 labelled "stratified population." The researcher then performs simple random sampling *within* each stratum. Actually, the researcher has another choice to make: whether to use proportional or disproportional stratified random sampling.

PROPORTIONAL STRATIFIED RANDOM SAMPLING

In *proportional stratified random sampling,* the same sampling ratio is used within each stratum. In our example, this approach produces the following result: the proportion of students with different majors in the sample is exactly the same as the proportion of students with different majors in the population; and the students within each stratum of the sample are theoretically representative of the students within the corresponding population stratum (e.g., the sociology majors in the sample are representative of sociology majors in the population), within the limits of sampling error. At the end of this study, the researcher's conclusions will apply both to "students in Dalhousie's Faculty of Arts" (since the sample as a whole is proportionately representative of the population, within the limits of sampling error) and "Dalhousie students majoring in sociology, psychology, English, or any other arts discipline" (since each stratum of the sample is representative of the corresponding stratum of the population, within the limits of sampling error).

But in an example like this one, the researcher has obtained stratified samples that are theoretically representative of each stratum within the population; however, his or her ability to make conclusions about each stratum, and especially to compare strata, is impaired. It all comes down to that qualifying phrase "within the limits of sampling error." The main problem arises from including the English majors, of whom only 10 are sampled. As our earlier discussion of sampling error revealed, any result based on a sample of only 10 is bound to be very tentative, since our 95 percent confidence range would require us to specify that the result could be inaccurate by plus or minus 30 percentage points, not a very precise conclusion. There are two ways to get around this problem: we can increase the overall sample size, so that even the smallest group is still large enough for analysis, or we can use *dis*proportional stratified random sampling.

DISPROPORTIONAL STRATIFIED RANDOM SAMPLING

When the researcher is primarily interested in *comparing* results between the strata rather than in making overall statements about "students in the Faculty of Arts," or when one or more of the subgroups are so small that a consistent sampling ratio would leave sample sizes in some groups too small for adequate analysis, a *disproportional stratified random sample* might be drawn.

Here, the researcher still begins by stratifying the population into subgroups of interest and then taking a random sample within each stratum. But a different sampling ratio is used within each stratum, so that equal numbers of students end up in each of the stratum samples.

So if the researcher wants a sample of 200 students from the population of 1000 students (i.e., an overall 1:5 sampling ratio), *proportional* stratified random sampling will yield 70 sociology majors, 60 psychology majors, 10 English majors, and 60 students with majors in "other" arts disciplines. But with *disproportional* stratified random sampling, the sample of 200 might include 50 majors of each type (to create an optimal comparison using equal numbers of students from each group), chosen by using different sampling ratios within each stratum. In such a case, overall statements about "Dalhousie students majoring in arts subjects" would be tenuous (since the sample as a whole is no longer representative of the university's arts students),[3] but the researcher *could* make statements *comparing* the subgroups, since each subgroup (or stratum) of the sample *is* representative of that subgroup in the population. In sum, we end up with the alternatives depicted in the bottom portion of Figure 4.1.

MULTISTAGE CLUSTER SAMPLING

Each technique discussed so far requires a sampling frame. But a sampling frame isn't always available. Does the lack of a sampling frame prevent researchers from drawing a probabilistic (and hence theoretically representative) sample? No. One probabilistic technique *doesn't* require a sampling frame. Known as *multistage cluster sampling,* this technique essentially involves random sampling of clusters within clusters until one reaches the desired unit of analysis.

Suppose we want to acquire a representative sample of people who live in California's Bay Area and that no sampling frame of such people is available. How can we find a sample of people who meet the "representativeness" criterion?

Multistage cluster sampling in this case begins by acknowledging that people (our unit of analysis) generally live in residences, that residences exist on blocks, that blocks are part of neighbourhoods, that neighbourhoods make up communities, and that "the Bay Area" actually comprises a collection of communities. Thus, if we first prepare a list of communities that make up the Bay Area (i.e., San Francisco, Oakland, San José, Marin County, etc.), and then take a random sample of these communities, that sample of communities is formally representative of the population of communities that make up the Bay Area. We can then get maps of each of our sample communities, divide them into neighbourhoods, and take a random sample of neighbourhoods within each community. Because the neighbourhoods are representative of the population of neighbourhoods in the communities from which they were drawn and because the communities were randomly chosen to be representative of all communities in the Bay Area, the neighbourhoods we've sampled must be representative of all the neighbourhoods in the Bay Area. Neighbourhoods comprise individual blocks, so we can randomly sample blocks within each of our sample neighbourhoods and then randomly sample residences within blocks; finally, we can randomly sample the people within the sampled residences.

By performing a random sampling within each cluster, we end up with a sample of people that is representative of the population of people in our sample residences, which in turn is representative of the population of residences on our sample blocks, which in turn is representative of the population of blocks in our sample neighbourhoods, which in turn is representative of the population of neighbourhoods in our sample communities, which in turn is representative of the population of communities that make up the Bay Area. Our sample of people is thus theoretically representative of people who live in the Bay Area—and we found them without a sampling frame.

While this approach can obviously get somewhat laborious, it *is* a good way to acquire a formally representative sample—an even better way to describe it would be to call it an "unbiased sample"—when no sampling frame is available. To acquire a representative sample of customers of McDonald's restaurants in North America one could sample provinces and states, then counties, then roads within counties, then McDonald's restaurants on those roads, and finally customers in those restaurants.

Multistage cluster sampling can be very useful, but it should be used only when a sampling frame is unavailable, since it's ultimately not as good as the other probabilistic techniques. To appreciate why it's not as good, we must go back to the concept of sampling error. Remember that there will always be *some* sampling error whenever we draw a random sample, although the bigger the sample, the lower that error is likely to be. For a simple random sample, we sample only once and can easily compute the probable degree of sampling error. But for a multistage cluster sample, we're actually taking samples of samples; since all sampling involves some degree of error, we thus *accumulate* error with each successive level of sampling.

In the McDonald's example, we take five samples (states/provinces, counties, roads, McDonald's restaurants, and customers), accumulating error at each stage. Thus, while our eventual sample is *formally* or *theoretically* representative, since the sample taken at each stage was random and hence *should* be representative, our *confidence* in the precision of our representativeness is less than it would be if we had sampled only once from some overall sampling frame. Indeed, with multistage cluster sampling, rather than stating that you've achieved a theoretically representative sample, you'd probably be better off stating that you have no reason to believe that your sample is *un*representative.

Although our examples have emphasized the sampling of *people,* the same strategies apply for other objects of interest. Suppose we want to do a content analysis of a representative sample of DVDs available (through video outlets) to people in B.C.'s Greater Vancouver Area. If a sampling frame (i.e., a list of all DVDs available for rental in Greater Vancouver) were available, we could draw a simple random sample or a systematic sample with random start. If we also knew what proportion of DVDs are classified "family," "adventure," "comedy," "horror," or "adult," and wanted to compare the content of these video types, we might use stratified random sampling.

But alas, there's no such sampling frame: we know because Ted's been there (e.g., see Palys 1984, 1986). One might therefore use multistage cluster sampling to acquire the sample of videos. This would involve first sampling communities within Greater Vancouver, then sampling video outlets within those communities, and then sampling videos within those outlets. This approach would allow you to acquire a formally representative sample of videos, even without a sampling frame.

Can Sampling Problems Be Overcome by Sample Size?

As noted earlier, probabilistic samples receive that name because the sampling techniques used to obtain them conform to the rules of probability theory, particularly its basic requirement that the probability that any given person or element will be selected must be known, or at least knowable. When the population is known and sampling is random, these techniques ensure a theoretically representative sample, within the limits of sampling error.

Sampling error in this context varies according to two factors: the nature of the procedure followed (it must be random) and the sample size. Assuming that the first criterion (random sampling) is met, then the larger the sample size, the smaller the sampling error and, hence, the more confident we can be that we've obtained a truly representative sample.

But if we violate that first criterion by failing to use a random sampling procedure, the principles and mathematics of probability theory cannot be applied because we have no idea of the likelihood that a given element will be sampled. As a result, we can't compute or estimate how much sampling error exists. Thus, as sample size increases, we have no way of knowing whether we can be more and more confident that our estimates of the population's characteristics are getting more and more accurate, or whether we're merely acquiring a bigger and bigger biased sample.

Huge samples in themselves—no matter how big they might be—do not ensure representativeness; it's *how* you sample that's most important. An excellent illustration of this point arose in relation to a 1992 State of the Union address given by then–U.S. president George Bush (senior). After Bush's speech, the CBS program *America on the Line* coupled its post-speech discussion with a "viewer call-in poll." Viewers who owned Touch-Tone phones were encouraged to call and offer their reactions to the speech through a computerized system that would compile all the responses. A total of 314 786 people phoned to express their opinions.

Now, 314 786 people is a lot of people, far more than the 1000- or 2000-person samples used in most national surveys. It's hard not to be impressed when a poll's source states that the poll captures the opinions of more than 300 000 people. But can this particular huge sample genuinely be considered representative of the broader population of Americans?

One way to address that issue considers it on a purely rational basis, asking whether there's any reason to believe that the sample *is not* representative. If there is, we should be able to at least speculate on its deficiencies. The CBS phone-in sample was clearly not randomly chosen; people "volunteered" themselves for participation in a very particular social context. In order to have participated in the poll, a person would have to have been home that evening, own a television, have had the television on, have enough interest in current affairs to have been watching a news-oriented program instead of whatever was on the other channels, be interested enough in politics to have listened to a presidential speech, care enough about having his or her opinion heard to have actually phoned the CBS number, understand English well enough to have understood the survey questions, and have been free to spend the required time on the phone answering questions. It's doubtful that people who meet all these criteria are representative of the general American public. Thus, despite the mammoth sample size, it seems doubtful that a sample of opinion

drawn in the manner of the CBS phone-in poll could be representative of the broader population.

We can also address the representativeness issue empirically. The ideal situation would be to have the results of a survey done at exactly the same time, in which the same questions were asked, but with a sample drawn randomly from the general population. Had such a survey been conducted that night using the same questions asked of the *America on the Line* phone-in sample, we could assess just how representative that 314 786-viewer sample might have been.

In fact, exactly such a random sample was drawn. Concurrent with its phone-in poll, CBS also commissioned a survey that used a randomly chosen sample of 1234 Americans, who were asked exactly the same questions as the phone-in sample. Table 4.2

Table 4.2

Is Bigger Always Better? Comparing Simultaneously Drawn Probabilistic and Non-probabilistic Samples

Question	Alternatives	Viewer Call-In ($N = 314\ 786$)	CBS Formal Poll ($N = 1234$)
Are you better off now than four years ago?	(a) better	29%	24%
	(b) worse	54	32
	(c) same	17	44
Are you worried about job loss this year?	(a) yes	64%	48%
	(b) no	36	52
Would you pay more taxes for free health care?	(a) yes	58%	46%
	(b) no	42	53
Does the president understand the middle class?	(a) yes	30%	43%
	(b) no	70	57
Are media exaggerating how bad economic conditions are?	(a) yes	39%	35%
	(b) no	51	64
Future of America's children? Will it be … ?	(a) better	21%	24%
	(b) worse	57	36
	(c) same	22	39

Source: Adapted from D. R. Monette, T. J. Sullivan, and C. R. DeJong (1994), *Applied Social Research: Tool for the Human Services* (Fort Worth, TX: Harcourt Brace).

shows the questions that were asked and the collective responses of both the randomly chosen sample and the much larger phone-in sample.

Monette, Sullivan, and DeJong (1994) note that, given the size of the random sample ($N = 1234$), we can compute that the probable degree of error involved is around plus or minus 3 percent. Thus, any difference between the random sample and the phone-in sample that was larger than 3 percent could not be attributed to chance variation alone, but must be due to something else—probably the different sampling methods used. As Table 4.2 reveals, only one comparison stayed within the range of 3 percent; the other 13 ranged from 4 percent to as much as 27 percent, with an average difference of approximately 14 percentage points between the two techniques.

Even more problematic is the fact that the two sets of results differ not only in *magnitude* but also in *kind*. The call-in results seem more pessimistic and critical. Those who phoned in reported feeling *worse* off than they had four years previously; were *worried* about job loss; wanted *free* health-care access paid for by taxes; felt that the middle class is *misunderstood;* believed that "America's children" faced an even more *dismal* future; and believed that media portrayals of bad economic times were *not* exaggerated. In contrast, the representative sample of Americans reported feeling that things were pretty much the *same* as they'd been four years earlier; were *not* worried about job loss; were *not* willing to pay more taxes to cover free health care for all; and expected *similar* futures for America's children. They agreed with the phone-in sample that the president didn't understand the middle class and that the media weren't exaggerating when they depicted times as tough.

As these results help reaffirm, anyone who claims to have generated a representative sampling of opinion without having used a probabilistic sampling technique is skating on thin ice. Yet such claims appear in the media all the time. Radio phone-in shows, lobbyists who generate letter-writing campaigns, and newspapers that encourage readers to clip a coupon and send it to some local official often argue that the sheer volume of replies allows them to legitimately claim they represent public opinion. Obviously, any issue that can stimulate 100 000 people to send postcards of complaint to their local MP must be more intensely felt and broadly contested than one that generates only 100 cards. But while those 100 000 cards may well indicate that an issue has captured public attention, it's sheer folly to say that the 100 000 people who sent in those cards somehow "represent" public opinion.

NON-PROBABILISTIC SAMPLING TECHNIQUES

Representativeness: An Overrated Concept?

The probabilistic techniques discussed above represent the optimal techniques *if* the researcher's objective is to draw a sample that's formally representative of some larger, well-defined target population. But for many reasons, acquiring a formally representative sample may be impossible and even undesirable. Indeed, if we were to offer a nominee for the "Academy of the Overrated," the "representative sample" would be near the top of our list. Let us tell you some of the reasons why.

Obtaining a "representative sample" of any target population is very expensive and time-consuming. Interestingly, the *easiest* representative sample to acquire would be one of Canadians, since we could just ask any national polling organization to administer a questionnaire or an interview on our behalf. The pollsters would contact a representative national sample of 2000 Canadians and administer our 20-minute questionnaire by telephone. At a cost of between $50 000 and $100 000, we could get answers to our questions within a week or two.

Costs and time required would escalate considerably if we wanted more than 2000 Canadians polled or if our questionnaire took longer than 20 minutes to administer. The costs would go through the roof if we wanted our questionnaires or interviews administered in person rather than over the phone, and we're not even sure the polling organizations could accommodate such a request. If we wanted to administer something other than an interview or a questionnaire, for example, to do observations or to acquire any other type of representative sample (e.g., of students, corporate executives, or people who buy lottery tickets), we'd be just plain out of luck. Still, we *are* in the truth business, so perhaps each social scientist *should* do his or her best to "go for the gold" when undertaking any piece of research. But we doubt it.

Representative samples aren't useless—far from it. When our research objectives are *descriptive,* that is, when we want to know something like "how Canadians feel about changes to the health-care system," "how Berkeley students feel about the prospect of tuition increases," or "how Manitobans feel about their provincial government's education policies," "representative sampling" is clearly the route to take. But social scientists are rarely content with description alone. Our goal is generally theory and understanding, and we can't think of one theory that aspires merely to describe some singular state of affairs. Theories deal with variable*s* (note the plural) and with the interrelationships among them. The objectives of theory are *relational* and *explanatory*. So if a theory posits that a relationship should exist between variable *A* and variable *B*, all we *really* need in order to test that theory is a sample whose members are heterogeneous with respect to those two variables.

Many theoretical and research efforts in the social sciences are oriented toward discovering *universals*, principles that hold true across all samples and all situations. As we argue earlier in this chapter, if we're looking at a universal process, then where or whom we sample doesn't matter; anyone will do.[4]

Cook and Campbell (1979) encourage us to ask what we end up with when we acquire a formally representative sample. They point out that even if one acquires a representative sample and hence generates results that can be generalized to the population as a whole, those results *won't* necessarily also hold for all subgroups within the population. For example, even if we find out the overall distribution of attitudes among Canadians about environmental regulation, there are no guarantees that the same distribution would characterize both the male and

the female subgroups, people of different religious or political persuasions, or people with different education or income backgrounds. And of course, differences in attitudes among different subgroups of the population are often of greater theoretical interest to us than is mere description of the population as a whole.

Thus, Cook and Campbell (1979) argue that we ought to distinguish between generalizing *to* populations of interest and generalizing *across* subgroups of interest. Ultimately, they maintain, the researcher who samples various "unrepresentative" (i.e., unique) groups of interest and then either demonstrates that the same results hold across all these groups or shows that—and perhaps explains why—results *differ* across groups is in a much more powerful theoretical position than is the researcher who can merely describe, in gross terms, the overall status of a variable in a population of interest.

Finally, many researchers view the emphasis on representative sampling as simply misplaced. Qualitative researchers have been the most vocal in this regard. Huberman and Miles (1994), for example, note that

> sampling choices within and across cases are powerfully determinative of just which data will be considered and used in analysis. Quantitative researchers often think randomly, statistically, and in terms of context-stripped case selections. Qualitative researchers must characteristically think purposively and conceptually about sampling. (441)

Morse (1994) adds simply that researchers should emphasize gathering data that are rich, suggesting that this goal is best achieved when sampling is driven by theoretical aspirations rather than by statistical requirements.

Indeed, we must remember the different role that theory plays in deductive and inductive research; then we must consider how those differences may play out in how we look at things like sampling issues.

In that regard, recall that in more deductive/quantitative approaches, one *begins* with theory;

hence it is theory that will tell us which samples and sites are relevant to look at. The universe (in its sampling sense) is defined by theory, and the trick with respect to sampling is to identify one that will be representative of the universe to which we wish to generalize.

In contrast, remember that more inductively/ qualitatively driven approaches aspire to *develop* theory. Thus, instead of the universe to which we wish to generalize being defined by theory, the whole challenge for the inductive researcher is to *find out* what the universe of generalizability is for whatever concepts emerged in the initial study.

Thus, inductive researchers are far more likely to begin with a unique sample or site of interest and then search for other unique samples that promise to broaden (or limit) whatever concepts emerged in the initial study. Sampling is driven less by a quest for "representativeness" and more by a desire to explore and elaborate. For that reason, the next sample and the next study are chosen by their heuristic value, that is, how challenging and useful they will be for theory development (e.g., Becker 1998).

The basic point should now be evident: the question of which sampling technique to use and the question of which people or objects to sample are complex ones that depend (like everything else) on your research objectives, the constraints of the situation, your theoretical mission, and the type of phenomenon you're looking at. At those times when a formally representative sample *is* useful and desirable, one or more of the probabilistic sampling techniques discussed above should be pursued. But when a formally representative sample is neither useful nor desirable or when such a sample is impossible to acquire, one of the non-probabilistic techniques discussed below may prove helpful.

Non-Probabilistic Sampling Methods

HAPHAZARD, CONVENIENCE, OR ACCIDENTAL SAMPLING

The simplest type of non-probabilistic procedure, known variously as *haphazard, convenience,* or *accidental sampling,* involves little more than "getting whomever you can." A university instructor might try to assess the reliability of an attitude scale by giving it to an undergraduate class on two separate occasions. Or, for a class project, you might go to your local video arcade to administer an interview or a questionnaire to whoever happens to be around. The only requirement for research of this type is to administer procedures to "a bunch of people" who are, ideally, somewhat heterogeneous with respect to the phenomenon of interest. Generally, samples of this type would be sought for "instrumental" research (e.g., research to complete a class requirement), for pilot research to pretest research instruments, or for research aimed at generating universals.

PURPOSIVE SAMPLING

A second non-probabilistic sampling procedure, known as *purposive sampling,* also doesn't aim for formal representativeness. People or locations are intentionally sought because they meet some criterion for inclusion in the study. Suppose you want to know how viewing films like *Kanehsatake* or *Atanarjuat: The Fast Runner* influences people's attitudes about Aboriginal peoples and First Nations rights. You could go to a location where one of these films is being shown and administer an attitude scale or a questionnaire to some people before they go into the theatre and to others as they leave. Or suppose you want to interview people who buy lottery tickets, attend fitness centres, or like to ski. To find such people, an obvious strategy would be to purposively sample people who are buying lottery tickets at different stores, interview people at various fitness centres, or administer your questionnaire to people who are waiting in line to buy lift tickets in Vail, Colorado. Such target groups are chosen for their theoretical or practical interest.

Sampling is always "purposive" to some degree, since identifying a target population invariably expresses the researcher's interests and objectives. Because they reflect our understanding of the phenomenon of interest, these purposive choices may indirectly reaffirm rather than challenge that understanding. Researchers studying illicit drug use, for example, are more likely to study people whose behaviour brings them into contact with official agencies (e.g., the police, coroners, treatment groups) than they are to study drug users with a productive and successful lifestyle. Researchers studying gambling are more likely to study people who frequent institutionalized gaming venues (casinos, bingo halls, racetracks) than they are to study gamblers who operate outside the law (e.g., by placing bets with "bookies") or people whose risk-taking isn't socially recognized as gambling (e.g., those who play the stock market). Researchers studying prostitution are more likely to study its more blatant forms (e.g., street prostitution) than they are to study its less obvious (e.g., some escort agencies) or more subtle (e.g., prostitution of one's principles) manifestations. Certainly such choices are defensible, yet we must remain clear about the inherent limitations to understanding they entail.

The researchers may also be interested in strategically sampling particular *individuals* in the target group or at the research site being studied. Such is especially the case with more inductive, exploratory research (where the researcher is trying to get a preliminary feel for the people or phenomenon being studied), but this approach is not limited to such research. In any field-based inquiry, researchers soon realize that prospective interviewees are *not* created equal: some are incredibly informative or provocative, others are unwilling to talk, still others can talk for hours without saying anything useful. Morse (1994) states that in general terms,

> a good informant ... has the knowledge and experience the researcher requires, has the ability to reflect, is articulate, has the time to be interviewed, and is willing to participate in the study. (228)

Morse (1994) also eschews the sampling of representative or "typical" group members in favour of *extreme* or *deviant case sampling*. For researchers interested in studying pain, she suggests, people who suffer excruciating pain, while atypical, may be of greater interest than some of the many people who suffer chronic pain. Her rationale: those with the greatest pain experience the phenomenon of interest

in "concentrated" form and hence may reflect processes of interest more obviously.

Not unrelated to the above is the practice of *intensity sampling,* which involves sampling people whose interests or vocation makes them "experiential experts" because of their frequent or ongoing exposure to a phenomenon. The American Psychological Association (APA) used this technique to develop its ethical guidelines by identifying and interviewing certain "high exposure" people, for example, journal editors, who review many manuscripts; members of university ethical review boards, who must constantly consider ethical issues; and authors of ethics texts. Similarly, if you want to study techniques of persuasion, the logic of intensity sampling would suggest that you sample people who make persuasion their business, such as lawyers, sales reps, and advertisers.

A third sampling method suggested by Morse (1994) is *maximum variety sampling*. Unlike random sampling, which emphasizes acquiring the "typical" respondent, maximum variety sampling emphasizes sampling for diversity. Suppose the distribution of ethnicity in the general population is 35 percent British, 30 percent French, 15 percent "other European," 10 percent Asian, and 4 percent Aboriginal, while the rest of the population comprises at least a dozen other ethnic groups, each constituting less than 1 percent of the population. A researcher sampling for statistical representativeness would use a probabilistic sampling technique, hoping to acquire respondents in numbers consistent with their presence in the population. But while such a sample would obviously be statistically representative, 80 percent of the respondents would be of European origin. And owing to the vagaries of chance, some smaller ethnic or cultural groups might be left out of the sample entirely. In contrast, a researcher engaging in maximum variety sampling might aim to sample members of *every* ethnic and cultural group. Such a strategy would clearly be beneficial if the researcher hoped to unearth either the *variety* of human experience and perception with respect to some phenomenon or some of the *commonalities* of that experience across diverse peoples.[5]

In sum, informants who are unrepresentative of the group as a whole, statistically speaking, may still provide useful information and provocative insights that help researchers understand a group, an organization, or a situation:

> The primary feature of all these methods is that the situation of the sample is determined according to the needs of the study, and not according to external criteria, such as random selection. Participants are representative of the same experience or knowledge; they are not selected because of their demographic reflection of the general population. (Morse 1994: 229)

Purposive or theoretical sampling thus merely extends the admonition that researchers should be guided by the objectives of the study and should recognize that while "representativeness" may at times be a crucial requirement, at other times kneeling before the gods of randomness impedes rather than facilitates understanding.

At their best, purposively sampled accounts provide rival or competing explanations of group processes that researchers can use to probe further. An intentional search for *disconfirming cases* (cases that are clearly inconsistent with the theory being tested or developed) will further enrich the researcher's pondering. The researcher must still consider the limitations of perspective inherent in any single role within a group, scrutinize each informant's motives (whether constructive or malevolent), and always look for independent sources of information (e.g., other informants, archival records) that help place an informant's contribution in some broader perspective.

THE SNOWBALL SAMPLE

Snowball sampling takes its name from the familiar experience of starting with a small snowball and, after rolling it down a hill or around in some damp snow, ending up with a huge ball that can serve as the base for a humanoid snow figure. By starting very small, you can still end up with something very big. In the sampling realm, snowball sampling involves starting with one or two people and then using their connections, and their connections' connections, to generate a large sample. This technique is especially useful if your target population is a deviant or "closet" population, or isn't particularly well defined or accessible.

Edna Salamon (1984) used the snowball procedure to good effect in her doctoral research on "kept women." Salamon wanted a sample of women who had received apartments, cars, trips, maintenance money, and so on in exchange for their camaraderie and involvement in an intimate relationship. But where does one acquire such a sample? There's obviously no sampling frame available. And there are no "kept woman clubs" to approach. Salamon was lamenting this problem to her hairdresser one day when he said "I know a few; I'll introduce you." He introduced her to a few kept women, each of whom introduced her to other kept women, each of whom introduced her to others, until she had acquired a sizable sample of kept women.

The main danger in using this procedure is that one's first snowball may well influence the shape of the snow figure that results. Executives who went through Harvard Business School probably best know other executives who also went through Harvard Business School; street prostitutes are probably more likely to know other street prostitutes than they are to know call girls, who travel in more exclusive company. In general, people are more likely to know people who have similarities with them. Indeed, this social dynamic makes snowball samples possible in the first place. So one must either remain cautious in generalizing results or conscientiously try to start several different snowballs in several different niches.

QUOTA SAMPLING

A final non-probabilistic procedure is *quota sampling*, a technique that made Gallup (as in Gallup Poll) a household word after George Gallup correctly predicted the result of the 1936 U.S. presidential election. Quota sampling is still used by some pollsters, especially marketing researchers who want a heterogeneous sample but don't need true representativeness (although quota sampling *is* formally representative to the extent that the distribution of characteristics in the sample is similar to the distribution of those characteristics in the population).

To do a quota sample, the researcher must first know something about at least the demographic characteristics of the population to be studied. Such information is usually provided by census data. Suppose that we want to ask people about child-rearing practices and that we know from earlier research that attitudes about these practices vary with the respondents' sex and educational background. The researcher would begin by acquiring census data that show how those characteristics are distributed in the population. Suppose we did so, finding the breakdown shown in Table 4.3.

For the sample to be formally representative, 30 percent of our respondents should be males who have completed high school or less, 10 percent should be females who have obtained some postsecondary education, and so on. As with stratified random sampling, quota sampling starts with a target population that has *known* characteristics. But with stratified random sampling, we'd now proceed to randomly select people from within each category: the quota sampler would merely go out and find (for a sample of 100, for example) 30 males with a high school education or less, 35 females with some postsecondary education, and so on. Since *any* 30 males with a high school education or less will do, the researcher might look for them in shopping malls, at pool halls, at union meetings, at laundromats, or just about anywhere.

The quota sampling technique assumes that all people within a given stratum are equal, that for example, all males with a high school education or less will have pretty much the same attitudes regarding the phenomenon of interest. While such an assumption may not be indefensible, it's still fairly tenuous. Quota sampling's major strength is that it ensures a heterogeneous sample with respect to relevant background variables.[6]

SAMPLING ISSUES IN COMPUTER-ASSISTED RESEARCH

The Internet as a Research Site

Just as the proliferation of the telephone in the 1930s and thereafter changed communication patterns and offered first minimal and then extensive new ways to conduct social research, bourgeoning use of the Internet and technological advances that make many different kinds of computer-assisted research possible behoove us to give special consideration to the current status of sampling issues that are arising and being addressed in relation to such research.

Demographics of Internet Connectivity

Worldwide personal computer use surpassed 1.1 billion in late 2006 (Computer Industry Almanac 2006). Both the Canadian and United States governments have made strong commitments to ensuring that all citizens have access to network technology such as the Internet. The express goal of the

Table 4.3
Hypothetical Population Breakdown by Sex and Education

	Completed High School or Less	Some Postsecondary	Completed Postsecondary
Male	30%	15%	5%
Female	35	10	5
Total	65	25	10

Canadian government is to make Canada "the most connected country in the world" (Dryburgh 2002). Just as hardware, software, and network capabilities influence the character and success of particular computer-assisted designs, understanding the differences in the socio-demographic profile and skill set of network computer users is also crucial for achieving success in computer-assisted social research (CASR).

U.S. Census Bureau figures as of August 2000 showed 51 percent of U.S. households had one or more personal computers, and over 80 percent of households had one or more members of the family who indicated that they used Internet-connected computers (Newburger 2001). In comparison, Statistics Canada data for the end of 2000 indicated 55 percent of Canadian households owned one or more personal computers and 82 percent had members who used Internet-networked computers.

Within North America, although people over the age of 65 and certain ethnic minorities appear to be slightly less likely to own a personal computer, age and ethnicity do not appear to be major factors in the determination of personal computer ownership. Quite predictably, socioeconomic characteristics do appear to exert more of an influence on an individual's likelihood of owning a PC. People with higher levels of education and higher incomes are more likely to own a personal computer. From a research standpoint this profile is both encouraging and discouraging. While the digital divide appears to be closing, large portions of the North American population still do not own a personal computer (ACNielson 2004; Weber 2004)

The question confronting researchers wishing to use the Internet to acquire samples that are not prone to coverage error is just how pervasive is the digital divide. While sociologists are just beginning to conduct research into this area (DiMaggio et al. 2001), the empirical CASR literature offers us a fairly clear picture of what the "average" Internet research participant looks like. However, the enormous growth of the Internet in the last ten years has resulted in two very distinct pictures: the pre-2000 participant and the post-2000 participant.

Findings from research conducted prior to the year 2000 indicate that the modal participant in Internet-based CASR were married, Caucasian, male, and between 18 and 59 years of age (Hewson et al. 1996; Krantz & Dalal 2000). They also tended to have significantly higher than average incomes (Buchanan 2000), more education (Schmidt 1997; Sheehan & Hoy 1999) and were more likely to have superior computer and technical skills (Binik et al. 1999; Coomber 1997).

By 2004, the number of Internet users had grown dramatically. However, 97 percent of Internet host computers are located in primarily English-speaking developed countries (Epstein & Klinkenberg 2001). Dahlen (2002) and Katz and colleagues (2001) have all found relatively equal distributions of users along sex lines. Bimber (2000) found that when sex differences in samples are found they are the product of socioeconomic factors, not gender. There is also an increase in the numbers of ethnic minorities using the Internet (Katz et al. 2001). And although Internet users still tend to be more economically advantaged, the range of incomes one sees among Internet users is increasing (DiMaggio et al. 2001). There is a trend in Canada and the United States of increased Internet use in households with incomes less than $35 000 per year (Katz et al. 2001). Large differences still remain when it comes to educational attainment (DiMaggio et al. 2001) and awareness of technology (Katz et al. 2001). Finally, while more people over the age of 65 are using the Internet, this portion of the population is still drastically underrepresented in Internet samples (Katz et al. 2001).

SOLICITING SAMPLES

To date researchers who have conducted research in networked environments have utilized both probability and non-probability sampling methods in order to access and study populations that are of interest to them. A variety of approaches have been used to obtain a probability sample from a networked environment. In the majority of studies three distinct sampling units are employed to construct sampling frames that can be used to generate a random sample: (1) published e-mail addresses,

(2) electronic subscription information, and (3) high-volume websites.

E-mail addresses are frequently compiled from conventional and electronic organizational directories, newsgroups, chat rooms, or peer-to-peer chat networks that function as the equivalent of a telephone book. Researchers select a sample from these directories and treat them as analogous to probabilistic samples of networked computer users.

Alternatively, electronic subscription groups are used as sampling units of networked computer users. Various organizations compile lists of subscription groups such as Internet service providers (ISPs), Usenet newsgroups, listserv mailing lists, and web-based discussion forum members. Rather than identifying individual users, researchers randomly sample topic-specific subgroups from these lists and then solicit subscribers of the selected groups in much the same way that stratified or cluster sampling is applied to the general population.

Finally, heavily trafficked websites are often used to construct sampling frames of the general Internet-using population (Koch & Emrey 2001; Ross et al. 2003). Researchers usually begin by selecting high-traffic or topic-specific websites. After these websites have been identified, advertisements are posted that direct interested visitors to a separate research site.

Targeted non-probability samples are drawn when sampling frames that list all of the members of the population are not available, or when judgment/purposive, snowball, or quota sampling techniques gain better access to targeted populations that are somehow deviant, stigmatized, or hard to reach (Barry 2001; Basi 1999). In order to obtain their samples, researchers place very specific advertisements in print, radio, and televised media; topic-specific listserves; newsgroups; discussion boards; chat rooms; instant messaging areas; and high-traffic websites.

CHARACTERISTICS OF INTERNET PARTICIPATORS

The academic literature on CASR access and protection cites two primary advantages of the Internet as a research site. Perhaps the most commonly cited access advantage of using the Internet for acquiring samples is that, since it is a truly global network, it is the most effective method for soliciting larger and more demographically and geographically diverse samples (Barry 2001). Additionally, many psychologists have found that Internet samples have more interest, provide clearer and more complete responses, and may be more informed about specific topics of interest than many of the student samples currently used in empirical psychology (Gosling et al. 2004; O'Neil & Penrod 2001; Petit 2002).

Researchers who require substantively, as opposed to statistically, representative samples have found that the Internet is an ideal environment for targeted sampling. It affords researchers a unique opportunity to access difficult, deviant, hard-to-reach, or stigmatized populations (Atchison 1996, 1998; Barry 2001; Fox, Murray, & Warm 2003). In addition it has been useful for conducting research with elite groups (Bauman et al. 1998) and physically handicapped, shy, and disorganized individuals (Gosling et al. 2004) who are notoriously difficult participants to solicit for focus group, interview, and other types of direct contact observation and data collection designs.

The importance of privacy and security for research participants is fundamental regardless of the medium of data collection. It only stands to reason that any environment where participants and researchers feel protected from violations of their privacy and security will be beneficial for sampling. Because many Internet-based CASR designs allow people to participate in relative anonymity, CASR provides just such an environment. Some research has indicated that the anonymity that it affords actually improves overall response rates (Kiesler & Sproull 1986; Sheehan & Hoy 1999).

A DIFFERENT WAY OF THINKING ABOUT COMPUTER-ASSISTED RESEARCH

Internets, Intranets, and the Wireless Globe

The statistics on computer ownership and Internet use provide powerful evidence that coverage error is an important consideration for researchers wishing to use "Internet users" as their population. Moreover, no matter how much the digital divide shrinks in the years to come, the size and fluidity of the Internet makes defining the boundaries of the population impossible.

There are many reasons to believe that Internet connectivity will continue to grow as it has until it pervades society—just as the telephone went from being an exotic tool of the wealthy to a standard appliance in virtually every home—but we also would suggest that treating "Internet connectivity" as synonymous with "opportunities for computer-assisted social research" is far too narrow a way of looking at the contemporary world and the role of computers and computer-assisted research within it. There are two things we must keep in mind. First, ownership of a computer is one thing, but access, either inside or outside the home, is quite another. It is hard to find a school, community centre, public library, corporate or commercial office, government facility, or social service agency in North America without networked computers. Second, although it is fashionable to talk of the Internet as the way we use networked computers, a sizable portion of computer networks are not connected to the Internet; instead they are connected via an **intranet**. At present reliable statistics are not available on the percentage of the North American population who have access to either Internet or intranet network–connected computers. Given the pervasiveness of technology in North American society it is reasonable to estimate that at least 90 percent of the North American population already has access to a network-connected computer. Furthermore, as the cost of technology continues to drop and wireless networking becomes ubiquitous, it becomes possible for researchers to bring networked technology into the field to access the remaining 10 percent.

Many social science observers have found it convenient to refer to research conducted over computer networks as Internet research. Accordingly, much of the empirical literature evaluating the reliability and validity of CASR has taken the Internet as both the start and endpoint of the research process. This approach was certainly understandable when the

Internet first surfaced, but it fails to appreciate the degree to which multiple forms of networked computer technology have penetrated North American society. We need to move away from the assumption that in order to participate in research conducted on or through networked environments people must own a personal computer. Furthermore, we need to stop thinking that the Internet is the only structure linking computers to one another. To this end it is important to start looking at computers and network technology as both an observation and data collection medium and a mode of contacting participants (Bradley 1999).

Soliciting Responses/Participation

MODES OF SOLICITATION

Market researchers have long been aware of the lucrative benefits of accessing computer-savvy populations. While there is much that social scientists can learn from the techniques that have been developed within the commercial sector, the constant, often harassing, attempts to access and research the computer-using population by market researchers and commercial enterprises has undoubtedly made potential research participants quite skeptical of solicitations that are represented as serious social research. Fortunately, reports from the empirical social science literature offer myriad possibilities when it comes to soliciting CASR participants.

For the most part the contact method used by researchers employing a particular computer-assisted observation or data collection approach mirrors the methods used in traditional designs. Researchers using more qualitative CASR designs have relied almost exclusively on direct personal contact to secure participation. In almost every case, they have located their samples in non-computerized environments and either brought the technology to the participant (Cooleya et al. 2001; Hampton & Wellman 1999) or directed the participant to the technology (Barrett & Barrett 2001; Hessler et al. 2003).

By far the most common single-method approach to soliciting responses is direct contact through e-mail. Another popular technique is placing advertisements with hypertext links on topic-specific websites.

Finally, many researchers have used the overlapping nature of network environments to their advantage when it comes to soliciting research participants. Combining targeted e-mail, Usenet and web advertisements and links, direct chat and instant messaging, search engine listings, personal contact, and advertisements in traditional print and televised media has proven to be quite successful for many researchers who make use of more structured observation and data collection designs (O'Neil & Penrod 2001; Pettit 2002; Ranchhod & Zhou 2001).

POSSIBILITIES FOR IMPROVING ACCESS AND RESPONSE

Since problems of access often start with problems in sampling, many researchers have argued that response rates can be dramatically improved if researchers employ targeted sampling techniques (Fricker & Rand 2002; Koch & Emrey 2001). Researchers have consistently found that targeted groups are more responsive to solicitation than general populations (Jackson & DeCormier 1999). In addition, it is increasingly possible to recruit specific subpopulations systematically within non-networked environments (Chen et al. 2001)—a process referred to as validated sampling (Fricker & Rand 2002). This approach is likely to be increasingly useful as networked computers find their way into all strata of family homes, educational institutions, commercial venues, corporate offices, and public facilities.

In times of declining research participation, a major challenge for any social researcher is to prevent participants from simply refusing to take part in our research. With the proliferation of unethical and poorly conducted network-assisted research, many computer users have begun to distrust network administered research (Kaye & Johnson 1999; Sheehan & Hoy 1999).

Several options exist to help rectify this problem. At a most basic level social researchers can take steps to distinguish ourselves from commercial, entertainment, and market researchers (Fricker & Rand 2002). This can be accomplished through the use of

digital confidentiality certificates or assurances (Sheehan & Hoy 1999), the implementation of anti-spamming legislation with built-in exemptions for legitimate researchers and charitable organizations, and the use of identifiable academic research domain names (Cho & Larose 1999). Several researchers have also recommended that participants be contacted prior to the start of the research (Bosnjak & Tuten 2001; Sheehan & Hoy 1999) preferably through non-networked channels (Mahotra & Peterson 2001). If personal contact is not possible, personalizing the electronic request has been shown to be a fair substitute (Schaefer & Dillman 1998).

The specific format of the research instrument greatly influences a respondent's ability to participate (Hampton & Wellman 1999). The inherent flexibility of computerized observation and data instruments offers hope in this respect. It is a relatively simple task for researchers to design shorter, simplified, and less obtrusive data collection instruments in order to improve response rates (Crawford et al. 2001). Additionally, designing the instrument so that less experienced users have an option to respond via mouse, keyboard, touch-screen, or voice activation is an increasingly realistic option. Furthermore, the plummeting cost of equipment makes it easier to bring the computer to the participants who do not have access to computers. Recently Chris attended the Vancouver International Jazz Festival where he participated in a computer-assisted self-administered questionnaire (CASQ) sponsored by a tobacco company. Instead of depending on participants approaching the company's kiosk, designers placed stand-alone terminals at strategic locations throughout the festival site. The terminals were set up so that participants only needed to know how to push a button in order to participate. In the two hours that he observed three of the terminals, more than 40 people from diverse backgrounds stopped to participate.

SUMMING UP AND LOOKING AHEAD

Consistent with the theme developed elsewhere in this book, this chapter argues that there is no one "best" sampling procedure. Rather, deciding which is "best" depends once again on one's research objectives and on the nature of the phenomenon being studied. The chapter therefore discusses a *range* of techniques, outlining their respective strengths and weaknesses. Each technique is classified as either *probabilistic or non-probabilistic* (see Table 4.4).

As we've seen, sampling strategies, along with the associated questions of sample representativeness and sample bias, also apply to sampling something besides people. We might want to sample objects (e.g., the products of a particular manufacturer, types of films) or a particular type of situation (e.g., marriage proposals, casual drug use, career decisions, interactions between the police and the community). In each case, we must consider the relationship between our sample of people, objects, or situations and the broader population from which the sample is drawn. We'll return to this point often in the chapters that follow.

We've also argued here that in its broadest sense, any knowledge we generate is merely a sample of all the knowledge we theoretically *could* generate. We must therefore remain aware of how our "common-sensical" (i.e., culturally provided) understandings of the world influence our identification (and hence sampling) of target issues and groups, which in turn influences the course of future knowledge, implicitly reaffirming the status quo.

Perhaps one of the biggest developments to hit the research world in the last few decades is the parallel development of the Internet and computer (digital) technologies, and we conclude this chapter by discussing some of the unique sampling issues that arise when one considers engaging in computer-assisted social research (CASR). We review what have now become the "standard" concerns to express surrounding coverage error, representativeness and the generalizability of findings, but suggest these problems are diminishing as the Internet and Internet accessibility become more pervasive. And while these concerns should not be dismissed by researchers wishing to make the Internet a central component in their research design, neither should their importance be overstated. Very little social research is built around questions that require perfect devotion to these requirements (Fricker & Rand 2002); concerns about the lack of universality of the Internet are well placed in a small range of research, but those concerns may be overstated and esoteric. Representative samples are still possible in many intranet situations or in situations where finite groups of interest define themselves by subscription, and as is always true, much of the best research that is done relies on located targeted groups of persons, which the Internet and search engines facilitate tremendously.

Table 4.4

Examples of Probabilistic and Non-Probabilistic Sampling Procedures

Sampling Procedures		
Probabilistic	**Non-probabilistic**	
Simple random sampling	Haphazard or convenience sampling	
Systematic sampling with random start	Purposive sampling	
Stratified random sampling		• extreme case sampling
	• proportional	• intensity sampling
	• disproportional	• maximum variety/diversity sampling
		• deviant case
Multistage cluster sampling	Snowball sampling	
	Quota sampling	

Finally, we also suggest that the research community needs to get past the narrow view of thinking of "Internet-based research" as the only way to acquire samples for computer-assisted social research. While the Internet is certainly how many people understand networked technology, very little attention has been paid to looking at the networked environment as a means to an end as opposed to an end in and of itself. For one thing, when it comes to using computer networks to access and research populations we need to move away from the assumption that in order to participate in research conducted on or through networked environments people must own a personal computer. We also need to recognize that the Internet is not the only structure linking computers to one another. To this end it is important to start looking at computers and network technology as both an observation and data-collection medium as well as a mode of contacting participants. We need to continue to develop new and efficient methods of contacting perspective participants and soliciting their participation. In order to do this we must start thinking outside the box. Network technology is pervasive in North American society; people do not need to use the Internet in order to be able to participate in social research.

With our discussion of sampling concluded, and our "getting started" and ethics chapters behind us, you now know enough to start thinking in general terms about putting a proposal together in which you set out a game plan for undertaking a piece of research. The next chapter outlines some of the issues you need to consider and articulate as you go through that process, while the rest of the book will help fill in what must for now remain blanks—the specific design and procedures you will create to answer your research questions.

STUDY QUESTIONS

1. How does the homogeneity or heterogeneity of the attributes of the phenomenon one hopes to study relate to the sampling issue?

2. "Any study that doesn't use a representative sample will inevitably produce findings that are not generalizable." Discuss this statement.

3. What does it mean to say that a sample is *representative* of some larger population?

4. What criteria have to be met for a sample to be considered a *random* sample? Why would you want a random sample?

5. Gwen wants to acquire a *random* sample of people who attend a very controversial film. Which of the following procedures would give her a *random* sample? (a) she rolls a dice and a "3" turns up. Gwen approaches the 3rd person in line and every 10th person thereafter; (b) Gwen goes down the line and arbitrarily picks people by whim; (c) Gwen's favourite colour is green, so she decides to interview every person who shows up wearing something green.

6. What is the relationship between *universe, population,* and *sample?*

7. Prepare a summary table of the sampling techniques discussed in this chapter. Begin by drawing four columns on a sheet of paper. Title the first column "Techniques"; in that column, list all the techniques covered in the chapter. Title the second column "Procedures"; in that column, describe in your own words the procedures involved in executing each technique. Title the third and fourth columns "Strengths" and "Weaknesses," respectively; in these columns, list situations for which each technique would be useful, along with the technique's advantages and limitations.

8. Alison wants to interview a representative sample of people who live in apartments in Vancouver's highrise haven, the West End. Unfortunately, no sampling frame is available, and it would be impossible to construct one. What sampling procedure would you recommend that she use? Why?

9. How does *quota sampling* differ from *stratified random sampling?*

10. Can an *unrepresentative* sample still be useful? If so, explain how.

11. You plan to study the department you're majoring in at your college or university. In particular, you want to examine the undergraduate curriculum to ascertain both how it came about and how it might be improved. You want to gather data via interviews. How do you decide whom to sample? Discuss some of your alternatives, describing their respective advantages and limitations.

12. This year's student council is evenly divided on whether the student-run cafeteria should be run on a not-for-profit basis (in order to minimize the cost of meals to students) or on a for-profit basis (with all the profits going to the student society's bursary program). Riaz decides to do a survey to determine the attitudes of the current student body toward these alternatives. He goes to the cafeteria at noon on a Thursday, numbers all the tables (from 1 to 250), randomly samples 50 of the tables, and interviews all the people sitting at those tables. He finds that 57 percent of the students interviewed prefer the for-profit alternative. How confident can Riaz be that this result is representative of the opinions of the student body? Could he be more confident in the representativeness of his results if he had interviewed people from 100 randomly chosen tables?

13. Chris takes a different approach to the problem outlined in Study Question 12. She approaches the college registrar for a list of all students who are currently enrolled; using a table of random numbers, she chooses one student from that list. When interviewed, that student expresses an opinion in favour of the for-profit alternative. Is that one student's opinion theoretically representative of the opinions of the entire student body? Explain why or why not.

14. Pat wants to do an interview study of "hockey fans." Suggest two probabilistic and two non-probabilistic techniques that might, under cer-

tain conditions (which you should specify), allow her to acquire such a sample. Discuss the advantages and limitations of using each of those techniques.

15. Identify a population of people that you are interested in knowing more about and devise a way to sample and solicit them that uses computer technology. Once you have devised your strategy explain how you think your strategy is an improvement over more conventional approaches that you could have used.

16. What is the digital divide and what role does it play in computer-assisted social research?

17. Is it ever possible to obtain a representative sample of respondents on the Internet? Why or why not? What are some *advantages* to seeking Internet-based samples?

18. Devise a creative way of getting your friends to participate in a small Internet survey. Why do you think that the strategy you have come up with would be particularly successful?

NOTES

1. The one exception to this rule is random digit dialing (RDD), a technique developed in the context of telephone survey research, where no explicit sampling frame exists. "RDD relies ... on a procedure that, when followed properly, includes all units or elements of the target population" (Gray & Guppy 1994: 141).

2. This statement assumes that the sampling procedure is probabilistic and has been executed appropriately.

3. Some researchers counteract this problem by computing a "weighted" mean, a number that's adjusted to reflect what the mean (or average) would theoretically be if groups were represented in the sample in the same proportions as they appear in the population.

4. Note, though, that it's very problematic to merely *assume* that a given process is universal. Ideally, one would first show that a certain principle operates in widely disparate groups,

to the point where its universality has been demonstrated. Only after *demonstrating* the process's universality could one legitimately proceed by sampling whomever one wishes.

5. Is maximum variety sampling thus just another name for disproportional stratified random sampling? No. Although the maximum variety sampler in our example has essentially stratified the population on the variable of ethnicity, there's no further requirement to randomly sample within each stratum. Indeed, maximum variety sampling aims to maximize the diversity of views that are heard; thus, instead of seeking the "typical" respondent within each stratum (as is the goal of stratified random sampling), researchers following a maximum variety strategy would probably still try to sample for maximum diversity within each stratum.

6. Although George Gallup made his name with this technique in the 1936 U.S. presidential election, and successfully used it again in 1940 and 1944, he suffered huge embarrassment in 1948, when he predicted that Thomas Dewey would be the next U.S. president. The American public voted instead for Harry Truman. Gallup subsequently abandoned quota sampling techniques in favour of probabilistic procedures.

CHAPTER 5

CONSTRUCTING A RESEARCH PROPOSAL

Coming up with a good research topic and generating researchable questions is just the beginning of the research process. Making it all happen means making contacts, getting approvals, perhaps seeking funding, and convincing others that your research is well considered, ethical, and viable. It does not necessarily mean getting every last little detail settled, although that depends in part on what sort of research you are doing—straight hypothesis testing can be specified in detail; more emergent and exploratory research will be more open-ended because of the collaborative elements that need to be worked out. Nonetheless, your professors, admissions committees for graduate programs, granting agencies, university or college research ethics boards, and your prospective participants all want to know, before they say "OK" to you, that you have some understanding of what you want to do, and that your project is reasonable, ethical, and has a chance of achieving its objectives. In the social sciences this assurance is achieved through the writing of a research proposal.

Despite the obvious importance of writing research proposals within the social sciences, there are very few books available to help researchers navigate the difficult terrain of writing a coherent and convincing research proposal. Many texts on social research gloss over the research proposal process, leaving the impression that researchers who have specific interests or questions that they wish to pursue simply go out and start researching. Furthermore, the final published research papers, articles, and reports that fill the shelves of university and college libraries are often so well polished and structured that it is difficult or impossible to piece together the underlying methodological decision-

making process that produced the published results. The intent of this chapter is to help you better understand what goes into a research proposal and to provide you with some practical suggestions for developing research proposals of your own.

WHAT GOES INTO A RESEARCH PROPOSAL?

A research proposal, like every well-written academic paper, has an introduction, a body, and a conclusion. A research proposal is just like a substantive position paper in that the goal is to develop and articulate an argument supporting the thesis that the proposed study and its guiding questions are important, relevant, and interesting, and that the techniques you have selected to go about answering these questions are sound enough to allow you to successfully complete the proposed study given your resources and limitations.

Just as there are many ways one could approach writing a term paper on contemporary applications of Marxist theory, there is no single way to write a research proposal. The single most important consideration that guides how a research proposal is structured and presented is the nature of the research questions that are being asked. The research question or questions provide a general framework for the design decisions that are likely to follow, since it is about finding the most complete answers to the research question(s) that the entire research process is directed.

While it is important to recognize that research questions, personal style, desired research method, and audience all will influence how you go about laying out your research proposal, several interrelated components are common to nearly all proposals. Within the social sciences research proposals contain a specific *research topic,* a critical discussion of academic *literature* relating to the research topic, a clearly stated and researchable guiding *research question,* a convincing *justification* for conducting the research; a discussion of the specific *research design* and *data analysis strategies* that will be used in order to address the research problem and answer the research question(s), and a tour of any *research ethics* issues that pertain to your research and how you have decided to address them.

THE RESEARCH PROPOSAL WRITING PROCESS

Generating a Research Topic

The first step in writing a research proposal is to select a research topic. Often the first time a student is asked to sit down and identify a topic to research is in an introductory research methods class. Many students in that situation have a difficult time finding a research topic and generating good researchable questions.

As you saw in Chapter 2, ideas about what to research can come from many places. Research ideas that are derived through deductive approaches are guided by theory. Inductive ideas emerge from interaction with and observation of social phenomena. The research process itself gives another set of sources, and sometimes topics fall in your lap because someone presents you with one.

The biggest trick at the beginning is to care about what you are researching. In this chapter we will draw examples from several research proposals that have been prepared for various purposes:

- A proposal by Bob Menzies and Ted Palys involving the history of psychiatry and the asylum as an institution of social control in British Columbia in relation to minorities

- A proposal by Tammy Dorward written as a thesis prospectus for her MA thesis involving the

way that "community" was defined and engaged in the development of Vancouver's Aboriginal Transformative Justice Services (VATJS)

- A proposal that Chris Atchison prepared as the prospectus for his doctoral dissertation regarding prostitution and the role of the male sex buyer

- A proposal prepared by Michelle McGinn and Ted Palys designed to secure funding for research involving the views and expectations of research participants regarding various research ethics issues

Placing Your Research Topic within the Academic Literature

With topic in hand, your next step is to address how others have thought about and researched it. While it is always important to pursue new, exciting, and novel topics, ideas, and questions, quite often it is helpful to ground your study within a larger framework in order to better understand how you can best go about producing researchable questions, selecting the appropriate methods and techniques for pursuing the answers to these questions, and analyzing the information that is produced from the careful execution of these techniques. The literature review provides you with an excellent opportunity to do exactly this.

A well-written literature review situates a project and provides clear evidence that allows the audience to better assess why the topic and research questions are important and how the proposed research fits into the larger academic context. In other words, your literature review should provide a clear and concise synthesis of the major trends in theory, research, policy, and practice, and it should identify the questions or areas of concern that are considered to be the most important or relevant for the community that is currently working in the area. You will recall from Chapter 2 that the point of a literature review is not to simply regurgitate what others have said about your topic but to think critically about what has been said and to identify and highlight the consistencies and disagreements in theory, research, policy, and practice that are evident. Once you have accomplished this you will be in a much better position to identify the flaws or gaps in knowledge that need to be remedied. It is by highlighting these flaws or gaps that you begin to lay the foundations for your own study.

In the case of McGinn and Palys (2005), the problem was that the existing literature featured a lot of talk and very little action when it came to understanding research participants' views of the research process and ethical issues therein:

> The Tri-Council Policy Statement on Research Ethics (TCPS), Canada's federal authority on research ethics, is not the only code of ethics to enjoin researchers and REBs to take a "subject-centered perspective" when they consider ethical issues in their research: "researchers and REBs must strive to understand the views of the potential or actual research subjects." (MRC et al 1998: i-7) Despite its centrality, a literature regarding participant perspectives on research is virtually non-existent.... The purpose of our project is both to begin and to promote research regarding participant perspectives on ethics issues. (2)

For Menzies and Palys (1999), however, quite the opposite was the case. There was already an extensive literature around the world that had begun examining psychiatric practice from a more patient-centred viewpoint, and many historical studies. The challenge for them was thus to specify where they fit in that existing domain of inquiry, as well as to identify what new contributions their proposed research offered:

> In undertaking this study, we will also be contributing to the wider historical investigation of institutional psychiatry in the province of British Columbia and Canada. In contrast to elsewhere in the country (e.g. Cellard, 1991; Dowbiggin, 1997; Mitchinson, 1991; Refvik, 1991; Shortt, 1986), a literature on the origins and development of British Columbian psychiatry and mental health has only recently begun to surface. To date, histor-

ical writing in this province has concentrated principally on criminally insane persons (Chunn & Menzies 1998), on the deportation of alien "lunatics" (Menzies, 1998), on life in the women's wards at the Provincial Hospital for the Insane (PHI) in New Westminster (Davies, 1989), and on the role of families in the involuntary commitment of women patients (Kelm, 1992). Given the immense importance of a system that has confined more than 100 000 British Columbians since its inception, and with the increasing availability to researchers of a rich historical data archive, much work remains to be done. As discussed above, in this project we propose to build on this emergent body of research by investigating one aspect of psychiatric history in the province—namely, the treatment and control of persons bearing the multiple stigma of mental disorder and racial/ethnic marginalization.

There are many ways to critically address the literature relating to your topic of interest. The approach you take to structuring your review is a matter of personal style, preference, and a consideration of your audience. While different audiences are likely to be partial to a particular style of writing over another or will be sympathetic to a particular perspective on social research, it would not be unusual for a literature to address some or all of the following basic questions:

- What have others said about this topic? Who are the major groups that have expressed an interest in the topic or issue?

- Are there particular problems or controversies surrounding the topic?

- What is the history behind these problems or controversies? How have they arisen?

- What theories have been developed around the topic and what do they say?

- What methods have been used to study the topic?

- What research has been done on the topic?

- What policies or practices have been developed in relation to the topic?

- Are there consistencies in existing theory, methodology, research, policy, and practice relating to the topic, or is there disagreement?

- Are there flaws in the existing theory, methodology, research, policy, and practice that you feel you can remedy through your proposed research? What are these flaws and how will your research resolve them?

Stylistically, the literature review is similar to a discussion paper like the ones you would write for a theory class, in that the objective is to critically synthesize and assess several related academic books or articles that have been written in your area of interest. Your literature review should be a free-flowing discussion of several choice books or articles that you feel are particularly useful for elaborating how others within the academy have addressed the topic.

Quite often students ask us how many pieces of literature or how many articles they need to include in the literature review of their research proposal. The answer to this question is not straightforward. The short answer is, you need enough books or articles to demonstrate that you have a good reading or understanding of the topic area. You need to show that you have given adequate attention to how others have addressed the topic within the literature. In some cases this may be 8 or 10 books or articles; in other situations it might be 30, 40, or 50. The advice we generally give our students is that the more they read the better they will be at identifying potential problems, directions, important areas to concentrate on, new research questions, and alternative methodologies. Further, it is important to understand that the literature review process is ongoing throughout the design, execution, and analysis stages of a research project. Good researchers are always going back and reading more on their topic and trying to find overlaps with others.

Poor literature reviews lose the reader in details and irrelevancies, give the impression the writer is meandering, don't seem to have any particular point

to them, and tempt the reader simply to skip ahead to the next section. A good literature review is just like the first chapter of a really good adventure novel: it provides the backdrop, introduces you to the main characters, and leaves you with a desire to see how the rest of the story unfolds. A core component of almost every academic article that is published is a literature review. It is a useful exercise to go and read journal articles from different disciplines to see how the literature is reviewed and presented within each of these disciplines.

Constructing Researchable Questions

In Chapter 2 you were introduced to the process of constructing researchable questions. They are clearly an important element, as developing/refining them further or actually answering them is where all of your research activities will be directed. It naturally follows that all of the research decisions that are outlined and discussed in the research proposal are contingent on whether and how they will contribute to answering your research question(s). You need to present your research question(s) in a way that helps you define the nature and scope of the research. Of course, one possible research question, particularly with more inductive/collaborative approaches, is always, "What should my research question be?" or "What other research questions should I include?" In such a case your proposal will outline what you will do and who you will talk to in order to make that happen.

Operating in relation to a well-developed literature and in the context of their own research programs that had been in place for several years, Menzies and Palys had a large and very specific list of things they wanted to know:

During the initial stages of this project, supported by [various research grants from SSHRC and Simon Fraser University], we have generated and have begun to address a range of questions that pertain to the social and psychiatric control of racial and ethnic minority group members. These include the following: With what frequency did

First Nations, Chinese, Japanese, Doukhobor and South Asian peoples enter the mental hospitals of British Columbia during the period under investigation? What were their patterns of age distribution, gender, marital status, education, occupation, and other socio-demographic attributes? What can be learned about their lives prior to therapeutic contact? Had they previous experience with mental, judicial or welfare institutions? What situations and events initiated their psychiatric confinement? What individuals and agencies were involved in the securing of their commitment to hospital? Did their racial and ethnic status contribute to prior life experiences and encounters leading to confinement? Did the reports of physicians, police and other authorities make reference to their minority identities or link these with behaviour and imputed pathologies? Once hospitalization had transpired, did racial and ethnocultural ascriptions figure into the profiles and accounts of these 200 patients? If so, how were these manifest in ward notes, official reports and correspondence? What was the apparent impact on the treatment of individual subjects? Was there evidence of differential treatment across the five minority groups comprising this study? And how did the patients respond? In their surviving notes and letters, or in the representations of their personal and legal advocates, did they articulate a sense of racial/ethnic identity or a sensitivity to partiality or prejudice in their institutional experience? Did race/ethnicity appear to impact their quality of life while under confinement, their length of hospitalization, or the conditions of release for those who were discharged? Finally, what knowledge can be garnered about the subsequent lives of those individuals who survived and returned to the outside world?

In contrast, Tammy Dorward's master's thesis was her first significant foray into the realm of research, although she had been interested in Aboriginal justice policy issues for some time. The literature in that area identified "broad community involvement and support" as a key element in the establishment of successful Aboriginal programs, but she found that most of the literature on that topic, and most of the programs that had been developed, involved reserve-based communities where the boundaries and citizenry of the community were fairly easily defined, and where the people all shared a similar core cultural heritage. But a growing number of Aboriginal people leave the reserve to study and work. Do they still have the rights that are guaranteed to Aboriginal peoples in Canada's *Charter of Rights and Freedoms*? Do they form a "community"? How would an Aboriginal program that set out to be "community-based" identify and involve them? Dorward's thesis became a case study examination of how one program in Vancouver dealt with those very issues with respect to the creation of Vancouver's Aboriginal Transformative Justice Services (VATJS), and gave her a clear research question and focus:

> Given the fundamental importance of the concept of "community" to both governance and justice, and the unique challenges that arise when that term is operationalized within the urban setting, my thesis will involve an examination of how the concept of "community" was conceptually and operationally defined in the course of developing the VATJS.

Providing Justifications for Your Research

While having an interesting topic and solid research question is the focal starting point of any good research proposal, the research question cannot be understood apart from the deeper reason or purpose of the proposed study. The research questions do not tell people who are reading your research proposal why the study needs to be conducted; they merely tell people what will be answered. When we say that you have to justify the study, what we're really saying is you have to demonstrate to your reader why they should care. You cannot just assume that because you feel something is important, relevant, or interesting that your audience will necessarily share your beliefs or passion. If you cannot convey to readers why they should care about the particular topic, then you're unlikely to get the support, guidance, advice, or funding necessary to realize your goals.

There are several ways that you can go about justifying your study. It is often impossible to know who is going to be reading your research proposal and even more difficult to know exactly how to engage them. Fortunately, you don't need to place all of your eggs in one basket when it comes to elaborating the justifications for your particular research design, topic, and questions. You can justify your study on a number of different grounds in an effort to engage as diverse an audience and range of sensibilities possible. The easiest way to do this is to return to the academic literature in order to draw specific connections between the proposed research and the development of a theory, method, policy, and/or practice.

One of the most common ways of justifying a proposed research study is to situate the research topic and questions within the theoretical literature in the area and to point to the contribution that the proposed research will make to the development of social theory. For instance, in his dissertation proposal that involved a study on prostitution and the role of the male sex buyer, Chris pointed out that by further describing, exploring, and understanding the population of men who buy sex, sociologists and criminologists would be better equipped to develop theories of masculinity and gender that were informed by specific empirical evidence rather than conjecture:

> Risk-based research authorizes researchers as expert speakers about sex buying at the same time as it de-legitimates male sex buyers as speakers and active subjects capable of framing the problems in different ways. Aside from the phenomenological investigation conducted by Holzman and Pines in the early 1980's, sociologically informed research into the nature of the socio-cultural context of sex buying has not received much attention within the theoretical or empirical literature on the client. The primary focus of [the proposed] research will be the development of a qualitatively and quantitatively informed understanding of risk decision making processes involved in the male purchase of sex. More specifically, … I hope to be able to obtain an interpretive understanding of the attitudes, behaviours and decision making practices of male sex buyers that is grounded in both an empirical investigation of self-reported attitudes and behaviours and an in-depth account of the lived experiences and varied and multiple socially and culturally informed meanings that male sex buyers attribute to the risk decisions that are pertinent to their purchase of sex.

Another potential way to justify the pursuit of a particular topic or a research design is to point to the methodological contributions that the design will make. Perhaps the way that you have chosen to pursue your investigation is methodologically different than the approaches that other people in the field have taken. For example, if all the studies on student satisfaction with their research methods classes are based on the analysis of aggregate statistics collected from year-end surveys that ask students to rank the performance of their professors and teaching assistants using fixed-response multiple choice questions, it is safe to assume that this method will produce a limited understanding of students' experiences with those classes. Such surveys are necessarily superficial in what they ask, and for privacy reasons never ask for details about the students that might be useful in understanding, for example, what sorts of professors, teaching styles, and classes appeal to what sorts of students. You could design a research project that puts a more qualitative spin on addressing student satisfaction. Instead of using an aggregate survey you could propose sampling a smaller number of students from the class and engaging them in lengthy in-depth interviews covering a variety of topics and experiences. This shift in method could offer a clear contribution to our understanding of student satisfaction with their classes.

You can also justify a study in terms of the policy applications that could emerge as a result of the data acquired from the study: by better understanding a particular topic and answering specific research questions, social policy in relation to the topic could be developed or changed. Menzies and Palys argued in their proposal that understanding history is its own reward, in part because many of the problems of the past still exist and beg attention:

> We believe that this project will make a significant contribution to the historical understanding of medical and social ordering in British Columbia. It will offer a unique approach to understanding the institutional treatment of racial and ethnic minorities in the province, and more generally across Canada. To the extent that problems of racialization and ethnocentrism remain entrenched in *fin-de-siècle* society, the work has both historical and contemporary relevance. It will help to expose both the manifest and implicit means by which the dimensions of race and culture get played out in the operations of our therapeutic and regulatory institutions. In addressing the practices of the past, we can learn much about the conflicts and prejudices that continue to plague British Columbian and Canadian social order as this century draws to a close.

Tammy Dorward was more explicit in identifying her policy interests, and more succinct in her statement of it:

> My goal will be to critically analyze the concept of "community" as it was developed and implemented in the development of the VATJS and to explore the implications of that concept, and my analysis of it, for future programme development.

For McGinn and Palys, the justification was a very basic one—that the dearth of research in the area required some basic exploratory work to identify what some important research questions in the area were:

> The purpose of our project is both to begin and to promote research regarding participant perspectives on ethics issues. We follow a collaborative approach and seek participant input from the outset.... Our hope is not only to provide an initial contribution to an area that begs attention, but also to help identify questions and offer interim observations that will encourage/promote others to become involved and contribute.

As you can see, there are a variety of ways to go about justifying researching a particular topic or researching specific questions within the body of your research proposal. While the approach you take is largely a matter of personal style, preference, and a consideration of your audience, it is wise to attempt to address the following general questions:

- Why is the topic worth studying?

- Why are the research questions that have been developed worth answering?

- What practical significance does the proposed study have?

- What will be accomplished by the completion of the proposed research project?

- In what ways does the proposed study contribute to the general understanding of the topic or to the construction of social theories?

- What contribution is the research expected to make to the advancement of knowledge or to the development of new methods?

- What contribution is the research expected to make to wider social policy or practice?

Locating Yourself within the Study

Quite often in academic writing we're encouraged to depersonalize how we present information and arguments. Most often this depersonalization manifests itself in the awkward third person language that we are encouraged to use when presenting an argument, writing a research proposal, or analyzing and presenting the findings of our research. For example, instead of saying, "I believe that this design will produce the most valid and reliable results," students are often encouraged to depersonalize the claim by saying, "It is believed that this design will ..." For some academic writers this depersonalization is seen as a way of ensuring that our projects remain free of bias, while others argue that by making our personal connection to the research more transparent we not only acknowledge our awareness of potential sources of bias, we avoid fraudulent disinterest and instead show how research doesn't have to be a cold and inhuman process.

Regardless of the stylistic position you adopt, or your discipline imposes, for your own academic writing, part of designing and conducting social research is being both critically aware and reflexive of your own position within that research.

When we say that you have to locate the study within your personal experience we are not saying that you have to write a tell-all autobiography confessing all your deep, dark inner secrets. We are simply suggesting that you share with the reader of your research proposal why the study is particularly important to you or how it relates to some experience you have had in your own life. There are a number if strategies that you can use to locate the study within your personal experience. One popular technique is to show how the proposed research fits into your ongoing research program or is related to experiences or insights you have gained from earlier achievements or involvement in the field under investigation. That was very much the case for Menzies and Palys in their study of asylum files:

> This study comprises the second stage in a wider inquiry into the medical and legal regulation of racial and ethnic minorities in British Columbian history. Following an initial compilation, during the summer of 1999, of selected case file documents for patients admitted from the inauguration of BC's mental health system up to 1942, we now propose to expand the research to include samples of five racial/ethnic patient populations (First Nations, Doukhobor, Japanese, Chinese

and South Asian) who were hospitalized through to 31 December 1950. The extension and finalization of these data sets are integral to the successful completion of this project. The work has become possible through the impending availability (as of late Fall 1999) at the BC Archives of a new data base including all public mental hospital files in the province that were closed through death or discharge between 1943 and 1969. The [proposed grant] will permit us to assemble and analyze a unique data base of clinical file records and institutional documents that will constitute the first historical study concentrating on the racial/ethnic dimensions of institutional psychiatry in Canada.

As another example, perhaps you are planning on applying for an honours or graduate degree program; you may want to indicate how your proposed research is designed to help build your knowledge base so that you can pursue advanced studies or research. Another popular method of connecting yourself with a proposed study is to point to the ways that a particular study is motivated by events in your personal life or experiences that you have had. For example, some of our students who have undertaken research on the social challenges faced by mentally challenged youth indicated in their proposals that their research interests were motivated by their own experiences growing up with siblings who are afflicted with a particular mental disability.

While it is certainly debatable as to how much researchers should have to reveal about themselves as a condition of the research process, when it comes to putting together a solid research proposal there are considerable benefits to being reflexive and transparent about where you fit into the research process. To this end we advise you to develop the style and technique that you are most comfortable with for elaborating on your own connection to the research within your research proposal. Regardless of the strategy you ultimately develop, it is important for you to remain conscious of the influences that your own experiences and position have on the research decisions that you make.

THE RESEARCH DESIGN: A ROADMAP TO SUCCESS

As you have seen, the research decisions that you make are influenced by a number of factors operating, sometimes silently, behind the scenes. The most important factor influencing your research decisions is your research question. After all, the whole point of conducting social research is to find answers to the questions we have about the social world. The underlying objectives of your questions (exploration, description, understanding, explanation, or transformation) serve as a signpost or route marker that guides you toward making particular design decisions. The questions will govern how complex the design has to be, including what the units of analysis of the study will be and which sampling strategy is best to study them, how the units should be measured or observed, and which type of analysis will produce the most valid and reliable answers.

The design section of the research proposal is where the pragmatic part of your research planning begins. It is at this stage of the research proposal that you elaborate on exactly how your research strategy will unfold. A clear research design provides a roadmap for people reading your research proposal, showing them the exact route you think you will take to arrive at your empirical destination. It also lets your audience know why you think that the route you have chosen is the best one to take and should follow from your statement of research objectives and your research question. Although whatever is most important will depend on your research and the issues that are unique to it, some core questions that are considered in many research proposals:

- Who or what will you study in order to collect the data necessary to answer your research questions?

- Will it be appropriate to select a sample? If so,
   - What sampling strategy will you be using?
   - What processes and procedures are involved in the sampling strategy that you plan on utilizing?

- How large will your resulting sample be?
   - How do you know that this sampling strategy and the resulting sample will be adequate to provide you with the information necessary to answer your research questions and meet your research objectives?

- If it is not appropriate to select a sample,
   - Why is a sample not appropriate?
   - What procedures will you use to select the units of analysis for your study?
   - How many observations will you be making?
   - How can you be sure that the type and number of observations that you intend to make will be enough for you to answer your research questions?

For Tammy Dorward, for example, who was interested in understanding how Vancouver's "Aboriginal community" came to be defined and involved in the process of creating the Vancouver Aboriginal justice program (VATJS), some preliminary discussions with persons who were involved in the development of the program and a perusal of some of the documentation available to her led her to identify the following as crucial to answering her research questions:

a) Examining archival data pertaining to the conception and design of the VATJS to consider how and by whom "the community" was conceptually and operationally defined.

b) Interviewing and surveying people involved in that process to see how they believe the concept was/should be defined. In an attempt to understand the diversity of views Aboriginal people may have regarding this topic, I am looking for a wide range of people from different categories:
   - Programme records regarding the initial Elder's Consultation lists the names of 32 participating Elders. I would like to begin by interviewing Elders, and would like to complete between 5-10 interviews
   - Community Council members and programme personnel (3-6 interviews)

- I also plan to survey people attending West Coast night [a weekly gathering at Vancouver's Aboriginal Friendship Centre], which will conclude with the question of whether the respondent would be willing to discuss the topic further in an interview (10–20 from this category)
- Students at Native Education centres (5-10 interviews)
- Others that are identified to me in the course of data gathering.

For McGinn and Palys, who were very much at the beginning of what could become an extended piece of work, a more flexible, exploratory approach was warranted to identify what might be some important questions to ask, followed by an effort to cast as wide a net as possible to gain some preliminary response to those themes identified in the first phase:

> In Phase I of the research, focus group interviews with purposive samples of persons who previously have participated in research will be conducted in which people are asked about their participation in and perceptions of different ethical issues in relation to the research process. We intend to use what we hear from those first targeted groups to develop more structured instruments to do the broader and more extensive web-based study described below in Phase II.

They also chose samples for the initial focus group research that were relatively easily available to them and that they also believed would be fruitful in helping them to meet their exploratory objectives:

> We believe this first foray will be most fruitful if we focus on groups who are frequently asked to participate in research and/or who live/work in a milieu in which research is common; the more experience they have, and the more different variations of approaches and procedures they have encountered, the greater the depth that will be possible in the conversation. Also, we are less

interested in the facts of their participation than their perceptions of it, and use "previous participation" or "being in an environment where research is frequently conducted" as criteria for participation because we want to go beyond "research" as an abstract process to one that has some concrete meaning for the participant, at least as a referent or departure point, from which to consider why they might or might not have participated.

The authors go on to outline how Palys would conduct focus groups with individuals from various niches within the criminal justice system—former prisoners, police officers, and lawyers—while McGinn would obtain various educational samples—parents of school-aged children, university students, and teachers. The benefits of visiting these particular niches are explained. In relation to the criminological samples, for example, they write:

> Focussing on these "criminological" samples has several research benefits. Certainly criminological research has been the focus of considerable controversy for the last decade in Canada and elsewhere (e.g., see Israel 2004a; Lowman and Palys 2000; Yeager 2004), with many of the debates between researchers and REBs residing in apparently different views by criminological researchers and REB members who have no experience in researching criminological issues over the expectations that criminological samples have of researchers and the institutions who employ them. To that extent, there is an urgency to examining this domain that is duplicated by few other areas.

One of the biggest challenges in research is determining how and where you can best approach prospective participants in your research so that they will agree to participate. Many projects that seem great on paper never get anywhere if the people are unwilling to participate and/or the data are otherwise unavailable. Indeed, the difference between "paper" research where everything always works wonderfully, and "real" research where one bumps into the vagaries of everyday life, is one of the reasons we try to have students do actual research projects rather than proposals whenever feasible. The lessons learned are invaluable for making one's next proposal better by more completely anticipating all the bases that need to be covered. Whatever your experience, one of the things you need to do in your proposal is not only to convey your plans, but to also give evidence showing they are feasible. In some instances this may be very easy—for example, you need access to a public setting and can gain that access precisely because the setting you need *is* public. But many other groups require special access, which brings in other issues—gatekeepers, greater ethical complexity regarding negotiation and consent, whether permissions have been obtained, and so on.

Sometimes, familiarity with the population that you are interested in through previous group membership can facilitate the design process. Your "insider" status may have provided you with a working knowledge of how the group is organized, how they talk, how to gain their trust, and how to handle yourself when you are interacting with them. If you don't have this type of avenue into a group you will need to invest more time in detailing how you will get beyond your "outsider" status and encourage people to participate.

Regardless of how familiar you are with the population you wish to research, you need to convey to your audience that you have given significant thought to how you are going to "sell your project" to your prospective sample and how you will manage your research if you are not successful in making the "sale." To do this, there are several interrelated questions that are helpful to think about and address within your proposal:

- Who is available for your study and how will you contact them?

- Once you have contacted people for your study, what procedures will you use to encourage them to participate in the study?

- How do you know that these procedures will work?

- What will you do if people refuse to participate?

Beyond knowing exactly how you are going to encourage people to participate in your research you have to remain conscious of the fact that as social scientists our research often involves inserting ourselves into the lives of real people. The relationships that we forge with the people who are kind enough to consent to participate in our research are not entirely neutral. As academic or social researchers we have a certain degree of influence and power within the research setting, if for no other reason than the fact that it is we who ask the questions and in some cases wear the funny white lab coats. It is also important to remember, however, that the power balance between the researcher and the participant is not one-sided. Most social research takes place outside the safe and secure setting of the university in environments that are more familiar to the participant than the researcher. As you saw in Chapter 3, in order to address potential abuses of the balance of power between the researcher and the participant, the social science community has developed a variety of ethical codes of conduct that people who conduct social research have agreed to abide by. Relevant issues must be considered in your proposal. These may include the following:

- How will you obtain the consent of your participants?

- Are you providing any guarantees and assurances to your research participants?

- Might your research have a foreseeable positive or negative impact on those you study? What is the nature of that prospective impact?

- What procedures will you have in place to ensure that your study will not bring about harm to those involved or related to the research?

- What procedures will you have in place to ensure that your research participant's privacy, confidentiality, and anonymity (if applicable) are respected and protected?

For example, for McGinn and Palys there were two main ethics issues to be dealt with in each of the two phases of their research (phase I involved focus groups; phase II involved a web-based survey): (a) consent, and (b) confidentiality, as well as recruitment issues that were relevant to the web survey. In regard to the focus group study, they stated:

Consent

The announced intent of the discussions with participant groups will be to "have a discussion about 'research participant perspectives' in which people who have participated previously in research, or who have opinions about the research they have seen carried on in their midst, can bring and share their experiences and views." At the first opportunity prospective participants will be given an information sheet that outlines [a lengthy description follows that identifies the purpose of the research; what their participation would involve; who they should contact to find out more].

We will ensure in each case that in order to participate persons will have to make a free choice as to whether to come to the group, so that consent will be implicit in attendance at the meeting and each person's voluntary choice to participate in the conversation. A verbal explanation of the project rationale will be given that will follow the points listed in our written project description above, and a discussion begun. Michelle and Ted will lead their respective discussions, and begin by asking whether anyone present has any objection to the discussion being recorded. It will be explained that the recordings will allow a transcript to be created that maximizes accuracy of recall. In the event there is an objection, anonymized written notes will be taken instead.

Confidentiality

Participants in group discussions will be told the obvious, i.e., that there are others in the room and

hence that there are limitations to how "confidential" anything might be among the persons in the room. Persons interviewed individually can be asked how confidential they would prefer the interview to be, and their wishes recognized. Our own intention is to anonymize transcripts and never use names in any presentations or reports that arise from this work because our interests are in the issues that are identified and not in the identities or personalities of those who contribute the information. Beyond that, we can only encourage group participants to be respectful of each others' sensibilities to the extent they would like others to respect theirs.

Because participants will be talking about research in which they have participated, confidentiality issues may arise for the persons who were in charge of designing and implementing those research projects. We will never ask for the names of those persons or, if given them, will not record them, as we have no interest in pursuing that end of the experience in this project; our interest is solely in their perspective on their research experiences.

In Chris's proposal, which involves conducting web-based surveys and some subsequent interviews with men who buy sex—behaviour that may be highly stigmatized in many contexts but is not illegal—he deals with a variety of ethics issues but identifies confidentiality issues as the most significant:

Every precaution will be taken to ensure that the participants' privacy and confidentiality are protected throughout the course of the research. While knowledge of the men's identities will be requested if they are going to participate in the semi-structured interviews, it will not be a requirement for participation in the self-administered questionnaire portion of the research. There will be no way in which to identify the participants who indicate that they wish to remain anonymous, providing they do not provide any identifying information within their responses.

All men who elect to participate in the self-administered questionnaire will be given instructions and options which attempt to ensure that their responses remain protected from third party interception. The men will be specifically instructed not to give any identifying information or to mark their responses in any way which may be used to identify them at a later date by either the researchers or any third party. In addition, they will be informed of the security risks associated with transferring information via the Internet and they will be provided with alternative submission options should they feel that electronic submission is too much of a risk. Specifically, respondents will be given two options for returning responses to the researchers. Questionnaires may be filled out and returned to the researchers while on the World Wide Web via a simple HTML form and a secure socket layer connection. If the respondents have serious concerns about the interception of their responses they may download and print a PDF hard copy of the questionnaire and return it in an unmarked envelope via conventional mail to the researchers at an address at Simon Fraser University.

MEASUREMENT AND DATA COLLECTION

With your sample and sampling strategy clearly defined and discussed, you need to turn your attention to issues of measurement and data collection. While identifying "who" or "what" you are going to study is vital to successful research, if you don't have a well-thought-out research instrument to guide or structure your observations or measurement you will not be able to answer your research questions, and all the thought and work that you put into your research plan up to this point will have been for naught.

The nature of the measures and instruments you develop in order to answer your research questions is heavily influenced by the research perspective you use to inform your research design. While a single research question can be answered in a variety of ways, once you elect to employ a qualitative or quantitative approach the specific measurement techniques that are available to you become more narrowly defined. For example, perhaps you are interested in understanding what motivates participation in extreme sports like base jumping, rock climbing, and long-board downhill skateboarding. Answers to this question can be found using a qualitative or quantitative methods or both. Perhaps you are interested in the qualitative meaning that participants attach to their extreme activities. In this case you would probably want to develop your research design around a qualitative case study of an extreme sports participant or a micro-ethnography of a particular extreme sports community. Conversely, you may think that it is more important to test a particular theory of adventure-seeking behaviour that has been developed by researchers who have looked at similar populations. In order to test this theory you may decide that a quantitative approach involving the use of a self-administered questionnaire or quasi-experimental design will provide the best answers to your question.

As you will come to understand as you read through the remaining chapters of this book, there are many qualitative and quantitative techniques available to you for finding answers to your research questions. Your goal in the methods and data collection section of your research proposal is to provide a convincing argument for why you feel that the particular measure you have developed and the data collection technique that you have selected are the best suited for your proposed research. Again, there is no template for how you should go about doing this, but there are several key questions that you need to consider in order to present a solid argument for the decisions you have made, including the following:

- What are the key concepts or variables in your study?

- How will you conceptually define and measure the central concepts or variables in your study?

- In what respect do your definitions and measurement techniques duplicate, build on, or differ from those used in previous studies of this topic?

- What specific data collection technique(s) will you use to collect the data necessary to answer your research questions and address your research objectives?

- Why have you selected the data collection technique(s) that you have?

- How do you know that the observation/measurement device you plan on using for your study will give you the best information or data for answering your research questions?

- Once you have completed your observations, what procedures will you implement to store the research data?

- What procedures will you implement to ensure that the data remain secure and confidential?

Proposals will vary in the extent to which measurement instruments can be specified. In more exploratory and inductive research you may be able to do little more than list a few themes that might be addressed for starters, with everything else to be determined on a collaborative basis depending on where your conversations with research participants lead you. In other areas you may be able to specify more concretely what you will ask. For example, even though McGinn and Palys's proposed research was more exploratory in its objectives, they already knew some issues they wanted to address in the focus group portion (phase I), simply because any code of ethics lists sets of principles and so they knew what was available. The big question they were posing was whether there were *other* issues or perspectives that ethics codes had not considered that should *also* be addressed. In any event, as an example, they said the following with regard to what participation in the research would involve:

Nature of Participation

Exploratory research requires a flexible and open-ended approach that is open to new directions, observations and issues as they arise. We propose to begin with a tentative overall guiding structure and sense of purpose that can be shared and be a starting point for discussions with participants. Our focus is on ethics issues that arise in regards to research participation, and the overall guiding framework we will begin with is to follow a chronological ordering through successive phases of the research process—access and recruitment, consent processes, expectations of confidentiality and so on—along with some more overarching considerations about relations among researchers, research participants, and REBs.

The proposal went on to list the areas McGinn and Palys knew they wanted to address, along with sample questions in each area. A requirement for participation in their research was that individuals must have had some prior research involvement they could reflect on (so that the interaction would deal with a particular research experience rather than research in the abstract), and the ordering of topics McGinn and Palys proposed to follow was created to reflect how the process would have been experienced from the research participant's point of view—starting with the way access was obtained and their participation sought, through the gathering of data and any follow-up.

ANALYSIS, EXPECTED OUTCOMES AND BENEFITS OF THE STUDY

Once you have presented a clear and well-defended argument for what or who you will study and how you will make your observations or collect the data necessary to answer your research questions, you need to shift your attention to thinking beyond the project to envision the type of analysis you will do and what some of the expected outcomes of this analysis are likely to be. Many students find this section of the proposal very difficult to write because they find it hard to envision what the data they will be collecting will look like, and they often have not yet been exposed to qualitative or quantitative data analysis. In order to begin to think about this you will want to read through the Chapters 11 and 12 to get a feel for how data is handled at the analysis stage.

By this stage in the proposal writing process you have already designed and discussed the data collection techniques that you plan on using to answer your research questions, so you should have a very clear idea of what the possible format of the information you will be collecting will look like. For instance, if you plan on using a self-administered questionnaire or quasi-experimental design in order to gather observations, you already know that the information you get back will be in a fairly structured format with many of the responses or observations already defined and ordered. Conversely, if you plan on conducting lengthy personal interviews, case studies, oral histories, or micro-ethnographies, you will most likely have to deal with large amounts of open-ended textual information.

Regardless of whether you have quantitative or qualitative data or both, making sense of it will involve a process of data reduction where you take the volumes of information that you have collected and organize and synthesize them into core components or themes that help you to best go about answering your research question(s). The point is to make the information accessible and understandable so that you can bring to light certain patterns that speak to your research questions. For the purposes of the research proposal you are generally required to provide your audience with some indication as to how you think you will go about doing this. In order to accomplish this there are several key questions that you should address in your research proposal:

◆ How will you organize the data to make them ready for analysis (e.g., transcription, data entry, coding, cleaning [correction/synthesis/editing])?

◆ How will findings be analyzed and reported (e.g., by hand or using a data analysis program)?

◆ What specific analysis procedures are you planning on using or what kind of analysis do you plan to conduct? Are specific hypotheses being tested? How do the analyses connect back to your research question(s)?

◆ What is the purpose of the analysis?

◆ What are the projected findings, conclusions, and implications of the proposed research?

◆ How will the findings be disseminated?

◆ What effect might your analysis have on or for the population that you are studying?

ACKNOWLEDGING POTENTIAL PROBLEMS, LIMITATIONS, AND DELIMITATIONS

Far too often both novice and experienced researchers construct research proposals that promise the moon and the stars without taking into account that there are likely to be methodological and practical constraints that will prevent the delivery of such lofty promises. A well-thought-out and convincing research proposal will clearly detail the potential *limitations* and *delimitations* of the project.

In the limitations section of your proposal, you acknowledge the potential weaknesses of your design that have been brought about by the compromises you have had to make in order to construct a realistic project. Limitations can include potential problems obtaining access to people or settings, possible respondent refusal, equipment failure or technological support issues, limitations on personal skills and expertise, restricted budgets and time frames, and cultural and linguistic barriers.

For example, perhaps you realize that to fully understand the effects of long-term exposure to images of gaunt and unhealthy women in fashion magazines on women's health practices a longitudinal study would be necessary. As a student who may be heavily burdened by a full course load and student loan debt you may not have the time or financial resources to conduct such a study, so instead you have opted to design your research around a less generalizable but more realistic qualitative cross-sectional design. It is in the limitations section of your proposal where you should acknowledge this fact but make the argument that in spite of this, the data that you will get from your study will be an acceptable first step in understanding some of the ways that these images are affecting women's health. By doing this you address potential criticisms before they are made and you lay the groundwork for your future, more heavily funded and supported, research design.

Many people reading this book will probably be familiar with legal contracts such as your video rental or cellular telephone agreement. These agreements are excellent examples of how lawyers place parameters on the rights and responsibilities of both the company providing the service and you, the consumer. In the research world these parameters are referred to as *delimitation*. The purpose of the delimitations section of your research proposal is to make it clear to your audience exactly what you will *not* be doing in the research. In most cases the delimitations that researchers place on their project address issues such as the range of behaviours or practices or information that will be included for, and excluded from, investigation; the particular participants or research sites that will, and will not, be observed; and the type of measurement or data collection techniques that will, and will not, be used. In short, any conscious decision that you make pertaining to the strategies, methods, and techniques you propose to use in order to answer your research questions usually involves making a decision about what strategies, methods, and techniques you will not use. The delimitations section of your research design is where you highlight and explain these decisions.

Think of this section as the cover-your-butt section of the design. Just as lawyers use fancy clauses to ensure that liability falls on certain parties in the event of a problem, the delimitations section of the research proposal makes it clear to the audience what will be excluded from the deliverables in your proposed project. In other words, the delimitations place limits on the scope of your proposed research. This way people can't come back to you after the research is completed and say, But why didn't you do this, that, or the other thing? If they do, you can simply say, "Because I said I wasn't going to do that."

SUMMING UP AND LOOKING AHEAD

Different fields of study within the social sciences will highlight particular aspects of the research decision-making process over others, and they will do this using their own unique language and style. In this chapter we have attempted to provide you with a general framework of questions and strategies for developing a research proposal that reflects both your own sense of style and substance while at the same time allowing you to address some of the common themes and questions that appear throughout the social sciences. Again, it is important to remember that since every research project is motivated by different topics, questions, perspectives, and techniques, there is no one-size-fits-all approach to research design.

What is important when you are writing a research proposal is that you remain flexible and willing to change as the design unfolds. The point is not simply to put together a proposal that looks like it might work, the point is to put together a well-thought-out design that demonstrates that you have given each step of the process careful thought and attention and that as a result you have produced a sound design that anticipates potential problems and incorporates methodological techniques that dramatically improve the chances that the research will be successful. It is impossible to anticipate all the potential road closures and detours that you may confront during the journey through conception, design, implementation, and analysis. Like any cross-country road trip, the process of research is full of twists and turns, bouts of car sickness, and truly amazing and serendipitous discoveries. The point is to prepare yourself for these possibilities by familiarizing yourself with the landscape and the roadways so that you arrive at your destination safely and securely with a whole bunch of interesting stories to tell.

The remainder of this book is dedicated to introducing you to the specific methods of data collection and analysis that are contained in the toolbox of the social scientist. As you read on, consider the various techniques that are presented and try to relate them back to topics that you think may be interesting to investigate. While you do this, ask yourself how each of the techniques could be integrated into research on a topic that interests you. Think about the relative advantages and disadvantages that each of the techniques could offer in exploring, describing, understanding, or explaining your topic. By doing this not only will you become a more critically aware consumer of the research and conclusions that are presented to you on an ongoing basis, but you will also be able to make informed decisions about the variety of methods that are available to you in your rapidly expanding social science toolbox.

STUDY QUESTIONS

1. Select a particular research topic that interests you and develop five researchable questions to explore, describe, understand, or explain something about that topic that interests you. Once you have done this make a list of the approaches that you could use to study each of your research questions.

2. Select a research topic or question that interests you and in 250 words or less provide a convincing justification for why this topic or question is important and why research needs to be conducted in relation to it.

3. Select three empirical articles from refereed journals in your field of study and identify at least three limitations and delimitations of each study.

CHAPTER 6

INTERACTIVE METHODS: SURVEYS, INTERVIEWS, AND ORAL HISTORY TECHNIQUES

Few processes are as fundamental to social science research as the person-to-person exchange of information. On the one hand it's so simple: you ask a question and you get an answer. On the other hand, that simple interaction has had enough written about it to fill a small library.

TYPES OF INTERACTIVE METHODS

The range of techniques that fall into the domain of "interactive methods" is incredibly large. Entire typologies have been created to categorize and organize the available techniques (e.g., see Campbell 1950; Denzin & Lincoln 1994, Fishbein 1967, Kidder & Campbell 1970; Oskamp 1977; Reinharz 1992). The main techniques subsumed under interactive methods are questionnaires and interviews—different ways of asking questions and getting responses, whether on paper or by voice. But as we shall see, there's slightly more to it than that.

Questionnaires and interviews are very similar devices. The only difference is that an interview involves an ongoing question-and-answer dialogue between researcher and respondent, while a questionnaire involves written responses to a document that is prepared ahead of time. The actual questions that appear on a questionnaire or in an interview don't *have* to be different, although they often are because of the different dynamics involved in an essentially solitary–written context (the questionnaire) versus a more social–verbal one (the interview).

At least three different types of questionnaires can be distinguished, on the basis of how they're administered. These include the self-administered questionnaire, where the researcher makes face-to-face contact with a single respondent who completes the questionnaire by himself or herself, and where the researcher may or may not continue to be present; the group-administered questionnaire, where a group of individuals is brought together to complete individual questionnaires in each other's company, typically under the researcher's supervision; and the mail-out questionnaire, where there is no personal contact between researcher and respondent (since the questionnaire is simply mailed or dropped off to the respondent), and hence no more instructions and explanations to the respondent than appear on the questionnaire itself. In each case we also have the computer-based equivalent these days; because of their novelty and because less is known about them at this juncture, we discuss them separately later in this chapter.

At least four different types of interviews have been identified: the telephone interview, otherwise known as the telephone poll or telephone survey; the in-person individual interview, where researcher and participant sit and talk eye-to-eye, usually in some relatively private setting; the focus group interview, in which the researcher acts as both moderator and interviewer for groups of respondents who articulate and discuss their views; and the oral history interview, where a flexible interview style is used to encourage people, usually specifically targeted respondents, to tell about some experience or other phenomenon of mutual interest to them and the researcher. Again, computer analogues to these face-to-face and mediated communications are becoming more pervasive; we discuss them later.

Questionnaires

Among questionnaire methods, whether the researcher is present (e.g., for group-administered questionnaires and some self-administered questionnaires) or not (e.g., for mail-out questionnaires and some self-administered questionnaires) will make a difference. Face-to-face contact typically provides two things: higher **response rates** and the chance to both clarify ambiguities or misunderstandings and monitor the conditions of completion.

THE DIFFERENCE (NON)CONTACT MAKES

The more that the sample's formal representativeness is a concern, the more important personal contact is. With personal contact, it's not uncommon that 80 percent to 90 percent of the people you approach will agree to participate; when a group of prospective respondents agrees to allow a researcher access to their group (e.g., when administering questionnaires to students in a classroom or to all persons who attend a meeting), response rates may approach 100 percent. In contrast, impersonal mail-out questionnaires more commonly result in response rates of between 10 percent and 40 percent. Lower response rates may not be a problem if the nature of the volunteer bias can be adequately assessed and/or if the researcher wants to obtain only a heterogeneous sample rather than a formally representative sample.

The fact that respondents answer questionnaires on their own poses special constraints the researcher must consider. First, respondents must be literate in the language used in the study, or they won't be able to read the questionnaire. Second, even if respondents are literate, the researcher must ensure that the vocabulary used in the questions is appropriate for the sample group being approached. Third, researchers designing questionnaires must

successfully anticipate possible ambiguities or misunderstandings. The questions themselves and the instructions to respondents must be clear.

Such considerations are vital in mail-out questionnaires or other self-administered settings where the researcher isn't there to offer clarification or resolve misunderstandings. But even if the researcher *is* there, many people will be reluctant to voice their concerns or confusion. The result will be missing data because of non-response or, worse yet, complete data that are unreliable and invalid because the question was misunderstood or responded to in a way only obliquely related to the real curiosities of the researcher.

An absent researcher cannot monitor other procedural aspects of the study. A mail-out questionnaire may be sent to a particular person, but someone other than the intended respondent may actually fill it out. Similarly, we can't know whether respondents took the task seriously, giving their most comprehensive and candid responses. Such problems are thought to be relatively uncommon, since people who aren't interested in and/or serious about the topic of study are likely to simply ignore the questionnaire and fail to return it. But to the extent that such tendencies *do* exist, they make the data less valid.

The researcher's presence in some self- and group-administered questionnaire studies allows him or her to make sure that the appropriate person(s) complete the questionnaire and to watch for cues that some individuals may not be taking the task seriously. But the researcher's presence may bring its own problems.

Higher response rates may benefit the researcher, but if they result from group pressures for conformity in participation, ethical issues arise. Further, participants who are implicitly or explicitly coerced into participation may sabotage the data, for example, by responding in a flippant, random, or neutral manner. Those who respond flippantly (e.g., by answering "as often as I can" in response to a question that asks them to indicate "sex," or "Mars" to a question about their birthplace) are easily identified. Those who intentionally respond randomly or neutrally are harder, if not impossible, to identify; their impact on the data will be to make significant group differences or correlations among variables less likely to be found.

COST AND EFFICIENCY

The major advantage of questionnaires is that they generate a substantial amount of data relatively quickly and cheaply, at least in some cases. This is particularly true of group-administered questionnaires, where it's not impossible to obtain dozens of completed questionnaires within a day (e.g., when administering questionnaires to students in classrooms or to people waiting in line to see a film).

Overall, questionnaires are an optimal alternative when your budget is limited, the questions you want to ask are relatively straightforward, and you're interested only in acquiring a fairly large, heterogeneous sample (rather than a formally representative one). Table 6.1 shows some of the advantages and disadvantages of the different questionnaire techniques.

Interview Techniques

TELEPHONE SURVEYS

Large-scale survey research formerly relied on face-to-face interviews with samples of people identified on a geographical basis, since this was the only way to acquire large representative samples of the general population. But from approximately the 1960s onward, those who enjoy gathering large sets of perceptual data turned more and more to telephone interview techniques. Several factors drove that transition.

The telephone went from a high-tech development that few people had to an essential tool of life in the industrialized world. Concerns that were voiced in the 1930s and 1940s about the selection bias involved in contacting samples via telephone (i.e., because only wealthier people had telephones) had all but vanished by the 1970s and 1980s. In such countries as the United States and Sweden, 94 percent to 99 percent of all households can now be reached by phone. In Canada, as long ago as 1987, the Canadian Radio-television and Telecommunica-

tions Commission released data showing that "98.5 per cent of Canadian households had phones, almost double the number in 1947" (see "Phone Has Become ..." 1989: F6).

There were other reasons that telephone surveys supplanted the in-person interview as the most commonly used survey technique. The costs of in-person interviews were rising rapidly, and telephone surveys offered an inexpensive alternative with little or no loss in response rates. Personal safety was also becoming a concern, particularly in urban centres in the United States. And these concerns went both ways. Respondents were becoming increasingly reluctant to allow strange interviewers into their homes but remained willing to "let them in" by phone. For their part, interviewers were becoming increasingly worried about their own safety as they walked the streets in some neighbourhoods, going door-to-door. Contact by telephone was safer for them, too.

The centralization of telephone interviewing also meant that research directors could take greater care in monitoring "quality control." Conversations between interviewers and respondents could be taped and critically analyzed for training purposes. And instead of losing prospective respondents for whom English was not a first or preferred language, a group of interviewers could be amassed who, collectively, could handle a broad variety of language situations in one centralized location (e.g., see Gorden 1980). The development of random digit dialing (RDD) techniques for a time made quasi-representative sampling a real possibility.

Nowadays, however, the telephone survey or poll is waning rapidly. RDD has become ineffective because a phone number is no longer tied to a particular family or social unit in a particular place; phone companies now let subscribers carry their phone numbers within the same area code so that the connection between localized neighbourhoods and phone exchanges is rapidly becoming a thing of the past. People also now have multiple phone numbers and multiple phones—cell phones, faxes, the home phone—which makes sampling difficult. In addition, far too many harassing phone calls from

Table 6.1

Advantages and Disadvantages of Different Questionnaire Methods

All Types of Questionnaires	Group-Administered Questionnaire	Self-Administered Questionnaire	Mail-Out Questionnaire
Advantages/Strengths			
Easy to offer respondent anonymity and for respondent to feel that anonymity is provided	Can clarify questions for respondents if they ask	If researcher is there, can respond to questions and clarify ambiguities	You can cover a large area for the cost of postage only
Good way to amass a lot of data quickly	High response rates, especially in "captive" settings	Medium response rates among questionnaire techniques	Good way to get a heterogeneous sample
Relatively inexpensive compared to interview techniques	Useful when population of interest works or resides in a certain location	Respondent can answer in privacy	Anonymity is maximized
Structured questions make for easy data coding and compilation	Easy for respondents to see that the process is anonymous	Good for sensitive issues where anonymity is provided	
Disadvantages/Limitations			
Literacy is required to complete questionnaire	Privacy may not be guaranteed if respondents are shoulder-to-shoulder	Researcher, if not present, cannot clarify ambiguities	Thick questionnaire and reminder mailings will add to postage costs
Vocabulary must be appropriate for full range of respondents	Respondents may be influenced by vocal respondents who make comments aloud	Misinterpreted questions and non-responses not caught by researcher until too late	Researcher cannot clarify ambiguities or misinterpretations
Researcher's data are limited to what's on the paper (i.e., no nonverbal or contextual cues)			Usually low response rates
			Can't tell whether it was the intended respondent who actually completed the questionnaire

salespeople phoning in the guise of a survey have made it more and more difficult for serious researchers to distinguish themselves from entrepreneurs. Although telephone surveys are still conducted, for more serious polling purposes they are a disaster waiting to happen. Thoughtful and forward-looking survey companies are hedging their bets and looking elsewhere.

FACE-TO-FACE INTERVIEWS

Although the interview is common to both qualitative and quantitative research traditions, the way it "looks" in a given research setting can vary considerably. How the interaction is formulated, the logic that guides how respondents are sampled, how the process is administered, and the sorts of objectives that characterize it all vary depending on the researcher's research objectives, theoretical interests, and epistemological stance.

HIGHER RATES OF PARTICIPATION Many of the disadvantages of questionnaires are handled admirably by the interview. Participation rates among people approached for a face-to-face interview are often around 80 percent or even 90 percent; this is comparable to some self- and group-administered questionnaires and considerably better than mail-out questionnaires. Thus, volunteer bias is generally less of a problem with interviews.

BENEFITS OF CONTACT The interaction of interviewer and respondent also offers benefits that can enhance the quality of the data gathered. The interviewer can ensure that the appropriate person completes the interview, can clarify immediately any confusion about particular questions, and can encourage verbally stingy respondents to embellish further. Also, since the interviewer asks questions and writes down responses, the respondent needn't be literate. And although some participants may feel less anonymity in the personalized interview setting than with the impersonal questionnaire, skilled interviewers can often build sufficient rapport to alleviate such misgivings. Finally, the rapport that's built may have longer-term benefits for researchers engaging in longitudinal research, since respondents may be more willing to participate in **panel studies** involving repeated interviews.

TIME AND COST The biggest disadvantages of face-to-face interviews are their cost and the time required to complete a large-scale interview study. While it wouldn't be unusual for a questionnaire study to cost $4 or $5 per participant or for a telephone interview study to cost $20 to $25 per participant, conducting the same study by face-to-face interview might well cost $50 or even $100 or more per participant. But comparing these estimates may be deceptive, since they reflect alternatives that aren't equally likely to occur. As quantitative researchers seeking large data sets have leaned more and more toward using telephone surveys, the realm of the face-to-face interview has, for the most part, been vacated to more qualitatively oriented researchers, who are more likely to do the interviewing themselves than to hire teams of research assistants to amass huge sets of aggregate data.

WHERE THE ACTION IS This very shift tells us something about how the process of face-to-face interviewing is conceived differently from questionnaires or telephone surveys. Large-scale quantitative researchers place great emphasis on the design phase of survey questionnaires; the "highest priced talent" *designs* the survey instrument, while the survey's actual *execution* is often relegated to the "lowest priced talent," that is, part-time assistants who often have little commitment to the data and may not even know who's sponsoring the study or what its purpose is (beyond what can be determined from the superficial content). In contrast, more qualitatively oriented researchers typically value the process of data gathering as much as the design of the research instrument itself. As a result, both the study's design and its execution are undertaken by the "highest priced talent."

Embedded here are two very different views of the data-gathering process. Recall that among quantitative researchers, the role of the researcher-as-expert is to determine what is important to ask; after that, *anyone* can gather data, as long as he or she is properly trained to be neutral, detached, and standardized in delivery. Qualitative researchers view the data-gathering process itself as informative, maintaining that one must be open to any new directions that may emerge in the context of the interview because of the unique perspective of the participant(s). Doing so effectively requires people who are familiar with the participants and with the phenomenon under study, and who clearly understand the research objectives so that they can make responsible decisions about what to do in the unique situations that emerge with every interview.

Because of other preferences held by those who engage in qualitative study (e.g., a phenomenological perspective, an inductive approach, an emphasis on case study analysis in context), face-to-face interviews look very different from telephone surveys or mail-out surveys simply because the qualitative researcher is much less likely to be trying to amass huge sets of standardized data for nomothetic analysis. Face-to-face interviews tend to be longer and more detailed, tend to seek greater depth of response, and tend to be more open-ended in their construction to allow for phenomenological input from respondents. They're also more likely to be situated in some context (e.g., an organization, a group, a limited geographical setting such as a neighbourhood) that plays an important role in the analysis.

HUMANIZING THE PROCESS This more intimate connection between the researcher and respondent may have many benefits associated with it, such as greater likelihood of developing rapport, but the interview's interactive nature also means that one must be more careful about *reactive* bias. Interviewees can be very attentive to cues that the interviewer emits, since they want to know whether they are "doing well" as participants. Thus, what you choose to write down out of their verbal responses and even your supportive and encouraging "uh-huhs" or nods of the head may be taken as cues about what the interviewee "should" be talking about. One must avoid leading the interviewee.

Finally, although a sensitive interviewer may reassure the respondent about confidentiality, interviews clearly generate less of a feeling of anonymity than do impersonal questionnaires. Considerable effort must therefore be made to ensure that rapport is created and that the interviewee legitimately believes there is no reason to feel threatened. We say "legitimately" here on the assumption that that is true. Obviously, where possibilities for repercussions exist—whether to the individual or to his or her group—because of the results of the study, ethical practice requires that respondents be informed of that possibility and that researchers build in safeguards to the extent possible.

DEALING WITH THE DATA Lastly, the interviewer must make some choices about how to retain

responses, and each choice has its advantages and disadvantages. If the choice is to write down verbatim responses to questions, the process can become quite tedious and may well interrupt the flow of the interview while the respondent waits for the interviewer to finish writing down each response. The researcher may therefore choose to write down only summaries or major points from the response, but then distortion may occur, or matters that are subsequently found to be important may be left out.

Another possibility is to tape (using audio or video recording) the interview. This approach frees the interviewer to pay attention to the interviewee, although some would advise that the interviewer should occasionally jot down notes in any event, because doing so helps the interviewer retain the flow of the interview, because most respondents expect you to write something down every so often, and because notes give you some backup in case a technical foul-up renders the tape useless and you must regenerate the content of the interview from memory. On the other hand, transcribing tape responses is expensive, and the permanence and unforgiving accuracy of tape may inhibit candour.

FOCUS GROUP INTERVIEWS

The focus group interview is essentially a group version of the face-to-face interview. Focus groups have an extensive history in marketing research, but have only more recently been discovered by the broader social scientific community (D. L. Morgan 1988; Morgan & Spanish 1984). Such groups normally involve a *target sample* or *purposive sample* of informants brought together to discuss the phenomenon in which the researcher is interested. As Fontana and Frey (1994) note, "The group interview is not meant to replace individual interviewing, but it is an option that deserves consideration because it can provide another level of data gathering or a perspective on the research problem not available through individual interviews" (364).

In marketing, a group of typical consumers might be brought together to discuss their preferences, what they value in an existing product, or what they might like to see in a developing product. General Motors, for example, might be interested in designing a new truck and might hire a research agency to bring together a group of truck owners to discuss what features they believe should be included in the design. Marketing researchers also have used focus groups to assess other products and their packaging, such as politicians.

In the social sciences, however, the "product" the researcher wants to develop may be a questionnaire or a completed study. The participants would be invited because of their relevance to the phenomenon of interest to the researcher. An early example of this (cited by D. L. Morgan 1988) would be Merton and Kendall's (1946) effort to evaluate the persuasiveness of wartime propaganda; more recently, Morgan and Spanish (1985) created focus groups to generate discussions concerning perceptions of risk factors involved in heart attacks, and D. L. Morgan (1986) brought together focus groups of widows as part of his investigation into bereavement. One can envision innumerable other uses, including government administrators discussing organizational processes or policy objectives, film directors discussing how they reconcile their own beliefs with the market-oriented pressures of funding agencies, and groups of parents discussing education policies in relation to their children's schools.

UNIQUE ADVANTAGES Such groups may serve several purposes for researchers. D. L. Morgan (1988) explains that focus groups can be used productively when

> orienting oneself to a new field; generating hypotheses based on informants' insights; evaluating different research sites or study populations; developing interview schedules and questionnaires; [and] getting participants' interpretations of results from earlier studies. (11)

Focus groups also may provide provocative and/or insightful information to the exploratory researcher who is looking for unanticipated consequences to organizational interventions; is interested in determining issues of importance to those in the

research setting or in acquiring new insights about the phenomenon from those who have experienced it; and/or is trying to develop research instruments (e.g., questionnaires, interview schedules, sampling strategies) that have integrity with respect to the phenomenology of those under study.

But the usefulness of focus groups is not limited to exploratory research. After a piece of research is completed, for example, and the researcher has analyzed and interpreted the data, this information might be imparted to additional focus groups for discussion. Such discussions may help the researcher gather alternative interpretations for further consideration and generate additional hypotheses and/or research questions on which to focus subsequent research. Indeed, it was for exactly this purpose that Merton, Fiske, and Kendall (1956) originally coined the term "focus group" (see Fontana & Frey 1994).

Although focus groups have much in common with the traditional in-person interview, D. L. Morgan (1988) argues that their inherent social dynamic gives them at least two unique advantages. First, instead of simply taking an inventory of opinion through individual interviews, the focus group setting places opinions "on the table" where differences between perspectives can be highlighted and negotiated. This process allows participants to embellish on positions, discuss related dynamics, and articulate the rationale(s) underlying their perspective. Blumer (1969) advocates identifying a small number of informed participants who are acute observers in any social setting of interest, and then states that "a small number of such individuals brought together as a discussion and resource group is more valuable many times over than any representative sample" (41). D. L. Morgan (1988) adds that a second major advantage of focus groups is the opportunity to "witness" (as opposed to "influence") extensive interaction on a topic within a relatively limited time frame.

AND UNIQUE COMPLICATIONS, TOO While some advantages accrue from the social composition of focus groups, this characteristic can also pose problems. Some people will be less comfortable than others in expressing their opinions publicly; people with more extreme or unique views may be reluctant to expose them to possible ridicule; and people will undoubtedly be more concerned about maintaining their image in a public setting than in a one-to-one interview. Fontana and Frey (1994) reaffirm Merton and colleagues' (1956) view that three skills are particularly important in the group interviewer's repertoire:

> First, the interviewer must keep one person or a small coalition of persons from dominating the group; second, he or she must encourage recalcitrant respondents to participate; and third, he or she must obtain responses from the entire group to ensure the fullest possible coverage of the topic. (365)

Thus, focus groups may be seen as a useful vehicle for encouraging the embellishment and negotiation of public opinion, while the traditional single-person interview or questionnaire acts as a complementary expression of privately held opinions or "secret ballots."

The focus group also accords a less central but no less important role to the researcher. In an interview involving one researcher and one participant, the respondent can look only to the researcher for direction. The researcher in the focus group setting generally plays a more facilitative and less directive role. Although the researcher can set up a structured situation, he or she typically acts only to initiate, prompt, and referee the discussion. Accordingly, one might infer that the results will be influenced more by the group than by the researcher.

In sum, focus group interviews are compatible with an array of research objectives, and while they possess their own limitations, they also offer unique strengths. They thus seem a currently under-utilized addition to the social science researcher's procedural repertoire.

ORAL HISTORIES

There are two types of oral history, only one of which will be considered in detail here. Be sure you understand the difference between them. The one

that receives only passing attention in this book is the type of oral history remembered and practised by Aboriginal peoples in North America.

ABORIGINAL ORAL HISTORIES Until relatively recently, most North American Aboriginal cultures were primarily oral cultures. Consistent with this emphasis, Aboriginal peoples made extensive use of oral history, where the role of particular individuals would be to remember certain stories about their people's history, rather like walking archives.

These memories weren't merely the recollection of stories, as might have happened when your parents told you a story when you were a child, but were in fact "lived memorizations" and verbatim accounts that would be repeated in the same manner 50 years from now as they would be today. Indeed, contemporary oral histories are often found to be identical to those recorded by anthropologists at the turn of the 20th century (e.g., see Mills 1994). Part of their integrity came from the fact that one of the "jobs" of each new generation required accurately learning and remembering the stories handed down by previous generations.

Another part of their integrity came through their having survived the rigorous process of ongoing challenges to their accuracy. Among the Aboriginal peoples of the northwest coast, for example, this process occurred in the context of the feast (potlatch) system. On appropriate occasions, each speaker recounted, in this most public of settings, the history of his or her clan, the boundaries of the clan's territories, and the way its crests and songs had been acquired. Anyone at the feast could challenge this oral history; the lack of challenge signalled acceptance that the account was valid (e.g., see Gisday Wa & Delgam Uukw 1992; Mills 1994).

We make these points for two main reasons. First, we want to encourage respect for the oral histories of Aboriginal peoples. Because of Europeans' and other non-Aboriginal peoples' reliance on written documentation and reverence for materials in written archives, many Europeans and non-Aboriginals have ethnocentrically assumed that no documentary history meant "no history" (e.g., see

Wolf 1982), and that oral histories are little more than some sort of quaint, ever-changing cultural fairy tale. This is far from the truth. Yet such views have been used by colonial powers to dismiss Aboriginal histories and thereby deny Aboriginal rights.[1] Second, we've made this point to put the oral histories we'll deal with in this chapter into perspective.

ORAL HISTORY IN SOCIAL SCIENCE Broadly defined, "history" is everything that happened before you read this sentence. And now even that sentence has receded into history. We can never know *everything* about history, but that hasn't stopped historians and the rest of us who are interested in history from trying to understand it. In trying to do so, we realize one of the challenges of understanding history: it isn't here anymore. We thus cannot study history directly, but must do so by looking at those pieces and remnants of history that remain.

WHAT'S IN THE BOX? Now, let's imagine that the history we *can* study is all contained in a huge box. Of all that happened in that huge period of time we know as "history," the only things we can base our study of history on are the things inside that box, because those are the only things that remain. And while many things get inside the box, many things do not. For example, last weekend, Ted's son Felix pitched an absolutely great game against the best team in his Little League; it was the only game that team lost all year. Felix was extremely happy about it, and Ted was glad he was there to see Felix play. It was an enjoyable moment for both of them as father and son.

But 100 years from now, when some historian sits down to write something about early 21st century humanity—even if he or she is writing about "father–son relationships in the early 21st century"— there isn't a chance in the world that this future historian will write about the day Ted's son pitched such a great game and Ted was there to watch. Why? Because that bit of human history, while as real as the fact that Ottawa is the capital of Canada, will never make it into the box of human events out of which future historians will manufacture history.

Or will it? Ironically, our describing that experience here makes it possible that some historian in 2107 actually *will* see some dilapidated old copy of this book and discover the fact about Felix and his dad and Felix's great day of pitching. Because we've put it in writing, a fact that would otherwise be recalled by no one besides Felix and his dad (neither of whom will be around by then) is now part of the contents of the box of study-able human history. It's actually a very interesting example of **selective deposit,** a phenomenon we'll discuss in more detail in Chapter 8. This term reflects the recognition that some things have a higher likelihood of being put into the box than others, and that some people and groups have better access to the box than others do. It's interesting, for example, that, in Ted's role as dad, he has very little likelihood of accessing the box. No one outside his immediate family will probably ever have any sense of him as a parent. But in his roles as university professor and author, he has somewhat more access to the box, as evidenced by this book, which is now part of the written historical record.

One of the tragedies of history is that so much that would be interesting to know will remain forever beyond our grasp because it was never placed inside the box. It's interesting to consider what sorts of biases have entered into that process. What people or groups have been systematically *less* likely to have had a chance to put something in the box? And what people or groups have had much *better* access to the box, allowing them to influence our sense of history by placing their experiences into the box?

Clearly, some people have had better access to the box than others. Governments, the rich, the powerful, the upper classes, and the educated have all had better access to the box than individual citizens, the poor, the vulnerable, the lower classes, and the illiterate. Similarly, because of the history of patriarchy in many non-Aboriginal traditions,[2] it is also the case that men—because until relatively recent times, it was primarily they who formed the governments, controlled the property and wealth, and had better access to education—have had better access to the box than women. When historians open the box to try to understand history, the "facts" they look at are therefore not *all* the facts, or even a representative sample of facts, but only the facts placed there by those who had access to the box. So when we try to look at what life was like in, say, 17th-century England or 15th-century Spain, we're relying most typically on the views of the rich, the powerful, and the educated and on the views of men. Even when we find material about others whose experience we also would like to understand—the daily life of the average 15th-century Spanish peasant, say—it's rarely through *their* eyes that we see the world around them, but rather through the eyes of non-peasants who had access to the box.

RECTIFYING THE IMBALANCE OF WRITTEN HISTORY

Oral history is partly a way of trying to deal with the problems of access just outlined. It recognizes and to some extent shares the general European bias in favour of written documentation, and therefore tries to get material into the box that wouldn't otherwise be there. Oral history is consequently seen by many as "an interview technique with a mission." Fontana and Frey (1994), for example, note that "oral history does not differ from the unstructured interview methodologically, but in purpose" (368), where the purpose is to take material that otherwise might have been forgotten and make it part of the written record. Reinharz (1992) adds that "oral history … is useful for getting at *people* less likely to be engaged in creating written records and for creating historical accounts of *phenomena* less likely to have produced archival material" (131; emphasis in original). By interviewing people about their past, we "recover" parts of history that might otherwise have been lost; by interviewing people about their present, we help ensure that their record is available for future generations.

Although examples of collected oral history narratives go back to antiquity, "its modern formal organization can be traced to 1948, when Allan Nevins began the Oral History Project at Columbia University" (Starr 1984: 4, cited by Fontana & Frey 1994: 368). That quotation, of course, has a certain delicious irony, since it's another example of how people with access to the box of history (like academics at prestigious universities) are the ones whose contributions we remember and can cite because they're part of the written record.

Because of the nature of the mission associated with oral history, you shouldn't be surprised to discover that the technique has been particularly popular among people who are on the margins of society—minorities, the poor, street people, and women, for example—and/or among those who are interested in engaging in research with such people. Oral history narratives exist *en masse* for many of the "common people" of history whose experience would otherwise be ignored or forgotten. Examples include collections in which people talk about their working lives (e.g., Terkel 1975), as well as more specific projects that focus on Pennsylvania steelworkers and their families, women working in Baltimore canneries (e.g., Olson & Shopes 1991), the experience of Blacks in the Vietnam War (Terry 1984), Palestinian women engaged in resistance activities (e.g., Gluck 1991), and a staggering array of other groups. No doubt many others haven't yet seen the light of day; as Fontana and Frey (1994) note, "often, oral history transcripts are not published but may be found in libraries, silent memoirs awaiting someone to rummage through them and bring their testimony to life" (368).

Recently, oral history methods have found particular favour among many feminist researchers, who see oral history methods as a way to rectify the gender imbalance in the largely male-dominated documentary archives of history. Gluck and Patai (1991) note that

> The first major body of literature on women's oral history appeared in late 1977 in a special issue of *Frontiers: A Journal of Women's Studies*. This ground-breaking issue served as the key reference on women's oral history for many years, and the suggested outlines for women's oral history interviews that appeared at the back of the journal were xeroxed, dittoed, and mimeographed by women in communities and classrooms around the country. (4)

Emphasizing the gathering of women's oral histories is thus a way to include women's voices in history: "Refusing to be rendered historically voiceless any longer, women are creating a new history—using our own voices and experiences" (Gluck 1984: 222). Reinharz (1992) suggests that women's oral history actually serves a threefold function: drawing women out of obscurity, repairing the historical record, and providing stories of people with whom women readers and authors can identify.

QUESTIONS ABOUT RESEARCH RELATIONSHIPS
While feminist engagement in oral history is thus rewarding in its own right, involvement in this massive oral history project has also prompted feminists to lead the way in contemporary reconsiderations of oral history in particular, interviewing in general, and, even more broadly, the whole set of relations between respondents and researchers. The concern is not only that men's voices dominate history, since this imbalance could be addressed simply by using techniques like oral history to rectify it, but also that the methods available to us now, since they were conceived in a traditionally male-dominated social science, are often particularly "male" in the way they're conceived, designed, and executed. Many feminist researchers who took the plunge into oral history research found that straight application of the methods they'd been taught in graduate school needed reconsideration. Minister (1991), for example, observes that

> the male subcommunication subculture is assumed to be the norm for social science interviewing ... If women aspire to become approved oral historians, they must learn to control topic selection with questions, must make certain that one person talks at a time, and must encourage narrators to "take the floor" with referential language that keeps within the boundaries of selected topics. (31)

Minister clearly doesn't intend to encourage women to aspire to those essentials. Instead, she argues that women must carve out their own version of oral history, a version that's more sensitive to, and a better reflection of, women's ways of communicating.

> We will not hear what women deem essential to their lives unless we legitimate a female socio-communication context for the oral history situation. As Sue Armitage says, "We will learn what we want to know only by listening to people who are not accustomed to talking." (31–32)

Anderson and Jack (1991) agree that more female-reflective approaches are required. They believe, for example, that men tend to look at the interview purely as an information-gathering session, so that designing an interview study becomes a strategic question of how best to order and compile questions and answers. In contrast, they believe women are more attuned to relationships and process and that woman-to-woman interviews must reflect that difference:

> Realizing the possibilities of the oral history interview demands a shift in methodology from information gathering, where the focus is on the right questions, to interaction, where the focus is on process, on the dynamic unfolding of the subject's viewpoint. (23)

A major problem crops up when interviewing women, according to Anderson and Jack (1991). Because men's experience has defined much of contemporary existence, women have become used to talking in dual narratives: using concepts that reflect men's cultural domination, but focusing on their own experience, which may or may not be adequately captured by those schemas. Feminist oral history researchers must therefore be particularly sensitive to reading between the lines:

> We need to hear what women implied, suggested, and started to say but didn't. We need to interpret their pauses and, when it happens, their unwillingness or inability to respond. We need to consider carefully whether our interviews create a context in which women feel comfortable

exploring the subjective feelings that give meaning to actions, things, and events, whether they allow women to explore "unwomanly" feelings and behaviours, and whether they encourage women to explain what they mean in their own terms. (17)

This process is clearly an interpretive one. However understandable the position, it's also fraught with complexity and paradox. At issue here is the question of "voice" and, especially, whose voice (if either) dominates the final look of the text that's produced from the interview. An excellent self-critical analysis by Borland (1991) of an oral history interview she did with her grandmother highlights the dilemma well. The article focuses on an experience for which Borland's interpretations of "what was *really* going on" and "what was *really* being said" were completely different from her grandmother's. Rejection of the interpretation by her grandmother after reading the first draft led to further discussion, further revising, and some movement on the parts of both women as they tried to reach jointly satisfactory resolution of the meaning of the original episode.

One of the central tenets of feminist research is that women must be able to say things in their own voice and that voice must be heard. Male-dominated science is seen as an inappropriate model to the extent that it embodies hierarchical relations between the researcher and those researched, where an "expert" researcher "extracts" data from "subjects" and then reinterprets it according to a "culturally sanitized" (i.e., male-dominated) "spin." Instead of treating each other like researcher and respondent, many feminists aim to do research in the same egalitarian and respectful manner in which one might interview one's friend or grandmother. Anderson and Jack's (1991) assertions seem to question that sort of face-value acceptance, seeing the task as one of reading between the lines and finding what the women being interviewed are "really" saying and what they "really" mean by it.

Many feminist researchers (including Borland 1991, as noted) have wrestled with these issues.

Their analyses can make us all aware of how our professional zeal may lead us to usurp others' voices and to take for granted some things that perhaps shouldn't be accepted. Black feminists, for example, argue that sisterhood has its limits if it means homogenizing women's experience in a way that doesn't do justice to the equally meaningful and simultaneously marginalizing experience of race (e.g., see Collins 1991; Etter-Lewis 1991; Fine 1994; Olesen 1994), while others make the same point regarding Latina (e.g., see Benmayor 1991), Aboriginal (e.g., see Greschner 1992; Monture-Okanee 1993; Petersen 1994), and Third World women (e.g., see Hale 1991; Patai 1991; Salazar 1991). All call for research considerations that acknowledge and respect cultural differences

Computer-Assisted Social Research

The Internet is expanding at an unprecedented rate; its growth has eclipsed all other technologies preceding it (Dahlen 2002). Between 1994 and 1998 50 million people logged on to the Internet worldwide; it took 38 years for radio and 13 years for television to acquire the same user base (United Nations 2004). It is clear that the Internet is the fastest-growing information and communications medium to date, and it will not be long before it is as common as the television or the telephone (Dahlen 2002). At present, Internet traffic doubles every 100 days; in December 2005 one billion people worldwide were online (United Nations, 2004).

Prior to the popularization of the Internet, Kiesler and Sproull (1986) provided a roadmap for using networked computers to conduct social science research. While they were optimistic about the potential of computer technology, they felt that "until such time as computers and networks spread throughout society, the electronic survey will probably be infeasible" (p. 403). The available statistics on the growth of computer technologies such as the Internet provide ample evidence that the technological revolution that we have witnessed over the past 20 years makes it impossible to ignore the research possibilities envisioned by Kiesler and Sproull.

PRACTICAL BENEFITS AND BURDENS

CASR brings with it a number of practical benefits and burdens. One of the most cited is the effect that implementing a computer-assisted design has on the speed and duration of the research process; CASR can be much faster than comparable traditional designs. In network environments the footwork of the design and administration process is done by network connections. Research teams can create, edit, and finalize the research instrument without the burden of scheduling and attending physical meetings, and the research team can administer the design without having to physically connect with the participant.

Once in motion, CASR allows researchers to move from observation to analysis much more quickly than conventional research designs. Finally, when research is conducted over wide area networks such as the Internet, observations can be made and data collected 24 hours a day, 7 days a week. This being said, in some cases the initial design and administration of the research can be prohibitively time-consuming. When the research team is inexperienced with the use of technology or the technological infrastructure for the research is not already in place, extra training and the installation and testing of hardware and software may be necessary. Furthermore, researchers who are new to the technology are more likely to make errors during the administration and observation stages that can result in even greater time delays in the research.

When it comes to the cost of materials and labour there are several distinct differences between CASR and conventional research methods. The hardware, software, and scripting that is required for the observation and data collection portion of a CASR project can cost researchers thousands of dollars. However, researchers can offset the software and scripting costs by using freely available open-source software and scripts instead of high-priced commercial applications. Furthermore, while equipment and design costs can be high, these costs are generally recouped

through savings on paper, postage, transcription, mileage, lodging, the renting of research venues, and repeated research. While it is uncommon to find hard-to-estimate human labour costs factored into discussions of many traditional data collection methods, the introduction of computer programmers and graphic and web designers into the CASR design process has made many social science researchers begin to account for the cost of labour. The hourly rate that most programmers and designers charge can reach as high as $120. The result is that in some situations CASR can be quite a cost-effective solution for the North American researcher. This advantage does however depend on researchers having enough experience with technology that they can implement solutions that require specialized user and programming skills.

It is important to recognize that there can be considerable start-up material and personnel costs associated with CASR, but repeated research is less costly since much of the investment is saddled by the first project and the cost of upgrading vital research materials is much less than first-time creation expenditures. Moreover, researchers should keep in mind that some research designs are more cost-effective than others. For example, the simple e-mail–based questionnaire, where questions are placed in the body of the e-mail, costs almost nothing to administer, while complex computer-assisted experimental and quasi-experimental designs that require special hardware and software can cost tens of thousands of dollars.

In addition to considerations of time and money, many CASR designs also dramatically alter the physical research environment. Research such as experimental, focus group, personal interview, or ethnography that would normally require a physical space can be conducted in a networked environment (Birnbaum & Wakcher 2002; Buchanan & Smith 1999; Evans et al. 2003; Karr 2000). Additionally, with the increasing availability and affordability of handheld and laptop computers and wireless networks, researchers are not confined to any one physical locale in order to collect and analyze data. However, problems associated with powering the computer can limit how long a researcher can stay out in the field. This is particularly challenging for researchers conducting research in remote settings. Moreover, while the introduction of computer technology into the research setting has enhanced our ability to use highly controlled experimental designs that can be reproduced with ease and precision (Karr 2000), the inability for the researcher to be physically present in some virtual experimental settings can be quite prohibitive.

For research designs that are not dependent upon the physical presence of a researcher, network-based CASR facilitates the solicitation and recruitment of large, geographically and demographically diverse samples (Fox et al. 2003; Gosling et al. 2004). These larger samples make it possible to amass large amounts of data in a relatively short time.

The benefits of bypassing physical and geographic limitations extend beyond the acquisition of research participants to the coordination of the research process itself. Team meetings and research coordination are much more efficient as investigators are able to conduct virtual as opposed to physical project meetings where they can communicate their progress and observations or make changes to the research design without introducing confounding variables to the procedure.

BURGEONING POSSIBILITIES

Although using computers and network technology to collect data and make observations is clearly not appropriate for all social science research situations, there are many examples of situations where implementing technology is a viable methodological option. In primary data collection the goal is to collect original information from an identifiable population; techniques used include self-administered questionnaires, face-to-face interviews, telephone interviews, panel studies, and focus group designs. All of these conventional approaches to the collection of primary social science data can be adapted to CASR designs. In fact, many of these methodological approaches have been adapted by social researchers.

The computer-assisted self-administered questionnaire (CASQ) comes in three main varieties—disk-based, e-mail, and web-based (Truell et al. 2002). Like its traditional counterpart, this mode of data collection is perhaps the most widely used within the social science research community. The oldest and most basic form of CASQ is disk-based administration. With this technique participants are given a floppy disk, CD, or portable drive that contains a questionnaire that can be completed on a personal computer (PC). Responses are either stored back on the disk or they are sent automatically across a network. With the increased availability of the World Wide Web (WWW) and e-mail, this mode of CASQ is not used as often; however, some researchers have found it a useful option for targeted populations (Hampton & Wellman 1999).

E-mail is one of the simplest and most used network information and communication components. Eighty-nine percent of networked communications is accomplished via e-mail (Jackson & De Cormier 1999). As a result, e-mail is seen by many as the most effective mode of CASQ (Hessler et al. 2003; Sheehan & Hoy 1999). E-mail questionnaires can be divided into three distinct types: simple e-mail messages with questions in the body of the e-mail text (either plain or XHTML formatted text), separate documents that are attached to an e-mail, and embedded URLs in the body of an e-mail message that direct the user to a web-based CASQ (Bradley 1999). In all of these variants of the self-administered questionnaire, responses are either sent directly back to the researcher via e-mail in text form or attached in a separate file, or they are received via a web-based interface.

The massive expansion of access to and use of the WWW in public (Internet) and private (intranet) networked environments over the past ten years, accompanied by improvements in user interface and scripting support, has made web-based CASQs a very popular format for the collection of social science data (Dahlen 2002; Gosling et. al. 2004; Ross et. al. 2003). Web-based CASQs generally come in three varieties: an open website where no control is placed over who can visit the site or complete the questionnaire, a closed website where visitation and participation is controlled by an access restriction protocol (e.g., password or identity check), and hidden surveys that appear on websites after some form of scripted trigger mechanism is enacted (Bradley 1999). All of these options involve user responses being sent via a web browser directly to a research server where the information is compiled in either text form or in databases.

Many researchers wishing to implement a more direct-contact or open-ended observation and data-collection technique have opted to use computers and network technology to conduct interviews, panel studies, and focus groups. Computer-assisted interviewing (CAI) allows an interviewer or participant to use a computer program to guide them through the interview process. In most cases the computer provides a series of structured questions to the interviewer or respondent and answers are recorded directly into a program or database (Peiris, Gregor, & Alm 2000). This form of interviewing is rapidly becoming the most dominant mode of data collection for interviewer-administered structured surveys (Couper 2000; Gravlee 2002). Several variants of CAI have been used by social science researchers, including interactive voice response (IVR; Corkrey & Parkinson 2002), computer-assisted personal interviewing and mobile computer-assisted personal interviewing (CAPI/MCAPI; Gravlee 2002; Hampton & Wellman 1999), computer-assisted self-interviewing (CASI; Barrett & Barrett 2001, Cooleya et al. 2001), and computer-assisted telephone interviewing (CATI; Corkrey & Parkinson 2002). In research settings where the researcher is interested in collecting observations from a panel of participants (Crawford et al. 2001; MacElroy 1999) or a focus group (Ozer 1999; Sweet 2001; Tse 1999) computer-administered designs have also been found to be quite useful.

The introduction of computers and network technology as a medium for data collection and observation allows us to move social research design into the 21st century. While the approaches to data collection and observation listed above are excellent examples of how computer technology may be adapted to traditional observation and data collection instruments, they have not begun to tap into the potential that new technology offers.

ASKING QUESTIONS

Once you've decided on the interactive technique most appropriate for your situation, you're ready to formulate specific questions. This step involves two considerations on your part. First, you need some sense of the content you want to include or address in your questions (or, conversely, how open and free-ranging you want an interview to be). Second, you need to create concrete questions that will "tap" into that content; to do so, you need some sense of the different ways in which questions can be posed.

Question Content

We can't begin to count the number of times we've read undergraduate research papers that feature a good introduction that contextualizes the issues well by summarizing relevant literature and identifying a reasonable research question, followed by a reasonable "methods" section that includes a copy of the research instrument—but where the two don't match! This situation leads to some very interesting "discussion" and "conclusion" sections: students end up going through some incredible verbal acrobatics trying to actually say something about their research question from their data. Asking the wrong questions is one of *the* most common mistakes novice researchers make.

An Iterative Process Starting with General Objectives

Your research questions and research objectives should come first: none of the subsequent decisions you must make will be optimal unless you have a clear sense of what you're trying to accomplish. Once you know that, designing a research project becomes a matter of taking a series of steps in which you follow an iterative process and become progressively more specific in elaborating and defining the matters of interest to you. And as long as each step follows from the one before, you're assured that your final step (the questions you ask and the data you gather) will be connected to your first (your objectives). Thus, when you write your final paper or report, your data will "speak" to your objectives.

Let's look at an example. Several years ago when personal computers were first appearing and various organizations were just starting to see the benefits of computerizing or implementing a computer to assist their activities, Canada's federal Department of Communications approached Ted and asked him to do a behavioural evaluation of the Mobile Radio Data System (MRDS), a computer-based communications system that the Vancouver Police Department had installed in their cars and that was at that time state-of-the-art. The federal government had promoted its development, wanted to evaluate it, and had already undertaken an engineering evaluation and cost-benefit evaluation of the system; now they wanted to know in more behavioural terms how it was used and what people thought of it.

But "doing an evaluation" is a rather amorphous objective. The first thing the research team had to do was to develop a clearer understanding of what "doing an evaluation" would look like in this context. Discussion among the research group, as well as with people from the funding agency (the federal government department) and at the research site (the police department), led to the identification of two key components they wanted to examine: (1) attitudes about the system; and (2) how the system was used in the process of the organization's activities.

The next step was to begin moving from abstract "issues" or "phenomena" and to start considering how exactly these abstract concepts took on life with this system in this context. Attitudes about what aspects of the system? And on what basis could you start to understand system use? The team did some exploratory research to help identify salient issues. The research included a reading of some of the relevant "trade" literature (i.e., policing magazines and

journals that included articles discussing similar information systems); going on ride-alongs with patrol officers, both to see how they used the system and to have a chance to talk with them about it away from more formal meetings at headquarters; undertaking informal target and focus interviews with different people in the police department—patrol officers, administrative staff, dispatchers—to gain insight into their opinions about the system; and some final brainstorming among the research team members to identify issues of particular interest to the group as academics: the big issue that interested them, and which had captured their interest in the first place, was to try and understand the *implications* of what were then the first glimmerings of what would later become a burgeoning permeation of computerized information systems throughout society.

You can see this process beginning to unfold in Figure 6.1, which shows the beginning objective (to evaluate MRDS) followed by the various types of evaluations that were included (Engineering; Cost-Benefit; Social/Behavioural) and the first iteration of the social behavioural evaluation that identified the three main issues to be addressed in the social/behavioural evaluation—system use, satisfaction, and implications. As Figure 6.1 shows, in the end the research team was able to undertake a multi-method evaluation that would give a comprehensive view of the system and those who used it. You can read Palys, Boyanowsky, and Dutton (1983, 1984) for a description of the whole study; what we'd like to focus on here is the process they went through to generate their attitudinal survey items.

Figure 6.2 shows how the three domains of interest were taken through further iterations to get to an eventual set of items. For the first area—attitudes—the research team found several salient elements that seemed to contribute to the variety of attitudes that officers held about the system. These included effects of the system on job satisfaction (for some the system enhanced it; for others the system detracted from it); beliefs about impacts of the system on job effectiveness (some believed it helped them in their jobs; others believed it did nothing or detracted); beliefs about impact of the

Figure 6.1
Beginning Survey Construction Process from the VPD/MRDS Study

Engineering Study		
Cost/Benefit Study		
Evaluate MRDS / **Social/ Behavioural Study**	**Attitudes**	• Self-administered survey • 207 officers • Structured observation • 88 ridealongs × 4 hours • Semi-structured interview schedule • Administered on ride-alongs
	Use/Behaviour	• Archival data supplied/generated by VPD • Memos from implementation • System use data • Exploratory interviews • VPD Admin • VPD Patrol • VPD Dispatchers • VPD Technical
	Implications	• Other archival/professional literature • *The Police Chief* • *Sheriff's Star* • *Law and Order*

Figure 6.2

Development of Items in Survey Construction Process from the VPD/MRDS Study

Category	Item	Statement
ATTITUDES	Job Satisfaction	MRDS has had a positive effect on my job satisfaction.
	Effectiveness	I think MRDS helps me be a more effective officer. / MRDS produces so much information it makes me a less effective officer.
	Safety	I think MRDS makes policing a lot safer. / MRDS can create a false sense of security with suspects.
	(In)dependence	I find that with MRDS I end up relying on the system more and more.
	Relations with Community	I find I check out a lot more people now than I did before MRDS.
	Overall	Overall I like MRDS.
	Ease of data access	With MRDS I get information much more quickly than with radio only. / I feel tied to my car with MRDS.
	Frequency of Access	With MRDS I probably investigate cars or people I otherwise wouldn't have bothered with.
USE/BEHAVIOUR	1-person vs. 2-person patrol	MRDS is of less use when I'm on patrol by myself than when I have a partner.
	(Non)Stressful Situations	MRDS is of less use in highly stressful situations.
	MRDS vs. Radio	I would rather work in a radio-only car. / [Situational scenarios also addressed this element]
IMPLICATIONS	Implications for officers: • Professionalism • Man/Machine • Autonomy/Self-Def'n	[See "attitudes" section; also arose in more depth in interviews; big differences among officers in how they saw themselves and how they related to the machine; some viewed it as a duller of instincts and human connectedness, while others saw it as something that gave them autonomy, control, professionalism]
	Relations within VPD	MRDS makes me more independent of the dispatcher.
	Relations between police	Ultimately I think MRDS dehumanizes policing.

system on officer safety (some believed it enhanced safety; others thought it undermined it); and so on. Note, by the way, that the reason these elements were identified is because they were aspects of the system on which there was variability—people had different views about these elements—and the exploratory research had given the research team reason to believe that they were important in understanding overall views of the system.

If you proceed to the next column of Figure 6.2, you'll see that the next step was simply to create items—in this case they created what are called "Likert-type" items (these are explained later in this chapter) that involve statements of belief that respondents indicate their level of agreement or disagreement with—that reflected those various elements.

When the eventual attitude scale was administered to 200 officers in the organization, the results allowed the researchers to report back to both the federal department and the local organization with answers to the question they had been posed. Why? Because each step of the iterative process was connected to the one preceding, which meant that the product at the end of this design process—the very specific and concrete items respondents reacted to—had a very clear and demonstrable connection to the objective that started it all off.

As you can see, we need to do much of our thinking *ahead of time* when it comes to designing a questionnaire or interview. That includes doing the literature review and exploratory research that will allow us to create an informed and useful research instrument. It's all time well spent because it ensures that our objectives are indeed addressed by the data we gather.

Having gone through these considerations so that we know what content we wish to include, we must next address how to ask those questions. We noted above that the items from the MRDS survey were Likert-type items, but there are in fact many different ways to ask questions. The following section covers some of the variety of alternatives that are available.

Question Structure

The main types of questions are open-ended and closed or structured questions. An *open-ended ques-*

tion might be "What do you like most, and what do you like least, about this text?" or "What would be your overall evaluation of this course, and why?" Even more open-ended might be a simple probe like "Tell me how you feel about the course so far." A *closed* or *structured question* on the same topic might be "Please rate the quality of the textbook on a 5-point scale running from 1 (dislike the text a lot) to 5 (like the text a lot)." As you can see, open-ended questions leave a lot up to the respondent; they really are open to a wide range of responses, depending on the respondent's own concerns. Closed or structured questions, in contrast, allow the respondent only a small range of responses (e.g., filling in a blank, checking off a point on a rating scale) and involve some *presupposition* on the researcher's part about which aspects of a given issue are important to address.

OPEN-ENDED QUESTIONS

STRENGTHS As with virtually every other method described in this text, one cannot say that either open-ended or structured questions are better on some overall basis. Each has advantages and limitations in any particular research situation. Open-ended questions are clearly superior if the researcher is interested in hearing respondents' opinions in their own words, particularly in exploratory research, where the researcher isn't entirely clear about what range of responses might be anticipated. For example, you wouldn't want to ask a question like "Which of the following attributes do you think is the *most* important for a professor to be concerned with when teaching a course on research methods: (a) punctuality; (b) wears nice clothes; (c) easy exams; or (d) other?" only to discover when you went to analyze the data that 87 percent of the respondents checked off "other."

In exploratory and pilot research, the responses to an open-ended question can be used to create the alternatives for structured questions in a later study with more descriptive or explanatory objectives. Open-ended questions are also useful when you want to determine the salience or importance of opinions to people, since people tend to mention those matters that are most important to them first (see Kahneman, Slovic, & Tversky 1982). In this sense, open-ended questions can also operate as "indirect" measures, generating answers that are minimally affected by external influence or by suggestion emerging from the structure of the research instrument itself.

But you shouldn't feel that open-ended queries are suitable only for exploratory and small-sample research. Even in larger-scale studies, respondents enjoy being offered at least a few chances to express matters in their own words; at the very least, a space should be designated at the end for "anything else you would care to add that hasn't been adequately addressed" or "any comments you might care to add about the questionnaire." When interwoven within a structured questionnaire, open-ended items can be a rich source of illustrative vignettes that can be included in a final report and can provide material that helps the researcher interpret responses.

Finally, open-ended questions are also useful when the choice would otherwise be to offer an extremely long list. There are at least several hundred different occupations, for example; it would seem silly to try to compile a huge list of these for respondents, and then expect them to hunt through the list for theirs. A far easier alternative is simply to ask "What is your occupation?" or "How would you describe your occupation?"

LIMITATIONS Of course, open-ended questions also have disadvantages. It isn't advisable to include too many of them in a single questionnaire; after two or three, each additional question makes the respondent more likely to abandon the questionnaire without completing it. (People often get "turned off" when what's advertised as a questionnaire turns into an essay exam.) In interviews, the more open-ended the question—and the more such questions one asks—the more one requires time, a relatively private setting, and good rapport between interviewer and respondent.

The biggest drawback to open-ended questions is that the responses become incredibly cumbersome as your sample size and/or the number of questions increases. How do you *deal* with all these open-

ended responses you've gathered? The uniqueness of each person's priorities, views, and means of expression can make it seem that you have as many different categories as you have respondents. Making comparisons between different people, whether in the content or intensity or priority of the opinion they express, can become very difficult. To do it properly, content coding schemes must be developed, and coders must be trained and their interrater reliability assessed. Because of these difficulties, researchers, especially quantitative researchers engaged in studies with larger sample sizes, have tended to rely on more structured response alternatives that come "precoded." It's a much more efficient process. The major challenge is to ensure that the structured device does justice to the opinions and feelings that lie behind people's responses. Open-ended questions in smaller-sample exploratory, pilot, or field research are extremely useful for developing sensitive questionnaires.

CLOSED OR STRUCTURED QUESTIONS

Closed or structured questions have their own advantages and disadvantages. If the researcher has done a good job of considering the range of alternatives that might be considered, respondents get to consider the whole range of alternatives before making their own judgments about what category to code themselves into. The fact that all responses follow a standard form (e.g., using the same set of categorical alternatives or the same rating scale) makes comparability among respondents easier, since quantification or categorization is generally inherent to the item's structure (e.g., it's both easier and clearer for us to be able to say that "64 percent of males but only 37 percent of females agreed with the proposal" or that "males gave an average rating of 3.6 while females gave an average of 5.6 on the 7-point scale" than to explain and justify verbally any differences between respondent groups). Computerized scoring and analysis of data are also made easier.

Closed questions are also particularly useful when one wants to cover a lot of ground in a questionnaire or interview, since one can ask many more structured than open questions in a given period of time.

But you're obviously making a choice: do you go for *breadth* (lots of questions but relatively superficial responses) or *depth* (fewer questions but more elaborate responses)?

COMBINING OPEN-ENDED AND STRUCTURED QUESTIONS

A useful strategy involves actually combining open-ended and structured items. When doing so, you would generally include the open-ended questions on a given topic first. Part of the rationale for using open-ended items is an interest in hearing the respondents' words and concerns in a way minimally affected by the researcher. Putting closed or structured items first can subvert this aim by focusing the respondent's attention on certain attributes of the topic.

One commonly used technique is known as **funnelling:** first asking broad, open-ended questions on a topic and following up with successively narrower, more well-defined structured questions. Successive funnels can set the pacing and break the monotony of similarly formatted questions. For example, we might begin with a very general query about your evaluation of this textbook. Then we might ask an open-ended question about the book's organization and flow and funnel down to queries about specific aspects of organization and flow. Next might follow a second funnel from an open-ended question about the clarity of explanations in the book to more specific questions about particular sections or explanations.

The Variety of Structured Questions

SINGLE-RESPONSE ITEMS

One way to present a structured question is merely to ask it, giving respondents an empty space in which to write their response. This type of question is called a *single-response item*. The following three questions are of this type:

1. In what year were you born? _____
2. What was your total family income last year (before taxes)? $_____
3. What is your official job title in this organization? _____

Each asks the respondent to supply a very specific piece of information. But there can be problems associated with this form, since people are sometimes reluctant to provide an exact number or a one-word response, especially to questions about age and income or to those that suggest more complex responses. Respondents may therefore be more likely to skip the question or to give a simplistic response that doesn't really capture their opinions on an issue. You're left with missing data in the first instance and with incomplete or invalid data in the second. Moreover, if people don't have an exact response readily available (e.g., few people know their total family income down to the last dollar), a false sense of precision may result. The answers may *appear* very precise but may really be just "ballpark" guesses. If people *are* willing and able to provide the information, *single-response* items offer both precision and great flexibility in how responses will be aggregated across participants (e.g., they can be grouped by $5000 increments, $10 000 increments, etc.). So if you *can* ask a single-response question, do so; if you suspect that people may be unwilling to respond or unable to give precise information, choose a *categorical-response item* instead.

CATEGORICAL-RESPONSE ITEMS

Categorical-response items present categories in which respondents may place themselves. The simplest type of categorical question is the *dichotomous item*. As the prefix *di-* suggests, such questions have only two response alternatives. For example, the question "What is your sex?" has only two possible responses for most situations: you can be male or female.[3] Similarly, we might ask, "If a referendum were held tomorrow for the reinstatement of capital punishment, would you vote for or against?"

Although there are many "natural" dichotomies (e.g., sex is dichotomized into male and female), *any* continuum can be dichotomized. Attitudes about the death penalty, for example, can be seen as a continuum ranging from extreme support to complete rejection, or they might be dichotomized, as they were above, into "for" and "against." Whether you use a continuum or dichotomy would depend on your research purpose.

Such reduction inevitably means a loss of information, and may distort the phenomenon under consideration. For example, there was considerable discussion in Canada in the 1980s about capital punishment. Ardent supporters of the death penalty unerringly pointed to opinion polls that showed that approximately 75 percent of Canadians expressed support in answering a dichotomous question on the subject. But a more detailed analysis (Palys & Williams 1983) showed that most proponents were guarded in their enthusiasm, exhibiting considerable ambivalence about the death penalty's prospective application. The media image of Canada's collective run "back to the noose" was anything but accurate. Consistent with Palys and Williams's (1983) analysis, and quite in contrast to earlier media reports, a proposal on the issue was soundly defeated when it came before Parliament.

Other categorical items offer more than two categories. Here's an example:

What was your total family income last year (to the nearest dollar, before taxes)?

      (a) less than $10 000
      (b) $10 000 to $19 999
      (c) $20 000 to $29 999
      (d) $30 000 to $39 999
      (e) $40 000 or more

Categorical items offer several advantages. First, respondents are often more willing to place themselves into categories (especially with sensitive topics like income) than they are to give exact responses. Second, accuracy is less likely to be affected by ballpark guesses, since the question itself asks people to place themselves in a ballpark. The main disadvantage with categorical items is that they are considerably less flexible than single-response items; one can always aggregate categories together, but categories can never be taken apart. This problem may not affect a given study, since you choose category intervals appropriate to your particular needs and interests, but you might find it hard to compare the results of different studies (e.g., if you used $5000

increments to code income, and another study used $3000 increments).

There are two characteristics of categorical items you should concern yourself with. First, the categories must always be *exhaustive,* that is, they must cover all possible alternatives. Second, for most questions, the categories should be *mutually exclusive:* there should be no overlap between categories, that is, there should be only *one* category per respondent that is appropriate. In sum, there should be an alternative, but usually only *one* alternative, for everybody. The "income" question we gave you earlier met both of these criteria: no matter what your total family income, there was a category—and only *one* category—into which you could place yourself. But consider the following question:

What was your age in years at your last birthday?

      (a) less than 20
      (b) 20 to 30
      (c) 30 to 40
      (d) 40 to 50
      (e) 50 to 60

These categories are *not* mutually exclusive: they overlap. A person who is 30 years old, for example, could legitimately check either "b" or "c." Nor are the categories exhaustive. Which alternative do 65-year-olds choose, for example? There's no place for them. If you understand the notions of exclusivity and exhaustiveness, you should be able to rewrite the question above so that it meets these criteria.

Although categorical questions must always be exhaustive, one type of categorical question, the *multiple-response item,* does *not* require the respondent to choose only one alternative. For example, you might ask a question like this one:

Which of the following have you done in the last month? (check all that apply)

      (a) gone out to dinner at a restaurant
      (b) seen a film at a cinema
      (c) seen a play at a theatre

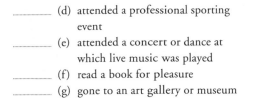

      (d) attended a professional sporting event

      (e) attended a concert or dance at which live music was played

      (f) read a book for pleasure

      (g) gone to an art gallery or museum

As always, the choice of issues to address will reflect your research objectives and/or theoretical curiosities, as will the content and range of alternatives offered. The above example might be appropriate for a marketing questionnaire or for a study of leisure preferences among members of some identified social groups.

A limitation of the response structures described thus far is that they look no further than simple dichotomies (did/did not; true/false; yes/no; no way/way) or category memberships (e.g., is or is not described by a given category). But in most situations, we are interested in embellished *continua* that are *scaled* by gradation.

RATING SCALES

A fourth type of structured question is the *rating scale,* which is extremely pervasive in social science research. As its name implies, such a question asks the respondent to rate some object on some attribute. Several types of rating scales are shown in Figure 6.3. The "satisfaction" scale used by T. Atkinson (1977) shown here is probably the most commonly used; it supplies verbal labels at either end of the scale, with numbers in between that the respondent would circle depending on the *direction* (or "valence") of his or her feelings (i.e., satisfied or unsatisfied) and on the *intensity* of those feelings (i.e., the number 7 expresses more intense satisfaction than the number 5).

There are many variations on this type of scale. Figure 6.3 shows a 1-to-7 scale, but there's nothing magical about 7-point scales. It's not unheard of to see 5-point, 10-point, or even 100-point scales. Some scales leave out the numbers entirely and merely present respondents with a line, and adjectives or descriptors at the ends; the respondent puts a stroke through the line at whichever point best rep-

resents his or her opinion. "Scores" or "ratings" are produced by measuring the distance from one end of the scale to the place where the stroke intersects.

The Cantril ladder (see Figure 6.3b), another type of rating scale, was first used in an international survey conducted some years ago (see Cantril 1965). Cantril was interested in people's evaluations of their quality of life. As a respondent, you would first have been asked to imagine and describe the *worst* possible situation in which you could see yourself. That situation would be considered a "1" on the scale. Next, you'd be asked to imagine and describe the *best* possible situation in which you could see yourself, one where all your dreams and aspirations were realized. That situation would be considered a "10." With the scale's ends thus defined, the next question was "Where on the scale would you say you are *right now?*" Note that Cantril's scale is known as a *self-anchoring scale,* since the end-points are personally defined (i.e., your best aspirations and worst fears will undoubtedly be different from those of others).[4]

A final example of a rating scale is the "faces" scale (see Figure 6.3c) described by Andrews and Withey (1976). Scales like these are particularly useful when dealing with children or with others whose literacy level might be questionable. The respondent is directed to "pick the face that best illustrates how you feel" about the attitude object in question; this scale is useful when the ratings being made are on a like–dislike or happy–sad type of continuum. But note that people other than young children may find the use of such a scale somewhat condescending.

OTHER STRUCTURED ITEMS

There are several other types of structured questionnaire items, all of which have their roots in some of the more formal attitude-assessment techniques we will discuss in the next section. We'll mention only two here.

LIKERT-TYPE ITEMS The first type of structured item is known as a "*Likert-type*" questionnaire item because its format is of the type included in an attitude scale developed originally by Rensis Likert

Figure 6.3

Three Samples of Rating Scales

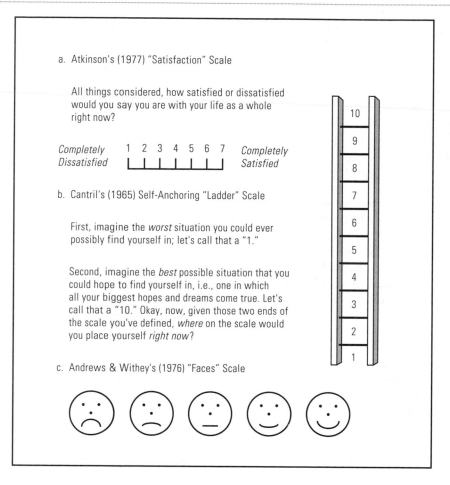

a. Atkinson's (1977) "Satisfaction" Scale

All things considered, how satisfied or dissatisfied would you say you are with your life as a whole right now?

Completely Dissatisfied   1 2 3 4 5 6 7   *Completely Satisfied*

b. Cantril's (1965) Self-Anchoring "Ladder" Scale

First, imagine the *worst* situation you could ever possibly find yourself in; let's call that a "1."

Second, imagine the *best* possible situation that you could hope to find yourself in, i.e., one in which all your biggest hopes and dreams come true. Let's call that a "10." Okay, now, given those two ends of the scale you've defined, *where* on the scale would you place yourself *right now*?

c. Andrews & Withey's (1976) "Faces" Scale

(see Likert 1932). Two attributes distinguish a "Likert-type" item. First, the item is an *assertion* (rather than a question). Second, the respondent's task is to indicate the extent to which he or she *agrees* or *disagrees* with the assertion. Typically, if Likert-type items are used, a number of them are given in succession on a questionnaire. Once respondents get used to using the agree–disagree format, which happens very quickly, they can deal rapidly with many different issues. The following is an example of a "Likert-type" item:

All things considered, I think the death penalty should be reinstated.

.... (a) disagree strongly
.... (b) disagree somewhat
.... (c) neither agree nor disagree
.... (d) agree somewhat
.... (e) agree strongly

The Likert-type item is useful if, instead of being interested in hearing the respondent's position in his or her own words, you're interested in the extent to which a person agrees or disagrees with a position formulated by the researcher. For example, rather than having the respondent explain his or her views regarding capital punishment, an item like the example above might be used to give a "bottom line" position, to see whether and to what extent the respondent will agree or disagree. You might then be interested in some of the reasons behind their (dis)agreement, and hence offer a number of alternatives (e.g., an item that states a moral argument for or against capital punishment, another item that expresses a vengeance theme, and so on) to be able to identify the logic that underlies different positions, or simply to distinguish between people who hold similar positions for different reasons.

SEMANTIC DIFFERENTIAL-TYPE ITEMS Finally, another type of questionnaire item provides for a *semantic differential–type* response. Osgood, Suci, and Tannenbaum (1957) developed an attitude scale they dubbed "the Semantic Differential." Devised to assess the *meaning* associated with particular attitude objects, it involved a set of bipolar adjectives (or dimensions) upon which any given attitude object could be described. For example, you might see the words "this textbook" (or some other object of assessment) printed at the top of the page, and your task would be to rate "this textbook" on a list of bipolar adjectives such as those shown in Figure 6.4a.

Although the original Semantic Differential still sees occasional use in attitude research, it's more typical to see its influence in the semantic differential–type response format. The respondent is asked to express his or her attitudes or feelings by providing ratings with respect to bipolar scales (i.e., opposing concepts, words, or phrases), where the two poles of

Figure 6.4a

Items from the Original Semantic Differential

Please rate *Research Decisions* on the following dimensions:

fair	__ __ __ __ __ __ __	unfair
good	__ __ __ __ __ __ __	bad
heavy	__ __ __ __ __ __ __	light
fast	__ __ __ __ __ __ __	slow
hot	__ __ __ __ __ __ __	cold

the continuum are separated by some odd number of spaces (usually, but not necessarily, 5 or 7) separated by colons. For example, we might be interested in obtaining your evaluation of your local medical clinic. Instead of using the Semantic Differential (with its given adjectival pairs), we might decide to adapt the format to more relevant dimensions. We might thus ask you to rate service provided by the medical staff at your local medical clinic on the dimensions depicted in Figure 6.4b. Note that one can use any opposing words, phrases, or other concepts that are of interest. Note also that the presentation of dimensions has been varied (i.e., the continuum's "good" end is sometimes on the left, other times on the right) in order to inhibit response sets.

Question Wording

Thus far, the discussion has emphasized determining both the general content and the structure of the questions. Another important aspect of the interview or questionnaire is the actual wording of the questions (e.g., see Sudman & Bradburn 1982).

A ROSE BY ANY OTHER NAME
Is there any difference to you between "forbidding" something and "not allowing" it? Empirical attention to the issue of question wording began in 1940, when the following two questions were asked of two comparable national samples of respondents:

> Do you think the United States should forbid public speeches against democracy?

> Do you think the United States should allow public speeches against democracy?

The two questions seem to be asking essentially the same thing, but one is positively worded and the other negatively worded. The percentage of people who *agree* with one item ought to be roughly equal to the number who *dis*agree with the other. That is, if 30 percent of the people say "yes" to the first item (that the United States should *forbid* such speeches), a similar percentage should say "no" to the second item (that the United States should *not allow* them).

Figure 6.4b

Items in Adapted Semantic-Differential Format

Please evaluate the level of service you receive from the medical staff at Everyperson's Medical Clinic on the following dimensions:

friendly	unfriendly
efficient	inefficient
can never get a quick appointment for urgent matters	they always find a way to fit you in
always in too much of a rush	always have time to talk and ask questions

But in fact, while only 54 percent said that the United States should *forbid* such speeches, a full 75 percent said that they should *not be allowed*. In hindsight, perhaps we can think about the two words and make some distinction between them, but who could have predicted such huge variation on the basis of what still seems little more than a difference of nuance? A swing of 21 percent on the basis of a small shift in wording makes any statements about the sampling error's being "plus or minus 2.5 percent, 19 times out of 20" seem downright trivial. If such enormous swings can occur because of relatively small wording changes, then perhaps *wording* is the more important issue to attend to.

One of the few studies to directly and comprehensively do so was completed by Schuman and Presser (1981), who go beyond single examples like "forbid versus allow" and ask broader questions about general types of wording shifts. For example, the forbid/allow variant is subsumed under the general category "changes in the tone of the wording." Their general finding, consistent with the forbid/allow example, is that small differences in wording can produce substantial swings in results. Ironically, however, and contrary to the common wisdom, the most blatant examples of biased wording were the *least* effective in influencing results. Schuman and Presser explain that "respondents seem to recognize and discount the more obvious instances of bias. By contrast, the more subtle changes in wording—such as the 'forbid/allow' variation—can have large effects on

responses" (see Institute for Survey Research [ISR] 1982: 1).

The authors note that one implication of this finding is that when researchers want to examine changes in attitudes over time by comparing newly acquired data to old, it's very important to replicate the original wording exactly. For example, when they replicated the forbid/allow experiment in the 1970s, they found the same 20 percent difference between the two wordings. But when they compared the results of the two *matched* sets of wordings (i.e., comparing the 1940 "forbid" data to the 1970s "forbid" data, and the 1940 "allow" data to the 1970s "allow" data), each matched set revealed about a 30 percent change in the direction of a more tolerant response. The importance of keeping wording constant is made clear, though, when one considers what conclusions would have resulted had *mismatched* wordings been used:

The two possible *mismatched* replications of the question (comparing 1940 data from the "forbid" version to mid-1970s data from the "allow" version, and vice-versa) would yield two very different results: evidence of either a slight (less than 10 per cent) increase in tolerance, or a whopping increase of 50 per cent. (2)

Clearly, then, question wording must be kept identical if a researcher wants to compare the results of two or more surveys. If a change of wording is necessary for some reason, the researcher should include both wordings on at least one occasion, so that an explicit comparison can be made that will allow an assessment of the effect of the wording change.

CONTEXT EFFECTS

Even with wording held constant, Schuman and Presser (1981) also reveal that *context effects* can exert a significant impact on the results of surveys. Responses to a question are influenced by the questions that surround that question, particularly by those that immediately precede it.

> The importance of such order effects was demonstrated by Schuman and Presser's replications of a 1978 ... survey question on whether a pregnant woman should be allowed "to obtain a legal abortion if she is married and does not want any more children." When this question was asked *alone,* responses were considerably more favourable than when it followed a question about allowing abortion if "there is a strong chance of serious defect in the baby." Thus, the context in which a question is asked also affects answers, and so context (as well as wording) should be held constant when studying trends. (ISR 1982: 2)

Indeed, context effects seem particularly worrisome because of consequent openness to manipulation. Pollsters typically provide probability theory esti-

mates of the accuracy of their results (e.g., accurate to within plus or minus 2 percent, 19 times out of 20) and occasionally give an item's exact wording (so that any obvious biases in the wording can be detected), but press releases and media accounts rarely show all the questions that were asked. This approach makes polling results and their revelation open to abuse. Table 6.2, for example, shows two hypothetical polls conducted by the hypothetical polling agencies for two of Canada's political parties, each of which is clearly interested in advancing and justifying its own agenda.

The hypothetical Liberal survey sets the stage by drawing attention to Canada's positive international image as an open, peaceful nation that values cultural diversity and human rights. The hypothetical Conservative survey begins by drawing attention to problems of conflict and expenditure that are stereotypically related to what many see as the downside of immigration, that an allegedly homogeneous "Canadian" way of life is being undermined by an open door that cannot effectively screen out the world's riffraff. Needless to say, the results that the two groups of respondents give to the final question, which is common to both surveys, will probably be rather different. But suppose both surveys were done with representative samples of more than 2000 adults from across the country. One can imagine

Table 6.2

A Series of Questions from Two Hypothetical Surveys

The Liberal Survey	The Conservative Survey
Do you support or not support the current role of the armed forces as primarily international peacekeepers?	Would you agree or disagree that many of our traditional values are now being undermined?
Do you believe or not believe that Canada should do everything it can to foster its international image as an open country that values human rights?	Would you agree or disagree with the view that Canada's levels of unemployment are still way too high?
Would you agree or disagree with the view that Canadians are a tolerant people who value cultural diversity?	Are you concerned or not concerned about current levels of expenditure for social welfare services?
Do you believe that current levels of immigration are (a) too high? (b) too low? or (c) about right?	Do you believe that current levels of immigration are (a) too high? (b) too low? or (c) about right?

the different headlines that would appear the next day, depending on which party actually conducted its poll and put the results in a press release, as is fantasized in Figure 6.5.

The more complete that researchers and pollsters are in reporting their procedures and making research materials available, the more fully their conclusions can be scrutinized and their work replicated by others.

OTHER ADMONITIONS

A number of sources are available that do a good job of explaining other considerations that should be kept in mind when wording questions (e.g., see Gray & Guppy 1994; Schuman & Presser 1981; Sudman & Bradburn 1982).

CONTEXT-APPROPRIATE WORDING When choosing the wording for questions, keep the age and education level of your target population in mind. A certain vocabulary may be appropriate for your university endeavours but may not be a language that your respondents understand. Still, the fact that most people haven't had your educational opportunities doesn't mean they're stupid. The challenge to communicate effectively is yours.

You should be sensitive to local jargon and be able to use terms that have well-defined local mean-

Figure 6.5

Hypothetical Headlines and Articles Based on the Results of the Hypothetical Surveys Reported in Table 6.2

Headline Emerging from the Hypothetical Liberal Poll	Headline Emerging from the Hypothetical Conservative Poll
"Immigration Levels OK," Canadians Say	**"Too Many Immigrants," Canadians Say**
A poll released today by Respected Pollsters, one of Canada's most successful polling firms, revealed that a majority of Canadians (57.3%) support current immigration levels. In the poll, conducted only last week, more than 2000 Canadians representatively sampled using scientifically accepted procedures were asked the following question:	A poll released today by Respected Pollsters, one of Canada's most successful polling firms, revealed that a majority of Canadians (57.3%) believe that immigration levels are "too high." In the poll, conducted only last week, more than 2000 Canadians representatively sampled using scientifically accepted procedures were asked the following question:
Do you believe that current levels of immigration are (a) too high? (b) too low? or (c) about right?	Do you believe that current levels of immigration are (a) too high? (b) too low? or (c) about right?
The Chairman and Research Director at Respected Pollsters noted that, for a sample of this size, the results will be accurate to within 2.5 percentage points 19 times out of 20.	The Chairman and Research Director at Respected Pollsters noted that, for a sample of this size, the results will be accurate to within 2.5 percentage points 19 times out of 20.

ings. For example, if doing research in a prison, instead of referring to "a prisoner who shares information with prison authorities," it would probably be appropriate simply to use the term "rat." Another technique involves first asking the people you interview what word *they* prefer to use for a given thing or behaviour. In a survey on sexual behaviour, for example, you might begin by asking respondents what words they use to refer to two people engaging in sexual intercourse. If a respondent says "make love" (or whatever), you would then use that phrase in any question about that behaviour, for example, "Do you think it is acceptable for two people to make love on their first date together?"

MINIMIZING BIAS Keep the questions neutral in order to avoid biasing responses. Do not use loaded terms. Referring, for example, to "dangerous" drugs, "disgusting" pornography, "hard-working" students, or "sensitive" erotica is tantamount to telling participants how you expect them to respond.

An interviewer's manner is also important for avoiding bias. The clichéd description of the ideal interviewer as tolerant, friendly, interested, supportive, detached, professional, and neutral is really quite accurate. The idea is to provide an environment that facilitates rapport and imposes as little as possible on respondents' views. To do this, you must be sincerely interested in understanding the interviewee's perspective and be able to consider the expression of your own views irrelevant.

This is particularly so when asking "threatening" questions, such as those involving illegal or socially non-desirable behaviours. Rather than asking respondents whether they have ever *used* illegal drugs like cocaine, for example, you might ask whether the person has ever *experimented* with the drug. And instead of asking "*Did you vote* in the last election?" you might ask "*Were you able to vote* in the last election?" Applying a more neutralizing spin in a question's preamble may also facilitate the reporting of undesirable behaviour.

AVOIDING AMBIGUITY Watch for *ambiguities* in the terms you use. Even though *you* may know what you mean, you must ensure that you and the respondent

are talking about the same thing. Many of the descriptions we ask people to offer of themselves contain inherently ambiguous labels. If we ask people whether they go skiing or have a drink "often," for example, "often" may well have different meanings for different people, or even for the same people for different behaviours. There are many other examples of ambiguous concepts. A question about "drug use," for example, is highly ambiguous. Do you mean Aspirin? Alcohol? Prescription drugs? Marijuana? Heroin? You must be very specific, or at least ensure that you and the respondent are on the same wavelength. But note that these issues are more problematic in the questionnaire than in an interview, since interviews allow for some clarification of ambiguities (assuming you catch them); in a questionnaire, they simply produce unreliability and inconsistency in responses.

MEANINGLESS RESPONSES Avoid questions that can be answered by the respondent without any knowledge about the topic, for example, "Do you agree with the prime minister's new foreign policy initiatives?" This question could be answered by someone who doesn't know who the prime minister is, let alone anything about his or her foreign policy initiatives. Rubenstein (1995) reports that when surveys include questions that ask respondents to express their opinion on nonexistent laws (e.g., a nonexistent *Public Affairs Act*), 25 percent to 35 percent express an opinion anyway, while the rest (65 percent to 75 percent) will volunteer that they have never heard of the act or say they have no opinion on it.

DOUBLE-BARRELLED ITEMS Avoid double-barrelled items, that is, two questions in one. For example, the question "Would you be upset if you found out that your 18-year-old son or daughter was smoking and selling marijuana?" is really asking about two things: smoking and selling. The respondent might not feel the same way about both parts of the question.

ACRONYMS Don't assume that people know acronyms, unless you're dealing with a very specialized audience and have done the preliminary exploratory work that allows you to feel confident that "everyone" in the setting is familiar with them. In other words, you should generally avoid questions like "What's your SIN?" or "Do you know anyone at VPD?" or "Would you rather be a PO, a PC, or work at the AG's office?" But if you're engaged in research with civil servants in Ottawa, they may well find it condescending if you don't use terms like PMO, DM or ADM, and DND.[5] In any event, watch what you take for granted.

ALWAYS DO A PILOT STUDY You should *always* do a brief pilot study or trial run before going out and administering your research instrument "for real." There are *always* things you take for granted without recognizing, and there are *always* surprises you never even considered when constructing the questionnaire. The time to catch these difficulties is *before* you commit major resources to duplicating the questionnaire or to time spent interviewing.

Asking Questions in a Virtual Environment

Despite the promising future that computer-assisted social research (CASR) may hold for social science observation and data collection, results from the empirical literature draw our attention to a number of problems and prospects related to instrument format and design, the use of technology in the research setting, and control over research data that must be addressed.

INSTRUMENT FORMAT AND LAYOUT

"Usability" is a term employed by graphic and web designers to refer to the importance of understanding the user interface instead of the system upon which the interface is run (Couper 2000; Fricker & Rand 2002). While computer-assisted instruments afford researchers greater latitude in how they ask questions, there has been little research into the effects of computerized question formats on participant response. In other words, we know very little about the usability of computer-assisted data collection instruments. The networked environment is qualitatively different from traditional research

environments. As a result, research participants have not had the opportunity to get used to changes in the appearance of the data collection instrument or response formats. This can be particularly problematic for novice computer users and aged participants. In experimental designs, problems with the research instrument can negatively affect the internal validity of the research results. In questionnaires or interviews, problems with the interface can result in higher levels of item non-response or sample attrition.

Conversely, computer-administered observation and data collection instruments also serve to enhance usability in three major ways: design, control, and accessibility. Researchers can take advantage of the graphic power that computers have to offer through design programs such as Macromedia Flash and scripting languages such as AJAX, Java, and ColdFusion to create attractive, interesting, and compelling research instruments (Fricker & Rand 2002; Petit 2002; Schmidt 2002). Doing so makes a whole new way of asking questions possible through the integration of audio and video media into the research instrument. For example, researchers can include a short multimedia clip in a structured interview or questionnaire and ask questions related to that clip. In addition, researchers can make response formats much more intuitive for participants. For example, instead of asking participants to rate their level of happiness using a nondescript numeric rating scale, it is possible to provide a series of detailed animations that change as the participant moves a slider up or down the scale.

Computerized observation and data collection instruments also afford the researcher an unprecedented amount of control over format and layout. CASR can facilitate more complex data collection designs. It aids in the measurement of ancillary information such as the time it takes for a participant to respond to particular items (Barrett & Barrett 2001). It is also possible to randomize the question order and precisely control the timing of questions or events in a structured interview, self-administered questionnaire, or experiment (Barrett & Barrett 2001; Schmidt 2001). Flexible ordering options can be implemented to reduce, or at least control for, order effects. Additionally, the strategic use of interface design and scripting allows researchers to incorporate adaptive questioning into the research instrument in a manner that is neither obvious nor disturbing to the research participant. With adaptive questioning, answers to specific questions help influence which subsequent questions will be asked (Bauman et al. 1998; Liu et al. 2001). The obvious advantages of this design feature are that individual respondents answer fewer questions that are irrelevant to them, and the complexity of the overall instrument is reduced for respondents since they no longer need to read and follow skip patterns and instruction sets.

In addition to enhancing the complexity of the data collection design, a well-constructed computerized instrument can help ensure that questions are completed and completed accurately (i.e., helps reduce invalid responses, item non-response bias, and interviewer error; Liu et al. 2001). Unlike a human interviewer who may forget to ask a specific question, with CAPI or CASI all questions are asked because the computer always follows the programmed routine (Peiris et al. 2000). In less structured interview and observation instruments, researchers can script in pop-up dialogue boxes that automatically request that the interviewer probe further if a certain number of keystrokes are not present in a particular answer or if the respondent has not given a very detailed response. Finally, in CASQs it is quite common for researchers to build in programmed checks of the responses provided to ensure that all required questions have been answered and that the information provided corresponds to the expected format.

Perhaps one of the most promising possibilities that computerized instruments offer in the way of format and design comes in the form of improved access. Multi-modal participant input devices can be created to facilitate the participation of people who have physical disabilities, limited reading or computer skills (Black & Ponirakis 2000), and attention deficits. Additionally, instruments can be customized to adapt to language and cultural differ-

ences. For instance, CASQ participants can be allowed to fill out forms presented in a number of different languages or the digital voice that is used in a CAI may be changed to one that the participant is more culturally familiar with (Black & Ponirakis 2000). It is also possible to build in instructions or construct elaborate help or frequently asked questions (FAQ) sections that can be made available to a research participant at the click of a mouse (Karr 2000). Finally, the instrument can also be set up to provide feedback or instructions to the respondent when he or she has problems navigating the instrument, filling out questions, or submitting responses (Bauman et al. 1998; Woong, Yun, & Trumbo 2000).

TECHNOLOGY AND THE RESEARCH SETTING

At present, the most significant technological limitations facing researchers wishing to use computers and network technology in the field are that handheld computers do not have sufficient disk-drive space and memory, secure wireless network access is sporadic, and the range of mobile research-related software applications is limited (Greene 2001; Woong, Yun, & Trumbo 2000). Experimental researchers have found that differences among computers in graphic display (Horswill & Coster 2001; MacInnes & Taylor 2001; Schmidt 2001), data processing speed and hardware timing (Eichstaedt 2001; Finney 2001), and keyboard and mouse performance (Eichstaedt 2001) hinder the experimental data collection process. They have also found that networked environments where participants do not interact directly with the researcher introduce many more uncontrollable environmental variables, thereby reducing the internal validity of the research (Ross et al. 2003; Wolfe & Reyna 2002). Some field researchers have expressed similar concerns that the use of technology in field research may influence a respondent's reactions, with a negative effect on data quality (Gravlee 2002).

A few researchers have found that the lack of physical presence in the research setting leaves them with less control over interactions with the participants or the setting (Epstein & Klinkenberg 2001;

Petit 2002). When conducting network-administered focus groups, differences among participants may be magnified and variations in the setting may be overlooked. It is generally not possible for the researcher or participant to pick up on audio or visual cues that emerge during the interview or observational process (Black & Ponirakis 2000). Because there is no visual contact the researcher is not privy to facial expressions and body language. Nor is the researcher able to pick up on voice tonality (Tse 1999). Furthermore, it is much more difficult to develop personal rapport in interview or focus group settings (Black & Ponirakis 2000). Not being able to have physical connect with the participant or pick up on context effects significantly limits the type and range of data that are available to researchers.

While there are certainly problems associated with implementing technology in the research setting, there are also some unique general and method-specific advantages. The provisional nature of digital research instruments makes it relatively easy to make changes or modifications on the fly without disrupting the flow of the research (Petit 2002). Additionally, some researchers have found that the speed (Gravlee 2002) and the privacy and flexibility (Black & Ponirakis 2000) of observation and data collection in computer-assisted settings increase respondent's willingness to participate in the process. In anonymous CASR environments participants are more likely to self-disclose (Epstein et al. 2001; Gravlee 2002) and are thus more likely to take part in studies of reactive, socially taboo, or highly sensitive topics. Several researchers have found that the social-desirability effects are lower in anonymous computerized environments (Evans et al. 2003; Fox et al. 2003; Gravlee 2002). Furthermore, in interview and observational designs the visual separation between the participant and the researcher can help to reduce potentially biasing interviewer effects. (Epstein & Klinkenberg 2001).

Some virtual environments have also been found to enhance existing face-to-face settings and activities. Virtual environments force researchers to rethink the nature of the field setting and our approach to selecting and studying such sites. The interactions that can be captured in the networked field setting are becoming more complex (Best et al. 2001; Ruhleder 2000). Networked field environments can be asynchronous or synchronous and they can contain an array of virtual social artifacts such as pictures, animations, movies, audio recordings, and documents.

HANDLING INFORMATION AND OBSERVATIONS

Technical problems can seriously interfere with the recording and storing of research data. They arise from many different sources, including network failures, software failures, and scripting errors. An unstable server or network connection often results in data loss or corruption (Bauman et al. 1998; Bosnjak & Tuten 2001; Campbell, Campbell, & Maglio 1999). Different versions of software have been found to create confusion among researchers and participants (Bradley 1999; Epstein & Klinkenberg 2001; Sheehan & Hoy 1999) that resulted in missing or incomplete observations and sample attrition. Finally, errors in scripting often lead to problems with the data. Instead of relying on trained researchers to record observations CASR relies on potentially "buggy" script. The former scenario is usually more readily detectable; the latter can be more difficult, if not impossible, to detect. Extensive pre-testing is costly and time consuming, but vital. Finally, problems with networks, servers, software, and scripting can also result when respondents intentionally or unintentionally bias research results by changing their answers, submitting answers on multiple occasions, or participating in portions of the research that are not applicable to them (Bauman et al. 1998; Sheehan & Hoy 1999; Woong, Yun, & Trumbo 2000).

Concerns are often expressed about respondents biasing research results by submitting answers on multiple occasions or without being part of the population of interest. Although this can be a very real problem, researchers have a number of methodological, scripting, and database options at their disposal to ensure that it is less likely to occur. For example, by using a combination of client and server-side scripting, secure relational participant and response databases, and randomly assigned numeric passwords it is possible to exercise complete control over the processing of questionnaire responses.

STRATEGY AND PROCESS

The most frequent situation in survey and interview research involves a researcher's approaching a respondent that he or she may never have (and in all likelihood hasn't) met before. Respondents know nothing about you or your study's purpose other than what you tell them, and their participation is a fragile gift that can be withdrawn at any time.

So far, we've concentrated on the discrete elements of questionnaires and interview schedules: choosing content, considering different ways to word and structure individual questions. Now it's time to consider the research instrument as a whole. How do you put a sizable number of these individual questions together in a way that will make the experience of completing the survey or interview as enjoyable and free of frustration as possible for respondents, while ensuring that your own objectives as a researcher—to maximize response rates, minimize error, and obtain candid responses—are also met?

General Organizational Issues

For the most part, general matters of organization are similar in the preparation of both questionnaires and interviews, but some elements are also clearly unique. For the questionnaire, because respondents must complete the document on their own, aesthetic concerns like the questionnaire's "look" and apparent ease of completion play an important role. For the interview, because the interviewer is present and there's a constant interchange back and forth between the interviewer and respondent, the choices the interviewer makes—whether and when to probe, how to rephrase a question, when to hold back and when to go ahead with a more intimate question—will have a big impact. In the discussion below, we will deal with general questions of organization that

are applicable for both interviews and questionnaires but will also occasionally pursue matters that are applicable only to one or the other.

AESTHETIC APPEAL

Many texts, particularly those that deal with more quantitatively oriented survey research, emphasize the creation of a questionnaire that is aesthetically inviting and easy to follow (e.g., see Gray & Guppy 1994). The general impression given by this literature is that if a questionnaire looks pretty and professional, is well laid out and easy to follow, doesn't include too many open-ended questions, and doesn't seem too big, you'll increase the likelihood of snagging a respondent. This view may be overly simplistic, but certainly if the converse is true—if your questionnaire is *not* well laid out, seems difficult to follow, has too many open-ended questions, and is big enough that it looks like it will take a sizable chunk of time to complete—only the most motivated of respondents will complete the questionnaire, and your response rates will suffer.

ANTICIPATING A CONVERSATION

Beyond the first impression, your next challenge is to organize the questionnaire or interview and its constituent parts so that it follows a logical sequence and, ideally, reflects and anticipates a social conversation. Numerous principles can be used to guide the sequencing of questions. If a chronological sequence is involved in the phenomenon being addressed (e.g., the way information is processed in an organization, the development of a romantic relationship from first date to some state of mutual commitment, questions on child rearing that ask about the different stages of child development), the questionnaire's sections can merely follow that chronology. Alternatively, questions can be arranged by topic, grouping together the ones that are thematically related, from general to specific, from most important to least important, and/or from least threatening to most threatening (Gray & Guppy 1994).

The big trick with creating a questionnaire is to try to organize it in a way that mirrors a conversation you might have with a respondent. The same is true of the interview, of course, but the very nature of the interview means that you can adapt somewhat to the unique social dynamic that arises with each respondent; in contrast, once the questionnaire is photocopied, you're stuck with the standardized setup you've created. Preliminary exploratory work, through exploratory interviews, focus group discussions, and/or participant observation, can play a crucial role in helping us know how best to organize our research instruments.

THE RESPONDENT'S PERSPECTIVE

It is that actual or imaginary *conversation,* preferably with an emphasis on the way the *respondent* would probably organize things, that should guide the structure of the interview or questionnaire, and *not* your anticipated analysis. Variables can always be reorganized when you start analyzing the data. Too many novice researchers let *their* perspective and interests dominate the interview or questionnaire, instead of putting their own structures "on hold" and letting the respondent's schema organize the show. Of course, you'll want to ensure that all the questions that are important to you are addressed. But the order in which they are addressed should be governed by the respondent's convenience, not yours.

SOCIAL CIVILITY: UNWRITTEN RULES

Perhaps the place to begin is by discussing briefly some of the unwritten "rules" of conversation, so that we can then consider how they'd apply to the questionnaire or interview setting. Imagine that you're at a party or some other social gathering. Somewhere between the chip dip and the petits fours you find yourself standing next to someone you've never met, and the two of you begin a conversation. Such conversations never begin with requests for intimate details. ("Hi. Did you ever consider suicide during your adolescence?") Instead, they usually start with an exchange of pleasantries and chitchat that does little more than serve as a warm-up and allow time to determine whether you'll pursue the conversation further. These beginning portions of the conversation typically deal with

basic, superficial details of our lives that we're prepared to share with anyone. ("So what do you do?" or "So are you here because you know the host or the hostess?") As long as the person you're chatting with isn't completely weird (in which case the exit/escape sequence is enacted), these initial moments often involve a search for common interests that can provide the basis for further conversation.

COMMON GROUND

Once the first "real" basis of conversation is tacitly agreed on (e.g., you find that you both like outdoor activities such as hiking and camping), the two of you will typically "go with it" for a while, perhaps comparing notes on favoured hiking trails or outfitters and/or trading stories. This sort of conversation can consume the whole evening if you find an intense compatibility of interest. More often, though, the first topic soon becomes exhausted; the conversation then either terminates or moves into another phase.

Phase 2 may simply be another topic, related to the first (e.g., you move on to canoeing) or not (e.g., you find that you also have a common interest in impressionist painters). But now that you've "checked each other out" and decided that you share some things in common and that you each seem like a reasonable human being, the exchange often moves to a more intimate level. Rather than dealing only with activities and interests, you start to ask about and share more in the way of feelings and opinions. Two people who hadn't met half an hour earlier are suddenly trading information about some frustrating aspect of child rearing, comparing their fears about having vasectomies, or talking about what dipsticks men (or women) can sometimes be.

OVERSTEPPING BOUNDARIES

Of course, few conversations ever go completely smoothly. At times, one person may feel comfortable enough to stretch the bounds to a more intimate topic or level: "So, I hear you and Kim separated recently; how's that going for you?" If such an attempt is made prematurely, the other person is caught off guard. Perhaps you've touched a nerve.

Perhaps your motives are unclear: are you asking to be caring, because you want to ask the other person for a date, or because you're about to disclose your own experiences (which the other person isn't yet ready to hear)? Whatever the reason, an avoidance ritual begins. Sensitive listeners notice these things—the slight blush, the superficial response, the subtle change of topic—and, respecting that they've crossed an inappropriate boundary, back off a bit. Later, when the other person understands our motives better or simply feels more comfortable with us, we or the other person may return to that issue, and this time the conversation will continue to flow. But for now, the matter is put on hold and another topic is addressed.

WITHDRAWAL

When conversations turn intense, we rarely terminate them abruptly. Instead, a "shutdown" sequence is often enacted: we withdraw gradually, often by returning to a more superficial level of conversation that reconnects us with what's happening around us. ("Oh ... I see some people are starting to dance; do you like to dance?") Sometimes this process marks the beginning of a new friendship or romance. Other times we merely go our separate ways and, despite having enjoyed the interaction, may never see the other person again.

Additional Considerations Unique to Research

A FORMAL INTRODUCTION

Many of these same "rules" are followed in organizing a questionnaire. Your first task in a questionnaire or interview should always be to introduce yourself with a brief statement about who you are and the purpose of your study. Any promises you're prepared to make, for example, that a brief summary of results will be sent to participants following completion of the study if they're interested, should also be made here. In the case of a questionnaire, respondents should be told whether they should write their names down or complete it anonymously; for interviews, or when respondents' names are obtained on a questionnaire, you should clearly specify what steps you will take to safeguard their confidentiality. This can all be accomplished in a few sentences or a short paragraph, for example,

> My name is Pat Wallace, and I'm a graduate student in sociology at Provincial University. This questionnaire is part of my master's thesis, which deals with how different parents teach "appropriate behaviour" to their children, so it includes a number of questions that ask about your parenting practices. The whole thing should take no more than about 20 minutes to complete. I hope you'll answer all the questions, but feel free to leave out any that you feel uncomfortable about. Finally, please note that responses to this questionnaire are intended to be anonymous. If you'd like to receive a brief summary of the results of the study after it is completed, please fill out the small card at the end of the questionnaire and submit it separately from your completed questionnaire. Thank you very much for agreeing to participate.

GETTING TO KNOW YOU

After the basic introduction, the first topic that's asked about is often relatively trite and superficial, devoted to acquiring preliminary information, for example, to ensure that the respondent is an eligible participant in the study and perhaps to ask about a few demographic details (although one generally avoids such "threatening" demographics as income and education at this point). Because respondents are often looking for cues, we give them signposts that tell them what we are doing (e.g., "First I need to ask just a few general questions so that we have a record of how many kids you have and how long you've been a parent"). The first section also sets the pace for the interview or questionnaire, establishing a rhythm of query and response, query and response.

TRANSITIONS

After passing this "getting to know you" phase, the interview or questionnaire bridges to the first set of questions about the main phenomenon of interest. Again, some sort of signpost is often given, both to keep the respondent informed and to provide a bit of a mental break before digging into the next section. For example, a transition might be "Okay, that completes the first section regarding some of your early experiences as a parent; now I'd like to ask a few questions on how you handle different kinds of situations that can arise with young children."

If only one set of questions deals with the main phenomenon of interest, the questions in the set would normally be ordered from least to most threatening; if there are several *sets* of questions, then the *sets* would also be ordered from least to most threatening. Each time there's a change of theme, another signpost should be offered to help make the transition.

LOOSE ENDS AND THE FINAL WORD

The final section of the interview or questionnaire should tie up loose ends and leave some positive resolution. For example, a final section often includes some "basic" demographic items that will help you describe the sample and perhaps engage in subgroup analyses. An additional benefit of including such items is that when dealing with populations with known characteristics, one can use responses to these questions to assess the sample's representativeness. In any event, the final section should leave respondents with a good taste in their mouths. Conclude with a thank-you, asking respondents (in interviews) whether they have any questions they'd like to ask and (for both interview and questionnaire respondents) whether they have anything they wish to add or further comments to make.

Perspectives on the Research Interview

Although the above discussion pretty much covers the "general organization" issues that pertain to the more structured survey methods, interview researchers, particularly those who engage in semistructured or unstructured interviews, have gone much further in analyzing the process of interaction in the interview setting. Some apparently hope merely to make prospective interviewers aware of the various cues respondents can give (e.g., nonverbal cues) as to whether they're feeling comfortable, becoming defensive, or whatever (e.g., Gorden 1980; Gray & Guppy 1994). Other texts are written more along the lines of a strategic manual, where the name of the game is to control the setting in such a way that the respondent tells all and feels comfortable about doing so.

A DRAMATURGICAL PERSPECTIVE

Berg (2001), for example, offers what he refers to as a "dramaturgical analysis of the interview," analyzing in detail the different roles that interviewer and respondent occupy and the expectations that each commonly has of the other. He also discusses how the researcher can get maximal information with minimal defensiveness through sensitive attention to both verbal and nonverbal cues. Resistance in the respondent is thus a challenge to be overcome. For example, Berg spends considerable time discussing the "evasion tactics" enacted when we step over the line and ask about things that are too personal or painful.

> Such evasion tactics may involve a word, phrase, or gesture that expresses to another participant that no further discussion of a particular issue (or in a particular area) is desired. Conversely, people also usually acquire the ability to recognize these evasion tactics and, in a natural conversational exchange, to respect them. (84)

But the interview isn't a "natural" encounter, and deferring to people's evasion tactics all the time would mean that much data of interest would be lost. Berg makes no bones about the mission:

> This sort of deference [ceremony] simply cannot be permitted during the course of a research interview. In fact, the emergence of evasion tactics during the course of an interview is among the most serious obstacles to overcome—but overcome them you must! ... The interviewer must maneuver around a subject's avoidance rituals in a manner that neither overtly violates social

norms associated with communication exchanges nor causes the subject to lie. (84)

For Berg (2001), the interviewer's role is a complex one; he argues that besides being an actor in the setting, the interviewer must also serve as director and choreographer. With respect to evasion tactics, for example, Berg advises that the interviewer must recognize them as they occur and should respond to them with deference, but must also look for a chance to return to that sensitive area. The strategy being advocated thus mixes sensitivity with persistence. By deferring to the evasion tactic, the interviewer shows that he or she is not insensitive to the respondent's feelings, earning "rapport points" by doing so. Berg suggests that the respondent will now be more likely to reply because the interviewer has shown that he or she knows when to back off.

FEMINIST VIEWS: A MORE EGALITARIAN EXCHANGE?

Such analyses, however insightful they may be about the subtle dynamics that pervade the interview setting, can also sound incredibly manipulative and exploitative. Particularly lamentable are the sorts of "strategic" analyses that treat the prospective respondent as a fish to be reeled in or a conquest to be mounted. Many feminist researchers have been particularly assertive about this issue, pointing out how often relations between interviewer and respondent are construed in a way that merely re-creates the inequity, hierarchy, manipulation, and exploitation that exist in the world (e.g., see Fonow & Cook 1991; Reinharz 1992). Thus, although the interview is seen as a very appropriate research tool—and, some would argue, a particularly *female* type of research tool because of the value it attaches to sensitivity, empathy, good listening skills, and the ability to deal with and talk about feelings (e.g., see Gluck & Patai 1991; Reinharz 1992)—the belief is that the whole interaction needs to be reconstrued.

Many feminist methodologists concur that the interview should be a more egalitarian exchange, guided by principles of mutual respect and collaboration. But feminist researchers differ considerably in how far they'd go in asserting that principle. Oakley (1981), for example, maintains that feminist interviewing should be characterized by openness, engagement, intimacy, self-disclosure, and the potential for developing a long-lasting relationship. Making friends with everybody would seem a formidable task, though, and could also limit the range of research one could conduct.

Others assert that an egalitarian exchange does not require promises of friendship or mutual self-disclosure as either conditions or preconditions for conducting a mutually respectful, mutually beneficial interview. Indeed, many argue that one reason people open up and "tell their stories" is precisely because they *are* strangers and *won't* be seen again. Zimmerman (1977) makes this point in her interview study of women who had undergone abortions:

> The interviewer was a stranger—not a part of the woman's world and someone she would not likely see again. The interviewer was also a professional who would not discuss the interview with anyone else. For these reasons, the women may have felt they could talk about their most private lives and feelings relatively freely. (210)

After summarizing some of the diverse opinions that exist on this issue, Reinharz (1992) concludes that "clearly, there is no single feminist perspective on researcher–interviewee relations and self-disclosure" (34). Yet the fact that such questions are being posed at all must be seen as a most healthy sign for social science. As Reinharz notes, these "ethical questions are heightened in feminist interview research because feminists try hard to avoid perpetuating the exploitation of women" (27). If only researchers of all theoretical persuasions were so concerned.

THE MEANING OF SELF-REPORTS

The techniques described in this chapter reflect social scientists' desires to systematically unearth people's perceptions via self-report. Whether we use an interview or questionnaire, and whether our items are open-ended or structured, at the heart of our efforts is the goal of acquiring whatever information people will tell us about their thoughts, feelings, beliefs, attitudes, opinions, or behaviours. Once we have our data the temptation is to feel that we have unearthed some inherent truth(s). And perhaps we have.

Still, self-report techniques are but one method and represent but one way of engaging truth(s). We must therefore try to contextualize these truths as we would any others. What exactly do we have when a respondent places a check mark on a rating scale, answers "yes" to item 16, or embellishes in great detail when we ask an open-ended query? Although many different issues apply to self-report measures as a class, two will be considered here: the dangers of literalist fallacies and the relationship between self-reported attitudes and related behaviours.

The Naiveté of Literalism

As the preceding paragraph implies, we commit a major interpretive error when we give self-reports (or any other type of data) the status of *prima facie,* or literal truth. Questions and rating scales are perhaps best seen as vehicles we create through which respondents can express their thoughts, feelings, and so on, making them visible to the researcher in the same way that smoke is used in wind tunnels to afford visibility to the air currents that exist but would otherwise go unseen. Two questions plague the researcher: what do those utterings and check marks mean, and how useful are the individual and/or aggregate ratings for the research objectives at hand?

This is not to say that we cannot believe what people say, even though we must sometimes be cautious about that, too. As Kelly (1955) suggests, "If you want to know something about someone, *ask them*—they might just tell you." And as Kidder and Campbell (1970) have found, measures of reliability and validity are maximized when questioning is direct. By and large, our own experience tells us that people who participate in research generally don't set out to deceive you. They may package their information to show their best side, but in general, people

seem motivated to put forth their views "truthfully" within the constraints you provide for their responses.

Most respondents in social science research, particularly the typical university student or average member of the North American population, appear to understand the tasks we give them. They understand order and magnitude (i.e., that 2 is larger than 1 but not as large as 6) and appear able to deal with rating scales.

But a problem arises when we try to make comparisons among individuals. Does the fact that one person checked 5 while another checked 6 mean that one's attitude is stronger or more extreme than the other's? Not necessarily. Quantitative researchers assume that people's ratings really take on meaning only when they're aggregated (i.e., when we compile the responses of many different people together). The belief is that our various individual propensities—to avoid extreme categories or rely on them heavily, to be cautious or audacious in our responses, to underestimate or overestimate our perceptions—will cancel one another out overall in the population, or will be equivalent overall in different groups we might wish to compare. This is the main reason that reliability and validity assessment almost uniformly relies on groups of individuals to assess or demonstrate their strengths; it is at that level that such power can be shown. Interpolating or extrapolating from aggregate to individual behaviour is courting trouble, and an example of **ecological fallacy.**

Attitudes and Behaviour

The question of meaning is not bypassed by focusing at the group level. Even when the attitudes or opinions of groups of individuals are assessed by interview or questionnaire methods, one must still consider what relation these measures, and people's responses, have to other indicators or measures of interest. One issue that has plagued researchers for years is the question of the relationship between what people *say* about their beliefs, attitudes, and/or opinions when you ask them and what they actually *do* when faced with real or simulated behavioural choices.

This area of inquiry was given a provocative initiation by LaPiere (1934), who performed a study in racist, ethnocentric middle America during the Depression years. LaPiere was interested in studying prejudicial behaviour toward minorities in real-world settings. Anticipating that there'd be a lot of it, he travelled around the United States with a young, foreign-born Chinese couple, carefully recording the number and nature of their interactions with the owners and employees of the hotels, auto camps, and restaurants they visited. He also varied the conditions of their approach (i.e., sometimes he did the talking, sometimes one of the couple did; sometimes he went in with them, sometimes they entered alone). In all, the trio travelled more than 15 000 kilometres, stopping at 250 different establishments, and during all that time, they were refused service *once*.

That original finding would have been heartening, given their expectations, were it not for the follow-up study LaPiere undertook once he and the couple returned home. Six months after completing his original study, LaPiere created questionnaires, which he sent to each of the 250 establishments they'd visited on their trip. Recall that when they actually visited the places, LaPiere found that 249 out of 250 places (or 99.6 percent) welcomed them, while 1 (or 0.4 percent) did not. The 128 replies he received in response to his questionnaire from those same establishments revealed a very different story.

His questionnaire asked "Will you accept members of the Chinese race as guests in your establishment?" In response, 118 (or 92.2 percent) said "no," while 9 (or 7.0 percent) said "it depends," and only 1 (or 0.8 percent) said "yes." Rather surprised by these results, since they were so opposite to the trio's experience, LaPiere wondered whether their own visits to those establishments might have affected the responses. Accordingly, LaPiere then sent the same questionnaire to 128 similar places they had *not* visited—but the results were the same.

LaPiere felt that his study revealed severe limitations to questionnaire responses. He did see some utility to them (e.g., in asking about beliefs), but the huge inconsistency he observed between the questionnaire and behavioural data led him to distrust self-reports:

> The questionnaire is cheap, easy, and mechanical. The study of human behaviour is time-consuming, intellectually fatiguing, and depends for its success upon the ability of the investigator. The former method gives quantitative results, the latter mainly qualitative. Quantitative judgments are quantitatively accurate; qualitative evaluations are always subject to the errors of human judgment. Yet it would seem far more worth while to make a shrewd guess regarding that which is essential than to accurately measure that which is likely to prove quite irrelevant. (LaPiere 1934: 237)

CONSIDERING (IN)CONSISTENCY

Although we agree with LaPiere's assertion that it's advisable to tackle what is most important rather than what is easiest, we question, as have others (e.g., see Oskamp 1977), whether or in what ways LaPiere was justified in calling the results of his behavioural and questionnaire studies "inconsistent." Certainly, we assess people's attitudes not only because we're interested in their attitudes per se, but also because we believe that knowing people's attitudes will help us understand and/or predict their behaviour (e.g., see Fishbein 1967; Oskamp 1977; Zimbardo, Ebbesen, & Maslach 1977). The relationship between the two is thus of interest to us and has been investigated extensively. For this text, the question becomes how we might gather attitudinal data so that attitude–behaviour links can be addressed. The literature on this topic notes five considerations to keep in mind when assessing the correspondence between attitudinal and behavioural data, considerations that indirectly offer advice on how to assess attitudes.

SITUATIONAL THRESHOLDS Consider the following scenario. You approach a woman at your local library as part of a study on attitudes about environmental issues and ask her first to rate her concern about the environment (i.e., an attitudinal measure) and then to tell you whether she attended last Saturday's "Walk for the Environment" (i.e., a behavioural measure). She indicates that she's "strongly" concerned about the environment but did *not* attend last Saturday's event. Is this an example of attitude–behaviour inconsistency?

Campbell (e.g., 1963) is among those who have suggested that situations like the above don't necessarily reflect inconsistency but, rather, indicate differences in situational thresholds. Expressing an attitude is much easier than doing a behaviour (which invariably requires some level of time, effort, money, etc.). If people do the easier thing but not the harder thing, their apparent "inconsistency" in behaviour may merely reflect the fact that they're prepared to go only so far; they surpass the first situational threshold but not the second. True inconsistency, according to Campbell, is evident only when a person exhibits the harder behaviour (i.e., goes on the "Walk for the Environment"), but fails to exhibit the easier one (i.e., does not express support for environmental issues). The literature reveals that such inconsistencies rarely occur (see Oskamp 1977).

DIFFERENT STIMULI Returning to LaPiere's (1934) study, consider the two stimuli with which the hotel and restaurant managers were presented. The attitudinal measure asked whether they would allow "members of the Chinese race" as guests. In contrast, the behavioural measure, in effect, asked whether they would allow as guests the two specific people with whom LaPiere showed up. Were the attitudinal and behavioural responses made to the same stimulus? If not, then it hardly seems fair to draw a conclusion of inconsistency.

And evidence certainly suggests that the two stimuli were indeed *not* the same. LaPiere notes the stereotypical and prejudicial attitudes of Americans at that time to many foreign ethnicities, including Chinese, and these are clearly reaffirmed in studies done during the same period by Bogardus (1925) and by Katz and Braly (1933). But LaPiere's two Chinese travelling companions were "a young Chinese student and his wife," who were both "personable, charming, and quick to win the admiration and respect of those they had the opportunity to

become intimate with." Further, although both were foreign-born, they spoke "unaccented English" (LaPiere 1934). Researchers who wish to predict reactions to a particular behavioural criterion should ask about that criterion in their attitudinal measure.

COMPETING MOTIVES Questionnaire items often query attitudes in the abstract: respondents are asked how they feel, in general, toward environmental issues, tax increases, or Latvians. In contrast, behaviours usually take place in the context of everyday life, where we face many situational contingencies and choose among alternative actions. The question "To what extent are you concerned with environmental issues?" asks in general terms for an expression of concern for the environment. In contrast, the behavioural criterion of, say, whether the respondent attends a meeting that evening concerning a local development project involves many situational contingencies (e.g., free time, the availability of transportation to the meeting) and competing motives (e.g., concern with environment balanced against interest in development; time at the meeting balanced against desire to go bowling or spend time with family).

AVAILABILITY OF ALTERNATIVES Questions asked in the abstract also ignore the fact that the lack of behavioural alternatives may foster what would seem to be inconsistent behaviour. You may not be particularly enamoured of your local morning newspaper, for example, but may buy it anyway because it is the only morning paper available. Similarly, some persons watch television programs they don't like only because they lack hobbies and other interests in their life.

"NORMATIVE" PRESCRIPTIONS OF BEHAVIOUR Many social situations prescribe particular ways of behaving as "appropriate"; individuals may suppress the expression of some attitudes in certain contexts. We're taught, for example, to be polite to people even if we do not particularly like them; and, in Canada in the 1990s, expressions of racism or chauvinism are seen as offensive and tasteless. Ironically, in 1930s America, the situation was quite the reverse; white hegemony dominated, and few thought it inappropriate to express racist and prejudicial attitudes as the questionnaire respondents did to LaPiere (1934). But when faced with a particular stimulus (like the couple LaPiere travelled with), people felt similarly free to "make exceptions" if they chose to, perhaps depending on such considerations as how "white" and counterstereotypical the couple appeared to be.

AVOIDING THE PITFALLS

These five considerations suggest that overall, in the aggregate, there are many reasons *not* to expect a one-to-one correspondence between attitudinal measures and behavioural criteria, even if both are valid. At the same time, the existence of such pitfalls indirectly suggests precautions the attentive researcher can follow to avoid them.

GENERAL INTERESTS? GENERAL QUESTIONS!
First, the evidence (see Fishbein & Azjen 1975) suggests that correspondence between attitudinal and behavioural measures is generally weakest when a single-item attitudinal measure (e.g., "To what extent are you concerned with environmental issues?") is correlated with a single behaviour (e.g., "Do you plan to attend Friday's meeting on environmental issues?"). Why? Partly because there's room for error in both. Psychometric studies show that the more times and the more different ways you express a question, the more reliable will be your characterization of the person on the issue at hand. The same is true in the behavioural domain.

Note that in each case we're looking at a general *domain* of interest to us (i.e., attitudes about the environment, behavioural manifestations of environmental concern), but sampling only one element of each. There are many different components to environmental attitudes, and there are many different ways to express one's environmental concern (or lack thereof) behaviourally. Just as we should be reluctant to generalize more broadly on the basis of a survey that samples only one person, we should also be reluctant to generalize about a person's attitudinal or behavioural leanings on the basis of one

question or one behaviour. To assess general proclivities, one must sample more broadly across both the attitudinal and behavioural domains.

SPECIFIC INTERESTS? SPECIFIC QUESTIONS! If a researcher is interested in predicting a very specific behaviour, the situation warrants a very pointed question that simulates the criterion setting as closely as possible, either by varying the actual setting or by describing a specific hypothetical scenario in a preamble. Some of the most successful efforts at predicting actual behaviour on the basis of attitude measures are pollsters' astoundingly accurate election predictions. Part of their success is attributable to appropriate sampling for such a research objective, that is, obtaining a representative sample of voters. But another factor is that respondents are asked a very specific question about their intentions about the behaviour in question (i.e., "How would you vote if the election were held today?"). Further, efforts are often made to simulate actual voting conditions as much as possible (e.g., by providing respondents with some way to cast a "secret ballot" where only aggregate results can be known).

CONSIDERING STEREOTYPING/PROTOTYPICALITY
Researchers should consider that people may hold many opinions about things with which they've had little experience. People do not refrain from having opinions about Iraq even though they have never been there, have never met anyone who lives there, and know little about the country and its history. The stereotypes people hold about other social groups (or social objects or social policies) may or may not be accurate in general and are always inaccurate when they deny the possibility of exception. Yet people often use stereotypes as a departure point when we ask them about some social category "in general."

So researchers should consider the relationship between the stimulus they provide and the particular behavioural criterion they have in mind. For example, Ted's research experience regarding "pornography" shows that survey questions must be very carefully worded because of variation in what "pornography" means to different people. Asking whether "pornography" should be censored, classified, or left unregulated, for example, leads to trouble. Some respondents think the question refers to material that has some sexual content, whereas others assume the researcher is referring to sexual material that depicts violence, particularly toward women (see Palys, Olver, & Banks 1983). The solution here is to (1) ask respondents to articulate their definition or sense of the term; (2) provide a definition for respondents; or (3) not even use the term but, rather, describe the scenario/stimulus you have in mind (e.g., video scenes involving female nudity; videos showing explicit sexual activity involving gay couples), since you're the one doing the research and hence have some objective in mind.

ASSESSING CONTINGENCIES Researchers can surmount the difficulties associated with "contextualizing" questionnaire responses by asking about the contingencies and competing motives that might intercede between attitude and behaviour. Fishbein and Azjen (1975) show strong correspondence between the two with only three intervening variables considered.

SUMMING UP AND LOOKING AHEAD

This chapter reviews techniques that involve interaction—sometimes immediate (as with an interview) and sometimes delayed (as with a questionnaire)—between researcher and participant. The advantages and disadvantages of each are discussed, and some of their similarities and differences noted. Considerable time is also spent outlining the various ways that questions can be phrased, some of the strategies and techniques used in the overall organization and implementation of a questionnaire or interview, and some of the obligations and responsibilities entailed in dealing with a respondent on a human-to-human basis.

The chapter places the techniques into three main groupings: *surveys* (which include the various types of questionnaire plus telephone surveys), *interviews* (including the face-to-face individual and focus group interviews), and *oral history methods.*

Survey techniques have been the favourite of quantitative researchers, largely because such methods embody many of the criteria that quantitative researchers believe are characteristic of "good science": a researcher-centred deductive approach, analytical distance from one's "subjects," a way to amass large quantitative data sets in order to identify patterns of relationships that hold across many individuals regardless of their circumstances, and so on. But ironically, what has been called "good science" by *quantitative* researchers has been considered "poor science" by many *qualitative* researchers. Similarly, much of what has been "good science" to qualitative researchers has been seen as inefficient and misguided by many quantitative ones.

There's probably a useful distinction to be made between a technique *itself* and how that technique has been used *in practice.* Once that distinction is made, it becomes clearer that the various clusters of researchers don't have big problems with the variety of methods represented in this chapter; rather, they differ in terms of how those methods have been designed and put into play. Many feminist and indigenous researchers, for example, criticize the quantitative survey for being little more than a re-creation of the non-egalitarian problematic that exists in the world (e.g., see Reinharz 1992; Smith 1999), while many others point out the crucial role that quantitative surveys have played in making people aware of the pervasiveness of such phenomena as sexual harassment and other violence against women).

The broader theme of this chapter, then, isn't that you must declare allegiance to one method (and the associated cluster of researchers) or another. Instead, look at the different methods as different ways of compiling and understanding people's views. As you engage a research area, different methods will be useful to you at different times, depending on your objectives in a given project. Nor do we want to leave you with the impression that the various methods are discrete entities that, like dinner entrées, must be chosen one at a time. It would be far better to approach them as a smorgasbord in which the particular combination of methods you use is up to you.

For example, in the police study described in this chapter (Palys, Boyanowsky, & Dutton 1983, 1984), the researchers used both interview and questionnaire techniques, knowing that they'd complement each other in supplying the information sought. Because the researchers came in after the system had already been in operation for more than a year, and the archival record on the system's development and implementation was at best sporadic, oral histories helped fill in the gaps, giving a more human face to the multiplicity of meanings that people place on a new technology. By doing target interviews with people throughout the organization, Palys and colleagues (1983, 1984) were able to get a good handle on the perceived positives and negatives of the data system they were evaluating. But because of the limitations of target interviewing, they weren't sure whether the views they were picking up were held broadly or just by a few vocal people. Accordingly, they used the results of the interviews to design a questionnaire that was meaningful to the people involved, both in how it was worded and in the issues it addressed.

The questionnaire's great strength was that it allowed the research team to gather a large amount of data to see how broadly certain feelings and views were held among patrol officers who used the system. But the limitations of self-administered questionnaires (where you can't ask many open-ended questions) meant that, while they could get a good sense of *what* people's attitudes were, they were limited in their ability to understand *why* the respondents felt that way. Another round of interviews with a cross section of the patrol officers allowed the researchers to ask for officers' interpretations of why those attitudes were expressed, and at least get a sense of why *some* people might feel that way. The study's strength was thus that it effectively combined *both* quantitative *and* qualitative methods, bene-fiting from their respective strengths and offsetting their respective limitations.

And, finally, some time was spent introducing network technology as an increasingly important means of conducting primary social research. We shouldn't look at CASR as a replacement for existing methods, instead we should see it as another tool in the proverbial toolbox that the 21st-century methodologist can utilize in order to better understand our social world. With the recognition that CASR is likely to continue to grow in popularity as a mechanism for collecting social science data, it is vital that serious academic efforts be made to assess the methods we use to acquire our data in this information age. To this end critical discussion of the use of computer technology in social science research needs to be expanded beyond the confines of specialized academic publications to the pages of books and journals with a broader readership. Furthermore, greater emphasis must be placed on educating the research community about computer technology in general and CASR in particular. With very few exceptions, most popular research methods textbooks in the social sciences pay only scant attention to computer technology and CASR, and quite often the discussions found in these books only illustrates the utility of CASR as a form of secondary data collection.

When it comes to the design and development if CASR, it is apparent that the most significant technical issue confronting the social science research community is the lack of standardization across hardware and software applications (Ranchhod & Zhou 2001; Smith 1997; Wolfe & Reyna 2002). The most significant practical issue relates to the underdevelopment of research-specific software (Tse, 1999). Until operating systems, hardware, and software are standardized and made more accessible, cost-effective, reliable and functional it may be necessary for the social research community to establish partnerships with software developers, network administrators, computer programmers, and graphic and web designers.

Similar issues will arise in subsequent chapters. Whether the topic is observational methods

(Chapter 7), archival techniques (Chapter 8), or the variety of experimentalist approaches (Chapters 9 to 11), we'll see that different clusters of researchers have tended to construe each set of methods in different ways, using them to largely different ends and eschewing the way others have used them. Our approach throughout will be to articulate their diversity in a way that will, we hope, help us understand how we can all benefit from it.

STUDY QUESTIONS

1. The president of your university is interested in assessing the attitudes of people in this province or state regarding postsecondary education. Unsure whether to do the study using mail-out questionnaires or a telephone interview, he or she comes to you for advice. What advantages and limitations do you see to each approach in this situation?

2. Compare the following in terms of their relative strengths and limitations: (a) in-person interviews and focus group interviews; (b) in-person interviews and telephone interviews; (c) mail-out questionnaires and in-person interviews; (d) in-person interviews and in-person questionnaires.

3. What is volunteer bias and why might it be problematic?

4. What does CASR stand for and what advantages and difficulties does it bring to the research process?

5. What advantages does the Internet offer as a place to conduct social research? What are some of its limitations?

6. While some groups we may wish to study are easy to find (e.g., practising physicians can be located through phone listings or medical association records), others are more difficult to locate (e.g., people who have tattoos). What possibilities does the Internet offer in terms of ways of locating people who share a particular pastime or identity? How would you go about

looking for a group of people who shared an interest in origami? What are your options?

7. Indicate the role that question wording and question context can play in the results obtained in a large-scale telephone survey. What is the magnitude of their effects, relative to the degree of sampling error that usually exists in most large-scale studies (which often have sampling error in the range of plus or minus 2.5 percent or 3 percent, 19 times out of 20)?

8. As a class project, have each person in class make five copies of each of the two versions of the immigration questionnaire shown in Table 6.2 (but with the labels "Conservative Party Survey" and "Liberal Party Survey" deleted). Add a few questions at the beginning and end asking for demographic information (e.g., age, sex, education, political affiliation) that will allow you to describe your sample. Have each person take his or her ten surveys home and administer them—in random order and without seeing which questionnaire any given person receives—to as heterogeneous a group of friends and relatives as possible. Bring your completed questionnaires back to class, and combine all the questionnaires into one large sample. Analyze the data to see whether question context really made a difference to responses to the final question. Have someone in your class e-mail me the results (palys@sfu.ca); they will be included in the next edition of this book.

9. Chris is conducting oral history interviews with women who worked in munitions factories in World War II. What are the relative advantages and disadvantages in this case of (a) taking general written notes during the interview and trying to write any "juicy" quotes down verbatim; (b) using a tape recorder to tape the interviews; (c) taping the interview and writing down key points as the interview proceeds?

10. What unique advantages do focus group interviews have to offer? What limitations do you have to be aware of? What can you do to try to minimize those limitations?

11. What is "selective deposit," and how is it related to the study of history? In what sense do oral history methods address some of the problems of selective deposit?

12. Look again at the section "Question Content" to see the steps involved in translating a general set of objectives into an inventory of concepts, and then into specific questions that ask about those concepts. Form a study group with other people in your class and consider how you might follow through those steps if you wanted to put together a questionnaire that could be used at the end of any course offered in your department to evaluate student satisfaction with the course and with the effectiveness of its instructor.

13. The president of your university wants to include both open-ended and structured items in the study described in Study Question 1. Which ones should be placed first? Why?

14. Create a small questionnaire on a topic of interest to you that includes one open-ended question and one of each of the types of structured items discussed in this chapter (i.e., a dichotomous item, a single-response item, etc.).

15. Jeff wants to include a question on income in his questionnaire. What are the relative merits of using a single-response item or a categorical-response item to get this information?

16. Indicate what is obviously wrong with the wording of each of the following questions, and then rewrite each question in an appropriate manner.

    a. How many times would you say you have purchased drugs within the last six months?

    b. Do you feel that pliobenthamiacine (PBM) should be made legal for over-the-counter purchase?

    ____ Yes
    ____ No

    c. Do you feel that the use of marijuana and cocaine should be decriminalized?

    d. How do you feel about the depraved individuals who use a dangerous drug like heroin?

    e. Finally, please indicate your age in years at your last birthday:

       1) ____ 20 years or less
       2) ____ 20 to 30 years
       3) ____ 30 to 40 years
       4) ____ 40 to 50 years

17. The discussion in this chapter about the research interview encouraged you to consider the relationship between researcher and researched. At one end of this continuum, we can consider our scientific aspirations, where part of learning the "tricks of the trade" involves knowing how to use what you know about the interview situation to get the most out of every interview, for example, by the way you design the situation, ask the questions, build rapport, and so on. At the other end, we've seen a view that the interview should be an egalitarian exchange of information between "friends." In a study group or in an essay, discuss the strengths and limitations of each of those views. Consider, for example, how these decisions relate to the qualitative– quantitative distinction and to your own view of research. Consider also the implications for knowledge that would arise if each view were "the" dominant mode of interviewing in your particular area of interest.

18. Compare and contrast the feminist and dramaturgical views of the interview that were discussed in this chapter.

19. When asked what political party she prefers in the next election, a respondent replies "the Green Party." But she doesn't make a financial contribution to the party when asked to do so. Is this an example of attitude–behaviour inconsistency? Suggest alternative interpretations.

NOTES

1. For a dismissive and self-serving treatment of oral history evidence in the Canadian legal system, see the original B.C. Supreme Court Decision of Chief Justice McEachern in *Delgamuukw v. British Columbia [1991] B.C.J. No. 525* and its analysis by Cassidy (1992) and Culhane (1998). For a termination of that policy by the Supreme Court of Canada and more respectful consideration of Indigenous oral history, see their decision in *Delgamuukw v. British Columbia [1997] 3 S.C.R. 1010.* For a paper that argues there is still a long way to go see Napolean (2005).

2. Many Aboriginal women argue that patriarchy is a uniquely European experience that did not exist among Aboriginal peoples, in North America at least, until the imposition of European systems of governance by such mechanisms as the *Indian Act* (1876) in Canada (e.g., see Greschner 1992; Monture-Okanee 1993).

3. One can imagine situations where this question could get much more complex, such as when hermaphrodites, transsexuals, or people undergoing sex changes are explicitly made a focus of study, but these situations are fairly rare and hence are ignored here.

4. Cantril also content-analyzed the descriptions people gave of their best and worst situations, comparing them across the 16 countries in the study. Cantril's (1965) book *The Pattern of Human Concerns* is an interesting blend of qualitative and quantitative analysis that offers a textured portrait of the varying contexts in which many of us live.

5. For the uninitiated, your SIN is your social insurance number; VPD is the Vancouver Police Department; and PO, PC, and AG refer to being a probation officer, police officer (or police constable), or working in the attorney general's office. As for the Ottawa-speak, the PMO is the Prime Minister's Office; DMs and ADMs are deputy ministers and assistant deputy ministers; and DND is the Department of National Defence.

CHAPTER 7

OBSERVATION AND ETHNOGRAPHY

Because observation is something that all of us do all the time, we must begin by dispelling the idea that observation as a research method involves no more than "just looking." Observation as a research strategy involves *looking with a purpose:*

> As members of society, we also make observations of the everyday world. These guide us in forging paths of action and interpreting the actions and reactions of others ... What differentiates the observations of social scientists from those of everyday-life actors is the former's systematic and purposive nature. Social science researchers study their surroundings regularly and repeatedly, with a curiosity spurred by theoretical questions about the nature of human action, interaction, and society. (Adler & Adler 1994: 377)

Two distinct versions of observation will be discussed in this chapter. One version, typically (but not exclusively) part of more quantitative traditions, asks simply how we can gather observational data in a reliable and valid manner that allows us to test hypotheses and develop theory. The second version, typically (but not exclusively) the province of more qualitative traditions, sees observation as a general-purpose strategy, often used in concert with other methods, through which one can attempt to understand the phenomenology of the "other." While we will try to keep the two apart for pedagogical reasons, you'll see that the two versions are in some ways best seen as endpoints on a continuum, with the border between them a rather hard one to demarcate.

QUANTITATIVE OBSERVATION

One definition of *observation* offered by Weick (1968) describes it as "*the selection, provocation, recording and encoding of that set of behaviours and organisms* in situ *which is consistent with empirical aims*" (360; italics in original). To aid digestion of that mouthful, let's break the definition into its component parts.

Selection reminds researchers that "observation" is *not* a process whereby everything that happens is somehow visually recorded by the researcher. Rather, one looks *for* something for some reason that imposes an order on what we see; the selectivity involves an "editing" or "filtering" of events, and we try to be self-conscious of how we do so and of the limitations it imposes.

Provocation is an optional element. Observation may be done obtrusively or unobtrusively, and may or may not involve some manipulation of the setting as is done in field experiments. Observational techniques may therefore be employed within a wide range of research contexts, since they're consistent with all research objectives from exploratory to the purely descriptive to more explanatory research.

Recording or *encoding* sees us gathering data for analysis, which involves a broad range of alternatives, from keeping ongoing field notes—an open-ended and less structured approach more commonly used in qualitative field research—to employing more structured observational coding schemes to categorize or count behaviours, as is more typical of quantitative research. Either way, though, "encoding" necessarily involves *simplifying* what we observe, and we must exercise care to ensure that the encoding process doesn't do an injustice to the process we're attempting to describe or understand.

The reference to "that set of behaviours and organisms" points to the desirability of observing *multiple behaviours* and *different measures of the same behaviour* in any given context.

Including *in situ* (a Latin phrase meaning "situated" or "in context") in the definition underscores the importance of observing behaviour *in context* or looking at "natural" behaviour.

Leaving the term *empirical aims* intentionally open-ended, Weick acknowledges that observation may serve many functions, from straight *in vivo* (a Latin phrase meaning "in life") description to the formal testing of hypotheses. Observation is consistent with many research traditions, and if one had to boil it down to a word, is almost synonymous with "empiricism"; it is what researchers do.

Within the quantitative tradition of observation, the preference has been for more structured observation used in concert with a deductive approach that relegates the act of observation to the testing of hypotheses or the gathering of data that are defined by the researcher as important.

Three issues are of particular importance to quantitative researchers within the observational realm. First, because of the high priority attached to generating reliable and valid measurement, it is important we discuss how to develop, assess, and implement a reliable and valid coding scheme. Second, because of the awkwardness that arises when we watch people instead of interacting with them, there is a worry that the presence of a known observer will result in **reactivity,** that is, that the participants' behaviour will be deflected from its "usual" course when research participants know they are being observed. And third, because quantitative researchers believe that there are costs and benefits associated with either extreme—getting "too close" and courting "over-identification" *or* remaining "too aloof" and heightening reactivity— attention is paid to the relation between the observer and those he or she is observing, and the implications this relation

may have for the data that are gathered. Each of these issues will be examined in turn.

Gathering Data: Checklists and Coding Schemes

Quantitative observational researchers are expected to begin with a clear sense of purpose and a well-developed coding scheme that will result in the accumulation of reliable and valid data. These criteria are met through use of standardized checklists and coding schemes. Deductive researchers construct such tools on the basis of theory and the literature, whereas inductive researchers incorporate issues and indicators that emerge from preliminary exploration. This section describes some of the types of coding schemes that have been constructed and briefly discusses the assessment of reliability and validity.

As a first dimension to consider, coding schemes might be conceived of as either *static,* where particular attributes of the setting are noted (e.g., age and sex of participant, public or private setting) or *dynamic* (i.e., focusing on behaviour and its unfolding). Dynamic coding schemes may include simple categorizations (e.g., whether someone gives change to a busker) or more complex ones (e.g., whether eye contact is made, how the initial verbal appeal is delivered, whether there is a movement to check for funds).

In general, coding schemes are one of two types: a **sign system** or a **category system.** With *sign* systems, the researcher essentially waits, noting each time a predetermined criterion behaviour occurs. For example, a researcher investigating the incidence of prosocial behaviour among children in a playschool setting might observe the children over the course of a day and (after having taken care to develop an operational definition of what kinds of acts will be considered "prosocial") note each time a prosocial act occurs. In contrast, *category* systems attempt to create a set of mutually exclusive, and exhaustive, categories into which any given behaviour might be classified. Thus, rather than checking off each prosocial act, the researcher might code on a minute-by-minute basis and, within each minute, code (at its simplest) whether the behaviours the children are exhibiting are prosocial or non-prosocial or (in a more complex coding scheme) whether the dominant behaviour was prosocial, affectionate, communicative, aggressive, or whatever.

A sign system would give a better indication of *how many* prosocial acts were witnessed (since every act is counted), whereas a category system would give a better indication of the *temporal flow* of the prosocial acts during the day (e.g., Was the amount of prosocial behaviour greater in the morning, when the children were fresh, or in the afternoon, when they were more tired? Was there more prosocial behaviour before they watched *Yu-gi-oh* or after?).

One classic example of a coding system used in structured observational research is a category system developed by Bales (1970) known as Interactional Analysis. Figure 7.1 shows the 12 categories it includes: they're intended to be mutually exclusive and exhaustive of all that might happen, in general terms, in a group. When engaged in discussion or a problem-solving task, each person who contributes to the group dynamic (whether verbally or nonverbally) has his or her verbal contribution coded according to one of the 12 categories. As a general framework, it offers a way to investigate such phenomena as differences between group members in participation styles, for example, or a way to look at changes in the group dynamic as a function of variation in the composition of the group, the nature of the problem, and/or the nature of the instructions. Bales's system has been one of the more popular coding systems for studying group dynamics and

Figure 7.1

Bales's (1970) Interactional Analysis: A Category System for Observing Interaction in Groups

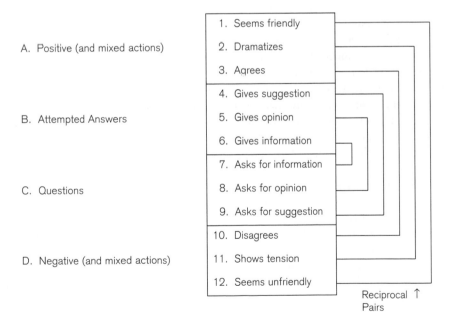

Source: Adapted from C. M. Judd, E. R. Smith, and L. H. Kidder (1991), *Research Methods in Social Relations,* 6th edition (Fort Worth, TX: Holt, Rinehart and Winston), p. 282.

has been in use for more than 35 years. There are many such systems that can be used *in toto* or adapted. In another domain, for example, Judd, Smith, and Kidder (1991) note that "at least 73 systems for observing young children are available in the literature" (283).

Assessing Reliability

Whichever alternative is chosen, researchers are obliged to consider the reliability with which their coding scheme can be implemented. If the coding scheme is sufficiently well defined, different individuals should be able to code the same material or events independently and come to the same conclusions. Thus, if we're using a sign system to code incidents of violence in a TV program, we're in big trouble if you count 3 incidents and another researcher counts 27 when we watch the same program. Clearly, the researcher should assess the reliability with which a coding scheme can be applied *before* doing the actual study, since doing the study is a waste of time if one cannot have any confidence in the reliability of the observational scheme.

In general, such an assessment is made by having different individuals code the same material independently. The reliability of the category coding scheme is the extent of inter-rater agreement. For example, in a one-hour observational period where two raters were using a category system to code the "dominant theme" in each one-minute period, what percentage of the time did the two raters make the same categorizations, and what percentage of the time did they differ? If the inter-rater agreement is above 80 percent, and especially if it's above 90 percent, then you're doing pretty well and can feel comfortable going ahead and coding "for real." If it's lower than that, a better coding manual and/or more training might be required. In either case, the data should be examined carefully to determine exactly where the disagreements are occurring; this approach will help highlight what aspects of the coding scheme or training program need to be rectified.

A number of factors are known to influence the reliability of coding schemes:

- The more *clearly defined* and *non-overlapping* the coding system, the higher the reliability.

- *The shorter the period of time* between the event and the coding of it, the greater the reliability of the recording; coding while observing is obviously optimal here.

- Reliability is lower when *inference* is required: observers can agree more easily whether people are "walking" or "running" (two overt behaviours) than on whether people are "happy" or "sad" (two emotional states or feelings that involve more inference) about heading to their destination.

- Reliability is higher when the *number of categories* is small. A larger number of categories generally requires finer, more difficult distinctions.

- *Coder training* will affect reliability. The researcher must determine just how much training is required in order to maximize the reliability of the observational scheme.

Reliability is particularly enhanced by a careful articulation of one's nominal definition of the construct(s) under consideration. For example, in one graduate-level methods class he taught, Ted informed students that they were going to study coding schemes the next week. In preparation, they were each to watch the first period of a hockey game that was to be broadcast that weekend, and were to come to class the next week ready to state how many violent acts occurred during that first period. When the students returned and gave their counts, the numbers ranged from zero to 140!

Clearly, "violent" meant different things to different people, so Ted asked the students to explain what the term had meant to them. The person who counted "zero" considered "violent" to be synonymous with "fights," noting that there were none during the period that was observed. For the person who counted 140, "violent" meant any non-accidental physical contact between players, and there were many incidents of bumping, boarding, and such during the period. Others argued for definitions that recognized professional hockey as a contact sport and hence focused on "gratuitous" contact as the defining aspect of "violence." Still others felt that, to meet their definition, the contact had to be gratuitous *and* outside the rules; these people focused on penalties emerging from contact (e.g., "tripping" would be a violent rule violation, but "too many men on the ice" would not). They spent much of the class discussing which definition was "best" for their purposes. Once they agreed on what definition to employ, each of the students independently counted incidents of violence in a video-taped period of hockey. This time, there was very little variation in their counts. In other words, their coding was now *reliable;* independent observers could code the same material and come up with essentially the same results.

There are several other comments to make about this example. First, recall the distinction between reliability and validity. Although the students had become *reliable* in their coding, the *validity* issue still remained. In one sense, all four of the definitions supplied were "valid." All you can do is choose definitions consistent with your research objectives and theoretical approach, and then articulate these choices for scrutiny by other researchers. The "best" choice will vary depending on the theory and objectives that guide you, as well as the context. If one player intentionally bumps another during a football game, we may consider it "nonviolent" because it is "within the rules" and "part of the game." But the same behaviour on an escalator at Sears might be considered "violent" because it's gratuitous in that setting. The challenge is to derive a definition that is useful in your research context and to articulate your choices so that others can judge the utility of your definition to them.

Threats to Validity: Dealing with Reactivity

Having developed a suitable coding scheme, the researcher sets out to implement it. One worry is whether the mere act of observation will somehow "change" their behaviour because of being observed. This is an issue of reactivity; that is, whether and

how the researcher's presence causes research participants to change from their "usual" or "normal" behaviour patterns because they know they're being watched.

It's certainly easy to think of many situations where this might occur, particularly when the behaviour being observed is a socially undesirable one that would not reflect well on the research participant. Parents whose child-rearing styles are being observed, for example, are probably less likely to engage in abusive behaviour when they're being observed; teachers are probably less likely to yell at their pupils; police officers are probably less likely to engage in civil rights violations.

Several factors, some of which the researcher has some control over, can minimize reactivity in most observational settings. An obvious one is the *conspicuousness of the observer.* All else being equal, a researcher who's in the middle of the action will be more conspicuous than one who stands discreetly at the edge of activity. Related to this are the *characteristics of the observer*, particularly the *similarity* of characteristics between the observer and observed. In general, the greater the similarity between observer and observed (in age, dress, race, for example), the less conspicuous the observer will be and, hence, the less reactivity will be generated. Observational research is thus a good time *not* to wear white lab coats, nor should a 40-year-old professor in a suit expect to fade into the woodwork when studying the Goth community. On the other hand, fraudulent behaviour stands out like a sore thumb. The professor might look transparently absurd if he or she died his/her hair black and acquired various piercings.

The *characteristics of the participants* also affect reactivity. Children, for example, seem to forget about an observer's presence a lot more quickly than adults do, although the novelty of being observed wears off fairly quickly for both groups. Indeed, another important principle is that *the longer the observational period, the more reactivity is reduced.* This is so for several reasons: (1) novel stimuli in a person's environment (such as an observer) dominate the person's attention initially but soon fade into the background; (2) rapport is often established between the observer and those being observed, so that the observer becomes a less threatening presence; and (3) although it's easy to construct and maintain an image for a short time, most people find it very hard to keep up a false front over the long term.

The *rationale for observing* given to participants also plays a role in the defensiveness they exhibit. For example, in an evaluation concerning the Vancouver Police Department's Mobile Radio Data System (which gives officers access to various data banks from a computer terminal located in patrol cars), Palys, Boyanowsky, and Dutton (1984) went out of their way to assure officers that it was the *system* rather than *them* that was being evaluated (although it took some time before patrol officers actually became convinced that this was the case). As well, the fact that several of the observers had prior policing interests and/or experience seems to have minimized reactivity (note that the factor used to their benefit was one of trying to maximize the similarity between observer and observed).

Palys and colleagues also were fortunate in that study to have a way of assessing the extent to which the presence of observers generated reactivity, since they were able to scrutinize computerized archival records of system use, thereby comparing in some ways how officers used the system when observers were present versus how they used it when observers were not. The differences turned out to be quite trivial, although officers had clearly minimized their frivolous use of the system (e.g., to send riddles and jokes to one another; to make arrangements for lunch) in the presence of the observers.

As this example suggests, *the nature of the phenomenon the researcher is observing* also will influence reactivity. The more deviant or stigmatized the

activity being scrutinized, the more reactive the situation, and the longer it will take to build appropriate rapport.

The Relationship between Observer and Observed

Weick (1968) and other sources in the more quantitative traditions (e.g., Babbie 1989; Judd, Smith, & Kidder 1991) suggest that a major element differentiating observational studies is the nature of the relationship between the observer and the observed. The continuum of roles that is envisioned, attributed variously to Gold (1958) and Junker (1960), can range from the **complete participant** to the **complete observer,** as depicted in Figure 7.2. We'll examine the two extremes of the continuum first, and then try to make some sense of the middle ground.

THE COMPLETE PARTICIPANT

With the "complete participant" role, the observer does not reveal himself or herself as a researcher. From the perspective of those being observed, the researcher *is* a participant. There are two ways this might occur.

THE *POST HOC* OBSERVER In the first, the observer *really is* a participant, with any efforts at "observation," in its empirical sense, done on a *post hoc* (a Latin phrase meaning "after the fact") basis. That is, someone who has been a participant in some social situation decides to write about it after his or her participation ends. Examples would include a politician who decides to write his or her memoirs after retirement; anyone sitting down at

Figure 7.2

The Traditional Observational Continuum: "Complete Participant" to "Complete Observer"

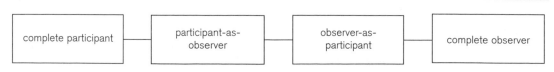

the end of the day to make a diary entry; or someone who has been a prisoner, a sex worker, or the head of a major corporation writing after the fact about his or her experiences. The defining aspect here is that as the process occurs, the person *is* a participant; only after the fact does he or she decide to reflect on his or her experiences and write an analytical account based on earlier observations.

This *post hoc* development of accounts has both advantages and limitations. Accounts produced by former participants can be very analytical and insightful; the information they provide often has all the immediacy, intimacy, and insight that can only come from direct involvement. Besides the interesting perspective these accounts represent in their own right, the heuristic benefit of providing them as raw data for subsequent analysis should also not be overlooked.

But the limitations to the "*post hoc* observer" role are several. First, ethical issues are raised by a transition from "complete participant" to later "writer/ analyst," since the "informed consent" provisions of ethical guidelines are clearly violated. Second, it's virtually a research truism that to minimize reporting bias and distortion in data gathering, the researcher should be prepared to systematically gather relevant evidence while the observation is in process. Observation as a social science research method requires preparation, attention to detail, and the systematic retention of notes. Because of the *post hoc* observer's after-the-fact change in role, his or her accounts are more likely to be subject to errors of memory or selective recollection of events (since he or she was busy participating at the time).

One also must consider the motives of those who adopt an observer role after the fact. Do they have a particular axe to grind or image to convey? It will surely be reflected in their accounts. "Complete participants" who wish to make the transition to "writer/analyst" should be particularly sensitive to the need for independent corroboration of their accounts (e.g., by compiling memos, tapes, or other documentation; interviewing other participants; compiling media accounts); such evidence may also help to jog one's memory or fill in gaps.

THE SURREPTITIOUS OBSERVER The second way to adopt the "complete participant" role involves the researcher entering a situation fully intending to engage in observational research, but doing so without ever telling those being observed what he or she is doing. Laud Humphreys's (1970) *Tearoom Trade*, noted in Chapter 3, would fall into this group. Another example is the classic study entitled *When Prophecy Fails*, by Festinger, Riecken, and Schachter (1956).

But as with the *post hoc* observer, the lack of informed consent and the presence of deception should wave red flags for you in the realm of ethical concerns. Key factors to consider here are (a) whether the situation is "public" or not, and (b) whether the data that are gathered involve identifiable persons. For example, few people have any problem with the idea of doing observational research on the way that people use public spaces such as waiting rooms, elevators, shopping malls, and parking lots. One can easily imagine other examples: examining crowd behaviour while attending a sporting event or music concert; spending time in courtrooms watching interactions among lawyers, judges, and court staff. In each case, the researcher participates as just another member of the crowd; the process of observing such behaviour doesn't seem like a violation of privacy, since one is examining only those actions people decide to reveal in public anyway. Further, because there's rarely any attempt to acquire people's names in this sort of setting, anonymity is preserved. In most such cases the people are not identified and cannot be after the study is over.

But what if the researcher wants to videotape the way people spontaneously order themselves as they enter buses or get on escalators. Some would be concerned about consent issues here because of the possibility of identifiability; others would have no problem with it as long as the only people who see the tapes are members of the research team so that confidentiality is preserved.

Also, we have glossed over any difficulties with separating "public" from "private" spaces, but is the line always so easily drawn? What about meetings of

Alcoholics Anonymous? They are open to anyone who wants to attend, but is the "open" invitation not implicitly limited to those with a drinking problem who want to seek help? Can the "open" invitation also be exploited by researchers, journalists, and so on? Lofland and Lejeune (1960) did exactly that in their study of AA and were chastised by some and praised by others when they published their work.

Similar questions are asked about cyber opportunities such as chat rooms, some of which are completely open; others require "memberships" that are simply a matter of registering, while others are more surreptitious and closed (see Atchison 1999 and Kitchin 2002 for discussions about these issues as they pertain to cyber-research). Is it acceptable for researchers to "lurk" in such cybersettings in order to observe the interaction and then to write about it without the consent of those involved? In the past one might have argued that the provision of confidentiality made surreptitious observation acceptable, but we have to be careful when we quote someone "anonymously" because powerful search engines such as Google now make it quite plausible that today's "anonymous" quote will be quite easily attached to a person via some cyber-group's electronic archive.

Social scientists continue to be divided about the wisdom of doing surreptitious research, as they have been for years. Some maintain that deception is never acceptable. Others argue that such an approach is reasonable as long as (1) the research question is of sufficient merit; (2) those being observed are not adversely affected or diverted by one's presence; and (3) appropriate precautions are taken to ensure confidentiality. Still others suggest that even those restrictions are too cumbersome and that when observational research is designed to expose and analyze abuses of power and other corruptive practices, anything goes (e.g., see Punch 1994 for a discussion of that perspective and Miller & Tewksbury 2001 for a broader discussion about the utility and ethics of covert methods). Perhaps intending to steer a midcourse, others have gathered data as "complete participants" but have then sought "informed consent" after the fact by informing those

involved of their motives and asking whether they might be permitted to use the data (e.g., Alfred 1976).

Finally, it has also been argued that from a purely scientific perspective, the "surreptitious observer" role cannot be dismissed, since it combines the dual advantages of being an observer (and hence being prepared, systematic, etc.) while also minimizing the reactivity of participants through the shared participant role.

When a decision is made to engage in surreptitious observation, other issues arise. For example, assuming a strictly participatory identity in the setting, while still maintaining your observational motives, requires you to assume multiple roles, a situation that can create role conflict (e.g., see Cicourel 1964; Marquart 2001; Riecken 1969). The problems are twofold. First, because (by definition) the "real" participants can't know that you're an observer, you can't take notes while observing. As a result, you must either make numerous trips to the bathroom in order to jot down notes or write down a choice quotation, or wait until the end of the day to write daily synopses. In the former case, if not perceived as having a bladder problem, you may be viewed suspiciously. In the latter case, the longer the delay between when you make your observations and when you actually write them down, the greater heed you must pay to distortions of recall or the bias of selective memory. Cicourel (1964) argues that such distortions represent one of the biggest problems in research involving the complete participant.

A second problem arises from the fact that, in order to continue the participant guise, you must *participate*. But by doing so, you potentially alter the very process you are trying to observe. When Festinger's graduate students joined a doomsday group in order to study them, it's possible that the mere act of their joining helped convince the original group members of the veracity of their vision. And once you've joined, what do you do when someone turns to you during discussion and asks, "So what do *you* think?" If you say something and people follow your suggestion, you may have influenced the group to go in a direction it might not otherwise have gone. If you say something and your suggestion is *not* followed, this sequence of events might be the beginning of disharmony or factionalism within the group. But if you *don't* say anything, you may engender suspicion about your presence or contribute to feelings of indecisiveness or ambiguity among members of the group. In sum, it's hard to know how to be "neutral"; this is one instance where politicians, many of whom seem quite expert at sounding like they're responding to a question while really saying nothing, may provide a useful model.

Finally, it should also be noted that there are many other settings where ethical concerns do not seem as problematic, even though participants in the research are never told that they have participated in a piece of research. Lyn H. Lofland (e.g., 1973), for example, has spent a considerable amount of time sitting in bus depots and other public places observing the way strangers use space in public settings. And John Lowman (1989), as part of his study evaluating the effects of changes in the "communicating" laws regarding prostitution, included simple counts of the numbers of prostitutes who could be observed working the streets both before and after the change in the law.

THE COMPLETE OBSERVER

At the other extreme of the continuum is the "complete observer" role. This position is epitomized by the researcher who identifies himself or herself as being engaged in observational research, and who either sets up a study in his or her own setting (such as a laboratory or clinic) or gains access to another setting (such as an organization or group) by seeking and obtaining the permission of someone appropriate. Once in the setting, the complete observer typically does his or her best to remain relatively inconspicuous, doing nothing other than observe with the full knowledge of all who are present that that's why the researcher is there.

OBSERVING ON HOME TURF There's an extensive tradition of observational research in the laboratory, particularly among experimental social psychologists and those who study child development. Such studies typically involve setting up a particular situation, with the observer then retreating behind a one-way glass to make notes or systematically code the behaviours that emerge. This method was particularly popular in the "group dynamics" domain, for example, where researchers would test theories about the dynamics of groups under varying conditions. There are two great advantages to this approach. First, it's ethically non-problematic (assuming participants aren't misled about the purpose of the research), because participants are informed from the start that they're participating in an observational study. Second, because it happens on the researcher's own turf in a predetermined manner, he or she is ready to observe, using checklists or other coding schemes that have been prepared ahead of time.

The biggest *dis*advantages associated with such research are the often artificial and decontextualized nature of the setting (if, indeed, any setting can be said to "lack" context), and the reactivity that's often involved when research participants know they're being observed. The artificial nature of such settings means that while they may be reasonable research sites for testing theoretical propositions (i.e., hypothesis testing)—since such testing requires only a setting in which the scope conditions designated by the theory are met—one must be cautious about generalizing one's results to other settings where different contextual conditions hold. And reactivity remains a problem no matter what one's research objectives are.

THE COMPLETE OBSERVER IN THE FIELD Besides considerations of reactivity, the complete observer in the field must first deal with problems of access. You must address the question of why any group or organization should let you—a stranger—observe its behaviour. Although we might like or hope for the prospective participants to trust us immediately because we are affiliated with a university and/or have a project due next month and/or are basically honest and well-meaning, reality is rarely so benevolent. Instead, the complete observer must be prepared to talk his or her way into the group.

Lofland and Lofland (1984) suggest that you'll be most effective in doing so if you come armed with connections, accounts, knowledge, and courtesy.

With respect to *connections,* Lofland and Lofland (1984) suggest that, if you're not connected with the target group or organization already, you'd do well to cast about among your friends and acquaintances to find someone who is and who would be willing to provide an introduction. They recount the experiences of Joan Hoffman (1980), who was herself a member of an elite family and who had attempted to talk to community elites who were serving on hospital boards:

> Introducing myself as a sociology graduate student, I had very limited success in getting by the gatekeepers of the executive world. Telephone follow-ups to letters sent requesting an interview repeatedly found Mr. X "tied up" or "in conference." When I did manage to get my foot in the door, interviews rarely exceeded a half hour, were continuously interrupted by phone calls ... and elicited only "front work" ... the public version of what hospital boards were all about ... By chance during [one] interview, my respondent discovered that he knew a member of my family. "Why didn't you say so?" The rest of the interview was dramatically different than all my previous data. (Hoffman 1980: 46; cited in Lofland & Lofland 1984: 25)

Even when you know no one in the setting, connecting with one person who can act as an "in" and/or "key informant" can make all the difference between getting a project off the ground and not. For Whyte (1943), in his classic *Street Corner Society,* for example, the person who made all the difference was "Doc." For Duneier (1999) in his study of sidewalk entrepreneurs in *Sidewalk,* it was seller of "black books" Hakim Hasan, with whom he struck up a conversation when he noticed Hasan was selling a book Duneier had written previously. For Horowitz (1983), the beginning came with a mixture of persistence and luck:

> I chose to sit on a park bench where many youths gathered from noon until midnight. On the third afternoon of sitting on the bench, as I dropped a softball that had rolled toward me, a young man came over and said "You can't catch" (which I acknowledged) and "You're not from the hood [neighbourhood], are you?" This was a statement, not a question. He was Gilberto, the Lions' President. When I told him I wanted to write a book on Chicano youth, he said I should meet the other young men and took me over to shake hands with eight members of the Lions. (7; cited in Berg 2001: 146)

Once a preliminary connection is made, Lofland and Lofland (1984) argue that you should also be prepared with *accounts,* by which they mean "a carefully thought-out explanation or account of the proposed research" (25). Use words and concepts that are meaningful to the prospective sample, and while you should be prepared to offer an academic justification for your project, that's probably not what's being sought here. Instead, you should be ready to offer a simple, straightforward, and honest explanation that addresses the question "Why are you interested in us?"

Ironically, Lofland and Lofland introduce "being knowledgeable" as a liability, though at times it can also be an asset, depending on the situation. A commonly used strategy is to represent yourself as a "learner," which, indeed, in some ways, you are (otherwise, there'd be no need to engage in the research). The advantages of taking that approach are twofold. First, it reduces the extent to which you might be perceived as threatening. Second, the process of "teaching" reveals much about a person's understandings.

But the role of "naive observer" can also be overplayed and can end up interfering with the acquisition of rich data. If you're perceived as unknowledgeable, you're likely to receive little more than what Hoffman (1980) referred to above as "front work," that is, superficial information of the type that usually appears in brochures or on guided tours. Particularly when people are very busy and/or are more senior members of the organization, you must demonstrate that you're worth their time and that they, in particular, are the only appropriate sources for what you need to know. Showing that you've done your homework, that you don't ask the same simple questions that everyone else asks, that you can speak "the language" of that profession, and that you know something about the phenomenon you wish to observe (but do not have too many preconceived notions and are willing to watch and listen) is a good recipe for being treated seriously.

Finally, Lofland and Lofland (1984) emphasize that you must show *courtesy* and respect in negotiating for entry. This means phoning ahead to make appointments at a time convenient to your guide(s); taking the time to tell everyone who's interested a little bit about your research, even if a given person isn't directly involved; and ensuring that you also get permission from dependent or subordinate populations as well as from those who act as gatekeepers (e.g., asking the kids for their permission and not just their parents and the daycare person).

MIXING PARTICIPATION AND OBSERVATION The two middle roles in the observational continuum are labelled **participant-as-observer** and **observer-as-participant.** As their titles suggest, both involve a mixing of the participatory and observational roles, with the difference based on which of the two predominates. This in itself may not be particularly clear-cut, and participant observers often float back and forth between the two, depending on the particular situation.

One perfect example of a mixture of roles was chosen by Muzafer Sherif in his famous "Robber's Cave" studies (see Sherif et al. 1961). Sherif was interested in studying group dynamics, particularly with respect to group formation, cohesiveness, and conflict, and used a boys' summer camp as the context in which to perform his research. As far as the boys were concerned, it was summer camp and nothing more. But for Sherif, it was also an opportunity to manipulate different aspects of the situa-

tion (e.g., setting up teams, facilitating the development of rivalries, setting up a situation where only through cooperation could an obstacle be overcome) to systematically investigate their effects. Everything that happened involved typical summer camp experiences; Sherif's interest was in making things happen at particular times rather than leaving them to chance.

The ideal from Sherif's perspective was to be a participant—to avoid reactivity effects and to be close to the centre of the action—while at the same time remaining detached from the action so that he didn't inadvertently influence it. If you were Muzafer Sherif, what role would *you* occupy in order to ensure that you didn't interfere unintentionally in the course of events? He obviously couldn't pretend to be one of the boys. He might have chosen to be a camp counsellor, but then might have become a special focus of attention for the kids. The brilliance of Muzafer Sherif is revealed in that, even if you were at the camp, you would probably have looked right past him. He was the janitor and part-time maintenance person, one of those invisible service people who are always there but in some way socially nonexistent or outside the action, perhaps raking leaves or picking up litter. His presence would likely go unnoticed.

In many ways, mixing the participant and observer roles surmounts the problems of each role in isolation. To the extent that the researcher's status as an observer is honestly presented, ethical concerns about deception or lack of informed consent are minimized. And to the extent that the researcher acts as a participant in the setting, reactivity is often reduced because, as a participant, he or she more quickly fades into the group.

MORE QUALITATIVE METHODS: PARTICIPANT OBSERVATION AND ETHNOGRAPHY

We now begin crossing the border to methods favoured by more qualitatively oriented researchers. Participant observation (a tradition in sociology) and ethnography (rooted in anthropology) are often used to try to get into the phenomenological world of the "other," that is, coming to *know* people who are different from one's "self." J. Lofland (1971) suggests that it's more characteristic in modern life for us to *know about* people and things than to *know* them:

> A significant feature of being a modern person—of living in what we call the modern world—is to *know about* a wide variety of other human beings but not to *know* them. To know about a category of human beings is to have it represented by second parties that such a category exists. We can know about Hottentots, Russians, presidents, delinquents, hippies, or whatever through newspapers, television, face-to-face reports, and other *mediated* means. (1)

But, adds J. Lofland (1971), "to know about—to know through stereotype and typification—is not enough. We want a more direct sense of what other people are about and what their lives are like than that provided by casual and unexamined typifications" (2).

The difference between "knowing about" and "knowing" is the difference between casual curiosity and the more systematic, strategic interest of social scientists. By arguing for direct contact, Lofland reaffirms that part of being a social scientist is to *interact* with the phenomena we wish to understand; as G. Morgan (1983b) phrased it, we "engage" them. We seek *direct* evidence from the world that bears on the theoretical issues that we deem—or that emerge as—important, and observation is a way to gather such data.

J. Lofland (1971) suggests that *knowing* requires the social scientist to be close to the people being studied in four respects:

> (1) He should have been close in the physical sense of conducting his own life in face-to-face proximity to the persons he tells about; (2) This physical proximity should have extended over some significant period of time and variety of cir-

cumstances; (3) The [researcher][1] should have developed closeness in the social sense of intimacy and confidentiality. He should have developed relationships that provided him reasonable access to the activities of a set of people through their entire round of life; (4) He should have conducted his recording activities in such a way that his reportage can give close and searching attention to ... the minutiae of daily life. (3)

Not all researchers would agree with Lofland. While Lofland's distinction between *knowing about* and *knowing* may be useful in reminding us of the limitations of what we think we know, many would question whether it's ever *really* possible to know (in the most profound sense) without having lived the life one aspires to understand. Can a non-Aboriginal person ever *really* understand what it's like to grow up as an Aboriginal person in Canada? Can a physically healthy person ever *fully* appreciate the life of the physically challenged? Certainly there are aspects of the experience about which we can gather information, but perceptions and understandings founded on a lifetime of experience are very hard to capture in even the most extensive research program. But to the extent that we *can* understand those others, Lofland's admonitions seem a reasonable set of criteria to adhere to, and they can be well met with participant observational and ethnographic methods.

QUALITATIVE ETHNOGRAPHY

Both participant observation and ethnography refer to methods whereby the researcher spends extensive time (e.g., months or years) in a setting trying to understand some aspect(s) of the setting from the perspective of those in it, often using a combination of methods (e.g., observation might be supplemented with interviews and archival analysis). But at another level, ethnography is so completely different in its history and in the way it's construed that it merits separate attention for the issues that have arisen in its development. By way of background, Vidich and Lyman (1994) explain that *ethnos,* a Greek term, denotes a people, a race or cultural group ... When *ethnos* as a prefix is combined with *graphic* to form the term *ethnographic,* the reference is to the subdiscipline known as descriptive anthropology—in its broadest sense, the science devoted to describing ways of life of humankind. *Ethnography,* then, refers to a social scientific description of a people and the cultural basis of their peoplehood. (25; italics in original)

The Challenge of Understanding an "Other"

The history of ethnography conveys much about the history of social science and its attempts to grapple with the understanding of an "other," that is, someone other than ourselves. Vidich and Lyman suggest that ethnography grew out of Europeans' interest in understanding the "primitive" cultures they encountered when Columbus stumbled across the "New World."[2] Trying to understand someone so completely different from oneself poses a very big problem. As Vidich and Lyman (1994) phrased it,

> in practice, it becomes this question: By which values are observations to be guided? The choices seem to be either the values of the ethnographer or the values of the observed—that is, in modern parlance, either the *etic* or the *emic* ... Herein lies a deeper and more fundamental problem: How is it possible to understand the other when the other's values are not one's own? (26)

THE EARLY ETHNOGRAPHER

Good question! Early cultural ethnographies (in the 15th and 16th centuries) by Europeans were done from a clearly European perspective, and evaluated indigenous practices and beliefs using a European yardstick. Most of these written accounts were produced by explorers, missionaries, and colonial administrators. Not surprisingly, when the implicit question was "how European" indigenous cultures were, the answer was "not very." Since the Europeans of that time saw themselves and their Christian religions as the epitome of "civilization," indigenous peoples were regarded as inferior, thereby

giving justification to the incredible greed and horrific treatment many of these "civilized" visitors exhibited toward their hosts (e.g., see Berger 1992; Churchill 1994; Wright 1992).

The beginnings of "modern" ethnography are typically said to have emerged in the late 19th and early 20th centuries, when anthropologists like Bronislaw Malinowski (e.g., see 1922) and Margaret Mead (e.g., see 1928/1960) actually left their homes and went travelling to see firsthand how these "others" lived.

> The field-worker, during this period, was lionized, made into a larger-than-life figure who went into and then returned from the field with stories about strange people. Rosaldo (1989) describes this as the period of the Lone Ethnographer, the story of the man–scientist who went off in search of his native in a distant land ... Returning home with his data, the Lone Ethnographer wrote up an objective account of the culture he studied. (Denzin & Lincoln 1994: 7)

Once again, the criteria for analysis were clear. The application of Darwinian evolutionary theory to social matters—an approach that placed humans at the top of the natural order and was conveniently adapted by Social Darwinists to place Caucasians at the top of the human order—allowed any concerns about social relativism to be easily placed aside. If "we" were the top of the human heap, then surely "ours" were the most appropriate criteria to be used in understanding and evaluating other cultures. Thus, "objectivity" meant employing European standards and imposing a European point of view. The scholar's challenge was to translate indigenous beliefs and practices into terms that Europeans could understand.[3] But when taken out of context that way, practices that might have played an important social role in indigenous cultures for thousands of years could appear quaint, trivial, and trite, if not completely beyond "rational" belief. The result made some people wonder how contemporary North Americans might appear if they were studied and written about in the same manner (e.g., see Miner 1956).

DISCOVERING THE "OTHER" AMONG US

The next "moment" of ethnographic history (to use Denzin & Lincoln's [1994] term) featured a number of American sociologists who began to practise a similar method to understand the "other" that existed at home. Although there were other isolated examples of this "urban ethnography," it was at the University of Chicago's sociology department in the 1920s through the 1940s (the "Chicago School") where this approach was practised with zeal. The names Robert Park, Ernest Burgess, W. I. Thomas, and Louis Wirth are prominent in such accounts. Central to their approach was the idea that American cities are brimming with heterogeneous peoples of differing lifestyles and worldviews, and that an understanding of American culture requires some understanding of that diversity. Park was the one to conceive of the "natural area" as the appropriate unit to be studied:

> Every American city has its slums; its ghettos; its immigrant colonies, regions which maintain more or less alien and exotic cultures. Nearly every city has its bohemias and hobohemias, where life is freer, more adventurous and lonely than it is elsewhere. These are called natural areas of the city. (Park 1952: 196; cited in Vidich & Lyman 1994: 33)

Park encouraged sociologists to undertake case studies of these natural areas. And he, along with his colleagues and students, did so *en masse* for more than three decades. Studies were undertaken of "the Jewish ghetto, Polonia, Little Italy, Little Germany, Chinatown, Bronzeville and Harlem, the gold coast and the slum, hobo jungles, single-room occupants of furnished rooms, enclaves of cultural and social dissidents, the urban ecology of gangdom, and the urban areas that housed the suicidal, the drug addicted and the mentally disabled, and on the social and economic dynamics of real estate transactions," to name only a few areas (Vidich & Lyman 1994: 33).[4] It was in keeping with this tradition that William Foote Whyte actually moved into an Italian-American neighbourhood to engage in research he called "participant observation" (see 1943).

Despite the differences between these two earlier moments of ethnographic history, they also shared a certain similarity. Underlying both was a sense of social scientific mission born from a kind of Euro-American imperialism that romanticized the "others" they scrutinized, while at the same time seeing their eventual passing as tragic, but inevitable, in the march of "progress" and assimilation. For anthropologists like Malinowski, the study of indigenous peoples was important primarily because it was a way to have a last brief glimpse of our own prehistory before it became ensnared by the inevitable onslaught of "progress" and "civilization" and faded into oblivion. For sociologists like Park, however much hobos or immigrants were lauded and romanticized, one senses the belief that the urban ethnographers' texts would ultimately stand as museum pieces once all lost their uniqueness in the "melting pot" that was America. This attitude calls to mind the Borg, an alien culture featured on the former TV series *Star Trek: The Next Generation*, whose slogan was "Resistance is futile; assimilation is inevitable."[5]

But assimilation, it turned out, was not at all inevitable. Although challenges to theories that touted its inevitability were first raised in the 1930s (even by Park himself), a third moment of ethnographic history laid these views to rest. Vidich and Lyman (1994) describe the process: "During the two decades after 1970, ethnological studies of African-American, Amerindian, Mexican-American, and Asian peoples also cast considerable doubt on whether, when, and to whose benefit the much-vaunted process of ethnocultural meltdown in America would occur" (37). Other studies would attempt to give a voice to other of society's underclasses, while also attempting to bring new levels of rigour to the process of qualitative analysis (e.g., see Becker 1958, 1963, 1979; Becker, Geer, Hughes, & Strauss 1961; see also Kidder 1981a; Smith & Manning 1982).

ISSUES OF "VOICE" AND "PRIVILEGE"

The issue in many ways became an issue of *voice*: minority ethnic and racial groups became tired of other people speaking for them. All had felt the injustice that the supposedly "neutral" sciences had imposed on them either by denying their voice entirely or, on those occasions when they were given one, by reinterpreting what they were trying to say. And while all were interested in participating in the contemporary world, all were also unwilling to leave behind their hyphenated identities as the price of admission. We saw the same theme evident in Chapter 6 with respect to feminist perspectives and the need to rectify the gender imbalance of written history.

Because of these concerns, many ethnographic researchers have great problems with the role continuum presented above under "Quantitative Observation," the one that runs from the "complete participant" through a mixture of roles to the "complete observer" (recall Figure 7.2). That continuum implies that one *can be* a "complete observer" devoid of any participatory interest. But as Atkinson and Hammersley (1994) point out,

> although it is important to recognize the variation to be found in the roles adopted by observers, this simple dichotomy is not very useful, not least because it seems to imply that the nonparticipant observer plays no recognized role at all ... In a sense *all* social research is a form of participant observation, because we cannot study the social world without being part of it. (248–49; see also Hammersley & Atkinson 1983)

This statement reflects the growing recognition that we cannot study the world without acknowledging the "we" that is doing the studying. As Denzin and Lincoln (1994) remind us, "any gaze is always filtered through the lenses of language, gender, social class, race and ethnicity. There are no objective observations, only observations socially situated in the worlds of the observer and the observed" (12). Our collective and individual biographies—whether because of the experience or the *lack* of experience (and hence perspective) they entail—cannot help but enter into and influence our work. Left at that, the challenge becomes one of trying to understand the role that biography might

play in our work, and either make an effort to counteract it or simply be upfront about its existence and let the reader decide what to make of it.

But the problem becomes magnified when we consider the power relations that have traditionally existed whenever we carry out a piece of research. We may try to be thoughtful about how we consider the research participant(s) we're observing and may do our best to listen to them carefully as they tell us about their world; at the end of the day, though, it's typically we alone who take the data home and "make sense" of it. The power of the text is ours:

> Many voices clamor for expression. Poly-vocality was orchestrated and restrained in traditional ethnographies by giving to one voice [that of the researcher] a pervasive authorial function and to others the role of sources, "informants" to be quoted or paraphrased. (Clifford 1986: 15)

Much attention has been paid in the ethnographic literature to this relationship between "self" (the observer) and "other" (the observed). bell hooks (1989) captures the attitude well:

> Often this speech about the "Other" annihilates, erases: "no need to hear your voice when I can talk about you better than you can speak about yourself. No need to hear your voice. Only tell me ... your story. And then I will tell it back to you in a new way. Tell it back to you in such a way that it has become mine, my own. Re-writing you, I write myself anew. I am still the colonizer, the speak subject, and you are now at the center of my talk." Stop. (70)

The concept around which much of the debate has centred is that of "privilege," a term that refers to the control that being the researcher gives over the content and form of the final text (for example, the book or article that emerges from a piece of research).[6] The very nature of the research and publication process gives us the last word. Recognizing that fact reminds us of the weighty responsibility and ethical obligations that being a researcher entails.

People entrust their views to us, and part of our moral obligation is to ensure that they are treated with respect, fairness, and a sense of justice. Indeed, many would argue that part of the academic mission is to facilitate our own obsolescence by helping create the social conditions in which people generally, and the disadvantaged in particular, can speak for themselves.

This does *not* mean we should avoid doing research with people who are different from ourselves, for example, that men should never do research about women or that non-Aboriginal people should never do research involving Aboriginal people. Nor does it mean we should systematically avoid engaging in interpretation because doing so is somehow inherently an act of academic imperialism. Michelle Fine (1994) argues that this would be tantamount to witnessing injustice without expressing outrage. The trick is to ensure that, when we *do* engage in such research, we are especially sensitive to issues of voice, going out of our way to make the research a collaborative enterprise, seeking input at all stages from those who will be most affected and whose perspectives we seek to represent. As Fine (1994) suggests,

> Those of us who do this work need to invent communities of friendly critical informants who can help us think through whose voices and analyses to front, and whose to foreground. (80)

Thus, for example, a non-Aboriginal social scientist should be able to do research dealing with Aboriginal issues—indeed, *not* doing research on so important a topic seems a tacit acceptance of injustice[7]—but the person who does so without seeking diverse and critical Aboriginal input at every stage of the process, from the design and conception of research to the final act of writing and interpretation, risks a myopic and potentially hurtful result (see also Smith 1999).

HOW AND WHAT DO YOU OBSERVE?

The sections above on quantitative and qualitative approaches to observation research urge us to con-

sider both the research role we occupy and the nature of the relationship that exists—or that we create—both between us as researchers and those we observe. Unless we do only the more contrived form of observation, the kind that occurs in situations that we construct and that occur on our own turf (which nonetheless has its own advantages and uses), both forms of observation must consider problems of access and/or the ethical issues that can be associated with observing others surreptitiously.

But assuming that we *do* get access to the setting or group that we wish to observe, the researcher's next challenge is to make specific decisions about what, and then how, to observe. A detailed inventory of all the various techniques and alternatives is beyond the scope of this text, but various sources offer us a few basic points to consider.

Options Regarding Structure

A first dimension of interest is in how *structured* or *unstructured* the researcher wants the observational process to be. At the more *un*structured end, the observer is *not* constrained by checklists and coding schemes, but rather reports, in narrative fashion, any observations relevant to the research objectives. This strategy provides maximal flexibility and can produce records with a comprehensiveness and richness not matched by other techniques. But any observation involves some degree of selection from all that occurs, and the danger with more unstructured schemes is that some portion of this selection may be unintentional and hence unacknowledged, implying unrecognized bias.

Of course, it's also quite possible to combine structured and less structured approaches during an extended field project. Indeed, many would argue that one should *begin* on a more unstructured basis during the preliminary, exploratory phases of observational research. During this period, one tries to contextualize the phenomenon of interest, gathering basic descriptive information that will inform subsequent analysis (e.g., How frequently does the phenomenon occur? Who's involved in the process? What other aspects of the process warrant scrutiny?).

The preliminary phase is also a time to sharpen research questions, to consult with people who are knowledgeable in the field along with those who are most likely to be affected, and to decide what particular types of data will be used as indicators for the key concepts of interest.

A primary hazard to avoid here is in *not* making the transition to more focused observation. Certainly a more focused research question facilitates this transition, as does the imposition or generation of theory. The danger, as Cicourel (1964) notes, is that without theory or a clearly focused research question, the researcher has no guide for his or her activity, in which case the method may amount to little more than a never-ending "pilot study" that accomplishes little or nothing.

Some Places to Start

Obviously, what one looks for will depend on one's particular research objectives and understanding of the phenomenon of interest. Nonetheless, an inventory of some "basic" attributes may be considered. Most generally, J. Lofland (1971) argues that, when you boil it all down, everything we call "social science" can be said to address one or more of the following three questions:

- What are the *characteristics* of a social phenomenon, the forms it assumes, the variations it displays?
- What are the *causes* of a social phenomenon, the forms it assumes, the variations it displays?
- What are the *consequences* of a social phenomenon, the forms it assumes, the variations it displays? (13)

As one might expect when all of social science is summarized in three sentences, Lofland's synopsis subsumes considerable complexity. Consider how time is represented in these questions. In pointing to *characteristics* or attributes of the phenomenon under study, Lofland is talking about *now,* the present. Implicit is a detailed and laborious description of the phenomenon as it is. Questions about *causes* direct our attention to the *past*. What are the antecedents of the phenomenon? Which of these are noteworthy in the generation or emergence or shaping of the phenomenon? Finally, questions about *consequences* direct us to the *future*. In what sense is the phenomenon itself an initiator or cause of subsequent events? How does variation in the phenomenon relate to subsequent variation in other phenomena of interest?

J. Lofland (1971) considers the delineation of *characteristics* to be qualitative analysis and the articulation of *causes* and *consequences* to be quantitative analysis. But what characteristics are of interest to us?

PARTICIPANTS

Since social science focuses on human behaviour, it seems reasonable to focus on the humans who inhabit our chosen milieu. Thus, as a minimum, you should describe participants in terms of demographics (e.g., age, sex), as well as other variables of interest that you note when observing, that appear in the literature as identified correlates, or that your particular theoretical dispositions dictate. *Who are these people?*

ACTS AND ACTIVITIES

What people *do* is clearly of interest to social scientists; their behaviour in the setting of interest will be one component of any complete observational account. Such behaviour may include anything from relatively brief, situationally constrained acts to elaborate activities that occur over more extended periods of time. What is happening? Involving whom? What aspects of the behaviour are of particular interest to you (e.g., the way strangers are socialized into the setting; the way friendships form; the informal social rules that guide action)? Observation that extends over time helps researchers identify regularities and idiosyncrasies in behaviour patterns that will in turn help focus subsequent research.

WORDS AND MEANINGS

Related to, but not necessarily synonymous with, what people do is what they *say*. This element of the observational process can obviously include a lot: for example, the attitudes and beliefs that are espoused during ongoing activity, the explanations and accounts that people offer for what they do and how they do it, and the personal and social meaning that people see in and derive from what they do.

There are many decisions to be made about how to capture speech. One choice will pertain to how passive or provocative the researcher chooses to be in relation to the participants. Will you listen to ongoing and spontaneous conversation, or will you actively question and unearth information of interest to you? These two stances should not be seen as mutually exclusive. You might, for example, wish to be more passive during the initial, exploratory phases of the research, in order to acquire information about spontaneous activities and utterings, but later take a more provocative role in asking questions or seeking explanations/accounts.

RELATIONSHIPS

The elements listed above focus on individuals, but people exist—both implicitly and explicitly—in relations with other people in the production of phenomena of interest. Many aspects of relationships might therefore be of interest to us in an observational setting. You'll want to know, for example, who's a "regular" in the setting and who's more transient or tangential. You also may wish to ascertain the formal and informal roles different people occupy in the setting, and what these roles mean to them. And of course, all of social psychology opens up to you when you begin focusing on relationships: Who talks to whom? How and with whom is information shared? How are individuals recruited or screened for participation in the setting? What power relations exist? How do friendships and animosities evolve? How is status reaffirmed? What brings these people together?

THE SETTING OR ENVIRONMENT

Action must happen somewhere, and the "somewhere" will tell you something about the individuals or group in question and potentially influence the action. What is the setting, and how is it perceived by both participants and the broader society? How do participants personalize and utilize the setting? To whom is the setting open, and to whom is it closed? How is accessibility conveyed? What objects are present, and what do their nature and position convey about the group or individuals being observed?

HISTORY

Social scientists rarely study situations that just appear. Our presence on-site often in itself signifies that the group or setting we're observing has been around at least long enough to have caught our attention. Many observers in the social sciences view a knowledge of the history of any setting or group as an integral part of understanding its current complexities.

Any study of history will be partly *descriptive* (e.g., certain persons or groups participated; certain events occurred on particular dates) and partly *interpretive* (e.g., we make inferences about why certain people were involved and the role they played, or we articulate what we feel is the broader significance of the processes we observed). Thus, historical accounts are themselves worthy of study *as* accounts, since they reflect the perspective of the person or group offering the account. It's no accident, for example, that the Euro-dominated societies of Canada, the United States, and Australia typically trace their histories to their "discovery" by, respectively, John Cabot (in 1497, although French Canadians more typically ignore Cabot and begin with Jacques Cartier in 1534), Christopher Columbus (in 1492), and Arthur Phillip (in 1788), as if no other cultures had ever visited these places before (although in fact that wasn't so; see Wolf 1982) and as if the land the European explorers found had been barren of any human population at the time (which it certainly was not). Who the heroes and heroines are, what events are identified as "important," and the nature of myths and legends all tell something about the individual, group, or setting under study.

At the same time, you should always be aware of history as a social construction, and its openness to revision. Although we can't recall the source, we have always been struck by the profundity of the statement "History is a justification of the present."[8] History is, virtually by definition, always written from the writer's vantage point. And since those in power are the ones who write mainstream histories, their samplings of past events comprise all those things that were "important" (from that perspective) in getting to where we are today. To the extent that certain events are impossible to ignore (such as world wars or changes of government), the "spin" placed on them typically makes "our" people the heroes and heroines, while others are ignored or their contributions minimized, and the vanquished are deemed unworthy of mention.[9] Current events and characteristics are assumed to be "natural" or "inevitable," and history is the name given to accounts of the glories and errors we encountered en route to the enlightened present. Still, as Yogi Berra is reputed to have said, "It ain't over 'til it's over"[10]— that is, no history can ever hope to be "complete" until there's nobody left on earth to write it. In the interim, social scientists should be as interested in and as cautious about historical accounts as they are concerning other data sources.

COMBINING ELEMENTS

The components listed above shouldn't be seen as an inventory of things to include or as a rigid outline for your ultimate report. To quote J. Lofland (1971), "what have been outlined ... [are nothing more than] ... *elements* with which to sort and classify observations and to build some *other kind* of analytic scheme for one's observational materials" (54; italics in original). The researcher's task is to ascertain what is important and what isn't, and then to build or test a theory or account of how the relevant elements interact over time to produce the phenomenon of interest.

This is not to minimize the importance of a clearly defined research question and set of research objectives. Indeed, the components discussed tie in with Becker's (1958) delineation of the phases of observational research. Two of the phases he notes are (1) selecting problems to study, concepts to employ, and indicators through which to opera-

tionalize the phenomenon and its attendant explanatory concepts; and (2) gathering descriptive and relational information concerning the frequency and distribution of the phenomenon under study. A central aim is the contextualization of the phenomenon under study, that is, determining where and how the phenomenon of interest fits into the social process being observed. This leads us to Becker's (1958) third phase, which involves (3) articulating individual findings *along with* a model of the organization (or group or process) under investigation.

In sum, Becker (1958) exhorts us to articulate our understanding of the process that the phenomenon under study is part of, since doing so will help organize our findings and indicate something of their meaning to both the participants and the researchers.[11]

Field Notes

Many novice researchers, as suggested at the beginning of this chapter, fail to distinguish "observation" from "just looking." "Just looking" is something we all do whenever we enter a setting. "Observation" is an empirical technique that involves looking for a purpose—one has an analytical interest and is prepared to gather "relevant" data, however those terms are defined.

In more formal/structured settings, the researcher's role is clear; you will arrive with clipboard and coding scheme in hand, and there will be predetermined rules you will have established (when you decided how to operationalize your variables of interest) that specify whom to observe and at what times. But even when all your formal data coding is done on prescribed sheets, we strongly advise that you either include a space for "comments" at the bottom of the sheet or have a small pad of paper at the ready. In some settings, a videotape may be made of the activity for future analysis. And in even less structured situations, the researcher who doesn't have easy access to paper and pen is a fool.

Even for structured observation methods, but especially for less structured ones like participant observation and ethnography, field notes are integral to observation. *No* observational session is complete until those notes have been done. The notes should specify the time and place of observation, the people present and their spatial distribution and interaction, and any other details the observer deems of interest. Field notes are normally very personal documents, and they have a crucial role, particularly in less structured observational research, because they're the raw data on which your analysis will be based. They are rarely shown to anyone but members of one's research group and would virtually never be published as is (see Malinowski 1967 for an exception). So feel free to insert comments, make queries to yourself, and speculate about what might be occurring.

Richardson (1994), for example, advises that when taking field notes, she distinguishes between several different types of notes via a shorthand she has developed for herself:

Observation notes (ON): These are as concrete and detailed as I am able to make them. I want to think of them as fairly accurate renditions of what I see, hear, feel, taste, and so on.

Methodological notes (MN): These are messages to myself regarding how to collect "data"—who to talk to, what to wear, when to phone, and so on. I write a lot of these because I like methods, and I like to keep a process diary of my work.

Theoretical notes (TN): These are hunches, hypotheses, poststructuralist connections, critiques of what I am doing/thinking/seeing. I like writing these because they open up my text—my field note text—to alternative interpretations and a critical epistemological stance. It is a way of keeping me from being hooked on my "take" on reality.

Personal notes (PN): These are feelings statements about the research, the people I am talking to, myself doing the process, my doubts, my anxieties, my pleasures. I do no censoring here at all. I want all my feelings out on paper because I like them and because I know they are there anyway,

affecting what/how I lay claim to knowing. Writing personal notes is a way for me to know myself better, a way of using writing as a method of inquiry into the self. (526)

Our systems aren't so differentiated, although we try to include the same variety of notes that Richardson (1994) reports. Ted simply distinguishes between things he's describing (on the basis of observing, hearing, etc.) and remarks he makes to himself that bear on personal feelings, tentative interpretations, questions to consider, future information to acquire, and so on. He just writes the former directly, enclosing the latter in square brackets to set them off as notes to himself. [For example, at this point in the reading, you might be remarking to yourself that you would benefit from borrowing one of the classic ethnographies referred to in this chapter from the library to see firsthand how the process of ethnography is often described.]

Regardless of the particular style you develop, such notes are important. Because they create an ongoing record or personal archive over the course of your study, they act as a diary of the process you've gone through. You can look back over them to see how your knowledge and understandings of the situation have changed over time, to check whether all your ongoing speculations have been tested, or to discover any discrepancies or inconsistencies that might have become evident over time.

Of course, it may not always be comfortable or feasible to actually take notes in the setting itself, although it's always advisable to at least jot down very brief notes or key words that will help you remember the chronology of the session. Whatever the case, always leave time at the end of each observational session to retire to a private location as soon as possible, *before* engaging in any other activities, to flesh out and organize the notes you've taken, which often are written all over the paper, in the margins, and with circles and arrows and perhaps little maps all around. And don't underestimate the length of time it'll take you to do so; many experienced observers suggest that you can expect to spend four hours formalizing your notes for every hour of observation (e.g., see Adler & Adler 1994; Berg 2007; Lofland et al. 2006). The longer you wait, the poorer the record.

If you make note-taking a habit, your skills will improve substantially with experience. For example, Ted now finds that as long as he's able to jot down a few notes and key words that reflect the overall chronology of a session, he can use them to generate an astonishingly detailed description of events that can leave people wondering whether the session was actually tape-recorded. A good place to practise such note-taking is in your classes. You probably take notes on lectures. If you do not already do so, try sitting down as soon as possible after each class and rewriting your notes, embellishing certain points. With practice, you should soon be able to virtually re-create the whole lecture, and you'll find your later notes far better organized and thoughtful than the ones made during class, where the lecture's pace can cause you to leave points out. The worst thing you can do (besides taking no lecture notes at all) is take your lecture notes and then not look at them again until it's time to study for your exams. By that time, the train of thought will have been lost, the squiggles and arrows that seemed so meaningful at the time will appear completely unfathomable, and you may have trouble following your notes, although they seemed perfectly logical when you first wrote them.

SUMMING UP AND LOOKING AHEAD

This chapter gives preliminary consideration to the extensive range of activities subsumed under the notion of observational research. We've seen that observational strategies are very flexible techniques that can be used in a broad variety of research settings. Indeed, "observation" is a highly generic term that can describe activities ranging from casual to formal and from structured to unstructured—activities that may or may not involve interaction between researcher and participants. The chapter emphasizes some of the many issues that weigh on the researcher up through and including the process of gathering data. Little is said, however, about how

to make sense of those data. These deficiencies are redressed in subsequent chapters.

We've seen in this chapter that an observational approach offers several advantages, not the least of which is that it often (although not necessarily) involves behaviour in its real-world context. But observation is rarely used alone. Instead, it is either a precursor to more intimate research, where the researcher starts by checking out the scene, or an important element in a comprehensive participant-observation or ethnographic situational analysis in which observation of behaviour *in situ* is combined with supplementary strategies (e.g., interviews, questionnaires, archival analysis).

The importance of supplementing observation with other techniques (especially self-report) cannot be overemphasized. Most obviously, it allows you to compare what people *say* with what they *do*. Sensitive observational study may greatly assist in the generation of new interpretive information that may didactically inform the overall analysis, which in turn may suggest further elements of the setting to observe in greater detail.

Finally, both quantitative and qualitative approaches to observation are discussed. Besides differing in their preferences for greater or lesser structure (which, respectively, facilitate the collection of either quantitative or qualitative data), the two approaches are also shown to differ significantly in the way they conceive of the observational setting itself. Quantitative researchers, particularly those rooted in positivist traditions, are more likely to see themselves as separable from the act of observation, such that issues of reactivity and stance are highlighted. But qualitative researchers see such divisions as artificial, and question whether the act of observation can ever be separated from the issue of who does the observing. Related to this are questions concerning the standards or criteria used to make judgments based on observational data. Recent postmodern trends challenge us to consider the implications of trying to understand the "other" without autocratically presuming that our particular way of knowing is necessarily "privileged" or "authoritative."

Many of these same issues emerge in the context of archival analysis, another form of observation, to which we turn in Chapter 8.

STUDY QUESTIONS

1. Louise wants to do an observational study of cocaine use among Toronto's upper class. But she's unsure about what role to adopt on the continuum from "complete participant" to "complete observer." (a) Discuss each of the possible roles in terms of the ethical issues and reactivity involved. (b) What other advantages and disadvantages do you see to the various roles in this situation? (c) Indicate how you might approach this situation, and what you might look for at your first cocktail party.

2. Anne-Marie is designing a study of how Vancouver's major newspapers go about investigating, defining, and portraying "crime news." The study will involve an observational component, and Anne-Marie recognizes that her study may induce some degree of reactivity among the sample group. She comes to you for advice. Explain what reactivity is and give two suggestions about what Anne-Marie might do to minimize reactivity in her study. In each case, explain why you believe the suggestion you make will lead to a decrease in reactivity.

3. What is the difference between a *sign system* and a *category system* in observational research? Show that you understand the difference by indicating how each would be used in coding a children's cartoon show for its violent content.

4. Several years ago, a study was conducted regarding the social content of video pornography. The study incorporated scene-by-scene coding of video content in terms of sex, aggression, and sexual aggression. Each scene was viewed and coded as to whether it included sex and/or aggression and/or sexual aggression, or none of these. (a) Did the video study utilize a *sign* system or a *category* system when coding scene content? Show that you

understand the difference between these two by explaining your choice. (b) Describe one way you could assess the reliability of the coding scheme.

5. Pick a social setting of interest to you (e.g., your classroom, a video arcade, a bowling alley, a bus), and approach it as an observer engaged in preliminary exploratory analysis. Keep field notes, and speculate on the "rules" that govern behaviour in that setting. Also consider the ethical issues involved in observing in such a manner.

6. Differentiating possible observer roles on a continuum ranging from *complete participant* to *complete observer* was standard for many years. Why is that continuum now seen as problematic?

7. How do the notions of *legitimation* and *representation* discussed in Chapter 2 relate to the issues of *privilege* and *voice* discussed in the current chapter?

8. *Can* men do research about women? *Should* men do research about women? Discuss this issue in a study group or in an essay.

9. Compare and contrast the qualitative and quantitative perspectives on observation. What similarities and differences do you see?

NOTES

1. Lofland actually uses the term "reporter" here, since this quotation is excerpted from a broader discussion about individuals who report in one way or another about life (e.g., social scientists, reporters, novelists, filmmakers).

2. We have some concerns regarding Vidich and Lyman's (1994) historical account, largely because it's both Eurocentric (i.e., conveying the idea that nobody but Europeans were ever interested in understanding the different cultures they encountered in their travels) and Americentric (i.e., adopting the perspective that anything important in history must somehow have involved the United States of

America). Those who attempt to avoid the mistake of citing an overly recent past have returned to the "classics" and traced the beginnings of ethnography to the ancient Greeks (e.g., see Atkinson & Hammersley 1994), who are often recognized as having offered the beginnings of Western European thought. But all the peoples of the world have been encountering other cultures for millennia (e.g., see Wolf 1982), and no doubt all have had curious individuals among them who were interested in "making sense" of how other people in other cultures live. The attributions Vidich and Lyman make should thus be viewed critically as embodying the perspective of two American researchers who implicitly accept the primacy of document-based European history. These limitations notwithstanding, Eurocentric views *have* dominated "the academy" (which is, of course, another European creation) for the last several hundred years and hence deserve consideration for the changes of method and sensitivity that have been evident over the years.

3. Although we continually refer to "Europeans" here, the term is actually shorthand for Western Europeans—or, more specifically, to Western European thought. The latter is generally considered to have originated in ancient Greece and refers to an epistemology that continues to dominate what we now know as the "Western" or "industrialized" world, that is, Europe, North America, Australia, and New Zealand.

4. The authors note references in their article for each of these areas of study. We have omitted them here in the interests of continuity and space, and because our intention is merely to convey the intensity and diversity of the collective research effort.

5. For non-Trekkers, we should note that the Borg were a particularly ruthless group of interplanetary travellers who shared a collective consciousness and took it upon themselves to either annihilate or assimilate everyone they came across.

6. We say "for example" here because there are many kinds of "texts" other than written ones. We may produce a film, for instance, or begin to represent ourselves as "experts" on a certain group (in conferences, workshops, or policy-making sessions) because of the access we have had to their lives. There may be good reasons to do so, but part of our interest as researcher/ citizens should be in trying to find ways to enhance opportunities for people—especially those who are disadvantaged and who lack access to media—to speak for themselves.

7. We say this guardedly, since there are many scenes of injustice in the world today and many important issues to be addressed; none of us, obviously, can address them all.

8. In the previous edition of *Research Decisions*, Ted asked for help in locating the source of this quote. University of Toronto sociology major Maria Nunes suggests it comes from Herbert Butterfield's (1931) *The Whig Interpretation of History*, which he criticized as little more than a "justification of the present." See, for example, http://news.bbc.co.uk/2/ni/ progammes/the-westminster-hour/4258793.stm

9. For example, many American histories of World War II depict Americans doing all the important things while the Canadians, French, British, and Russians contribute valiantly in their shadows. (When of course *we* all know that the *Canadians* were the centre of everything!) And imagine how different the history you learn in school would be if the Nazis had won the war. Of course, control over history goes two ways. On the one hand, those in power can look back and write history in a manner that justifies their existence, so that their being in power is clearly "natural" and "inevitable." On the other hand, those who successfully argue for a different history may well succeed in changing the future, to the extent that they may bring to light events that question the legitimacy of those in control to remain so. The success of the feminist critique of male-dominated history, for example, while

it has produced "better" history (because of filling in gaps that were previously ignored), has also reaffirmed women's growing social empowerment to those who might otherwise have been resistant to it.

10. Yogi Berra is a former player for the New York Yankees and former coach/manager of the New York Mets, two professional baseball teams in the United States. Berra's quotation is commonly used in sportscasts these days whenever a team makes a dramatic comeback, emerging victorious at the last possible moment. Each mention reaffirms the qualities of tenacity and persistence and their value in sport.

11. Becker (1958) goes on to describe a fourth phase, in which the problems of inference and proof are addressed. This issue has broad applicability and is discussed in Chapters 10 to 12.

CHAPTER 8

UNOBTRUSIVE AND ARCHIVAL METHODS

Chapter 6 included a discussion of numerous interactive methods, while Chapter 7 focused on a broad range of observational techniques, varying from simple observation of ongoing social processes to detailed participant observation and ethnographic studies that involve extensive contact in getting to know an "other."

This chapter extends the notion of observation to understanding people and culture through the things we produce. Since producing things is part of what we do, *analyzing* the things we produce is another way to learn about us (and others) as people. By examining things people produced long ago, we can also understand something about our past, the "we" who lived before.

More specifically, this chapter considers the variety of material that we can look at, other than ourselves, to help us understand both our current and past selves. Such materials include archival data (e.g., government statistical reports and secondary data archives), contemporary products (e.g., newspapers, television, web pages), and a wide variety of historical material (e.g., old newspaper reports, books, historical documents). Both qualitative and quantitative techniques will be considered.

UNOBTRUSIVE MEASURES: MINIMIZING REACTIVITY

In 1966, a rather significant monograph titled *Unobtrusive Measures* (Webb et al. 1966) was published. In it, and in a subsequent edition (Webb et al. 1981), the authors argue that the choice of operationalizations/indicators for our attitudinal and behavioural variables of interest has, by and large, tended to emphasize self-report and straight obser-

vational methods (e.g., attitude scales, interviews, questionnaires, and observation of ongoing behaviour in the lab or field). Although not disparaging of these techniques, the authors point out that all of these "direct contact" techniques share the problem of "reactivity" or "centre of attention" effects, because the respondent or participant in such research is typically aware of being observed. Even a multimethod approach is limited if all the methods used are subject to reactivity. Consequently, the authors argue, we should expand the scope of our choice of indicators to include what they call "unobtrusive measures." Aptly enough, the subtitle of their book is *Non-reactive Research in the Social Sciences*.

Unobtrusive Measures offers a compendium of techniques and measures that are less influenced by the intrusion of the researcher. These techniques are non-reactive because (1) the "data" are typically produced without thought that the "evidence" might someday be scrutinized by social scientists; and (2) generally, the researcher arrives on the scene after, and sometimes *long* after, the "participants" have left. These techniques cast the researcher in the role of a detective perusing a scene and attempting to infer individual and collective attitudes and behaviours on the basis of the evidence that has disappeared or remains.

Unobtrusive measures are generally divided into two categories: *physical trace* and *archival* measures, although it might be argued that the latter are merely a special case of the former. The next section gives a brief overview of the physical trace and archival measures described most comprehensively by Webb and colleagues (1981), and then examines in greater detail an archival measure found throughout the Western world: the crime statistic.

PHYSICAL TRACE MEASURES

When people engage in virtually any kind of behaviour, they generally leave behind some sort of evidence of that behaviour. The evidence may be that something is *missing* from the scene that was there before or that something is *present* in the scene that was not there before. These two states of affairs correspond to the two general classes of physical trace measures delineated by Webb and colleagues (1966, 1981). **Erosion** refers to some sort of wearing away or removal of products or materials because of our physical presence or activity, while **accretion** refers to some sort of addition to or building up of products or materials because of our physical presence or activity.

To illustrate the two, one can do no better than observe the master of inference at work. In "The Red-Headed League," Sherlock Holmes observes a man who has walked into his office. Within seconds, Holmes turns to Dr. Watson and comments that his "only" deductions prior to hearing the man speak are that "he has at some time done manual labour ... that he is a Freemason, that he has been in China, and that he has done a considerable amount of writing lately" (Doyle in Dougle 1892/1980). Both Dr. Watson and the stranger are astonished by these statements—all of which turn out, of course, to be correct—until Holmes explains the basis of his inferences. The statements regarding manual labour, Freemasonry, and China were based on what Webb and colleagues (1966) would call accretion measures, since in each case Holmes observed instances of materials being present that spoke of prior activity. The inference that the stranger had done manual labour was based on the observation that the muscles of one hand were significantly more developed than those of the other, while the conclusion that the fellow was a Freemason came from observing a particular pin he was wearing. As for the statement about visiting China, Holmes, who had done prior research on tattoos, knew that the design and coloration of the stranger's tattoo could only have been created in China.

In contrast, the inference that the man had done a considerable amount of writing recently was based on an erosion measure. Specifically, Holmes observed that one cuff and elbow of the stranger's suit were worn to the point of being shiny, and that the worn spots coincided with the spots where one's clothing would make contact with a desk.

Of course, physical trace measures can offer information about more than a particular individual. Webb and colleagues (1981) discuss a variety of erosion measures that have been used in social science and applied settings. Examples include

- using the rate of tile replacement in a museum as an index of exhibit popularity;
- assessing the wear on library books as an index of reading consumption (since just looking at loan records can't tell you whether the book was read or used as a doorstop); and
- using naturally eroded paths between apartment buildings as an index of interaction among apartment dwellers.

An even greater variety of accretion measures has been reported. Particularly pervasive is the graffiti seen on exterior walls and in washrooms around the world, which has been analyzed for what it reveals about our social attitudes (e.g., see Webb et al. [1981], as well as Mockridge's *The Scrawl of the Wild* [1968]). Other examples include

- using the setting of buttons on car radios as an indicator of listening preferences;
- looking at smudge, fingerprint, and dirt accretion on books as an indicator of reading consumption;
- analyzing the imagery presented on vases, paintings, and other objects of art (e.g., murals) as an index of cultural attitudes and character; and
- scrutinizing garbage to reveal consumption practices, as well as to reveal activity described in memos, notes, and early drafts of written material.

Certainly Webb and colleagues' (1981) motives are provocative. Their stated overall aim is "to inspire researchers to get out of the rut of routinized research measures, [and] to brainstorm a wide range of possibilities before narrowing down on the feasible few for the actual research" (12).

The primary advantages of physical trace measures are their inconspicuousness and their anonymity. Traces are generally not produced with the idea that, at some future point, they will be analyzed in some way by a social scientist. Often they are clearly anonymous; for example, worn-out paths may reveal aggregate patterns of activity without the possibility of identifying particular footprints.

But for certain indicators in this category, invasions of privacy and issues of confidentiality and lack of informed consent must in fact be considered; after all, many people would be offended if they found that someone was going through their garbage. Another disadvantage of physical trace measures centres on the sometimes unknown representativeness of the information that survives. The problems here are twofold: *selective deposit* and *selective survival.*

To fully understand these terms, you must begin by appreciating the difference between two kinds of history. On the one hand, there are all the events of our collective history, that is, everything that has ever happened up until the very moment that you read this sentence. The second kind of history is the history we create, that is, the sort of material you read in history books. One might hope that the latter would be a representative reflection of the former, but it isn't. This is so for several reasons, not the least of which is that all the "facts" of history are not equally accessible to us. People who are interested in writing histories are constrained by the nature of the evidence that remains.[1] It thus behooves us as social scientists to consider the relationship between what was and what remains, so that we can better appreciate the limitations to our understanding that are engendered by the gaps between the two.

Selective deposit addresses one of these limitations by referring to the fact that, of all the individuals and societies that have ever existed on this planet, some individuals and some societies are more likely than others to have placed their beliefs and experience into the historical record. If we want to have some picture of how people lived and what they looked like during the Renaissance, for example, we are likely to be looking primarily at the experience of the wealthy: there were no cameras at the time, and the wealthy are more likely to have commissioned art in their likeness. Similarly, while royalty and others who held power would have been able to express their opinions and worldview through official proclamations and documents, the lower classes probably didn't have the same opportunity to make their positions heard.

While the notion of selective deposit reminds us that some people are better able to place things in the historical record to begin with, it's also the case that, among those things that are initially put into the historical record, some have a better chance of surviving the ravages of time than others. This process is referred to as **selective survival.** Once again, it is the wealthy and powerful who seem to have the advantage.

For example, suppose we want to gather data about life expectancies in 14th-century France. While it may be the case that virtually everyone who was buried there at that time was provided with some sort of grave marker showing his or her name and years of birth and death (i.e., selective deposit was equal), the marble and brass tombstones and sarcophagi of the wealthy would have survived longer than the wooden crosses of the poor.[2] Similarly, since more aggressive peoples often destroy as many cultural remnants as possible of those they conquer, historical evidence of the victors frequently survives while that of the vanquished does not. For example, evidence of the Spanish in the post-Columbian Caribbean survives, while much of the historical evidence of the Carib people—who inhabited what is now known as the Dominican Republic and other Caribbean islands (e.g., Cuba) until they were virtually annihilated by the Spanish—does not.

At the same time, it would be shortsighted of us to think of "archives" in nothing more than historical terms. One of the things that the joy of finding some old treasure trove of artifacts (or some empty space where they might have been but were lost) should sensitize us to is what we can be doing right now to preserve artifacts that have great social value, as the information we are producing now is the history of the future.

Reading through old documents that were produced more than a century ago is quite an incredible experience. Ted did just that with colleague Bob Menzies in a study of asylum files that went back to 1879 (see Menzies & Palys 2006). The candidness of the file reports was striking, and the opportunity they had to look at them in the aggregate—allowing them to see how minority patients were dealt with relative to "white" ones, how women were dealt with and discussed as opposed to men, and how the files reflected changing mores and other societal changes that had implications regarding insanity and its treatment. Such files are more than simply "data"; they are a part of our cultural heritage and experience from which we can learn about ourselves.

In that regard we have to comment on a truly regrettable tendency that is having and will have a profound effect on possibilities for future analysis. This involves the notion of selective survival, and is reflected in our shortsightedness with respect to the retention of archives. An excellent example of this was brought to our attention by criminologist Ron Melchers of the University of Ottawa, who noted that the City of Ottawa was considering destroying a century's worth of records regarding juvenile fire setters. A concerned archivist who had recommended they be permanently archived had brought them to Melchers's attention when his recommendation met with resistance from the Fire Department—which saw them as having no value and was not legally required to consider any broader social concerns—as well as the city's Access to Information and Privacy Office, which apparently saw them as easier to dispose of than to consider how the rights of the individuals in the files and the greater social interest served by social research might be reconciled. It is fascinating also that Professor Melchers received no help from his REB—they simply said that privacy law in Ontario would never allow the

use of these files for research without the consent of the persons named in the files, which shows an astonishing trivialization of the value of research and unwillingness to find ways to reconcile these considerations.

The general impression one gets from such cases is that rather than being seen as a social resource that has value as both a historical artifact and potential research resource, archives are seen as complicating and a problem—complicated rights claims to deal with, complicated ethical issues to consider and resolve, and retention of a history that can come back to haunt you if and when someone were to sue or make other claims against an organization. One sees this even with research ethics boards at universities, who one would think would have some larger perspective about the historical value of retaining documents. Far more attention is paid to how long one "must" keep records until one can dispose of them than is paid to their long-term value as a social archive. If academic institutions are so shortsighted about such issues, small wonder that others whose social mandates do not involve a research component care even less. Fortunately there are persons like Professor Melchers and the City of Ottawa archivists who are sensitive to these issues and ready to speak up. In the end the two of them orchestrated a very hopeful resolution to this: the City of Ottawa is now in the process of establishing a permanent mechanism—the *City of Ottawa Archives Ethics and Advisory Circle*—for better involving the research community in discussion and advice regarding the appraisal of collections for their research and historical value and the reconciliation of the ethical issues involved in prospectively making available those collections that are retained.

ARCHIVAL MEASURES

Archival measures comprise any information that is contained in "hard copy" records or documents.[3] And while they may include such materials as written or taped records of speeches, photographs, newspapers, books, or private materials such as diaries and letters, probably the biggest class of archival materials includes the running records and statistical compendia produced by all levels of government and many public agencies. One could argue that archival measures are nothing more than a particular type of accretion measure, since the documents referred to are indeed products of human activity, but they are sufficiently different and voluminous to be treated as entities worthy of consideration on their own.

Numerous advantages accrue from studying archival materials, not the least of which is that an inspection of historical evidence encourages us to think in terms of social *process,* reminding us that things were not always as they are now and suggesting, therefore, that this is also not how they always must be. Many archives also allow longitudinal analysis, and because they already exist and may cover an extensive time span, allow longitudinal analysis to be done *now;* that is, one needn't wait for 20, 40, or 100 years for the process to unfold.

Further, archival sources *exist;* they are a concrete artifact that was prepared in some bygone time. That assertion may sound obvious, but it implies that we and others *can* go back to a given document or archive again and again to subject it to greater or different scrutiny, unlike the oral history of the Beothuk people (the original inhabitants of Newfoundland), for example, which died with the last of the Beothuk in 1829 (see Upton 1988). We may disagree on our interpretation of what a document means, but at least we are working with the same document. While mass death from plagues or diseases brought by colonists wrought havoc with oral cultures, document-based cultures have their own sources of disaster—more than one archive has burned in a fire, been destroyed in an earthquake, or been scattered to the wind by a tornado or hurricane.

An advantage of archival study is that conducting such research typically costs much less than many other research methods. And as with other unobtrusive measures, archival data are generally less influenced by reactivity than interactive techniques. But one should always consider the reactivity of one's archival source rather than merely assuming that

reactivity is absent. *Hansard* (in Canada) and *The Congressional Record* (in the United States) contain speeches that may not have been prepared with the knowledge that a social scientist might peruse them, but that *were* prepared (and, in the case of *The Congressional Record,* were also later edited) for public consumption in a political context. The same is true of political memoirs and of many institutional records, where contemporary standards of "political correctness" undoubtedly influence what is committed to paper.[4] Personal diaries and letters, in contrast, may have been prepared for a limited audience or with the thought that no other person would ever read them. Minutes of meetings for some organizations will be complete and thorough; others may worry about the role such documentation can have in law suits.

Archival sources are subject to the vagaries of selective deposit and selective survival. The researcher's task is always to consider how such availability will influence the conclusions. Some examples of selection are fairly blatant: government archives are more likely to be available than those of smaller groups or individuals. But others are more subtle. Cook and Campbell (1979), for example, point out the bias toward "outcome" rather than "process" data in many series put together for monitoring purposes. The existence of such tendencies in historical sources reaffirms the value of having one's research question *guide* the research, lest one be seduced into believing that the *available* data are necessarily the most *important* or *relevant* data. Researchers must be sensitive to the ways in which data availability constrains their conclusions and the range of theory that can be developed, while also recognizing the value in the treasure they have found.

Finally, researchers who delve into the archives should be on the lookout for possible shifts in how particular data series are defined and in the procedures for recording or saving material. If the series is local enough to have been prepared by a single person, then one must consider that any changes following his or her retirement might reflect little more than the presence of a different recorder, rather than changes in the phenomenon of interest. Similarly, policy shifts in recording practices, or computerization of a previously manual system, may produce differences in what otherwise look like continuous and comparable time-series data.

In sum, archival data can be treasure troves of information that tell about society. They are necessarily secondary data that are unlikely to have been prepared for research purposes. This is both their limitation and strength; the information was prepared by someone else, and for some other purpose than for supplying evidence that might be useful to a researcher. The influence of the data's *context of production* must be considered (although this is no less true of any other data-gathering technique). The intermediary process between event and datum, or between having the thought and putting it to paper, must be considered and articulated.

This chapter scrutinizes examples of research that use several different kinds of data archives. First, we'll consider one you've probably seen on the TV news or read about in newspapers or magazines. This topic has also received attention in one way or another from researchers in sociology, criminology, psychology, anthropology, economics, and education, to name but a few of the fields. The data series we refer to are crime statistics.

An Example:
The Construction of Crime Data

Although several varieties of crime statistics are produced by criminal justice agencies, "crimes known to the police" typically receive the greatest attention from academics, the media, and the general public. Every month, in every jurisdiction in North America (in fact, in most of the industrialized world), the police compile and send off their statistics to their respective federal governments, who dutifully publish these figures, along with computed crime rates. Periodically, articles appear in the media about how the crime rate is up or down, along with various pet theories to account for this change. Many sociologists, criminologists, and others analyze these statistics to try to find out whether crime is up or down, and why; comparisons are made between various

cities and countries. Crime statistics undoubtedly rank with the consumer price index and unemployment rates as one of the primary indicators of our quality of life. But what do they mean? And how are they compiled?

Perhaps the best way to begin answering these questions is to introduce the notion from test theory that every observed score (O) is a function of a "true" score (T) plus some degree of error[5] (e), that is,

$$O = T + e$$

Ideally, we attempt to reduce error to zero so that $O = T$. That is, we want our observed scores (i.e., the crime rates published by the federal government) to reflect nothing but the "true" situation (i.e., the actual amount of crime that exists in reality). The problem, of course, is that we can never know reality directly; if we could, we wouldn't need crime statistics. Still, that should not stop us from considering the possible strengths and weaknesses of the measures we *do* choose. Thus, in assessing any measure, from crime statistics to survey results, we need to consider how systematic error might have been introduced in our measurements.

One way to do so is to look at how a given statistic is constructed. A simplified model of how crime statistics are constructed is shown in Figure 8.1 (adapted from Skogan 1975). The process begins with the generation of a "true score," that is, the occurrence of a "criminal event," a behaviour contrary to the laws of Canada.

Even in making that opening statement we're already in hot water, since the more we emphasize a country's laws as the defining measure of "real" crime, the more guilty we are of subscribing to status quo definitions of good and bad. There will no doubt be good reason for our choice, but we have to understand that along with acceptance of this definition comes an *ideological* choice. Many would argue, for example, that certain behaviours we now define as "crimes" (e.g., drug possession, illegal acts committed by the police when trying to catch elusive criminals) should not be so defined or that many behaviours we do *not* currently define as crimes (e.g.,

Figure 8.1
The Process by Which a Crime Statistic Is "Constructed"

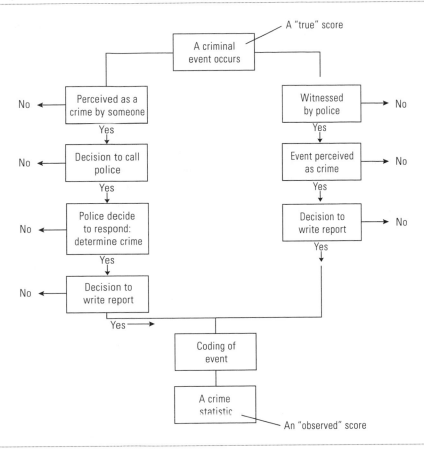

Source: Adapted from W. G. Skogan (1975), "Measurement Problems in Official and Survey Crime Rates," *Journal of Criminal Statistics, 3,* pp. 17–32.

violations of worker safety regulations, some "civil" matters) *should* be so defined. The law is a human creation and thus reflects society, culture, and values. An extensive discussion of such issues is beyond the scope of this book (but see Lowman & Palys 1991). What's important for now is that you appreciate the connection between theory and method, ideology and data.

WE START WITH A "TRUE" SCORE

For exposition's sake, let's accept "contemporary Canadian law" as our referent for "reality." We begin with an act, a "true" score, to see what filters it must

pass through before it becomes a "statistic" (i.e., an "observed" score).

Basically, this process begins in one of two ways. Either the "crime" is perceived as such by a private citizen or it is noted in some other way by the police. Let's deal with those two separately.

WAS THE EVENT PERCEIVED AS A CRIME?

Going down the left-hand side of Figure 8.1, we see that the first step in the process lies with the community: someone must first perceive the event as a crime. If no crime is perceived, nothing is likely to be done. There are a variety of reasons why the citizen might not perceive a "criminal" act as such, including the following:

1. The act may be so subtle that no one knows it happened. Did you lose the $20 or was it stolen? Computer crime or skilled embezzlement may not be detected.
2. The act may be witnessed, but the victim or witness may not realize the act is illegal. There are more than 40 000 laws in Canada's *Criminal Code*; do we all know all of them?
3. The victim/witness may perceive the act as questionable but still within the bounds of "legal" behaviour. For example, it's not always clear to observers when spanking becomes child abuse, or when we cross over from "rip-off" to "fraud," or whether a hockey fight constitutes an assault.

People's tendencies to perceive a given event as a crime also may vary depending on cultural factors (e.g., among different ethnic groups), as well as spatially and over time. For example, one study (Dutton et al. 1982) involved visits to communities ranging from extremely remote to highly urban in eight different provinces where policing was provided by the RCMP. The concept of "assault" clearly varied considerably by place; a certain amount of "roughness" was tolerated in a mining town like Flin Flon, Manitoba, for example, that would likely have been treated as "assaultive" in a suburb like Burnaby, British Columbia. The upshot is that comparability of data regarding criminal and/or deviant behaviour across time, space, and cultures can be extremely problematic.

WERE THE POLICE CONTACTED?

If an act *is* perceived as criminal, the next step in its becoming a statistic is that the police must be contacted. It's obviously difficult to ascertain from police records why people *don't* phone the police. But some hints have been forthcoming from victim surveys, where individuals who report having been victimized to the interviewer are then asked whether they contacted the police—and if not, why not.

Table 8.1 shows the results that were obtained in one U.S. study. These data suggest that citizens who feel victimized will impose their own set of filters in determining whether the matter warrants attention,

Table 8.1

Reasons Cited for Not Reporting Victimizations to the Police

Reason	Personal Crime (%)	Household Crime (%)
Nothing could be done, lack of proof	30.8	36.1
Not important enough	25.6	30.1
Police would not want to be bothered	6.2	8.9
Too inconvenient or time-consuming	3.1	2.4
Private or personal matter	5.6	5.4
Fear of reprisal	0.8	0.4
Reported to someone else	15.9	3.2
Other, or not given	12.0	13.4

Source: National Association of Criminal Justice Planners/National Criminal Justice Information and Statistics Service (1979), *Criminal Victimization in the United States, 1977* (Washington, DC: National Association of Criminal Justice Planners/National Criminal Justice Information and Statistics Service), p. 70. Reprinted with permission.

and if so, whether it's specifically *police* attention (as opposed to medical attention, for example) that's warranted.

In sum, not all crimes are enumerated in crime statistics reports because, for varying reasons, the crime may not have been reported in the first place. It's usually these unreported crimes that are referred to as the "dark figure" of crime (e.g., see Skogan 1975).

DID THE POLICE RESPOND?

When a crime *is* reported, the ball is in the police's court. The first decision they make is whether to respond to your call. They must decide whether they agree that the matter is one for the police, and then whether it's possible or worthwhile to send someone out to the scene. In many instances, the police won't respond at all.

WAS A REPORT WRITTEN?

If police *do* respond, one of the things they determine is whether or not a crime has been committed. But even if they agree that one has, officers have considerable discretion in deciding whether to write a report and whether to recommend the laying of charges.

Research by Black (1970) and by Black and Reiss (1970) shows that a variety of extralegal factors influence officers' decisions about whether to write a report. The officers in those studies were *less* likely to do a report when the relationship between perpetrator and victim was close, since they believed that such cases would less frequently make it to court.[6] Officers were *more* likely to write a report when the victim was deferential or of high status.

THE POLITICS AND POLICY OF CRIME DATA

Crime reporting and hence crime rates are sensitive to policy shifts, some of which can be self-serving. Seidman and Couzens (1974) perused reports for the Washington, D.C., police, concluding that a decrease in crime rate that city had appeared to enjoy was primarily a product of the police chief's orders to get the crime rate down, a task that was most easily accomplished by underreporting and down-

grading crimes. Skogan (1975) notes that these tactics are particularly prevalent in those urban centres where police chiefs are evaluated by their ability to reduce the crime rate.

Policy changes may occur for other reasons as well. Priorities may change because of both political pressures and pragmatics (e.g., courts getting full). In British Columbia, for example, it is not unusual for the Crown to issue informal policy directives (e.g., don't bother me with charges for marijuana possession where the amounts are small; report *all* wife assaults) that police are expected to honour. As a result, some authors (e.g., Ditton 1979) argue that crime statistics have *nothing* to do with the amount of crime that "really" exists, instead reflecting little more than shifting foci of social control. Certainly police efforts in the area of victimless crimes bear only a tangential relationship to the amount of that crime that exists; a case can be made that this statement is also true of some crimes involving victims (e.g., wife assaults).

Crime statistics also change when record-keeping practices change. In London, England, for example, "robbery" statistics formerly included only those cases where the robbery was certain or probable; "suspected" robberies were written in a separate book. But then a policy change called for *all* robberies, whether suspected or certain, to be recorded; a 220 percent increase in the "crime rate" was subsequently observed (Skogan 1975). Similarly, a shift in recording policies in New York City helped the robbery rate the next year go up 400 percent, while assaults with a weapon rose 200 percent, larcenies went up 700 percent, and burglaries rose by 1300 percent.

And of course, a big policy change occurs when the law changes. Resulting shifts in the crime rate may thus not reflect *any* change in behaviour; rather, they may merely reflect a change in the breadth or existence of a criminal designation or in the evidentiary rules that make cases more or less likely to be investigated and prosecuted.

Although this discussion has so far focused primarily on the left-hand side of Figure 8.1, many of the same arguments hold with respect to the right side of the figure, which refers to proactive efforts by the police to control crime. Suffice it to say that there will be much crime that the police will not witness and that much of the crime that *is* witnessed will be either ignored or not formally reported.

HOW DO WE COUNT?

Whether the reporting source is a police officer or a citizen, some events will pass through the various filters noted above and be considered worth recording as an official crime statistic. Here we come to a bit of a problem: coding the event. Remember that we want to enumerate the amount of crime that exists in our society. To do so, we must agree on how to count, and such agreement is a lot harder to reach than one might expect. Brantingham and Brantingham (1984) offer the following example to illustrate the complexities involved:

> Two men go on a crime spree. They enter a convenience store, rob the proprietor and three customers, shoot a police officer who attempts to apprehend them, knock cans and bottles off the shelves, and set the store on fire as they leave. (51)

How many crimes are involved here? An ambitious Crown attorney might find 16: (1 murder + 4 robberies + 1 vandalism + 1 arson + 1 weapons charge)? 2 defendants = 16 crimes. At the other extreme, one might argue that because there was only a single event, there must be a single crime—or perhaps two crimes, because there were two perpetrators. But if we decide to call it only one crime, what do we call it? The first one (i.e., robbery)? The last one (i.e., arson)? The most frequent one (i.e., robbery)? The most serious one (i.e., murder)? Another possibility is that we could count the number of victims (one proprietor, three customers, one police officer), and hence count five. So which is it? One? Two? Five? Sixteen? Something else?

Since 1962, Canada has joined the United States and much of the rest of the industrialized world in adopting Uniform Crime Reporting (UCR) procedures in an effort to standardize (or make more reliable) reporting across jurisdictions and police forces. The general rules are as follows: for crimes of violence, one counts the number of victims; for crimes of property, one counts the number of events; and for multiple offences, only the most serious offence is recorded. In our example, therefore, the local police would tell Statistics Canada that one murder had been committed.[7]

The use of this scoring system has several implications. First, since Canada did not use UCR procedures until 1962, you're courting difficulty if you compare pre-1962 and post-1962 crime figures, and potentially also those before and after 1990 (see note 7). It also suggests that crime rates overstate the relative frequency of violent crimes relative to property crimes, and that crime rates are an understatement of the number of offences reported to the police.

As Skogan (1975) suggested, the advent of UCR brought greater reliability but sacrificed an already tenuous validity in the process. On the other hand, there is evidence that we should *also* be concerned with the reliability of UCR reporting. The British Columbia Police Commission audited UCR in 1979 among different police forces in the province and found reasonable comparability on homicide, sex offences, robbery, breaking and entering, and *nothing* else.

FINAL COMMENTS ON CRIME STATISTICS

Crime statistics released by a government agency look terrifically official and precise. They're frequently perceived as "objective" indicators of crime. By now you should realize that this is *not* exactly the case: crime statistics (like any other statistics) are the result of a human process. As Skogan (1975) states,

> *Every statistic ... is shaped by the process which operationally defines it, the procedures which capture it, and the organization which interprets it.* (17; italics in original)

In other words, every statistic, regardless of whether it is the crime index published by Statistics Canada or a self-report to a survey, is in some sense a *social construction* that comes into being as a function of various psychological, sociological, and organizational processes. One of the big difficulties with archival statistics is that because of their assumed/perceived "objectivity," their reliability and validity often have been subjected to less scrutiny than is the case with perceptually oriented survey measures.[8] To the extent that they have been assessed in this way, their validity and reliability appear questionable. More to the point, we must consider what they mean, as we must do for any data.

Those who frequently use crime statistics argue that even though crime statistics are invalid, they're nonetheless useful. Brantingham and Brantingham (1984), for example, compare them to a bathroom weigh scale that's miscalibrated and always reads 10 kilograms too light. The weight readings are incorrect (i.e., invalid), they say, but could still be used to measure *changes* in weight or to compare different people, since the error is constant. But the errors in crime statistics do *not* appear to be constant. The various "scales" in North America are miscalibrated to varying unknown degrees; even given scales in given locations change their degree of miscalibration over time. Comparisons are still possible, but they must be done with some sensitivity to the changing context(s) in which crime statistics have been produced and with some understanding of how far any comparisons can be stretched (e.g., see Brantingham 1991).

But to the extent that crime statistics *don't* show the amount of crime in an area, what *do* they show? Various arguments have been put forth. Some authors (e.g., Ditton 1979) argue that crime statistics show little more than social control policies; that is, crime statistics are an indicator of police priorities and activity more than of crime per se. Certainly this argument is easy to support when considering victimless crimes, and there's evidence that the same is true to varying degrees with respect to certain crimes involving victims (e.g., assaults, wife assaults). But such an argument becomes more difficult to make with other crime categories, such as murder, where the proportion of "social control" versus "real crime" probably tips in favour of the latter.

Crime statistics also reflect public confidence in and expectations about police performance. Some events are so trivial they'd probably *never* be reported, while some events are so serious that they'd virtually *always* be reported. But there's a big grey area between those two extremes, where "confidence in the police" can play a significant role in whether the police are informed. Evaluations of a crime prevention program known as Operation Identification (OI),[9] for example, often find an *increase* in the crime rate after OI is introduced to an area. Apparently people are more likely to call the police, since they've been told that the probability of recovering stolen goods is enhanced (Lowman 1983).

This is not to say that all official crime statistics produced to date should be scrapped or that people who produce them should be looking for other jobs. Instead, crime statistics should be treated the way we treat all other data we gather: as a social product that is related to, but is only an imperfectly mirrored reflection of, the phenomenon it aims to describe. Indeed, the trick is to understand the crime statistic (or whatever other data you gather or produce) as a part of the phenomenon you're scrutinizing.

A splendid example is provided by Lowman (e.g., 1984, 1989; Lowman & Fraser 1995), whose research on the prostitution issue has focused on time series data concerning charges and convictions, but treats those data as a subset of a larger information pool that includes interviews with women who work as prostitutes and with criminal justice personnel, longitudinal observation of the solicitation and control processes, content analysis of media attention to the issue, and other archival analysis. The result not only contributes to the academic theoretical literature but also informs relevant policy matters.

The limitations of crime statistics, as well as a desire to get some idea of victimization rates, have led investigators to look to other techniques, such as self-reports of criminal activity and victimization surveys, to complement official archival sources. Victimization surveys, in particular, have received considerable attention in recent years.

Alternative Views of Crime: Victimization Surveys

A discussion of victimization surveys might seem an odd inclusion in this chapter, since surveys were dealt with in Chapter 6's look at interactive techniques. But including them here allows us to make several important points. First, we wish to reaffirm that *every statistic is a social construction*. Although we personally have less of a problem with self-report information (e.g., interviews, attitude scales) than with archival statistics of the Statistics Canada genre, perhaps because we "produce" the former ourselves, one should always keep in mind the strengths and limitations of one's data and consider the various sources of bias or error that might exist.

Second, "used" survey data have themselves become an important source of archival data for social scientists. When major studies are done, the raw data are frequently made available to qualified researchers in anonymized form for secondary analysis. Other investigators can then peruse these data for far less than the cost of generating them.[10]

LIMITED TO CRIMES WITH VICTIMS

Victimization surveys have their own limitations, which are a product of the way the information is gathered. Figure 8.2 will help focus our discussion. Once again, our diagram begins with a "true" score (i.e., a "crime" that occurs). The first filter through which the event must pass is that the crime must involve a victim, since a victimless crime is unlikely to be reported in the survey.[11]

FINDING THE RESPONDENTS

Next, the victim must be interviewed. Victimization surveys typically seek representative samples of target populations, usually the residents of a given urban centre. Of course not everyone will be interviewed. But as long as all people and all victimizations have an equal probability of being selected, a representative picture of victimizations can emerge. Unrepresentativeness occurs when all victimizations do not have an equal probability of being selected. So we must consider these systematic sources of bias.

Figure 8.2

The Construction of Crime Statistics via Victimization Surveys

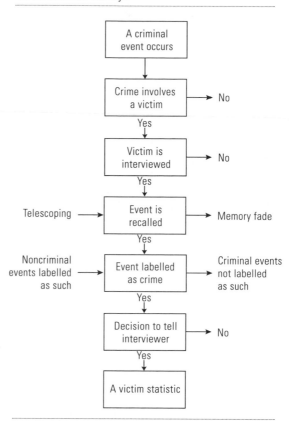

One type of person (and hence crimes against such people) that will not appear in victimization surveys is the nonresident victim (i.e., commuters, transients, tourists). We interview people from a particular area, but not everyone who was victimized there is from that area. Skogan (1975) notes that an average of 13 percent of the daytime population in U.S. cities are commuters, in addition to varying numbers of tourists and transients. People in these categories can be victimized and can even report their victimizations to the police, but they won't be around to be interviewed later.

RECALL: MEMORY FADE AND TELESCOPING

Given that the victim *is* interviewed, the event must first be recalled. One must guard against two problems here. One is **memory fade,** the tendency for events to be forgotten. Memory fade has been investigated in two ways. In one strategy, *known victims* (as revealed by police records) are interviewed to see if their victimizations are reported to the interviewer; overall, such studies suggest, about 75 percent of known incidents are recalled. Given that *known victimizations* are generally of higher saliency (they were considered important enough to have been reported to police), the implication is that memory fade for less serious incidents is probably greater. In the second strategy, investigators ask a sample of respondents about victimizations and plot these against time. Monthly crime rates decrease visibly as you go back in time, especially after three to six months, which suggests that memory fade has occurred.

While memory fade refers to the tendency of events during the sample period to drop out, **telescoping** refers to the propensity of respondents to bring events that were *outside* the sample period into it. In answer to a query about victimizations within the last year, for example, respondents may include events that actually happened more than a year ago. Part of the reason may be that people are responding to implicit or explicit demands to report victimizations if you've contacted them about, and they've consented to, a victimization survey. Another reason may be the generally fuzzy definition of "a year ago" as a boundary for thought; an event may be described as "about a year ago" regardless of whether it was really 10, 12, 14, or even 16 months ago. This problem of telescoping is reduced by **bounding** (e.g., instead of saying "in the last six months," you might cite a more memorable event, such as "since Christmas") or by successive administrations of the survey (where the sample period is bounded by the prior visit). Victims require signposts to guide their recall. (The degree of error in unbounded situations is 17 percent to 21 percent.)

LABELLING THE EVENT AS A CRIME

As Figure 8.2 shows, the next step involves labelling the event as a crime. The victim must categorize the event both as a crime and as belonging to a particular crime category. But this may or may not be the "right" crime category, and the event might or might not "really" be a crime. The evidence suggests, though, that this isn't an especially big problem. In a pilot study in San Jose, California, legal authorities and respondents classified an event in the same category 88 percent of the time (Skogan 1975).

BUT WILL YOU TELL THE INTERVIEWER?

Next, even if the event *is* accurately recalled and labelled, the respondent must decide whether to tell the interviewer about the event. In validational studies where known victims (i.e., people identified through prior reports filed with the police) are interviewed, decisions about whether to tell the interviewer seem to be affected by some of the same variables that influence decisions about whether to report the incident to police. One of these is the relational distance between victim and perpetrator. "Known victim" respondents recalled and reported victimizations by strangers 75 percent of the time, those by acquaintances 58 percent of the time, and those by relatives only 22 percent of the time. Rapes were reported very cautiously; in one pilot survey in San Jose, California, *all* rapes were described as "attempted" (Skogan 1975).

JUST ANOTHER "TAKE" ON CRIME

Recall Skogan's (1975) statement, cited earlier with respect to crime statistics of the UCR variety: "*Every statistic ... is shaped by the process which operationally defines it, the procedures which capture it, and the organization which interprets it*" (17; italics in original). The previous section should have demonstrated that this warning applies equally to victimization surveys. Neither type of data gives the truth about crime, although each contributes a truth. In G. Morgan's (1983b) terms, each engages crime, giving its own particular "take" on the phenomenon.

Content Analysis of Archival Data

Another "archive" we can examine includes many other kinds of products, such as newspapers, institutional/agency files, textbooks, speeches, films or videos, television programs, diaries, and letters, that, while they may not have been produced explicitly for the purpose of research, may nonetheless provide useful data. Any of these materials can be analyzed for content. The next section illustrates the steps involved in doing so.

DEFINING THE FOCUS

Content analysis requires the researcher to have some clear idea of what he or she is after. However the focus is derived—from the researcher's personal interests, from theory, or from exploratory study—the researcher must begin with a clear specification of objectives.

For Simon Davis (1990), the interest was in looking at mate selection. Previous research had indicated that the selection of opposite-sex partners often follows traditional sex-stereotyped roles. In Davis's terms, stereotypical media portrayals have a long history of emphasizing women as "sex objects" (attractive, alluring, seductive), while for men, the emphasis has been on portraying them as "success objects" (intelligent, wealthy, professional). In keeping with this pattern, the evidence on mate-selection practices had found that men emphasized physical appearance more than women as a factor in mate selection, while women emphasized personality, commitment, and financial security. Davis (1990) wondered whether this was still the case in the more progressive 1990s: "Were traditional stereotypes still in operation, that is, [were] women being viewed as sex objects and men as success objects?" (45).

THE RESEARCH SITE

Davis's research question could have been addressed in many ways. He could have created a survey or interview study in which he asked people the sort of characteristics they were looking for in the "ideal mate," or he could have approached married or cohabiting couples and asked them to explain what it was about the other person they had found so appealing. But if men were most interested in ensuring that they coupled with a woman who looked good on their arm, would they admit it? And if women most valued someone who was smart and successful, thereby providing social status and financial security, would they confide that to him? Davis was worried about the "social desirability" bias that might permeate these methods. Accordingly, he looked for a research venue where social desirability influences would be minimized.

The location he decided on was the newspaper, specifically, the "personals" columns, where many people advertise for a prospective partner or mate. It seemed to meet the criteria: here, men and women seek mates; in the process, they must decide which aspects of themselves they think are most "relevant" to specify, as well as which aspects of the prospective mate they feel are most important. Even better, they're doing so because they really do want to find a partner; they're unlikely to be thinking about the possibility that some social scientist might ever read their ad as part of an analysis of factors involved in mate selection.

Of course, many different kinds of newspapers and magazines include such "personals" in their classified advertising. Many cater to specific audiences, such as lesbians, gays, executives, or people who seek sexual kinkiness. Although the mate-selection practices shown by such groups may be of interest, Davis chose to stay with more "mainstream" ads, particularly those that involved prospective heterosexual relationships. Accordingly, the newspaper he scrutinized was his city's main daily newspaper, which in Davis's words is perceived as a "conservative, respectable journal" (1990: 45), rather like the Victoria *Times Colonist*, the *Winnipeg Free Press*, the *Toronto Star*, or Montreal's *La Presse*.

Many city libraries keep old copies of the local newspaper as part of their document archive, and it was to the city library that Davis went to check for old editions of his local paper, the *Vancouver Sun*. A preliminary examination of these papers revealed that, although one can place a personals ad on any day of the week, Saturday was clearly the "big" day for such ads: 40 to 60 ads appeared every Saturday, as opposed to between 2 and 4 ads a day during the week. So he decided to focus only on Saturday editions. Of the 52 Saturday editions in the year before he started the study, Davis chose to randomly sample six from throughout the year, subjecting *every* ad in each of those editions to analysis. The random sampling would ensure that the editions he analyzed could be considered representative of the issues published during that year; at 40 to 60 ads per weekend edition, he could expect to end up with 200 or 300 ads, which seemed a reasonable number to analyze. But how to analyze them?

OPERATIONALIZING THE VARIABLES OF INTEREST

Davis had stated that he was interested in this notion of women (in men's eyes) as "sex objects" and men (in women's eyes) as "success objects" (which he defined as involving financial and intellectual accomplishments). But how do you analyze the typical personals ad for those elements? That is, how do you determine whether any given ad is or is not an example of those phenomena?

Davis approached this question by looking for particular words that could be taken as indicative of the concepts of interest to him. First, he decided to analyze only that part of the ad in which the ad's writer specified what attributes he or she sought in a prospective mate. Within that portion, he decided (after reading many ads to see what kinds of words and phrases were typically used) on the codes shown in Table 8.2.

Three other attributes the ads were coded for included the sex of the ad's author; the age of the ad's author, but only if a *specific* age was indicated; and the ad's length (expressed as the number of lines).

Note, by the way, that the first nine codes fall neatly into the general categories Davis had been talking about with respect to his primary study objectives. The notion of the "sex object" is reflected by the first four categories—words or phrases that mention "physical attractiveness," "physique," or "sex" or that request a "picture." The notion of the "success object" is addressed by the "employment" cluster contained in the next three categories—"profession," "employed," and "financial"—as well as the

"intellectual" cluster represented by the categories "education" and "intelligence."

The remaining four categories—"honest," "humour," "commitment," and "emotion"—all related to a "personality" cluster that had been found in the literature to be more commonly concerns of women; hence, although they were of interest to gather data about, they didn't explicitly relate to the focal concepts of "sex object" and/or "success object."

Davis's elaboration of categories took what had been a very ephemeral idea—the notions of "sex object" and "success object"—and began translating them into fairly concrete, operational terms. Certainly one positive outcome of doing so would be that coding could probably be done with a high degree of reliability, since such categories reduce the amount of inference required of the coder.[12] Note also how his study design involved a step-by-step approach, in which each step builds on the one preceding; as a result, the data address his objectives adequately and clearly.

You should see, for example, that if we were to now go ahead and code the various ads to ascertain how often ad authors of each sex used terms like "attractive," "professional," and "well educated," we should have a fairly clear answer as to whether men are indeed more interested in meeting "sex objects" as defined in this study and whether women are more interested in meeting "success objects" as defined in this study. And that's exactly what Davis (1990) went on to do.

AGGREGATING AND ANALYZING THE DATA

With his 13 coding categories in hand, Davis could use them to code the various ads. One problem he anticipated was that a few particularly zealous "sex object" seekers or "success object" seekers could really throw off the data if they said the same thing a dozen different ways; that is, if each of the 13 phrases were counted as an instance of the phenomenon of interest, the total number would inflate the average for their group (i.e., for men or for women). Accordingly, Davis decided to code each of the categories as either "present" or "absent." Operationally,

Table 8.2

Coding Scheme Used by Davis (1990) for an Analysis of Mate-Selection Patterns Evident in Personal Newspaper Advertisements

#	Code	Explanation
1	Attractiveness	Coded when the author of the ad indicates that he or she seeks someone who is *pretty, attractive, handsome,* or *good-looking.*
2	Physique	Similar to category 1, but focused more on the body than on the face; relevant key words here would include *muscular, fit and trim, good figure,* or *well-built.*
3	Sex	Used when reference is made in the ad to desirability of *high sex drive, sensuous, erotic;* or where there is a clear message that author wants to find someone interested in engaging in sexual activity (i.e., *lunchtime liaisons–discretion required*).
4	Picture	Some ads request that respondents send along a photo of themselves, while others do not. Davis (1990) assumes that if a picture is requested, appearance is important.
5	Profession	Used when the author indicates that prospective partner should be a *professional person.*
6	Employed	Coded when the ad specifies that the person should have a *steady job* or *steady income.*
7	Financial	Used whenever the ad indicates that the person sought should be *wealthy, financially stable,* or *financially secure.*
8	Education	Coded whenever an indication is given that the prospective mate should be *well read, college educated,* or simply *well educated.*
9	Intelligence	Key words for this category include a request for someone who is *intelligent, bright,* or *intellectual.*
10	Honest	Coded when the ad requests someone *honest* or states that respondent should have *integrity.*
11	Humour	Coded when reference is made to the desire for the prospective mate to have a *sense of humour,* to be *cheerful,* or to enjoy a good laugh.
12	Commitment	Used when author explicitly indicates that he or she seeks a liaison that would be *long-term, might lead to marriage,* or similar phrasing.
13	Emotion	Used when there are indications of the desirability of emotional expressiveness, such as *romantic, expressive, sensitive,* or *responsive.*

Source: Based on S. Davis (1990), "Men as Success Objects and Women as Sex Objects: A Study of Personal Advertisements," *Sex Roles: A Journal of Research, 23,* pp. 45–46.

this meant that he would sit down with each ad, ask whether each of the 13 categories was evident, and then code it on a purely yes-or-no basis.

Thus, if an ad said that its author was looking for someone "with a great body," that ad would be coded as a "yes" for the "physique" category. If another ad expressed its author's interest in someone who was "muscular, fit, with great body tone, and curves and bulges in all the right places," that ad, too, would be coded as a "yes" for the "physique" category, even though its author repeated essentially the same thing four times in succession.

Davis then went through each of the randomly sampled Saturday editions, finding a total of 329 ads. He decided to omit one of them from the analysis (noting the decision in his article) because it involved a gay relationship rather than the heterosexual relationships on which he had decided to focus. Of the 328 remaining ads, 215 (or 65.5 percent) were placed by men, while 113 (or 34.5 percent) were authored by women.

Because he had coded for the age of the person in each ad, he was also able to tell us a bit about who these people were: the average age of those who reported it was 40.4 years, with very similar average ages for the men (40.7 years) and the women (39.4

years) who had included that information. The biggest problem here was that a full half of the women (50.4 percent) and almost a third of the men (32.6 percent) did not report their *exact* age.

Once all the ads were coded, Davis had only to begin making the appropriate comparisons. His first analysis scrutinized the differences between men and women in each of the 13 categories. These data are reported in Table 8.3: where Davis found significant differences, we've shaded the side with the significantly higher percentage. Most (10 out of 13) of the individual comparisons were statistically significant

Table 8.3

Gender Comparison for Attributes Desired in Partner

Variable	Gender		Chi-Square
	Desired by Men (*n* = 215)	**Desired by Women** (*n* = 113)	
1. Attractiveness	76 (35.3%)	20 (17.7%)	11.13(*)
2. Physique	81 (37.7%)	27 (23.9%)	6.37(*)
3. Sex	25 (11.6%)	4 (3.5%)	6.03(*)
4. Picture	74 (34.4%)	24 (21.2%)	6.18(*)
5. Profession	6 (2.8%)	19 (16.8%)	20.74(*)
6. Employed	8 (3.7%)	12 (10.6%)	6.12(*)
7. Financial	7 (3.2%)	22 (19.5%)	24.26(*)
8. Education	8 (3.7%)	8 (7.1%)	1.79(ns)
9. Intelligence	22 (10.2%)	24 (21.2%)	7.46(*)
10. Honest	20 (9.3%)	17 (15.0%)	2.44(ns)
11. Humour	36 (16.7%)	26 (23.0%)	1.89(ns)
12. Commitment	38 (17.6%)	31 (27.4%)	4.25(*)
13. Emotion	44 (20.5%)	35 (31.0%)	4.36(*)

Note: (*) means that the difference between the male- and female-authored ads was statistically significant at the p < .05 level; (ns) means that the comparison was non-significant, that is, the difference observed was no greater than what you would expect on the basis of chance variation alone.

Source: S. Davis (1990), "Men as Success Objects and Women as Sex Objects: A Study of Personal Advertisements," *Sex Roles: A Journal of Research, 23,* p. 47. Reprinted with kind permission from Springer Science and Business Media.

(i.e., the differences were found to be larger than would be expected on the basis of chance variation alone; see Chapter 12); all the differences, significant or not, were in the anticipated direction. Thus, for the "sex object" cluster, men were more likely than women to specify that they were seeking someone who was attractive, had a nice physique, and/or was interested in sex, and were more likely to request a picture of the respondent.

For the "success object" cluster, women were more likely than men to express a preference for someone who was a professional, employed, and/or financially secure. The data on the "intellectual" cluster were a little less clear: there were no statistically significant differences between the sexes in the extent to which they mentioned the desirability of "education" (although women had the higher percentage again), yet the category "intelligent" was noted significantly more often by women than men.

As for the "personality" cluster, women were more likely than men to specify attributes that fell into all four of these categories. But the size of the difference was statistically significant only for "com-mitment" and "emotion," and not for "honesty" and "humour."

Another way to look at these data is to group them into the overall categories of interest, for example, to aggregate all the "sex object" categories—appearance, physique, sex, picture—to create one overall index. This is shown in Table 8.4, which reaffirms the overall differences between male-authored and female-authored ads that were already evident when we scrutinized the individual categories. Men are shown to be more likely than women to state in an ad that they're seeking someone who's physically attractive; women are more likely than men to say that they're seeking someone who's financially stable and well educated.

Alas, despite all the gains that have been made in the realm of sexual equality, Davis's (1990) data seem to show that many men and women still follow very traditional patterns when seeking a mate.

CAVEAT AND CRITIQUE

Or do they? Probably the most positive element of Davis's (1990) analysis is the use it makes of an

Table 8.4

Gender Comparison for Physical, Employment, and Intellectual Attributes Desired in a Prospective Partner

Variable	Gender		Chi-Square
	Desired by Men ($n = 215$)	Desired by Women ($n = 113$)	
Physical (aggregating variables 1–4)	143 (66.5%)	60 (44.2%)	15.13(*)
Employment (aggregating variables 5–7)	17 (7.9%)	47 (41.6%)	51.36(*)
Intellectual (aggregating variables 8–9)	29 (13.5%)	31 (27.4%)	9.65(*)

Note: (*) means that the difference between the male- and female-authored ads was statistically significant at the $p < .05$ level.

Source: S. Davis (1990), "Men as Success Objects and Women as Sex Objects: A Study of Personal Advertisements," *Sex Roles: A Journal of Research, 23,* p. 48. Reprinted with kind permission from Springer Science and Business Media.

unobtrusive archival measure to scrutinize "real" processes involved in searching for a mate (i.e., the people who placed the newspaper ads were in fact searching for partners) and the avoidance of reactivity that this approach allows. But we should still be careful about how much confidence we place in the conclusions.

Davis (1990) expresses caution related to the apparent age of his sample. Having determined that the average age of those ad authors who cited their exact age was around 40, he suggests that the results may merely reflect the particular age cohort represented in the ads. Just because the 40-ish people who placed these ads seem to follow very traditional patterns of mate selection does not mean that people of other cohorts—those in their teens and 20s, for example—also do so.

One must also question the representativeness of those who use ads as a way of selecting mates, rather than more conventional means such as introductions through friends, meeting at social events such as parties, and/or meeting at venues of common interest such as the gym, library, or opera. Indeed, the fact that those who placed ads were in their 40s and were still (or newly) unattached may suggest that ads are a venue for mate selection largely for those who are unable to meet people through conventional means and/or for those who are still unattached precisely *because* they have a rigidly sex-typed and traditional conception of roles and desirable attributes. People who are more socially skilled may have met someone already, and hence do not need to place an ad.[13]

As this implies, those who chose mates *not* because they sought someone with a great body or a large bank account, but because they sought a well-rounded person who combined many positive attributes, may well be sitting out there happily ensconced in and enjoying their relationships, and may never even have considered placing a personals ad. Thus, although Davis's (1990) findings are indeed consistent with his hypothesis regarding differential bases for mate selection, they may well have emerged precisely because people who seek mates for the attributes he hypothesized are the people who

end up placing personals ads and not because they're at all representative of the way men and women in general seek and select mates.

OTHER USES OF CONTENT ANALYSIS

Davis's (1990) study shows one way to do a content analysis of archival material, but the range of what can be analyzed in that manner is limited only by your imagination. Newspaper articles are a popular target for content-analytic procedures: since this medium has now been around for at least a century, one can learn much from them about media images and about how commonly certain activities caught public attention in days gone by. Lowman and Fraser (1995), for example, included a content analysis of 100 years of newspaper coverage regarding the prostitution issue.

Other media, of course, can also be content-analyzed. Some years ago, for example, Ted engaged in some research for the Fraser Committee on Pornography and Prostitution concerning the social content of video pornography. The question was "What sorts of materials are available to the average video renter who wishes to rent a sexually explicit tape from his or her local video outlet?" A five-person team content-analyzed more than 100 such videos on a scene-by-scene basis in order to ascertain the extent to which they included violent, sexual, and/or sexually violent content (see Palys 1986). Similar methods have been used to content-analyze television programs for violent content.

Just about anything can be content-analyzed. Some researchers have content-analyzed children's textbooks to examine how the portrayals of women in such books have changed over time. Others have examined the artistic imagery on ancient vases for themes of power and achievement. Other sources of data for content analysis have included bumper-sticker messages, institutional/agency files, speeches, films, television programs, diaries, letters, and even T-shirts.

Qualitative Analysis of Archival Data

But engaging in more quantitative content-analytic procedures is not the only way to approach archival data. More qualitatively oriented researchers often approach the analysis of archival materials through less structured and more thematic means. An excellent example of such methods is offered by Trigger (1988), who examines the portrayal of Aboriginal peoples in histories of Canada written from 1744 to the present.

As we were growing up, our social studies and history classes in elementary and high school had astonishingly little to say about Aboriginal peoples. Despite the fact that Aboriginal peoples flourished on Turtle Island (the North American continent) for at least 10 000 years before the arrival of European explorers, the history of Canada that we were taught began with John Cabot's arrival in 1497 on the continent's eastern shores.

And, of course, anything important that has happened since then that was written about also focused primarily on Europeans or (later) Euro-Canadians. We were offered information about Champlain's sojourn in Acadia, how the voyageurs opened up the Great Lakes and associated river systems, how Henry Kelsey was overwhelmed by all the buffalo on the Prairies, how Simon Fraser bravely made his way down the river that would later bear his name, and how Captain Cook was the first seafarer to show up on the west coast, very close to where we now make our homes. If the "Indians" showed up at all in these histories, it was to sit quietly on the shore watching Jacques Cartier arrive, martyr Father Brébeuf in Quebec, paddle canoes for the voyageurs, stage a "rebellion" on the Prairies, engage in occasional "massacres" of European settlers, and sit awestruck when the great Iron Horse came through to join Canada from sea to sea. In sum, they were alternately (if not inconsistently) portrayed as bloodthirsty and passive, when they were portrayed at all.

We've since learned, but only because we made it our business to do so, that that history was deficient in many ways: what we were taught was a largely narcissistic and self-serving account written by Europeans and Euro-Canadians for themselves. Trigger (1988) played an important role in sensitizing us to that when he set out to ascertain whether written history was "always" the way we had learned it or whether history had literally "changed" depending on the nature of the relationship between Aboriginal and non-Aboriginal peoples at different times. He addressed that question by examining written histories of Canada from as far back as he could find them. In addition to offering an important perspective on historical study and Canada's Aboriginal peoples, his work serves as an example of a relatively unstructured qualitative thematic analysis of this unique archival material.

The earliest written history Trigger found was authored in 1744 by Pierre-François-Xavier de Charlevoix, a French Jesuit priest. Charlevoix lived extensively among different First Nations during a four-year stay in Quebec and on a two-year trip from Quebec to New Orleans and back. His descriptions of the Aboriginal peoples he encountered are by and large very positive. He considered the continent's natives to be every bit as rational as the Europeans, perceiving them as skilled traders and valuable military allies who did especially well when dealing with Europeans who underestimated them (Trigger 1988).

Charlevoix's accounts were an influential source for later histories in English, for example, those written by George Heriot in 1804 and William Smith in 1815, that continued to portray Aboriginal peoples in a positive fashion. This was particularly so after the Iroquois were instrumental in defeating the French—a defeat that ensured the British would remain the dominant European power in North America—and during the American Revolution, when the Iroquois again fought beside the British against the upstart Americans.

At least that was true of *English* histories; the depiction of Aboriginal peoples in *French* histories changed dramatically after France's 1759 defeat on the Plains of Abraham: "The image of native people in contemporary French-Canadian folklore ... kept alive the memory of Iroquois attacks against missionaries and European settlers during the seventeenth century" (Trigger 1988: 21).

One highly influential history was written by François-Xavier Garneau in 1845. "This book was written explicitly to be a history of the French-Canadian nation and sought to glorify the struggle of a people to survive and maintain their cultural identity in the face of the British threat" (Trigger 1988: 21–22). The Indians,[14] particularly the Iroquois, whose alliance with the British helped bring about the fall of New France, were clearly among the enemy.

Trigger notes that, unlike Charlevoix, Garneau had had little experience with Aboriginal peoples, so there was little to inhibit him in developing his accounts of French valour in the face of tremendous adversity. He depicted Aboriginal peoples as savage and backward; described them as constantly engaging in scalping, torture, and massacres; and charged them with sexual promiscuity, mistreating their children, and enslaving their women.

Garneau's history in turn influenced subsequent generations of French-Canadian historians, such as Jean-Baptiste Ferland, Etienne-Michel Faillon, and Henri-Raymond Casgrain (who were all priests, and hence added a more embellished role for the church in bringing "civilization" to the New World). "This gave them an additional motive to stress the vices of native people, whom they generally portrayed as dirty, immoral, cruel, and animal-like prior to their conversion to Christianity" (Trigger 1988: 22).

The latter part of the 19th century saw publication of Darwin's (1859) *On the Origin of Species*; evolutionary theory was subsequently applied to Aboriginal/non-Aboriginal differences, with French historians Benjamin Sulte and Lio-Adolphe Groulx asserting the biological superiority of the French over the Indians and Métis, an assertion that was used to further justify their oppression.

Although the British histories took longer to arrive at a similarly negative tone, they soon did so nonetheless. As long as the Indians were of use to the British—as trading partners, guides, hunters and fishers, and military allies—the depictions of Aboriginal peoples in written Canadian histories remained positive. But after the War of 1812, there was no longer any military threat, and the Europeans' interests in the fur trade waned; consequently, the Indian became of little use to the British, who now saw Aboriginal peoples as little more than an impediment to the acquisition of land for settlement and cultivation. By 1855, John McMullen's

History of Canada showed that the British had quickly and conveniently forgotten how instrumental the Iroquois were in the establishment of British North America; their role in those struggles was now depicted as marginal. In the words of Trigger (1988), McMullen went out of his way to depict Aboriginal peoples

> ... as primitive and animal-like. Particular emphasis was placed on their cruelty, dirtiness, laziness, and lack of religion, while their love of freedom, which Heriot and Smith had praised, was now dismissed as being wild and primeval in nature. Indians were frequently asserted to be incapable of becoming civilized and hence doomed to perish with the spread of European civilization. (Trigger 1988: 23)

Such portrayals further "legitimized" the minimization of the important role that Aboriginal peoples had played in the history of the country—how could peoples so "backward" and "uncivilized" ever have been involved in nation-building?

At the same time that Canadian colonials were relegating Aboriginal peoples to the broom closet of history, exploiting their lands, and creating treaties only to violate them, Canadian historians were writing self-adulatory accounts of how well we were treating our "native wards." John Castell Hopkins's 1901 *Story of the Dominion* "informed readers that in Canada, Indians had never suffered from racial antagonism, treaty breaking, removal from their reserves, abuse by greedy Europeans, or failure to receive legal justice" (Trigger 1988: 23):

> These interpretations of Canadian history required great self-deception, or hypocrisy, on the part of writers whose governments were treating their former allies with much the same mixture of repression and economic neglect as American governments were treating defeated enemies. (24)

Trigger notes that English-Canadian histories written in the first decades after 1900 all but abandoned the Indian, apparently accepting the view that they were "a primitive and static people who were doomed to disappear" (24). French-Canadian histories, on the other hand, continued to lament the losses of the past, with Aboriginals simultaneously and contradictingly being portrayed as lazy, immoral, unorganized, and uncivilized until "saved" by the Jesuits and Christianity, and among the primary architects of France's military misfortune.[15]

More recently, Trigger (1988) suggests that Canadian and Native histories seem to have fallen into one or the other of two camps. The first continues the tradition of the past 100 years but with a somewhat less overtly racist edge:

> Although the more obviously pejorative stereotypes have largely been excised from historical works ... the neglect of native peoples has persisted in mainstream Canadian historical studies, French and English. In most works, it has become fashionable to point out that European settlers learned how to use canoes, snowshoes, local foods, and herbal medicines from the Indians and that the Indians had a religion adequate to their needs and were often better nourished than were European settlers. Such observations, for all their good intentions, leave native people far from centre stage; indeed, they continue to treat them more like props than like actors. (24–25)

The other view of history that is now being seen is one that avoids sole reliance on the typically self-serving accounts of missionaries and colonials, instead subjecting such accounts to critical analysis through the use of a broader array of sources. Interestingly,

> ... this renewed interest in the role of native people in North American history corresponded with their growing importance in modern society. After World War II native populations, which had continued to decline into the 1920s, began to increase rapidly both on reserves and in the cities. In the 1960s native groups became politically active and started to demand the right once more to control the resources necessary to shape their own lives. Their struggle against poverty and gov-

ernment tutelage was accompanied by a cultural renaissance that witnessed native painters, singers, and actors gaining worldwide recognition. (Trigger 1988: 36)

These factors—coupled with the need to deal with growing Aboriginal social problems and political unrest and with the advances Aboriginal peoples were making through the courts, in international forums, and in government circles, as well as with the growing numbers of Aboriginal academics and Native leaders who have captured Canadian attention—have all rekindled an interest in Native history that is not based solely on documents created by missionaries and colonial agents.

But while much is changing, much remains to be done. As Trigger (1988) reminds us,

> ... only as these studies progress will we be able to distinguish systematically between the manner in which previous generations of Euro-Canadians treated native peoples and the false consciousness that justified their actions and coloured the historical records they produced. This in turn is a necessary preliminary to a deeper and more genuine understanding of native history. In spite of the progress that has been made so far, there are strong reasons to believe that entrenched European stereotypes continue to distort our understanding of native peoples and their history. (40)

LESSONS FROM TRIGGER

Trigger's (1988) study represents a different kind of "content analysis" than was implemented by Davis (1990); the former researcher relies less on coding schemes and checklists and more on a well-defined research question and a thematic reading of his sample materials. In the process, he also shows how easily history can become little more than a justification of the present, although the paper is also replete with indications of ways we can decolonize our minds and practices.

One lesson we have seen before: Skogan's (1975) admonition that "*Every statistic ... is shaped by the process which operationally defines it, the procedures which capture it, and the organization which interprets it*" (17; italics in original). Although initially asserted in an article on police crime statistics, Skogan's comment is equally applicable to historical accounts, reminding us that researchers must always be critically aware of the processes and perspective embodied in their sources and of the contexts in which those accounts were produced.

Missionaries believed in the divine inspiration of their activity and had a strong need to justify its rightness and success. There is evidence that many overestimated their success at conversion. Further, most of the documents available for analysis were prepared by missionaries "for publication in tracts designed to encourage European donors to support their work; hence, few failures [or doubts] are discussed at length" (Trigger 1988: 32), and negative portrayals of the Indians would help underline the magnitude of the challenge facing them. Trigger advises that one should always be on the lookout for independent sources for corroboration, and concludes that "it appears that what historians ... have concluded about missionary successes in New France is largely a reflection of the hopes and fears of the missionary chroniclers and of what modern scholars wish to have been the case" (32).

About the accounts of colonial writers, Trigger is no more flattering. He approvingly cites Jennings's (1975) work, which

> forced American historians to recognize that those settlers who initially recorded relations between native people and Europeans often either did not understand why Indians acted as they did or else had vested interests in misrepresenting their behaviour in order to portray self-seeking and exploitation by Europeans in a benevolent or at least an innocent fashion. Historians since the seventeenth century, especially those who were naturally predisposed to idealize Euro-American history, have tended to accept these accounts at face value. One role of [current historical research] is therefore to free mainstream North American history from its legacy as a colonial ideology. (Trigger 1988: 36)

Trigger's advice is "to learn to combine the study of written documents more effectively with data provided by ethnology, historical linguistics, ethnosemantics, archaeology, and oral traditions, as well as with the analytical perspectives of economics and ecology" (35).

This is good advice, with applicability beyond the restricted range of Aboriginal history per se. Indeed, it is advice that has already been offered in this text in another form: the need for multimethod inquiry, as well as the need for listening to a range of "voices" when constructing analytical accounts. Certainly the most biting aspect of Trigger's historical critique is the extent to which, except for the earliest histories and some of the most recent ones, Aboriginal "voices" have been completely missing from historical accounts.

EVALUATING SOURCES

Trigger's (1988) article is also a reminder that any source must be held up to the light in any comprehensive effort to understand the situation it purports to explain. In a discussion of participant-observation research, Lofland and Lofland (1984: 51) offer several basic "questions or tests that can be used to evaluate your own perceptions and the perceptions of other people" (see Table 8.5).

Not all these questions are directly applicable to the sorts of archival data that Trigger has analyzed, but most are. And collectively, they argue for the need to generate something of a "credibility" index when scrutinizing any archival or verbal account. Doing so will not guarantee the credibility (or lack thereof) of evidence; one can imagine situations where an apparently antiseptic source is nonetheless biased or where a supposedly "dirty" source embodies self-correcting mechanisms that effectively counteract the bias that might otherwise have prevailed. But these are wise principles to consider.

SUMMING UP AND LOOKING AHEAD

This chapter focuses on data sources that are growing in importance to many social scientists as they broaden their investigative strategies beyond

Table 8.5

Questions or Tests to Pose When Critically Analyzing Perceptual Evidence

1. Directness of the report:

   Is this account based on direct perception, or does it come second-, third-, or fourth-hand? If the latter, is it therefore to be treated with caution as fact, even if it is accurate as image?

2. Spatial location of the reporter:

   Even if firsthand, was my (or my reporter's) spatial location such that this perception might be accurate in some respects but still skewed or partial?

3. Social locational skewing of reported opinion:

   With regard to reports of opinion, what might there be about the relation between me and the reporter that might lead him or her to lie, distort, omit, falsely elaborate, or otherwise be less than accurate?

4. Self-serving error and bias concerning reports:

   From what I know on other grounds about my own or the reporter's commitments, values, and announced biases, are there reasons to be suspicious of the content of this report? Does it fit all too conveniently with what I want to believe, or what the reporter might want to believe, about people and events? That is, is it self-serving and therefore to be regarded with caution?

5. Previous plain error in reports:

   From what is known about my or the reporter's previous perceptions, am I an accurate observer/listener? Is the reporter? Have I or the reporter made errors in the past, even though these are not self-serving errors?

6. Internal consistency of the report:

   Is this report consistent within itself? Are there spatial–temporal factors stated at one point that contradict spatial–temporal assertions at other points? Were the events of this report possible within the time and space constraints given in the report or known about on other grounds? Do the people involved unaccountably contradict themselves within this report?

7. External consistency; agreement among independent reports:

   Is this account consistent with other accounts of the same events or experiences? Have I assembled enough independent accounts, subjected them to the above questions, and then compared them for degree of agreement? On points of remaining disagreement, have I made sufficient effort to speak with more participants in the event or persons involved in the experience—persons who are otherwise qualified reporters—in order to arrive at a truthful account?

Source: J. Lofland and L.H. Lofland (1984), *Analyzing Social Settings: A Guide to Qualitative Observation and Analysis,* 2nd edition (Belmont, CA: Wadsworth), p. 51. Copyright 1984. Reprinted with permission of Wadsworth, an imprint of the Wadsworth Group, a division of Thomson Learning: www.thomsonrights.com. Fax 800-730-2215.

interviewing or direct observation to include a historical dimension in their research and/or to take advantage of existing archival sources. After first differentiating between "physical trace" and "archival" evidence, the chapter shows some of the various ways social science researchers use and try to understand archival data.

The first type of data considered in detail are "official crime statistics," which are analytically deconstructed in an effort to show how a statistic of this sort is produced and to show the many qualitative elements contained in its construction. The reason for doing so is not to cast any sort of pejorative light on crime statistics per se, but rather to make the point that the same range of considerations should be implemented when one considers *any* set of archival statistics, no matter what government, agency, organization, or institution produced them. At the root of this view is the idea that we must always be prepared to ask questions about what the numbers *mean,* an approach that requires understanding something about the procedures and perspectives that combine to produce them.

This point is driven home in the section that attempts to deconstruct the kinds of "crime statistics" that are generated via victimization surveys. Part of our mission here is to dissuade you from any idea that the name of the game is simply to decide which version of crime statistics is "better" or "truer" in its representation of crime. Victimization surveys and police (UCR) crime statistics are simply different "voices," each of which offers a different "take" on crime. That section also aims to draw your attention to the many secondary data archives that are available to all researchers, including those who aren't in a position to acquire half-million-dollar grants.

Content analysis of archival materials is then discussed, using Davis's (1990) study of mate-selection criteria evident in personals ads featured in a local newspaper to show the procedures involved in such research. Attention is also drawn to the broad range of materials that can be subjected to this more quantitative form of analysis, including virtually everything from antique vases to bumper stickers and T-shirts. The dénouement of his (and our) analysis again involves taking a step back and asking just what the numbers mean, thereby reinforcing the point again that one should never simply take one's numbers at face value. Any data series is partly descriptive and partly interpretive; the thoughtful researcher pays heed to both aspects.

Finally, research by Trigger (1988) is used to illustrate a more qualitative form of archival analysis, one in which the researcher is *not* armed with checklists and coding schemes, but begins with a well-defined question that's used to focus analysis of a sample of material defined by the research question as relevant. In Trigger's case, the question concerned the variability that has existed in historical accounts of Canada, particularly with respect to the inclusion and representation of Aboriginal peoples in those accounts.

Although not in itself directly concerned with inquiring about the "facts" of Canadian history, Trigger's research sensitizes us to the way in which historical accounts can be self-serving accounts that do little more than justify the context in which they are produced.[16] The raw data of history are yet another archive that deserves exploration, and part of the researcher's task must involve an effort of deconstruction as part of exploring what those data mean, that is, considering the processes and perspectives embodied in their construction.

The message that arises from these four excursions into the world of archival analysis is clear. Just as we saw in earlier chapters that questioning (in Chapter 6) and observation (in Chapter 7) give one a "take" on reality (rather than "truth" itself), unobtrusive and archival measures must also be considered in the light of the methodological and organizational procedures and assumptions by which they were produced. Each technique and each data source offers only a slice of truth—using a certain implement to reveal a certain perspective. Ultimately, the researcher's task is not only to uncover these truths but also to articulate the perspectives that gave rise to them.

Of course, gathering data is not an end in itself, nor can it ever occur in a vacuum. Inductive perspectives notwithstanding, one never "just" gathers data in the hope that some self-evident truth will emerge. Even inductivists begin with an orienting strategy (see Wagner 1984) or some preliminary "commonsensical" understanding that leads them to focus on certain bits of information to the exclusion of others (e.g., see Campbell 1978). At the other extreme, deductivists are guided to particular variables by whatever theory they attempt to test or impose.

In both cases, the data that *are* gathered will be influenced by considerations of ethics and by situational constraints. No researcher can research everything, nor can one avoid pragmatic considerations in a world where research funding and data accessibility are limited. Researchers must decide what data to use;

those who await "perfect" data are in for a very long wait, and will probably never do any research at all. It's no sin to use "imperfect" data; the sins arise when one begins to assume that the *available* data are necessarily the most *important* data and/or fails to continue asking about the meaning of the data and about the organizational, cultural, and/or methodological context in which they were produced.

Data are gathered for some purpose, a purpose that, as discussed in Chapter 2, may range from pure exploration to explanation. Whether for theory generation (inductive research) or for theory probing and testing (deductive research), the business end of the research process generally involves gathering information about "what is happening" and, perhaps more important, about why or how it's happening that way. Generating and testing such explanations or theories involve not only gathering data, but gathering them in a context and according to a plan, a plan that helps researchers choose among rival plausible explanations concerning what, how, and why. Doing so involves considerations of *research design,* a topic to which we will now turn in greater detail.

A certain logic underlies matters of research design, a logic that applies broadly to both quantitative and qualitative techniques and perspectives. This logic is best appreciated in highly structured situations where social scientists are given complete license to create a situation that meets their inferential needs. Accordingly, we'll begin our discussion with a detailed examination of the logic underlying the highly structured laboratory experiment. Successive chapters move through progressively less structured situations to ethnographic studies and case study designs. As you read Chapters 9 to 11, pay particular attention to the *logic* that underlies how inferences are made in the different settings.

STUDY QUESTIONS

1. Differentiate between *erosion measures* and *accretion measures,* and give an example of each.
2. Skogan (1975) states that *"every statistic ... is shaped by the process which operationally defines it, the procedures which capture it, and the organization which interprets it"* (17; italics in original). In what sense is this claim true of the crime rate estimates produced by the police for Statistics Canada? In what sense is it true of the crime rate estimates that are produced by victimization surveys?
3. Some criminologists (e.g., Ditton 1979) argue that crime rates based on police data have nothing to do with crime and everything to do with police involvement in social control activities. To what extent do you agree or disagree with that perspective?
4. In what ways do crime statistics exemplify the advantages and limitations of archival data cited in this chapter?
5. Three people go on a crime spree. They break into a sporting-goods store and steal several shotguns, shoot and kill the store's owner, steal a nearby car, drive the wrong way down a one-way street to make their getaway, and then speed off down the highway. How would these activities be coded using the UCR system of crime-counting?
6. A researcher wants to evaluate the impact of a Canadian law that changed in 1962, and decides to use a time-series design. What difficulties do you see immediately with a study of that type?
7. *Memory fade* and *telescoping* are both problems that must be dealt with in victimization surveys. Describe what each problem is and how each can be dealt with.
8. This chapter has subjected crime statistics to considerable scrutiny aimed at demonstrating the relationship between particular events and our archival record of them. Try to apply the same type of scrutiny to any other archival statistic(s) of interest to you (e.g., suicide rates, unemployment rates, hospitalization rates, abortion rates, or rates of adolescent drug use).
9. Crime statistics suggest that about 90 percent of the crimes that are committed in Canada each year are nonviolent, while about 10 percent are violent. Does the coverage of crime news in your local newspaper reflect that state

of affairs? Using Davis's (1990) study, reported in this chapter, as a guide, design a content-analytic study to answer that question.

10. Trigger's (1988) study focuses intentionally on the written record of historical analyses created by settlers of European descent. But how is the study of Aboriginal peoples affected by the processes of *selective deposit* and *selective survival?*

11. Compare some of the advantages and disadvantages you see with doing more quantitative analyses such as Davis's (1990) version with more qualitative analyses such as Trigger's (1988)?

12. You are approached by another student who has been assigned an archival research project that looks at the portrayal of people who used marijuana during the late 1800s. They have been instructed that possible sources of data include records of parliamentary debates, pamphlets produced by local church groups, and personal correspondence between local politicians. (a) What cautionary note would you give this student regarding the pitfalls associated with selective deposit/survival? (b) How could they overcome these pitfalls/weaknesses?

13. Find out which newspapers your college, university, or municipal (public) library keeps and how many years' worth of issues they've retained. Design a quantitative and/or qualitative study that compares the way newspaper reports from different time periods treat an issue of interest to you. For example, you might look at (a) how women are portrayed in articles from the 1960s, 1970s, 1980s, and 1990s; (b) how environmental issues and/or environmental activists are portrayed in the 1960s and in the 1990s; or (c) whether the composition of the newspaper's front page is different now than it was at the turn of the 20th century.

14. A central theme of the chapter is the need to critically examine all sources of data to understand its strengths and limitations. What are some of the considerations that Lofland sug-

gests we should pose when examining perceptual evidence?

15. How does Trigger's (1988) analysis relate to Michel Foucault's power–knowledge themes, discussed in Chapter 1?

NOTES

1. There are, of course, other limitations that we have alluded to elsewhere in this text. For example, one limitation comes from the social position of those who write histories; in this regard, it is often the case that "history is a justification of the present," in that the elements of our collective history that we look at are those that speak to how we got where we are today. That is, historians write about those aspects of history that are relevant to *them*. Another factor, in many ways related to the first, concerns the beliefs that historians have about the "usefulness" or "preferredness" of certain forms of evidence over others. For example, European traditions place great emphasis on documentary (written) evidence, which, coincidentally, benefits their own views of history and disadvantages other, more oral, cultures (e.g., see Wolf 1982).

2. Actually, we don't have a clue about burial practices in 14th-century France. We created this example simply for purposes of illustration. An alternative possibility is that the wealthy (who were more likely to be literate at that time) may have written their years of birth and death on their tombstones, while the poor (who were less likely to be literate) did not. If that were the case, then it would be an instance of selective deposit rather than selective survival.

3. In keeping with the issues of selective deposit and survival addressed in the previous paragraphs, remember the limitations that arise from focusing only on written materials here. Oral histories are an equally important source of historical information, as discussed in Chapter 6.

4. This example should sensitize us to the need for understanding something of the context in which different documents are created. Novice archival researchers are often astonished at the sorts of negative views of different groups that exist in official documents from earlier in the 20th century and before, when imperialism and colonialism were at their heights and when ethnocentric and arrogant views of "others" could be expressed with the "certainty" that no one of "their" ilk would ever read the documents. While some people may hold similar views today—and evidence of racism and intolerance is certainly everywhere—such views are much less likely, given the advent of "freedom of information" legislation and the like, to be expressed in institutional materials. Thus, even a given type of archival material, institutional records, for example, may suffer differing degrees of reactivity at different times.

5. The error that is "added" may be positive or negative; that is, error can sometimes reduce and sometimes inflate scores from the "true" value.

6. A recent study by Rigakos (1994, 1995) in a Vancouver suburb is of interest here. He interviewed members of that suburb's primarily male police force and found that they, too, expressed the common belief that women "typically" would not show up in court or would refuse to testify about assault or violations of court injunctions. But when queried in detail, the officers in this study revealed that such cases were in fact quite rare, with the few that did occur having taken on a sort of "legendary" status. Rigakos (1994, 1995) interprets these data as evidence of male officers' insensitivity to the plight of women in abusive relationships and the justification that these "legends" give for their continuing inaction.

7. Note that counting procedures have again changed recently, with the current move being toward a more incident-based approach (see Lowman & Palys 1991).

8. This has not been the case with crime statistics, however. As this chapter shows, such statistics have been subjected to considerable theoretical and empirical scrutiny (see Lowman & Palys 1991 for a more extensive review).

9. Operation Identification, a police program for preventing burglaries, operates on the assumption that clearly recognizable goods are less desirable for thieves because such goods can more easily be traced as stolen and hence are "hotter." Residents are encouraged to borrow an engraver from the police and to engrave an identifying number (e.g., their social insurance number or driver's licence number) on their valuable goods.

10. Note that there's a built-in bias in such archives, since they're more likely to represent research that is substantially funded and is conducive to recording on magnetic tape or CD-ROM.

11. People are unlikely, for example, to spontaneously admit to having consumed illicit drugs or to having solicited the services of a prostitute. On the other hand, many studies of self-reported criminality have been undertaken. When the three types of data—official crime statistics, victimization surveys, and self-report crime surveys—are studied together, a fascinating overall picture emerges (e.g., see Lowman & Palys 1991).

12. Although the coding method was concretized to the extent that reliability should be high, it's unfortunate that Davis didn't take the extra step of undertaking a reliability analysis.

13. We don't mean to suggest this as a characterization of *all* people who place personals ads, since many reasons might drive one to try using this method of meeting a potential mate. But it seems plausible that such people are *among* those who place ads and that there may be enough of them to produce the results Davis (1990) observed.

14. As Kline (1994) and Palys (1996b) have shown, part of European ideology has involved depicting North America's diverse Aboriginal

peoples as a singular, homogeneous "other," known collectively as "Indians." When we use the term "Indians" in this section, it's only because we're recounting a source that saw Aboriginal peoples in that way—an erroneous and self-serving European construction. When using our own voices, we use terms like "Aboriginal peoples," "indigenous peoples," or simply "First Nations," since these are more consistent with Aboriginal peoples' understandings of themselves and are more

respectful of their special status as the indigenous inhabitants of this continent since time immemorial.

15. It doesn't say much for the French, of course, if so "inferior" a people did such a good job of facilitating the demise of the French colonies in North America.

16. Foucault's writings (explored in Chapter 1) are highly germane here; Trigger's (1988) analysis is easily construed within Foucault's power–knowledge framework.

CHAPTER 9

MANIPULATIVE CONTROL AND THE LOGIC OF EXPERIMENTATION

Thus far in this book, we've discussed general approaches to science, some of the ideals cherished by members of the scientific community, and some of the variety of ways in which information about humans is gathered. The techniques considered thus far have been discussed largely in terms of their use in *exploring* and *describing* phenomena of interest. Important though those activities may be in any systematic program of research, they don't exhaust the range of possibilities.

Any curious human explores when he or she pursues the impulse to try to understand something new. But such exploring is not, in and of itself, science. Pollsters may follow scientific procedures when they describe public attitudes for the media, but merely taking a poll to find out what people think is not, in itself, science. For members of the scientific community, exploration and description are important precursors—but precursors nonetheless—for the *real* stuff of science: examining *relationships* between variables and formulating *explanations* regarding their occurrence.

Don't get us wrong. The methods we've discussed so far *can* be used in the context of relational and explanatory analysis; they *produce* the data on which explanations are based. It's just that having such data in and of themselves is not enough. The bigger question, which we'll pose in this and the next two chapters, involves how we can either structure or take advantage of the existing structure of these data so that our inferences about "what's going on" are both reasonable and justifiable.

These issues of inference are addressed in a group of research approaches that we discuss in this and the next two chapters. They include: the classic experiment (Chapter 9); quasi-experimentation (Chapter 10); and

case study analysis (Chapter 11). We suggest the three share a common underlying logic that involves eliminating *rival plausible explanations* to make reasonable inferences about "causes" and other processes, but vary in the degree to which they emphasize either **manipulative control** or **analytic control** to do so.

RELATIONAL AND EXPLANATORY OBJECTIVES

Recall J. Lofland's (1971) statement (Chapter 7) that science ultimately boils down to three types of questions: those regarding *characteristics, causes,* or *consequences.* The preceding chapters on data-gathering techniques were oriented more toward using the various methods to reliably and validly describe *characteristics* of phenomena of interest.

In terms of the time frame each type of question addresses, describing the characteristics of things focuses most explicitly on the "present" portion of the time continuum. Now we expand our coverage to include the *antecedents* (causes) of our phenomena of interest, as well as their *implications* (consequences) for other variables of interest. Our focus now turns to the task of examining *relationships* among variables and *explaining* how particular variables combine and interact to produce phenomena of interest.

Explanation, in its social scientific sense, involves making non-tautological and non-trivial assertions about the dynamics of some phenomenon of interest. As Silverman (1985) states, "explanation is never fundamentally concerned with particular elements or units, but with the articulation of the relation between elements" (34). In sum, our quest for explanation brings us to *relational* research: the question of what variables "go with" what other variables. More to the point, how do particular sets of variables come together to produce the phenomenon of interest to us?

Whether our prospective insights into the phenomenon have emerged from inductive, exploratory research, from the tenets of our deductive theorizing, or from the literature, our task now is to develop our theorizing by examining relationships between variables. Thus far in this text, we've focused primarily on the *nouns* of our theoretical propositions—how can we describe the phenomenon of interest to us, and how can we operationalize the variables that we feel may have explanatory utility? Now we want to ask in what ways variables *combine* to *produce* or *generate* or *cause* a phenomenon to occur; that is, we want to focus on the verbs.

It is this last verb—"cause"—that has preoccupied philosophers and researchers for centuries. Of all the types of relationships that might exist among variables, *causal relationships* have received the most attention. Things happen. Why? Who or what caused them to occur? The process of generating *explanations* was seen as a matter of articulating the sequence of events that in some sense caused a phenomenon to occur. And *theory* was what glued it all together. But how can one ask questions about causal relationships among variables?

INTRODUCING EXPERIMENTALISM: AN EARLY EXAMPLE

Let us begin by telling you a story about a little study (reported by Cook & Campbell 1979) that was done in France in 1648, a full 200 years before John Stuart Mill formalized the empirical principles that play such a major role in the research we do today. The experiment was initiated by Blaise Pascal, a mathematician and physicist whose name may be familiar to you from the term "kilopascal," which is a metric unit for measuring air pressure.

Just to set the stage, you should know that the "Torricellian vacuum" was a phenomenon known to the physicists of Pascal's day, as well as to Pascal himself. What *is* a Torricellian vacuum, you ask? Well, to make one, you need a dish or bowl; a tube that's closed at one end, open at the other, and more than 76 centimetres (30 inches) long; and a lot of mercury (the element, not the planet). Step one is to pour some mercury into the bowl; step two is to fill the tube with mercury. For step three, you invert the tube full of mercury so that the closed end is at the top and the open end is sitting inside the bowl of mercury. What happens when the tube is inverted? You might think that all the mercury would just drain out, but it doesn't. The level of mercury in the tube will fall a bit, but the mercury won't just run out. When the mercury level in the tube falls, a vacuum is created in the top (closed) end of the tube: *that's* a Torricellian vacuum!

The people of 1648 knew that the Torricellian vacuum existed, and that when you inverted the tube, the mercury didn't just fall out, but they weren't especially clear on *why* it worked. Pascal developed the theory that the reason the mercury stayed in the tube was because of atmospheric pressure, more specifically, because of the mass of the air pressing on the mercury in the bowl. How could he determine whether his theory was correct? The reasoning Pascal followed was this: *if* his theory was correct, the column of mercury should become shorter if it was taken to a higher altitude (where the weight of the air pressing down on the mercury in the bowl would be less simply because there's less of it). So he asked his brother-in-law, a man named Perier who happened to live in a mountainous region in France, to help test his theory.

On Saturday, September 19, 1648, Perier and a few friends set out with two Torricellian tubes, two bowls, and a lot of mercury, with the intention of scaling a local mountain that was about 900 metres (3000 feet) high. At the foot of the mountain, they set up both tubes and found that the mercury in each stood at the same height: 712.22 millimetres (28.04 inches). One of the tubes was left standing: a Father Chastin remained behind, watching to see whether the mercury level in it changed over the course of the day. The rest of the group packed up the second tube and scaled the mountain. When they reached the top, they again set up the tube.

They found, just as Pascal's theory had predicted, that the column of mercury now measured just 627.63 millimetres (24.71 inches), much less than it had 900 metres (3000 feet) below.

Just to be sure, the group made multiple measurements at that higher altitude, under a variety of conditions: on both sides of the mountaintop, inside and outside a shelter located there. In all cases, the level of mercury in the tube remained the same. Setting off down the mountain again, the group stopped partway down to take yet another measurement; this time they found the height of the column of mercury to be 676.9 millimetres (26.65 inches), that is, intermediate to the readings taken at the top and bottom of the mountain. When they finally returned to the base of the mountain, Father Chastin reported that the mercury level in the tube that he'd been watching hadn't changed all day. And when they again set up the second tube beside the first, they found once again that both tubes showed the same original measurement: 712.22 millimetres (28.04 inches). In sum, all the observations supported Pascal's theory.

Although contemporary notions of experimental design have really become formalized only within the last century or so, Pascal's relatively simple study bore many of the features of contemporary experimentalist practice. The most important aspect of Pascal's study was that he decided to actually experiment, to test out his theory. It was classical deductive reasoning that suggested that *if* the theory were true, *then* some real-world predictions should follow; clearly, when the data were gathered, they would serve to either support or refute his theory.

Note also how important it was for Father Chastin to remain at the base of the mountain with one of the tubes. What would have happened if they'd brought along only one tube, using it to take measurements at both the bottom and the top of the mountain? Would it have made a difference in the inferences they could have made? Clearly it would have. Perhaps the changes they observed were due to changes in the weather or to the sun's position in the sky (i.e., time of day). However, such climatic or temporal changes would have affected *both* tubes.

That is, if the sun's position, for example, was causing the mercury to take on a certain level, both tubes would have shown the same effect; but they didn't. In fact, the two tubes were apparently equal in all respects except one, the altitude. When the tube stayed in one place, the level stayed the same. When the second tube was moved to a different altitude, the levels changed in the direction predicted by Pascal's theory. Furthermore, when the tube was measured in a variety of positions—but with altitude all the while being kept constant (i.e., at the top of the mountain)—the levels didn't change.

We have here many of the basic attributes of contemporary experimental design, including the following:

1. A variable (i.e., altitude in Pascal's study) or set of variables whose effect we wish to assess. This variable is known as the **independent** or treatment **variable.**
2. Some way to measure the effects of the independent variable; this second variable (in Pascal's study, the height of the column of mercury in the tube) is known as a **dependent** or outcome **variable.**
3. Some *comparison,* from which changes can be inferred and, one hopes, attributed to the treatment (Pascal's study achieved this aim by taking measurements at high and low altitudes).

With regard to the third attribute, it should be noted that not all forms of comparison are equally useful to the researcher. Comparing the criterion measure at two points in time (e.g., before and after some event of interest) may allow assessment of the degree of change, but isn't particularly useful for isolating the locus (or source) of that change. In contrast, comparing the criterion measure in two situations that differ only in the presence or absence of some event of interest allows us to assess not only the degree of change that has occurred, but also something of the source of that change. In a study like Pascal's, comparing measurements on the same tube at different points on the mountain would tell us that change had occurred, but wouldn't help us isolate whether the change was due to changes in altitude, instrumentation, time of day, or some other factor. In contrast, comparing two tubes that were exposed to identical conditions *except* changes in altitude means that any changes in mercury levels could only be due to the changes in altitude.

Finally, note that while the observed data could be said to *support* Pascal's theory, to *be consistent with* the theory, and/or *to be not inconsistent* with it, we *cannot* say that the experiment *proved* Pascal's theory. There may have been other variables present of which we were not aware, and there may be other competing theories that would also have made the same prediction in this instance.

THE TERMINOLOGY AND LOGIC OF EXPERIMENTATION

Moving now to a hypothetical example within the social sciences, suppose we want to know whether watching a series of films about immigrants' contributions to Canadian culture will affect people's attitude toward immigration policies and current immigration levels. Assuming that we've followed the procedures described earlier in this text and have constructed a reliable and valid measure of this attitude, one way to assess the impact of exposure to the films would be to measure the preliminary attitudes of a group of individuals regarding current immigration levels; show this group of people the series of films; and measure the group's attitudes once again, in order to see whether any change in attitude had occurred. This process is illustrated in Figure 9.1.

Figure 9.1

Diagram of One Way to Assess Change in Attitudes (One-Group Pretest/Posttest Design)

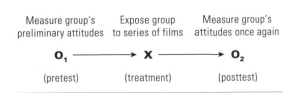

Measure group's preliminary attitudes	Expose group to series of films	Measure group's attitudes once again
O_1 $\longrightarrow$	X $\longrightarrow$	O_2
(pretest)	(treatment)	(posttest)

Independent and Dependent Variables

Note that our hypothetical study has two key variables, as did Pascal's study. The first variable is the one whose impact we want to assess, namely, the exposure to a series of films. The second variable is the one we measure in order to see whether any effect has indeed occurred, namely, attitudes toward current immigration levels. Note that the choice of which variable to impose or manipulate (i.e., exposure to the films) represents a decision we make *independently* of the actual execution of our study. This variable whose impact we are trying to assess is thus known as the *independent variable* or the *treatment variable*.

How about the other variable in our study, the attitudes that we are attempting to measure? What level or values will they take on in the actual study? We can't really answer that question until we actually do the study, since the values that variable takes on will *depend* on who is in our subject sample, what their attitudes are, and how potent or effective the independent variable actually is in causing change. Rather than being independent of the actual execution of the study (as was the case with the films), the values that the attitude variable takes on are very much *dependent* on what happens during the actual execution of the study. This variable is known as the *dependent variable* or the *outcome variable*.

Internal Validity

Suppose that we do the study and find that, following exposure to the films, there *is* a change in our dependent measure. What can we conclude from that observation? We might *like* to conclude that the change we observed was attributable to the independent variable of interest (i.e., the film series). But how confident can we be in drawing that inference?

It's time to introduce a major concept: the **internal validity** of a study. This term, coined by Campbell and Stanley (1963), refers to *the extent to which differences observed in the study can be* unambiguously *attributed to the experimental treatment* *itself, rather than to other factors.* In other words, to what extent can we be confident that the differences we observe are caused by the independent variable per se, rather than by **rival plausible explanations**?

After defining the term, Campbell and Stanley (1963) delineate a number of "threats" (i.e., concerns) that one should keep in mind when assessing internal validity. A number of these are relevant to our hypothetical research design.

SOME THREATS TO INTERNAL VALIDITY

HISTORY The first potential threat to internal validity is **history,** which refers in pretest/posttest designs to the specific events occurring between the first and second measurement in addition to the independent variable. In other words, what else might have happened between the pretest and posttest that might also account for the results that we observed? In our hypothetical study, *many* events other than the film series might have occurred that could also have led our respondents to change their attitudes. They might have seen newspaper articles or TV shows about immigration successes or have been exposed to classroom materials dealing with immigration policies. How do we know it wasn't one of those *other* factors or variables that caused a change in attitude, rather than the films we showed? In the research design we have right now, there's no way we can tell for sure.

MATURATION Another type of threat to internal validity noted by Campbell and Stanley (1963) is **maturation,** defined as processes within the research participants themselves that change as a function of time per se (not specific to particular events), such as growing older, more tired, more hungry, and so on. In other words, sometimes changes occur merely because of biological processes that happen over time, and we must be careful to recognize those processes and their effects when we're assessing the effects of other independent variables.

For example, suppose we come to you with a pill and suggest it will help children learn to walk. In order to demonstrate the effectiveness of this pill, we

first acquire a sample of year-old children, none of whom can walk. We give each of the children (or their parents) a box of the pills, with the instruction that the children are to take one pill a month for a year. One year later, we come back and find that every single one of the children (now two years old) knows how to walk. The design would be like that depicted in Figure 9.2. Were the pills effective? Maybe. But a rather compelling rival plausible explanation would be that it wasn't the *pills* that caused the change, but rather maturational change within the children (i.e., physical processes like bone development, physical competence, coordination) that now allowed them to walk. In other words, they probably would have learned to walk anyway, with or without the pills.[1]

The above example may seem fairly obvious, but it shows how maturational processes can threaten internal validity. Sometimes, though, the effects of maturational processes are more subtle and, consequently, ignored. Returning to our immigration example, suppose we start by giving a questionnaire in the morning about immigration policies (i.e., our pretest), spend a solid eight hours showing various films to our research participants, and end the day by again giving the questionnaire on current immigration policies (the posttest). In the end, we find that our participants show more hostile attitudes and appear to be more critical of immigrants. Can we conclude that exposure to the films caused the change in attitude?

The films *may* have caused the change. And historical factors wouldn't be a threat to that conclu-

Figure 9.2

A Pretest/Posttest–Only Design Showing Effects Pertaining to Maturational Processes

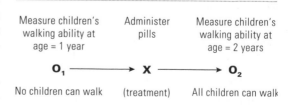

Measure children's walking ability at age = 1 year	Administer pills	Measure children's walking ability at age = 2 years
O₁ ⟶	**X** ⟶	**O₂**
No children can walk	(treatment)	All children can walk

sion, since our participants have been insulated from other events (e.g., news media reports). But look what we've done. We've required our participants to put in a long day, given them no opportunity to have lunch, and kept them busy doing our questionnaire and viewing our films. What happens to people in that type of situation? Many people get tired and hungry; over the course of a long, demanding day, they may also become more impatient, terse, and grumpy. Because of these physiologically based "maturational" changes, in other words, we might expect that by the time of the posttest, participants will have become slightly more hostile in their responses to our questions. Can we therefore conclude that the *films* caused the change to more critical attitudes? Although we might like to do so (given our interests), we would also have to consider (as a rival plausible explanation) that maturational changes may have caused the change.

TESTING A third threat to internal validity is **testing,** specifically, the effects of taking a test on scores in the second testing. Such effects can operate in several different ways. Having taken a test, you may become sensitized to the issue involved in a way that you wouldn't have been otherwise. Suppose somebody gives you a questionnaire regarding your attitudes about current immigration levels. The mere fact that you were administered the questionnaire may lead you to be more sensitive to, or more likely to pay attention to, related material that's presented in the press, on TV, on the radio, or in your classes. When you then receive the posttest after the administration of the independent variable, and it turns out your attitudes have changed, researchers can't be sure whether the change was produced by the independent variable or by the greater sensitization to issues induced by the pretest. Consequently, this phenomenon, known as *pretest sensitization,* is a threat to internal validity. Why? Because it offers a rival plausible explanation for the source of change.

Another way in which testing can threaten internal validity is through *practice effects.* If we were trying to assess your abilities, for example, it would

be difficult to know in the posttest situation whether you had improved purely because of the practice the pretest gave you or because of the independent variable we had imposed on you.

STATISTICAL REGRESSION (REGRESSION TOWARD THE MEAN)

A related yet very different threat to internal validity is known as **statistical regression** or **regression toward the mean.** Recall that, with testing, we were talking about *real* change occurring between pretest and posttest (e.g., because of practice, sensitization to issues, or greater motivation); in such a situation, the threat to internal validity relates to uncertainty about whether the independent variable or the testing effect was the source of the change.

With statistical regression, we also observe a change, but in this instance, the change is more apparent than real. We know that any measuring we do is subject to a certain amount of random error, no matter how many precautions we take to minimize it. Many (if not most) times, these positive and negative chance influences will be distributed equally across a group, or across time for a particular individual, so that in the long run, the *average* score of a particular individual or group will be a good indication of their "true" score. But on any given occasion, chance events may "stack up" in a positive or negative direction. Also known as *regression toward the mean,* statistical regression refers to the propensity of extreme scorers on the first testing to score closer to the mean (average) of the group on the second testing. This phenomenon occurs because chance events are unlikely ever to stack up to precisely the same degree on two successive occasions.

Let's take LeBron James as an example. In case you haven't heard of him, LeBron James plays for the Cleveland Cavaliers, a National Basketball Association (NBA) team. An astoundingly good basketball player, he dominates a game in the manner of a Michael Jordan or a Magic Johnson, averaging roughly 30 points a game. But even LeBron James has good games and bad games. Basketball fans know that James is a great basketball player because they observe his performance over the course of a whole season. But in the social sciences, we rarely have the luxury of such extended observation. Instead, our situation is often more like that of the person who goes to only one basketball game in which LeBron James happens to be playing.

Suppose this person goes to this basketball game to assess how good a basketball player LeBron James is. And suppose James has a great night: he can't do anything wrong, and he ends up scoring 50 points. If, on the basis of that single assessment, our observer concludes that "LeBron James is amazing; he gets 50 points a game," basketball fans know that the observer is *overestimating* James's "true" ability. But (and here's the important part) what if the same observer goes to see LeBron James play in a *second* basketball game later in the same season? The last time he or she saw James, the basketball player scored 50 points, but his *average* is about 30 points a game. Now, if you were a betting person, would you bet that on this second occasion LeBron James will (1) do even better than he did last time, (2) do the same as he did last time, or (3) do worse than he did last time?

If you picked (1) or (2), please send us your name and address: we could use the money. James *may* get 50 points or more in this second game, but the likelihood is much higher that he will perform more consistently with his average or typical performance and get something closer to 30 points. This is true *not* because James has changed or because of anything special that might have happened between the two games, but purely because the first performance was atypically high due to chance factors. This phenomenon—the tendency of extreme scores to move ("regress" is the technical term) closer to the mean on a subsequent testing—is known as *statistical regression* or *regression toward the mean*. The more extreme the first score, the greater this propensity.

Regression toward the mean threatens internal validity whenever a group is picked *because* of the extremity of their scores on a pretest. For example, suppose that in the study concerning attitudes about current immigration levels, we decide to administer our immigration questionnaire to 100 people and

then pick the 20 people from that group who were apparently *least* in favour of current immigration levels (i.e., the 20 people with the lowest scores on the pretest) to see whether exposing them to our film series will lead them to temper their attitudes somewhat. Although we're confident about the reliability and validity of our scale, there will *always* be *some* degree of error in the scores. And as argued above, the odds are high that to the extent that we've erred in assessing our group's attitudes toward current immigration levels, the errors among the *lowest* scorers will likely be errors of *under*estimation (e.g., see Figure 9.3). Since on a second testing, the *chance* errors that contributed to the extremity of those low scores are unlikely to stack up to the same degree as before, the scores on the second testing will be less extreme (i.e., closer to the mean of the group). Thus, it will *look* as though there's been attitude change (because the average score changes), but all we've *really* witnessed is that phenomenon known as regression toward the mean. And we'll be uncertain as to what extent the change we observe is attributable to the independent variable (i.e., the film series) or to the regression artifact. As Cook and Campbell (1979) say,

> statistical regression (1) operates to increase obtained pretest-posttest gain scores among low pretest scores, since this group's pretest scores are more likely to have been depressed by error; (2) operates to decrease obtained change scores among persons with high pretest scores since their pretest scores are likely to have been inflated by error; and (3) does not affect obtained change scores among scorers at the center of the pretest distribution since the group is likely to contain as many units whose pretest scores are inflated by error as units whose pretest scores are deflated by it. (52–53)

History, maturation, testing, and statistical regression are the only threats to internal validity we will deal with at this time. But keep in mind that **selection** biases (see Chapter 4's discussion of sampling) and **instrumentation** changes (see Chapter 8's discussion of archival methods) may also threaten internal validity. Those interested in further reading

Figure 9.3

The Different Propensity of Scores from Three Areas of the Normal Distribution for Regression toward the Mean

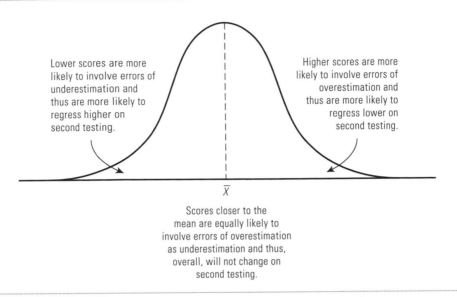

Lower scores are more likely to involve errors of underestimation and thus are more likely to regress higher on second testing.

Higher scores are more likely to involve errors of overestimation and thus are more likely to regress lower on second testing.

$\overline{X}$

Scores closer to the mean are equally likely to involve errors of overestimation as underestimation and thus, overall, will not change on second testing.

should consult Campbell and Stanley (1963), or Shadish, Cook, and Campbell (2001).

The main point here is that, in any study, one should always ask *why* a particular result was observed. Did the independent variable produce the result, or could it have been produced by something else? In our hypothetical study, how confident are we that the changes in attitudes regarding current immigration levels were produced (caused) by the film series and not by something else? Given the *one-group pretest/posttest design* we have so far, we can't be very confident at all that the film series caused the change; in other words, we have low internal validity. There are just too many *rival plausible explanations* (i.e., alternative factors that might also account for the observed result). Somehow we have to overcome that problem.

CONTROLLING FOR RIVAL PLAUSIBLE EXPLANATIONS

As noted earlier in this book, there are some significant differences between how members of the scientific community and laypeople go about making sense of the world around them. How many times have you seen people, including you, make comparisons on some variable of interest at two points in time, and then attribute the change to some intervening factor, when in fact it could have been caused by any number of things? How many times have you heard "The crime rate is up; it must be because of ..." followed by the person's pet peeve or interest (e.g., our permissive society, too many marijuana smokers, the recession, the moon in Aquarius, changes in the ozone layer), or "She's really changed since she met Larry"? Such implicit or explicit causal statements *may* be right, but they may *also* be wrong. Social scientists are interested in ascertaining *which* of those rival plausible explanations is correct, and under what conditions. But how can we do that?

CONTROL AND COMPARISON GROUPS One answer comes in the form of a **control group,** which is a second group added on to the design we already have. The control group starts off the same as our first group (the experimental group) and is treated identically to the experimental group in *all* respects *except* the control group doesn't receive the independent variable. This gives us the design shown in Figure 9.4: the *pretest/posttest control group design*. In our hypothetical study, our control group would receive the pretest and the posttest at the same times as the experimental group, but *wouldn't* be exposed to the film series. Instead, the control group might quietly sit and wait, watch a travelogue about a surfing contest in Waikiki, or do something else that kept them busy for the same amount of time and at the same type of activity as the experimental group but that wasn't directly related to attitudes regarding immigrants or immigration policies.

Suppose we do this study and obtain the results shown in Table 9.1. The control group's scores have changed slightly, but nowhere near as much as those of the experimental group. Now can we confidently assert that the changes in attitudes in the experimental group were a function of the film series rather than of rival plausible explanations?

Our internal validity in this case is actually fairly high. The best way to see this is to *try out* some rival plausible explanations to see what happens. Could the experimental group's attitudes have changed because of *historical factors?* Maybe, but probably not. Why? Because the control group (as a group) was subject to those same historical factors, and their scores didn't change much at all. Could *maturational factors* have entered in? Maybe, but the control group had the same time delay between pretest and posttest, and it didn't cause them to change. Well, how about the effects of *testing?* Once again, pretest sensitization can't account for the results, because it would have had an equivalent effect on the

Figure 9.4
A Pretest/Posttest Control Group Design

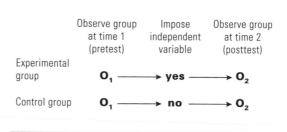

control group, and they didn't change at all. So why did the experimental group change their attitudes? Given that the experimental and control groups were equal to begin with (as shown by their similar pretest scores), and given that they were treated alike in every respect except for the imposition of the independent variable, the most likely explanation is that any change in the experimental group that wasn't observed in the control group must have been a function of the one element on which they differed, the film series.

The control group doesn't always have to be a "do nothing" group. *Control* groups are simply *comparison* groups that help us isolate and assess the impact or influence of particular variables. Accordingly, the nature of a control group will depend on what you're trying to assess, within the constraint of ethical considerations. Let's take two examples.

In the first example, imagine that you want to assess the effects that viewing explicitly sexual films has on those who view them. Your experimental group will thus comprise people to whom you show a sexually explicit film. In order to assess the effects

Table 9.1
Hypothetical Results for the Pretest/Posttest Control Group Design in Figure 9.4

	Pretest Scores	Impose Independent Variable	Posttest Scores
Experimental group	Average score = 43.6 →	yes →	Average score = 58.6
Control group	Average score = 44.1 →	no →	Average score = 46.8

of the film per se, you must choose an appropriate comparison group, a group that's similar to the experimental group in all respects, except that this group doesn't view a film with sexually explicit content. Let's say that the sexually explicit film you're showing is 30 minutes long. The procedures require that you welcome your experimental group to the lab, explain the nature of their participation, answer any questions, take them to the viewing room, and then give them a posttest measure. What would be an appropriate control group?

One possibility is simply to have a control group of people who come in, complete a pretest, sit around for 30 minutes, and then complete a posttest. But such an approach creates more differences between the experimental and control groups than mere exposure to a sexually explicit film. Those who watch the sexual film have a whole range of experiences besides watching the film itself; for example, they receive the degree of attention (including instructions and explanations) accorded to people who are central to the research, and their attention is focused by a TV or film screen that they've been asked to watch.

A control group that comes in and does nothing, therefore, not only doesn't see the sexually explicit material, but also doesn't receive the same degree of attention from the experimenter and doesn't have their attention monopolized by a screen. Thus, when you come to the end of the study and want to evaluate internal validity, you can't tell for sure whether any differences between the two groups are due to the film, the attention paid to people, or to diverting their attention to a screen. A better procedure would involve giving everyone in the control group the same attention you give those in the experimental group, and showing them a film, too, but ensuring that it contains absolutely no sexual content. In that way, you duplicate all aspects of the experimental group's experience except for the one element whose effects you wish to test: that is, the effects of viewing a sexually explicit film.

For the second example, consider someone who has developed a new drug, treatment program, or counselling approach that is used for people in need

(e.g., for depressed patients). At the moment, suppose that these people receive "Don't Worry, Be Happy" (DWBH) counselling that focuses on the counterproductiveness of compulsive worrying. People who use that method have a decent success rate, but you think that your program may be better, so you set out to evaluate its effectiveness. Your experimental group will thus comprise people who receive your new program. But what is an appropriate control group here?

A "do nothing" control group would be problematic in two ways. First, it would be a problem for the same reason noted in the preceding paragraph regarding the assessment of the effects of the sexually explicit film, that is, "attending a counselling program" and "doing nothing" differ on many more variables than just the content of the program. To counteract that, you might have the control group come in for equal periods of time and engage in some other form of interactive activity (e.g., playing table tennis for an equivalent time period).

But ethical issues arise whenever you engage in research with people in need. "Doing nothing" may be a violation of your ethical obligation to ensure, to the best of your ability, the well-being of people under your care. Because of this, researchers in this situation will often use the "best known treatment" or "usual treatment" (the DWBH counselling, in this instance) as their basis of comparison.

The research question then changes from "Does the new program *work?*" (a question that implies a comparison between giving the program and doing nothing) to "Does the new program work *any better* than what we do already?" (a question that implies a comparison between giving the new program and giving the old one). Often in such instances, the evaluation will measure many more variables than simple "treatment success," thereby allowing comparisons between treatments on other dimensions. It might be found, for example, that the new treatment is no different from the existing treatment in terms of success of treatment, but that it achieves that success at significant cost savings, allows clients to go home more quickly, has fewer side effects, or is less intrusive.

EXPERIMENTALIST LOGIC IN A NUTSHELL

As the above discussion reveals, the logic of experimental design goes like this: *if* you have two (or more) groups who are equal to begin with and if you treat them equally in all respects *except* one (that being exposure versus non-exposure to the independent variable), any subsequent differences between the groups must be attributable to the one variable on which the groups differed. *Control* and *comparison groups* play a valuable function in empirical research by allowing one to isolate a particular reason behind any change that is observed. They're called "control" groups because they help control for rival plausible explanations.

ENSURING INITIAL GROUP EQUIVALENCE

One point was glossed over in the preceding discussion. Thus far, we've said that *if we can assume our experimental and control groups were equal to begin with* and if we use appropriate controls, high internal validity will result. The italicized phrase refers to the **assumption of pretest equivalence.** But it includes a very big "if." How reasonable is the assumption that our groups are, in fact, equal to begin with?

SELECTION BIASES In some instances, the assumption of pretest equivalence can't be made at all. This is typically the case in many *existing groups* situations. For example, suppose we want to evaluate whether jail or the imposition of a fine is more effective in reducing recidivism (i.e., reducing the likelihood that people will re-offend). To do this, we get a sample of 1000 people who have been sentenced to jail and 1000 people who have been fined, and then see how many in each group recidivate during a two-year follow-up period. Would comparing these two rates tell us the relative effectiveness of the two sanctions in reducing recidivism? No. Why not? Because the two groups likely differed on many attributes other than type of sanction; that is, they probably also differed in terms of offence committed, prior record, or other variables that are also plausible alternative influences on our dependent variable.

The same is true whenever groups are formed on something other than a chance basis. Allowing *self-selection* or *volunteer selection* (i.e., letting people choose the groups in which they want to be), for example, can be problematic. Suppose we want to evaluate the effectiveness of a "defensive driving" course. We offer such a course to 16-year-olds at a local high school; some students sign up for it, whereas others do not. Two years after the course is completed, we compare accident records for all those students who in fact received their licence, and find that those who took the course have been involved in significantly fewer accidents than those who didn't. Was the course effective? Well, maybe. But it's also possible that the two groups were not equal to begin with. Those who "self-selected" themselves into the course may have done so because of a greater concern over safe driving and, hence, might have been expected to have fewer accidents whether or not they took the course.

The opposite might happen when group membership is *mandatory*, for example, where people charged with impaired or dangerous driving might be sentenced by the courts to take a safe-driving course. In this instance, we might well find that the "experimental" group does more *poorly* than a control group of other drivers picked at random—not because the course is poor, but because the process of group assignment created an experimental group that included those with poorer driving records and less apparent intrinsic motivation to drive carefully.

In either case, differences in motivation or concern may "cause" any subsequent differences in accident rates, rather than the driving course per se. Selection biases threaten internal validity by making the locus (i.e., source) of the observed change more ambiguous (i.e., increasing rather than reducing the number of rival plausible explanations).

In sum, selection biases form another possible threat to the internal validity of experimental research. So how can we ensure that our assumption of pretest equivalence is tenable, thereby enhancing internal validity? There are two major ways to do so: *random assignment* and *matching*.

RANDOM ASSIGNMENT Given that you have a group of people ready to participate in your research, **random assignment** is achieved by letting "chance" be the *sole* determinant of which group (i.e., experimental or control) any given person is a member of. You might, for example, cut a deck of cards before each person comes to see you, with a red card indicating that the next person will go into the control group and a black card meaning he or she will go into the experimental group. Or you might flip a coin or use a table of random numbers. *Any* purely chance process is fine. Any procedure that's *not* a chance process (e.g., using existing groups, letting participants choose the group in which they want to be, putting the neediest or the first to arrive in the experimental group) is inferentially problematic.

Random assignment, coupled with adequate group sizes (e.g., at least 30 per group), allows you to assume, with a reasonable degree of confidence, that the two (or more) groups, on average, are fairly equal on all pre-experimental variables. Another way of looking at it is to assert that you have no reason *not* to assume that the groups are equal to begin with.

To illustrate this process, we'll share with you an exercise Ted did recently with an undergraduate methods class that had about 90 people in it. Since he wanted to split the students into two equivalent groups, the size of the class ensured that he met the "adequate group size" criterion. Thus, random assignment should have created two approximately equivalent groups.

Ted began by giving the class a short questionnaire that included several types of items: (a) several *demographic* items (e.g., age, sex, number of siblings, birthplace); (b) several *opinion* items (e.g., Do you believe in God? What are your views on Aboriginal self-rule?); and (c) finally, a couple of *silly* items (e.g., Do you like cats? Write down the first number between 1 and 99 that pops into your head). A total of 82 students completed the questionnaire.

Ted's first step was to take these questionnaires and number them from 01 to 82. Then he used a table of random numbers (for an example of such a table, see Appendix A) to assign the respondents to two separate groups. The big test was to see whether the "average" persons in each of the two groups *really were* equal in all respects, given that Ted's sample size was sufficient (which it was) and that the process of assigning persons to groups was totally random (which it was).

As expected, and, in fact, even better than anticipated,[2] the two randomly created groups were nonsignificantly different in *every* respect. The average ages in groups 1 and 2, for example, were 22.3 and 22.0, respectively—not significantly different. Similarly, the average numbers of siblings in the two groups were 2.1 and 2.3, respectively, and the average heights were 174.2 centimetres (68.6 inches) and 175.2 centimetres (69.0 inches), respectively; the difference within each of those comparisons was statistically nonsignificant (i.e., the differences were no greater than you would expect on the basis of chance variation alone). With respect to attitudes regarding the death penalty, the average positions were 3.4 and 3.3, respectively, on the 5-point rating scale for the two groups; again, the difference was statistically nonsignificant.

Some of the other variables were categorical. For example, 42 of the students indicated that they'd been born in British Columbia (B.C.), while 40 had been born elsewhere. After being randomly assigned, 21 people born in B.C. and 20 people born elsewhere ended up in each group. In response to the "Do you believe in God?" question, 50 students answered yes, 14 said no, and 18 were agnostic. After people had been randomly assigned to the two groups, the yes/no/agnostic breakdowns in each group were 24/7/10 and 26/7/8, respectively; again, the difference between groups was nonsignificant.

We won't belabour the point by going through the rest of the comparisons; suffice it to say that the exercise was quite consistent with the idea that if group size is adequate and if participants are assigned to groups randomly, the groups you end up with have a very high probability of being nonsignificantly different from one another, *overall* or "on the average," in every respect, from their "average" attitude about nuclear disarmament to their average shoe size. And if they're similar overall in all respects, those variables have been equalized (or "held constant across groups") and hence can't threaten internal validity.

This finding is related to what we've found to be a common misunderstanding that novice researchers have about threats to internal validity, a misunderstanding that warrants explanation here. Let's take the example we used earlier that involved seeing whether exposure to a certain film series might change people's attitudes about appropriate levels of immigration. To do so, we randomly assign a large number of people to one of two groups: the experimental group views a film series that shows some of the many immigration successes we see in Canada; a control group, in contrast, sees a film series dealing with traffic safety (i.e., a topic that has nothing to do with immigration issues). In the end, we find that the group who viewed the immigration film series expresses significantly more positive attitudes toward Canada's immigration policies than the group who watched the unrelated films. When we use this example in our classes, we invite criticism of the design; more than one student has said, "But what if there are a few recent immigrants in the experimental group; wouldn't they be more positively disposed to immigration anyway?" or "What if there's someone in there who had a recent negative experience with an immigrant; wouldn't that bias the results?"

The point to consider is that while such people certainly exist, and may well find their way into our study, random assignment allows you to assume that these people will be *equally distributed* across all the groups in the study. Thus, while the experimental group may have some relatively recent immigrants in it, random assignment allows you to assume that there are probably just as many recent immigrants in the control group. Similarly, the two groups will also be equal in terms of the overall positivity or negativity in their experiences with immigrants. Thus, even though we can think of lots of possible "contaminants" that might threaten the internal validity of our design, the question is always whether, overall, we have any reason to expect that such people will

be *differentially* assigned to either of the two groups. No matter how many such "contaminants" we can think of, as long as the two (or more) groups are equally affected by their presence, then the two groups remain "equal overall to begin with," and internal validity is not threatened.

Note that the power of random assignment (discussed in more detail in Campbell & Stanley 1963; Cook & Campbell 1979; and Kerlinger 1973) allows an alternative to the pretest/posttest control group design. This new design, which is called the *posttest-only control group design*, is illustrated in Figure 9.5. The pretest is considered redundant in this design, since one can *assume* that the groups are equal to begin with; thus, this design circumvents the problems associated with pretest sensitization (which cannot occur if there is no pretest).

In sum, random assignment is a very powerful research procedure that directly addresses the crucial experimental assumption that your experimental and control groups are equal in all respects *before* you impose or administer your independent variable— the assumption of pretest equivalence. But random assignment has some limitations. Chance does occasionally play little tricks on us. Even though you flip a "fair" coin ten times, and it *should* come down heads about half the time, and it usually does follow that pattern (or close to it), it may well happen that heads comes up every time—or never. Similarly, if we randomly assign people to groups, we assume that the groups are equal in all respects, but occa-

Figure 9.5

The Posttest-Only Group Design

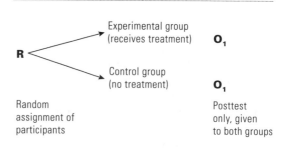

| R | Experimental group (receives treatment) | O_1 |
| Control group (no treatment) | O_1 |

Random assignment of participants | Posttest only, given to both groups

sionally it might not work out that way. Thus, if we rely on random assignment, we'll generally be in fine shape but may occasionally be surprised.

The likelihood of being surprised in that way, however, is strongly related to group size. If our group size is small (i.e., fewer than 30 per group, and especially 10 or fewer per group), the chances rise of our getting an uneven ("skewed" is the technical term) distribution of characteristics between groups. Thus, researchers who rely on random assignment to create equivalent groups with small sample sizes are playing with fire, although even in that case it is noteworthy that the researcher is letting nothing other than chance influence assignment to groups and thereby creating a "fair" test and avoiding "stacking the deck" in one direction or the other. But what can you do if you have no choice but to use small samples and/or if you're unwilling to put your faith in chance? A second technique for ensuring group equivalence is known as *matching*.

MATCHING While random assignment allows you to *assume* pretest equivalence, the **matching** process intentionally *creates* equivalence. In our study regarding attitudes toward immigration policies, for example, we may choose to match the groups on their pretest scores *or* (more typically) on some variable(s) we know to be related to attitudes regarding immigration policies (e.g., political conservatism, attitudes toward minority groups). To show you how this would be done, let's use the example of matching groups on political affiliation.

To begin with, we have a bit of a procedural problem, because we obviously first need to know all our research participants' expressed political preferences. If we can get this information, we can look for matched pairs of individuals (e.g., two New Democrats, two supporters of the Bloc Québécois, two Liberals, another two New Democrats, etc.). For each pair, we might flip a coin to assign one individual to the experimental group and the other to the control group. In this way, we'd be guaranteed groups that are constituted equally with respect to political affiliation, and hence (since political affiliation is related

to views regarding immigration policies) on pretest attitudes regarding immigration policies as well.

While the strength of matching lies in the fact that using this technique *ensures* pretest equivalence, its main weakness lies in the pragmatics of using it. Good matching technique requires that we identify "good" variables on which to match and that the information on which we're basing our matching is available. Achieving both of these conditions is often easier said than done.

In addition, matching very quickly gets out of hand if you try to match participants on more than one variable. For example, suppose we want to match respondents on sex, education, religion, political preference, and income. In order to create matched pairs on all five variables, we might have to find two "male Protestants with less than grade 10 education who vote Conservative and make between $20 000 and $30 000 per year," two "female Catholics with some university education who vote NDP and made more than $30 000 last year," and so on, depending on the particular people in our sample. Needless to say, this becomes a very complex and difficult task.

Random assignment, in contrast, is easy. Theoretically, one can use random assignment to create groups whose average units are essentially equivalent with respect to sex, age, political affiliation, attitudes regarding immigration policies, how they feel about their mothers, authoritarianism, height, how long it has been since their last bath, and all other variables, both interesting and mundane. In sum, matching (at least within the controlled experiment) hardly seems worth the effort, and might be justified only when sample sizes are too small for random assignment.

EXTERNAL VALIDITY Our focus so far has been entirely on *internal validity*: the extent to which *differences between groups* can be unambiguously attributed to the experimental treatment. But there are three other types of validity on which any given study can be evaluated: **external validity, ecological validity,** and *statistical conclusion validity*. (Note that there are numerous other types of validity we haven't yet considered; some will be addressed later in this book, whereas others are included in more specialized texts.)

External validity refers to the *generalizability* of results beyond the specifics of the study. As you now know, doing research involves applying relatively abstract, theoretical concerns to very concrete situations. Suppose our theoretical interest is in assessing the relationship between "anxiety" and "performance." Following the literature in this area, we might say that there is a curvilinear relationship between these two concepts (see Figure 9.6): performance is optimal when anxiety is at a moderate level and poorest when anxiety is either very high *or* very low.

Our *theoretical* interest lies in the relationship between *all* types of anxiety and *all* types of performance, in *all* situations and across *all* people. But in any given study, we obviously can't include all types of anxiety and all measures of performance; nor can we include all situations or all people. Rather, we must become very concrete in how we assess these variables. For "anxiety," we might choose to focus on the anxiety that some students feel when they write exams, and we might operationalize "anxiety" as the

response people give when asked "Please rate how anxious you feel right now, on a 10-point scale," as they sit down to write their final exam in this research methods course. For "performance," we might decide to look at the grade the students receive on that final exam. Our sample of research participants might include all students taking your research methods course this semester.

Suppose that, having done the study just described, we do indeed find the curvilinear relationship between "anxiety" and "performance" we hypothesized. What have we found? In a literal sense, all we have found is that when one class of this semester's research methods students sat down to write the final exam, their self-reported levels of anxiety were curvilinearly related to their grades on the exam. But, ultimately (theoretically), that's not what we're interested in; our study was just one of many possible studies we could have done to assess the *theoretical* anxiety–performance relationship in which we're interested. Thus, we'd want to know whether the results we observed were obtained merely because of the specifics of our study or whether they reflect the more general relationship between anxiety and performance.

In sum, we are interested in the *generalizability* of our results to other people, situations, and times. Would we have obtained the same results if we'd done the study with other students? In other courses? In other semesters? If we'd taken physiological rather than self-report measures of anxiety? If we'd looked at anxiety in a job interview or before giving a speech rather than in an exam situation? Or if we'd used a measure of performance other than grades? These are obviously all empirical questions that could eventually be addressed in other research. In the interim, they suggest that we'd be wise to consider the limitations of what we've achieved and to be cautious in our extrapolations.

Before concluding this discussion, let us reaffirm that *external validity* refers to the extent to which one's results are generalizable beyond the specifics of the current research project. It *doesn't necessarily* have anything to do with how *representative* one's sample

Figure 9.6

The Theoretical Relationship between Anxiety and Performance, According to the Yerkes–Dodson (1908) Law

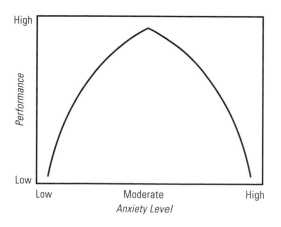

is. Suppose we acquire a sample of male first-year university students who play on the football team. We prick each one with a needle on the baby finger of his right hand. Each time we do this, the finger bleeds. Now, male first-year university student football players probably aren't representative of anyone other than male first-year university student football players, but the *result* that we observe here (i.e., they bleed when we prick their fingers) is probably *generalizable* to many other kinds of people as well; hence, we could say that the result or finding has high external validity. But if we ask all these football players how they feel about Canadian foreign policy regarding Libya, the results we obtain will probably *not* be generalizable to other groups; hence, external validity on that question would be low. External validity doesn't *necessarily* depend on the representativeness of the sample per se; rather, it depends on the nature of the phenomenon with which one is dealing and on one's research objectives.

ECOLOGICAL VALIDITY As we've seen, the question of *external validity* is essentially a theoretical one. Our particular experiment is basically a sample of all the experiments that could have been done to assess the theoretical relationship under investigation, so the issue that concerns us is the representativeness of our particular experiment with respect to that theoretical universe. But there's another type of validity—*ecological validity*—that's a little more pragmatic in its sensitivities and that's especially relevant when there's a particular kind of situation to which we are interested in generalizing. It can be considered a type of external validity, since it also addresses issues of representativeness and generalizability, although it does so in a slightly different way.

The term *ecological validity*, first used by Brunswik (1955), refers to the representativeness of the treatments and measures you use in relation to the particular milieu to which you wish to generalize. For example, let's return to the anxiety–performance study described above. In the earlier example, we were interested in the *theoretical* connection between anxiety and performance: the particular experiment we did was therefore one of many studies that could have been done that embodied the key constructs specified by the theory.

But suppose we now want to take a more *applied* approach and are interested in studying anxiety and performance in the classroom. We might very well end up designing the very same study—one that looks at the relationship between pre-exam anxiety and exam performance—but our analysis of it would be quite different. Here, instead of asking how well the experiment's conditions represent the theoretical universe, our question becomes how well the situation represents the kinds of situations to which we're interested in generalizing, that is, how well does the experiment represent the *ecology* of our situation of interest?

In this example, ecological validity would be fairly high, since we're using real students who are experiencing real anxiety of a type that commonly occurs in classrooms and who are engaged in an ecologically relevant task (the exam) with real consequences (their final grade) on the line. But it's easy to imagine other studies that aren't so clearly connected to their real-world counterparts.

For example, consider one line of research in which researchers were interested in learning about how we form our impressions of people. Typical studies in that area investigate how we combine information about people, how we resolve conflicting information about people, and how different aspects of our history or character affect the impressions people have of us. One series of studies investigated the way that wearing glasses can affect impressions.

More specifically, experiments have shown that people who wear glasses are typically judged to be more sincere, wiser, more honest, and more intelligent, *ceteris paribus*, than those who do not wear glasses. The experiments demonstrate that if you show photos of people either wearing glasses or not wearing glasses to the typical sample of volunteer undergraduate research participants and ask them to rate the people in the pictures on myriad different dimensions (like intelligence, sincerity, and honesty), participants will quite reliably rate people with glasses more highly on those dimensions than people who don't wear them.

The nice thing about using an experiment to test this effect is that taking that approach offers tremendous control over the situation: you can actually have participants rate the *same people* with and without glasses, thus controlling for other differences, such as attractiveness. Now, if you wear glasses as well as contacts, does this mean you should wear your glasses to job interviews to get an edge over all those people with 20:20? At first glance it would seem so. The results of those studies, in addition to being *internally* valid, were also very high in *external* validity: different researchers in different settings at different times using different subject groups have produced the same result again and again and again. However, the experiment isn't particularly *ecologically* valid. Recall that we're trying to learn about how people really form impressions about others. But there are actually very few situations in which people are required to form impressions based on a single variable alone. Even if we must generate an impression from just looking at a photo of someone, we instantly see not only whether he or she wears glasses, but also his or her attactiveness, approximate age, style (e.g., hair, jewellery, tattoos, etc.), demeanour, and other factors, any or all of which might also influence the impression we form. And how often do we really make judgments on the basis of just a picture alone? When we meet people at parties, are introduced by good friends, or learn about them in job interviews, we also can talk to the person; hear about his or her attitudes and values; glean more information from the way he or she dresses, acts, and talks about himself or herself; and so on.

Thus, while the "glasses" experiments may have high *internal* validity, and their results may have fairly good *external* validity, they may well have poor *ecological* validity, because the experiments fail to simulate the kinds of situations we're most interested in understanding. That state of affairs creates a certain irony: it becomes possible to create knowledge that's true in *theory* but misleading in *practice*.

The results of the glasses experiment show that glasses *can* make a difference, but whether they *do* make a difference in a real-world evaluative situation is another issue entirely.

Indeed, some years later Michael Argyle of Oxford University—a primarily laboratory-based experimental social psychologist who was beginning to consider the role of context in experimentation—extended the basic "glasses effect" research in an interesting way. Instead of making "glasses versus no glasses" the *only* piece of information that raters knew about a person, Argyle *began* by gathering the "first impression" data (showing that he could replicate the well-known "glasses effect"), but then simply let the scene run further: the people in the pictures started talking about their interests, values, and experiences. The end result? Not surprisingly, under those conditions there was *no* "glasses effect."

The "glasses effect" is "true," in the sense that it can be reliably replicated by any experimenter who wants to perform the study, but it's true *only in particular circumstances* within the strict confines of the laboratory, that is, when "glasses versus no glasses" is the *only* information people have on which to base their judgments. As soon as they have access to other information they can use, the "glasses effect" no longer occurs; what previously seemed like such an important variable (when it was the only variable under consideration) fades into nothing. Because of this, many authors (e.g., Manicas & Secord 1983; Palys & Lowman 1984) suggest that while the purely theoretical "can" questions are eminently suitable to experimental analysis, an experiment may *not* be a particularly useful launching point for the "does" questions unless ecological validity—how well our research conditions represent the important elements of the context to which we wish to generalize (e.g., see Palys 1978; Palys & Lowman 1984)—is explicitly considered.

Statistical Conclusion Validity

Suppose you watch someone who has a $1 coin. He flips it once and get tails. He flips it again ... and get tails. Once again ... and it's tails. Another flip ...

another tail. Another flip … another tail. If he continues flipping the coin and continues getting tails, at some point you'd probably begin to suspect that the coin is rigged, that he's not reporting truthfully, or that he's not flipping correctly. Ted has in fact done just this in his undergraduate research methods class on a few occasions. Students usually start voicing suspicions after the fourth or fifth tail in a row. Why do you think that happens?

From experience, we "know" that there are two possible outcomes when we flip a coin: heads or tails. The probability of getting tails on any given flip of the coin is 1 out of 2. The joint probability of getting tails twice in a row is 1 out of 4. For three in a row, it's 1 in 8. The event "four tails in a row" has a joint probability of 1 in 16. And the joint probability of getting five tails in a row is 1 out of 32.

When Ted starts flipping a $1 coin in his class, people seem to assume that he's flipping a "fair" coin and that he's accurately reporting what he sees. There's nothing unusual about a coin coming up tails when you flip it. Nor is there anything especially atypical about getting two tails in a row. Three in a row might be worth a chuckle, but still represent no particular problem. But four in a row? Suddenly people start to wonder. That *is* a fair coin, isn't it? Five in a row? What's going on? Note that we *start* by supposing that "nothing special" is going on, that chance alone is operating, and that the rules of probability theory apply. When what we see deviates only slightly from what we'd expect by chance alone, we might find the oddity interesting or cute, but we don't question our assumptions. There comes a point, though, when what we observe is a little *too* atypical; that's when we start to question whether it's really chance alone that's operating or whether something else is going on.

Researchers in the social sciences go through much the same sort of process when they come to the end of a piece of research. Suppose we did the "attitudes about immigration policies" study described earlier; suppose further that at the end of the research, we want to compare the attitudes of those who were exposed to the film series to the attitudes of those who were not. What are the alternatives? One alternative is that there's no difference between the experimental and control groups. If that happens, we'd probably say that there was no evidence that the film series had any effect.

But we shouldn't be too surprised if the mean scores of the two groups aren't *exactly* the same, since we might expect a certain amount of variation just by chance alone. In other words, the average scores in the two groups might not be 4.64 and 4.64, but they might be 4.64 and 4.65. That does not seem like much. How about 4.64 and 4.70? 4.64 and 4.90? 4.64 and 5.34? At what point are we no longer prepared to write off the difference as mere chance variation? At what point, in other words, do we decide that the difference is sufficiently large that chance variation *alone* can't account for it and that something else must therefore be going on? Where do we draw the line?

Social scientists rely on elementary probability theory to help them make this decision. Many statistical tests (e.g., *t*-tests, chi-square, analysis of variance) are designed to tell us the exact probability of obtaining the results we observe *if* chance alone is operating. For social scientists, this information is crucial, since the central issue is not the mere magnitude of differences between groups but the probability of observing that magnitude of difference *if* chance alone is what's operating.

Recall that the students in Ted's classes tend to get suspicious about his coin flipping when the probabilities reach in the neighbourhood of 1 in 16 (.06) or 1 in 32 (.03). In the social sciences, researchers agree that the odds must be at least 1 in 20 (i.e., .05) or *less* (i.e., .02, .01) before we can say that something other than chance must have been operating to produce the observed results. Only at that point, in other words, are researchers prepared to say that a difference they've observed is *statistically significant*.

Why .05? Why not .10 or .01 or some other level? Although Sir Ronald Fisher (1925) is generally credited with fixing .05 as the required probability for considering a difference statistically significant, Cowles and Davis (1982) identify Karl Pearson as having played an important role with his development of the chi-square "goodness of fit" test in the

1890s, since this test was the first to allow the computation of the exact probability that observed deviations from expected (theoretical) distributions could be attributed to chance variation. Pearson and his contemporaries exchanged views concerning which value to use as a cutoff for statistical significance. Articles by various authors (see Cowles & Davis 1982) in the first two decades of the 20th century gradually homed in on .05 as the consensus choice. Fisher (1925), whose contributions in research design and in developing the analysis of variance earned him senior academic status, may thus be seen as having given his blessing to a well-established tradition. Ultimately, the choice of .05 was relatively arbitrary; it simply represents the consensus of turn-of-the-20th-century academics.

The subjective appeal for this choice is certainly reaffirmed in Ted's experiences with the coin-flipping exercise. Students quite reliably get suspicious after about four or five successive "tails" flips— the probabilities of which are .06 and .03, respectively—suggesting that the .05 level *does* correspond reasonably well to people's intuitive sense of when a given observation is sufficiently "special" or "atypical" or "unique" to get excited about. And while the choice of .05 per se is merely a tradition or convention, its value rests in the very fact that it *is* a tradition, generally considered to be beyond the control of the experimenter/researcher. As such, .05 is an independent arbiter that impartially distinguishes between observations that are statistically significant (and hence deserve further scrutiny) and those that aren't (and hence can be written off to chance variation).

In this sense, statistical significance is an all-or-none event; either a result *is* statistically significant or it *isn't*. Hockey provides a useful analogy here: when Jarome Iginla of the Calgary Flames skates down the ice, "success" is defined as shooting the puck into the opposing team's net. Either Iginla scores a goal or he doesn't; if he *doesn't,* it doesn't particularly matter whether his shot hits the goal post or misses the net by a metre (although our hearts may flutter a bit more in the former instance). Similarly, observations that have a probability of occur-

rence of .05 or less are considered statistically significant; if the probability level is any higher (regardless of whether the observed probability level "hits the goal post" at $p = .06$ or "misses by a metre" at $p = .20$), the results are still considered within the range of what could be expected on the basis of mere chance variation.

What, then, does it mean to say that your data are statistically significant? All it means is that if chance alone was operating, the probability of obtaining the results you did is equal to or less than 5 in 100 (i.e., $p \leq .05$). In other words, your results are sufficiently unique to suggest that chance alone cannot account for them. And if chance alone cannot account for the results, something else must be going on. Statistical significance does *not* imply that what you've found is important. Nor does it imply that your study is internally valid, since the statistics are blind to the adequacy of your design (at least in terms of its internal validity). Importance and internal validity are both separate issues; neither is indicated by statistical significance alone.

AN EXAMPLE: ASSESSING THE EFFECTS OF VIOLENT PORNOGRAPHY

The rest of this chapter will be devoted to fleshing out the abstract concepts we've been discussing. To that end, we'll be examining a particular study—one experiment in a program of primarily experimental research aimed at assessing the effects of viewing violent pornography—in considerable detail.

We've picked this experiment for several reasons. First, the issue of violence against women is very important, and violent pornography has been cited by various theorists as one of many factors that exacerbate that phenomenon. Second, the experimental research that's been done in this area, primarily by Ed Donnerstein of the University of Wisconsin and Neil Malamuth of the University of California at Los Angeles (UCLA), adheres particularly well to experimental principles. Third, these researchers and their research have been quite influential in the social policy arena, Donnerstein and Malamuth have served as expert witnesses in courts, testifying about the effects of viewing violent pornography, and both have also testified before federal commissions in Canada and the United States that have looked into whether and to what extent pornographic materials should be the subject of legal censure.

In 1994, Malamuth gave evidence in *Little Sister's v. the Queen,* a case heard in the British Columbia Supreme Court. From the start there was every indication that, no matter what the outcome in the provincial Supreme Court, the case would eventually proceed to the Supreme Court of Canada, which it did.

The case concerned Little Sister's Book and Art Emporium, a retail establishment in downtown Vancouver that sells primarily sexually oriented material (mostly books and magazines) to a largely homosexual (both gay and lesbian) clientele. Materials destined for Little Sister's from other countries are often impounded at the border by Canada Customs officials, who then notify Little Sister's, who must then go through an extensive legal and bureaucratic process in an attempt to have the material released. Indeed, such seizures happened so often, and so much *more* often than they happen to bookstores and video outlets that deal primarily in heterosexual material, that Little Sister's decided to take Canada Customs (and the federal government) to court, alleging that the store is a victim of homophobic harassment and that this process of prior restraint is inexcusably contrary to the Canadian Charter of Rights and Freedoms. The federal government acknowledged that its procedures *were* contrary to the Charter, but argued that such procedures are necessary whenever there's no other way to prevent the harms that would result from the proliferation of such pornographic material.

This large, complex case occupied considerable court time. One issue that had to be considered centred on the question of whether exposure to gay sexual material, especially violent gay sexual material, creates harms, in particular, by somehow promoting sexual violence. The federal government hired Malamuth, one of the foremost experimental researchers in the field, to make its case, a task that he tackled by relying almost exclusively on the exper-

imental evidence that he and his colleagues had generated over the previous decade or so. Ted offered to help Little Sister's (which had a shoestring budget and relied extensively on volunteer help) by writing an opinion on Malamuth's opinion (see Palys 1994).

The way Ted approached that task was *not* to question Malamuth's qualifications or the quality of the research that he and his colleagues had done. Malamuth is clearly well respected in the field of experimental social psychology, and his research is exemplary within that tradition. Indeed, a large part of Ted's written opinion involved showing how carefully constructed the research was. At the same time, Ted expressed concerns about how Malamuth and his colleagues interpreted the results of their research. Ted reexamined their research using the various concepts we've discussed in the chapter (although so far at a largely theoretical level), as well as posing questions about the meanings we attribute to our research.

Isolating and Operationalizing the Variables

The laboratory experimenter's challenge is to contrive a situation where the effects of a single variable can be isolated and observed without changing the very nature of what is being looked at. As we've seen, experimental social psychologists approach this problem in much the same way that physicists or chemists might seek to observe a single electron or observe a chemical reaction in a contrived situation ostensibly free of worldly contaminants. Implicit in this view is the idea that the thing being observed may be changed in *magnitude* by its removal and relocation into the laboratory, but not in *character*.

People who want to ban (or strictly regulate the distribution of) violent video pornography argue that allowing it to be available creates social harms, primarily by increasing the likelihood that those who are exposed to it will themselves engage in sexually violent behaviour, for example, pedophilia and rape. Looking at such behaviour directly, either in the lab or anywhere else, would clearly be unethical. So researchers who want to test this hypothesis have looked at other kinds of aggressive behaviour, with the understanding that the behaviour investigated in the lab, the act of giving small electric shocks to a stranger, although clearly far removed from the brutality of a sexual assault, is nonetheless comparable to such an assault in essence: both behaviours are manifestations of the concept "aggression"; and the two behaviours differ only in magnitude, not in kind. The primary *dependent variable* in the "effects" research area is thus the average level of electric shock that one person is prepared to deliver to another person.

The key "causal" variable (or *independent variable*) of interest in the effects literature is exposure to pornography, especially violent pornography. In order to assess pornography's effects on the *dependent variable* (the level of aggression exhibited against a stranger), the logic of the experiment requires the researcher to create two conditions (in the simplest case) that are identical in all respects except one: the presence or absence of the variable whose effects one wishes to test. Most of the effects literature involves more complicated designs, but the fundamental principle that drives such studies involves comparing two or more groups that are equivalent in all respects, on average, on every variable except one.

A Paradigmatic Effects Study

A "typical" design in the effects area is offered by Donnerstein and Berkowitz (1981). That study is paradigmatic insofar as its operational choices have been replicated dozens of times in subsequent research; it provides the standard against which subsequent research is often judged. Malamuth cites the study frequently and favourably.

THE SAMPLE

The research participants in Donnerstein and Berkowitz (1981) were all male, undergraduate, introductory psychology student volunteers, as is true of most studies in this area. Eighty males took part in this study. When each participant showed up for his appointment at the lab, he was told that another person (always a woman) also had an

appointment and that the two of them would be participating in the study together.

PROCEDURES AND DESIGN

Following introductions, the experimenter turned on a tape recorder. The taped instructions revealed that one of the two participants would be a "learner," whose job would be to try to remember certain word pairs; the job of the other would be to assist the experimenter. An allegedly random draw was then held to determine who would play each role. But unbeknownst to the male participant, the draw was actually rigged: the woman always became the learner, while the man always became the experimenter's assistant. The woman, as you may suspect, was actually an employee or a confederate of the experimenter's. She was trained to respond in the same preprogrammed manner each time the experiment was run.

With the pair's roles determined, the experimenter next stated that the woman would be given some time to study the word pairs before a "test" was given. The man, in the interim, was to spend his time writing a brief essay about the possible legalization of marijuana. When he finished, the woman was brought back into the setting, where she was supposed to evaluate the essay. She remained on the other side of a partition, though, and wasn't supposed to communicate directly with the man. Instead, she communicated *in*directly, by written note and through the delivery of some electric shocks via finger electrodes placed on the man's hand. Her evaluation of the essay was unambiguous; her written evaluation stated that the essay was terrible, and when faced with the choice of how many electric shocks to deliver to the man, she delivered 9 out of a possible maximum of 10.

This little interchange served two experimental goals. First, it helped reaffirm the "reality" of the electric shocks to the male participant. This was important, because the man would soon have an opportunity to deliver electric shocks to the woman, and the experimenter needed the man to believe that any shocks he delivered were real. Second, this interchange—known among effects researchers as the *anger manipulation*—has become a virtual requirement of effects testing, since it seems that unless the woman first angers the man, no effects of exposure to violent pornography are observed.[3]

After the anger manipulation is performed, the woman is allowed further time to study. Noting that this studying will take some time and that the male participant now has nothing to do, the experimenter says something along the lines of "By the way, a friend of mine down the hall is preparing some film clips for another experiment, and he needs people to make some ratings of them. Since we have some time to kill, would you be interested in going down the hall and helping him out for a few minutes?" Virtually all participants agree to do so.

At this point the manipulation of the independent variable occurs. Participants are *randomly assigned* to one of four experimental conditions; the only difference between the conditions is the type of film clip to which participants are exposed. In Donnerstein and Berkowitz (1981), two of these clips portrayed (1) a *nonsexual and nonviolent* clip of a talk show, and (2) a *sexually explicit but nonviolent* depiction of a man and a woman engaging in mutually consenting intercourse. Each video segment was about five minutes long. The other two clips were of similar length; both involved a scene in which three people—a woman and two men—are studying together when the men begin to make sexual advances toward the woman. She resists but is raped. The difference between the third and fourth films was not in their visual content (which was identical), but in the voice soundtrack: in one version (3), the woman protests at first, but soon begins to enjoy the process (a rape myth depiction; the "*sexually violent/positive outcome*" condition); in the other (4), the woman resists at first and throughout the process, experiencing all the horror of a sexual assault she is powerless to stop (the "*sexually violent/negative outcome*" condition).

Thus, the *independent variable* in the study was the "exposure to a film" at one of four "levels," one corresponding to each of the four conditions above. The *dependent variable* was the average level of shock delivered by participants from each of the four groups. Technically speaking, this design is a *randomized non-pretested comparison group design*, as is represented in Figure 9.7.

After viewing one of the four film clips and completing a few rating scales (consistent with the cover story that was offered), the male participant returns to the first experimenter, who is now ready to receive him. By this time, the woman has completed her studying and has had some electrodes attached to her fingers. The man, adopting his assigned role of assistant to the experimenter, begins assessing whether the woman remembers the word pairs she has been studying. Whenever she makes a mistake, the male participant's job is to determine how many electric shocks she should receive and then to deliver them. Of particular interest to the experimenters was the average number of electric shocks that the male participants would deliver (i.e., the *dependent variable*) and how (if at all) that number would vary depending on the type of film clip the participant had viewed.

Figure 9.7

The Randomized Non-pretested Comparison Group Design Used in Donnerstein and Berkowitz (1981)

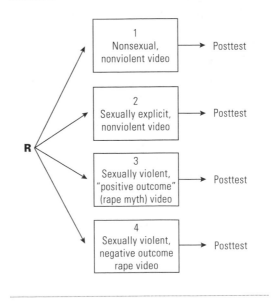

STATISTICAL CONCLUSION VALIDITY

Recall the basic logic of experimentation: *if* the groups are all equal to begin with, any subsequent differences in the dependent variable (here, the average shock level) among the groups must be due to the one variable on which their experience varied (here, the type of film to which they were exposed). We must first, therefore, try to find out whether there are in fact any "differences" to worry about. If there are no differences among the groups, then there's nothing further to explain. In this instance, where we have one dependent variable and four levels of the independent variable, the appropriate statistical procedure to use is the analysis of variance, and the appropriate test of significance is the *F*-test.

When Donnerstein and Berkowitz (1981) tested their results in this way, they found that after being exposed to the anger manipulation, the two groups who viewed the sexually violent film clip (whether it was accompanied by a "positive outcome" or by a "negative outcome" soundtrack) administered a significantly higher average level of shock than did either the group of participants who viewed the sexually explicit but nonviolent depiction or the group who viewed the nonsexual and nonviolent talk show clip (see the graph of these results in Figure 9.8).

Having found a significant result, we next examine the validity of that result. This involves asking whether the appropriate statistical test was used and whether the test was a "fair" one, that is, one that didn't "stack the deck" in favour of one outcome or the other. As Chapter 12 will show, the analysis of variance is indeed the appropriate test here. As for whether the researchers "stacked the deck" in favour of finding a certain result, this ends up being a very technical question; while it's important for the advanced student to consider, it would only detract from our discussion of other issues here.

ASSESSING INTERNAL VALIDITY

The differences in average shock level between the two groups who saw the sexually violent video clips and the other two groups—who saw, respectively, a sexually explicit but nonviolent video and a neutral

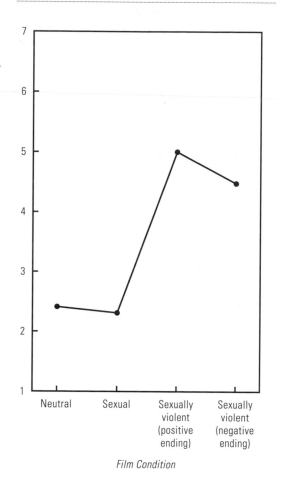

Figure 9.8

Graphed Results from Donnerstein and Berkowitz (1981), Showing Mean Shock Level Administered by Each Group

Film Condition

video—were statistically significant. But remember that a result's statistical significance does not imply anything about that result's importance. Nor does it necessarily imply that the independent variable had an effect. It means only that the degree of difference between the two groups is greater than one would expect on the basis of chance variation alone. If chance alone cannot fully account for the difference, clearly something else must be going on. But what is the "something else"?

After reading Donnerstein and Berkowitz (1981), we might like to suggest that the differences between the groups are a reflection of the effects of viewing the films. But we must assess the study's internal validity before taking our best guess in that regard. Let's consider the various threats to internal validity that were explained earlier in the chapter to see how well Donnerstein and Berkowitz (1981) controlled for them.

IF THE TWO GROUPS ARE EQUAL TO BEGIN WITH ...

A first possible threat is *selection*. This threat would strike right at the heart of the design, since it undermines a fundamental element of experimental logic: the assumption that the two groups are equal to begin with. If the groups are not equal to begin with, any after-the-fact differences may merely reflect the before-the-fact differences.

We can indeed assume that the four groups in Donnerstein and Berkowitz (1981) were identical to begin with. Why? Since participants were assigned on a purely *random* basis to one of the four conditions, we have no reason to believe that, before viewing the videos, one group (overall) was any different from any other (overall). People who have more or less proclivity to violence, more or less experience with having viewed video pornography, more negative or more positive attitudes toward sexual material, or whatever other individual difference variable that we can think of will all have been equally distributed across the groups. We might feel more comfortable if the researchers had assigned 30 or more participants per group rather than 20, but there's still no reason to assume that the deck has been stacked in favour of one group any more than any other. So selection doesn't seem to be a threat to the internal validity of this design.

... AND ARE TREATED IDENTICALLY IN ALL RESPECTS ...

Several other threats can also be ruled out. *History* cannot be a threat, because every effort was made to treat everyone identically in all respects except for the level of the independent variable they received.

They all came to the same lab, met the same female confederate and the same experimenter, heard exactly the same tape-recorded instructions, and received the same evaluation of their essay by the confederate, all according to the script laid out by the researchers. Even the four levels of the independent variable were administered in similar ways: all four groups were asked to do "a favour," all four groups had to go down the hall to meet another experimenter in another room, all four groups saw a video of similar length (with only the content varying), and all four groups completed a series of rating scales after they saw the film.

The whole experience occurred within an hour for each participant, so *maturation* seems unlikely to have entered in as a threat. In any event, to the extent that there *were* any maturational influences, such as the participants' getting more tired as the experiment progressed, these would have been equal, overall, across all groups.

Testing couldn't have been a threat, because there was no pretest. Similarly, *statistical regression (regression toward the mean)* couldn't have been a threat, because neither group was selected on the basis of any sort of extreme score.

Taken together, the preceding paragraphs suggest that the internal validity of the Donnerstein and Berkowitz (1981) study is quite high. Although we cannot be positive, because there might have been some threats we haven't considered, it seems that the only difference between the four groups was in the content of the film they viewed. And if that's so, it must be because of the content of the films that they reacted differently to the confederate when given an opportunity to administer electric shocks.

EXTERNAL VALIDITY: REPRESENTATIVENESS ISSUES

Although their theoretical interests are in the effects of exposure to violent pornography on "people," Donnerstein and Berkowitz (1981) conducted this study, as is the case with most of the experimental research in this area, using a specific type of research participant: male, undergraduate, introductory psychology students who volunteered to take part in the study. Because such a group is obviously anything but a "representative sample" of the general population, many critics of the effects literature (e.g., see Byrne & Kelley 1989; W. A. Fisher 1986) question the *external validity* (generalizability) of the research results. Can *any* result obtained with such a sample be generalized to the broader population of interest (i.e., all people, or even all males)?

We do *not* see that criticism as particularly relevant here. Even if we acknowledge that students are *not* typical of all people, so that the question of who is sampled becomes an important one, a criticism based on their being "unrepresentative" is empty unless we identify the nature of the sampling bias that exists and then consider the possible implications of that bias for the results the researchers obtained.

In that regard, we can expect several differences between male, undergraduate, introductory psychology students and the general male population. Not only have such students received more extensive formal education than the average population member, but we might also speculate that they might be less likely to use "physical" means to solve conflicts or achieve goals, and perhaps be more introspective about their behaviour and the motives underlying it, for example. But if that's so, it might be argued that these people may be even *less* likely than the general population to engage in aggressive and assaultive behaviour. Indeed, the upshot of the sample's "unrepresentativeness" is that if it can be demonstrated that even such a relatively well-educated and literate group can be affected by exposure to violent pornography, then this study's results may well be, if anything, a *conservative* estimate of the extent to which such effects will exist in the population as a whole (Malamuth [1989: 183] makes a similar argument). In sum, although external validity is ultimately an empirical question worth considering, no immediate issues of external validity seem inherently problematic to this study's conclusions.

CONSIDERING ECOLOGICAL VALIDITY

The laboratory experiment involves creating a contrived setting designed to provide a "pure" test of a theoretical proposition among a designated sample of research participants. This contrived setting can pose a problem when researchers engage in experimental research that is later used to influence social policy. The problem arises when, in the interests of experimental purity, researchers (1) create situations that are related only obliquely to situations in the world that the researchers are ostensibly trying to help us understand, and (2) create misleading results because of the way in which they virtually *create* the very effects they're allegedly trying to *test*. These considerations have been embellished in greater detail elsewhere (see Palys 1989; Palys & Lowman 1984), but also deserve some attention here.

Laboratory experimentalists are taught several basic principles for use in designing an experiment. Two of these, both rooted in the F-ratio[4] (the statistic typically used to compare groups), are (1) the principle of *maximizing between-groups variation* (i.e., the degree of difference between experimental and control groups), to make as clear a differentiation between conditions as possible; and (2) the principle of *minimizing within-groups variation* (i.e., the degree of "natural" and "random" variation that exists within the groups being tested), to make as "sensitive" a test of the hypothesis as possible.

In studies like the one being considered here, researchers accomplish the former goal by choosing the most gruesome "violent pornography" they can find, choosing sexually explicit material that is extremely explicit and not at all violent, and making the "neutral" material as devoid of sexual and violent content as they can. They accomplish the latter goal by using relatively homogeneous populations of respondents (e.g., male, undergraduate, introductory psychology student volunteers) and by attempting to exert experimenter control over the situation to standardize conditions as much as possible (e.g., by using tape-recorded instructions to minimize any variations in the reading of the instructions, variations of the sort that would otherwise happen over time if the experimenter were to read the same instructions again and again; and by having the woman confederate send her insulting statement about the male participant's essay via written note so that the message remains exactly constant across all tested groups).

A third principle of experimentation advises experimenters to *control all available response alternatives* so that any impetus to behaviour that is created by the conditions of the experiment is harnessed in the service of the dependent variable. Underlying this view is something of a "hydraulic" model of human behaviour: the belief is that if a stimulus can effectively energize a behavioural response, the astute experimenter will "dam up" all behavioural alternatives but one, so that the magnitude of all behavioural impulses will be visible in the chosen place. In the context of the effects literature, where the interest has been in determining aggressive impulses, this has meant that participants have been given only one way to express themselves: by delivering electric shocks to the woman on the other side of the partition.

All of these principles have been employed in the studies described in the effects literature produced by Donnerstein, Berkowitz, Malamuth, and their colleagues. Indeed, they are widely represented as principles of "good experimentation" (e.g., Aronson & Carlsmith 1968; Festinger & Katz 1953; Kerlinger 1973; Rosenthal & Rosnow 1984), and they do make great sense *if* one is addressing a purely theoretical question of interest, where the central issue for the researcher is whether a theoretically hypothesized relationship *can* be given empirical life.

But when we make decisions about cases in court or try to develop social policy, we're interested not *solely* in questions of theory, but also in their implications for practice. The interest of the court, for example, in *Little Sister's v. the Queen,* as Ted understood it, was not in the answer to the question "*Can* exposure to aggressive pornography increase the likelihood of subsequent harm?" but rather in the answer to the question "*Does* it do so?"

Those are two very different questions. The first is more purely theoretical. To ask whether something *can* happen is to ask simply whether a particular phenomenon can be generated, that is, whether there is any evidence that a specified theoretical linkage can occur. The second is a more contextualized and applied question; it asks whether, in the real world, the conditions exist in which the phenomenon of interest occurs. Think back to the studies reviewed earlier in this chapter about the effects of wearing glasses. The early experimental research showed that wearing glasses *can* affect the impressions that other people derive of you. But later research showed that it generally *doesn't,* unless that's the only piece of information that people have of you, a condition that rarely applies outside laboratory experiments. In sum, it's not inconsistent or implausible for the answers to those two questions to be "Yes, it *can*" but "No, it *doesn't.*"

Donnerstein and Berkowitz (1981) clearly show that, under certain conditions, viewing violent pornography *can* affect the likelihood that people will engage in aggressive behaviour. But in order to address the question of whether it *does* have such an effect, we must consider the study's ecological validity, asking how well the experiment's conditions approximate or represent the actual conditions in the world in which pornography is consumed. Stated another way, we must ask whether, in the interest of living up to experimentalist ideals, Donnerstein and Berkowitz have made the situation into something *other than* that which they set out to investigate. For example,

1. While the aggressive behaviour that's of interest to us is *severe* (e.g., violence in the form of sexual assault and other sexual abuses), ethical requirements constrain laboratory investigation to behaviour that's relatively *trivial* (small electric shocks that cause minimal pain and no long-term trauma or damage) and hence probably result in an overestimate of the extent to which people are prepared to engage in the more severe forms of such behaviour.

2. While aggressive behaviour is *discouraged* in society (e.g., one is subject to arrest and imprisonment for behaviour such as sexual assault), the experiment requires it to be *encouraged* in the experimental setting by an experimenter who, as an authority figure, represents the interests of legitimate science.

3. While in the real world we have many *alternatives* about how to respond when we're angered (e.g., by withdrawing from the situation, by talking to the person who has angered us), the effects researchers offer their research participants *only one way* to communicate any displeasure they may feel: by imposing an electric shock to the fingertips of the woman on the other side of the partition.

Whether singly or in combination, the compromises demanded by experimental requirements have an effect: they force us to change the very nature of what we're investigating in order to achieve manipulative control; that is, we wind up making the situation into something other than what it normally is. Are such shifts non-problematic? Or do they "create" effects that wouldn't otherwise exist?

At least two studies have investigated the impact of some of the above factors. Regarding caveat 3, for example, Fisher and Grenier (1994) wondered what would happen if research participants were given a broader array of response alternatives than just delivering shocks. They discovered that when response alternatives were given, the vast majority of respondents—no matter which film they'd been exposed to—chose to *talk* to the woman who'd angered them, rather than to deliver electric shocks.

Regarding caveat 2, relevant evidence has been supplied by Malamuth (1978). He describes this research in a later publication (1984) as follows:

Following exposure to these [visual] stimuli, all subjects were insulted by a female confederate and then were placed in a situation where they could aggress against her via the ostensible delivery of electric shocks under one of two assessment conditions. Half of the subjects were assigned to read a communication that suggested it was "permissible" to behave as aggressively as they wished (disinhibitory communication); the other half were given a communication designed to make them somewhat self-conscious about aggressing (inhibitory communication) ... The results

revealed no significant differences in aggression following the inhibitory communication. (35)

In sum, as soon as conditions in the experiment start to better approximate those in the real world, that is, when people have alternative ways of responding and when aggressive responses are discouraged, the findings of the laboratory-based research appear to vanish, and no effects are found.

At the same time, by creating a set of conditions under which effects of viewing violent pornography *were* observed, Donnerstein and Berkowitz (1981) *have* helped to show some of the parameters that might affect the likelihood of aggressive behaviour in the world, for example:

1. One element of their research was that students were, by the nature of the situation, actually *encouraged* to aggress. This should attune us to the need to ensure that people are discouraged from believing that aggression is a legitimate way to respond to angers and frustrations in the world.
2. Similarly, Donnerstein and Berkowitz's (1981) study involved a situation where respondents experienced *no consequences* for their aggression, either to themselves (in the form of punishment) or to their victims (in the form of pain and trauma). This suggests that those who see sexual assault and violence against women as behaviours they can engage in with impunity may be more likely to engage in such behaviour. And this in turn should sensitize us to the need for competent investigation and prosecution of assaultive behaviour, so as to maximize deterrence. Similarly, it suggests that greater emphasis should be placed on educating people about the experience of assault victims, particularly in terms of the pain and suffering that they have had to endure.
3. Further, the Donnerstein and Berkowitz (1981) study, coupled with Fisher and Grenier (1994), shows that aggression is more likely to occur when there are no behavioural alterna-

tives available or when none are *perceived* to be available. This should sensitize us to the need to encourage people to recognize that there are a variety of ways to deal with frustration and anger other than through aggression; people who know no other way of responding may well continue to aggress.

In sum, this analysis suggests that looking for effects of certain images per se is probably a fruitless task. Instead, we've suggested that any effects are mitigated by other variables, such as the meanings that are attached to our behaviours and the context in which those behaviours occur.

THE FRAGILITY OF MEDIA INFLUENCE EFFECTS

It seems fairly clear from the literature that any "media effects" that can be attributed to the message or content of violent pornography per se are, in the grander scheme of things, a fairly trivial influence. Even Malamuth (1989), who has built much of his reputation on demonstrating these effects, recognizes that the media may not even be a particularly important element in the behavioural equation:

As with many behaviours, it is apparent that anti-social behaviour against women is a function of many interacting causal factors. It is very difficult to gauge the relative influence, if any, of media exposure alone. However, by itself, it is likely to exert a small influence, if any. (198)

CONTEXT, MEANINGS, AND BEHAVIOUR

The experimental paradigm is typically silent with respect to variables of the sort that qualitative social scientists cherish most dearly, for example, the *meaning* of images to people and the role that culture and individual differences can play in the generation and interpretation of images.

In this regard, Abramson and Hayashi (1984) offer a comparative analysis of Japanese and American pornography, attitudes about sex, the role of sex in the media, and so forth. They note, for example, that Japanese laws and mores completely prohibit images that many North Americans would find relatively tame (e.g., neither pubic hair nor adult genitalia may be shown), while at the same time allowing a variety of images that many North Americans would find horrendous (e.g., the admonition against showing pubic hair has resulted in the proliferation of sexualized images of prepubescent girls):

Of particular note in Japanese pornography (film and novel) is the recurring theme of bondage and rape. Although movies are much less explicit than their American and European counterparts, the plot often involves the rape of a high school girl ... In fact, one of the best ways to ensure the success of a Japanese adult film is to include the bondage and rape of a young woman. This juxtaposition of sexuality and aggression is evident in almost all forms of Japanese sexual material, including cartoons, films, and sexological museums. (178)

Given these differences, if it were in fact the case that sexually violent themes and images in and of themselves somehow "cause" greater aggressiveness, sexual aggression would be rampant in Japan—and at higher levels than in the United States. But despite the pervasiveness of such sexually violent material, rates of sexual assault and other forms of sexual abuse in Japan appear to be far lower than those in Western countries.

In comparison to Western nations, Japan has a substantially lower incidence of rape: in the United States there are 34.5 reported rapes per 100,000 population; in England, 10.1; in West Germany, 10.7; in France, 3.2; and, in Japan, 2.4 ... The discrepancy in the incidence between the United States and Japan cannot be attributed to variance in the laws because the laws are basically the same (although prosecution rates may vary).

If there is a direct connection between the prevalence of rape imagery and rape behaviour, Japan should have an overwhelming occurrence of rape. As indicated in the preceding paragraph's rape statistics, it does not. Consequently, it is our suggestion that mediating circumstances are involved, especially in the form of internal constraints to maladaptive behaviour. (181)

These observations about the importance of culture in the rules of sexual practice and the interpretation of sexual and sexually violent images are particularly germane to the court case involving Little Sister's Book and Art Emporium. Since Little Sister's caters primarily to the homosexual community, another question of interest in considering this case concerns whether—and if so, to what extent—any of the findings reported in the effects literature are applicable to that community.

EXTERNAL VALIDITY REVISITED: GENERALIZING TO WRITTEN MATERIALS AND TO THE GAY COMMUNITY

All the experimental effects research has involved video materials and mixed-sex dyads. Can the results of that research be generalized to exposure to written materials? And would the effects observed among mixed-sex dyads also be seen if same-sex dyads were involved? These questions clearly concern the *external validity* of the research. Malamuth was asked by the Department of Justice to comment on that issue with respect to the Little Sister's trial.

GENERALIZING TO WRITTEN MATERIALS Malamuth begins by acknowledging that no available data reflect directly on the issue of whether the results from video research can be generalized to exposure to books and magazines. But he then speculates that the potential harms he discusses may occur just from exposure to the written word. He predicates this suggestion on his belief that the important element is the *message communicated,* rather than the medium of communication.

The type of analysis being offered here is certainly consistent with Malamuth's more quantitative approach. Just as he refrains from looking into the meaning of sexual/pornographic stimuli to the consumers of such materials, so also does Malamuth emphasize the concrete, externally visible stimulus (the overt message), apparently assuming that the

message itself has some objective meaning that is uniform to all. Stating that the important element is the *message communicated* downplays any consideration of the person who receives the message, any attribution of meaning to its content, and any situational and/or cultural factors that might enter into its interpretation.

Our own sense is that several differences between written and oral media may be recognized. First, while video pornography is often consumed in social settings (see Palys 1984), written pornography (books and magazines) is more likely to be consumed by one individual at a time. Second, one needn't be literate to watch a video, but literacy is required for reading a book. In both cases, one could envision that these variables (i.e., solo versus social consumption; literacy requirements and the propensity to read books, especially as related to educational attainment and cultural differences) might make a difference in who seeks out each type of pornographic material and also in the range of interpretations that are made by that selection of people.

GENERALIZING TO THE GAY COMMUNITY Regarding whether the results of the effects research can be generalized to the gay community, Malamuth suggests that any effects that are observed for heterosexual pornography among members of the heterosexual community will in all likelihood be the same for homosexual pornography among members of the homosexual community. Although he acknowledges having no data that bear directly on this issue, he bases his speculation on the answers to three questions: (1) Are the messages in homosexual pornography basically the same as those in heterosexual pornography? (2) Are the minds of homosexuals basically the same as the minds of heterosexuals? (3) Are there problems of sexual conflict within the homosexual community? In all three cases he answers yes and, hence, concludes that the same processes prevail among the homosexual community as among the heterosexual one.

Although Malamuth is correct in saying that no existing data bear directly on this issue, the most closely related finding we know of (concerning male–male aggression following exposure to violent pornography) would urge more caution in reaching such a conclusion. Summarizing the findings from his and Donnerstein's (1984) laboratory research, Malamuth notes that "the data show that exposure of male subjects to aggressive pornography increases aggressive behaviour against *female* but not male targets" (35).

Besides that result, the problem with Malamuth's responses is his tenacious belief in the objective qualities of messages. When he asks whether homosexual pornography and heterosexual pornography are basically the same, Malamuth is led by his belief in the "objective," observable content of messages to answer yes. To Malamuth, the question "Are homosexual minds and heterosexual minds basically the same?" involves only knowing whether the basic physiological material and information-processing capacities of homosexuals and heterosexuals are the same; he concludes that, at that level, there are no differences between the homosexual mind and the heterosexual mind. And, of course, he's right.

But Malamuth misses the point. Although the superficial content that appears in some heterosexual pornography and some homosexual pornography may be similar, the *meanings* associated with those images, and hence their relationship with behaviour, may well be considerably different. In this regard, we must remember that the historical experience of homosexuals and heterosexuals has been very different. While heterosexuals have enjoyed feeling "normal" about their sexuality, the gay community has endured many years of being considered "deviant" and/or "unnatural." Because being homosexual has been an unwarranted source of stigma for many years, many gay people still feel reluctant to "come out of the closet." Given homosexuality's historical status as an oppressed lifestyle (e.g., through institutional harassment and "gay-bashing"), one might anticipate that gays' marginalized status would have left a greater sense of shared community and interdependence among homosexuals than among heterosexuals. Some authors have also argued that, when it comes to matters of sexual violence, the situation in homosexual relations is unique in the sense that it might be more inherently egalitarian

because of the gender similarity of the two people involved (e.g., see Brock & Kinsman 1986).

Taken together, all these differences between homosexuals' and heterosexuals' life experience would leave us surprised if the two communities did *not* attach different meanings to sexual practices and sexual images. There's clearly a need for more research in that area, particularly by gay researchers, to articulate these issues. In the interim, the safer course would be to assume, on the basis of gays' significantly different social history, that differences in meaning do exist.

A third element considered by Malamuth was whether there is any evidence of violence in the gay community; to this question he also answers yes. And indeed, the gay community, like any other community, is not immune to sexual violence. But to assume that the same dynamics must therefore characterize both homosexual violence and heterosexual violence seems inconsistent with the feminist literature that Malamuth suggests informs his analysis. For example, to the extent that sexual violence between men and women involves not only violence but *gender* violence, embedded in a history of patriarchal relations, how could patterns of sexual violence among same-sex partners (who are equal in overt gender status) be a product of the same dynamic? Overall, the biggest threats to homosexuals involving violence probably involve people from *outside* the gay community (harassment—and worse—from the intolerant and from gay-bashers) more than people from *inside* it.

Final Comments on the Effects Research

In offering the preceding detailed analysis of the Donnerstein and Berkowitz (1981) study, we have several aims: we hope we've shown how analyzing and critiquing a piece of research involves considering it in the light of the concepts (e.g., statistical conclusion validity, internal validity, external validity, ecological validity) introduced in more abstract form in the earlier part of this chapter. You should now be able to go through any example of experimental research and do the same.

You also should consider experimental research in the terms introduced much earlier in the text, particularly in terms of notions of engagement. As we've noted several times before, doing a piece of research involves *engaging* a phenomenon of interest, and the results that one acquires will bear the imprint of the tools we use to engage them. We are reminded of the analogy that G. Morgan (1983b) offered regarding the various ways one can engage an apple: by looking at it, touching it, eating it, comparing it to other fruits, and so on. Each is simply a different way of engaging an apple, and the "truth" that emerges from each method of engagement is no more and no less true than any other; each just gives its unique glimpse into the apple's qualities.

Similarly, we can engage phenomena by observing them, interviewing people about them, gathering archival information about them, or experimenting with them. Seen in this way, the experiment, as a way of understanding, is no more right or wrong than any other means of gathering data; it has unique strengths and weaknesses, and the thoughtful researcher must consider these when interpreting an experiment's results.

SUMMING UP AND LOOKING AHEAD

When people construct an experiment, they're usually doing so because they're interested in assessing the *causal* impact of one variable (the *independent* or *treatment* variable) on another variable (the *dependent* or *outcome* variable). Philosophically, the criteria governing when you can legitimately infer that a causal relationship has occurred are delineated by John Stuart Mill (1843/1965). Mill states that one must meet three criteria:

1. *temporal precedence* (i.e., since we believe that causes come before effects, we must demonstrate that change in the variable we think is a cause did indeed come before its alleged effect);
2. existence of *a relationship* (i.e., if the alleged cause really *is* a cause, changes in it should be

associated with subsequent changes in its alleged effect); and
3. *elimination of rival plausible explanations* (i.e., one must rule out the influence of all possible variables *other than* the one being considered as a source of causal influence).

The traditional experiment elegantly addresses these three criteria. Inherent in the traditional conception of the experiment is the idea that the experiment happens *because* and *when* you want it to happen. Thus, you are able to prepare suitably *reliable* and *valid* measures of your *dependent variable,* and can measure it at appropriate times. In the same vein, you *make* the experiment happen by manipulating the *independent* variable and assessing its effects. Thus, the *temporal precedence* criterion is addressed: because you "cause" the cause to occur, you are able to assess whether the level of the dependent (effect) measure is different only *after* the imposition of the independent variable.

Of course, we'd expect to observe a certain amount of variation (i.e., change) in the dependent variable over time purely as a function of chance. The first question of interest to us after completing a study, therefore, is whether any change we observed is greater than we would have expected on the basis of chance alone. This question concerns the *statistical significance* of the results. If the change we observe is statistically significant, we will have demonstrated the *relationship* criterion that Mill espoused: we will have demonstrated that a change in the independent variable *is* associated with a change in the dependent variable and that the latter change is greater than might be anticipated on the basis of chance variation alone.

Remember, though, that finding statistical significance in our results *doesn't* immediately allow us to say that the *independent variable* caused the change. All we know at this point is that chance alone wasn't the cause of the change. But what was? That's an *internal validity* question. We must consider rival plausible explanations as well, such as history, maturation, testing, and other threats to internal validity.

According to the logic of experimentation, if two groups are equal to begin with and if they are treated identically in all respects *except* for the presence or absence of the independent variable, any subsequent differences between those groups can be accounted for only by the influence of the independent variable. And while *control groups* exist to ensure that the groups are "treated identically" in all respects, recall that either *random assignment* or *matching* allows us to ensure that the groups were indeed equal to begin with.

Even if we can meet Mill's criteria, we face the question of whether the results we've observed are *generalizable* beyond the specifics of the study. Can the results be generalized across *time, people,* and *settings?* This, of course, is a question of *external validity.*

And finally, the concept of *ecological validity* raises questions about how well an experiment captures or represents the setting to which we wish to generalize. It's an important element for considering whether theoretical processes that *can* happen actually *do.*

The last part of this chapter analyzed a particular example of experimental research—Donnerstein and Berkowitz's (1981) experiment to assess the effects of viewing violent pornography on its viewers—in order to show how the abstract concepts described earlier in the chapter can be used to design, analyze, and critique a particular piece of research. The case is also made that, far from being a "privileged" mode of creating knowledge, the experiment, like any other method, is a tool that engages phenomena in a particular manner, with unique strengths and weaknesses in the way that it does so.

STUDY QUESTIONS

1. Explain how Pascal's study in 1648 embodied the basic logic of experimental design.
2. Yasmin feels she has developed a cure for the common cold and wants to test it out. Fifty cold sufferers come to her office one Monday; each receives her treatment. A week later, they all come back, and Yasmin finds that 44 of them (88 percent) no longer have colds. She concludes that her cure is indeed very effective and cites an 88 percent cure rate. Would you agree with her conclusion? What *rival plausible explanations* would you entertain? How might you *control* for these?
3. Bill is a cautious fellow who wants to buy a safe car. He reads some published statistics that compare all the various models of cars in terms of the frequency with which they are involved in accidents. On learning that the BMW 735i sedan (a very expensive car) has the lowest number of accidents and the lowest number of fatalities, he goes out and buys one, believing that he will be safer. From an empirical perspective, would you agree with the logic underlying his decision? Why or why not?
4. Recall the selection biases discussed in Chapter 4, "Sampling," and the problem of changes in *instrumentation* or data-gathering procedures discussed in Chapter 8, "Unobtrusive and Archival Methods." In what way might these operate as threats to internal validity?
5. Students who take our undergraduate research methods courses receive tutorials (small group "help" sessions where attendance is optional) in addition to the weekly lecture. Since we've often wondered how helpful the tutorials are to students, we've constructed an evaluation to find out. All semester long, attendance is taken at the tutorials. At the end of the semester, we use the attendance reports to construct three groups: those who always or almost always came to tutorial (e.g., missed no more than two tutorials over the semester); those who never or almost never came to tutorials (e.g., came to two or fewer tutorials over the semester); and those who fell in between (i.e., came sometimes). We then compare the average final grades in the course for the three groups. Suppose that this semester, we find that those who always or almost always came

to the tutorials had the highest average grade, those who came part of the time had the next-highest average grade, and those who never or almost never came received the lowest average grade. Suppose further that the differences between the groups are statistically significant.

   a. Name the *independent variable* in this study.

   b. Name the *dependent variable* in this study.

   c. What does it mean to say that the differences between groups are *statistically significant?*

   d. Evaluate the study's *internal validity,* identify what threat(s) to internal validity you believe might be present, and state how you might redesign the study to control for those threats.

   e. Show that you understand the concept of *external validity* by identifying our external validity concerns in this study.

   f. Evaluate the study's *ecological validity.*

6. Jill intends to perform an experiment in which she'll compare whether "factual" appeals or "emotional" appeals are more effective in changing people's attitudes regarding nuclear disarmament. About 100 people have volunteered to participate in her study, and she wonders whether *random assignment* or *matching* would be the better procedure to use in assigning participants to groups. Compare the relative advantages of these techniques in Jill's situation, state which you would recommend, and explain how you would do it.

7. Why are control groups called *control* groups, that is, what do they *control for?*

8. People are different from one another. In what sense, then, can random assignment or matching be said to *equalize* groups?

9. Jerry reads the Malamuth and Donnerstein (1981) study regarding the effects of viewing pornography on aggression, and says, "Yeah, but I'll bet some of the people in the control group were consumers of pornography *before* they participated in the study. Wouldn't that undermine differences between the groups and mess up their conclusions?" How would you respond?

10. Bob, the head coach for Little League, has developed a series of clinics to teach the kids the essentials of base running. A total of 60 kids end up playing on league teams. Always seeking a challenge, Bob identifies the 20 kids who had the slowest times during the tryouts and makes them the "experimental" group, which is then exposed to his base-running expertise. Another 20 kids are randomly chosen to be the "control" group, that is, they are not given any particular instruction in base running. In order to equalize the amount of attention the two groups receive, however, the control group is given extra practice at bunting, a skill that has no relation to base-running speed.

    After two weeks, the kids are assessed again. Bob finds that the base-running times of those in the experimental group have improved significantly, while times of the control group have remained unchanged. He concludes that the techniques utilized in his base-running clinics are indeed effective.

   a. Name the *independent variable* in Bob's study.

   b. Name the *dependent variable* in Bob's study.

   c. Indicate what *threat(s) to internal validity* Bob should be concerned with here.

   d. Indicate what Bob's *external validity* concerns might be in this situation.

11. Differentiate between *random selection* and *random assignment.* Which is more relevant to internal validity and which to external validity? Explain.

12. Just because an experiment shows that a phenomenon *can* occur in the lab does not mean that it *does* occur in the world. Would you agree or disagree with that statement? Explain.

NOTES

1. We also cannot say for sure that the pills *weren't* effective. They may actually have been helpful, but the research design described here doesn't allow us to assess that. This design produces low internal validity because it leaves us with ambiguity over whether the change was due to the pills, maturational factors, the two combined, or something else.

2. Actually, although the odds *were* on Ted's side, there were no guarantees. Long shots *do* occasionally come in, and if we had more information on the groups of students, we'd probably find *some* differences somewhere. When we engage in many comparisons, a certain number will appear significant simply because of chance variation alone. Welcome to probability theory. Read on to find out how the scientific enterprise tries to deal with this situation.

3. It was in Donnerstein and Berkowitz (1981) that the anger manipulation was tested for the first time. We've left out that half of the experiment in our description here in order to simplify the discussion.

4. Because we haven't yet discussed much in the way of statistics, we keep our treatment at a relatively conceptual level here. The analysis of variance and the *F*-test are discussed in greater detail in Chapter 12.

CHAPTER 10

QUASI-EXPERIMENTATION, EVALUATION RESEARCH, AND THE MOVE TO ANALYTIC CONTROL

STRENGTHS AND LIMITATIONS OF LABORATORY EXPERIMENTATION

Discussing the logic of experimentation was a convenient way to tell you about some very basic empirical concepts (e.g., operationalization, internal validity, external validity, statistical significance) that are relevant to all experimental and experimental*ist* inferential research. But not all interesting phenomena can be re-created and/or observed in the laboratory. Nor would we necessarily *want* to spend all our time in the lab. No one method can claim to be *the* royal road to truth. Every method engages the world in its own manner, with its attendant strengths and weaknesses. The researcher's task is to weigh those various advantages and limitations, and then choose the methods best suited for the research question at hand.

So what are the advantages of laboratory experimentation? The lab offers maximal manipulative control over the experimental situation; hence it is ideally suited to situations where creating or simulating the phenomenon of interest is conceptually defensible and causal inference and precision are the highest priorities. In the lab, we can randomly assign our participants to the various experimental and control groups and hence ensure that the crucial experimental assumption of pre-experimental equivalence is met. Note also that since we create these groups, we can construct situations ideally suited to the research questions we wish to pose. And of course, because these experiments occur on our own turf, when we want them to, we are best prepared to

measure the dependent variable with instruments of demonstrated reliability and validity.

This creative power has other benefits as well. In the laboratory, situations can be intentionally created that do not yet exist in the world, as can situations that we hope will not exist. As an example of the former, we might use the lab to do preliminary testing of emergent technologies or different organizational structures before they're foisted on users in the field. As for the latter, we wouldn't intentionally make a real airplane carrying real people crash, but we can use lab simulations to assess and/or train those who might have to deal with such events (e.g., see Palys 1978).

Finally, it could probably also be stated that the laboratory experiment is ideally suited in many ways for addressing strictly theoretical questions, perhaps more so than practical or applied research questions. Given that various authors (e.g., Kerlinger 1973) have affirmed that theory is the goal of science (as opposed to "truth" or "knowledge" or "facts" per se), this suggests that the lab plays an important role in social science. Note also that much theorizing is of the *ceteris paribus* variety (implying that theories assert the relationships among variables of interest, all else being equal), and laboratory experimentation is one manifestation of that logic. If a theory suggests that variable A should or might have a certain effect on variable B, for example, then one could observe variable B in a lab situation where all variables except variable A are held constant or otherwise controlled (e.g., by random assignment to groups). Variable A, of course, would be present in one group (the experimental group) but not the other (the control group). By doing so, we would have investigated the effects of variable *A* on variable *B*, *ceteris paribus*.

As long as our interests are purely theoretical, and as long as we limit our interpretation to this generic *ceteris paribus* situation, the laboratory can serve a useful role. But if we're more interested in contextualized behaviour in that open system we call the world, the lab's role may be more limited (e.g., see Manicas & Secord 1983). Researchers who extrapolate answers to applied questions from their theory-based lab research may be on tenuous ground, since all else is never equal in the real world; every setting embodies its own unique context (e.g., see Palys & Lowman 1984).

Until relatively recently, many social scientists believed that the controlled lab situation allowed a "pure" test of the relationships among variables in a vacuous, context-free situation (e.g., see Festinger 1953). But in the early 1970s, various European authors began to challenge this view (e.g., see Israel & Tajfel 1972). They asserted that since all behaviour occurs within a context and since "laboratory behaviour" is still "behaviour," attention is warranted to the context within which lab behaviour occurs and to the relationship between the lab context and the context of the "real world" (see especially Tajfel 1972).

Argyris (1975) and Brandt (1975) were among those to agree that the laboratory does indeed embody a social context, but both authors suggest that in many ways that context is the "wrong" one. They depict the experiment as embodying the most imperialist of tendencies—a centralized authority (the experimenter) defines the game and decides the rules, participants are often kept in the dark as to the experimenter's full motives and methods, the role of "subject" is to accept the experimenter's definition of the situation and respond within those constraints, and the preferred epistemology underlying the experiment is one that embraces the utility of manipulative control. Too centralized; too controlling; too hierarchical; too secretive; too minimizing of participants' views and interpretations. The authors remind us of our social responsibilities and

suggest that such control-oriented methods encourage control-oriented policy (see also Latour 1987); instead of empowering, such methods and policies are arguably exploitative.

More recently, Manicas and Secord (1983) took up the torch in their articulation of the contemporary critical realist perspective in social science. They agree with those who assert that the laboratory is a place to test theory (e.g., Kerlinger 1973; Mook 1983), since it's a closed system in which basic structures of individual human behaviour (e.g., competencies, abilities, powers) can be investigated. But there's a bigger question: Do our interests lie exclusively with the concoction of theories of lab behaviour per se, or are we also interested in theorizing about life in its broader context? If the latter, then Manicas and Secord (1983) assert that it's a whole new ball game. In sum, they argue that traditional experimentalists are accurate in their analysis (as it pertains to lab behaviour), but myopic (because the conditions they study exist only in the lab).

As this summary suggests, some of the major questions about laboratory research revolve around the notion of exactly what lab behaviour means. But the lab has even more clear-cut limitations. Not the least of these is that there are many phenomena that we would prefer to attend to *in vivo* (a Latin phrase meaning, literally, "in life"). Not all phenomena can be transported into the lab, nor can all be scrutinized conveniently in the typical hour-long laboratory session (e.g., the aging process, the development of criminal careers, observations of social change, the impact of deinstitutionalization, etc.). And when the mountain can't come to us, then we must go to the mountain.

GOING TO THE MOUNTAIN

Not even 30 years ago, most researchers in the social sciences felt that "going to the mountain" meant that one had to throw principles of experimentation, and hence opportunities for causal inference, out the window. Only in the lab could one gather "clean" data in well-controlled situations created at the whim of the experimenter; the field necessarily involved "dirty" data subject to too many uncontrolled influences. Aspects of the experimental method that were seen as integral to experimentation—random assignment to groups, for example—were seen as impossible to duplicate to any significant degree outside the lab. Hence, the notion of "field experimentation" was seen as a virtual contradiction in terms, and "evaluation research" (e.g., studies that attempt to assess the effects of a particular program or legislative changes) was seen as a necessarily subjective, qualitative, and error-prone task. There was a clear hierarchy of methods, with the experiment at the top and case study methods at the bottom.

Field Experimentation

At the risk of oversimplifying, let us suggest that there are really two basic ways to approach the challenge of doing experimental research in the field. The first involves *field experiments,* which are little more than experiments (in the traditional sense of the word) that happen to be done in the field rather than in the lab. In all other respects, one follows the same procedures: manipulating independent variable(s), operationalizing and measuring the dependent variable, randomly assigning participants to groups, testing for statistical significance, and assessing internal and external validity. The second type of field research is used to make causal inferences when you are unable to or don't wish to manipulate the independent variable (i.e., its timing and coverage are beyond your control) or to randomly assign participants to groups. This approach is known as **quasi-experimentation.**

Donald T. Campbell and Quasi-Experimentation

THE "TRAPPINGS" VERSUS THE "LOGIC" OF EXPERIMENTATION

The individual who played the most significant role in formulating the quasi-experimental perspective was the late Donald T. Campbell, formerly of

Northwestern University just outside Chicago.[1] His classic article "Reforms as Experiments" (1969b) really broke the ice, although its themes had been the subject of discussion for some years before it was published (e.g., see Campbell 1957; Campbell & Stanley 1963).

Campbell's contributions are twofold. First, he supplied a vocabulary and a set of dimensions on which research might be evaluated (e.g., the terms "internal validity" and "external validity" were coined by him). Second, he argued that researchers should not confuse the trappings of experimentation with its underlying logic. He noted that random assignment to groups, for example, is not an end in itself, but an efficient vehicle for achieving experimental objectives (i.e., ensuring groups are equal to begin with; eliminating or controlling for certain rival plausible explanations). Thus, while he agreed with the traditionalists who argued that random assignment to groups is frequently difficult in field settings, he disagreed with their conclusion that experimentation in field situations is therefore impossible.

Recall that not too long ago, social scientists believed that causal inference is possible only in situations where you can manipulate the independent variable and employ random assignment. These two attributes were seen as prerequisites for causal inference, and studies that didn't involve them were considered a distant second best. Instead, Campbell argued that we should keep our objectives in mind and that if particular vehicles for achieving these objectives are not available, then we should not throw our hands in the air in frustration but, rather, look for alternative methods to meet those objectives.

THREE CRITERIA FOR INFERRING CAUSALITY
Many of our contemporary conceptions of science emerged from the philosophizing of such people as David Hume (an 18th-century Scottish philosopher) and John Stuart Mill (a 19th-century English philosopher). Mill spelled out three criteria of causality that are still very influential today. In order to be able to infer the existence of a causal relation-

ship between two variables (let us generically call them X and Y), Mill (1843/1965) stated that at least three conditions must be satisfied. One must demonstrate that

1. the presumed cause (X) came *before* (i.e., was "temporally precedent" to) the effect (Y);
2. the presumed cause and effect are indeed related to each other (i.e., the presence or absence of X is associated with an increased likelihood of the presence or absence of Y); and
3. the relationship between X and Y is not explained by the presence of other plausible causal agents.

As Chapter 9 shows, these criteria are admirably met by traditional experimental design. The temporal precedence criterion is met by the fact that one manipulates the presumed causal variable (i.e., the researcher "causes" the presumed "cause" to occur) and is there waiting to measure changes in the dependent (or "effect" or "outcome") variable. The existence of a relationship between X and Y is demonstrated by an observed difference between the "experimental" or "treatment" group and the "control" group. The final criterion, the absence of rival plausible explanations, is addressed by the concept of internal validity. You can see, therefore, why (1) manipulation of the independent variable, (2) the existence of experimental and control groups, and (3) random assignment to groups were thought to be integral prerequisites of experimentation, since they directly and elegantly addressed Mill's criteria.

ADAPTING CAUSAL CRITERIA TO FIELD SETTINGS

Campbell (1969b) encouraged us to go a step further. He recognized the importance of being able to do research in the "real world," arguing that we'd all be a lot better off if we could somehow *evaluate* the effects of legal reforms and other social changes— that is, become more of an "experimenting society" rather than operating chiefly on the basis of intuition and subjective self-interest. To do so, he suggested, we would first have to stop confusing the *trappings* of experimentation with its *logic*. He argued for an extension of this logic in his development of quasi-experimental design. To quote one of his former colleagues at Northwestern:

> the assumption of [quasi-experimental design] is that the experimental method has much broader application than its laboratory version suggests.... What is important is *not* [the] ability to manipulate and assign randomly, but the *ends* these procedures serve ... The problem then becomes one of providing the proper translation rules to get the social scientist out of the lab and into the "real world," while retaining some of the strong inference characteristic of the laboratory setting. (Caporaso 1973: 6–7; our italics)

Thus, if manipulation of the independent variable and random assignment to groups become difficult to accomplish in field settings, we should not resign ourselves to the feeling that causal inference is thus impossible, but rather should look to the underlying logic of experimentation for alternative procedures that will fulfill these same experimental objectives. According to Campbell (e.g., 1969b), the temporal precedence criterion of causality (i.e., cause before effect) is relatively easily dealt with in many field situations by the acquisition of time-series data. With respect to the inability to randomly assign participants to groups, Campbell (1969b) notes that

> the advocated strategy in quasi-experimentation is not to throw up one's hands and refuse to use the evidence because of this lack of control, but rather to generate by informed criticism as many appropriate rival hypotheses as possible, and then to do the supplementary research ... which would reflect on these rival hypotheses. (413)

An Example: The Connecticut Speeding Crackdown

Perhaps the best way to explain this approach is by example. Toward this end, we can do no better than to tell you about Campbell's evaluation of the impact of the Connecticut speeding crackdown, the published version of which (Campbell & Ross 1968) was written to emphasize the methodological principles involved in the research more than the actual findings. But first, some background.

During 1955, 324 people died in traffic accidents on Connecticut's highways. A record number of deaths had already occurred as the 1955 Christmas season approached. On December 23, 1955, then-governor Abraham Ribicoff announced a new crackdown on speeders. Like many others, Ribicoff believed that excess speed was a major cause of traffic fatalities and that the point system that had been in effect in Connecticut until that time was ineffective in keeping speeders in check. In its place, Ribicoff announced that henceforth, all people convicted of speeding on the highways would have their licences suspended. There would be a 30-day suspension for the first offence, a 60-day suspension for a second offence, and an indefinite suspension, the exact duration of which would be the subject of a hearing after 90 days, for a third.

There were, in fact, fewer deaths on the highways of Connecticut in 1956; "only" 284 persons died, 40 fewer than had been killed on the highways in 1955. Ribicoff was most pleased with this decrease, arguing that the saving of 40 lives was well worth the inconvenience to individuals who had been guilty of speeding. The Connecticut crackdown was the subject of considerable national attention because of its apparent success, and Governor Ribicoff proudly accepted awards from such agencies as the National Safety Council for his efforts.

Campbell and Ross (1968) do not question Governor Ribicoff's statements that the saving of 40 lives was "worth it," since the relative worth of 40 lives versus inconvenience to speeders is obviously not an empirical question, but rather one of value and philosophy. Instead, the two researchers addressed themselves to the question of whether Ribicoff was correct in identifying the crackdown as the causal agent in the change that was observed or whether some other rival plausible explanatory factor(s) might have accounted for the results.

WAS THERE A CHANGE IN THE DEPENDENT VARIABLE?

The first thing to establish in doing such an evaluation is whether there is any evidence at *all* that the crackdown was effective. The answer to that one is fairly obvious, since we've already told you that there were 40 fewer deaths in 1956 than in 1955. So change did occur, and it was in the predicted direction (i.e., fewer rather than more deaths). This is immediately evident in the simple before–after "gee whiz" graph[2] shown in Figure 10.1.

WAS THE INDEPENDENT VARIABLE REALLY MANIPULATED?

The second thing you'd want to establish is whether a speeding crackdown really did occur, as Governor Ribicoff said it did; that is, is there evidence that the independent variable of interest really *was* manipulated? If it *wasn't*, then one could hardly argue that *that* was the variable causing the change. This may sound somewhat obvious, but much of politics is theatre, and it's not uncommon for politicians to say something will happen when in fact it doesn't. On some occasions this failure occurs at the political level, for example, when the proposed change does not make it to or survive the legislative process. On other occasions, the institutions or bureaucracies that are *supposed* to carry out the change in policy can be quite inventive in finding ways *not* to do so (e.g., by finding loopholes in the policy, giving the matter low priority, or moving discretion to another bureaucratic level).

The evidence generally supports the notion that a crackdown really did occur, just as Governor Ribicoff had said it would. To ensure compliance among judges, Ribicoff went on public record to state that judges who did not follow his directive of suspending speeders would find that they wouldn't be reappointed next time their positions came up for renewal. The number of licence suspensions for speeding in the first six months of the year went up dramatically, from 231 in 1955 to 5398 in 1956 (an increase of more than 2000 percent). Figure 10.2 shows the significance and abruptness of this change.

Figure 10.1

Traffic Fatalities in Connecticut before and after the Crackdown

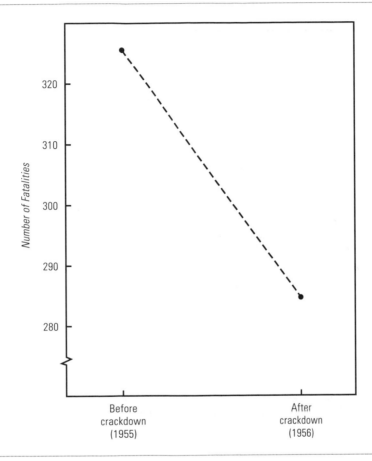

Source: D. T. Campbell and L. H. Ross (1968), "The Connecticut Crackdown on Speeding: Time-Series Data in Quasi-Experimental Analysis," *Law and Society Review, 3,* p. 38. Reprinted by permission from Blackwell Publishing.

But there also appear to have been some changes in how speeders were treated by both the police and the courts. Figure 10.3 shows there was a noticeable decrease in speeding violations expressed as a percentage of all traffic violations. This decline may indicate that the crackdown was effective and fewer people were speeding. But it could also mean that police officers had become less likely to ticket speeders, knowing that the inevitable punishment for the ticket would be a licence suspension (i.e., they may have given a larger "grace" region before actually giving a ticket) and/or had become more likely to give speeders a ticket for something other than speeding (e.g., exhibiting undue care).

Similarly, Figure 10.4 reveals a noticeable increase in the percentage of speeding violations that were

Figure 10.2

Percentage of Licence Suspensions as a Result of Speeding, by Year

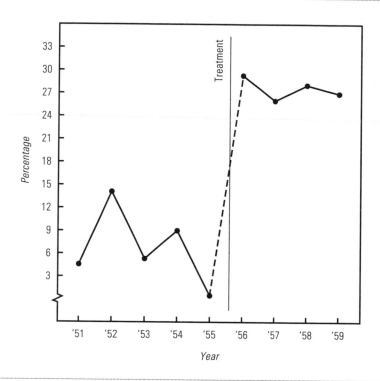

Source: D. T. Campbell and L. H. Ross (1968), "The Connecticut Crackdown on Speeding: Time-Series Data in Quasi-Experimental Analysis," *Law and Society Review, 3,* p. 48. Reprinted by permission from Blackwell Publishing.

ultimately judged "not guilty." Perhaps alleged speeders became more likely to fight their tickets in court, since avoiding a licence suspension is worth taking up time for; perhaps, too, judges became more likely to dismiss charges on minor technicalities, given the harsh punishment they'd otherwise be obliged to bestow.

Despite the caveats suggested by these two findings, the huge size of the crackdown (Figure 10.2) relative to the minor shifts observed in Figures 10.3 and 10.4 nonetheless convinced Campbell and Ross (1968) that the independent variable really was manipulated quite dramatically.

So what do we know at this point?

First, we know that there really was a change in procedures. The independent variable really was manipulated. Second, we know an attendant change in the dependent variable occurred *after* the independent variable was manipulated; that is, a decrease in deaths was observed *after* the speeding crackdown came into effect. In investigating the assertion that "the Connecticut speeding crackdown caused a substantial decrease in the highway death toll," we have so far established two of Mill's criteria: (1) the presumed "cause" *was* temporally precedent to the alleged "effect"; and (2) the cause and effect *did* covary in time. It is Mill's *third* criterion that's missing at this point: we haven't yet demonstrated

Figure 10.3
Speeding Violations Expressed as a Percentage of All Traffic Violations, by Year

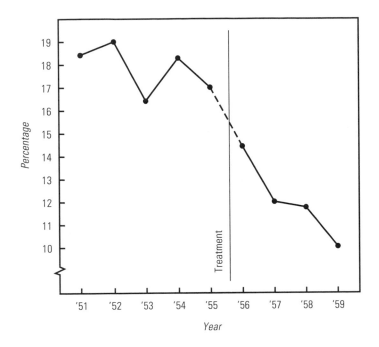

Source: D. T. Campbell and L. H. Ross (1968), "The Connecticut Crackdown on Speeding: Time-Series Data in Quasi-Experimental Analysis," *Law and Society Review,* 3, p. 49. Reprinted by permission from Blackwell Publishing.

that the observed change in the dependent variable was not caused by some plausible factor(s) *other than* the crackdown. Now *that's* the tough part!

In traditional laboratory experimentation, we simultaneously eliminate numerous rival plausible explanations by randomly assigning participants to groups (thereby ensuring pretest equivalence) and by creating a control group that is equivalent to the experimental group in all respects except for the independent variable. But that luxury obviously isn't available to us here. So what can we do?

ELIMINATING RIVAL PLAUSIBLE EXPLANATIONS

At this point, Campbell (1969b) encourages us to make a cognitive shift in our approach to experimen-

tation. What is our objective in this situation? The answer: we want to rule out rival plausible explanations. But how do we do that here? The answer: by starting off with the *assumption,* on the basis of the data shown in Figure 10.1, that the prevailing evidence suggests the crackdown *was* effective, and then systematically *deriving,* and then *testing, all* the plausible rival hypotheses we can think of.

In other words, Figure 10.1 can be viewed as the result of a one-group pretest/posttest research design that shows that there was an effect associated with the change in the independent variable. But what might have caused that change? The independent variable, that is, the crackdown, may have caused it. Okay, but what *else* might have caused the change?

Figure 10.4

Percentage of Alleged Speeding Violations Ultimately Judged "Not Guilty," by Year

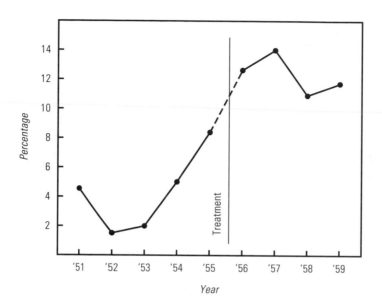

Source: D. T. Campbell and L. H. Ross (1968), "The Connecticut Crackdown on Speeding: Time-Series Data in Quasi-Experimental Analysis," *Law and Society Review, 3,* p. 51. Reprinted by permission from Blackwell Publishing.

Let's go through our list of threats to internal validity.

How about history (i.e., events that occurred between the pretest and the posttest other than the independent variable)? Yes, there are some possibilities here. Maybe 1955 was a particularly rainy or snowy year and/or 1956 was a particularly dry year, so that the difference in death rates was due to differences in road conditions rather than to the crackdown. All right, *go check it out*. Look up the meteorological records to see whether the "weather" explanation is plausible. Campbell and Ross (1968) did just that and found no appreciable difference in weather for the two years in question. One rival plausible explanation is eliminated.

Well, how about car safety? Maybe there was some dramatic change in car design on the 1956 models that led to the decrease in traffic fatalities. Again, *check it out*. Upon doing so, Campbell and Ross (1968) found that no such change had occurred. Two rival plausible explanations have now been eliminated.

How about road quality, then? Is it possible that the state poured a lot of money into highway improvement at that time, perhaps paving over many gravel roads or turning two-lane highways into four-lane divided highways? If so, we might suspect that the lower death rate was merely a reflection of better roads. But on checking it out, Campbell and Ross (1968) found that there were *no* atypical expenditures on Connecticut's highways budget. A third rival plausible explanation has now been ruled out.

You've probably caught the general drift by now. The emphasis is on *informed critique* as a source for generating rival *plausible* explanations, each of which is then tested by gathering whatever data are appropriate. The resulting analysis will leave you with either (1) *no* rival plausible explanations remaining, in which case we might assert that the crackdown itself is the most compelling explanation, or (2) *some* (or many) rival plausible explanations remaining, in which case we can do no more than list what these might be. The researcher's task is to take a comprehensive inventory of these and to test them out as thoroughly as possible.

The relatively simple comparisons we've noted above can also be supplemented with more elaborate quasi-experimental designs, depending on the types of rival plausible explanations one is attempting to assess and/or on the specifics of the situation. A relatively exhaustive inventory and delineation of these designs can be seen in Cook and Campbell (1979). This discussion will focus on a class of techniques known as **interrupted time-series designs.**

Time-Series Designs

Look again at Figure 10.1, which displays the basic data from Campbell and Ross's (1968) quasi-experiment. As is the case for any one-group pretest/posttest design, there is much that the design does not control, and there are many plausible explanations one must address. We have done so on a limited basis with some of the "history" threats above. But with this type of archival data, maturation and statistical regression are among the main threats.

In particular, regression artifacts must always be considered when we see a change reported. Campbell (1969b) makes the point well in his facetious advice to "trapped" administrators: to look good, all you have to do is pick the worst administrative unit under your control as the target for your "experimental" program, and then wait for a year; there's a high probability that your performance will improve

just because of regression toward the mean (but you, of course, take all the credit).

Even when such an approach isn't being taken by administrators for self-serving reasons, "extreme circumstances" often give birth to programs at short notice. When the media headlines scream "Worst Crime Wave Ever" or "Unprecedented Slaughter on the Highways," politicians and civil servants may use their discretionary funding to show that they're doing something and to reassure the public that everything's under control. Of course, it's exactly such circumstances that are most often associated with regression artifacts, in which case the situation will in all likelihood improve by next year, whether or not anything is done.

So one of our *first* concerns with the Connecticut speeding crackdown data should be the question "How typical was 1955?" A "treatment" as severe as the Connecticut speeding crackdown would most likely arise in the kind of extreme conditions most conducive to regression artifacts, and we were told that 1955 involved a "record high" number of highway traffic deaths. How could we address that threat to internal validity? The answer: by gathering time-series data that *show* the maturational trend of the data.

The interrupted time-series data are shown in Figure 10.5. You can see where our 1955–56 pre–post comparison graph (Figure 10.1) fits into the picture. Figure 10.5 suggests that regression is indeed a plausible concern; 1955 *was* an atypically high year, and the years from 1956 onward reveal a successively decreasing trend. What kinds of historical factors might be relevant besides those already considered? To address this issue, one can extend the *single* time-series design noted above into the *multiple* time-series design shown in Figure 10.6.

Multiple Time-Series Designs

The *multiple time-series design* attempts to use similar and/or nearby units as a sort of quasi-control, since even *nonequivalent* control groups may provide *some* useful information. While acknowledging that the control series is non-equivalent, one would still

Figure 10.5

Single Time-Series Data on Fatality Rates

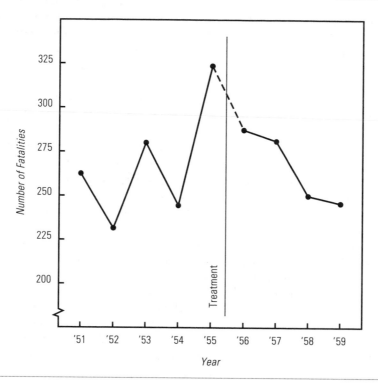

Source: D. T. Campbell and L. H. Ross (1968), "The Connecticut Crackdown on Speeding: Time-Series Data in Quasi-Experimental Analysis," *Law and Society Review, 3,* p. 42. Reprinted by permission from Blackwell Publishing.

attempt to match it as closely as possible with the treatment series. In Figure 10.6, the control states comprise four states that neighbour Connecticut and, hence, involve roughly similar topography, road conditions, and perhaps even citizenry (New Englanders). The smoothness of the control series, incidentally, is accounted for largely by the aggregation of four states: chance deviations on a state-to-state basis tend to cancel one another out. Note also that Figure 10.6 provides a bit of support for *both* the "regression" *and* the "crackdown" explanations. On the one hand, 1955 *was* quite an atypical year; on the other hand, the trend in the control states is for continually increasing numbers of traffic deaths, while the Connecticut trend following the crack-

down is for a decrease. Besides providing some degree of control over history threats (e.g., given sufficient proximity, to control for weather changes), multiple time-series may also (in some circumstances) control for *instrumentation* threats (i.e., changes in the measurement instrument or in the data-gathering procedure). This is not the case in the present data, since each state keeps its own books, but might be relevant in situations where all the control units (e.g., states) share the same record-keeping procedures (e.g., UCR crime rate statistics) and all make a change in procedure at the same time.

The final data Campbell and Ross (1968) share with us (in Figure 10.7) de-aggregate the control series of Figure 10.6 into separate states. Once again,

Figure 10.6

Multiple Time-Series Data on Fatality Rates, with Aggregated Comparison Group

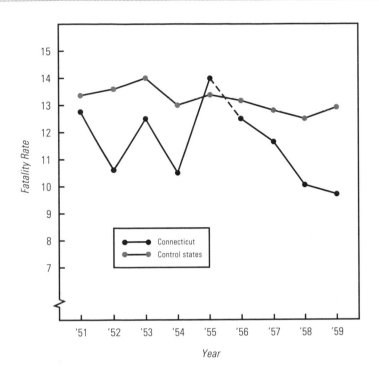

Source: D. T. Campbell and L. H. Ross (1968), "The Connecticut Crackdown on Speeding: Time-Series Data in Quasi-Experimental Analysis," *Law and Society Review, 3*, p. 44. Reprinted by permission from Blackwell Publishing.

the evidence is mixed, but it offers some support for a real effect over and above a regression artifact. The trend in most states is for a continuation of or even a slight increase in the number of highway deaths. The most similar profiles came from Massachusetts and Rhode Island. In both cases (and particularly with Rhode Island), increases in 1954–55 are followed by decreases in 1955–56. But in both cases, the trend rises again shortly thereafter. In contrast, the Connecticut trend is for a continuing decrease, leading Campbell and Ross (1968) to argue that while *some* of the change in the dependent measure is probably attributable to regression toward the mean, there's also evidence to suggest that the crackdown did indeed have an effect.

REVIEWING THE LOGIC OF QUASI-EXPERIMENTATION

In sum, there are several steps to follow in executing a quasi-experimental design. First, ask yourself whether there really was a change in the independent variable. (For example, Campbell and Ross [1968] looked to see whether there was any evidence that a "crackdown" on speeders had indeed occurred.) Second, ask whether there was also a change in the dependent variable—and if so, whether that change occurred after implementation of the independent variable. (For example, Campbell and Ross [1968] compared the number of traffic deaths in 1955 and 1956 and found that there was indeed a decrease.)

Figure 10.7

Multiple Time-Series Data on Fatality Rates, with De-aggregated Comparison Series

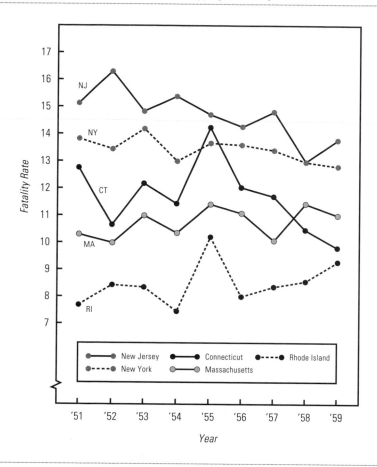

Source: D. T. Campbell and L. H. Ross (1968), "The Connecticut Crackdown on Speeding: Time-Series Data in Quasi-Experimental Analysis," *Law and Society Review, 3,* p. 45. Reprinted by permission from Blackwell Publishing.

If the answer to either of these first two questions is no, there's little sense in going further.

But if both answers are yes, then there are more questions to ask. A relationship evidently exists between the putative causal (independent) variable and the effect (dependent) variable, but *what factors other than the independent variable might also have accounted for the observed relationship?* Here, Campbell and Ross (1968) affirm, you must be your own best critic—if you aren't, you can be certain someone

else will. You must delineate *plausible* alternative explanations and doggedly pursue the relevant data that will allow you to test each of those alternatives.

If you follow these steps, in the end you will be able to formulate a reasonably good answer to such questions as "Did the new legislation have some effect?" or "Did the program cause a change?" And while this approach lacks the simplicity and elegance of the "true" experimental design and its almost formulaic ability to control for rival plausible explanations, certainly the importance of such a task makes it worth doing anyway.

APPRECIATING THE SOCIAL DYNAMICS OF FIELD SETTINGS

Earlier in this chapter, we looked at the logic underlying quasi-experimentation, in particular, the notion of ad hoc elimination of rival plausible explanations. Although interrupted time-series designs were the only ones discussed, many other possibilities exist that are applicable to a wide array of situations. These are discussed most comprehensively in Cook and Campbell (1979) and Shadish et al (2001).

Before concluding this chapter, there are two further issues to discuss: some threats to internal validity particularly relevant to fieldwork; and the "politics" of evaluative research, in terms of both the political dynamic inherent in the evaluative process and the political choices implicit in one's choice of variables.

New Threats to Internal Validity

As you'll recall from Chapter 9, a threat to internal validity occurs whenever any variables other than treatment variables obscure the source of change. To put it another way, research is often done in order to isolate the effects associated with a particular independent variable or merely to determine *which* "causal" variable was the source of observed change in the dependent variable. The fewer rival plausible explanations that exist, the clearer the source of change. The frontiers of ignorance are pushed back another inch.

Chapter 9 describes several classes of threats, including history, maturation, testing, regression toward the mean, and selection. While these threats should still be considered in quasi-experimental research, several other classes of threats to internal validity become particularly relevant to the evaluative setting in the field. We will discuss five of these: diffusion of treatment, compensatory equalization, compensatory rivalry, resentful demoralization, and mortality.

DIFFUSION OR IMITATION OF TREATMENTS

Within the confines of the laboratory, it's generally fairly easy to isolate experimental and control groups from each other. Even when participants know that there are other groups, they probably won't know much, if anything, about how their own experience differs from what's being experienced by others. Their participation is usually short-lived, and lines of communication between participants in different groups are rare or nonexistent. From the experimental perspective, this is as it should be, since clear inference requires clear isolation of groups.

In the field, however, it's not unusual to be faced with intact groups that can't be isolated from one another. Instead of having two (or more) comparison groups that are clearly different on the independent variable being considered, we may find that the boundaries between the groups are or become somewhat blurred. For example, if the groups are differentiated by their access to varying sets of information, any communication between groups about the nature of this information will make each group a little more like the other(s). This **diffusion of treatment** (sometimes called *imitation of treatment*) will act to minimize the groups' separation and heighten their similarity. The independent variable, in other words, doesn't have a real opportunity to "work." If this occurs, you might be left concluding—perhaps erroneously—that the treatment variable is ineffectual, when in fact it might have been quite efficacious had it just been given a reasonable opportunity.

Similarly, when the intact groups are neighbouring cities, provinces, or states, those affected by one state of affairs (e.g., a new law) may travel to the neighbouring community to overcome any perceived inequity. For example, when abortion laws become more restrictive, it's rarely clear whether the number of abortions in the affected area actually decreases; instead, those who seek abortions may merely use other methods or may travel to places that have more tolerant policies. Depending on the nature of the treatment under study, diffusion of treatment may artifactually inflate or reduce the "true"[3] impact of the independent variable.

COMPENSATORY EQUALIZATION

Similarly, **compensatory equalization of treatments** may act to obscure differences between groups, leading to an erroneous finding of "no difference." Cook and Campbell (1979) suggest that this problem arises when the treatment involves goods and/or services deemed desirable, and where there is a large disparity between groups. Administrators, those charged with implementing the treatment, or some of the recipients may reroute some goods or provide access to services among some or all members of the disadvantaged group in an effort to alleviate disparity.

For example, when in 1994 Quebec and Ontario dramatically reduced the amount of provincial tax they were charging on cigarettes, it wasn't unusual to find that smokers in neighbouring provinces would go there for cigarettes or that friends would send cigarettes by mail. Although legal authorities tried to thwart such activities, the practice probably continued. Any attempt to evaluate the effects of that policy change would need to assess whether the degree of compensatory equalization was sufficiently widespread to be problematic with respect to internal validity.[4] Diffusion of treatments is the result.

COMPENSATORY RIVALRY

New programs and legislative changes are much more public than experiments occurring in laboratories. If it's known that an evaluation is in progress, one may see **compensatory rivalry** by the respondents who are receiving the less desirable treatment(s). Knowing that one is in the disadvantaged group may spur a competitive spirit to overcome adversity and perform well. This is particularly likely to be the case in situations where the group already perceives itself as a group (e.g., work teams, crews, classes) and has a lot to lose if a difference is revealed.

This threat to internal validity has also been dubbed the *John Henry effect* (see Cook & Campbell 1979), after the legendary individual who, when he learned that his performance was to be compared to that of a steam drill, worked so hard that he outper-

formed the drill but died in the process. As a threat to internal validity, compensatory rivalry obscures "real" differences between groups.

RESENTFUL DEMORALIZATION

In contrast, if it's known that an evaluation is in progress, individuals who are in the disadvantaged group may respond with **resentful demoralization** if they perceive the result as adverse and inevitable. They may not even try to compete, and they may even intentionally reduce their performance. In this instance, the researcher may *overestimate* the actual potency of an independent variable.

MORTALITY

Although mortality is a threat to be considered in laboratory research and was featured even in earlier treatments of internal validity (e.g., Campbell & Stanley 1963), we chose to leave its delineation to this chapter on field experimentation, where it's most relevant. **Mortality,** in the present context, refers to a situation in which some individuals drop out of the research before it's completed. Single-session, short-term laboratory experimentation virtually precludes mortality as a problem. But in the field, where time-series data and a succession of follow-ups are more likely, the mortality problem increases in relevance. Some individuals who are recorded as participants at the beginning of the study do not return to receive the dependent measure at follow-up; for example, they drop out of therapy, choose to resign from the group, move to another jurisdiction, are released on parole, join another club, get lost, or die.

The problem is one of *selection bias,* and the questions to address are (1) Who are those that drop out? (2) In what ways, if any, do they differ from the remaining individuals in the group? (3) What is the relationship between (a) the variables on which those who drop out and those who remain differ and (b) the dependent measure? To the extent that there *are* differences between those who depart and those who remain, one's external validity may become limited, and comparisons within and between treatment groups (internal validity) will suffer. This is particularly so if there is *differential mortality* between groups, a situation that happens often, since those in the control group have the least reason to return and are participating only as a favour. Whenever mortality occurs, one must question not only the representativeness of those who remain, but also people's reasons for leaving. Conscientious researchers anticipate this possibility and gather sufficient pretest information to deal with this eventuality.

As the above discussion suggests, many new problems await one in the field. But why do these things happen? On some occasions, the vagaries of chance just seem to stack up against you, and Murphy's law[5] rules the day. But much also happens because of the human motives and emotions that are awakened by the particular topic of study. Welcome to the politics of evaluation research.

The Politics of Evaluation Research

Field research is more blatantly a part of the phenomenon it investigates than laboratory-based research. Certainly, the negotiation of design and measurement techniques for evaluation research is an interpersonal as well as a cognitive process, and the consequences of one's decisions and findings may be more visible. For these and other reasons, field research is a different kind of animal.

Chapter 3 discusses some of the ethical and moral decisions that researchers face when negotiating the terms under which a study will be conducted. Here, we'll discuss evaluative research within a political context, attempting to make explicit some of the roles researchers play within that process. In keeping with this book's general theme, the emphasis is less on telling the prospective researcher what to do than on articulating the decisions the researcher must make; these decisions should most certainly be made as a result of conscious choice rather than out of habit or naiveté.

Weiss (1975) identifies three major areas in which evaluation researchers should be aware of political considerations. First, she notes, programs aren't the result of some anonymous individual exclaiming, "Gee, why don't we give *this* a try?"

Quite the contrary: "they [have typically] emerged from the rough-and-tumble world of political support, opposition and bargaining; and attached to them are the reputations of legislative sponsors, the careers of administrators, the jobs of program staff, and the expectations of clients" (14). In sum, many, if not all, *programs are political creatures.*

PROGRAMS ARE POLITICAL CREATURES

This reality has several implications. First, researchers should realize that the program's official goals are not necessarily a reasonable statement of its initiators' actual goals. In an effort to appease various interest groups and to sell the desirability of program implementation, legislators and policymakers may make inflated and even grandiose claims that go beyond the capacity of any given program. A basic goal of public housing, for example, is to provide decent accommodation to those who might otherwise be disenfranchised. Yet what one hears in the news is that "public housing will not only provide decent living space; it will also improve health, reduce crime, and lead to improved school performance" (Weiss 1975: 16).

At the same time, public articulations of goals and objectives may also *omit* mention of many other goals that were considered when the program was formulated. These might include the desire to avoid layoffs of bureaucratic personnel, a desire to extend political power and influence, and/or the need to be perceived by the public as *doing something* about some area of social concern. Researchers must also realize that the perception of project goals will not necessarily be consistent throughout all levels of program implementation. As Weiss (1975) notes, "what the [government] writes into legislation as programme objectives are not necessarily what the secretary's office or the director of the programme see as their mission, nor what the state or local project managers or the operating staff actually try to accomplish" (16).

Thus, evaluation researchers must appreciate that there *are* political dynamics to the process of program development and implementation, and they must make sure that their evaluations and reports *speak* to the various constituencies. This is not to say that researchers should become co-opted by political considerations. Rather, they should be *independent* evaluators who *realistically* examine the program or phenomenon from the perspective of multiple constituencies. Above all, you don't want your report to be ignored or shelved with the comment "But that's not what we were trying to do!" You want to avoid being accurate but out to lunch.

We would also argue that *science* should be perceived as one of your constituencies; that is, you should not forget your academic heritage. Indeed, for us, the opportunity for academic payoffs is a prerequisite for involvement in evaluative research. Thus, an evaluation of a police department's computerized database system not only produced information that was useful to the police department and federal Department of Communications (Palys, Boyanowsky, & Dutton 1983), but also provided the basis for a broader discussion on the implications of computer technology for decision making (Palys, Boyanowsky, & Dutton 1984). Similarly, an evaluation of the social content of video pornography (Palys 1984) not only was useful to a federal committee investigating pornography and prostitution in Canada (Special Committee 1985), but also spoke to methodological issues concerning the role of context in behavioural research (Palys & Lowman 1984).

THE POLITICS OF THE DECISION-MAKING PROCESS

A second major way that Weiss (1975) notes that politics enter the evaluation research process requires an appreciation for the *politics of higher-echelon decision making*. To begin with, the funds that pay for evaluation research rarely come from the particular program being evaluated. More frequently, these funds originate from more senior bureaucratic levels, which are less concerned with program and organizational survival than those on the front lines. In this sense, one might think that senior decision makers might be more likely to consider the research evidence more dispassionately. But they have their own constituencies with whom they must deal and to whom they're accountable.

In sum, the decisions of senior decision makers ostensibly go beyond considerations of program effectiveness per se.

> Their decisions are rooted in all the complexities of the democratic decision-making process, the allocation of power and authority, the development of coalitions, the trade-offs with interest groups, professional guilds, and salient publics ... [The research evidence] will not be the sole basis for a decision, and legitimately so: other information and other values inevitably enter a democratic policy process. (Weiss 1975: 17)

The researcher, in other words, *can* make some reasonable statements about how things *are,* but affirmations about how things *should be* enter moral rather than empirical grounds. Researchers *can* expose fallacious belief, and they *can* unearth some historical or contemporary consequences of particular strategies of action. But in arguing over the desirability of different social futures, they are just one of many voices in the democratic decision-making process.

THE POLITICAL STANCE OF THE EVALUATION ITSELF

As Weiss (1975) points out, the third major way politics intrudes into evaluation research is in the stance of the evaluation itself:

> Social scientists tend to see evaluation research, like all research, as objective, unbiased, nonpolitical, a corrective for the special pleading and selfish interests of program operators and policymakers alike. Evaluation produces hard evidence of actual outcomes, but it incorporates as well a series of assumptions; and many researchers are unaware of the political nature of the assumptions they make and the role they play. (19)

As noted earlier, one of the differences between the laboratory and the field is that the latter is a more interpersonal and visibly consequential process. Although one rarely sees evaluation research on the evening news, it *is* a matter of some significance in the milieu under consideration. The researcher is a professional, but often an outsider, brought in to evaluate. His or her mere presence on the scene has several implications: it suggests that the researcher accepts the legitimacy of the goals and objectives being pursued. It also implies that the rationale underlying the program is a reasonable one. If it wasn't, why bother to evaluate the program? The researcher's presence alone gives an aura of legitimacy. All the above suggest a status quo orientation. Furthermore, the money to do the evaluation will probably have come from an "establishment" source, and those to whom the researcher will have access and who will read the report are most likely to be members of that group.

Typical design considerations also often promote a status quo view. Researchers should be aware that, when they limit their selection of independent variables to a particular set, they're implicitly stating that other variables are irrelevant or unchangeable. It's no accident that biogeneticists offer genetic solutions, economists see economic solutions, and lawyers offer legal solutions. Obviously, one must limit one's choice of variables in order to actually *do* a finite piece of research. But most evaluations limit their comparisons to those who receive the program and those who don't, ignoring (both in the design and in the final report) the social-structural conditions within which the program operates—and thus implying that these conditions are a constant.

Researchers have also been employed as the heavy; they were particularly useful (and used) in the conservative climate of recessionist restraint and fiscal retrenchment in the late 1970s and early 1980s. Most programs that have been evaluated show little or no direct effect in the social areas they have been designed to address (Weiss 1975). For example, consider a study like Campbell and Ross's (1968) classic evaluation of the Connecticut speeding crackdown. Campbell clearly selected that program as the one to write about because it allowed him to illustrate principles of quasi-experimental design. Governor Ribicoff conveniently made his pronouncement at the end of the calendar year, thus

affording an easier year-to-year comparison. The change he introduced was implemented swiftly, intensely, and pervasively. And even in that situation, the picture *could* have been more clear-cut, since regression artifacts were never completely dispensed with as a rival plausible explanation.

So how much *can* be expected of any more modest program? One more hour of counselling isn't going to eliminate crime, and one more housing development is not going to eliminate poverty. Nor is one more program of any kind going to alleviate all our social ills. So why are some programs picked for evaluation and others not? "The evaluation researcher—now that somebody was paying attention to findings—was cast in the role of political hatchet man" (Weiss 1975: 23). Evaluations of particular programs have often been treated as synonymous with evaluations of the *objectives* that underlie them. Rather than leading us to seek alternative ways of pursuing worthy social goals, evaluations often lead decision makers to cut funding for certain programs as a class and hence for the goals that those aim to reach. The political dilemma has been a real one for many researchers, who feel uncomfortable seeing programs that address important social objectives being terminated without replacement.

SO WHAT CAN A PERSON DO?

Weiss (1975) offers three pieces of advice for dealing with this array of potential pitfalls and complexities. First, she suggests that program goals be put "in sensible perspective," a task, we have argued, that requires attention to the plurality of goals represented by multiple constituencies. If one is going to believe in the virtues of heterogeneity and tolerance, then one must tolerate heterogeneity of perspectives and address these in the context of one's research design. Certainly one must consider alternative models of social justice to the utilitarian one that so pervasively guides evaluation research (e.g., see House 1976; Pepinsky 1987; Rawls 1971).

Weiss's (1975) second piece of advice is "to evaluate a particularly strong version of the program before, or along with, the evaluation of the ordinary levels at which it functions" (23). Clearly, such an approach would represent a fairer test of the efficacy of any given piece of social tinkering at its best. It is also consistent with Campbell's (1969b) notion of the "experimenting society," where we essentially adopt a local "pilot policy" approach to assess the prospective large-scale effect of policy alternatives. The articulation (and hence greater accountability) of social objectives that such a society would require might promote a welcome dialogue. But in practice, this advice brings us back to the status quo orientation inherent in the evaluation process when researchers limit themselves to the perspective of the funding agency. As Henry (1987) argues, even when one is critical of or attempts to set oneself apart from some other group, any discussion in that group's terms serves only to reaffirm its perspective—and hence its power.

This brings us to Weiss's (1975) third admonition, which is to do something *other than* evaluation research. She may be overly narrow in her implied definition of evaluation research as in-house evaluation bound by the perspective of the funding agency. But we concur with her statement that too often

> we concentrate attention on changing the attitudes and behaviour of target groups without concomitant attention to the institutional structures and social arrangements that tend to keep them "target groups." ... There may be greater potential in doing research on the processes that give rise to social problems, the institutional structures that contribute to their origin and persistence, the social arrangements that overwhelm efforts to eradicate them, and the points at which they are vulnerable to societal intervention. (24)

Our caveat to Weiss is that we perceive her extolled goals to be "evaluation research" as well, and thus to be no more or less likely to represent or support the "status quo" than the model she rejects. More directly, we believe that a plurality of perspectives should be fostered, at whatever level of analysis. This approach leads us (in different terms) to argue for the development of social theory, that is, "to think in new categories and suggest different orders

of intervention" (Weiss 1975: 24). Certainly, there are literatures that assess social structures on dimensions that are more conducive to independence from the status quo, for example, the literature that assesses social and economic policy from a "social control" perspective (e.g., see Lowman, Menzies, & Palys 1987).

SUMMING UP AND LOOKING AHEAD

Chapter 9 shows the logic underlying traditional laboratory experimentation; the current chapter encourages you to consider the principles underlying the inference process and to translate those to the investigation of behaviour in the world. But "quasi-experimentation" often retains some of the vestiges of the laboratory, particularly (1) the nomothetic testing of differences in central tendency between groups; (2) a unidirectional view of causality, where independent variables impose their effect on dependent variables; and (3) the positivist notion that "proportion of variance accounted for" is synonymous with "explanation" (i.e., successful prediction *is* explanation).

We now intend to push Campbell's contribution further, showing in the process that the three dimensions noted above are also mere trappings of traditional research rather than inherent in the empirical process. In doing so, we'll offer a rapprochement that attempts to reconcile what have been seen as largely mutually exclusive and competing epistemological models. The central theme in the upcoming chapters is that, regardless of the particular level of analysis we adopt, and regardless of whether our research is consistent with or critical of the status quo, there *is* a general set of epistemological principles that provide a useful guide for our research by facilitating inference about the loci of stability and change.

STUDY QUESTIONS

1. What are some advantages and disadvantages of laboratory experimentation?
2. State John Stuart Mill's three criteria for inferring the existence of a "causal" relationship,

and explain how these criteria are met by the traditional experiment.

3. In traditional laboratory experimentation, internal validity is maximized by randomly assigning participants to groups and by creating control groups that are equivalent to the experimental group(s) in all respects *except* for the independent variable. But those luxuries are frequently not available in field settings. What substitutes for them in quasi-experimental research, and how do those alternatives address the elimination of rival plausible explanations?

4. What is the difference between *manipulative* control and *analytic* control? What are their similarities?

5. According to Donald T. Campbell, why must researchers always be *particularly* vigilant about checking for *regression toward the mean* (otherwise known as *statistical regression*) when evaluating the effectiveness of social programs?

6. What advantages do *time-series* and *multiple time-series* designs have over a simple *pretest/posttest* design?

7. Field researchers often face evaluation research situations in which they must deal with intact groups who know about and can share information regarding the evaluation. What new threats to internal validity arise from this state of affairs? Explain how these *are* threats to internal validity, and in each case suggest how the researcher can prepare for or deal with those problems.

8. Photo radar has been touted by governments as an effective tool for getting drivers to reduce their speed and thereby reduce accidents. However, critics argue that it does nothing to the accident rate and is really nothing more than a "cash cow" to generate revenue from speeding tickets. Photo radar was introduced in British Columbia on August 2, 2000. In the first month alone (August), more than 49 000 speeding tickets were sent out to speeders caught by photo radar. Danielle and Sanjeeta undertook a study to determine whether the advent of photo radar was indeed effective in reducing the number of accidents on B.C. roads as the police had suggested.

Danielle and Sanjeeta approached the government-run Insurance Corporation of B.C. for relevant accident data and took the only data they were offered, which showed accident records for August 1999 and August 2000 for ten regions of the province (areas around the province's ten largest business centres) in which photo radar was used in the first month of operation. These data revealed that, in every one of the ten jurisdictions, there were fewer accidents after the introduction of photo radar (in August 2000) than in the same month the previous year (August 1999). Danielle and Sanjeeta did the appropriate statistical test on the data and found that, overall, the reduction in accidents was statistically significant.

a. What is the *independent variable* in Danielle and Sanjeeta's research?

b. What is the *dependent variable*?

c. What are two *rival plausible explanations* (RPEs) that you believe may threaten the internal validity of their research? What data you would ask for/obtain to address those RPEs?

d. What is *external validity*? Give two specific concerns Danielle and Sanjeeta might have regarding the external validity of their study.

e. Would a *time-series* or *multiple time-series* be useful for Danielle and Sanjeeta? What advantages might if offer them?

9. In what sense is evaluation research part of a political process? What can the researcher do to avoid being or becoming a mere pawn in that process?

NOTES

1. Professor Campbell then spent many years at Lehigh University in Bethlehem, Pennsylvania. He was a great man who was very generous

with his time to younger scholars like Ted, who had the honour of spending some of his first sabbatical with him. Campbell passed away in the spring of 1996, at the age of 81.

2. The "gee whiz" graph is a mainstay of many advertising campaigns because the existence of change is so obvious and convincing (Huff 1954). Of course, as researchers we need to go beyond such hype and consider the evidence for change and its causes.

3. Note that "true" here implies an attempt to get back to the *ceteris paribus* purity of the laboratory experiment. The researcher's task is to decide whether the nature of the diffusion is indeed threatening to the research objectives or whether the diffusion itself is merely a part of the real world process, where *ceteris* is never *paribus*. A time-series design that incorporates some measure of the rate of diffusion will be most helpful in either case.

4. Because the changes occurred in only those two provinces, the possibility of doing a rather nice quasi-experiment presents itself. The dependent variables of interest could be twofold: (1) the effects on smuggling that the policy change was designed to bring about, and (2) the effects on smoking rates (since many had argued that lowering prices would encourage greater tobacco consumption) that the policy change was designed to bring about.

5. Murphy's law, a rule originated by engineers, states that if something *can* go wrong, it will.

CHAPTER 11

ANALYTIC CONTROL IN QUALITATIVE CASE STUDY ANALYSIS

Several methodological features of qualitative approaches have been outlined so far in this book: we've noted that qualitative research is typically inductive and places a high value on preliminary exploration (Chapter 2), extols the virtues of target or purposive sampling (Chapter 4), and emphasizes that one should maintain flexibility and reap the advantages of more open-ended research instruments (see, for example, Chapters 6, 7, and 8).

Qualitative researchers also were described as particularly interested in the *processes* through which phenomena are produced. Phenomena are scrutinized by these researchers with an eye toward how they "unfold" and "evolve," and this view is reflected again in the belief that sensitive inductive research should similarly "unfold" and "evolve" as more and more is understood about the phenomenon or research site under consideration.

As the above summary implies, the process of gathering and analyzing qualitative data can be a challenging business. Since decisions about research instruments and research designs are *not* all made ahead of time but must be continually reconsidered as the work progresses, much depends on investigator competence in the field.

The ad hoc aspects of the qualitative research decision-making process also make it more difficult to describe how to do well. Although we've explained in earlier chapters how qualitative researchers might approach an interview or ethnographic study, the ways that your strategies might change as the research evolves become very situation-specific. Thus, instead of simply dealing with a decision *situation,* where we can discuss the relative advantages and disadvantages of choosing from among the various options open to you, we're given the task of describing an infinite number of possible decision *sequences,* each of which may make sense only when considered as a whole in its unique context.

It would be nice if one could point to examples of qualitative research in which the author(s) self-consciously discussed the decision points they faced, and how and why they made the decisions they did, but there have been few such accounts. Instead, romanticized tales of anthropologists in exotic locales maintaining their field notes under an oil lamp at the end of each day (e.g., see Clifford & Marcus 1986), the **chutzpah** of the urban sociologist studying gang members and social misfits whom many would fear to approach (e.g., see Duneier 1999; Miller & Tewksbury 2001), and the legendary status that some qualitative analyses have acquired—Malinowski's (1922) *Argonauts of the Western Pacific;* Mead's (1928/1960) *Coming of Age in Samoa;* Whyte's (1943) *Street Corner Society;* Goffman's (1961) *Asylums;* and Becker's (1963) *Outsiders,* to name but a few—combine to promote a certain qualitative mystique.

Even recent articles find it difficult to refrain from referring to the "art" of gathering qualitative data (e.g., Fontana & Frey 1994) and to the general lack of clear criteria by which to evaluate the adequacy of qualitative analysis (e.g., see Huberman & Miles 1994). Many other descriptions of qualitative methods avoid the task entirely by doing little more than tell you to find an interesting research site, empathize with the people there, and write down everything you can in your field notes. The impression given is that if you've spent enough time and gathered enough data, your dedication ultimately will be rewarded with the insightful analysis that inevitably emerges from such rich data.

However well-intentioned those recommendations may be, they do little to raise the confidence of the novice, who would probably prefer to receive more in the way of guidelines before heading out to the field. It's a bit like telling aspiring physicians in medical school about the "art" of proper diagnosis, and then sending them out the door to diagnose and heal people; the advice, while both direct and true, doesn't help very much if you're still unclear about what to do. This chapter (1) examines some of the characteristics and techniques of qualitative data analysis, (2) considers some of the ways in which those characteristics and techniques can help achieve the varying objectives of qualitative researchers, and (3) provides examples—both real and fictitious—that illustrate some of those analytical methods. This approach is not intended to refute the idea that some part of any research project is "artful" in its completion, but should at least take the discussion from the realm of the mystical into areas where guiding principles and the wisdom of exemplars can be learned (and learned from) and where challenges to our competence can be identified.

QUALITATIVE ANALYSIS AS AN ITERATIVE PROCESS

One characteristic of qualitative study is its iterative nature. An **iterative process** is one that is cyclical but not merely repetitive. Instead, the term also connotes increasing sophistication or change, as in a feedback loop, where each successive pass is different from the one preceding. In that sense, to describe a process as iterative is to suggest more the form of a spiral than that of a circle, with each cycle taking us a little further in some identifiable direction.

Successive *iterations* in qualitative research are evident at both the data gathering and data analysis stages. With respect to data gathering, the length of time one spends at the research site and with partic-

ipants is often quite extensive, so that *repeat* visits and *re*-interviews are commonplace. Indeed, it's largely for this reason that the admonition to allow one's analysis to evolve makes sense.

Consistent with this notion of successive iteration is the distinction Huberman and Miles (1994) make between "loose" and "tight" qualitative designs:

> [Loose designs] work well when the terrain is unfamiliar and/or excessively complex, a single case is involved, and the intent is exploratory and descriptive. Tighter designs are indicated when the researcher has good prior acquaintance with the setting, has a good bank of applicable, well-delineated concepts, and takes a more explanatory and/or confirmatory stance involving multiple, comparable cases. (431)

They add that data gathering can be most voluminous during early iterations, when the design is loose. Since one's efforts are still largely unfocused, few decisions can be made about what is and isn't "important" to save, and one should err on the side of inclusiveness until those criteria are decided. But as the research progresses, one becomes more and more selective, since decisions can now be made about what's "relevant" to the objectives of the study and what's not. The process is iterative to the extent that as one visits and re-visits the research site, and interviews and re-interviews those who reside there, each repetition comes with an increasing backlog of understanding and should be designed to take you closer to an increasingly well-defined goal.

A helpful aspect of the Huberman and Miles (1994) distinction is that it also speaks to the question of research objectives and notes how those will shift over time: from exploratory and descriptive to explanatory and/or confirmatory. And despite the qualitative admonition to maintain extensive field notes, the researcher should be thinking from the start about *data reduction*.[1] Exploration and description are not, after all, simply ends in themselves; they're the processes through which one identifies those elements that are important to investigate further, and the description one engages in should be of those elements that are most integral to developing explanations about the phenomenon of interest.

From Description to Explanation

IDENTIFYING PATTERNS, THEMES, AND CLUSTERS
Huberman and Miles (1994) suggest that preliminary description often involves *noting patterns* and *themes* that are observed in the setting and/or revealed in interviews, and *clustering* similar people, events, or processes together to begin making categories and help one see connections among objects/people/events. A variety of analytical techniques can be used to help you identify patterns, themes, and clusters.

TELLING A STORY Lofland and Lofland (1995) suggest that one technique is to try to write a story that summarizes in, say, a page or less, "what is going on here" or "how X happens." Outlining the plot and characters through such an exposition can be most informative in letting you know what you know, as well as what you don't know, thereby helping you identify where gaps still exist that must be filled in by further data. Remember that the "explanation" you're trying to develop is a detailed and compelling analysis of how a certain phenomenon is produced; what better way to begin than by engaging in the reality check of trying to offer such an explanation at the start?

Writing successive stories as you spend more and more time in the field can also be an invaluable source of archival information. If you look at all your stories together at a later point in the process, you're probably more likely to recognize the understandings you brought to the research site. You can then evaluate not only how your understandings developed over time, but also how your initial understandings may have constrained what you *could* find because of where you initially looked.

USING METAPHOR Although preliminary descriptions and explanations are bound to be fairly concrete, this is also a time to try to begin thinking about the processes involved in more abstract and conceptual terms. This level of theoretical abstraction helps connect you with the literature (and, indeed, helps identify what literatures are "relevant" to your situation) and is what will ultimately make your account "meaningful" or "interesting" from a social scientific perspective. One way to engage this conceptual realm is to use *metaphors;* these will get creative juices flowing and possibly connect you with other concepts and conceptual networks that can prove useful in identifying further lines of inquiry.

For example, if we were trying to explain the process of writing a book, we might try to imagine how writing a book is like playing a game of baseball. The team's manager (the author) must choose the starting lineup (the preliminary list of chapter titles) and develop strategies (explanations) that use his or her players (the author's strengths and weaknesses) most effectively in order to win the game (complete an informative and readable book). But does that metaphor in itself capture all that went into writing a book?

Having established the baseball metaphor, we can then look to other elements of the metaphor and ask whether they have analogues within the process we are trying to explain. For example, how do the rules of baseball fit in? Who are the opposing managers and the umpires? Is there a seventh-inning stretch? Extending the metaphor, we can recount that in writing a book, the author must also consider the rules of the game (expectations readers have about what sorts of elements will be included; constraints regarding page length that are imposed by the publisher), and he or she must be prepared to deal with the opposing managers (critics who operate from different sets of assumptions and understandings regarding what research is all about and who want the game to go "their" way) and the umpires (independent reviewers) over judgment calls and rule interpretations that may emerge.

Of course, other metaphors might be even more useful. Perhaps it would be better to compare "writing a book" with "preparing a meal" or "giving birth." Each approach would no doubt shed a slightly different light on the process of writing a book, and which is "best" depends in part on what you know and what you've experienced. For example, the two of us have coached, played baseball, and prepared many meals; hence we have some understanding of what those processes involve. But neither of us has given birth, and therefore would be more limited in how thoroughly we could explore that metaphor. And while just about any metaphor will do in order to get one's creative juices flowing, it's probably also true that in a given situation, some metaphors will have more potential than others because of their intrinsic similarity (or not) to the process you want to describe (e.g., we'd have a somewhat harder— although not impossible—time working with the metaphor "writing a book is like doing the laundry").

COMPARE AND CONTRAST Not unlike the use of metaphor is the tactic of making *contrasts and comparisons*. This activity can take many different forms, but the most common are *within-case* and *between-case* comparisons, where the "case" might be a particular person, setting, event, or process. If looking within a particular individual, for example, you might find it useful to compare how he or she acts in the company of strangers as opposed to that of friends, under stressful conditions as opposed to more relaxed ones, or when the person knows that she or he is being monitored as opposed to when she or he does not.

When *multiple* cases are available for comparison, whether explicitly (because we're dealing with multiple cases in the research setting) or implicitly (because there are other case studies in the literature that we can compare our setting to), a consideration of how the cases are similar to or different from one another may help attune us to useful explanatory concepts. These cases may be conceptualized either fairly concretely (e.g., what principles does Ingrid employ when making discretionary choices, as opposed to Su Mei?) or on the basis of other clustered categories of analytical interest (e.g., how does the experience of visible-minority employees seem to differ from that of the majority?).

Indeed, concrete comparisons are often the springboard from which clusters and their more conceptual category designations are derived. After comparing Ingrid's style to Su Mei's, we might also note that Ingrid's style is shared by Pat, Riaz, and Lewis, while Su Mei's style is emulated by Barinder, Jane and Simon. This observation may help us develop categories that are useful for describing differences (e.g., we believe that the style used by Ingrid et al. is more "autocratic," while that used by Su Mei et al. is more "consultative"). At the same time, constantly having to ask "Where does *this* one fit?" spurs us to both develop and hone those categories so that we can be rigorous in our use of them (e.g., isolate specific examples of each decision-making style to remind ourselves and eventual readers of what we mean).

EXAMINING RELATIONS AMONG CONCEPTS/ VARIABLES With clusters of individuals and preliminary conceptual variables of interest isolated, one then can examine *relations* among those concepts in the context of varying events. For example, the notion of "decision-making style" that we derived from comparing Ingrid and Su Mei may attune us to other dynamics within a research setting. We might start to notice that Su Mei's consultative style involves more ongoing contact and communication with those she supervises, while Ingrid's more autocratic style is associated with greater connectedness to the more senior administrators within the organization.

This observation may in turn help us "make sense" of other phenomena in which elements of decision-making style are influential *variables* to consider. For example, it might help explain why Su Mei is more popular among those she supervises than Ingrid is among her subordinates, or help us understand "similarities of decision-making style" as an *intervening variable* (e.g., it may account for why Ingrid regularly receives more positive performance evaluations from Pat, who shares Ingrid's leadership preferences and tends to see Su Mei as "indecisive" and "not in touch with senior management").

DRAWING PICTURES Field notes and developing analyses also will benefit from efforts to represent your understandings visually. Doing so may be as simple as trying to draw some boxes on a page, and then trying to fill them with grouped exemplars of the differing constructs you have been identifying. Drawing circles around related boxes may then help you to identify meta-constructs (at an even higher level of abstraction or generality). Or you might draw arrows to represent directions of influence or use them to show links between different groups or processes. Similarly, flow charts of processes, or maps of the physical environment, may help you articulate relations between groups (of people or constructs or whatever) or may lead you to reconsider these relationships in otherwise unanticipated ways.

COUNTING Despite the fact that we're talking about *qualitative* data analysis here, there's still a fundamental role to be played by *counting*. As Huberman and Miles (1994) remind us, counting helps keep us honest, while simultaneously helping us avoid some of the more insidious biases that can creep into our conclusions, such as the following:

◆ data overload in the field, leading to the analysts thus missing important information, over-weighting some findings, skewing the analysis

◆ salience of first impressions or of observations of highly concrete or dramatic incidents

◆ selectivity, overconfidence in some data, especially when trying to confirm a key finding

◆ co-occurrences taken as correlations, or even as causal relationships

◆ false base-rate proportions: extrapolation of the number of total instances from those observed

◆ unreliability of information from some sources

◆ overaccommodation to information that questions outright a tentative hypothesis (438)

For example, once we've refined our definitions of "decision-making style" and decided on the sorts of events we'll consider "autocratic" or "consultative," we may then want to systematically count all the various decisions by Ingrid and Su Mei that we've witnessed. On doing so, we may find that Ingrid isn't as autocratic as she at first seemed; after reviewing our field notes, we may realize that our categorization of her was unduly influenced by her actions during one particularly dramatic and memorable crisis.

Counting therefore helps us assess the *representativeness* of the phenomena we believe we are witnessing (e.g., just how often *are* significant decisions made? What proportion of the time are those decisions autocratically or consultatively derived?). Counting is also a way to look at how well our initial speculations about the relationships among variables are actually supported by data. For example, is it really the case that Su Mei engages in more frequent interaction with those she supervises, while Ingrid interacts more frequently with more senior administrators? If so, our speculation that that pattern is related to why Ingrid receives the more positive performance evaluations may have some merit and will deserve further scrutiny; if not, we'll have to begin looking somewhere else.

And finally, since the act of counting requires categorization, having to decide whether to count an event as a *this* or a *that* will have the positive effect of always demanding that we define and redefine our categories. Over time, this steady refinement will in turn require us to reexamine whether our preliminary categories are workable or not, adequate or in need of revision; it may also suggest other possibilities that might be even more useful. This result will be particularly likely if we ensure that we remain attuned to **negative cases,** that is, cases that don't "fit" the categories we've identified or that don't follow the pattern of relationships we imagine are there.

CONSTRUCTING EXPLANATIONS

Atkinson (quoted in Lofland & Lofland 1995) offers an appropriate summary that reflects the challenge of constructing explanations:

Making it all come together ... is one of the most difficult things of all ... Quite apart from actually achieving it, it is hard to inject the right mix of (a) *faith* that it can and will be achieved; (b) recognition that it has to be *worked* at, and isn't based on romantic inspiration; (c) that it isn't like the solution to a puzzle or math problem, but has to be *created;* (d) that you can't pack *everything* into one version, and that any one project could yield several different ways of bringing it together. (181; *emphasis* in original)

The various techniques described above should prove useful in generating descriptions and explanations in your qualitative research. At the same time, through such techniques as counting, and the successive iterations involved in developing theoretical constructs, speculating on relationships, and testing both, you can help ensure a high standard of rigour in your analysis. But while adopting those techniques can do much to enhance both the quality of your analysis and your confidence in its validity, you must always consider (as should any researcher doing any kind of research) that the explanation you've created is a constructed one and not the only "valid" description that could be drawn from your data.

CAN QUALITATIVE CASE STUDY BE "SCIENTIFIC"?
Although the above discussion affirms that qualitative analysis can be systematic and rigorous, the question of whether qualitative case study can meet the validity criteria of "science" with respect to *causal* analysis has been the topic of considerable debate. Some authors have suggested that the question itself is meaningless. Huberman and Miles (1994), for example, note that the very possibility of undertaking causal analysis in the context of qualitative research "is often attacked from both the right ('Only controlled quantitative experiments can do that') and the left ('Causality is an unworkable concept in human behaviour—people are not billiard balls')" (434).

Of those who *have* engaged the debate, both the nature of their arguments and the resolutions they've

offered are illustrative. For example, Donald T. Campbell, a formidable individual in 20th-century social science who also happens to have had more quantitative roots, initially rejected outright the idea that case study analysis could ever be done in any manner that might warrant the label "scientific." His classic monograph with Julian Stanley, for example, asserted that

[case] studies have such a total absence of control as to be of almost no scientific value ... Such studies often involve tedious collection of specific detail, careful observation, testing, and the like, and, in such instances, involve the error of *misplaced precision* ... It seems well-nigh unethical at the present time to allow, as theses or dissertations ... case studies of this nature. (Campbell & Stanley 1963: 6–7; italics in original)

The lack of control Campbell and Stanley (1963) cited here results largely from the problem of having too *many* possible explanations and too *few* observations against which to assess the comparative plausibility of those explanations. Quantitative statistical perspectives, which extol the virtues of aggregate analysis, require that you have more observations (i.e., cases, respondents) than you have explanatory variables. At the very least, the number of cases should be twice the number of variables; ideally, the ratio should be more like ten to one.

But at the time, Campbell believed that those ideal ratios were completely absent in the case study. Later, in retrospect, he explained why:

The caricature of the single case study approach which I had in mind consists of an observer who notes a single striking characteristic of a culture, and then has available all of the other differences on all other variables to search through in finding an explanation ... That he will find an "explanation" that seems to fit perfectly is inevitable, through his total lack of "degrees of freedom." (It is as though he were trying to fit two points of observation with a formula including a thousand adjustable terms, whereas in good science, we must have fewer terms in our formula than our data points.) (Campbell 1979b: 54)

We observed an example of what Campbell seems to have had in mind here when a local man received considerable media attention on the occasion of his 109th birthday. Interviews always seemed to include the inevitable question "So why do you think you've lived so long?" As methodologists, we shuddered. The situation involves one case (i.e., $N = 1$), one datum (i.e., the man is 109 years old), and a virtual *lifetime* of explanatory variables from which to pick the one we think explains his longevity.

Scientifically speaking, there's absolutely no way to decide in such a situation whether any one explanation for the man's longevity (e.g., because he had a wonderful wife) is any more or less plausible than any other (e.g., because he had a shot of Scotch every night before going to bed). In those circumstances, *any* account that attempts to explain a case study phenomenon is free to serve the interests of the explainer, because no logical criteria are available for us to choose from among the many equally plausible rival explanations that might be offered. Campbell was thus correct in saying that "case studies" of that sort can never meet the criteria of valid inference. But was he correct in characterizing *all* case study research in that way?

Life as a Case Study

An interesting implication of Campbell's preliminary analysis would be that much of what we experience in life can *never* be analyzed "scientifically" (Campbell & Stanley 1963); after all, what is life but a never-ending case study? Think about what you see in the newspapers and on the TV news every day:

◆ The Internet creates a global communications network that is faster and more accessible than anything that has existed before. How did it arise? What are its effects?

◆ The stock market reaches record highs with each passing week. Why?

◆ Right-wing political parties have replaced left-wing political parties in several provincial legislatures and state governments. Why?

◆ Aboriginal rights groups protest a federal change of policy that occurred without their participation and consent. Why?

The facts of our less newsworthy lives similarly beg for explanation: Why did the professor give me a C+ on that paper? Why does my partner all of a sudden seem so uninterested in me? Why am I still working on a degree in social work when I'd really rather be an architect? *Most of our lives* are spent dealing with case studies, where $N = 1$ (e.g., one person, one policy, one country, one issue, or one crisis). Does this mean that it's theoretically *impossible* for us to make any rigorous analytical sense of these situations?

The error of Campbell's earlier criticism (Campbell & Stanley 1963) was later addressed by several authors with the recognition that not only *can* we make rigorous sense of given case studies, but that we do it all the time. Indeed, many individuals do so—and do so very well—as part of making a living. Michael Scriven (1976), for example, points to a variety of professions whose practitioners *routinely* make rigorous decisions about the "causes" underlying specific case study phenomena:

◆ The historian attempts to explain why King John signed the *Magna Carta* at Runnymede in 1215.

◆ The coroner must ascertain the cause of death for each individual corpse.

◆ The physician, in order to prescribe an effective treatment, must diagnose why that rash appeared on your forearm.

◆ The engineering troubleshooter must ascertain why the bridge fell down during a recent flood.

- The mechanic must figure out why your car doesn't start.

- The detective seeks to determine "whodunit."

- The transit investigator must determine why one subway train crashed into another.

If "scientific" case study analysis were impossible, how could these people make sense out of these case study situations? And why are some people better at it than others?

Causal Checklists and the Modus Operandi Method

As Scriven (1976) describes it, common to all these occupations is an underlying logic to their inquiry, which he refers to as a **modus operandi method.** The analytical challenge common to all the examples noted above is to identify a cause or a set of causes for a given phenomenon. But where and how do we begin?

Invariably, we begin by relying heavily on existing knowledge, whether derived from the more formal literature or from our "common sense." We never enter a situation devoid of theoretical constructs: there's no such thing as "immaculate perception." Campbell (1969b) metaphorically describes knowledge as a ship rotting at sea—we know the ship is rotten, but we can't merely take it apart and reconstruct it or we'd sink! Thus we're left to change the ship one plank at a time, relying on all those other old planks (some rotten and some not) to keep the structure together and afloat as we replace its parts, eventually creating a whole new ship. New knowledge can't be created unless we trust a good portion of the knowledge we already have.

The "knowledge" we do have may vary from scientific to intuitive, but whatever its nature, Scriven (1976) says that we'll use it in "problem" situations as a source for generating "causal checklists." For example, suppose your car doesn't start and your mechanic now has the task of fixing it. Fixing the car requires first diagnosing why it does not start. The mechanic approaches your car knowing that numerous factors must combine in order for a car to start: among other things, there must be gas in it, the key must be turned, the ignition system must function properly, the battery must not be dead, spark plugs and points must be clean and properly set, and so on. In order to determine why your car doesn't start, the mechanic begins with what Scriven calls a "presence or absence check" to see whether each of the causal requirements is met.

In research jargon, the mechanic seeks to generate and consider *rival plausible explanations* that might account for the phenomenon of interest. Is there gas in the car? Are the plugs and points okay? Is the battery charged? If all but one of the causal requirements are met (e.g., the battery is dead, but there's gas in the car, the points and plugs look fine, etc.), then *that* is the probable cause. If *none* of the causal requirements appears to be absent (i.e., everything in the initial checklist seems fine), we may try to expand the list of possibilities by considering more remote alternatives, by applying causal lists from analogous phenomena, or by asking other knowledgeable people to suggest further possibilities.

In the event that *more than one* plausible factor emerges, Scriven (1976) suggests that we look for a modus operandi (MO) to help identify the actual cause, just as a detective might identify a criminal by the characteristic manner in which a crime is executed. Scriven (1976) goes on to explain that "the MO of a particular cause is an associated configuration of events, processes, or properties, usually in time sequence, which can often be described as the characteristic causal chain ... connecting the cause with the effect" (105).

Of course, one must have—through prior research or experience—a reasonable understanding of particular MOs and a decent list of rival plausible causes. Given that one has such a list, Scriven says, the following procedures apply: first, check for the presence or absence of each plausible cause in this situation. If only one plausible cause is present (or, in some cases, if only one is absent), the factor that's present (or absent) is the most likely cause; if more than one plausible cause is present, check for the presence of complete MOs. If only one MO is present, the cause associated with that MO is the cause in this case. If no recognizable MOs are present, none of the factors in the preliminary causal list is the cause; look for others. If more than one MO is evident, the causes that produce those MOs are likely co-causes.

Although the above account may be helpful the next time you try to figure out why your toaster isn't popping, the important point for the purposes of this book is that the logic Scriven (1976) espouses is not particularly distant from the experimentalist logic of inference discussed in Chapters 9 and 10. Once again, the technique involves systematically generating and considering rival plausible explanations, looking for relevant data that will help you compare their relative plausibility, and trying to isolate the most likely causal factor(s). The name of the game is to achieve control over rival plausible explanations. But instead of using *manipulative control* as one might do in an experiment, you exercise *analytic control* to achieve the same effect (see Palys 1989).

Examples like the above may well have played a role in Campbell's reconsideration of the possibility and plausibility of case study analysis, and he later (e.g., 1979b) revised his position. Scriven's (1976) comments show that engaging in case study analysis involves more than merely explaining *one datum*. Although the physician begins with one phenomenon to be explained (e.g., the fact that you have a pain in your stomach), a "good" explanation and effective treatment require that a *whole set of related data also* be considered (e.g., exactly where the pain is located, whether the pains are acute or chronic, your eating habits, how much stress you've been under, and so on) and that any explanation you offer must be consistent with the *complete web* of evidence. Taken together, these examples leave us to conclude that rigorous case study analysis does seem to be possible.

At the same time, two aspects of the above examples must be noted. First, the "causes" being assessed address only the most mechanistic meanings of that term. Second, the operating principles of toasters and cars are well known, so that "searching through rival plausible explanations" may be less clear-cut in

the social sciences. How well Scriven's (1976) modus operandi method can translate to the social sciences—where the challenge is to understand the dynamics of a *human* milieu and where, in any event, most social scientists consider "cause" in a much less determinative fashion—needs to be considered.

RIVAL PLAUSIBLE EXPLANATIONS IN THE CASE STUDY CONTEXT

In a particular social science research situation, a specific list of rival plausible explanations to consider may or may not exist; if it does exist, it may or may not be well developed. We've reviewed Campbell's (e.g., 1957; Campbell & Stanley 1963) efforts to articulate general classes of threats to internal validity in quantitative experimental research (e.g., selection, history, regression toward the mean; see Chapter 9). Later efforts (e.g., Cook & Campbell 1979) discuss threats that are uniquely problematic in quasi-experimental field settings (e.g., compensatory equalization and compensatory rivalry; see Chapter 10).

In the qualitative case study realm, rival plausible explanations must also be considered, but to date little effort has been devoted to systematically articulating threats in the manner of Campbell. A creative example to the contrary, however, comes from Howard Becker. Besides his other talents, Becker is also a photographer. He became curious about photo archives as a source of historical data, which in turn led to his writing an essay that considers the "truth value" of photographs, "Do Photographs Tell the Truth?" (Becker 1979).

At one level, Becker (1979) argues, *every* photograph is "true," insofar as any picture results from a purely mechanical/chemical process that occurs when rays of light reflect off the object in front of the camera and strike the film, thereby recording an image of the object. But, Becker notes, one could equally well assert that every photograph is to some degree "false," since one could easily have taken a very different photograph of exactly the same scene, a photo that might have resulted in a totally different set of inferences being made. How can we decide which of those two characterizations is more appropriate for any given photograph?

Becker's (1979) discussion focuses chiefly on an explicit consideration of reasons why a particular photo might be *false:* (1) the photo was faked (e.g., retouched, contrived); (2) the photographer was more interested in esthetic concerns (e.g., impact, genre) than in creating a historical record; (3) the photo inadequately samples events (e.g., focusing on unrepresentative parts of the action); and/or (4) censorship, whether externally or internally imposed, was involved. Each of these threats to the validity of an image has a parallel in interactive research: (1) data might be "fraudulent" in the sense that respondents may distort the representation of their beliefs or behaviour; (2) researchers may give an unrepresentative edge to their work by limiting it to a particular ideological genre; (3) data may be sampled inadequately; and/or (4) censorship, whether self-imposed or externally imposed, may influence the range of inferences.

In telling you about Becker (1979), we are not aiming to encourage you to consider the truth value of photographs per se; rather, we hope to draw your attention to the *process* he followed, exactly the process that any researcher should follow when examining his or her data. More specifically, the researcher is compelled not only to try to create an account that "explains" the data, but also to try to consider all the various reasons why that account might *not* be true. In qualitative data analysis, these requirements appear not only when considering the "truth value" to ascribe to any particular datum, but also when engaged in negative case analysis in the context of *analytic induction*.

Analytic Induction

Although notions of inductive analysis have a lengthier history in philosophy, analytic induction was first described as a social science technique by Znaniecki in 1934 (according to Berg 1989) and is now a standard inclusion when qualitative techniques are outlined (e.g., Denzin 1989; Manning 1991; Silverman 1985; Strauss 1987; Vidich & Lyman 1994). Denzin (1989) describes analytic induction as a procedural analogue to experimenta-

tion that borrows the notion of experimental and control groups to direct attention not only to instances of the phenomenon under study, but also to non-instances, that is, occasions when the phenomenon does not occur. Vidich and Lyman (1994) explain further that

> distinguishable from deductive, historical-documentary, and statistical approaches, analytic induction [is] a "non-experimental sociological method that employs an exhaustive examination of cases in order to prove universal, causal, generalizations." The case method was to be the critical foundation of a revitalized qualitative sociology. (39)

In the context of inductive research, the process begins when the researcher attempts to formulate some generalization or theory to capture the data that were observed (recall Wallace's wheel from Chapter 2). Having formulated a theory, the investigator turns it back on the data in order to systematically test how well the theory actually accounts for the data. Particular attention is to be paid to negative cases, since the times you're wrong can provide particularly rewarding information about how to improve your theory. Lindesmith (1952) describes this process:

> the principle which governs the selection of cases to test a theory is that the chances of discovering a negative case should be maximized. The investigator who has a working hypothesis concerning his data becomes aware of certain areas of critical importance. If his theory is false or inadequate, he knows that its weaknesses will be more clearly and quickly exposed if he proceeds to the investigation of those critical areas. This involves going out of one's way to look for negative evidence. (492)

Kidder (1981a) offers a most explicit articulation of analytic induction in terms of the underlying logic it shares with experimental and particularly quasi-experimental approaches.[2] Her article "Qualitative

Research and Quasi-Experimental Frameworks" reviews several classic studies from the qualitative archives, illuminating how the qualitative procedures may be translated in terms of an underlying quasi-experimental framework and vice versa. In the discussions of Becker (1963) and Cressey (1953) that we offer below, we rely heavily on her analysis.

The basic challenge to the inductive analyst is to offer a general account, or theory, that accurately describes all known instances and non-instances of the phenomenon under study. Becker (1963), for example, in his study of marijuana users, ultimately concluded that there were three prior conditions that all had to be present before an individual would become a regular marijuana user: (1) the person must learn the "proper" smoking techniques that allow an effect to be produced; (2) the person must learn to identify the relatively subtle effects that the drug produces; and (3) the individual must come to define those effects as enjoyable. As Kidder (1981a) describes it, the adequacy of that explanation was tested by assessing the extent to which all known cases (of regular marijuana use, and of non-interest in its use) could be fit into a cross-tabulation like that shown in Table 11.1.

Becker's (1963) analysis can be restated as a formula, where PC stands for "Prior Condition": PC1 + PC2 + PC3 = Regular User. Thus, in all cases where Becker found that a person was a regular marijuana user (i.e., phenomenon present), all three of those prior conditions were present (i.e., upper left-hand quadrant of Table 11.1). And in any case where a person was *not* a regular marijuana user (i.e., phenomenon absent), at least one of those prior conditions was missing (i.e., bottom right-hand quadrant of Table 11.1).

Also deserving of consideration are the remaining two cells of Table 11.1, both of which would be examples of *negative cases,* that is, where Becker's account didn't hold. The bottom left-hand corner would include instances of users (i.e., phenomenon present) who had *not* gone through all three phases specified by Becker. The top right-hand corner would include individuals who *had* gone through all three phases, but even so did not become regular marijuana users.[3] Cases in these two cells would clearly show the analysis to be inadequate or incomplete, since they'd reflect instances in which the theory was "wrong." The analyst's task is thus to formulate progressively better explanations that will empty the cells of negative cases and fill the cells that are consistent with the theory. The final score, in other words, must be 100 to nothing, or the researcher must go back to the drawing board and try again.

The actual process of offering, testing, and revising one's analysis is splendidly demonstrated in Cressey's (1953) study of embezzlers: as Kidder (1981a) notes, Cressey expressly articulates the four successive explanations he tried en route to arriving at a fifth explanation he found satisfactory.[4] On the basis of prior literature and research dealing with white-collar crime, Cressey (1953) relates that he began his investigation thus:

> The first hypothesis ... was that positions of financial trust are violated when the incumbent has learned in connection with the business or profession in which he is employed that some forms of trust violation are merely technical violations and are not really "illegal" or "wrong," and, on the negative side, that they are not violated if this kind of definition of behaviour has not been learned. (27)

Table 11.1

Depiction of Classification of a "Successful" Analytic Induction

		Phenomenon	
		Present	Absent
Prior Conditions	Present	100%	0%
	Absent	0%	100%

Source: Adapted from L. H. Kidder (1981b), *Research Methods in Social Relations,* 4th edition (Orlando, FL: Holt, Rinehart and Winston).

But it took only a few interviews with inmates (convicted embezzlers) for Cressey to realize that the initial hypothesis was inadequate. In terms of Table 11.1, he came across *negative cases* where the phenomenon was present (i.e., the person had embezzled), but the prior conditions specified by the preliminary working hypothesis were absent. Many interviewees indicated that they'd known full well at the time of the embezzlement that their behaviour was wrong and illegal (instances reflected in the lower left-hand quadrant of Table 11.1).

Cressey (1953) went back to the drawing board, returning with Hypothesis 2: "Positions of [financial] trust are violated when the incumbent defines a need for extra funds or extended use of property as an 'emergency' which cannot be met by legal means" (27). Subsequent interviews with embezzlers showed that many of them were well described by the second working hypothesis, since there were many examples of such "triggering" incidents (i.e., hypothesized prior conditions present, phenomenon present). But negative cases were also revealed. Some embezzlers admitted taking funds even when no "emergency" situation existed (i.e., phenomenon present, but hypothesized prior conditions absent). Others indicated that there were occasions where emergencies arose when they did not embezzle (i.e., hypothesized prior conditions present, but phenomenon absent).

Accordingly, a third hypothesis/explanation was formulated: "It shifted the emphasis from emergency to psychological isolation, stating that persons become trust violators when they conceive of themselves as having incurred financial obligations which are ... nonsocially sanctionable and which ... must be satisfied by a private means" (Cressey 1953: 28). An example of this situation might involve an individual who accumulates large gambling debts with a bookie; because such financial obligations are "nonsocially sanctionable," the person might find it difficult to approach a bank manager for a loan.

The revised hypothesis was checked against all cases to date, as well as new ones; once again, Cressey (1953) discovered that it fell short. Negative cases

came to light where the situation that triggered the embezzlement couldn't really be considered a "financial obligation" (i.e., phenomenon present, but hypothesized prior conditions absent) or where the existence of "nonsocially sanctionable" financial obligations wasn't fulfilled by means of embezzlement (i.e., hypothesized prior conditions present, but phenomenon absent). A new explanation was required.

Cressey's (1953) fourth hypothesis differed from the previous one by "emphasizing this time not financial obligations ... but nonshareable *problems*[,] ... that is, ... the subject could be in financial difficulty not only because of an acknowledged responsibility for past debts, but because of present discordance between his income and expenditures as well" (29). Although more successful than all prior attempts, the fourth explanation also revealed negative cases. Cressey (1953) then came to his final revision:

> Trusted persons become trust violators when they conceive of themselves as having a financial problem which is nonshareable, are aware that this problem can be secretly resolved by violation of the position of financial trust, and are able to apply to their own conduct in that situation verbalizations which enable them to adjust their conception of themselves as users of the entrusted funds or property. (30)

The adequacy of this final explanation was tested against all cases for which he had gathered information, and no negative cases were found. The explanation also held when he tested it with 200 other cases compiled by another researcher, and again with another sample of embezzlers interviewed by Cressey himself in a different penitentiary.

In sum, by paying particular attention to negative case analysis in the context of analytic induction, Cressey (1953) was able to formulate an explanation that accounted for all cases, thereby promoting theory development in the area of white-collar crime. Note also that the power of Cressey's analysis was enhanced by the fact that he didn't just content himself with having "explained" the data from his own study, but also tried to use the explanation on *new* cases. Analytic induction is done poorly when one fails to include all relevant cases (e.g., one notices only data that support one's contentions) and one makes no effort to apply the explanatory scheme to information beyond the data used to generate the theory.

Although Cressey (1953) is presented here as an analytic "success," he can be faulted on at least two points: his successive revisions to the theory represented the mere addition of caveats rather than true revision, and his theoretical conclusions are overly limited by the fact that only *convicted* embezzlers were included in his samples. We don't know whether people who get away with embezzling differ in some way from Cressey's samples. It may be, for example, that our "commonsensical" conception of embezzlement as a financially motivated activity makes it more likely that individuals who embezzle for those reasons will get caught. If so, empirical scrutiny of only those who have been caught would simply reaffirm our original understanding about the phenomenon. People who embezzle for completely different reasons may be less likely to get caught because we don't treat them seriously as suspects; hence, they wouldn't end up in prison samples like Cressey's, posing a challenge to his theoretical formulations.

Finally, although analytic induction clearly declares itself to be an inductive technique, more recent formulations have tended to place greater emphasis on the inevitable interplay between induction and deduction, as well as that between theory and data. Strauss (1987), for example, reflects on that in an allusion to his earlier monograph with Glaser on the discovery of "grounded theory" (Glaser & Strauss 1967). He notes: "Because of our earlier writing in *Discovery* (1967) where we attacked speculative theory—quite ungrounded in bodies of data—many people mistakenly refer to grounded theory as 'inductive theory'... But as we have indicated, all three aspects of inquiry (induction, deduction, and verification) are absolutely essential" (12).

AN EXAMPLE: SHERLOCK HOLMES AND "THE ADVENTURE OF SILVER BLAZE"

It's hard to convey the richness of analytic induction in the context of qualitative research, if for no other reason than that the space-saving figures and tables of aggregated quantitative data must be replaced by verbose descriptions of the rationale by which conclusions are generated. Studies that appear in journal article format must fit within the 30- to 35-page limit most journals impose. Many of the classic examples such as Cressey (1953) therefore appear in book-length form, making them tough to summarize in a section of a chapter.

We therefore needed a briefer example of an analysis that illustrates something of the ongoing interaction between theory and data, and induction and deduction, required for a comprehensive analysis. Fortunately, such analyses are prevalent in fiction, where, for example, sleuths sometimes show admirable methodological acumen. In this realm, one can do no better than to look at that master of sleuths, Sherlock Holmes. From Conan Doyle's many suitable stories, we've chosen to focus on "The Adventure of Silver Blaze."[5]

The Phenomena: A Disappearance and a Murder

Silver Blaze is a racehorse, a particularly excellent one who has won many races and prizes for his owner, Colonel Ross. The adventure begins when we find that Silver Blaze has disappeared from his stables and that his trainer, John Straker, has been murdered. Although such a disappearance and murder would likely have been newsworthy in any event, they are particularly so for having occurred within a week of the running of the Wessex Cup, for which Silver Blaze was the favourite until his disappearance.

Holmes, along with many other Britons, has been reading about the case with interest in some of the daily papers. The story begins with his realizing that his preliminary working hypothesis has been refuted. As Holmes describes it,

"I made a blunder, my dear Watson—which is, I am afraid, a more common occurrence than anyone would think who only knew me through your memoirs. The fact is that I could not believe it possible that the most remarkable horse in England could long remain concealed, especially in so sparsely inhabited a place as the north of Dartmoor. From hour to hour yesterday I expected to hear that he had been found, and that his abductor was the murderer of John Straker." (Doyle, in Dougle 1987: 185–86)

With two days having passed since the horse's abduction and Straker's murder, Holmes thus realizes that the case isn't as straightforward as it first appeared and, hence, that immediate closer attention is warranted. The disappearance and the murder are thus the phenomena that await explanation, and Sherlock Holmes applies his investigative techniques to that end. Will he be successful in time for Silver Blaze to run in the Wessex Cup?

Gathering Preliminary Data

Holmes is often regarded as the master of *de*duction, but it's noteworthy that he begins his efforts at explanation in this case by following the *in*ductive practice of gathering data first. His preliminary information regarding Silver Blaze has been based largely on archival sources, primarily the treatment of the case appearing in the daily newspapers. While such sources can be important, Holmes also recognizes their shortcomings:

> "The tragedy has been so uncommon and so complete, and of such personal importance to so many people that we are suffering from a plethora of surmise, conjecture and hypothesis. The difficulty is to detach the framework of fact—of absolute, undeniable fact—from the embellishments of theorists and reporters. Then, having established ourselves upon this sound basis, it is our duty to see what inferences may be drawn, and which are the special points upon which the whole mystery turns." (Doyle, in Dougle 1987: 185)

Accordingly, Holmes also supplements his examination of newspaper accounts with direct communication with Colonel Ross, who has invited his involvement in the case, and Inspector Gregory, the member of the local constabulary to whom the case has been assigned.

Two stables are approximately two miles (three kilometres) apart in the otherwise minimally populated moor around Tavistock. Silver Blaze had been housed at King's Pyland; Desborough, his primary rival in the Wessex Cup, is kept at Mapleton Stables under the management of Silas Brown. Silver Blaze had clearly been the early betting favourite. Besides horse and trainer, Straker's wife, a maid, three stable boys, three other horses, and a dog all make their home at King's Pyland.

Security precautions had been taken as the race approached, with the three stable boys rotating through successive eight-hour shifts in the locked barn: while one was on duty, the other two slept in the loft above. The maid brought meals to the stable for the lads. On the night in question, she was carrying a dinner of curried mutton to the barn when a stranger, later identified as Fitzroy Simpson, suddenly emerged from the darkness. He offered a bribe to the maid and to Ned Hunter, the on-shift stable boy, apparently wishing to obtain inside information concerning Silver Blaze's fitness for the upcoming race, but fled when the two refused his money and Hunter set the dog on him. A note of clarification to Holmes from the inspector reveals that Hunter had locked the stable door behind him before giving chase and that the open window isn't large enough for a person to pass through.

John Straker, the trainer, seemed rather excited when told about these events, and must subsequently have had trouble sleeping: his wife saw him getting dressed and heading out to the barn at 1:00 a.m., despite the rain. Mrs. Straker awoke at 7:00 a.m. to find that her husband had not returned. On going outside, she and the maid found the barn door open, Hunter in a drug-induced stupor, the other two boys still soundly asleep in the loft, and Silver Blaze gone. About a quarter of a mile (half a kilometre) away from the stables, John Straker's coat was found hanging from a tree branch, flapping in the breeze. Close to it lay the trainer's body.

> "His head had been shattered by a savage blow from some heavy weapon, and he was wounded in the thigh, where there was a long, clean cut, inflicted evidently by some very sharp instrument ... In his right hand he held a small knife, which was clotted with blood up to the handle, while in his left he grasped a red and black silk cravat, which was recognized by the maid as having been worn on the preceding evening by the stranger who had visited the stables." (Doyle, in Dougle 1987: 189)

When he regained his senses, Hunter agreed with the maid that the cravat was indeed the one worn by Simpson the night before. He also believed that the stranger must have drugged his food while distracting him with questions about Silver Blaze and the race. Analysis later revealed that his curried mutton was indeed laced with powdered opium, although the people in the house ate the same dish with no apparent effect. A check around the Tavistock area, including an examination of Mapleton Stables, showed Silver Blaze nowhere to be found. But some gypsies who had been seen camping in the area had apparently vanished the day after the crime became news.

Preliminary Induction

The gathering of preliminary data, as Scriven (1976) reminds us, is never done with "immaculate perception." The person who goes about gathering data will bring "commonsensical" or "informed" understandings to the situation, no doubt influenced by ideological and/or theoretical leanings. The data that are gathered, and the interpretations as to what those data mean, influence the range of alternative explanations considered. Preliminary induction involves drawing inferences from one's data to create a plausible account of the causal agent(s) or sequence of events that "produce" the phenomenon.

For Inspector Gregory, suspicion fell immediately on Fitzroy Simpson, the stranger who had appeared on the night of the murder. Witnesses (the maid and stable boy) placed him at the scene of the crime, and his intentions appeared to be less than honourable. Hunter indicated that Simpson had had an opportunity to drug his curried mutton, and John Straker was found with Simpson's cravat in his hand.

Simpson was easily found in one of the villas near Tavistock the day after the crime, and new evidence seemed consistent with the idea that he might have committed the crimes. Apparently Simpson is "a man of excellent birth and education, who had squandered a fortune upon the turf, and lived now by doing a little quiet and genteel bookmaking in the sporting clubs of London. An examination of his betting book shows that bets to the amount of five thousand pounds had been registered by him against the favourite" (Doyle, in Dougle 1987: 189). Further, his clothes were wet from being in the rain the night before, his red and black cravat was indeed missing, and he was in possession of a lead-weighted walking stick, which might conceivably have caused the head injuries from which the trainer died.

Analytic Induction: A Dialectic of Theory and Data

Preliminary induction from the above data might be sufficient to generate the theory that Fitzroy Simpson was the murderer of John Straker and the abductor of Silver Blaze; however, the process of analytic induction requires that the investigator or researcher pay attention to *all* relevant data, particularly to *negative* evidence that could serve to disconfirm one's theory.

The inspector was sufficiently confident in his theory to arrest Fitzroy Simpson, but Sherlock Holmes's attention to the case brings with it a healthy air of skepticism over whether the theory has yet been exposed to adequate scrutiny. In explaining his thoughts on the matter to his colleague and biographer, Dr. Watson, Holmes states,

> "I am afraid that whatever theory we state has very grave objections to it ... The police imagine, I take it, that this Fitzroy Simpson, having

drugged the lad, and having in some way obtained a duplicate key, opened the stable door, and took out the horse, with the intention, apparently, of kidnapping him altogether. His bridle is missing, so that Simpson must have put this on. Then, having left the door open behind him, he was leading the horse away over the moor, when he was either met or overtaken by the trainer. A row naturally ensued, Simpson beat out the trainer's brains with his heavy stick without receiving any injury from the small knife which Straker used in self-defense, and then the thief either led the horse on to some secret hiding place, or else it may have bolted during the struggle, and be now wandering out on the moors. That is the case as it appears to the police, and improbable as it is, all other explanations are more improbable still." (Doyle, in Dougle 1987: 189–90)

Holmes begins by questioning whether all evidence to date is indeed consistent with the theory, a reflection of proper negative case analysis. He wonders first why Straker's body was covered with considerable blood and bore a knife cut, suggesting a struggle, while Simpson's clothes had no bloodstains and showed no signs of struggle. But Dr. Watson notes that the blows to the head might have caused involuntary convulsions, which in turn may have led Straker to have cut himself with his own knife. Holmes next notes that Silver Blaze is still missing; he asks how a stranger from London could know enough about the local area to keep a horse hidden on an apparently barren moor. The Inspector suggests that Simpson might have passed the horse over to the gypsies, who have now vanished, adding that Simpson was *not* a stranger to the area, having stayed there for significant periods during two prior summers.

But Holmes isn't convinced. He suggests that the Inspector's case is still circumstantial, at best:

"A clever counsel would tear it all to rags ... Why should he take the horse out of the stable? If he wished to injure it, why could he not do it there? Has a duplicate key been found in his possession?

What chemist sold him the powdered opium?" (Doyle, in Dougle 1987: 191)

The inspector responds to each query, but the responses are weak insofar as none has any sort of concrete manifestation. Perhaps he took the horse out so no one would hear the creature when the injury was done, or perhaps the motive was indeed abduction rather than injury. As for the key, perhaps it was acquired during one of his previous summer visits, and he probably threw it away once the crime was committed. The opium was probably bought in London, making it difficult to trace.

Holmes becomes more skeptical than ever at this "shadow" evidence. He gives the coup de grâce by noting two events that, to him, make the current theory untenable and direct attention elsewhere. First, Holmes knows that opium powder has a very distinctive flavour, and he considers it too large a coincidence that the maid just happens to have served a curried mutton that night, a dish that would conveniently hide the taste of the opium. Clearly, Simpson could not have caused the particular choice of dinner that night; the perpetrator must therefore be a person in the house who could make such a choice. Further, Holmes notes that although the dog barked loudly when Simpson paid his evening visit to the maid and the stable boy, it did *not* do so when the murderer/abductor arrived at the stable later that night. This fact suggests that the dog must have known the intruder, again focusing attention back on the members of the Straker household.

Another theory is clearly required, and with his attention now directed toward the Strakers, it's time for Holmes to gather more evidence. Holmes first turns his eye to the murder victim, John Straker, asking what objects were in his pockets on the night of the murder. These include numerous items, the most noteworthy of which are a candle, some papers, and the knife that had apparently caused Straker's leg wound. Curiously, the papers include a bill for a very expensive dress from a London milliner; the invoice is made out to a Mr. William Darbyshire. Holmes is informed that Darbyshire is apparently a friend of Straker's and that letters to him are occasionally received at the Straker home. As for the knife, closer inspection by Watson reveals that it is a very small, delicate, razor-sharp knife of a type used for cataract operations, leaving Holmes curious as to why Straker would have possessed such a knife and why he would have taken such a thing along as a weapon against an intruder, when larger kitchen knives were just as easily available.

Because the data that Holmes uncovers suggest that the murder/abduction was an "inside job," Holmes's attention clearly turns to the Strakers, for only they could have chosen the menu that allowed the stable boy to be drugged. Although both may have been involved, only John Straker meets all the criteria of being able to determine the meal to disguise the opium, clearly having a key to the stable, being able to handle the horse he trained, and being known to the dog so that it would not bark and wake the sleeping stable boys when he arrived to do something to the horse. But what was he intending to do? How? Why?

After identifying John Straker as having had less than honourable intentions, Holmes wonders whether Mrs. Straker was also involved; he looks for a motive for the crime. His inductive leap emerges from examining the invoice to William Darbyshire that is among Straker's personal effects. Why would Mr. Darbyshire have millinery bills delivered to the house of John Straker? Could John Straker and William Darbyshire have been the same person? Perhaps Mr. and Mrs. Straker have been living beyond their means, using double identities, and were led to the crime by a need to meet debts created by an extravagant lifestyle.

To pursue this lead, Holmes employs a technique of indirect questioning to discover whether the dress billed to William Darbyshire had indeed been intended for Mrs. Straker:

> "Surely I met you in Plymouth, at a garden party, some little time ago, Mrs. Straker," said Holmes.
> "No, sir; you are mistaken."
> "Dear me; why I could have sworn to it. You wore a costume of dove-coloured silk, with ostrich feather trimming."

> "I never had such a dress, sir," answered the lady.
> "Ah; that quite settles it," said Holmes. (Doyle, in Dougle 1987: 192)

And indeed it did. But if Mrs. Straker isn't the woman for whom the dress was intended, then who is? If William Darbyshire was indeed John Straker, is there *another* Mrs. Darbyshire/Straker? Or a mistress, perhaps?

The Master of Deduction

Holmes has arrived at a theory that offers some consistency with the evidence gathered to date. Certainly none of the evidence has yet been demonstrated to be *inconsistent* with the theory that John Straker, due to financial pressures from some possible parallel life he was leading, was involved in some despicable plot to abduct or injure Silver Blaze in order to gain funds, whether through bets or through bribery. But at this point Holmes goes beyond the domain of analytic induction alone: he now also starts including the deductive mode that so characteristically distinguishes him from most other fictional sleuths. More specifically, Holmes begins to hypothesize about data that *should* exist *if* his theory is true.

Straker's possession of a surgical knife leads Holmes to speculate that Straker may have been intending to somehow surreptitiously injure Silver Blaze temporarily so that the horse wouldn't be able to race. If that was so, Straker probably led Silver Blaze to the depression on the moor where the murder subsequently took place in order to ensure that any cries from Silver Blaze wouldn't wake the stable boys who were asleep in the loft and to ensure that he wouldn't be seen perpetrating this deed. And if that was so, other evidence of that action should be found. Straker's coat, presumably removed in order to better perform the "operation," and an abundance of hoof- and footprints in the vicinity of the body were certainly consistent with Holmes's theory, although not definitive. Recalling that candles were found in Straker's pocket, and surmising that he would have required a light of some sort in order to undertake an operation, Holmes hypothesizes that *if* his theory is correct, other evidence of candles or matches should be present at the scene. But neither Watson nor the inspector is aware of Holmes's deductions as Holmes begins to closely scrutinize the area where the body was found:

> Stretching himself upon his face and leaning his chin upon his hands, [Holmes] made a careful study of the trampled mud in front of him.
>
> "Halloa!" said he, suddenly, "what's this?"
>
> It was a wax vesta, half burned, which was so coated with mud that it looked at first like a little chip of wood.
>
> "I cannot think how I came to overlook it," said the Inspector, with an expression of annoyance.
>
> "It was invisible, buried in the mud. I only saw it because I was looking for it."
>
> "What! You expected to find it?"
>
> "I thought it not unlikely." (Doyle, in Dougle 1987: 193)

Holmes next turns his attention to Silver Blaze. If Straker abducted him but was then killed, Silver Blaze must have run off somewhere. But if so, why hasn't he been found? Holmes heard the inspector express the belief that the gypsies might have found and taken him, but views this idea as being based on a convenient but inaccurate stereotype. And even if they had done so, surely it's absurd to believe that gypsies could have walked off with and sold the most famous and sought-after horse in England without anyone's noticing. On the basis of his knowledge of horses, Holmes speculates with Watson on Silver Blaze's location:

> "The horse is a very gregarious creature. If left to himself his instincts would have been either to return to King's Pyland, or go over to Mapleton. Why should he run wild on the moor? He would surely have been seen by now ..."
>
> "Where is he, then?"

> "I have already said that he must have gone to King's Pyland or to Mapleton. He is not at King's Pyland, therefore he is at Mapleton. Let us take that as a working hypothesis and see what it leads us to." (193)

But the inspector had already stated that he checked for 100 yards (90 metres) in all directions from the crime scene and was unable to find any further tracks. Still, acting on his theory and looking for indicators that could further test that theory, Holmes continues:

> "This part of the moor, as the Inspector remarked, is very hard and dry. But it falls away toward Mapleton, and you can see from here that there is a long hollow over yonder, which must have been very wet on Monday night. If our supposition is correct, then the horse must have crossed that, and there is the point where we should look for his tracks." (193)

Holmes brings along one of Silver Blaze's horseshoes, and evidence soon turns up that provides some support for Holmes's theory. Hoofprints are indeed found, indicating that Silver Blaze did walk in the direction of Mapleton. In the process of following them, Watson chances on a second pair of prints—from a human's square-toed boots—that are seen to come from Mapleton and to intersect with the horse's hoofprints; horse and human travel in parallel toward King's Pyland for a short while, after which they reverse ground in tandem and head back to Mapleton.

On the basis of these new observations, found serendipitously while following through with an investigation of implications (i.e., hypotheses) that flowed from his theory, Holmes induces that someone from Mapleton must have come on Silver Blaze as he wandered on the moor after running from Straker and, having begun to return Silver Blaze to King's Pyland, suddenly had a change of heart, succumbing to the temptation to take advantage of the act of fate that had brought Mapleton's main rival to its doorstep and taking the opportunity to hide the horse in the Mapleton stables until after the Wessex Cup. The most likely candidate is Silas Brown, the trainer of Desborough and the manager of Mapleton Stables; only he would have known how to disguise or hide a horse, and only he would have the authority to bring a new horse in to the stables unchallenged.

If that theory is true, Brown would have to have been the first to rise that day. When they arrive at Mapleton, Holmes checks his reasoning indirectly, by querying a groom who, seeing Holmes and Watson coming, has directed them to be gone:

> "I only wished to ask a question," said Holmes, with his finger and thumb in his waistcoat pocket. "Should I be too early to see your master, Mr. Silas Brown, if I were to call at five o'clock tomorrow morning?"
>
> "Bless you, sir, if anyone is about he will be, for he is always the first stirring. But here he is, sir, to answer your questions for himself." (194)

Holmes's first hypothesis is thus supported, and a second is as well when Silas Brown strides toward him wearing square-toed boots that match the unique footprints Holmes and Watson observed on the moor. Resistant at first, Brown admits to having hidden Silver Blaze after Holmes describes the events in such detail that Brown believes Holmes must have witnessed the entire scene. Empathizing with Brown's having succumbed to serendipitous temptation without original criminal intent, Holmes provides Brown with a way to show his remorse: by promising to care for the horse and to ensure that the animal appears at the Wessex Cup on racing day.

Back at King's Pyland, feeling confident that his theory is most plausible but still wanting to ensure that all loose ends are covered, Holmes generates two further hypotheses that suggest two final tests of the theory. First, if Straker had been intending to administer a delicate but impairing incision to Silver Blaze, Holmes speculates that Straker would probably have practised on other animals at the stables,

and his eyes "[fall] upon the sheep." Accordingly, he questions one of the stable boys:

> "You have a few sheep in the paddock," he said. "Who attends to them?"
>
> "I do, sir."
>
> "Have you noticed anything amiss with them of late?"
>
> "Well, sir, not of much account; but three of them have gone lame, sir."
>
> I could see that Holmes was extremely pleased, for he chuckled and rubbed his hands together.
>
> "A long shot, Watson; a very long shot!" said he, pinching my arm. "[Inspector] Gregory, let me recommend to your attention this singular epidemic among the sheep. Drive on, coachman!" (196)

With all but Holmes baffled at the meaning of that interchange, Holmes and Watson leave to test a further hypothesis. Promising Silver Blaze's owner that they'll see him and the horse on racing day, Holmes takes a photo of Straker along to London.

The one portion of the theory that Holmes has not yet tested involves the question of motive. We do not yet know whether John Straker and William Darbyshire were indeed the same person, and whether Straker's extravagant lifestyle led him to attempt to solve his financial problems by fixing the Wessex Cup against Silver Blaze. Taking Straker's photograph to the milliner at the address on William Darbyshire's invoice confirms Holmes's suspicions.

A Satisfying Resolution

On the day of the Wessex Cup, Silver Blaze does indeed appear; moreover, he wins the race. But with Silver Blaze safely found and returned, all of those present are still at a loss as to the identity of Straker's murderer. It is thus with no small sense of satisfaction that Holmes fills in the last piece of the puzzle: the murderer was none other than Silver Blaze!

"The horse!" cried both the Colonel and [Dr. Watson].

"Yes, the horse. And it may lessen his guilt if I say that it was done in self-defense, and that John Straker was a man who was entirely unworthy of your confidence." (198)

Holmes continues with his litany, which is consistent with all the evidence, both inductively and deductively gathered. He recounts the evidence concerning Straker's double identity and the extravagance of his lifestyle. The choice of curried mutton to drug Hunter, the dog that didn't bark, and Straker's possession of the cataract knife are all explained. As for the trainer's death, Holmes describes the chain of events:

"Straker had led the horse to a hollow where his light would be invisible. Simpson, in his flight, had dropped his cravat, and Straker had picked it up with some idea, perhaps, that he might use it in securing the horse's leg. Once in the hollow he had got behind the horse, and had struck a light, but the creature, frightened at the glare, and with the strange instinct of animals feeling that some mischief was intended, had lashed out, and the steel shoe had struck Straker full on the forehead. He had already, in spite of the rain, taken off his overcoat in order to do his delicate task, and so, as he fell, his knife gashed his thigh. Do I make it clear?"

"Wonderful!" cried the Colonel. "Wonderful! You might have been there." (200)

Dénouement

Sherlock Holmes's approach in this tale provides a splendid example of qualitative case study analysis, even though the flow of the reasoning is more characteristic of the realm of fiction than of the realm of social science research, where "truths" are neither so singular nor so straightforwardly amenable to analysis. "The Adventure of Silver Blaze" illustrates

the issue of access, which in Holmes's case is facilitated by his considerable reputation and by the invitation he receives from Colonel Ross to participate in the investigation. Although Holmes's initial information comes from the newspaper, he is clearly aware of the strengths and limitations of such data, and he uses this appreciation to whittle down the set of data that are "relevant" and that call for explanation. Further evidence is gained by visiting the actual scene of the events and by supplementing the archival data with interview data from a purposive sample of respondents who are identified as the investigation evolved.

The gathering of preliminary data is followed by attempts at induction, with inferences regarding particular data combining to generate a preliminary theory. Unlike Inspector Gregory, Holmes doesn't fall into the trap of prematurely accepting an induced theory, but continues to engage in a dialectic of theory and data that specifically includes generating and considering evidence that might disconfirm the theory. The process of analytic induction leads to the generation of a theory that is consistent, or at least not *inconsistent,* with all available evidence. Holmes then deduces the evidence that *should* exist *if* the theory is true, so that actual observation of concrete evidence (as opposed to the "shadow" evidence accepted by Inspector Gregory) will allow him to test the adequacy of his evolving theory.

In the process of undertaking these hypotheses and gathering relevant data to support or refute them, Holmes evinces a splendid understanding of how unobtrusive measures can be used to illuminate human (and equine) behaviour. His speculation regarding Silver Blaze's whereabouts is a beautiful example of how one must look in "visible" places for relevant data; while the inspector was unable to find hoofprints on the hard ground for 100 yards (90 metres) in all directions around the crime scene, Holmes speculates on *one* direction—toward Mapleton—and identifies a distant low-lying area between the crime scene and Mapleton as the likely location (because of its softness) for finding hoofprints *if* his theory is true. Besides thus providing a test of his speculations, Holmes is also rewarded with the serendipitous discovery of Silas Brown's boot prints, which help round out the sleuth's theoretical descriptions of the events of that fateful day.

SUMMING UP AND LOOKING AHEAD

This description of Sherlock Holmes's methods should show you why Donald T. Campbell was led to change his mind about the "impossibility" of "scientifically adequate" case study analysis. His earlier comments (e.g., Campbell & Stanley 1963) about case studies involving merely one observation (e.g., a murder), yet having myriad prospective explanatory variables (e.g., possible perpetrators or "causes") from which to choose, clearly do not appreciate the complexities of case study analysis. As Scriven (1976), Campbell (e.g., 1979b), and others (e.g., Rosenblatt 1981) subsequently told us, "singular" phenomena typically involve a whole set of related observations that are evident or identified by the researcher (e.g., all the clues in the mystery), and *the whole set* must be accounted for by the theory or theories proposed.

The strong logical ties underlying the whole continuum from quantitative experimental study to qualitative case study analysis are also clearly revealed. Particular data are gathered from the literature, from an experiment, from a case study, or from our personal life experience in order to generate a theory or theories that offer a plausible explanation for the occurrence and/or non-occurrence of the phenomena under study. Negative cases are particularly sought; more data are gathered, and their (in)consistency with the theory is scrutinized. Ultimately, the research task, whatever form it takes, is a dialectic process involving theory and data, where the goal is to generate and decide on the relative plausibility of prospective competing explanations.

Of course, the example of Silver Blaze falls short in some ways as an illustration of research logic. Holmes's appeal to distill his preliminary information about the case down to "absolute, undeniable fact" (Doyle, in Dougle 1987: 185) may make sense to us in the context of the mysteries surrounding Silver Blaze, but it also implies a *realist* perspective that may be less clearly applicable in most social science settings, where the reality of "facts" and the inferences one can draw from a given datum are more tenuous and negotiable. We see a hint of this in Inspector Gregory's stereotypically guided speculation about the possible role of the gypsies in Silver Blaze's disappearance, since it suggests that social psychological and/or ideological considerations might influence how likely we are to broach particular data and to be compelled by particular explanations. We attempt to incorporate these matters into the *Research Decisions* cauldron in the epilogue to this book. In the interim, Chapter 12 considers issues involved in quantitative data analysis.

STUDY QUESTIONS

1. Explain what is meant by an *iterative* process. Give an example of an iterative process beyond those given in this text.

2. Consider a decision you made recently (e.g., whether to go to university, what university to attend, whether to start or end a relationship), and reflect on the process that led to that decision. Write a brief summary of that decision-making process. Now invent a metaphor and try to apply it to that decision; for example, how is making a decision about what university to go to (or whichever decision you picked) like cleaning your house or apartment? Or like eating Cheerios for breakfast? Then try the same approach again, this time using another metaphor. Does using the metaphor bring to light aspects of your decision-making process that you hadn't included in your first summary? Which of the two metaphors did a better job of doing so? Speculate on why you think that might have been the case.

3. What are some of the "insidious biases" that Huberman and Miles (1994) suggest must be avoided in qualitative analysis? What are some

of the things you can do to try to avoid each one?

4. Rahim has been engaged in an ethnographic study of the Toronto Raptors of the NBA this semester. His research question focuses on the different ways that players maintain hope in the face of consistent and recurring defeat. He has kept field notes of his observations throughout the semester and supplemented them with interviews of coaches and players. But it is now nearing the end of semester, and Rahim simply does not know where to start in analyzing the mounds of data he has collected.

   a. In what ways might "telling a story," using "metaphor," "comparison and contrast," and/or "drawing pictures" help him to start organizing his data?

   b. When Rahim comes to us, we also tell him "counting" is a technique he might find useful. "What?" responds Rahim. "I was doing *qualitative* research, not *quantitative*!" How would you respond to Rahim's objection? What functions can counting serve in qualitative research?

5. Explain the process of *analytic induction* in your own words, using Wallace's wheel of science (from Chapter 2) to organize your explanation.

6. Why did Donald T. Campbell think, in his earlier articles on experimentation (e.g., Campbell & Stanley 1963), that "rigorous" case study analysis is impossible? How might Michael Scriven (1976) and Louise Kidder (1981a) have tried to change his mind?

7. You go home at night after a long evening in the library, looking forward to listening to some music while enjoying a nightcap of milk and cookies. But the stereo doesn't work! List the rival plausible explanations you might consider in determining why your stereo isn't working, and state how you might decide from among them which is most plausible.

8. If you like to read novels, check out Robert Pirsig's *Zen and the Art of Motorcycle Maintenance* (New York: Morrow, 1979). In the context of an absorbing tale about someone who's trying to find himself, it also includes a splendid running commentary on case study methods.

9. Experiments emphasize manipulative control; case study analysis emphasizes analytic control. Discuss the relative merits and demerits of the two approaches as routes to understanding.

10. Choose any of the Sherlock Holmes stories other than the one featured in this chapter, and consider Holmes's investigative process from the perspective of qualitative case study designs.

11. We offered several examples of professionals who are required to engage in case study analysis (i.e., physicians, mechanics, coroners, engineering troubleshooters). Can you think of other occupations that make the same demand? If you know someone in any of those occupations, interview him or her about the way he or she tries to isolate causes. Does he or she follow the logic outlined in this chapter? Explain.

12. Select an article from a recent issue of a newsmagazine that purports to be "analytical" about current events (e.g., *Maclean's, Time, Newsweek*), and consider the way the article's author develops his or her analysis. Is the logic of the analysis evident? Does the writer follow the steps required for rigorous case study analysis?

NOTES

1. Huberman and Miles (1994) note the common plea of researchers who gather 1000 pages of field notes, interview transcripts, and photocopied documents and then ask "What do I do with all these data?" Huberman and Miles approvingly cite Kvale (1988), who suggests that the ideal is to do one's research in such a way that one won't have to ask that question in the first place!

2. Kidder's academic pedigree is noteworthy, since she was a student of both Donald T. Campbell

and Howard S. Becker while undertaking her doctorate at Northwestern University.

3. Consider who such negative cases might be. The bottom left-hand corner seems particularly unlikely to have anyone in it, since if a person couldn't smoke "correctly," was unable to perceive the effects, or didn't see the effects as enjoyable, one wonders why that person would continue using the drug. For the top right-hand corner, one could imagine that a person may have met all three prior conditions but be deterred from using the drug on a regular basis due to other factors (e.g., perception of personal weakness, worry about the illegality of the behaviour and/or possible criminal sanctions involved). When considering Becker's results, one should appreciate that at the time the study was done (i.e., the 1960s), marijuana use was perceived somewhat differently than it is now in the "Just Say No" generation. Becker's findings may thus have been coloured by the relative ignorance that existed about marijuana in the late 1950s and early 1960s, prior to its broader acceptance and use in the mid- to late 1960s and in the 1970s. Whatever the influence, the central point here is that external validity concerns are as relevant to qualitative data analysis as they are to quantitative data analysis.

4. Although the references we cite in this section will be to Cressey (1953), we are relying heavily on Kidder's (1981a) account (see particularly pages 241–44).

5. We'll try to provide enough information from the story to allow you to follow the gist of this mystery and Holmes's resolution of it; however, we strongly advise that you secure a copy of the story and read it before reading the analysis that appears here. A video of the story is also available, in a series produced for the British Broadcasting Corporation (BBC) by Granada television in Great Britain; these star Jeremy Brett, who, in our opinion, gives a terrific portrayal of Holmes

CHAPTER 12

A CONCEPTUAL INTRODUCTION TO QUANTITATIVE DATA ANALYSIS

Our lives are full of numbers. The moment we're born, the person attending measures our height and weight. We count our teeth as they start to grow, and every child must be asked his or her age a million times. Soon, we move on to grade 1, then 2, then 3, and our efforts are evaluated with numerical grades or As, Bs, and Cs. Our education includes knowing various units of measurement (e.g., cups or litres, pounds or kilograms, dollars, miles or kilometres, hours). As we grow up, we become more interested in the world around us. We turn on the nightly news and discover that the Dow Jones Index went up 14 points, only 32 percent of the national voting population supports the current government and its policies, the rate of violent crime has dropped 3 percent since last year, the median housing price went up by $4000 in the past 12 months, and the Vancouver Canucks defeated the Detroit Red Wings 7–4.[1]

Numbers are a fact of life. They are also a tool of social science in the same way that they are a tool of everyday life: they help us describe, make comparisons, and express relationships. Of course, they can also be used to distort, mislead, and stonewall. Indeed, one of the implications of entering the information age seems to be that *everybody* can now point to *some* data *somewhere* that "proves" the correctness of his or her view of the world. So it makes sense to try to understand data and how they're used.

Data needn't be intimidating, although many people seem to find them so. Indeed, some people assert—sometimes even with a sense of self-righteous pride—that they aren't "numbers" people. As Toronto statistician Chuck Chakrapani com-

mented in a CBC-TV report, it's interesting how many would never boast about being *illiterate* brag about being *innumerate.*[2] Don't get us wrong. You can do perfectly good, interesting, and valuable research *without* getting into razzle-dazzle multivariate statistics, as we hope the earlier chapters in this book have shown. But any researcher who skips through the data section of an article or a report and takes the writer's conclusions at face value, and any citizen who uncritically accepts the reportage offered in contemporary media, is doing himself or herself a disservice. Any competent researcher and citizen needs to understand some statistical basics, and that's what this chapter will attempt to offer at a conceptual level.

This chapter will address the sort of data that are characteristic of quantitative research, that is, structured, systematically derived data amenable to aggregation and analysis.[3] We'll consider two ways to represent and examine those data: through **descriptive statistics,** which present the data in summary form, and through **inferential statistics,** which analyze sample data to reveal relationships among variables and to make inferences about populations. You'll see that the latter may be used inductively, to suggest possible relationships, or deductively, to test hypotheses. This chapter will emphasize the conceptual underpinnings of numbers and some of the statistical procedures to which they might be subjected. The aim is not to turn you into a statistician, but to discuss some statistical fundamentals in a way that will help you understand the statistics you will likely be getting either in lab periods or some other course.

VARIABLES AND CONSTANTS

In order to discern what it is about numbers that might interest us, we must take a step back and talk about the concept of **variables.** Stated simply, a variable is anything that varies. The opposite is a *constant*, which is something that *does not* vary. In your research methods class, for example, most likely all of you sitting in the chairs are students; that is, the social status of "student" is a constant in your class. Presumably all class members are also human beings, so we might say that "species" is also a constant in your class. But there are many *variables* in your class as well. The sex of your colleagues is a variable, for example (unless you attend an all-male or all-female educational institution), because your class includes both male and female students. Other variables might include students' declared majors, whether they are enrolled part-time or full-time, their ages, their ethnicities, their vocational aspirations, their attitudes on social issues, and so forth. The whole task of social science is to *explain* variations (e.g., why are the proportions of males and females so different in computing sciences compared to sociology?) in relation to other variations (e.g., variation in life history, competencies, aptitudes, interests).

As soon as you begin attaching numbers to things, several other processes are automatically activated. Numbers imply classification, for example, since the simple counting of objects implies that the objects are part of the category whose frequency you are counting. This is sometimes a relatively simple process, for example, your fingers and toes or the numbers of males and females in your class. But on other occasions, the boundaries that define a category may be rather more blurred; one must decide, for example, whether a death was an "accident" or a "suicide" or whether the punishment a parent delivers is "a spanking" or "physical abuse."

This chapter won't discuss the constructionist aspects of how social categories are derived, why some areas of life are more or less fully enumerated than others, or the social and political dynamics by which particular categories are negotiated (but recall, for example, Chapter 1; see also Lakoff 1987). But

don't forget that such issues permeate this chapter. Numbers always have an aura of precision about them; behind every number is a social process that has caused that number to exist (e.g., see Chapter 8's section on crime statistics). Maintain the same healthy skepticism about numbers that you do about any other information you might be presented with.

LEVELS OF MEASUREMENT

The types of descriptive and inferential statistics to use in any situation depend to some degree on the types of variables with which you are dealing, which in turn is a function of how you've gone about measuring them. Remember that social science research involves a continuing interplay between theory and data. The variables that interest us are theoretical constructions—abstractions we draw from our experience—that we feel are useful in describing and interpreting human activity. But empirical research cannot be done in the abstract.[4] We must give our variables empirical meaning by operationalizing them for a given research context. The correspondence rules by which those operationalizations are imposed (i.e., the way we take observations and change them into variables for analysis) define the type of measurement taken.

Nominal or Categorical Measures

The simplest way to measure an object is simply to categorize it, that is, say what it is and what it is not. Examples of categorical variables include sex (male or female), whether one owns or rents one's abode, a student's choice of academic major, and whether a person is in a treatment group or a control group. In each case, any assigning of numbers to those categories would be completely arbitrary. We can code oranges as "1" and apples as "2," but that makes no more or less sense than coding apples as "1" and oranges as "2." The different values the variable can take on (e.g., apples or oranges, for the variable "fruits found in lunchboxes") are merely different from one another; one value doesn't embody or possess *more* or *less* of the variable under consideration.

Apples and oranges, for example, are just different fruits, with neither being any more or less of a fruit than the other.

Ordinal Measures

A second level of measurement we can impose is called *ordinal measurement* because the numbers ascribed to our classification possess order. That is, not only are the values *different* from one another (as was the case with categorical variables), they also embody differences of *magnitude* with respect to the variable under consideration. For example, full-time faculty members in North American universities are classified into three categories: (a) assistant professors, (b) associate professors, and (c) full professors. There's an underlying sense of *order* to these categories; each successive category is "higher" in the academic hierarchy than the previous one. Numbers imposed in order to code and analyze the distribution of "academic rank" are somewhat arbitrary—we could equally legitimately call the categories 1, 2, and 3; or 3, 2, and 1; or 5, 10, and 15—but they aren't *totally* arbitrary, since using 1, 3, and 2 would destroy the underlying order we see.

At the same time, the limits of ordinal measures also are evident. In the real number system, the distance or interval between 1 and 2 is equal to the distance between 2 and 3, but that property does not hold for an ordinal variable like academic rank. The numbers are merely rankings; the order is important, but the distance between ranks is not constant. Another example might be "order of finish" at a track meet. Runners come in first, second, third, and so on; the order is important, but the distance between the first and second runners may not be the same as the distance between the second and third.

Interval-Level Measurement

When the property of equal distance *is* met, *interval-level measurement* is said to exist. In the monograph that originally differentiated these measurement types, Stevens (1951) gave thermometer readings as an example. Note that a temperature of 30° Celsius is *different* from a temperature of 20° Celsius (i.e., it meets the requirement of categorical measurement). It's also *higher* than 20° (i.e., there are magnitude relations, as in ordinal measurement). But a new criterion applies: one can also say that the *interval* between 20° and 30° is equal to the interval between 10° and 20°, or that 1° is of equal magnitude at any point in the scale. On the other hand, certain limits are imposed because the scale does not have a "true" zero point.

In the social world, suppose we ask a university's faculty members to indicate which they value more highly: the research or the teaching component of their jobs. To express their answers, we give them a five-point scale with the following verbal designations: (1) research is much more valued than teaching, (2) research is somewhat more valued than teaching, (3) research and teaching are about equally valued, (4) teaching is somewhat more valued than research, and (5) teaching is much more valued than research. Psychometric research (e.g., see Altemeyer 1970; Dawes 1972) has shown that people can use such scales quite easily and that unless the verbal designations are very poorly chosen, they use such scales in a manner consistent with at least interval-level properties.[5]

Ratio Measurement

The final level of measurement noted by Stevens (1951) is called *ratio-level measurement,* and the prototypical example is that of a ruler measuring distance or length. Ratio measurement embodies all three previous levels of measurement. A distance of 3 centimetres is *different* from a distance of 2 centimetres. We can also say that it's *longer* than 2 centimetres. Further, the differences between the points are meaningful: the interval between 1 centimetre and 2 centimetres is the same as the interval between 8 centimetres and 9 centimetres.

A notable new property of ratio-level measurement is that the scale has a true zero point; in other words, the number zero *means* something: namely, that there's none of the quality being measured. This property allows us to say, for example, that 2 centimetres is twice as long as 1 centimetre, or that the ratio of 2 centimetres to 1 centimetre is the same as the ratio of 8 centimetres to 4 centimetres (i.e., both are 2:1). Note that this situation differs from that in the thermometer example. The zero point on most thermometers is arbitrary: zero degrees, whether on the Celsius scale or the Fahrenheit scale, doesn't mean a total absence of heat or molecular activity. So one cannot say, for example, that 80° Fahrenheit is twice as hot as 40°, or that the ratio of 80° to 40° is the same as the ratio of 30° to 15°.[6] Other examples of ratio scales include measures of time, mass, and volume.

Levels of Measurement and Statistical Analysis

Stevens (1951) argues that it's important to differentiate between these levels of measurement because the range of mathematical operations one can legitimately perform on one's data is limited by the level of measurement. With nominal/categorical data, for example, it's reasonable to create frequency distributions and to indicate the most frequently occurring (or modal) categories, but it makes no sense to compute an "average" when the numerical coding of categories is completely arbitrary to start with (e.g., an "average" sex of 1.2). At the other extreme, with ratio-level data, one can meaningfully employ a wide range of mathematical operations.

There was a time when social science researchers bowed to Stevens's (1951) typology with the reverence otherwise reserved for works of scripture. But much has changed in the decades since that article was written. The onslaught began with a humorous article by Lord (1953) that focused on the relative merit of performing various statistical analyses with the numbers on football jerseys.

The numbers on football jerseys are obviously categorical: the fact that a quarterback wears number 12 while a halfback might wear 33 conveys no information at all about who is the better player. Computing average jersey numbers or comparing the average jersey number of one team to that of another would be a mathematical absurdity, according to

Stevens (1951). But the central character of Lord's (1953) fictitious story—a certain mathematics professor at an unnamed university—does exactly that (in secret, of course) when the players on the university team complain that the other teams laugh at them because their numbers are "too low."

To address this question, Lord's hypothetical professor does what to Stevens (1951) would have been unpardonable: he compares the mean (average) football number on his team to those of other teams and finds that his team's numbers are indeed significantly lower than those of their opponents. But given the particular question being posed, comparing the "average" jersey numbers actually made reasonable sense. The moral of Lord's (1953) story? One can do anything one wants with numbers, since the numbers themselves haven't a clue what's "being done" to them, but it's up to the researcher to make decisions about the range of operations that are meaningful to perform on given data in a given context. If the question (to continue Lord's example) is whether one team's numbers are significantly lower or higher than another team's numbers, computing the mean (average) numbers and comparing them is a meaningful and reasonable thing to do. But if the question were something like "Which team is 'better'?" then comparing the average number on football jerseys would be meaningless and absurd, since football numbers bear no relation at all to the underlying variable "athletic prowess."

One can indeed fault Stevens's (1951) scheme for the qualities ascribed to various measures, since the level of measurement is *not* inherent in the data itself; rather, one must always consider the use to which the data are being put. For example, Stevens argues that the ruler is a perfect example of a measurement scale (for distance or length) with ratio properties. In social science, though, our interests are *not* with the empirical variables per se, but with the underlying *theoretical* variables they're thought to represent.

As long as distance per se is all that interests us, in other words, the measures do have ratio-level properties. But rarely are we interested in distance per se in social research; instead, we're interested in distance as an operationalization or indicator of some theoretical variable of interest (e.g., social distance or interpersonal closeness). And it's the range of operations we feel comfortable using *when the measure is used as an indicator for the underlying theoretical variable of interest* that will influence the range of mathematical operations we can legitimately perform on the data.

Thus, using a ruler to measure height is one thing, but using the same ruler to measure the distance between two people as a measure of how much they like each other is something else. The first has ratio properties; the second likely does not. As this example reaffirms, the property lies not in the measure itself, but in how the measure is used.

This isn't the place to get into a lengthy review of statistical debates on the range of statistics that might legitimately be employed with any given type of data. Suffice it to say that numerous **"Monte Carlo" computer simulations** have shown that many statistical techniques, and certainly the ones in this chapter, can be quite robust to violations of the theoretical assumptions underlying them. One needn't, therefore, be as rigid as Stevens proposes, although one also shouldn't jump to the opposite conclusion, that "anything goes." These days seem to emphasize letting the nature of one's research questions guide one's data analysis, with the caveat that the researcher must consider how meaningful the analysis is, given the type of data and the theoretical use to which they are being put.[7] The question for us, then, is what those uses might be.

DESCRIPTIVE STATISTICS

A very basic use of statistics is to summarize one's data. Instead of saying that we have this marble, and this marble, and this marble, and so on, we can much more succinctly say that we have 10 red marbles and 12 blue ones. Such brevity is admired in the social sciences, where the nature of the scientific task requires us to *describe,* in conceptual terms, the nature of our social universe.[8] Descriptive techniques fall into three general categories: depictions of the *distributions* of each variable, statistics that convey the *central ten-*

dency of each distribution, and statistics that convey the *variability* or *dispersion* that exists in each distribution. Within each of these three categories various techniques may be most useful, depending on such considerations as level of measurement.

Depicting Distributions

The first and most straightforward step we can take toward summarizing our data is to create *frequency distributions* to summarize the number and percentage of persons occupying each of our analytical categories. Indeed, whenever you finish gathering and coding your data, the first thing you should do is prepare frequency tables for each of your variables, to better visualize how they are distributed. To illustrate the various types of descriptive techniques available to you, we'll continue the example of the faculty members at a fictitious university, which we will call Provincial University. Tables 12.1 to 12.4 show frequency distributions summarizing the number of male and female faculty members (Table 12.1), the number of faculty members at each rank

Table 12.1

Distribution of University Faculty by Sex

Sex	Frequency	%
Male	240	60
Female	160	40
All faculty	400	100

Table 12.2

Distribution of University Faculty by Rank

Rank	Frequency	%
Assistant professor	170	42.5
Associate professor	130	32.5
Full professor	100	25.0
All faculty	400	100.0

Table 12.3

Distribution of Responses to Question Regarding Relative Priority of Teaching as Compared to Research

Response	Frequency	%
Research valued much more highly	50	12.5
Research valued somewhat more highly	75	18.8
Research and teaching equally valued	150	37.5
Teaching valued somewhat more highly	75	18.8
Teaching valued much more highly	50	12.5
All responses	400	100.1

Note: Total percentage deviates from 100.0 as a result of rounding.

(Table 12.2), responses to a question about the relative value faculty members ascribe to the teaching and research components of their job (Table 12.3), and the numbers of years faculty members have been employed (Table 12.4).

These four tables collectively demonstrate a number of different aspects of frequency distributions. Note that frequency distributions are appropriate for data at all levels of measurement: sex (Table 12.1) is a categorical variable, academic rank (Table 12.2) is an ordinal variable, responses to the query about research and teaching priorities (Table 12.3) may be treated as an interval-level variable, and number of years of employment (Table 12.4) represents a ratio-level variable. Because each of the tables shows the distribution for one variable at a time, they're called *univariate frequency distributions* (*uni* = one; *variate* = variable).

A second thing to consider about Tables 12.1 to 12.4 is how they are presented. Each table has a number to identify it and a title that describes its contents. Each table also has clearly labelled columns, the first naming the category being described (under Sex, Rank, Response, and Years Employed). Also included in each of the tables is a column titled *Frequency* which indicates the number of observations that fall into each of the categories listed, and another indicating the percentage (%) of the total sample that is described by those categories.

The bottom row of each table shows totals for each of the columns.

You can see from the bottom line on Tables 12.1 to 12.4 that 400 faculty members were involved in this fictitious sample and that complete information was obtained on all four variables for all 400 faculty. If data are missing for any of the variables, you'd normally include a category called "Missing" to show the completeness of your information. If total percentages deviate from 100 (as occurs in Table 12.3), you'd also note the reason why (e.g., because of rounding errors or because respondents were allowed to check more than one category).

The differences between the tables are also noteworthy. Table 12.4 is the only table to give *cumulative frequency* and *cumulative percentage* (*cumulative %*) across categories. These are included for Table 12.4 because it summarizes a sufficiently large number of categories and because there's a clear ordering on the "years employed" variable, from lowest to highest. Thus, it can be seen that approximately one-eighth (12.0 percent; $N = 48$) of the faculty have been employed at the university for four years or less; or it can be computed that approximately half the faculty (49.25 percent; $N = 197$) have been employed at the university for 15 years or more.

But using year-by-year categories in Table 12.4 leaves us with 25 different categories! Such a detailed inventory may be of interest in some situations, but

Table 12.4

Distribution of Number of Years Employed at Provincial University

Years Employed	Frequency	Cumulative Frequency	%	Cumulative %
1	13	13	3.25	3.25
2	12	25	3.00	6.25
3	12	37	3.00	9.25
4	11	48	2.75	12.00
5	11	59	2.75	14.75
6	9	68	2.25	17.00
7	9	77	2.25	19.25
8	8	85	2.00	21.25
9	12	97	3.00	24.25
10	13	110	3.25	27.50
11	16	126	4.00	31.50
12	17	143	4.25	35.75
13	19	162	4.75	40.50
14	20	182	5.00	45.50
15	21	203	5.25	50.75
16	23	226	5.75	56.50
17	23	249	5.75	62.25
18	25	274	6.25	68.50
19	25	299	6.25	74.75
20	23	322	5.75	80.50
21	19	341	4.75	85.25
22	18	359	4.50	89.75
23	16	375	4.00	93.75
24	13	388	3.25	97.00
25	12	400	3.00	100.00
All faculty	400		100.00	

Table 12.5

Distribution of Years Employed at Provincial University, Using Five-Year Intervals

Years Employed	f	Cumulative Frequency	%	Cumulative %
1–5 years	59	59	14.75	14.75
6–10 years	51	110	12.75	27.50
11–15 years	93	203	23.25	50.75
16–20 years	119	322	29.75	80.50
21–25 years	78	400	19.50	100.00
All faculty	400		100.00	

hardly serves the purpose of data summary. Thus, you'd normally collapse so many categories into perhaps five to eight *aggregated categories* or *class intervals,* as has been done in Table 12.5. Category ranges should be of equal size (those in Table 12.5 all involve a 5-year range), should be based on an easily comprehended unit (e.g., 5 categories of 5 years each, rather than 7 categories of 3.57 years each), and should represent the full range of data. But note that such aggregation is achieved only at a cost; we've lost information on exact years of employment.

A second way to depict a frequency distribution is to graph it. Figure 12.1, which shows the distribution of the sex of the faculty members, is a simple *pie chart.* Such charts are best suited to situations in which a small number of categories are distributed reasonably equally (to avoid having many "slivers" of pie that are too small to be easily labelled) or for displaying how some entire entity (100 percent) is divided by category frequency.

Figure 12.2 uses a *bar graph* to show the distribution of academic ranks among the faculty in Provincial University (or PU), whereas Figure 12.3 shows a *histogram* of responses to the query regarding the relative value attached to teaching or research. Note that all three figures are numbered, and each has a title that identifies the variable being shown. Each

Figure 12.1

Faculty Membership by Sex

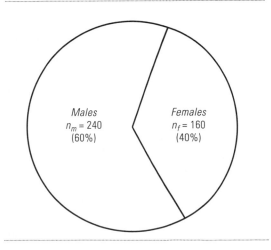

Figure 12.2

Faculty Membership by Academic Rank

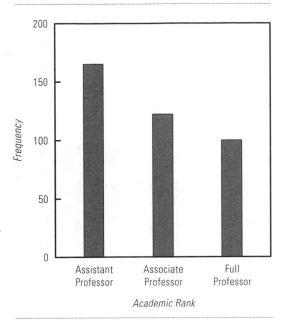

segment of the pie, and each bar of the bar graph and the histogram, is also clearly labelled.

A fourth form of graph, known as a *frequency polygon* or *line graph,* is particularly useful when there's a relatively large number of categories. Figure 12.4 shows the distribution of the numbers of years of employment among university faculty members (using the data supplied in Table 12.4), while Figure 12.5 depicts a bar graph of the categorized years-of-employment variable (using the data supplied in Table 12.5). Once again, note that all figures are clearly numbered, titled, and labelled.

Measures of Central Tendency

After depicting the distribution of each variable, whether through frequency tables such as Tables 12.1 to 12.5 or graphically as in Figures 12.1 to 12.5, the researcher is then ready to begin describing the distributions statistically. First to be considered are measures of *central tendency,* or the "typical"

Figure 12.3

Response to Query Regarding Relative Priority Attached to Teaching as Compared to Research

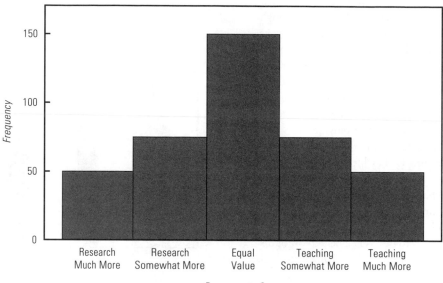

Response to Query

datum for each variable. The three available to you are the mode, the median, and the mean.

THE MODE

The mode identifies the score or scores that are "typical" in the sense that they represent "the most frequently occurring category." Thus, at PU, the modal faculty member with respect to the sex variable is a male, and the modal academic rank is that of assistant professor. As for the query about the relative value attached to research and teaching, the modal response was that the two are valued equally. And finally, more of the current faculty were hired 18 or 19 years ago than at any other time. As these examples suggest, the mode can be used to describe data at any level of measurement.

One potentially erroneous interpretation regarding these modal data should be pointed out. Given the *univariate* modes described in the previous paragraph, it may be tempting to say that the most "typical" faculty members are male assistant

professors who were hired 18 or 19 years ago and who value teaching and research about equally. But such is not necessarily the case. Indeed, there may not be even *one* person who has all those attributes. *Multivariate* patterns are not simply a reflection of their univariate components, as we shall see shortly.

THE MEDIAN

The second statistic for revealing central tendency is the median. This statistic identifies the "typical" datum as that which splits the distribution in half: 50 percent of the sample data lie above it, and 50 percent lie below it. The median is thus the middle score, which you can calculate with the right formula. But note that the median is not always a meaningful statistic; the idea of a "median" sex, for example, seems absurd, since the "typical" case cannot even exist. Indeed, the median is useless with nominal-level variables, because the order that is required to have a midpoint is absent. Medians can thus be used only with ordinal-, interval-, or ratio-

Figure 12.4

Distribution of Number of Years Employed

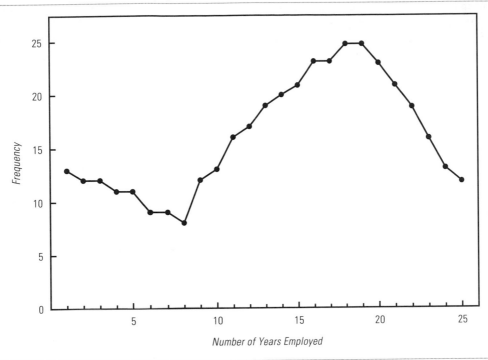

Number of Years Employed

level data. Returning to the data presented in Tables 12.2 to 12.4, you should see that the median academic rank at PU is a relatively junior associate professor (since the middle case is only 7.5 percent beyond the assistant professor category), the median opinion on the attitude item is one of valuing research and teaching about equally, and the median number of years employed at PU is 15.

THE MEAN

The final measure of central tendency to consider is the mean, or what you may know as the arithmetic average. It is computed by simply taking the sum of the values and dividing by the total number of scores. Thus, for example, if your midterm marks in the five courses you're taking were 76, 79, 82, 93, and 81, the mean would be the sum of those marks (76 + 79 + 82 + 93 + 81 = 411) divided by the number of courses ($N = 5$), or 411/5 = 82.2.

Since a mean is computed by adding and then dividing numbers, it has little meaning if the numbers are assigned arbitrarily. Thus, the mean has even more limited utility than the median when it comes to the kinds of variables for which it may be meaningful. Certainly it would be meaningless for nominal variables (e.g., a mean sex?), and it should be used cautiously or not at all with ordinal data (depending on the degree of arbitrariness of the coding scheme). Problems are fewer with interval data and nonexistent with ratio-level data. Thus, if the five responses to the attitude item (Table 12.3) were coded 1 through 5, we could say with little discomfort that the mean response is 3.0 (research and teaching equally valued). And you should be able to calculate (from Table 12.4) that the mean length of employment at PU is 14.3 years.

In sum, the mode, the median, and the mean are three descriptive statistics; each gives a picture of the "central tendency" of the distribution of scores you've obtained. Each expresses an "average" or "typical" score in its own way: for the mode, central tendency is identified as the most frequently occurring score; for the median, the typical score is the one that lies on the 50th percentile, splitting the distribution in half; for the mean, central tendency is defined as the arithmetic average. Let's review the results we obtained with the variables we observed at PU.

Sex is a *categorical* variable, so the only measure of central tendency that seems appropriate to use is the mode. The modal faculty member at PU is a male.

Our attention then turns to academic rank. Using the mode, we find that the most frequently occurring academic rank is that of assistant professor. The *ordinal* nature of the academic-rank data also leads us to use the median. But the median gives us a different indication of central tendency—that of junior associate professor—than does the mode.

Since responses to the query concerning the relative value associated with research and teaching

Figure 12.5

Bar Graph of Years of Employment in Five-Year Intervals

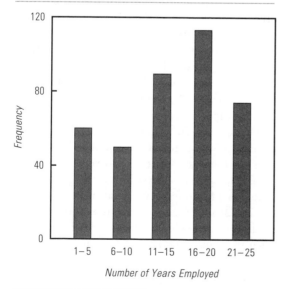

represent an *interval*-level variable, mode, median and mean are all appropriate statistics. Here, all three statistics point in the same direction: "equal value associated with research and teaching."

The last variable on which we have information is "years of employment at PU." Because this is a *ratio*-level variable, mode, median, and mean are all appropriate statistics. But here they give three different answers regarding the "typical" faculty member. The *modal* faculty member was hired 18 or 19 years ago (see Table 12.4); the *median* faculty member was hired 15 years ago; and the *mean* faculty member was hired 14.3 years ago.

Why do the mode, the median, and the mean point sometimes in the same and sometimes in different directions?

CENTRAL TENDENCY, SYMMETRY, AND SKEW

In order to answer that question, we have to consider one more characteristic of distributions: *symmetry* versus *skew*. A symmetrical distribution is any distribution in which the two sides are essentially mirror images. Thus, the three distributions shown in Figure 12.6(a), Figure 12.6(b), and Figure 12.6(c) are all symmetrical, even though their shapes are otherwise very different.[9] Whenever we have a symmetrical distribution (as was the case in Table 12.3 and its counterpart, Figure 12.3, with respect to the attitude variable), the mode, the median, and the mean will all lie in exactly the same place. When our distributions are *asymmetrical*, or "skewed," the situation changes.

Look at the three graphs included in Figure 12.7. You should recognize immediately that Figure 12.7(b) shows a symmetrical distribution, while Figures 12.7(a) and 12.7(c) show skewed distributions. In order to distinguish between the two kinds of asymmetrical distributions, mathematicians use the convention of describing the direction of the skew based on where the distribution's thinner end, or "tail," is. Thus, Figure 12.7(a) is referred to as a "positively skewed" distribution, since its tail is at the positive end of the number line; Figure 12.7(c) is referred to as a "negatively skewed" distribution, since its tail is at the negative end of the number line.[10]

Figure 12.6

Three Examples of Symmetrical Distributions

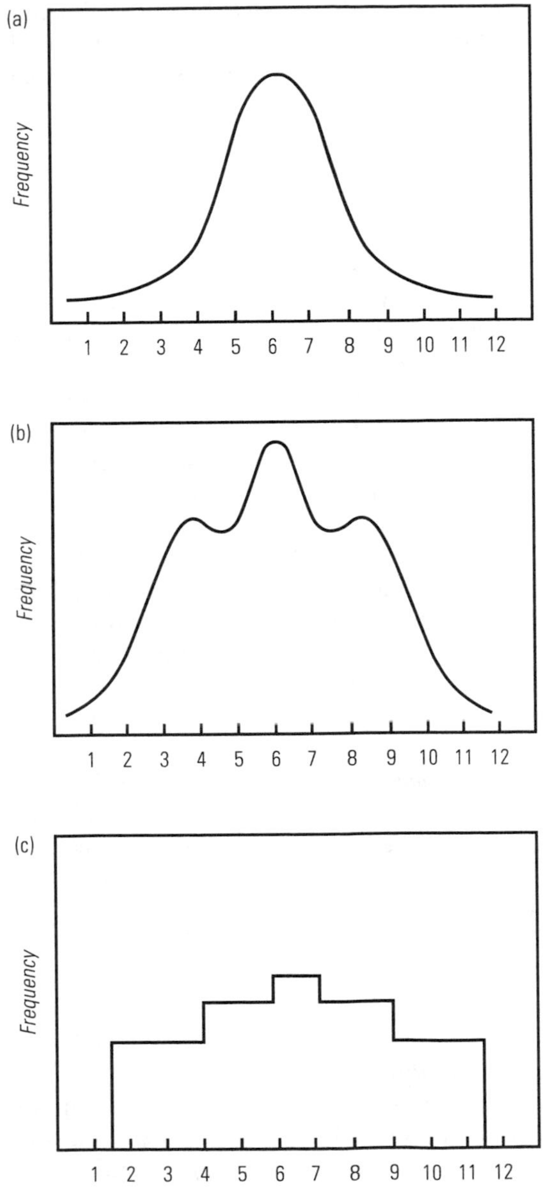

(a)

(b)

(c)

Figure 12.7

Examples of (a) a Positively Skewed Distribution, (b) a Normal Distribution, and (c) a Negatively Skewed Distribution

(a)

Mode ↑ $\overline{X}$
Median

(b)

Mode
Median
Mean $(\overline{X})$

(c)

$\overline{X}$ ↑ Mode
Median

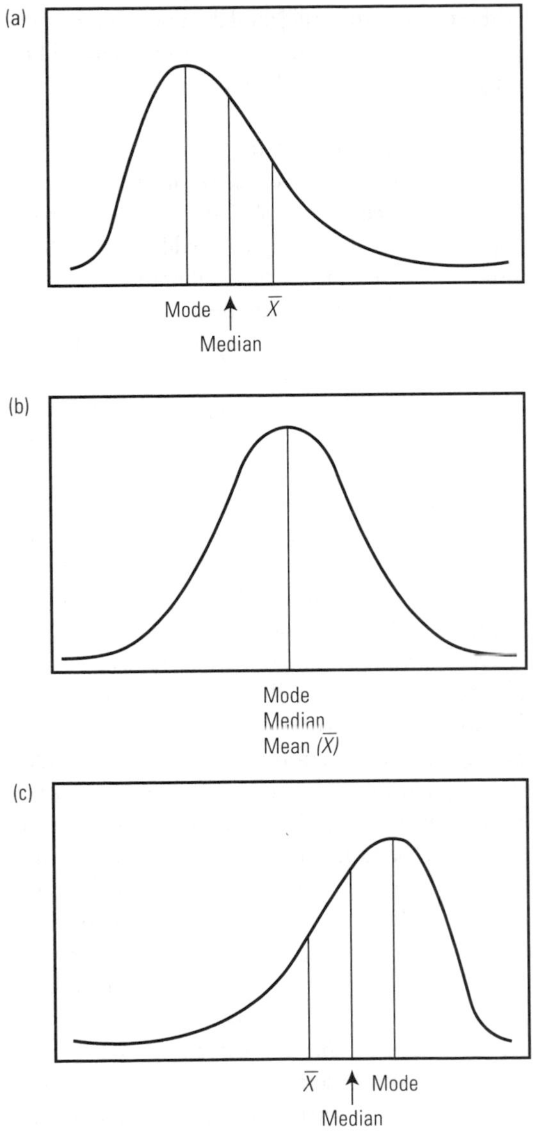

As noted above, when distributions are symmetrical, the mode, median, and mean will all lie in the same place; Figure 12.7(b) illustrates this situation.

But when distributions are asymmetrical, or skewed, the situation changes. Since the mode is by definition the most frequently occurring score, it remains at the highest "bump" in the distribution. The mean and the median, though, will be differentially affected by the extreme scores that lie at the distribution's "skew" or "tail" end. The mean, which is particularly affected by that tendency, will be "pulled" farthest away from the modal value. The median also will be affected but less so; it normally will lie between the mean and the mode.

HOW TO LIE WITH STATISTICS

While the statistics we have been dealing with thus far have been extremely "simple," they're also extremely important. *Any* data analysis should begin with an inspection of raw univariate distributions so that you can see how the variables are distributed and choose accordingly the type of statistics you report. In general, the more the better. Modes can be reported for any type of data. Medians are appropriate when the data have at least ordinal qualities; they are also the "better" statistic with interval- and ratio-level data when the distribution is skewed, especially when there are a few extreme scores. Means should always be cited for interval- and ratio-level data, but should be used more cautiously with ordinal-level data and with highly skewed distributions.

Not showing univariate frequency distributions and being selective in the statistic to report are favourite techniques of those propagandists who use statistics to provide distorted images. The whole idea of using statistics is to concisely summarize a set of data; implicit are the ideas that such summarization is a relatively neutral process and that summary statistics give a representative picture of the data as a whole. People's general faith in those suppositions allows the unscrupulous to manipulate statistics to their own ends. For example, tourist or investment brochures may extol how splendid an area Upper Oceana is, noting that tourism and property costs are very reasonable despite the fact that most Upper Oceanans live in comparative opulence—the average annual income is in fact a whopping $95 455 per year! Sounds great, eh? If only the rest of us were so well off! The impression we get is that the average Upper Oceanan is doing very well financially; perhaps some are doing better or worse, but the average

standard of living, at least as measured in economic terms, seems quite high.

But examining the entire distribution of incomes leaves us with a rather different impression. It seems that for every Upper Oceanan who has an annual income of $1 000 000, there are 10 others who earn a measly $5000 a year. Thus, it turns out that the "average" (i.e., the mean) masks a situation where a few individuals live in wealth, while the majority live in poverty. Generally speaking, the median should be reported along with the mean, since the median is less distorted by deviations from symmetry. Examining the univariate distributions is always a wise move, as is presenting them in a research report.

Examples of individuals and groups using statistics to mislead and distort are so numerous that they could easily fill a book. Indeed, readers interested in an enjoyable and thoughtful book on that topic should have a look at Darrell Huff's *How to Lie with Statistics* (1954; reissued in 1982 and 1993). In very readable fashion, Huff does an excellent job of explaining basic descriptive statistics and showing how they're often misused to distort and mislead. An awareness of such tricks should be part of everyone's education as a citizen and consumer. As a social scientist, your job is to appreciate such techniques as things to *avoid;* as a prospective member of the social science community, your task is to be open and complete in your descriptions and analysis of data.

Measures of Variability

Measures of central tendency convey one aspect of the nature of the distribution: the "typical" or "average" score. But distributions can also differ in their *variability*.

While measures of central tendency attempt to describe a distribution in terms of *similarities* (by focusing on a "most common" or "typical" score), measures of variability focus on *differences* among the scores (by attempting to generate measures of *dispersion*). So variability represents a key stepping stone in our analytic venture, since it's the basic "stuff" that social science is trying to explain.

THE RANGE

The most basic expression of the degree of dispersion that exists is given by the *range*. When dealing with categorical or ordinal variables, where any numerical coding that's involved is relatively arbitrary, providing the range involves giving a full enumeration of all the categories in which observations were obtained. This allows critical readers to inspect your categories to see what range of categories has been included. You also can articulate the range of frequencies that exist in your categories: this will tell your reader whether there is an approximately equal distribution of people across categories or whether they are more prevalent in one than another. Of course, such information can also be made available in tables or graphs of univariate frequency distributions.

With interval-level data, where the numbers begin to have some intrinsic meaning, the range is expressed as the difference between the maximum and minimum values. Thus, the range of responses on the "years employed" variable (see Table 12.4) was 24 years—from the most recent hiring, 1 year ago, to the earliest, 25 years ago.(i.e., 25 − 1 = 24).

Although the range is an important statistic to report, it's not sufficiently definitive. The difficulty is revealed by inspection of Figure 12.8, which shows two different distributions superimposed on each other. The distributions are symmetrical, have the same mode, median, and mean; and have exactly the same range, but only a cursory visual inspection is needed to see that they're still very different. One of the distributions is very dispersed, with scores spread across the whole range. The other is much more compressed, with a huge majority of scores squished in very close to the distribution's mean, a pattern that reflects very little variation.

Another problem with the range as a descriptive statistic is that it only takes one weird/extreme score to change it dramatically and thereby give an unrepresentative impression of the degree of variation that exists. For this reason, many researchers prefer to use a measure known as the *interquartile range* (IQR)

The "quartile" part comes from the fact you begin by dividing the distribution into quarters. If we look at the distribution of scores in Table 12.4

Figure 12.8

Two Distributions with Identical Ranges but Different Degrees of Dispersion

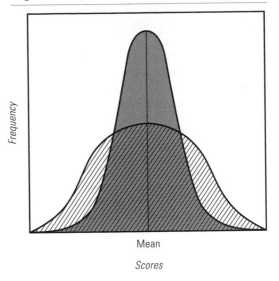

Scores

regarding "years of employment," for example, we can see that the 25 percent point (marking the "1st quartile") comes in the category of people who have been at PU for "10 years"[11]; the 50 percent point (marking the "2nd quartile" or median) comes in the category "14 years"; and that the 75 percent point (marking the "3rd quartile") comes in the category "20 years."

The "inter" part of the term comes from our desire to look at the distance between the first and third quartile points, that is, we want to lop off the extreme scorers in the top 25 percent and bottom 25 percent of the distribution and then look at the range that describes that middle 50 percent.

The IQR for the data in Table 12.4, therefore, is 20 − 10 = 10 years. In and of itself, this statistic is not particularly meaningful, but it would be, for example, if we wanted to compare the distribution of years of employment at PU to that at other universities. This brings us to yet another limitation of both the range and the interquartile range as descriptive statistics: although they are useful for comparing relatively similar types of distributions using similar units and similar categories, they are relatively meaningless in and of themselves and cannot be used to compare different distributions.

STANDARD DEVIATIONS AND VARIANCES

The challenge, therefore, is to develop a statistic that not only can convey differences in variability between similar-based distributions such as the two superimposed in Figure 12.8, but also has broader utility across a wider range of distributions.

The place mathematicians began to look for this statistic was at the concept of deviations from the mean, which seems reasonable enough, given that the variability we are trying to get a handle on involves variability around that central point. We can follow through the logic of it by starting with a distribution of scores, computing its mean, checking out how much each score we have deviates from the mean, and then maybe finding an "average" deviation around the mean.

Table 12.6 shows two distributions of scores,[12] under the left-hand columns "Thin" and "Dispersed." Both columns have the same range (i.e., in each the lowest score is 1, and the highest score is 9), and the mode for each distribution is 5. We'll leave it to you to do the computations that show that they also have the same median and mode (5.0 in each case). The table's third and fourth columns show how much each of the scores deviates from the mean of its group; at the bottom of each of those columns you can see the sum of the deviations about the mean. Funny thing—the total works out to zero in both cases!

Indeed, it turns out that this will always be the case, since the mean is in fact the numerical value for which the sum of deviations is zero: all the pluses and minuses will inevitably cancel one another out, and they'll always add up to zero. Just adding up deviations from the mean would thus seem to be a dead end; they don't do the job we require of them.

Not being the sort of folk who give up quickly, however, and always ready with a handy technique to take care of inconvenient things like pluses and minuses that cancel one another out, mathematicians next looked at the possibility of taking the absolute magnitudes of the deviations (i.e., ignoring the sign of the difference), but that didn't work out very well in more complex algebraic calculations. Then they came up with the possibility of *squaring* all the deviations about the mean. The nice thing about squaring each deviation is that it makes every number a positive number (i.e., −5 squared and +5 squared both equal 25); it also gives greater weight to deviations the farther they are away from the mean (i.e., a 1-unit distance, whether plus or minus, when squared, gives 1; 5 points of distance, whether plus or minus, when squared, gives 25). Columns 5 and 6 of Table 12.6 show what happens when we begin looking at the squared deviations; the sum of the squared deviations is given at the bottom of each column for the respective distributions. Do we have success?

The sum of the squared deviations about the mean is indeed greater for the dispersed distribution than it is for the thinner one. But our success is more apparent than real. Although the sum of the squared deviations about the mean is indeed successful at differentiating between the two distributions shown in Table 12.6, it turns out that other examples can easily be invented that make our success short-lived. More specifically, note that the dispersed distribution and the thin distribution in Table 12.6 have exactly the same number of people in them. What would happen if we took the thin distribution and simply doubled the number of scores we have? The range would be the same; the mean, median, and mode would all be the same; and the form of the distribution would be the same, but suddenly our sum of the squared deviations would be twice as large, suggesting that the thin distribution is even *more* variable than the dispersed one! That's a problem.

Fortunately, the problem is short-lived as well. The hint for a solution comes from the fact that our problem seems to be related to the number of observations. The solution comes when, instead of merely summing all the squared deviations about the mean, we then proceed to divide that sum by the number

Table 12.6

Describing Thin and Dispersed Distributions

Scores		Deviations from Mean		Squared Deviations	
Thin	Dispersed	Thin	Dispersed	Thin	Dispersed
1	1	−4	−4	16	16
2	2	−3	−3	9	9
3	2	−2	−3	4	9
3	3	−2	−2	4	4
4	3	−1	−2	1	4
4	3	−1	−2	1	4
4	4	−1	−1	1	1
4	4	−1	−1	1	1
5	4	0	−1	0	1
5	4	0	−1	0	1
5	5	0	0	0	0
5	5	0	0	0	0
5	5	0	0	0	0
5	5	0	0	0	0
5	6	0	+1	0	1
5	6	0	+1	0	1
6	6	+1	+1	1	1
6	6	+1	+1	1	1
6	7	+1	+2	1	4
6	7	+1	+2	1	4
7	7	+2	+2	4	4
7	8	+2	+3	4	9
8	8	+3	+3	9	9
9	9	+5	+4	16	16
Sum = 120	Sum = 120	Sum = 0	Sum = 0	Sum = 74	Sum = 100
$N = 24$	$N = 24$			Mean = 3.08	Mean = 4.17
Mean = 5.0	Mean = 5.0			$\sqrt{3.08} = 1.75$	$\sqrt{4.17} = 2.04$
				S.D. = 1.75	S.D. = 2.04

of observations, thereby giving us the *average* squared deviation about the mean. Once we do that, everything in the hypothetical examples works out splendidly. We see that the average squared deviation about the mean is substantially larger for the dispersed distribution in Table 12.6 than it is for the thin one (4.17 versus 3.08, respectively)—just as, logically, we feel it should be. And if you take the thin distribution and double the number of observations we made, it turns out that, when we divide that doubly large sum of squared deviations by the

doubled number of observations, we still end up with exactly the same average squared deviation. Once again, this is consistent with the logical notion that indicators of the form of a distribution, in terms of its variability, should not be influenced by other considerations such as sample size.

If you follow the reasoning above, you now understand the basis of two incredibly important statistics that form the basis of analysis for a wide array of statistical techniques. The summary statistic we ended up with above—the average of the squared deviations—is known in statistical parlance as the *variance* of a distribution.

As for the second statistic of importance, the one weakness of the variance as a measure of dispersion is that it's expressed in *squared* units rather than in our original scale of measurement. To make our statistic more meaningful in our original context, recall that we originally squared all the scores to get around the problem of having the pluses and minuses cancel each other out. Thus, to get back to our original units of measurement, all we need do is take the *square root* of the variance statistic. Given that we originally squared the deviations and, after finding their average deviation from the mean, are now taking the square root, our new statistic simply reflects the average deviation about the mean that is present in our distribution. That statistic is called the *standard deviation*. We will hear of it again.

INFERENTIAL STATISTICS

As the previous section stated, the notion of variability is a crucial one in social science. It's the variance in life that we spend the most time trying to explain: Why are things one way one time and a different way another time? To use the example of the faculty at Provincial University once again, it's all well and good to say that the largest number of faculty members are assistant professors, but an *understanding* of university life requires that we explain why some people are assistant professors, others are associates, and still others are full professors. And while it's nice to know the distribution of length of employment, things become even more interesting when we start asking why members of some social groups seem more or less likely to get hired than others, why and how these propensities might change over time, why more or fewer people are hired in one year than in another.

The rest of this chapter discusses two general classes of statistics that examine such relationships: *measures of association* (i.e., where the question of interest is in how two or more variables "go together" or are associated with one another) and *measures of difference* (i.e., where the general question of interest

is typically whether the means of two or more groups differ). This distinction is to some degree contrived, but as you'll discover near the end of the chapter, it's a useful pedagogical distinction to make at this time.

Examining Relationships among Categorical Variables

CROSS-TABULATION AND CONTINGENCY TABLES

The researcher who's interested in examining the relationship between two nominal or categorical variables will normally begin by cross-tabulating them, that is, creating a celled matrix or contingency table where the joint (or bivariate) frequencies are shown. For example, the Provincial University (PU) scenario involves two categorical variables: sex (male or female) and academic rank (assistant, associate, or full professor). The *univariate* frequency distributions for those two variables were depicted in Tables 12.1 and 12.2; their *bivariate* frequency is illustrated in Table 12.7. Such bivariate tables are a purely descriptive technique but are an important prerequisite for *inferential* analysis.

Like other tables, this one has an identifying number, a title that denotes its contents, and clearly labelled variable names and attendant levels. Across the table are three columns, each signifying an academic rank. At the bottom of each column are the (univariate) column *marginals* (i.e., totals): 170, 130, and 100 for the three ranks, as in Table 12.2. The two rows, labelled on the left side of the table, signify sex. On the table's right-hand side are the (univariate) row marginals: 160 females and 240 males, as in Table 12.1. The total number of faculty members, 400, is shown at the bottom right-hand corner of Table 12.7; there, we crosscheck to ensure that the total number of faculty members by rank (170 + 130 + 100) is the same as the total number by sex (160 + 240).

Within each cell of the table are the bivariate frequencies; that is, the number of people who manifest the joint characteristics of a given sex at a given rank. The number 90 in the top left-hand corner, for example, shows that there were 90 female assistant professors on the faculty at PU. You can see that the number of female faculty members decreases as you

Table 12.7

The Cross-tabulation of Sex by Academic Rank for Provincial University Data

		Academic Rank			
		Assistant professor	Associate professor	Full professor	Row marginals
Sex	Female	90 Ex = 68	50 Ex = 52	20 Ex = 40	160
	Male	80 Ex = 102	80 Ex = 78	80 Ex = 60	240
	Column marginals	170	130	100	Total = 400

go up the ranks (90 assistants, 50 associates, 20 full professors), while male faculty members are spread evenly across the ranks (80/80/80). It's also easy to compute that while roughly 53 percent of all assistant professors are female (i.e., 90/170 × 100), only 38 percent of associate professors and 20 percent of full professors are females; conversely, 47 percent of assistants, 62 percent of associates, and 80 percent of full professors are males.

Inclusion of a bivariate frequency distribution (also called a *contingency table*) is a very helpful way to summarize and represent your data. In this case, we immediately get the impression that sex and rank are associated at PU: female faculty members seem especially underrepresented at the senior levels of the academic hierarchy.

Another appropriate way to represent the data would be to use a grouped or clustered bar graph. Figure 12.9 shows such a graph for the "Rank by Sex" data of Table 12.7.

THE CHI-SQUARE DISTRIBUTION

But a social scientist researching this situation would not stop there. He or she would first want to know whether the joint variation of sex and rank we observe is still within the realm of what we might expect from mere chance variation or whether it

exceeds those bounds. This is a question of the *statistical significance* of the results. In order to determine it, we need some sort of measure by which we can decide how likely or unlikely we are to obtain

Figure 12.9

Sex and Academic Rank of Faculty at PU

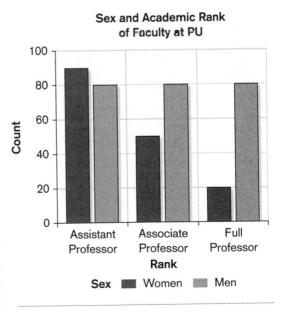

NEL

the particular distribution we observe. This is given by a statistic known as *chi-square,* which allows us to assess whether two categorical variables are associated beyond what would be expected on the basis of chance variation alone. Doing so requires us to first compute a chi-square statistic to describe the particular pattern of frequencies and then compare our chi-square statistic to the chi-square distributions to see how likely that particular chi-square value is to be observed.

The chi-square statistic describes deviations between what we'd *expect* (on the basis of chance, i.e., if the two variables were indeed independent) and what we actually *observe*. To compute the expected values, we take the univariate marginals (i.e., row and column totals) as givens. An *expected frequency* is then computed for each of the cells, depending on the relevant column and row marginal for each cell. In essence, we thus say, "Given that there are more male (240) than female (160) faculty members, and given that there are more assistants (170) than associates (130), and more of both than full professors (100),[13] how many female assistant professors would we expect there to be if there were no association between rank and sex?"[14] We do that by taking the column marginal for assistant professors (170), multiplying that by the row marginal for females (160), and dividing by the total number of observations (400) to get the expected frequency of 68 that you see in Table 12.7 in the "female/assistant professor" cell. Thus, if there were *no* association between sex and rank, we'd *expect* there to be 68 female assistant professors; in fact, we observe many more (*n* = 90).

The same procedure is followed for each and every cell. To obtain the number of expected female full professors, for example, you'd take the row marginal for females (160), multiply by the column marginal for full professors (100), divide by the total number of observations (400), and get 40— many more than the 20 female full professors we actually observe. We'll leave it to you to check our calculations on the other four cells; just follow the same rules noted above (i.e., relevant column marginal, multiplied by relevant row marginal, divided by total number of

observations). You can check your calculations by summing your expected frequencies for each row and column; they should add up to the actual marginal totals (since the marginals are treated as givens). For example, note that the expected frequencies for males in each of the cells in that row (102, 78, 60) add up to 240, which is indeed the total number of males we have; similarly, the expected values for the associate professor column (52, 78) add up to 130, which is indeed the total number of associate professors among the faculty at PU.

We now have *two* different bivariate frequency distributions: one of *observed* frequencies and another of *expected* frequencies. The chi-square statistic involves a comparison between the two. To compute it, we first take the *difference* between what we expected and what we observed for each cell. For example, in the "male/assistant professor" cell, we observed 80, but would have expected 102 if there were no relationship between sex and rank and if nothing other than chance had been operating—a deviation of 80 − 102 = −22. But note that if we observed 22 *fewer* male/assistant professors than expected, then, given the marginal, we must have had 22 *more* female/assistant professors than expected; indeed, that is the case (i.e., 90 − 68 = 22). We once again have the problem that a simple summation of all the deviations will add to zero; the mathematical solution, as with the variance statistic, is to square those deviations to get rid of the pluses and minuses. Thus, for the "male/assistant professor" cell, our squared deviation statistic is $(-22)^2$, or 484.

At the same time, we must also acknowledge that a deviation of 22 will be differentially "surprising," depending on the number we expected in the cell. If we had expected 500 people in the cell, for example, a deviation of 22 people might not seem especially large; if we had expected 50, on the other hand, a deviation of 22 is quite substantial. To take into account the relative magnitude of the deviation, we take the squared deviation statistic we computed above (484) and divide it by the expected value for that cell (102), to come up with 4.7.

The final step is to *sum* these individual cell statistics across all six cells, in order to create our final chi-square statistic for our contingency table. You should compute these values and the total for yourself, but the values we obtained (running from left to right across successive rows of Table 12.7) are 7.1, 0.1, 10.0, 4.7, 0.1, and 6.7, which sum to 28.7.

But what exactly does 28.7 mean? Is that big? Small? Surprising? Expected? We must take our sample statistic and compare it to the appropriate chi-square distribution in order to answer those questions. Appendix B shows a listing of critical values for different probability levels; pay particular attention to the .05 and .01 levels. These are values that our sample's chi-square statistic must *meet* or *exceed* before we're prepared to say, with 95 percent or 99 percent confidence, that the deviation between expected and observed values in our distribution was *statistically significant* (i.e., greater than one would expect on the basis of chance variation alone). But Appendix B gives a lengthy list of such criterion values. Which ones are "ours"?

DEGREES OF FREEDOM Note the column at the left of Appendix B, the one titled *df* (*degrees of freedom*). The reason we need that column recalls the problem we faced in calculating deviation statistics. The magnitude of a chi-square statistic will be sensitive to the number of cells included in the analysis. Our example table had two rows and three columns (or six cells), and we derived a chi-square value of 28.7. Would a table with three rows and four columns (i.e., 12 cells) have resulted in a higher chi-square value merely because of a greater number of cells? The answer, all else being equal, is yes. Thus, we must take the *size* of the contingency table into account, and we do so by considering the number of degrees of freedom it possesses.

Degrees of freedom (*df*) is a very hard concept to nail down, although you see it whenever an inferential statistic is being discussed. At its core is the notion that the theoretical distribution will vary in form depending on the number of parameters that are free to vary. With contingency tables, where the distribution of data is framed in terms of certain numbers of *rows* and *columns,* the *df* we have are constrained by the fact there are two rows and three

columns in our table; the number of cell values free to vary, given the marginal values, is relatively small.

The process might be illustrated by telling you how we went about creating that contingency table, in order to have an example that we could use as an illustration. Our earlier presentation of the univariate frequency distributions at PU (Tables 12.1 and 12.2) had established our givens (i.e., the observed univariate marginals). Because we wanted to create a situation where sex *is* related to rank, we first decided that we'd put most of the "female" observations into the "female assistant professors" category. We could have chosen any number from 0 to 160 to put in that cell, but we chose 90.

Then we went to the next cell. What limitations did we have? We know (from the given marginals) that there are 160 females, and now we also "know" from our choice above that 90 of them are assistant professors; thus, when we went to create a number for the "female/*associate* professors" cell, we could choose any number from 0 to 70 (since $160 - 90 = 70$) as the number for the cell. Like the first (female/assistant) cell, it had constraints but was still *free to vary*. We chose to put the number 50 in that cell.

The process continued: we went to the third cell—female full professors. But here our choices are no longer free to vary. Given the female row marginal of 160, and given our two choices in the female/assistant (90) and female/associate (50) cells, the number in the third cell *must* be 20—the *only* number that can go there if the marginal is to remain as set.

And the same is now true of all the other cells. There were 90 female assistant professors; if the column marginal for assistants ($n = 170$) is to remain, there *must* be 80 male assistant professors. Given there are 130 associate professors, and 50 of them are female, then there *must* be 80 male associate professors. Similarly, the number of male full professors *must* be 80.

In sum, as we went through the process of creating the above example, there really were only two cell values where we could make choices when setting the observed cell values. Mathematically, one says that in this 2×3 contingency table, despite the fact that there were six cells, we "really" had only two *degrees of freedom* that we could vary. After those two, *every* choice was "determined," *given* the marginals.

A formula has been derived that allows you to easily determine the degrees of freedom for a contingency table. Take the number of rows (2 in our case) and the number of columns (3 in our case), subtract 1 from each (i.e., $2 - 1 = 1$; $3 - 1 = 2$), and then multiply those two numbers together (i.e., $1 \times 2 = 2$). Mathematically, the formula is $df = (R - 1)(C - 1)$, where R is the number of rows, and C is the number of columns.

Thus, we now know that the particular values that are "ours" in Appendix B are the ones associated with $2df$; our chi-square value must meet or exceed 5.99 in order to be considered "statistically significant" at the 95 percent level of confidence (i.e., because the probability of observing our results on the basis of chance alone is less than 5 percent, or $p < .05$) and must exceed 9.21 in order to be considered statistically significant at the 99 percent level of confidence (i.e., $p < .01$). Both of these values are in fact handily exceeded by our chi-square statistic of 28.7. Thus, we can say with 99 percent confidence that the suggestion that rank and sex are *not* associated at PU is probably false. The likelihood of our observing these results by chance variation alone is so improbable that we reject the "null" hypothesis—that rank and sex are *not* related—and infer that sex and rank probably *are* related.

INTERPRETING THE RESULT So what does our finding really mean? No matter how we slice it, males appear more likely to have been promoted up the ranks than females. Is this indicative of biased promotional practices at PU? Is this yet another social example of how an "old boys' network" can make it hard for women to succeed? Certainly the data presented are consistent with that explanation; this is exactly the sort of bivariate distribution one would expect if discriminatory promotional policies were in place. But are there rival plausible explanations to consider?

One such explanation might assert that the significant association between sex and rank we observe is in fact not a result of discriminatory *promotional* policies, but rather the legacy of discriminatory *hiring* practices that acted to keep women out of university and graduate schools, and hence out of the academy, for many years. Thus, since women at PU may not have been adequately represented on the faculty until recently, perhaps those who are at PU are still at too junior a stage of their careers to warrant promotion.

If that were the case, then we'd expect to see it in our data. For example, we'd expect there to be a significant association between sex and length of employment, such as seems apparent in Table 12.8. We can see that the propensity to hire female faculty members has changed considerably over time. Of those still remaining from the hirings of 21 to 25 years ago, only 21.8 percent of the faculty hired were female,[15] while in succeeding five-year categories, the hiring rate for females went up to 34.5 percent, then 47.3 percent, then 50.9 percent, and finally to 54.2 percent. We'll leave it to you to work out whether the chi-square value for that contingency table is indeed significant. If it is, any interpretation must still consider the impact of *mortality* on the results.[16]

Even if we could take the bivariate frequencies of Table 12.8 at face value, the hypothesis that *promotional* practices are discriminatory has not necessarily been negated. We cannot simply ignore the earlier finding, which revealed proportionately fewer women appearing in the higher ranks. With this additional finding of differential likelihood of hiring females over time, several rival explanations remain plausible: (1) promotional practices favour males, (2) former discriminatory hiring practices mean that few women have been on faculty long enough to warrant promotion, (3) both of the above statements are true to some extent, or (4) neither of the above statements is true, and some other variable(s) account for the result. For example, it may be that promotional and hiring policies have always been equitable,[17] but the problem may lie elsewhere, for example, not enough women had access to university, entered graduate school, graduated with doctoral degrees, or whatever.

Table 12.8

The Cross-tabulation of Sex by Length of Employment at Provincial University

		Length of Employment					
		1–5 yrs.	6–10 yrs.	11–15 yrs.	16–20 yrs.	21–55 yrs.	
Sex	Female	32	26	44	41	17	160
		Ex = 23.6	Ex = 20.4	Ex = 37.2	Ex = 47.6	Ex = 31.2	
	Male	27	25	49	78	61	240
		Ex = 35.4	Ex = 30.6	Ex = 55.8	Ex = 71.4	Ex = 46.8	
		59	51	93	119	78	Total = 400

The next step in any comprehensive analysis would be to seek out data that bear on those various explanations. You might, for example, attempt to gather archival data on the comparative success ratios of male and female applicants for promotion, or the comparative research and teaching records of male and female faculty members at the time they were considered for promotion, to check for any evidence that more stringent criteria were imposed on female candidates than on males. Or you might want to consider whether the criteria themselves favour males over females, given existing social structures and vocational constraints. Alternatively, you might turn your attention to graduate-school admissions records or to proportions of male and female job applicants over time. Each set of data would shed further light on the dynamics of this microcosm of society and how it has changed (or not changed) over time. The only constraints will be the availability of data and the analytical intelligence of the researcher.

OTHER MEASURES OF RELATIONSHIPS FOR CATEGORICAL DATA

Many other statistics can also be computed for cross-tabulation; Norusis (1993) provides a full list of them. She also explains why some might be desirable by describing the limitations of the chi-square statistic:

The chi-square test is a test of independence; it provides little information about the strength or the form of the association between two variables. The magnitude of the observed chi-square depends not only on the goodness of fit of the independence model but also on the sample size. If the sample size for a particular table increases n-fold, so does the chi-square value. Thus, large chi-square values can arise in applications where residuals are small relative to expected frequencies but where sample sizes are large. (208)

In sum, while the chi-square test may allow you to reject the null hypothesis of independence, it does not in itself do a particularly good job of informing you about the degree of association that exists between two variables. The chi-square is also very n-sensitive; the larger your sample size, the more "easily" you'll be able to obtain statistical significance, even when the degree of association between the variables is actually rather small.

But what other kinds of statistics are there for this situation? Norusis's (1993) inventory includes examples that range from measures of the degree of association between two categorical variables all the way up to interval data. These latter inclusions stray a bit too far for us at this point in the discussion, so we'll limit the following discussion to a few statistics that we see as more likely to be of interest with categorical data.

Your choice in what further statistics you might look at should be governed by the kind of information that's most suitable for your situation. Norusis (1993) explains why:

> Indexes that attempt to quantify the relationship between variables in a cross-classification are called *measures of association.* No single measure adequately summarizes all possible types of association. Measures vary in their interpretation and in the way they define perfect and intermediate association ...
>
> A particular measure may have a low value for a given table, not because the two variables are not related but because they are not related in the way to which the measure is sensitive. No single measure is best for all situations. (209)

STRENGTH OF ASSOCIATION There are two general classes of statistics that address the degree of association in cross-tabulations. The first has paid homage to the widespread use of the chi-square statistic by attempting to modify the statistic in a manner that will be less influenced by sample size and more reflective of association.

One of these, the *phi-coefficient,* takes the chi-square statistic, divides it by N, and then takes the square root of that quotient. By doing so, it attempts to take sample size into account and establishes a statistic that can range from zero to approximately 1.0. The *coefficient of contingency* and *Cramer's V* do essentially the same but use slight modifications of the sample size element of the computational equation. In the case of a 2 × 2 table, all these statistics are pretty well equal in magnitude to the Pearson's r (correlation coefficient) that would be computed on the same data. For our rank/gender cross-tabulation (which of course is *not* a 2 × 2 table), the three statistics are 0.267, 0.259, and 0.268, respectively, all of which were statistically significant ($p < .05$), as was the case with the chi-square statistic.

REDUCTION OF ERROR The second type of test statistics are those based on the concept of "proportional reduction of error" (PRE).

> These measures are all essentially ratios of a measure of error in predicting the values of one variable on knowledge of that variable alone and the same measure of error applied to predictions based on knowledge of an additional variable. (Norusis 1993: 211)

To take our rank/gender example again, you start by saying, "If I don't know what sex a particular faculty member is, and I want to predict what rank he or she holds, what prediction would I make, and how often will I be incorrect in my prediction?" Then you continue: "Okay, now what prediction would I make if I *am* told the *sex* of the person whose rank I am trying to predict, and what is the likelihood of me being wrong now?" And finally, "To what extent (if at all) will my predictions in the second case be better than my predictions in the first case?"

The first statistic considered is Goodman and Kruskal's lambda statistic. In answer to the first question, Goodman and Kruskal assert that the logical prediction to make is whatever category is the modal one. In our rank/gender data, for example, the largest number of people in the sample were assistant professors (170 out of 400 faculty members), that is, 42.5 percent of all faculty members, or 0.425 of the sample. If we were to just guess "assistant professor" every time we were asked to guess an individual's rank without knowing what sex he or she is, we thus would be "correct" 42.5 percent or 0.425 of the time. The probability of being wrong is then given as $1 - 0.425 = 0.575$. File that number in your head as p_1.

The next question is what prediction we'd make if we *knew* the sex of the person. Answering it requires us to identify the modal category within each sex and to make that prediction for that sex. The situation is a bit odd for the males in our fictitious example, given that we have exactly the same number of men (80) at each rank, which means that any one of the three ranks could be used as our basis of prediction. Regardless of which category we decided to guess, we would end up being right about a third of the time, that is, 33.3 percent, or 0.333 of the time for *all the males*, or 0.200 of the *sample as a whole* (because the 80 men who comprise any one category represent 20.0 percent of the entire sample of 400 faculty members). For women, the modal category is "assistant professor," so if we predicted that category for every woman we would be correct 56.25 percent, or 0.5625 of the time among all females, or 0.225 of the sample as a whole. In combination, our "correct" guesses for the men and women faculty members, respectively, would cover 0.200 + 0.225 = 0.425 of the sample as a whole; conversely, this means we will still be wrong in our prediction 1 − 0.425 = 0.575 of the time. File that number in your head as p_2.

If you compare p_1 (0.575) to p_2 (0.575), you can see immediately that, although the chi-square and other measures of association were statistically significant, in fact our ability to predict rank from sex has not been enhanced at all. When we ignored the sex of the faculty member, we were wrong in our prediction 0.575 (or 57.5%) of the time. Now that we have taken sex into account, we are still wrong 0.575 (or 57.5%) of the time. Because the numbers are identical, it's fairly obvious the lambda statistic will be non-significant, but just for the record we'll note that the way you compute the lambda statistic is to calculate the degree of improvement in prediction:

$$\frac{p_1 - p_2}{p_1} = \frac{0.575 - 0.575}{0.575} = \frac{0.000}{0.575} = 0$$

That is, our predictive ability has improved by 0.0 percent, and that value, 0.000, is our lambda statistic. The statistics can range from 0 (where taking one variable into account offers zero improvement in prediction, as was the case in our example) to 1 (where taking the independent variable into account allows perfect prediction).

Finally, note that the extent to which your predictability will be enhanced will vary depending on which variable you are predicting from and which you are predicting to. In the example above, we tried to predict the rank of the person in two situations: where we did not know the sex and where we did. Our predictability did not improve at all, in part because so many of the faculty members at PU are assistant professors. What would happen if we went the other way and asked whether knowing the rank of a faculty member would help us predict gender?

Remember the place to start is by asking what prediction we would make knowing nothing about the faculty member. At PU, the largest number of faculty members are men, who comprise 240 out of 400, or 60.0 percent of all faculty members. Thus, if we know nothing about the faculty member, we should guess "man," and we will be right 60 percent (or 0.600) of the time. Conversely, we will be wrong 1 − 0.600 = 0.400 of the time. That is p_1.

What do we predict if we know the rank of the person? For assistant professors, the modal category is "woman" (90 out of 170, or 0.529). If we guess "woman" for all assistant professors, we thus will be correct 52.9 percent of the time across all assistant professors, or 22.5 percent across the sample as a whole (90 out of 400). For associate professors the modal category is "man" (80 out of 130 or 0.615), so that if we guess "man" for every associate professor we will be correct 61.6 percent of the time across all associate professors, or (80 out of 400 = 0.200) for 20.0 percent across the sample as a whole. Finally, for full professors the modal category is "man" (80 out of 100, or 80%). If we always guess "man" when we know the person is a full professor, then we will be right 80% of the time across all full professors, or (80 out of 400 = 0.200) for 20 percent of the sample as a whole. In combination, our "correct" guesses across the three ranks will be 0.225 + 0.200 + 0.200 = 0.625 for the sample as a whole; the flip side is that we will still be wrong 1 − 0.625 = 0.375 of the time. That number is p_2.

Now if you compare p_1 (0.400) to p_2 (0.375), you can see our predictability is something other than zero (as we computed above), although it is still quite small. When we compute the lambda statistic this time we get

$$\frac{p_1 - p_2}{p_1} = \frac{0.400 - 0.375}{0.400} = \frac{0.025}{0.400} = 0.0625$$

That is, our lambda statistic is 0.0625, which means that our predictive ability has improved by 6.25 percent. However, the probability of this occurring if nothing other than chance alone were operating is 0.443,[18] which means that the enhancement in predictability is no greater than one would expect from chance variation alone (i.e., $p > .05$).

Examining Relationships among Continuous Variables

THE LIMITS OF CONTINGENCY TABLES

The chi-square statistic discussed above is a useful measure of association when dealing with two categorical variables where each has relatively few levels. Although it's possible to use this type of statistic with larger numbers of categories, you need reasonably large expected cell frequencies in order to do the analysis with some degree of mathematical integrity; thus, sample size requirements rapidly become prohibitive as the size of the contingency table increases. For example, the contingency table involving sex and rank was a 2×3 table with 6 cells; with a minimal requirement of 5 to 10 expected observations per cell (or 30 to 60 observations in total), the 400 observations we had were clearly adequate to perform the analysis.

But suppose we want to look at the relationship between the length of time faculty members have been employed at PU (originally reported in Table 12.4, these data range from 1 to 25 years and thus have 25 levels) and their opinions on the relative value of teaching and research (see Table 12.3; the scale has 5 points and thus 5 levels). We *could* cross-tabulate those two variables, but the contingency table would be 5 rows deep by 25 columns wide—

125 cells! With the requirement for minimal expected frequencies of 5 to 10 per cell, we'd need somewhere in the order of 600 to 1200 observations before the statistical analysis became meaningful. Suddenly, our 400 observations look very puny.

Of course, we could always collapse cells in order to help our data fit the statistical requirements. Instead of the 5 levels on the opinion item, we could collapse down to 3: (a) research valued more than teaching (i.e., categories 1 and 2), (b) research and teaching equally valued (category 3), and (c) teaching valued more than research (categories 4 and 5). Similarly, we could group "years of employment" data into 5 levels of 5 years each (as was done in Table 12.5). These two steps would reduce our 5×25 (or 125-cell) table down to a 3×5 (or 15-cell) table, which would clearly be more reasonable, given our total number of observations.

But while we *can* do that, most researchers would be reluctant to do so, other than for simplifying, illustrative purposes. We'd lose too much information. Another alternative would be preferred: the *scatter-plot diagram*. Then we could go further, assessing whether the relationship between variables is linear by using the *Pearson product–moment correlation coefficient* (otherwise known as Pearson's *r*).

SCATTER-PLOT DIAGRAMS

A scatter-plot diagram is a graph that depicts the status of each respondent on the two variables whose association we're interested in assessing. It offers the great advantage of allowing us to "see" the nature of the relationship that exists between the two variables. Scatter-plot diagrams are a useful way to see what *kinds* of relationships might exist between your variables. Figures 12.10(a) through 12.10(h) show some of the variation we might see; for discussion purposes, note that for each of the diagrams we've created a "best" regression line or have placed a "balloon" around the entire set of data points in order to visually illustrate the amount of variation in scores that exists around the regression line.

The first dimension to consider is whether the relationship appears to be *linear* or *curvilinear*, or whether there is no apparent association at all.

Figure 12.10

Scatter-plot Diagrams of Eight Different Relationships between Two Variables

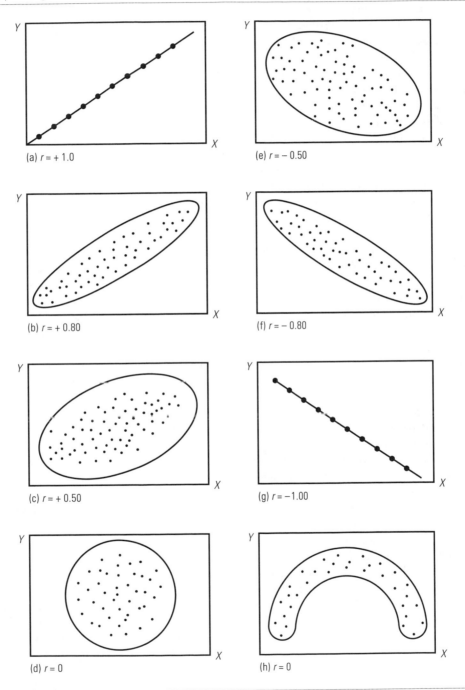

(a) $r = +1.0$

(b) $r = +0.80$

(c) $r = +0.50$

(d) $r = 0$

(e) $r = -0.50$

(f) $r = -0.80$

(g) $r = -1.00$

(h) $r = 0$

Figure 12.10(h) shows a curvilinear, inverted-U-shaped relationship. As an example of this sort of relationship, consider the data from the PU faculty members. It's conceivable that a curvilinear relationship exists between academic rank and the relative importance attached to the teaching and research aspects of the job. Assistant professors may value research more highly because they see it as an important element in tenure and promotion considerations. Associate professors may then pay greater heed to their teaching role, but full professors will undoubtedly include those whose research interest has won them international recognition for their work (since this is a prerequisite for promotion to full professor). We don't know how widely that pattern actually occurs, but it seems a plausible curvilinear relationship.

Other sorts of curvilinear relationships are also possible: U-shaped, circular, or any of myriad others. A consideration of those relationships is clearly important, since they're orderly and no less meaningful than linear relationships, although a detailed consideration of how to investigate them is beyond the scope of this chapter.

Figure 12.10(d) shows no relationship between the two variables at all. Points are strewn all over the scatter plot. These are of no great interest to us here, either.

The remaining scatter plots *do* concern us here. All depict *linear* relationships, albeit with varying strengths of association.

In distinguishing between those scatter plots, the first dimension to consider is that of the *direction* of the relationship: Are increases in one variable associated with increases or decreases in the second variable? The relationship is considered *positive* or *direct* if *in*creases in one variable are associated with *in*creases in the other; the relationship is considered *negative* or *inverse* when *in*creases in one variable are associated with *de*creases in the other. Figures 12.10(a), 12.10(b), and 12.10(c) represent positive or direct relationships, whereas Figures 12.10(e), 12.10(f), and 12.10(g) represent negative or inverse relationships.

The second dimension of interest is the *magnitude* of the relationship. The highest-magnitude relationships are depicted in Figures 12.10(a) and 12.10(g), where all points fall along the same straight line (known as the *regression line*). Next are the relationships evident in Figures 12.10(b) and 12.10(f), where there's a little dispersion around the line, but where the "balloon" fits quite tightly. Figures 12.10(c) and 12.10(e) are still lower in magnitude; there's still a definite direction to the mass of points—positive in Figure 12.10(c); negative in Figure 12.10(e)—but there's also considerable dispersion around the regression line.

QUANTIFYING THE RELATIONSHIP: PEARSON'S *r*

Not surprisingly, mathematicians have sought ways to quantify the direction and strength of the relationship between two quantitative variables. Karl Pearson's work around the turn of the 20th century resulted in the development of a statistic known as the Pearson product–moment correlation coefficient, or, more briefly, as Pearson's *r*.[19] Note that Pearson's *r* describes only linear relationships.

There are two components to any correlation coefficient: a sign and a number. The *sign* indicates the *direction* of the relationship: a plus (+) sign indicates a *positive* or *direct* relationship, and a minus (–) sign indicates a *negative* or *inverse* relationship. The *number* component is defined so that its range is between zero and one.[20] Zero is used when there is *no* linear relationship; 1.0 describes a *perfect* linear relationship, where every data point lies on the same straight line.

Figures 12.10(a) to 12.10(g) have been labelled with rough approximations of the Pearson correlation coefficients that might describe those data. You can see that Figures 12.10(a) to 12.10(c) differ from Figures 12.10(e) to 12.10(g) insofar as *r* values for the former all show a "+" while all the latter begin with a "−". Note also that the magnitude of the relationship decreases as one goes from the perfect relationship in Figure 12.10(a) ($r = +1.0$) to that in Figure 12.10(b) ($r = + 0.80$) to that in Figure

12.10(c) ($r = + 0.50$), and similarly as one goes from Figure 12.10(g) ($r = -1.0$) to Figure 12.10(f) ($r = -0.80$) to Figure 12.10(e) ($r = -0.50$).

The sign and numerical components together allow us to make immediate comparisons between relationships in terms of both their direction and their strength. For example, the relationships depicted in Figures 12.10(e), 12.10(f), and 12.10(g) are all similar in direction but different in magnitude; those in Figures 12.10(b) and 12.10(f) are identical in the strength of the relationships but opposite in direction.

A COMPUTATIONAL EXAMPLE It's fairly easy to compute a correlation coefficient for any given set of paired observations. We won't show the formula's derivation here, but conceptually, it can be understood as a weighted count of how often data points fall in quadrants "b" and "c" versus quadrants "a" and "d" of Figure 12.11.

Table 12.9 shows the computational sequence for a set of data involving the midterm and final exam grades for eight students taking a course in research methods. As you can see, the formula requires you to compute a number of different terms along the way. Generally speaking, the formula takes the scores on each variable, transforms them into

Figure 12.11

Four Quadrants of a Scatter-plot Diagram

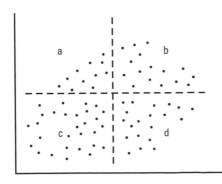

"standardized" scores (so that the variables don't have to be on the same scale or expressed in the same units), and then compares how variation in one variable coincides (or does not) with variation on the other.

The correlation coefficient of $r = + 0.85$ derived in Table 12.9 indicates a strong relationship between performance on the midterm and performance on the final: those who do well on the midterm generally do well on the final, while those who perform poorly on the midterm tend also to do less well on the final. But the relationship isn't perfect, suggesting also that some changes take place: some students who do well on the midterm are perhaps overconfident, don't study as much for the final, and therefore blow it; others take their poor midterm performance to heart, work harder, and improve on the final; or illness that affects some students during one exam is not a factor during the other. Measurement error also occurs: tests are imperfect, thus allowing regression toward the mean to occur.

The next question is whether the correlation we observe is greater than what we would have expected on the basis of chance variation alone. Once again (as with chi-square), this is a question of the *statistical significance* of the results.

We use r distributions in the same way as chi-square distributions. Appendix C shows a listing of criterion values for r, the Pearson correlation coefficient.

Once again, the criterion value depends on *degrees of freedom*. For correlations, the number of degrees of freedom is equal to the number of *paired observations* minus two. Thus, for our data, we have $8 - 2 = 6df$. Appendix C shows that for $6df$ we require a computed correlation of $r = 0.7067$ or higher in order for our relationship to be considered significant at the .05 level, or $r = 0.8343$ for the .01 probability level.[21] Our obtained correlation of $r = +0.85$ exceeds both those criterion values: we can therefore say with 99 percent confidence that the two sets of scores are related beyond the level one would expect on the basis of chance alone.

Table 12.9

Computing a Correlation Coefficient

Student	Mid-Term Score (X)	Final Exam Score (Y)	X^2	Y^2	XY
Wenona	18	18	324	324	324
Barry	19	23	361	529	437
Rajesh	30	25	900	625	750
Ali	33	28	1089	784	924
Sakura	27	34	729	1156	918
Chris	32	38	1024	1444	1216
Shihong	41	37	1681	1369	1517
Alexis	47	42	2209	1764	1974
$N = 8$	$\sum X = 247$	$\sum Y = 245$	$\sum X^2 = 8317$	$\sum Y^2 = 7995$	$\sum XY = 8060$

Computation

1. Take the sum ($\sum$) of the X scores: $\sum X = 247$
2. Square the sum of X: $(\sum X)^2 = (247)^2 = 61\,009$
3. Square each X score. Take the sum of those squared X scores: $\sum X^2 = 8317$
4. Take the sum of the Y scores: $\sum Y = 245$
5. Square the sum of Y: $(\sum Y)^2 = (245)^2 = 60\,025$
6. Square each Y score. Take the sum of those squared Y scores: $\sum Y^2 = 7995$
7. Compute cross-products by multiplying each X score by its associated Y score. Take the sum of those cross-products: $\sum XY = 8060$
8. Note the number of paired observations: $N = 8$
9. Insert the computed figures into the following formula to compute r, the correlation coefficient:

$$r = \frac{N\sum XY - (\sum X)(\sum Y)}{\sqrt{[N\sum X^2 - (\sum X)^2][N\sum Y^2 - (\sum Y)^2]}}$$

$$= \frac{8(8060) - (247)(245)}{\sqrt{[8(8317) - 61\,009][8(7995) - 60\,025]}}$$

$$= \frac{64\,480 - 60\,515}{\sqrt{[66\,536 - 61\,009][63\,960 - 60\,025]}}$$

$$= \frac{3965}{\sqrt{(5527)(3935)}} \quad \frac{3965}{\sqrt{21\,748\,745}}$$

$$= \frac{3965}{4663.6} = +0.850$$

10. Compute the degrees of freedom, which is given by the number of paired observations minus 2, that is, $df = N - 2 = 8 - 2 = 6$.
11. Determine whether the observed correlation is statistically significant by inspecting the critical values listed in Appendix C, for the appropriate degrees of freedom. You should see that for 6df, the critical values that must be exceeded are $r = 0.7067$ and $r = 0.8343$ for $p < .05$ and $p < .01$, respectively. In our example, where $r = 0.850$, we would conclude that our correlation is indeed statistically significant at $p < .01$; that is, the correlation is greater than we would expect on the basis of chance alone, suggesting that the two variables are indeed associated.

THE PROPORTION OF VARIANCE
ACCOUNTED FOR: r^2

While the correlation coefficient (r) conveys the magnitude and direction of a relationship between two variables, we'll also note here (but won't go into the proof) that the proportion of variance that's shared by two variables is equal to the square of their correlation coefficient. Thus, if we determine that the correlation between two variables is $r = 0.90$, then we also immediately know that $r^2 = (0.90)^2 = 0.81$ (i.e., that 81 percent of the variance in one variable is shared by the other).

Besides understanding the inherent relation that r and r^2 have with each other, a consideration of *how* they're related may give you a slightly different take on correlation coefficients. Figure 12.12 plots the relationship between r and r^2. You can see that correlations in the neighbourhood of 0.10 to 0.30 look fairly puny in this light, since even a 0.30 correlation between two variables means that they share only a paltry 9 percent of their variances in common (since $0.30^2 = 0.09$). Even a correlation between X and Y of $r = 0.50$, which many researchers would normally get very excited about, means that X accounts for no more than a quarter (25 percent) of the variance in Y; this still leaves another 75 percent of the variance in Y that is *not* yet accounted for. Not until correlations get into the 0.71 ballpark do you begin to account for even half of the variance in Y. Thus, while the unsquared correlation coefficient (r) may be useful in indicating direction, it may well give an impression of a stronger relationship than would be

Figure 12.12

An Illustration of the Relation between r and r^2

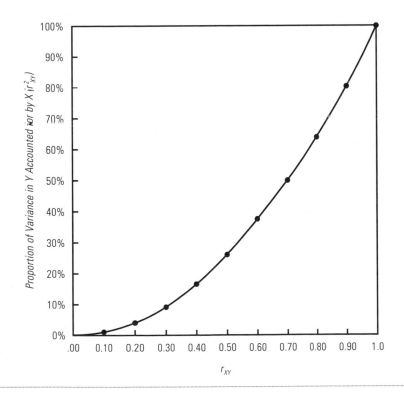

the case if you were to pay greater heed to r^2 and its proportion of variance interpretation.

WHAT CORRELATION COEFFICIENTS DO *NOT* TELL YOU
You've computed a correlation between two variables and found it to be significant. What does this mean? Literally, it means that the two sets of data you've correlated are associated more closely than you would expect on a purely chance basis. But before you jump to the conclusion that you've unearthed some immutable truth, look at some of the reasons you might have obtained the correlation coefficient you did. Consider the following:

1. *Whether the theoretical variables are related.* The discovery of a significant correlation is an *empirical* finding, which you may or may not be able to generalize to the theoretical domain. First, there's a question of the relationship between your theoretical variable and your operational one; that is, the epistemic relationship between the two. Second, as is true of any empirical finding, its *external validity* (or generalizability) must be considered; this is a separate sampling issue.

2. *Whether the association is a causal one.* Every methods textbook will tell you that *correlation does not mean causation.* The fact that two variables happen to "go together" doesn't in any way mean that there's necessarily a causal connection between the two of them. It *may* be that the first variable causes the second; it *may* be that the second variable causes the first; or it *may* be that both variables are influenced by some third variable that you haven't yet recognized. Other variables may "share variance" with both sets of scores, such that the correlation you observe may not reflect a "real" association between the two variables you are investigating, but merely the variance they share with that third variable. There's undoubtedly a correlation between the number of fire trucks that appear at a fire and the amount of damage done, for example, but this doesn't mean that the fire trucks cause the damage or that the damage causes the trucks. It's more likely that a third variable (the size of the fire) influences both.

A similar situation might be evident in the example of midterm and final exam scores. The correlation *may* reflect consistency in the evaluation of "competence in research methods" (as we hope), but it may also just reflect similarities in test-taking behaviour (which is independent of research methods competence per se). Many social beliefs are clearly supported by people's erroneous belief that correlation implies causation. For example, the occasional covariation of visible-minority status and "low levels of social achievement," however selectively that observation is obtained in the first place, is often used to try to justify the racist belief that visible minorities in some way "cause" their "inferiority," when instead social structures, racism, and institutionalized poverty are often causes of both. The tendency to blame the victim is another manifestation of confusing correlation with cause. Victims might in some cases be the architects of their own misfortune, but just as clearly might not.

The example above urges you to be cautious about jumping to conclusions when you find a significant correlation. Similar caution is warranted when you *don't* find a significant correlation. Pearson's r is designed to test for a very particular type of relationship between variables—a linear one. Just because a correlation is not significant does not necessarily mean that a patterned, orderly relationship does not exist. When looking at correlations, you should always look at scatter plots to avoid indulging in interpretations that may turn out to be nonsensical.

Examining Differences between Categories

A SLIGHTLY DIFFERENT WAY OF MAKING COMPARISONS
Thus far in our look at inferential statistics, we've emphasized techniques for measuring association. Let us now introduce another set of techniques that

tackle another very basic task one is often faced with in the social sciences, that is, making comparisons.

To explain how that is done in different situations, consider a situation in which you, as a student, might often find yourself. Suppose you complete two midterm exams, later finding that you scored 22 out of 27 on the Anthropology 101 midterm and 41 out of 55 on your Philosophy 330 exam. Did you do better in anthropology or philosophy? To answer that question, you might look for some common ground on which to compare the two scores, perhaps by translating your scores into percentages. On doing so, you find that your anthropology grade was actually 81.5 percent, while your philosophy score was 74.5 percent. Comparing the two, you infer that your performance was better in anthropology than in philosophy.

Social scientists who analyze such data would actually take the analysis a step or two further, as we'll soon see. But first we'd like to draw your attention to exactly what you did when you tried to compare your midterm exam grades in that way. You created an abstract, hypothetical situation in which a crucial element that made the two grades incomparable in the first place—the fact that one exam was marked out of 27 while the other was marked out of 55—was negated by looking at a theoretical distribution of numbers (who said you had no understanding of statistical concepts?) called percentages. Neither of the exams was actually marked out of 100. But you took the 22 out of 27 in anthropology and said, "Well, *if* this exam had been marked out of 100 points, and my performance and the marking remained constant, what would I have received as a grade?" And you came up with 81.5 percent. The same process with the philosophy grade led you to conclude you would have received a grade of 74.5 percent on that hypothetical exam. By establishing a common ground, you made the two grades comparable.

When we describe percentages as "theoretical," it isn't because percentages are unreal or completely abstract. Rather, the term implies that there's no particularly good reason, other than as a completely arbitrary standard of judgment on which people have agreed, to look at percentages or to have defined percentages as necessarily being a score out of 100. There's no law of mathematics stopping us all from deciding tomorrow that percentages will henceforth be computed with a base of 1000 rather than 100 (although a desire for linguistic integrity might lead us to call them "permillages" rather than "percentages") or even with a base of 472, if we so please. Percentages (or other such standardized ratios) may be arbitrarily defined, but given that we have defined them that way, the results we garner through them are anything but arbitrary.

Members of the social sciences go through a somewhat similar process, but they take a few more details into account. Since you've already learned the hard part—characteristics of distributions, and particularly the concepts of standard deviations and variance—the rest will be easy.

Z-SCORES AND THE NORMAL DISTRIBUTION

In the same way that percentages provide a common ground for comparing grades, social scientists have looked for a common ground on which to compare different distributions of scores. The creation they came up with is known as the *normal distribution*. It's "normal" in the sense that it's typical of many distributions we come across in everyday research; indeed, after more than a decade of gathering all sorts of data—from exam grades to attitude scores to aptitude measures to behavioural indices—we never cease to be amazed at how often one encounters distributions that are roughly normal in their form. There's a central tendency where scores cluster more closely together than anywhere else along the frequency distribution; as one moves farther and farther away from that mean/median/modal point, one sees fewer and fewer scores, until they disappear into infinity. Figure 12.13 depicts a standard normal distribution.

In the same way that "percentages" were arbitrarily defined as being out of 100, the standard normal distribution was also given some characteristics on a relatively arbitrary basis. The distribution's mean was set at zero, while the standard deviation was set at 1.0.[22] Of course, no such choice

Figure 12.13

A Standard Normal Distribution, Showing Proportions of Cases Falling at Different Distances from the Mean

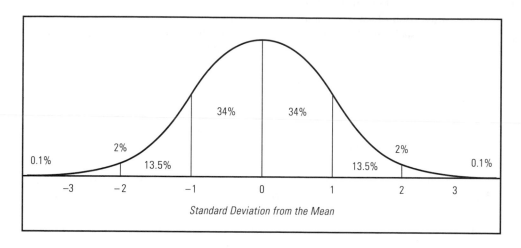

is *completely* arbitrary. Making percentages out of 100 rather than of 472 certainly makes computation easier, as does setting the normal distribution with a central tendency (i.e., mean) of zero and with variability (i.e., standard deviation and variance) of 1.0.

Once the normal distribution is defined, it becomes possible to calculate, for a particular observation at a given distance from the mean, the probability of getting an observation at least that far from the mean. This requires first that we have some measure of deviation from the mean. Since we've already discussed the notion of a standard deviation, it should come as no surprise that social scientists seized on the "standard deviation unit" as the ruler to use for any given distribution of scores. They could have called these "standard deviation units" or "SDUs" (or maybe FREDs or WILMAs). But being the conservative lot that they are, mathematicians decided to call deviations computed in terms of standard deviation units "*z*-scores."

Let's return to the example of your midterm exam grades. A social scientist wouldn't be content with merely using percentages as a common ground of comparison. Treating those percentages as comparable assumes that both exams were equally difficult

and that both professors (or their teaching assistants) marked with equal stringency. But as you may well have found in your own courses, that may be a tenuous assumption. So a social scientist would be interested in knowing whether the scores on that anthropology midterm are approximately normally distributed—and, if so, what the mean and standard deviation of the distribution are.

Suppose it was a particularly difficult exam, so hard that the mean score among your classmates was 15 out of 27, with a standard deviation of 10. That means that your score of 22 was actually 7 points above the mean, or 7/10 = 0.700 standard deviation units above the mean. In other words, your *z*-score on that exam would have been +0.7 (the "+" signifies your score was above the mean; recall that the mean of the distribution is zero, and that deviations from it can be in a positive or negative direction).

Next we'd want to gain the same information for your philosophy midterm. Suppose that it, too, was a fairly difficult exam. Most of your classmates managed to pass, since the mean and median were both 30 out of 55, but very few of them did either very poorly or very well: the standard deviation was a mere 8.0. With a mean of 30 and a standard deviation of 8.0, your score of 41 was, in fact, $11/8 = 1.375$ standard deviation units above the mean; in other words, you achieved a z-score of $+1.375$. Thus, when we compare your performance to that of your classmates, we find that you actually scored somewhat better in philosophy (with a z-score of $+1.375$) than you did in anthropology (where your z-score was $+0.700$), even though your percentage grade in philosophy (74.5) was lower than the one you received in anthropology (81.5).

The process is similar in many ways to what you did in translating your two grades into percentages. In looking for a common ground, you chose percentages, which are arbitrarily established to be expressed out of 100. The logic was essentially to say, "*If* both exams had actually been based out of 100, what would my two scores have been?"

The social scientist, however, says, "*If* the scores on both these exams were drawn from normal distributions, then what is their comparative likelihood of being drawn?" By referring your grades to the normal distribution, we could compute exact probabilities for obtaining at least any given score, or we could give percentile estimates of where you (or any other person) stack up in the distribution. But we'll leave that technique for your course professor to cover if he or she thinks it is useful. We now turn to a situation where we have two variables of interest— one categorical and one continuous—and we seek to determine whether the categories differ in their status on the continuous variable.

COMPARING MEANS THROUGH THE *T*-STATISTIC

In looking at your score on the anthropology exam, we tried to understand it by placing it in its distributional context. But social scientists, and particularly quantitatively oriented ones, aren't often interested in single scores. Scores are interesting only as parts of distributions. Similarly, samples are interesting only when they're linked to the populations from which they were drawn.

In comparing distributions, we're usually interested in whether the means differ: the t-statistic is the measure that mathematicians have invented for us to

use in this instance. People seem to rest so much easier when abstract concepts are reified—we relate so much better to Santa Claus than to the abstract ideals of harmony and sharing. Perhaps the t-test is little more than a tentative concrete response to the question "How big is big?"

One person who tried to answer that question was W. S. Gossett, who worked as a chemist at the Guinness Brewery in Dublin, Ireland, in the late 1800s. Apparently company policy forbade the publication of research, so Gossett published under the pseudonym "Student," which is why the t-distribution is known as Student's t-distribution and its descriptive statistic as Student's t (e.g., see McGhee 1985). The story begins where the standard deviation left off.[23]

When the question under consideration was the extremity of your anthropology exam score, we first found out where your score stood relative to the mean of the distribution of scores (i.e., we took the difference between score and mean). We then determined what the standard deviation of the distribution was, using that as a kind of ruler with which to measure your score in standard deviation (or z-score) units.

When a social scientist wants to know whether any two groups differ, the question is phrased in terms of whether there's a difference between the two group means. Not surprisingly, therefore, step 1 in computing a t-statistic involves finding the difference between the two means. But once we know the difference, how do we know whether it's a "big" difference or whether it might be expected to occur through chance variation alone?

Gossett grappled with that question by asking us to assume the null hypothesis, that is, that the two groups we're dealing with are actually just samples from the same population. Suppose we have a distribution that is normally distributed and that comprises an infinite number of observations. We randomly sample one group of five observations and compute their mean score, sample another group of five observations and compute *their* group mean, and then compare the two means to see how close they are to each other. Then we take another two samples of five observations each, computing and comparing their group means, then another two samples, and another two, until we've made an infinite number of comparisons. If we looked at those comparisons, we'd see that purely on the basis of chance variation, group 1 sometimes scored higher than group 2—sometimes by a little, sometimes by a lot—while other times group 2 scored higher than group 1. We could begin creating a frequency distribution of all of those differences.

Because the two samples were always drawn from the same population with the same population mean, we'd expect that over the long run the most frequent difference we'd observe would be zero and that frequencies would diminish as one moved away from that central tendency. Indeed, with extensive repeated sampling (as is done in Monte Carlo simulations), it can be demonstrated that a frequency distribution of differences between two sample means will be normally distributed, with a mean around zero, regardless of whether the population from which the observations are drawn is normal. If that's the case, it should be possible to determine the probability of *any* given difference, as long as we take into account the particular distributional characteristics we're working with. The *t*-statistic that Gossett developed was intended to provide us with exactly that information.

But how extreme is any given *t*-score? Not surprisingly (we hope), we determine that fact by checking our *t*-score against the Student's *t*-distributions, the critical values of which are reproduced in Appendix D. Just to put some flesh on this search, let's return to the example of the faculty members at PU.

Suppose we're interested in comparing 10 male and 10 female faculty members in terms of the relative value they attach to the research and teaching aspects of their job. Table 12.10 shows these hypothetical data; the females have a mean of 2.3 on the 5-point scale, whereas the males have a mean of 3.4. As this suggests, the female faculty members have a mean opinion that's on the "teaching valued more highly" end of the scale, whereas the male faculty members have a mean that's closer to the "research valued more highly" end of the scale (recall Table

12.3). The difference between them is thus 3.4 – 2.3 = 1.1 scale points. But is that difference "significant," or is it within the realm one might expect on the basis of chance variation alone? The computations necessary for deriving a *t*-statistic are shown in Table 12.10; we compare that *t*-value to the critical values summarized in Appendix D.

Enter the appropriate figures into the following formula for the computation of *t*:

As with chi-square and *r*-values, critical *t*-values take into account degrees of freedom, which, in this case, are determined by sample size. This is because, all else being equal, two samples of 5 people each are much more likely to have divergent group means than are two samples of 100 people each. The various *t*-distributions reflect this, as do the critical values listed in Appendix D.

Thus, we first compute degrees of freedom, which, for the *t*-test, are given by the formula $df = N_x + N_y - 2$, where N_x is the total number of observations in one group, and N_y is the total number in the other. When the sample sizes of the two groups are equal, the formula is more simply stated as $df = N - 2$, where N is the total number of observations in the two groups taken together. Since we sampled 10 female and 10 male faculty members, for a total $N = 20$, our degrees of freedom equals $20 - 2 = 18$. Accordingly, we must look at the line for 18df in the list of critical values given in Appendix D; there, we see that the critical value for *t* to be significant at the .05 level is 2.101, while the critical value at the .01 level is 2.878. Thus, the difference between male and female faculty members on the attitude variable, which resulted in a *t*-score of 2.31, exceeds the criterion for $p < .05$ but doesn't exceed the criterion for $p < .01$.

Limits of Two-Variable Analyses

ERROR RATES WHEN UNDERTAKING MULTIPLE ANALYSES

Researchers rarely do studies that involve only two or three variables. It's far more common to have several independent variables, several dependent variables, or a dozen or more questionnaire or observational variables. As the size and complexity of your

Table 12.10

Computing the t-Statistic

The distribution below shows responses for 10 male and 10 female faculty members to the query whether they value the research or teaching aspects of their role more highly; possible responses were (1) teaching much more highly valued; (2) teaching somewhat more highly valued; (3) teaching and research equally valued; (4) research somewhat more highly valued; (5) research much more highly valued.

Males (X)	Females (Y)	X^2	Y^2
2	1	4	1
2	1	4	1
3	1	9	1
3	2	9	4
3	2	9	4
4	2	16	4
4	3	16	9
4	3	16	9
4	4	16	16
5	4	25	16
$\sum X = 34$	$\sum Y = 23$	$\sum X^2 = 124$	$\sum Y^2 = 65$
$N = 10$	$N = 10$		
Mean = 3.4	Mean = 2.3		

Computation

1. Take the sum of the scores in group 1 (males): $\sum X = 34$
2. Square the sum of group 1 scores: $(\sum X)^2 = 1156$
3. Square *each score* in group 1, and take the sum of those squared scores: $\sum X^2 = 124$
4. Note the number of scores in group 1: $N_x = 10$
5. Compute the mean score for group 1: $\overline{X} = 3.4$
6. Take the sum of the scores in group 2 (females): $\sum Y = 23$
7. Square the sum of group 2 scores: $(\sum Y)^2 = 529$
8. Square *each score* in group 2, and take the sum of those squared scores: $\sum Y^2 = 65$
9. Note the number of scores in group 2: $N_y = 10$
10. Compute the mean score for group 2: $\overline{Y} = 2.3$
11. Enter the appropriate figures into the following formula for the computation of t:

$$t = \sqrt{\left[\frac{\left(\sum X^2 - \dfrac{(\sum X)^2}{N_x}\right) + \left(\sum Y^2 - \dfrac{(\sum Y)^2}{N_y}\right)}{N_x + N_y - 2}\right] \times \left[\frac{1}{N_x} + \frac{1}{N_y}\right]}$$

$$= \sqrt{\left[\frac{\left(124 - \dfrac{1156}{10}\right) + \left(65 - \dfrac{529}{10}\right)}{10 + 10 - 2}\right] \times \left[\frac{1}{10} + \frac{1}{10}\right]}$$

(continued)

Table 12.10

(continued)

$$= \dfrac{1.1}{\sqrt{\left[\dfrac{(8.4) + (12.1)}{18}\right] \times \left[\dfrac{2}{10}\right]}}$$

$$= \dfrac{1.1}{\sqrt{(1.14)\,(0.2)}} = \dfrac{1.1}{\sqrt{0.228}} = \dfrac{1.1}{0.477} = 2.31$$

12. Compute the degrees of freedom by taking the number of observations in group 1, plus the number of observations in group 2, minus 2, i.e., $df = N_x + N_y - 2 = 10 + 10 - 2 = 18$.

13. Determine whether the observed correlation is statistically significant by inspecting the critical values listed in Appendix D, for the appropriate degrees of freedom. You should see that for 18df, the critical values that must be met or exceeded are $t = 2.101$ and $t = 2.878$ for $p < .05$ and $p < .01$, respectively. Thus, our observed difference in the current example would be considered statistically significant at $p < .05$, but *not* at $p < .01$.

data collection increase, one possibility is to do more two-group comparisons via the *t*-test or more bivariate (i.e., two-variable) correlations to take the additional variables into account.

But as the number of variables increases, the number of possible comparisons that can be computed increases dramatically. With two groups, for example, only *one* possible comparison (i.e., group 1 versus group 2) can be made. With three groups, there are *three* comparisons possible (1 versus 2; 1 versus 3; 2 versus 3). But with four groups, there are suddenly *six* comparisons possible (1 versus 2; 1 versus 3; 1 versus 4; 2 versus 3; 2 versus 4; 3 versus 4). And by the time we reach ten groups, there are *45* different two-group comparisons that can be made! Substitute "variables" for "groups" and "correlations" for "comparisons" and you can see that the same is true for correlation coefficients.

You could always just go ahead and do each of those individual comparisons or correlations. But statistically that approach poses a problem. To understand why, recall that the notion of "statistical significance" suggests that we find a point on the distribution under consideration (i.e., chi-square, *t*, *r*) where we can feel confident that a difference is "real" or "reliable." We can never be certain that a difference is real; we can only be confident to varying degrees. Traditionally, the social sciences have adopted $p < .05$

as the default criterion, that is, the criterion to use unless there's some reason, articulated beforehand, to do otherwise. We choose that level because 95 percent confidence (i.e., in all likelihood being "right" 95 out of 100, or 19 out of 20, times) represents "good odds" that our decision to treat a difference (or correlation) as real is appropriate.

The other side of that figure, however, is that on approximately 5 out of 100 occasions, or in 1 out of 20 situations, we'll be *wrong*—we'll proclaim a result to be reliable when in fact it is not. If we're making only one comparison or a few comparisons, we're prepared to live with that uncertainty. But if 20 or 50 or 100 comparisons are made, the odds are high that some of the comparisons we observe to be "statistically significant" will in fact be spurious. If only a few of those comparisons are significant, we probably shouldn't be terribly excited by them; they're probably mere ephemeral shadows that will disappear next time we look at them. If you compute 100 correlation coefficients, for example, the odds are that around 5 of them will emerge as statistically significant purely on the basis of chance variation alone. Accordingly, researchers must be particularly cautious when interpreting the results of numerous tests on the same set of data.

There are at least three ways around this problem, however. The **Bonferroni technique** involves splitting the adopted probability required for significance across the entire range of comparisons to be made (e.g., see Kirk 1968; Pedhazur 1982). For example, if you're adopting a significance level of $p < .05$ and plan to undertake 10 separate t-tests (or chi-squares or Pearson correlations), the Bonferroni procedure involves merely spreading the .05 (known as the *experiment-wise error rate*) across the 10 comparisons, with the result that a $.05/10 = .005$ significance level would have to be achieved on any given comparison before you'd be prepared to consider it "reliable." This approach makes for rather conservative testing (since a .005, or 5/1000, criterion is a very stringent one), but this is considered preferable to engaging in "much ado about nothing."

Alternatively, if you're in the luxurious situation of having a very large number of cases (e.g., 10 times as many cases as you have variables), your data are amenable to a procedure known as **jackknifing.** There are several ways to do this, but the simplest is to randomly split your sample of cases into *two* samples, do the analyses you want to do separately in the two samples, and then focus only on those results that emerge as statistically significant in *both* data sets.

The logic of this approach is that while some correlations or comparisons may well turn out to be statistically significant on the basis of chance error when one is doing a large number of these calculations in one sample, it's highly unlikely that specific chance occurrences will replicate on a second occasion. Only those with some substance to them will do so, and hence only those that can pass the significance hurdle *twice* are thought to warrant further consideration and discussion.

The third alternative is to learn some more techniques that have been developed precisely in order to overcome that error rate problem. The analysis of variance (ANOVA), for example, is conceptually akin to doing multiple t-tests on a given set of data, but controls for error rate in the process. Similarly, multiple regression analysis has been developed to deal with situations in which one is attempting to correlate many variables with some criterion (dependent) measure. But these techniques are beyond the scope of this book, so you'll have to await further courses in statistics to see how they work.

SUMMING UP AND LOOKING AHEAD

This chapter has been one of the more difficult ones in this book to write, in large part because keeping it true to the book's themes has involved an articulation of the logic underlying selected quantitative techniques, more so than describing how to do them. As the book's title suggests, the overall emphasis is on looking at research as a *decision-making* process, and it's impossible to make decisions unless you know what conceptual issues lie underneath. Accordingly, we've avoided the sorts of "If you see X, do Y" dicta one sees in many methods and statistics texts, and although we've avoided offering purely mathematical proofs, we've tried to explain the resulting formulas in terms of the logic through which they were derived.

The chapter begins with a discussion of *variables* and *constants* and then introduces the notion of *levels of measurement,* explaining the differences between nominal, ordinal, interval, and ratio scales. One's level of measurement influences, to some degree, the range of statistics with which a variable may be analyzed. At the same time, it is not the empirical variable per se, but the underlying *theoretical* variable that's most important to consider when identifying our level of measurement—and hence which particular statistical operations are appropriate.

A number of *descriptive techniques*—frequency distributions, pie charts, bar charts, histograms, frequency polygons—are then discussed as ways of presenting distributions of obtained data. The task is to explain how one describes those distributions statistically. Indicators of *central tendency* include the mode, the median, and the mean; each is an appropriate summary statistic in some situations, but each can also be misused. Also included is a discussion of descriptors of distributional *variability,* including the range, the standard deviation, and the variance.

The focus then turns to *inferential statistics* that can be used to examine the relationships among variables. A distinction is made between those statistics that focus on the degree of *association* among variables (e.g., chi-square, correlation) and those that focus on examining the *differences* between groups (e.g., *z*-scores, *t*-tests). These tests are called inferential statistics because we're ultimately less interested in the sample per se than in using the sample as a vehicle through which to make inferences about populations.

First, the section on inferential statistics looks at examining relationships among categorical variables. The *cross-tabulation* or *contingency table* is a way to represent such *bivariate* relationships, while the *chi-square* statistic is the appropriate measure of the extent to which observed cell frequencies deviate from those expected on a purely chance basis. Comparing a computed chi-square statistic to its chi-square distribution gives the probability that the deviations we observe would occur on the basis of chance alone. Using the concept of *degrees of freedom* and Appendix B, you can determine the criterion value your chi-square statistic must meet or exceed in order to be proclaimed significant. A "statistically significant" result implies 95 percent or 99 percent confidence in stating that the distribution was unlikely to have been obtained by chance variation alone, suggesting that the two categorical variables are indeed associated with one another.

The chapter then scrutinizes ways to examine the relationship between two continuous variables. The *scatter-plot diagram* can be used to illustrate such bivariate distributions, and the *Pearson product–moment correlation coefficient* describes the direction and magnitude of a linear relationship. The critical values in Appendix C, along with the degrees of freedom, determine the particular criterion value that must be matched or exceeded in order for the correlation to be declared significantly greater than zero.

But a significant correlation coefficient does *not* tell us whether the underlying theoretical variables are, in fact, related or whether the association, however strong, is a causal one. A nonsignificant *r*-value doesn't necessarily mean that there's *no* relationship between the variables. Pearson's *r* tells you only about significant *linear* relationships; other curvilinear relationships may or may not exist and must be tested for separately.

Attention then turns to techniques that emphasize the assessment of difference; these normally involve looking at differences between groups (a categorical variable) on some continuous variable, that is, a comparison of group means. The *t*-statistic and *t*-distribution are useful in comparing two group means. But while a significant *t*-score leads us to conclude that the two groups do indeed differ, discerning the reasons *why* they differ remains an analytical (rather than purely statistical) task. Rival plausible explanations must be considered.

With the analysis of your data behind you, it's time to start writing it all up in a final research report. The next chapter looks at how to do that.

STUDY QUESTIONS

1. Differentiate between *variables* and *constants*. Show that you understand the difference between them by identifying three variables and three constants that might be used to describe the people in your research methods class.

2. Give examples of one variable at each of the four levels of measurement, and explain in your own words why that is the correct label for each.

3. "Measures of length and distance are ratio-level variables no matter what theoretical variable they are being used as operationalizations for." Would you agree or disagree? Explain.

4. Prepare a brief questionnaire that includes variables at all four levels of measurement. Designate your variable names, and state explicitly what level of measurement you feel each is being measured at. Invent responses; then prepare frequency distributions and compute summary statistics for each.

5. Perform appropriate bivariate analyses on the data gathered for Study Question 4.

6. For what kinds of variables (or levels of measurement) are the mean, median, and mode considered appropriate descriptors of central tendency?

7. In a recent edition of your local newspaper, look for an article that offers statistical information. Would you consider the data well presented? Why or why not?

8. Why is the standard deviation a "better" indicator of dispersion than the range, for interval- and ratio-level variables?

9. Acquire data from the relevant person at your educational institution (e.g., Office of Analytical Studies, Personnel Office, Faculty Association or Union) regarding your university or college faculty (e.g., information concerning distributions of sex, visible-minority status, rank, salary levels, years employed, etc.), and undertake an analysis of those data. Are they consistent with the view that you're attending an egalitarian educational institution? Offer rival plausible explanations, and indicate the sorts of data you might seek or generate to look into the matter further.

10. Encourage the professor in your research methods class (if he or she does not do so already) to tell you not only the class mean on your most recent or next quiz or exam, but also the standard deviation. What was your grade on that exam? What z-score would that be?

11. Hollie gets 87 percent on her final exam in Syrian Epistemology, where the mean of the class was 80 percent with a standard deviation of 5 percent; she manages to get 93 percent in Neo-Gregorian Chants, where the mean of the class was also 80 percent with a standard deviation of 15 percent. In sum, she scored above the mean in both cases. Compared to her respective classmates, however, did she do better at Syrian Epistemology or at Neo-Gregorian Chants?

12. Why do we need to know the degrees of freedom in our data before checking whether the chi-square or r- or t-value we have is significant?

13. Why is a high, statistically significant r-value not necessarily indicative of a causal relationship between the two variables being correlated?

14. A researcher computes bivariate correlations between pairs of variables by hand and ends up with correlation coefficients of -0.46, $+0.52$, $+0.83$, -1.04, and -0.87.
    a. Which of those r-values *must* be incorrect? Why?
    b. Of the remaining values, which represents the strongest association between two variables?
    c. For the correlation coefficient you chose in 14(b), what proportion of variance do the two variables share?

15. A researcher asks a sample of 47 males and 52 females whether they support the idea of censorship for sexually violent films. Among the females, 37 say yes, 11 say no, and 4 are uncertain. In contrast, 22 of the males say yes, 19 say no, and 6 are uncertain. Create a contingency table to depict these data. Do the necessary computations to learn whether there's a significant association between sex and opinions regarding censorship in that sample.

16. A graduate student wants to test out the notion that there is an inverted-U-shaped relationship between anxiety and performance (i.e., whether performance is lowest with either very low or very high levels of anxiety, and highest with moderate levels of anxiety). Given that the relevant data are gathered, would the Pearson correlation coefficient offer a useful way of testing whether the hypothesized relationship is indeed found? Why or why not?

17. A student gathers data on 15 variables from a sample of 100 shoppers at a local mall and proceeds to intercorrelate all the variables, resulting in a total of 105 different correlation coefficients having been computed. Although disappointed at the fact that not many of the relationships prove to be statistically

significant, he's pleased to see that 7 of them are, and he writes up an analysis that focuses on those 7. Is that a reasonable thing for him to do? What if he increases his sample size to include 200 shoppers?

18. What is the *Bonferroni procedure,* and when might you use it?

NOTES

1. If you haven't already surmised, this last example should clearly show that all the statistics cited here are fictitious.
2. Dr. Chuck Chakrapani is CEO of Millward Brown, a marketing research firm.
3. Although such data may also appear in qualitative research, qualitative researchers typically place greater emphasis on target sampling and flexibility in data collection, rather than on standardizing data collection and the opportunities for aggregation and comparison that such standardization allows.
4. You may well quibble about that statement, since there are many instances of legitimate scientific research that has taken place nowhere but in the mind of a scientist. Albert Einstein, for example, was well known for his reporting of the thought experiments that culminated in the development of the general theory of relativity. But this shouldn't detract from the general applicability of the assertion we're footnoting: the social sciences have taken great pride in their emphasis on the need to engage the world and gather data.
5. Altemeyer's (1970) research was done with adult university students; some authors therefore suggest that greater skepticism is warranted (i.e., not assuming greater than ordinal-level measurement on such scales)

when dealing with samples of young children, the cognitively challenged, or dyslexic or innumerate people.

6. The Kelvin scale, in contrast, *is* an example of ratio-level measurement, since its zero point represents absolute zero or a total absence of molecular motion.
7. This is not to say that "anything goes"; students are advised to follow the general principles of analysis stated here until they know enough about statistical and measurement issues to know when deviations from the "rules" are permissible.
8. This brings us back to the whole question of *categories,* discussed earlier in this chapter, and to the philosophical issues that underlie the choice of one summarizing/categorizing scheme over another, for example, Why are marbles worth describing? And why is describing marbles by their colour any more or less meaningful than describing them in terms of size, hardness, or whatever?
9. Figure 12.6(a) shows what's known as a "normal" distribution. Such distributions are of considerable theoretical importance, since most of the inferential statistics we'll discuss are based on the assumption that the scores for any variable are normally distributed in the population. We'll consider the normal distribution in more detail shortly.
10. Another mathematical convention is that smaller or negative numbers go to the left end of any graph, and positive and larger numbers go to the right. When discussing theoretical distributions, mathematicians generally assume that values can range from negative infinity (at the left end of the x-axis, or abscissa) through zero (in the middle) to positive infinity (at the right end of the x-axis).
11. Just in case it is not immediately evident what we are doing, note from the "Cumulative %"

column of Table 12.4 that 24.25 percent of the sample has "9 years" of experience or less. By the time we get to the end of the group that has "10 years" of experience, we have included 27.50 percent of the sample. Thus, the 25 percent point comes among those people who are in the "10 years" category.

12. The technique we're using here is to take a situation where we "know" what the answer "should" be—because we start with a situation that has been constructed to deal with a certain type of problem—in order to try out different possibilities to see what will give us an acceptable answer. In this case, we've created the example in Table 12.6 to show how misleading the range can be and to pose the problem of how we can differentiate between two distributions that have identical characteristics in many respects (e.g., same range; same mean, median, and mode; same number of observations), but that are so clearly different in their dispersion.

13. This in itself should give us pause, since rather than taking them as givens, one might wish to pay separate scrutiny to why the male:female ratio deviates from 50:50 and why the rank structure is the way it is.

14. The chi-square statistic, like all the others we'll be discussing in this chapter, requires that we express our hypotheses (e.g., that there is a significant relationship between sex and rank) as *null hypotheses* (i.e., that there is *no* relationship between sex and rank). The reasons for this will be expounded shortly.

15. The figure 21.8 percent is not in the table. We computed it by noting that in the column "21–25 Yes," there was a total of 78 hirings, 17 of which were women. This works out to $(17/78) \times 100 = 21.8\%$. We'll leave it to you to check whether the percentages we've shown for the remaining four columns are correct.

16. Recall from Chapter 10 that *mortality* refers to people who drop out of the sample and, hence, out of the analysis. All we have to go on here is the hiring history of those men and women who are here today. It may be that there were many more women (and/or men) who were hired but who died, moved to other universities, or entered other professions. A more complete analysis would thus require going back over archival hiring records to see to what extent "mortality" existed, and particularly whether rates of mortality were essentially similar or significantly different for the men and women who were hired.

17. Our definition of equity here assumes that in an egalitarian setting, the characteristics of the sample (e.g., faculty members) will be representative of the distribution of those characteristics in the broader society. For example, if 50 percent of the people in Canada are female, then, if this were a completely egalitarian society, one would expect that approximately 50 percent of the university faculty would be female, 50 percent of the engineers would be women, and so on.

18. We derived this number from an SPSS printout we undertook to double-check all our calculations.

19. Our understanding is that the letter r was chosen because it is the first letter in the word *relationship*.

20. This is arbitrarily done, in the same way that we arbitrarily set percentages to be based out of 100, or the way we set probabilities to run from zero to one.

21. Criterion values are expressed only in terms of the *magnitude* of the relationship; the direction doesn't matter.

22. Incidentally, this implies that the variance is also 1.0, since the variance is the square of the standard deviation.

23. Budding historians are asked in advance to forgive us for the story that follows, which is best described as an academic "docudrama" rather than a historically accurate rendition of discovery. Our interest was in articulating a logical progression of thoughts that would help illuminate the nature of the statistic being discussed. Our description may or may not actually represent the flow of Gossett's thinking when he developed the t-statistic.

CHAPTER 13

WRITING YOUR RESEARCH REPORT

You're in the home stretch now. You worked out your research question, you designed the research and made a proposal that satisfied you and others in your attention to ethics issues, you gathered all the quantitative and/or qualitative data, you did some preliminary analyses that led you to believe you have some understanding of your data, and now you're ready to write it all up.

There are many splendid books and chapters within books that offer advice about how to write research reports. For example, Howard Becker's *Writing for Sociologists* (1986) is a great one that continues to be used widely. Another is Harry Wolcott's (1992) *Writing Up Qualitative Research*. Psychologists can consult the *Publication Manual* published by the American Psychological Association (1994). *The Elements of Style* (1999), by William Strunk Jr. is another classic. In chapters, Lofland and colleagues (2006) offer useful advice on writing in *Analyzing Social Settings*, as does Berg (2007) in *Qualitative Research Methods for the Social Sciences*. And of course, more and more resources appear every year on the Internet.[1]

Although we will duplicate some of their coverage, our intention here is to concentrate on more general organizational considerations that you should keep in mind when writing. These considerations apply to your final research report, whether it's a term research project for a course, an article for publication, or a report you're writing as a consultant or agency researcher. This chapter emphasizes linkages between sections of your paper and will discuss ways you can organize them to maximize readability, continuity, and consistency. We also do an intensive case study of a paper written by a former student to

illustrate how at least one well-done paper exemplifies the principles discussed in the chapter.

GENERAL CONSIDERATIONS/PRINCIPLES

Purpose and Audience

Before you begin writing, it helps to consider in general terms your purpose in doing the research and why and to whom you are writing this report. By "purpose" we mean reasons such as, Did you set out to test a theory? To resolve a controversy that had appeared in the media or in the literature? To gather data that would have implications for policy development? To evaluate a program? To do preliminary exploration in an area that had received little research attention? Whatever the case and it may well be that more than one of these applies to you—your understanding of what you are trying to accomplish has implications for the way you present what you did and what you found.

Hand in hand with purpose are considerations regarding your intended audience. Knowing a bit about your audience is crucial in order to effectively "speak" to them through your paper, in the sense of using a language/vocabulary that is appropriate to them and anticipating and addressing their concerns.

Making It "Interesting"

"Speaking" to your audience means making it "interesting" for them, so start by whetting that interest, by explaining why reading your paper is the most important thing a member of your intended audience can do at that particular point. But how do we make a paper "interesting"? Murray Davis (1971) has written on exactly this topic. Actually, his particular focus was on what makes different *theories* "interesting." To address the topic he first determined which theories were most frequently represented in sociology textbooks—and took these as his sample of theories that were considered "interesting" enough to write about—and then considered whether there were any discernible differences between the theories that appeared frequently in texts and others that covered similar ground but did not garner the same attention.

Davis opens by suggesting we need to reconsider theoretical/methodological lore, which tells us the theories that get the most attention are those that best explain data. In fact, the truth is much more "interesting" than that:

> It has long been thought that a theorist is considered great because his theories are true, but this is false. A theorist is considered great, not because his theories are true, but because they are interesting. (309)

Davis's introduction is an example of a principle he explains in the article, that is, that one way to catch the readers' attention is to challenge what they believe to be true, or what the literature believes to be true, in the general form of "One state of affairs *seems* to be the case, or is *believed* to be the case, but in fact *something else* is true." Much of his article involves the elaboration of that basic principle in a variety of different scenarios, for example, what seems stable is actually changing; what seems disorganized and chaotic is actually highly structured and predictable; phenomena that seem very diverse are in fact all essentially similar. And this holds for their opposites as well, that is, something that always seems to be changing is in fact very stable, what seems structured and predictable is actually highly chaotic and disorganized, and some things that seem very similar need to be distinguished.

If there is a general message here about what makes something interesting, it is that readers are captivated when we challenge what they know, when we give them information that encourages a new way of thinking about an issue, or when we inform them on a topic they know little about. The question for you as an author therefore becomes one of how best to present your research so that readers see the value it might have for them. We'll address that question below, when we discuss the kinds of things you should be considering in each of the sections of your report.

General Shape of the Paper

"Speaking" to your audience and making your writing "interesting" for them also require you to organize your thoughts and message so that your paper is delivered concisely and effectively. The two of us sometimes think of writing as a big puzzle where we have all the pieces—or at least *think* we have all the pieces—but are not quite sure how they best go together to say what we want to say. At some level, the organizing schema that is "best" will vary from paper to paper, and it is up to you to find—sometimes by trial and error—the best way to tell your story in a way that is meaningful to you and your readers. However, there *is* a general organizational style that works well in the area of social science research.

Any good research paper will involve a judicious mixture of breadth and focus, something that arises from the fact that all research involves the interplay between theory (the general and abstract) and data (the specific and concrete). In considering how to organize such a mixture, it's useful to think of the general shape of the research paper as an hourglass: broad at the top, narrow in the middle, and then broad again at the base. Translated into writing, this means it is often best to start with very broad ideas at the top of your paper, get more focused as you move toward the concrete and specific elements involved in your particular research project, and then broaden out again to your conclusions and the implications they have for the more general concerns that brought you to do the paper in the first place.

One More Time

A final principle we'll leave you with is this: "It ain't over till it's over." In other words, you have to allow time in your writing for the redraft to get it right.

Writing is a bit like driving to a place you've never visited before. Some general principles and a roadmap will help get you there, but it's not until you've arrived and have a clear sense of your destination that you can begin to determine the "best" route and where you can flatly and easily reject some possibilities as "dead ends" or "the wrong direction." However, that is sometimes easier said than done when it comes to writing, where we often discover new things as we try explaining to someone else what we think we know. Gaps in our understanding begin to appear. We realize that the flow of logic we thought was so impervious to criticism is more porous than we imagined. Or we find the order in which we decided to tell the story turns out not to work that well after all. Finding any of these out is not a bad thing. It's actually one of the reasons we enjoy writing—not *really* knowing what we think about something until we have written it up and worked through all the details (e.g., see also Richardson 1994).

The main implication is that we need to think of writing from the very start as something other than a one-shot deal. To use the driving analogy again, think of your task as one of describing the best route to this new destination. The major accomplishment of your first draft is simply that it's done—and "getting there" is in itself no small feat—but that first draft still contains all the wrong turns, misreading of maps, dead ends, and so on. It's a route that got you there but is by no means the most direct route. Now, there *are* times when you might actually want to describe that *whole* journey, for example, when you're 80 and explaining in your memoirs all the trials and tribulations you faced *en route* to those

great ideas that brought you the Nobel Prize, but in most cases the rest of the world just wants to know what your point is, how you came to that conclusion, and what it means for them. To do that, we need to take our first draft and start whittling it down to the essentials, the basic information the reader needs to know to understand and travel the route.

The message here is that good writing is a *process* that will always take more than one draft, and this is true regardless of how good and experienced a writer you are. It normally takes no less than 5, and often more than 10, drafts before we think of our work as done; Ted has the record between us with 26 drafts of a report that he and a colleague prepared regarding confidentiality issues. First drafts stick out like a sore thumb: they wander all over the place; they sound like you are making it up as you go along; and they're generally pretty boring because it's never really that clear where you're taking the reader. How many drafts do you need to do? As many as it takes. There *does* come a point of diminishing returns, where you're better off getting the paper out there to have other people read it, but a big part of good writing is being supercompulsive about wanting to get it right. And as Howie Becker said the time you learn the most about writing is not when you write, but when you *rewrite*.

Generally speaking, the idea is to say what you need with as much economy as possible, but doing so—making every word count—is a very time-consuming process. It reminds us of a quotation from Pascal, who wrote a long letter to his friend and concluded by saying, "I have only made this [letter] longer because I did not have the leisure time to make it shorter."

Being concise takes time; allow for at least one more draft than you do now.

TELLING A STORY

With these general principles in mind, we can get more detailed about the particular sections that likely will comprise your research paper. In addition to giving you general advice that you can incorporate into your own research papers, we will work through an example to see how some of the principles come to life in an actual paper. Rather than going through something that one of us wrote, we will focus on a paper written by Patricia Ratel entitled "One Day at a Time: Single-Parent Mothers in Academe." She wrote it a few years ago when she was a student taking a research methods course, similar to the one that this book was designed for: a one-semester research course with a requirement for each student to do a modest, original research project by the end of semester. We'd like to thank her for giving us permission to reproduce her paper in its entirety (see Appendix F) as well as allowing us to dissect it.

We title this section "Telling a Story" because there are many parallels between writing a research report and writing a story or screenplay. Novelists, playwrights, and screenwriters will all tell you that every story has three parts to it: a beginning, a middle, and an end. Those same parts exist in every research report as well. Let's wander through each of those sections and discuss the kinds of considerations that are involved.

Beginning

The *Introduction* is where the characters are introduced and the stage is set; your "characters" will be things like articles from the literature or perspectives on a problem (which typically are tied to sources in the literature). Which characters are appropriate for you to introduce will depend on the research questions that guided your research and what you want your report to focus on now that you're finished.

We make a distinction here between "your research" and "your report" because the two are not the same. During the research design and data-gathering process there's always a tendency to gather more data than you will actually use. The common view is "better too much data than too little," so we always stretch a little further than we originally intended to ensure we've covered all our bases and have some sense of the broader context in which

our core research fits. Because of this, it is typical that you do *not* describe all of your research or detail all of your findings in your report, in the same manner you will not cite everything you read or discuss everything you thought while you were doing the research. The journey that research involves can be a lengthy one with assorted side trips and dead ends, but the objective of your final written report is to tell a focused, concise story. The only things that appear on paper are things that help that story get told. Get to the point.

If you are writing a relatively short research report, like a journal article or term project (i.e., anything up to about 25 double-spaced pages), then your cast of characters will be lean; no one should be introduced who does not have an important role to play. Longer projects, such as honours or graduate theses, which can be anywhere from 50 to hundreds of pages long, allow commensurately more room for character introduction, in part because you are allowed in those contexts to tell a more elaborate and complicated story. However, you should still be judicious about what is included, and everything that appears in your final draft should be there for a purpose. This requires having a preliminary sense of what your paper is about because that is a prerequisite to being able to decide what is "relevant" and "necessary" to include.

FRAMING THE RESEARCH

One of your first tasks in the introduction, as we alluded to above, is to show the readers that your paper is an "interesting" one they should read. The general principle we derived from Davis (1971) was that readers' interests are triggered when we can challenge what they know, offer a new way of thinking about an issue, or inform them on a matter they know little about. Some of the specific ways these justifications play out include the following:

1. "The common wisdom says" or "Everyone knows" X is true. But is it?

   So much of what we "know" is based on "the common wisdom" or what "everyone knows," which often turns out not to be true at all. If your research was designed to shed light on such a state of affairs, and particularly if your findings *do* challenge people's assumptions, then inform readers of that right from the start.

2. Some people think X is true. Some people think Y. What is going on?

    Controversy is interesting. If you've been doing research in an area where there has been considerable debate about what is "true" and/or where there has been disagreement over the "appropriate" thing to do, then offering your report as an effort to better understand and perhaps resolve the controversy is another way of capturing your reader's attention.

3. Our policies (and/or procedures) about X assume that Y is the case. But is it?

    Policies and procedures always involve under-standings or assumptions about (1) the nature of the problem the policy was designed to address, (2) the people for whom the policy is intended, (3) those who will be responsible for implementing the policy, and (4) what options led this particular policy initiative to be considered the "best" way for dealing with the situation at hand. If our research was designed to address these assumptions, then one way to frame our research is to identify the assumption and assert our interest in testing it out, for example, by seeing whether the people who apply for a program really are of a certain type or whether the treatment (or supplement or method) really is the best one available, and so on.

4. X is a phenomenon we know little about. It is interesting because …

    There are many things in the world that catch our interest but that we don't know much about. It may be a relatively new phenomenon or a bourgeoning phenomenon that is only now starting to appear on our radar screen. If your research pertains to such a phenomenon, then your introduction should describe what we know about it and supply any information about the pervasiveness of the phenomenon and/or the attention the issue has been receiving.

5. A theory suggests a certain phenomenon is interesting.

    Those taking a more deductive approach may be engaged in explicit theory testing and may well have decided to investigate a particular phenomenon because it so clearly embodies the conditions addressed by the theory and, hence, is conducive to testing hypotheses derived from the theory. If that is the case, then your introduction should explain the theory and articulate the connection you see between the theory and the research setting or phenomenon.

The challenge Ted gave his students in the semester Patricia Ratel was enrolled was to follow Lofland and Lofland's (1984) dictum to do a piece of exploratory interview-based research by "starting from where you are"; that is, students were encouraged to take an element of their own life and then try to place it in larger context by looking at what that element meant to others in the same position. Ratel was a single parent at that time, and like many others in that situation, she often felt overwhelmed by the challenge to be both a great parent and a great student. In very basic terms, she wanted to know how other women managed it—if indeed they did. The fact that she was experiencing the life herself gave her some "inside" knowledge of the situation that would help in formulating a research question that could be addressed in one semester. Knowing other women in the same situation meant she had ready access to an interview sample, and the fact she was "one of them" no doubt contributed to the feelings of trust it became evident they had for her.

Although Ted wasn't teaching them explicitly at the time, it happens Ratel used two of the techniques in her introduction that we mentioned above to help make her paper "interesting." See if you can pick them out. Here is her first paragraph:

Single parenthood is becoming increasingly pervasive in Canada. Statistics Canada (1984) reports that the number of lone-parent families increased by 10% in the preceding decade. Although some of these families are headed by males, the vast majority (82.6%) are headed by females. Indeed, as a demographic category, "single mothers" comprise 11.3% of the total population, and every indicator suggests this will continue. Until recently, very little was known or understood regarding the dynamics of their particular niche, but recent studies have enhanced our knowledge in a variety of areas.

You can see Ratel begins and immediately rouses our interest by (1) noting the *growing pervasiveness* of the "lone-parent" family and (2) pointing out how, notwithstanding its pervasiveness, *little is known* about life in this demographic category.

In the process, she also notes that the vast majority of "lone-parent families" are headed by women. This allusion is what we call a "hook," a reference that gives us some information and seems pretty innocuous at the point it's mentioned but is actually laying the groundwork for a revelation that will come later. In this case, what we will find is that Patricia's research will not focus on the "lone parent" but on a particular kind of lone parent: the single-parent woman. Putting the gender hook in at the start alerts the reader; when she tells us later that it is single-parent *women* she will be interviewing, it will be no surprise.

Ratel also immediately begins to funnel us down from broader issues to the specifics of her research project. She does so by going from a mention of "families" to more specific mention of "lone-parent families" and then gets even more specific by her reference to lone-parent families headed by *women*.

The end result is that, in less than 100 words, Patricia already has nailed down her general topic area, justified its importance, and started pointing us in the direction her research will take. The challenge for her now is to take some inventory of what we know about this particular category of family already, as well as what we don't know. Figuring that

out will help direct the research. Patricia continues to set the stage:

> Statistically speaking, the majority of single mothers in Canada live in poverty. Twenty per cent of all single mothers earn less than $5,000 per year, while 37% earn less than $15,000 per year, and these women have the lowest income growth rate in the country (Statistics Canada, 1984, p. 5). Norton and Glick (1986) compared single and two parent families on a variety of social and economic variables, and were led to conclude that:

> > By most objective measures, the vast majority of these families hold a disadvantageous position in society relative to other family groups. They are characterized by a high rate of poverty, a high percentage of minority representation, relatively low education, and a high rate of mobility. In short, they generally have little equity or stature in society and constitute a group with unusually pressing social and economic needs. (p. 16)

Other researchers have examined the economic pressures associated with single motherhood and have demonstrated that a number of factors, unique to today's economic environment, play a distinct role in perpetuating the poverty of these women. In most instances it is the woman who is least able to support the family, and yet, in eight out of ten cases it is the woman who assumes this responsibility. Inflation, high unemployment, job discrimination, lack of prior job experience, rising costs of adequate childcare, and inconsistent or non-existent child support all contribute to the feminization of poverty. (Grief, 1986)

In many instances, single mothers are maintained solely by the state, and their existence is meager at best. In other cases women seek employment and some degree of self-sufficiency. However, Pett and Vaughn-Cole (1986) suggest that most single mothers acquire low status positions because of socialization processes and are fearful of taking the risks associated with pursuit of an education, career opportunities, or non-traditional jobs that would prove more lucrative. The researchers highlight this as one of their most troubling findings as it implies a *cul-de-sac* of serious and continued economic deprivation. They argue for changes in both public policy and public attitudes to facilitate the development of educational training programs and the provision of adequate financial support and childcare systems for the economically insecure and depressed single mother. (p. 110)

Several important things are going on in this quotation. First, Ratel continues to show her command of the literature. Part of what impressed Ted about her paper when he first read it was the diversity of literature she considered and brought to bear on her topic in a very short time: everything from Statistics Canada census data to the results of interview and survey-based research in both Canada and the United States.

Second, although you don't know it yet, Ratel has taken you by the hand and is leading you down a path that leads directly to her research. Each time she mentions a study, she is doing so with a purpose: identifying and highlighting factors that should (and will) be addressed in her research. For example, the paragraphs above show that a big concern is where single-parent mothers get the money and resources to meet their parental responsibilities. The hook is in: the next place we see "financial issues" should be in her research design.

Third, she is starting to introduce a particular perspective, one that helped frame her research (e.g., in terms of what questions she asked) and that she will want you to consider when she presents her own data. The studies Ratel cites clearly show that single-parent women tend to live in poverty and often are "maintained solely by the state" (i.e., on welfare/social assistance), but Patricia is starting to place another question in your head regarding how these mothers can ever get out of that situation. Right

now, single-parent motherhood not only means being poor, it means being poor forever—note her use of the image of a *cul-de-sac* (dead end) in the discussion of one study. Clearly, we want to find a way out of that, not only for the good of the women and their children, but for society's benefit as well. Ratel starts to move us now to the experiences of women who mix other roles with motherhood. Since there is no literature that deals specifically with single-parent mothers in academe, she looks at neighbouring/related literature, that dealing with the experience of single-parent mothers who are *employed*.

We won't analyze each and every paragraph of Ratel's paper; you can see the whole thing in Appendix F. Our purpose here is to identify some guideposts to see why her paper *is* a good paper as you read through it. Suffice it to say for now that her introduction proceeds to review findings in the "parenting" literature, with particular emphasis on research that deals with single-parent families and/or that compares the experiences of lone parents with those of parents with partners. Note the issues that appear: Ratel cites findings showing that single mothers who work suffered from reduced emotional and physical well-being as a result of trying to juggle multiple roles; that their personal lives often suffer as they are forced even to give up time for sleep and relaxation; that children of single parents are often given considerable responsibility; that this delegation of responsibility can lead to the children of single parents "growing up faster" than other children; and that "social support" networks of friends and family are crucial facilitators of success.

You should see, therefore, that part of what makes Ratel's paper a good one is that her introduction immediately explains what makes her research "interesting" and then cites relevant literature in a very complementary and strategic way, that is, by attuning us to issues and factors that are important to tell us about and hence will find their way into her research. Her introduction has been a story that took us from some very general statements about the bourgeoning pervasiveness of single parenting in Canadian society to some very specific findings. She ends her introduction by telling us about the unique contribution her research will bring to the literature:

> Although the research in this area offers insight to the phenomenon of single parenthood, an investigation of the unique experiences of single mothers attending university has apparently not been undertaken. The present research represented an attempt to remedy this shortcoming. More specifically, the purpose of this study was to undertake an exploratory examination of the single mother experience in the academic context, by investigating a sample of women's lives in terms of their financial situations, their physical and emotional well-being, their social support systems, their academic experience, and the effects of their circumstances upon their children.

Perfect. Not one element of her statement of research is a surprise. Every single one was introduced previously. Our reaction to reading it is nothing but "Of course. How logical. It would be silly to do anything else." That's exactly what we want the reader to feel.

Middle

The middle of the paper is normally the largest part—as in any film or novel—because it is the place where the plot thickens as we articulate all the specifics of our research. This includes a *Methods* section, which describes *what we did* (our procedures, including any research instruments) and *with whom or with what we did it* (our research sample), and a *Results* section, which outlines *what we found* (the data). Let's consider each in turn. We'll do so by focusing on Ratel's paper regarding single-parent mothers but use her example to draw more general advice for you to keep in mind when doing those sections of your paper.

METHODS

There are two main subsections to Ratel's methods section. In the first she tells us who she needed to talk to, and it's no surprise that she wanted to interview women who are both students and single-parent mothers. But we need more detail than that to be able to critically evaluate the quality of the data she gathered and to make decisions regarding such dimensions as the generalizability of her conclusions. Let's see what she said.

The Women

As the research undertaken was exploratory in nature, a purposive sampling technique was utilized. This proved to be advantageous for several reasons. First, I was able to interview women whom I knew and, as a relationship of trust had been previously established, the participants were willing to grant me access to their lives. As I share their status, I believe they felt comfortable discussing their situations with me. Knowing that I had similar experiences gave the women confidence in my ability to report on the phenomenon and encouraged open disclosure.

The first thing Ratel notes is her sampling technique, which she describes as "purposive." That is useful, but we need to know more in order to evaluate whether such a choice is a good one or a bad one. Recall that one of the main themes in the chapter on sampling (Chapter 4) is that there is no one "best" sampling technique; the appropriateness of any choice is a function of several factors, not the least of which is how well it matches your research objectives. Patricia clearly hits a bull's-eye when she notes that her objectives in this research were exploratory, for which purposive or target sampling is an appropriate choice.

Patricia also considers the implications of her sampling decisions for the validity of her data, suggesting that her pre-existing knowledge of and friendship with the women, as well as the fact that she shared their status, likely enhanced their trust in her and would have been associated with open reporting and valid data. It is good of Patricia to report her views of this, but as independent critical readers we also need to be skeptical in taking comments like these at face value. Just because she says everything was wonderful does not make it so. As researchers, we always need to be our own best critics and not be too Pollyannaish about how wonderful and open everyone was with us; our problem is that we don't know enough yet to be able to speculate on whether Ratel is being reasonable or naive in her observations. What led Ratel to her conclusion? Is there any independent evidence of rapport, such as disclosure of information that one would not normally disclose unless one trusted the interviewer? We can't say one way or the other at this point, so we'll have to simply place our concerns "on hold" and hope that more information surfaces.

We don't have long to wait because Ratel continues to explain the logic underlying her choice of sampling strategy and the benefits of having proceeded in that way:

> The second reason a purposive sampling method was chosen was to ensure some variation within such a small sample. The ages of the women ranged from twenty-four to forty-one. Three of the women had one child, two were rearing three children, and the remainder had two children. One of the women had just started her first semester at university, while another woman had been in attendance for six years; the other women had been pursuing their education between two and four years. Furthermore, the women represented a variety of faculties, including business, education, psychology, criminology, anthropology, and fine arts. The experience of single motherhood also varied. One woman had been separated only a year; another had been on her own for twelve years.

> A total of nine women were approached and agreed to be interviewed. One interview was deleted from the analysis as the process was treated lightly and the resulting responses were flippant and dubious at best. Another respondent was lost because of concerns with confidentiality and the possible repercussions of involvement in the study. The analysis below focuses on the remaining seven participants.

Ratel concludes that first subsection by getting very specific about the number of interviews conducted. She is also forthright—as she should be—about having deleted one case because of her belief that the responses were insincere and invalid and about having lost a second respondent because of that person's concerns regarding confidentiality. And although we always regret losing participants, the reasons two of them were lost in this study actually reflect well on Ratel: we now have evidence that she is *not* a Pollyanna in her interpretation of respondent rapport and can recognize a lack of rapport when she sees it.

Losing the second respondent may have been a disappointment, but there are several things we learn from that as well. In general terms it helps to reaffirm the importance of confidentiality to research on sensitive topics. But beyond that, it also reflects positively on Ratel for acknowledging and accepting her respondent's right to withdraw participation. In research such as this, where Ratel is not just a "researcher" in their lives but also someone whose relationship with them outside the research context ranges from acquaintance to friend, it is particularly important for respondents to feel comfortable exercising freedom of choice; it is clear Ratel fostered that attitude and respected their wishes.

We end that subsection with a good sense of Patricia's respondents. It appears in some ways they are a unique group—as any nine single-parent women at any university or college in the country surely would be—while at the same time they show some degree of diversity and are not "atypical" in any clearly exceptional way.

Depending on the type of research you have done, a description along the lines of Ratel's may well be sufficient. Those who engage in research involving more structured approaches in which larger samples were acquired no doubt will have included some demographic questions that would allow your sample to be described quantitatively in tabular form, following protocols for the presentation of tables that are outlined in Chapter 12. This is where those tables should appear.

Having described *whom* she interviewed, Ratel's next task was to describe the interviews themselves:

The Interviews

Interviews were conducted within the women's homes, and each lasted between three and four hours. The interviews proved to be an emotionally turbulent process for the women. It is difficult to encapsulate, in a few brief lines, the underlying essence of the interviews except to state, without reservation, that the women who approached the exercise seriously were forthright and honest in their responses.

Again, it is good that Ratel chose to tell us how the interviews went, and it is immediately evident from the fact that the interviews were three to four hours long that these were not superficial chitchat. And although we always have to read a paper with a critical eye, Ratel has already started to build credibility with us through her earlier judgments about response validity. An important element of her work is the way that it mixes conceptual/analytic observations with concrete referents in a recurring pattern of concept/evidence/concept/evidence. We see the same thing here: a conceptual conclusion about how "forthright" she found the women followed immediately by examples of revelations that support that conclusion. The sorts of disclosures she cites do not seem the type people would make if they did not trust Ratel or were trying to keep the conversation safe and superficial:

The women discussed personal and intimate aspects of their lives. Since some of the women spoke of involvement in criminal and deviant behavior, confidentiality was a significant concern. The women were fully informed of the nature of the research, who would have access to it, and how the information would be used. Anonymity was guaranteed by ensuring that there would be no means of identification incorporated in the paper. In some instances excerpts were deleted from the report to protect the participants from any possible reprisals.

In addition to providing examples of sensitive information being disclosed to her (indicating a level of trust that Ratel has inspired), we are also learning about Ratel's professionalism in the area of ethics. As a researcher you always aspire to go beyond superficial chat, but when people reward you with their trust and start to disclose information that could cause them trouble or embarrassment if it were revealed to a third party, then you have to be ready to deal with that, and Ratel clearly was. Her description shows she was upfront about how the information they supplied would be used; Ratel goes beyond making generic statements about how information will be kept confidential to actively employ data-management strategies, for example, being sensitive to and keeping any information out of the written record that could cause the person to be identified, to protect the interests of her research participants.

Ratel closes this section with procedural information that informs her reader about how the questioning proceeded and the steps she took to maximize the validity of the data and ensure that her eventual reporting of the data would be accurate:

The research took the form of open-ended interviews. The women were informed of the general area of inquiry and presented with the specific topic areas for discussion. Following an introductory explanation and the gathering of demographic details, the women were free to discuss the issues as they saw fit. Notes were taken virtually verbatim and interjections were made only when it was necessary to elicit more details or to ensure a thorough understanding of the comments. This method was adopted in an attempt to ensure that my influence on the reporting was minimal. I was aware that I held particular opinions and speculations that emanated from my own experiences, and felt it imperative to maintain a receptive but neutral stance while conducting the interviews.

One of the things you should note here is that Ratel's methods section is actually very short—six paragraphs and less than 600 words—but the amount of information packed on that page is considerable. The important thing is that all the decisions she made about how to proceed were defensible, and we come away understanding what she did and why.[3] In that sense, she has successfully spoken to us as researcher/readers by anticipating and addressing our concerns and giving us sufficient information that we can make our own decisions about whether we agree. We finish the section curious what came out of it. The next section considers these results.

RESULTS

Ratel's study was by no means a large one. She interviewed nine women, with the typical interview taking 3 to 4 hours to complete—that is, about 30 to 35 hours of interviewing in total. If transcribed it would cover dozens upon dozens of pages. Just imagine how much more data larger studies would produce. There is no way you can report all that data. The challenge to the researcher is now to prepare a summary of the data that continues to inform us.

There are at least three basic principles that can guide the writing of a good *Results* section. First, it helps to summarize data and organize them thematically in a way that connects the results to your research questions. The organization of the results section as a whole, and every table and statement within it, should be presented in a way that explains why the data are of interest; the data should also explicitly connect to whichever research question or other methodological matter the data address.[4] Second, you should present data summaries concisely, for example, by not using three tables when you can collapse them into one. Third, avoid redundancy. For example, if something is already in a table, then do not also summarize it in the text, and vice versa.

Ratel's data presentation follows these three principles. Organized by theme, her headings are "Financial Circumstances," "Physical and Emotional Stress," "The Children," "Social Support," and "Academics." Are you surprised by any of these? You shouldn't be. The hook for each one was set in the introduction, where previous research was cited that

identified the first four factors as important domains to consider when examining the processes and impact of lone parenting. The fifth—academics—is the unique element Ratel brought to this project, and it is fitting that she concludes with it.

By organizing her results section using themes first identified in the introduction, Ratel is making it easy for the reader to make connections with that material. This transparency will pay dividends in the final part of her research report—the *Discussion and Conclusions* section(s)—when Ratel gives final consideration to what we can learn from her research, which will involve considering her results in the context of existing literature.

Within each of the themes identified, the results will again be organized in a manner that best explains to the reader what you have by connecting back to thematic hooks that were included earlier and forward to issues you want to address in the discussion section, which will conclude your report. The way you present data will depend in part on the type of data you gathered. For quantitative data, you should follow the principles discussed in Chapter 12 regarding the proper formatting of tables. Ratel's data were more qualitative, and we can look to see how she handled that type of data.

We won't examine *all* of Ratel's results in detail, but consider this one small section from her discussion of "Physical and Emotional Stress" as it plays out in the mothers' lives:

> All the women interviewed stated emphatically that they were physically exhausted. The multi-faceted nature of their lives, the adoption of three separate and distinct roles (i.e., wage earner, student, and mother) created demands on their time and energy that were difficult to manage. Inevitably, the women sacrificed their own well-being to meet these demands. Collectively, they reported that they are in poor physical health and pointed to lack of sleep, lack of exercise, and inadequate diet as the key contributing factors. The women contend with some anxiety because of their financial situations, but also must face the pressures associated with the academic environment, as well as

meeting the challenge of raising their children alone. There is a distinct cyclical element to this situation in which the inability to cope with the physical demands manifests itself in an inability to deal with the emotional stresses. This in turn takes a toll on their physical well-being. As Karen stated:

> I was on anti-depressants for the first year I was in school. I came very close to having a nervous breakdown, twice actually. I have a prescription for Valium but I'm trying not to rely on the drugs any more. I live on coffee and cigarettes; I'm always exhausted. After I deal with the kids at night, cook and clean, read bedtime stories, you know … I have to work until two or three in the morning because it's the only time I have to study. I get up at 5:30 in the morning so I can have a half an hour to myself before the kids get up and I start all over again. Occasionally, I force myself to back off and get some sleep. As soon as the semester starts, I'm counting down the weeks hoping I can make it through to the break. People tell me I don't deal with the stress appropriately, that I should get some exercise and get some more sleep. I know they're right but I have to laugh. Who's got the time? They just don't have a clue what I'm dealing with here.

Note here that Ratel presents data in two ways: (1) by summarizing what the women said and expressing it in a more aggregated form in her own words and (2) by including quotations from particular interviews. Her results section includes somewhat more of the former than the latter; each of the five subsections is thick with summary and yet contains only one or two quotations. This is Ratel's choice, and although it is entirely appropriate and defensible, others might encourage a blend that includes more of the women's own words.

Note also that Ratel does an excellent job of picking quotations that illustrate the themes she identifies in her own summary narrative. For example, in the portion of her "Physical and Emotional Stress" section quoted above, the part written by Ratel makes several points: the women are exhausted, they burn the candle at both ends, they don't sleep or eat well, and it all takes a toll on their health. The quotation that follows gives the words of a particular respondent ("Karen"), and what is she saying? That she's exhausted, burns the candle at both ends, doesn't sleep much, and that it all takes a toll on her health.

What you should see here is that Ratel is maintaining the pattern of concept/evidence/concept/evidence that we noted above regarding her methods section. In addition to giving us a feel for who these women are and how they speak, each round of concept/evidence establishes more and more credibility for Patricia as an observer. When she says that respondents told her they are so consumed by the combined demands of academe and parenthood and have little time for sleep, she follows up with a quotation that illustrates that observation. We see she is not making it up; she is not exaggerating; she is simply representing what she hears and identifying patterns and themes that really exist.

Read the following example, which we made up, and contrast it with Ratel:

> The women all relied heavily on superstition and saw conspiracies everywhere. With all of life's forces beyond their control, the end result, not surprisingly, was a sense of abandonment and alienation that manifested itself in apathy toward the other women whom they previously thought of as sisters. For example, one woman stated:
>
> > My mother always told me that "what goes around comes around," so I guess I've always tried to go out of my way to treat others how I would like them to treat me. I know some of the others view it differ-

ently, and they have every right to, but that's just how I always thought of it, I suppose.

If we were to read a paper that included something like the above, our reaction would be "Huh? Are you kidding?" Is it reasonable to see a phrase such as "what goes around comes around" as evidence of "superstition"? Or to pull the phrase "I know some of the others view it differently" out of context and infer that the woman was seeing "conspiracies"? Or to see the source's acknowledgment that women all have a right to their own opinions as "apathy"? We think not. And on the assumption that the kinds of examples a researcher will give are in all likelihood the *best* examples from the interviews that *most clearly* illustrate the concept offered by the researcher, then our fictitious researcher is on truly thin ice. There are just too many other ways to look at that quotation, and we begin to have doubts about everything else the researcher claims. If we can't agree with the researcher on the matters for which evidence is put forward, how can we ever trust his or her claims on other summary statements where we don't have direct access to the data to know what misinterpretations may be operating? We can't. Contrast this with Ratel's clear connections between conceptual assertions and data. You believe Ratel because she demonstrates to you that her observations are credible and the inferences she draws reasonable.

Another notable aspect of Ratel's results section is the manner in which she identifies her respondents, where each quote is attributed to a particular person. The names are, of course, fictitious, as she makes clear in a footnote, consistent with her pledge to maintain confidentiality. However, use of a name does two things. First, it maintains a human touch; the respondent is "Karen" rather than "Subject 28" or "Respondent A." Second, with respect to our methodological concerns, it helps us to keep track of who is being quoted throughout the paper.

To appreciate this point, you should consider the presentation of results from a sampling perspective.

With quantitative data presented in tabular form, for example, survey data showing the distribution of responses or the mean or median response to a particular questionnaire item, the summary data that appear in the table "represent" the sample in the sense that everyone who is part of the sample is contained in the distribution and have had their data included in the computation of the mean. We paid a certain price for that. Everyone accepted that their views would only be expressed as a check mark indicating a preference between predetermined categories, and we lost all the texture and nuance that comes when we hear people speak in their own words. What we gain in return is the ability to make charts and graphs that can easily and succinctly summarize people's views.

When we stay with qualitative data, as Ratel did, we have the great advantage of getting all that texture as we read the words of the women, but, because we cannot quote everything every woman said, we present only "illustrative" quotations where Karen (in this instance) presents a view that "stands for" the sample. The thing you have to demonstrate when you present data of that sort is that you are not simply selectively presenting one individual's opinions that you happen to like and that you are sampling more than one point of view.

One way to do this is to do as Ratel has done: provide a source for each quotation. Citing pseudonyms allows us to see in the paper as a whole who is being quoted at different times, without violating any confidences. Another problem with our fictitious quotation, therefore, is that we simply attributed it to "a woman" but did not attribute a particular source. How can you tell whether the next quotation comes from the same woman, who we may be quoting again and again, or someone different? In our case you can't, but note that in Ratel's case every quotation is given a source, and it allows us to see that she is offering quotations from various women and not simply quoting one again and again.

If there is an aspect of Ratel's write-up other authors might do differently, or that Ratel might have done differently had longer papers been allowed, it would be to include more than one quotation per section to illustrate statements. The way Ratel has done it also is a defensible and appropriate choice. However, presenting quotations on a given theme from more than one respondent allows us to get a greater sense of diversity among the sample. The use of one quotation at a time leaves an impression of homogeneity among respondents, that is, that they all shared a particular view. And that may well be the case, as Patricia's frequent reference along the lines of "All of the women indicated that ..." would suggest. Even there, however, some degree of redundancy—two or three different women perhaps, all stating essentially the same point—helps to *show* the homogeneity or heterogeneity of views and gives the reader a better opportunity to make up his or her own mind whether the researcher/author has adequately captured those views.

Certainly any good results section with qualitative data will have both types of statements that Ratel includes—summary statements in her own words and quotations that contain the verbatim words of respondents—and the challenge to the researcher is to find a judicious blend that most effectively summarizes the data. There are fewer formulas here than is the case with quantitative data (see Chapter 12), which is both refreshing and threatening. The challenge to you, the researcher, is best met by being forthright and transparent with enough information that the reader can decide for himself or herself whether your summaries and interpretations are plausible. Your job is to inspire confidence. Ratel is an example of someone who has done an excellent job of achieving exactly that.

End

DISCUSSION AND CONCLUSIONS

Remember the image of the hourglass that we mentioned earlier? In the introduction, you started off broadly at the top end of the hourglass by connecting with the literature and noting the big social issues and concerns that got you interested in the subject matter. Also in the introduction, you started

getting more and more specific about your interests. In that section you ended by outlining the more concrete and narrow focus of your particular research project.

The methods and results sections represent the middle portion of the hourglass, where all you're writing about is what you encountered in your research. Your challenge is to do as good a job as possible with your research participants on the topic you have chosen to study. It's not that we don't care about the bigger issues at that point; it's just not the time to be discussing them.

That time comes in the discussion and conclusion sections, which sometimes are combined, depending on the preference of the author and the dictates of the situation. You have several loose ends remaining to be tied in these sections: (1) giving a brief statement of how your results "speak" to your research questions; (2) what the implications of these results are for the bigger issues that made this research "interesting" for you in the first place; (3) tempering your inferences with critical reflection on the strengths and weaknesses of the research; and (4) any final statements you want to make about your research and its implications. All four are expected to be done in a straightforward manner with a minimum of flourish or hype.

We can examine the final discussion and conclusions section of Ratel's paper in light of these elements. She begins with a one-paragraph version of the introduction that restates the purpose of the research and the bigger picture it was designed to address:

> The structural characteristics of Canadian society are changing rapidly, and the family unit has seen many transformations in the last twenty years. Nonetheless the traditional nuclear family still predominates, although any imaginable configuration can be found in contemporary society. One of the prevalent trends altering the face of Canadian families in the last two decades is the growing pervasiveness of the single parent. The majority of single-parent households are headed by women and, although we know something of

them in the aggregate from statistical surveys, very little research has been done that shows the human face of this group. The purpose of this research was to do so by exploring the circumstances of a small and yet diverse sample of single mothers attending university, and examining some of the factors that shape their experiences.

This statement of the purpose that guided the research is followed by a succinct summary of how the results of the research speak to that purpose:

It is apparent that the women contend with a variety of problems that are unique to their status. The women live in or near poverty, accrue large debts to pursue their goals, and suffer debilitating physical and emotional stress as they attempt to maintain three separate and distinct life roles. They have a limited amount of social support, and their children are subjected to a number of pressures, including some dereliction. Their education is of paramount importance as their overriding goal is to better their life chances and remove themselves from the experiences common to most single mothers.

Ratel also connects the results of her research to the results of other research she had cited in the introduction. First, she notes the many ways in which the results of her research parallel the kinds of findings that are out there in the "single-parenting" literature:

The literature revealed that the majority of single mothers are struggling financially. Those who adopt dual roles by entering the work force are subjected to elevated levels of stress. It was acknowledged that the well-being of single mothers is correlated to the amount of social support they receive. Furthermore, a distinct relationship was found between their physical and mental well-being. Generally, the children experience some temporary emotional and behavioral problems while adjusting to the breakup of the family, and the demands placed upon their

mothers served to enhance the need for emotional independence.

If the results of Ratel's research were *at odds with* the research literature, then her next task would be to consider what differences between her research/ sample/context and that other research might account for any differences in findings. However, her research is quite *consistent with* the extant literature. This has two main implications: (1) her research adds evidence that speaks to the generalizability of those original findings; (2) notwithstanding the uniqueness of her sample—in this case, nine women trying to complete degrees at a medium-sized university on Canada's west coast at the turn of the 20th century—the experiences and views of the respondents are similar to the views presented by other single-parent mothers in other places at other times working in other milieux.

Having placed the hook at the end of the introduction that a unique contribution of her project was its focus on the dynamics of a single-parent mother's life in an academic context, Ratel now reconnects with that theme by summarizing what she learned and can now add to the literature:

Although there are a number of obvious similarities between single mothers generally and those in the academic setting, the pursuit of an education clearly aggravates the pressures and problems normally experienced by single mothers. The endeavors undertaken create a situation in which each factor plays upon and exacerbates the rest. This experiential dynamic is unique to the women in this study, and its comprehension necessary for a thorough understanding of the phenomenon in question. Figure 1 depicts the interaction between the five variables examined in this study and demonstrates the complexity created with the adoption of this status. The cross-impacts make more transparent that adding a single element— attending university, in this case—adds not just a single element or impact to one's life, but a whole new set of pressures that affect and are affected by every other element of one's life.

The "star" diagram Ratel includes as her Figure 1 (Figure 13.1) is not intended to represent any earth-shattering theory. Rather, it graphically illustrates her conclusions that the academic status of these women is not simply one more factor in a set of already complex lives but one that adds stress almost exponentially because of the interaction of that status with stresses already associated with every other element of one's life.

In a final paragraph, she considers some implications of her research, particularly with respect to social justice issues. These connect back to another hook that appeared in the introduction regarding the long-term sense of futility and frustration that arises among single-parent women, who fight an uphill battle trying to do nothing more than better their situation and provide a better future for their children:

> The research unearthed a number of structural elements that contribute directly to the problems encountered by these women: a lack of financial support, a lack of affordable childcare, and provincial policies that are antagonistic to their endeavors. The most pertinent example is the

Figure 13.1

Illustration of the Complex Web of Interrelationships among the Factors Examined in This Study

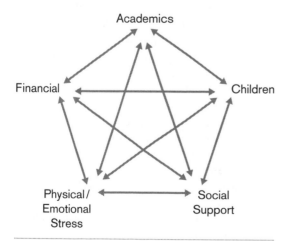

absence of maintenance in the majority of cases. Only two women in this study received financial assistance from their estranged partners, and in both cases the support was minimal and sporadic. This situation exists despite the fact that these men have a legal responsibility to support their children; despite existing legislation, little enforcement takes place. As Lou so aptly stated, "It's as if they want you to fail, as if they'd like to see you end up back on welfare!" Indeed, some women would argue that an insidious patriarchal conspiracy is at work. I find this contention to be excessive, although the general status of women in our society is not an irrelevant consideration. In the last two decades women have made some progress in altering their position in society, but substantive equality has not been realized. Motherhood is not a prestigious occupation; women who bear children are not generally honored and held in high esteem. Women with dependent children are a low-status and relatively powerless group and therefore, the ambivalence of legislators and policy makers is not unduly surprising. One cannot help but wonder how different the situation might be if it were reversed. Current indicators suggest that the trend of lone parenting will continue, and the plight of single mothers must be addressed. It is hoped that the current study will serve to enlighten readers and promote some understanding in this regard.

TRACKING

Although there are many situations where readers of this book may find specific aspects of the structure and organization of Ratel's paper useful to emulate, our broader purpose is simply to show you a well-organized paper that achieves what it set out to do, and where pretty much every word is there for a purpose.

This paper was excellent given the demands of the situation for which she was researching and writing. It would have been done differently if it were undertaken as an honour's or master's thesis, for publication in a journal (or newspaper or policy document), or if Ted had allowed longer papers. Theses would allow opportunity for more elaborate description of the research itself, more extensive consideration of its theoretical and policy implications, and more detailed reflection on methodological decisions. Policy documents would probably go into less detail regarding the specifics of the research but involve more detailed consideration of the advantages and limitations of different policy approaches.

We also hope that you come away with a sense of why you cannot expect to do a good job of a paper with only one draft. In addition, we have tried to emphasize the interconnectedness of the parts of Ratel's paper:

- The introduction leads us to the research question, lays the groundwork for the methods section, interests us in the outcomes of certain data, and provides the framework that we will want to return to in the discussion and conclusion section.

- The methods section is connected to the introduction insofar as it addresses the research question(s) introduced there and tells us how they will be answered, thereby providing fodder and direction for the results and discussions sections that follow.

- The discussion and conclusions section connects back to the introduction by offering answers for the research issues introduced there, being integrated with the literature cited there, and commenting on the bigger context first considered there. It connects back to the methods and results sections because it arises from and incorporates the data and data-gathering procedures outlined there.

A colleague of ours—John Lowman—uses the word "tracking" to describe this aspect of the rewriting process. He is referring to that one aspect of redrafting: ensuring that what you have written "tracks" correctly, so that all the essential elements of

your paper follow from each other and speak to each other following a logical flow. No information is missing that is required to maintain the flow; nor is there any superfluous information since these are tangents and distractions.

FINISH AT THE BEGINNING

The last thing you write is the element that goes first: the *Abstract*. Abstracts are brief summaries of your paper—normally no more than 150 words—that give an overview of your study's objectives, sample, research site, method(s), main finding(s), and, depending on your objective and the venue of publication, sometimes an implication or two of the findings for policy or practice. The reason for waiting until you finish the paper to write the abstract is that it needs to reflect what is in your paper, and since the paper itself will change to some degree as you redraft and hone its content, it's not until you've finalized the paper that you can summarize it.

There are really two main purposes an abstract serves when it's published in a journal or book. The first is that it gives readers a quick fix on the general thrust and implications of your research; this allows them to decide whether the paper is relevant to them and whether they want to spend time on the whole article. The second is that many researchers catch up on the literature by going through compendia of abstracts of recent research in order to locate articles that look interesting which they can then locate in the library, so your abstract must be both concise and self-sufficient.

SUMMING UP AND LOOKING AHEAD

The primary purpose of this chapter is to give you some advice on how to write a research report, something many readers of this book will be doing in conjunction with a course on research methods where this book is being used. A central theme of the chapter is that although each part of the paper has a unique purpose and provides unique information, the various parts all are linked and interdependent

Figure 13.2

Components of a Research Report

ABSTRACT

- ◆ Offers an overview of the research in no more than 150 words.
- ◆ Usually written last to ensure it reflects the content of the final research report.
- ◆ Should include an overview of your study's objectives, sample, research site, method(s), main finding(s), and, if appropriate, a statement of its implications for policy or practice.
- ◆ Must stand alone sufficiently well that readers can look at it and determine whether it speaks to issues of interest to them.

INTRODUCTION

- ◆ Provides the overall context for the research and describes why it might be "interesting" to persons who engage in research and/or develop policy and/or develop theory.
- ◆ Moves from more general to more specific and provides a justification for the research.
- ◆ Includes a focused and critical review of the literature that "sets up" the research by identifying themes that will be addressed in the research and considered in the discussion/conclusion.
- ◆ Concludes with a specific statement of the purpose of the research and any specific research questions being posed.

METHODS

- ◆ Offers an overall description of the research procedures.
- ◆ Outlines and justifies choices made with respect to sampling of research participants and setting.
- ◆ May include copy of research instrument if a standardized protocol is being followed or may simply include it as an appendix.

RESULTS

- ◆ Presentation of research findings.
- ◆ Organized thematically to reflect research question(s) and any other issues set out in the Introduction; this section anticipates the Discussion section.

DISCUSSION/CONCLUSIONS

- ◆ Begins with a summary statement of the research question or purpose of the research and gives a succinct answer to that question.
- ◆ Integrates the current study into the extant literature. Consistencies are noted and discussed in light of the generalizability of findings this reveals. Inconsistencies are also noted, and the researcher speculates on what the sources of these differences might be. Original contributions of the current research are highlighted.
- ◆ Engages in final consideration of the strengths and limitations of the research, often with an eye toward making suggestions for further research that will address any limitations/gaps that are identified.
- ◆ Concludes with general discussion of the implications of the research for other research, related policy, and so on.

insofar as each part sets up, anticipates, and speaks to issues that are raised in other sections.

The parts of a research paper and the roles each part fulfills are depicted in Figure 13.2. The way linkages can be accomplished between the various sections of the report is shown in the examination of a research paper by Patricia Ratel, a former student of Ted's, who did the research and paper several years ago when she was enrolled in a research methods course. We'd like to end by thanking Patricia once again, both for having done such a great job with the paper and for having given us permission to reproduce the paper and analyze it in detail in this book.[5]

With this chapter finished and your term research projects complete, it is time to pull some themes together and draw the book to a close, which we do in the next chapter.

NOTES

1. For example, Strunk's *The Elements of Style* is available online at www.bartleby.com/141/; there are also many guides to writing research papers you can find online if you apply your favourite search engine using terms such as "writing," "how to," "guide," and "research."

2. This quote comes from Blaise Pascal's *Les Lettres Provinciales*, Letter XVI, 1657 (London: Penguin Books) p. 257. We thank Esther Berry of the University of Sydney for solving the mystery of the source of this quote.

3. Because Ratel's questioning was open-ended and largely respondent-driven, she has given us as much detail as we need here and in the introduction to understand the process she followed. Researchers who use more structured methods and do surveys or interviews with preset questions normally would include a copy of their research instrument as part of their report, usually in an appendix.

4. The corollary here is that you should *only* report data that bear on your research questions and cut out the excess. This does not mean you should "hide" data that do not say what you like; that would be dishonest. We often gather more data than we actually need—you should not feel compelled to report every single datum you gather just because you gathered it.

5. Patricia Ratel completed her B.A. and M.A. in criminology at Simon Fraser University and went on to do policy-based research for the government of British Columbia. When we spoke with her recently to ask permission to include her paper in this book, we asked whether she knew anything more about the women who took part in her research. You may be interested to know that only two of the nine women who participated were actually able to finish the degree they were working on at the time Ratel interviewed them.

CHAPTER 14

EPILOGUE: MAKING RESEARCH DECISIONS IN "INTERESTING" TIMES

This chapter is our last chance to draw together some of the major themes in this book. It provides an opportunity to look back at what we've covered as well as to open the door to issues that appear to be growing in importance and receiving more and more attention in learned debate because of their implications for the research enterprise.

RESEARCH AS A DECISION-MAKING PROCESS

This book is titled *Research Decisions* to affirm that doing research is a decision-making process. A fundamental characteristic of research is that it is done "systematically," but that doesn't mean pulling out a copy of the rules or applying some algorithmic procedure; you must make *decisions* about how to design and execute any given piece of research. This process involves determining what you think is important; articulating your objectives; considering the advantages and limitations of the various research techniques and research designs available to you; considering what your choices will allow you to say about the world; and anticipating the impacts your research might have because of how it is done and what it can reveal. The challenge is always to mix strategy and values to come up with the best ethical research you can do, given your research objectives, the attributes of the phenomenon under consideration, and the context in which you operate.

One aim of this book has been to provide information about some of the many alternatives available to you, as well as about some of the implications of those choices—not merely decision rules or lists of what you should and shouldn't do in given situations if you want to engage in social research. As

we've argued in this book, "knowledge" is not an ever-growing pile of facts that accumulate in libraries; all knowledge embodies perspectives and understandings, can be both empowering and/or oppressive, will reflect the relations of power that exist within science and within the broader society that is its context, and, as such, will change in focus and interpretation over time. However, the researcher is not merely buffeted about by external forces; there is agency, too—researchers make choices about the directions they will pursue and the means by which they will do so, and policies regarding academic freedom have endured to ensure that constraint on that is minimal.

This recognition that researchers play an active role in the way they engage the world reaffirms that knowledge is a product of individual *and* social processes, and implies that fully understanding knowledge and "facts" and contributing to their generation requires us to understand both the context in which knowledge is produced and the people who produce it. Perhaps not surprisingly, when we scan for emerging and important social trends, we focus on shifts in the identity of those who participate in the research enterprise, and changes in the context in which they work.

RESEARCH TECHNOLOGY AT THE DAWN OF THE 21ST CENTURY

In the early years of the 21st century begins we find ourselves confronted with many scary and exciting prospects and possibilities brought about by the unprecedented growth of technology. Everywhere we look we see technology being infused into the very fabric of society and our daily lives. More and more people are using technology as a way to extend the range of their communities and to enhance their social lives. Cell phone technology, text messaging, direct chat programs, voice over IP (VOIP), web cameras, Internet sites and blogs, and many other network- and non–network-based communications technologies are bringing people together and allowing them to share thoughts and experiences in a way that they have never been able to in the past. In this new world of technology, the bounds and bonds of geography seem less important and less prohibitive than at any other time in human history.

Despite the exciting changes that have been brought about by the various technological innovations we have witnessed over the past 20 to 30 years, technology has not fundamentally altered the problems that confront the human race. We are still plagued with poverty, crime, gender discrimination, political turmoil, environmental degradation, racial and ethnic discrimination, sexual discrimination, and disparities in income and wealth. While all of these problems persist, how we think about them and how we actually go about researching and answering the questions that we hope will help us find resolutions is changing as a result of the growth and development of technology.

One of the more interesting by-products of the tremendous technological growth that we have witnessed is the proliferation of data, both in what we produce and what we have access to. In this new digital age, instead of producing raw goods, more and more we find ourselves producing information or data as a commodity. Data are everywhere and take many forms—medical records, legal records, online libraries, websites, records of our shopping and purchasing patterns, banking information, online dating or myspace.com profiles, scores of video games, e-mail, text messages, telephone records, music downloads. Much of our modern economy is constructed around the production, ownership, management, and utilization of this data. The most powerful people in the 21st century will be those who have the ability to gather, manage, and interpret various forms of data in a timely and efficient manner. An important issue is just how democratized and open, or proprietary and centralized, access to that information will be.

The clear trend in the computer industry is toward convergence, portability, and ease of use. It is increasingly common to see cellular phones, video game and entertainment centres, household appliances, and automobiles equipped with features of our home computer, such as web browsers, e-mail, audio and video players and recorders, and text messaging programs. In order to make these convergent technologies more portable, companies are developing the ultra mobile PC (UMPC), a small tablet-based personal computer that will allow users to access important data, entertainment, and communications features from anywhere on the planet. In order to reduce the size of these devices and to make them easier to use, the UMPC will be equipped with touch screens and voice-recognition software in place of the traditional keyboard.

The continued development of these portable devices will have many implications for how we conduct social research. Instead of dragging around suitcases full of hardware for recording, transcribing, storing, and transmitting our observations, we will be able to manage our data with a single device. Touch screens and voice recognition will enhance our ability to collect more complex and fluid forms of data such as interviews, field observations, and other potential audio/video-based data, since the costly and time-consuming process of manually recording data and transcribing these data will be eliminated.

One of the by-products of the trend toward developing multifunctional devices and the UMPC has been the manufacture of smaller, faster, and more reliable high-capacity storage solutions. Already it is possible to store the entire contents of your home computer on a device that fits on your key-ring. Having access to smaller, faster, more portable, and higher capacity storage devices will allow us to transport larger and larger audio, video, and textual data to and from any research setting we choose.

In order to make it easier for people to stay connected no matter where they move, live wireless networks are being expanded. In the next few years most major North American, Western European, and Asian cities will have fully implemented citywide wireless networks. As these wide-scale high-speed wireless networks become more pervasive, the cost of using them will continue to drop so that more and more people will have the same levels of access regardless of their social position. The increasing availability of high-speed wireless networks will undoubtedly have the most visible impact on the way that we conduct social research, as we will be able to relocate our research settings at will without disrupting our ability to maintain an uninterrupted connection to our established research network or to research participants within this network. In addition, they will make the collection and transmission of larger audio and video data from a variety of research settings easier, quicker, and more cost-effective. The implications of this for research designs that involve video ethnography, recorded focus groups, interactive surveys, and complex experiments are far-reaching.

It is also the case that as we write this, the bounds of the Internet are the bounds of electricity—one look at all the lights in a NASA satellite night photograph will show you where computer technology can go (see, for example, http://antwrp.gsfc.nasa.gov/apod/ap040822.html). But those are not the only places that humans are. Ongoing developments in satellite-based wireless and the invention of inexpensive computers with their own built-in and renewable power sources mean that the Internet will soon be able to go wherever people want it to go and places where we do not want it to go.

The obvious implication for social researchers of these ongoing and imminent advances will be an unprecedented ability to explore, describe, understand, and explain the world we live in. We can share our observations with researchers around the globe at the click of a mouse. As technologies converge and become more ubiquitous, social researchers will have even greater access to increasing numbers of individuals, groups, organizations, and social artifacts. We will have an increasing flexibility in how we go about investigating the social world as the range of techniques for collecting, storing, and analyzing data will become virtually limitless.

The challenge for those of us studying and working within the academy is to find more effective ways of using technology and making it more accessible not only within the academic setting but more directly in the populations with whom we wish to work and study. The key is to develop an academic culture that appreciates and efficiently integrates technology into our daily lives and into the way that we teach, learn, and do research both inside and outside of the academy, and engages in ongoing research and self-reflection about how that proceeds.

THE KNOWLEDGE FACTORY

While technological developments offer opportunities for broader outreach and ease in the acquisition of information from a broad array of participants, whether this inclusiveness will result in greater social participation and an enduring appreciation for a diversity of world views and research perspectives or more narrowly conceived mechanisms that preclude challenge to the existing order is an open question. In the academy we see that diversification with respect to its members has been accompanied by a greater centralization of control on the part of government both for itself and its contemporary partners—university administrations and business.

The processes and developments of the *Tri-Council Policy Statement* (TCPS) on ethics in research involving human participants contribute to that view. Its administration is effectively shared by government, who controls the funds, creates the structures, and appoints all the members; university administrations, who have agreed to implement the policy and advise on its development; and business, who by and large are the people chosen as "community members" to serve on REBs. As we saw in Chapter 3, the TCPS promises respect for disciplinary variation and epistemological diversity, but as yet—eight years after its initial implementation—it still falls short of being open and inclusive. Instead, researchers across the country—and especially more qualitatively oriented researchers and those who work with deviant and stigmatized groups—have suffered from the biomedical emphasis that guided the TCPS's creation, ended up dominating its pages, and led to research ethics review boards that allow members to make decisions about areas of research for which they have no expertise (SSHWC 2004).

Instead of engaging in "sensitive and thoughtful ethics review," a monolithic bureaucracy has turned to checklists and "best practices" that by some committees are formulaically applied, with the onus on those researchers who differ from a mythic norm to explain or comply, even when their proposals involve issues that have been debated at length in discipline-based forums. Instead of offering mechanisms that would constrain REBs, make them more accountable to actually following policy, and ensure proposals are evaluated by persons competent to do so, a federally appointed advisory body looking into procedural issues is suggesting the opposite—that REBs should have *more* discretion and *more* power (Subgroup on Procedural Issues for the TCPS 2005).

The emphasis on biomedical and technology-driven research is consistent with a further development that was put in place subsequent to the TCPS being enacted—the granting councils re-creating themselves as "knowledge councils" as opposed to their former identity as "granting councils" (see SSHRC 2004). With it comes the view that knowledge is no longer an end in itself; now the measure of knowledge is its ability to generate revenue in the short term; and the granting agencies are, in their own view, the appropriate ones to coordinate that. As the Minister of Industry stated,

> We need to ensure that the research and development efforts of universities and government find their way into the marketplace, and that venture capital support is available to entrepreneurial growth companies that are adept at creating and exploiting new markets and technologies. We need to support the development of knowledge-based companies that will specialize in commercialization of science and technology and programs to help Canadian companies bring their research to market. (Emerson 2005)

The Minister went on to describe in glowing terms how a new "culture of research entrepreneurship" is emerging in Canada, and that the role of the councils is to promote that development.

We do not object to those aspirations, and said very similar things ourselves in the preceding section where we described in positive terms the research possibilities that are blossoming in the wake of new technological developments. The question is one of balance and of ensuring not only that more commercial types of research are promoted and facilitated, but that so, too, are other forms of research such as critical research that asks us to reflect on these directions, and to consider other priorities and points of view. The Canadian Association of University Teachers (CAUT) submission expressed similar concerns:

> CAUT warned that at a time when the autonomy of the university and the integrity of scholarly research are already threatened by the increasing privatization and commercialization of universities' facilities, resources and production, SSHRC has a responsibility to protect the integrity of scholarly research from political and commercial pressures. ...
>
> CAUT suggests, in its response, that the proposals go too far in trying to please political authorities. "We are gravely concerned that the proposed 'transformation' is one more step towards diminished autonomy for academic research and university-based researchers," said CAUT executive director James Turk. ("CAUT Critical of Proposed SSHRC Transformation" 2004)

Will the academy's commitment to both critical and basic research be undermined because it conflicts with the interests of the groups that evaluate the "relevance" of proposed research before it can be evaluated via peer review for merit? With regard to critical research, the CAUT (2004) submission states, "Arguably, one of the most important functions of humanities and social science scholarship is its engagement in social and political critique. Bonds established between SSHRC research funding and a government agenda to increase the role of the private sector in public institutions will directly compromise this work."

Viewing the *Tri-Council Policy Statement* (TCPS) on ethics in this context reaffirms it as a most significant development in the Canadian research enterprise. Critics from the social sciences were concerned the TCPS was an inappropriate intervention of government to a problem that didn't exist (e.g., Palys 1996a) and violated the more arm's length relationship that postsecondary research and teaching institutions had had with government. Autonomy—both of the university from government intervention, and of university faculty/researchers from their university administrations—that had been considered a prerequisite for academic freedom of discovery was being undermined by an appeal to "ethics," except that ethics seemed to have little to do with it. Instead, centralizing ethics regulation was another step in the progressive centralization of authority that saw the federal government exert managerial control of the research enterprise and more securely place its direction in the hands of university administrations and business.

Just as having political and business interests pre-screen proposals for "relevance" undermines emphasis on assessed merit via peer review, we are concerned that imposing what may be a biomedically appropriate model of *a priori* ethics review on the more diverse social sciences and humanities can amount to prior constraint—censorship—over free speech (see also Hamburger 2005), something that should be anathema to the granting councils, and especially SSHRC, but which instead they defend and support. Ethics review and regulation has become a whole new industry, and the way it thus far has been implemented raises many questions about whether academic freedom and the research interests and perspectives of those who practise critically motivated research will survive.

This threat to survival is not because those researchers and their perspectives are "unethical"; it arises simply because ethics resolutions that make sense in one context (e.g., the biomedical one), where the relationship between researcher and participant is between strangers, short-term, finite, and quasi-contractual, can create *un*ethical resolutions when they are applied formulaically to other domains such as many forms of field research, where the relationship between researcher and participant is more typically long-term, evolving, collaborative, and based on mutual trust.

As an analogy, it is fundamentally true that we as a society value the rule of law and the principles upon which the criminal justice system is based. However, we do not impose its rules of procedure and evidence on the way that family members relate to each other: we do not require the child we believe broke the window to be informed of his or her rights or be provided with legal counsel before being asked how it happened, nor do we require proof beyond a reasonable doubt, nor do we provide any opportunity for appeal, and so on. Indeed, it would be an absurdity to make such an imposition. This is *not* because the principles that underlie the criminal justice system are somehow flawed or that family life is inherently unjust, but because the criminal justice system presumes a certain situation and relationship and can be highly *in*appropriate and *un*just when applied to other contexts.

The TCPS offers nothing new in the way of ethical principles or analysis. Its impact lies in the centralized structures for ethics review it requires that provides opportunity for an epistemological tyranny of the majority to exist, while simultaneously, in its worst manifestations, bestowing a moral/ethical licence for censorship that has few if any checks and balances against institutional and governmental myopia.

AN ENDURING DIALECTIC

When we look at the current context of academic social research we see the formation of a dialectic between a burgeoning technology and a growing centralization of control. The big question for us is whether the synthesis of this relationship will result in a one-size-fits-all academy that co-opts the potential of emergent technology in order to place greater technocratic controls over academic freedom or a broad and diverse research enterprise that draws upon the emancipatory potential of technology to extend the boundaries of the pursuit of knowledge. We vote for the latter.

If there is a *Research Decisions V* at some point in the future, it will provide the opportunity for us to revisit these issues and to assess how this dialectic is developing. We do not believe that the tensions that we have outlined in this chapter will be resolved conclusively in the near future. Nor will they, we hope, be resolved without the active contributions of members of the academic community who realize the value of defending the freedom of researchers to push the boundaries and challenge conventions through the creation and implementation of innovative social research.

APPENDIX A

TABLE OF RANDOM NUMBERS

Abridged Table of Random Numbers

73	17	86	15	27	10	42	72
64	46	07	88	76	45	61	55
19	09	22	09	35	99	76	34
08	72	60	22	84	17	81	39
90	09	97	61	90	37	23	52
34	43	09	17	30	20	59	61
02	48	34	21	18	03	99	61
45	90	33	88	89	70	04	80
03	61	05	61	77	70	17	47
05	56	83	78	26	48	35	06
15	86	60	14	49	10	51	17
38	07	45	88	06	06	29	92
60	22	86	92	52	31	00	47
81	94	25	53	73	89	42	62
87	97	01	09	03	40	86	12
17	35	11	60	12	23	83	26
71	27	96	45	07	60	71	82
66	38	80	72	74	42	21	53
94	84	69	37	69	35	59	32
03	26	07	66	93	88	48	54

Source: B. Sommer and R. Sommer (1991), *A Practical Guide to Behavioral Research: Tools and Techniques,* 4th edition (New York: Oxford University Press). Copyright © 1997 by Oxford University Press. Used by permission of Oxford University Press, Inc.

APPENDIX B

CRITICAL VALUES OF CHI-SQUARE

df	\multicolumn{5}{c}{Level of Significance for a Nondirectional Test}
	.10	.05	.02	.01	.001
1	2.71	3.84	5.41	6.64	10.83
2	4.60	5.99	7.82	9.21	13.82
3	6.25	7.82	9.84	11.34	16.27
4	7.78	9.49	11.67	13.28	18.46
5	9.24	11.07	13.39	15.09	20.52
6	10.64	12.59	15.03	16.81	22.46
7	12.02	14.07	16.62	18.48	24.32
8	13.36	15.51	18.17	20.09	26.12
9	14.68	16.92	19.68	21.67	27.88
10	15.99	18.31	21.16	23.21	29.59
11	17.28	19.68	22.62	24.72	31.26
12	18.55	21.03	24.05	26.22	32.91
13	19.81	22.36	25.47	27.69	34.53
14	21.06	23.68	26.87	29.14	36.12
15	22.31	25.00	28.26	30.58	37.70
16	23.54	26.30	29.63	32.00	39.29
17	24.77	27.59	31.00	33.41	40.75
18	25.99	28.87	32.35	34.80	42.31
19	27.20	30.14	33.60	36.19	43.82
20	28.41	31.41	35.02	37.57	45.32
21	29.62	32.67	36.34	38.93	46.80
22	30.81	33.92	37.66	40.29	48.27
23	32.01	35.17	38.97	41.64	49.73
24	33.20	36.42	40.27	42.98	51.18
25	34.38	37.65	41.57	44.31	52.62
26	35.56	38.88	42.86	45.64	54.05
27	36.74	40.11	44.14	46.96	55.48
28	37.92	41.34	45.42	48.28	56.89
29	39.09	42.69	46.69	49.59	58.30
30	40.26	43.77	47.96	50.89	59.70

The table lists the critical values of chi-square for the degrees of freedom shown at the left for tests corresponding to the significance levels that head the columns. If the observed value of χ^2_{obs} [the observed value of chi-square] is greater than or equal to *the tabled value, reject* H_0 *[the null hypothesis]. All chi-squares are positive.*

Source: Sir R.A. Fisher and F. Yates (1974), *Statistical Tables for Biological, Agricultural and Medical Research,* 6th edition (Harlow, Essex, U.K.: Addison Wesley Longman), Table IV. Reprinted by permission of Pearson Education Limited.

APPENDIX C

CRITICAL VALUES OF *r*

df = N – 2	Level of Significance for a Nondirectional (Two-Tailed) Test				
	.10	.05	.02	.01	.001
1	0.9877	0.9969	0.9995	0.9999	10.0000
2	0.9000	0.9500	0.9800	0.9990	0.9990
3	0.8054	0.8783	0.9343	0.9587	0.9912
4	0.7293	0.8114	0.8822	0.9172	0.9741
5	0.6694	0.7545	0.8329	0.8745	0.9507
6	0.6215	0.7067	0.7887	0.8343	0.9249
7	0.5822	0.6664	0.7498	0.7977	0.8982
8	0.5494	0.6319	0.7155	0.7646	0.8721
9	0.5214	0.6021	0.6851	0.7348	0.8471
10	0.4973	0.5760	0.6581	0.7079	0.8233
11	0.4762	0.5529	0.6339	0.6935	0.8010
12	0.4575	0.5324	0.6120	0.6614	0.7800
13	0.4409	0.5139	0.5923	0.6411	0.7603
14	0.4259	0.4973	0.5742	0.6226	0.7420
15	0.4124	0.4821	0.5577	0.6055	0.7246
16	0.4000	0.4683	0.5425	0.5897	0.7084
17	0.3887	0.4555	0.5285	0.5751	0.6932
18	0.3783	0.4438	0.5155	0.5614	0.6787
19	0.3687	0.4329	0.5034	0.5487	0.6652
20	0.3598	0.4227	0.4921	0.5368	0.6524
25	0.3233	0.3809	0.4451	0.4869	0.5974
30	0.2960	0.3494	0.4093	0.4487	0.5541
35	0.2746	0.3246	0.3810	0.4182	0.5189
40	0.2573	0.3044	0.3578	0.3932	0.4896
45	0.2428	0.2875	0.3384	0.3721	0.4648
50	0.2306	0.2732	0.3218	0.3541	0.4433
60	0.2108	0.2500	0.2948	0.3248	0.4078
70	0.1954	0.2319	0.2737	0.3017	0.3799
80	0.1829	0.2172	0.2565	0.2830	0.3568
90	0.1726	0.2050	0.2422	0.2673	0.3375
100	0.1638	0.1946	0.2301	0.2540	0.3211

If the observed value of r *is greater than or equal to the tabled value for the appropriate level of significance (columns) and degrees of freedom (rows), reject* H_0 *[the null hypothesis]. The degrees of freedom are the number of pairs of scores minus two, or N – 2. The critical values in the table are both + and – for nondirectional (two-tailed) tests.*

Source: Sir R.A. Fisher and F. Yates (1974), *Statistical Tables for Biological, Agricultural and Medical Research,* 6th edition (Harlow, Essex, U.K.: Addison Wesley Longman), Table VII. Reprinted by permission of Pearson Education Limited.

APPENDIX D

CRITICAL VALUES OF *t*

df	Level of Significance for a Nondirectional (Two-Tailed) Test				
	.10	.05	.02	.01	.001
1	6.314	12.706	31.821	63.657	636.619
2	2.920	4.303	6.965	9.925	31.598
3	2.353	3.182	4.541	5.841	12.941
4	2.132	2.776	3.747	4.604	8.610
5	2.015	2.571	3.365	4.032	6.859
6	1.943	2.447	3.143	3.707	5.959
7	1.895	2.365	2.998	3.499	5.405
8	1.860	2.306	2.896	3.355	5.041
9	1.833	2.262	2.821	3.250	4.781
10	1.812	2.228	2.764	3.169	4.587
11	1.796	2.201	2.718	3.106	4.437
12	1.782	2.179	2.681	3.055	4.318
13	1.771	2.160	2.650	3.012	4.221
14	1.761	2.145	2.624	2.977	4.140
15	1.753	2.131	2.602	2.947	4.073
16	1.746	2.120	2.583	2.921	4.015
17	1.740	2.110	2.567	2.898	3.965
18	1.734	2.101	2.552	2.878	3.922
19	1.729	2.093	2.539	2.861	3.883
20	1.725	2.086	2.528	2.845	3.850
21	1.721	2.080	2.518	2.831	3.819
22	1.717	2.074	2.508	2.819	3.792
23	1.714	2.069	2.500	2.807	3.767
24	1.711	2.064	2.492	2.797	3.745
25	1.706	2.060	2.485	2.787	3.725
26	1.706	2.056	2.479	2.779	3.707
27	1.703	2.052	2.473	2.771	3.690
28	1.701	2.048	2.467	2.763	3.674
29	1.699	2.045	2.462	2.756	3.659
30	1.697	2.042	2.457	2.750	3.646
40	1.684	2.021	2.423	2.704	3.551
60	1.671	2.000	2.390	2.660	3.460
120	1.658	1.980	2.358	2.617	3.373
∞	1.645	1.960	2.326	2.576	3.291

The value listed in the table is the critical value of t *for the number of degrees of freedom listed in the left column for a directional (one-tailed) or nondirectional (two-tailed) test at the significance level indicated at the top of each column. If the observed* t *is greater than or equal to the tabled value, reject* H_0 *[the null hypothesis]. Since the* t *distribution is symmetrical about* t *= 0, these critical values represent both + and – values for nondirectional tests.*

Source: Sir R.A. Fisher and F. Yates (1974), *Statistical Tables for Biological, Agricultural and Medical Research*, 6th edition (Harlow, Essex, U.K.: Addison Wesley Longman), Table III. Reprinted by permission of Pearson Education Limited.

APPENDIX E

CRITICAL VALUES OF *F**

Degrees of Freedom in Denominator	Degrees of Freedom in Numerator													
	1	**2**	**3**	**4**	**5**	**6**	**7**	**8**	**9**	**10**	**20**	**50**	**100**	**∞**
1	161	200	216	225	230	234	237	239	241	242	248	252	253	254
	4052	**5000**	**5402**	**5625**	**5764**	**5859**	**5928**	**5980**	**6022**	**6056**	**6208**	**6302**	**6334**	**6366**
2	18.51	19.00	19.16	19.25	19.30	19.33	19.36	19.37	19.38	19.39	19.44	19.47	19.49	19.50
	98.50	**99.00**	**99.17**	**99.25**	**99.30**	**99.33**	**99.34**	**99.36**	**99.38**	**99.40**	**99.45**	**99.48**	**99.49**	**99.50**
3	10.13	9.55	9.28	9.12	9.01	8.94	8.88	8.84	8.81	8.78	8.66	8.58	8.56	8.53
	34.12	**30.81**	**29.46**	**28.71**	**28.24**	**27.91**	**27.67**	**27.49**	**27.34**	**27.23**	**26.69**	**26.30**	**26.23**	**26.12**
4	7.71	6.94	6.59	6.39	6.26	6.16	6.09	6.04	6.00	5.96	5.80	5.70	5.66	5.63
	21.20	**18.00**	**16.69**	**15.98**	**15.52**	**15.21**	**14.98**	**14.80**	**14.66**	**14.54**	**14.02**	**13.69**	**13.57**	**13.46**
5	6.61	5.79	5.41	5.19	5.05	4.95	4.88	4.82	4.78	4.74	4.56	4.44	4.40	4.36
	16.26	**13.27**	**12.06**	**11.39**	**10.97**	**10.67**	**10.45**	**10.27**	**10.15**	**10.05**	**9.55**	**9.24**	**9.13**	**9.02**
6	5.99	5.14	4.76	4.53	4.39	4.28	4.21	4.15	4.10	4.06	3.87	3.75	3.71	3.67
	13.74	**10.92**	**9.78**	**9.15**	**8.75**	**8.47**	**8.26**	**8.10**	**7.98**	**7.87**	**7.39**	**7.09**	**6.99**	**6.88**
7	5.59	4.74	4.35	4.12	3.97	3.87	3.79	3.73	3.68	3.63	3.44	3.32	3.28	3.23
	12.25	**9.55**	**8.45**	**7.85**	**7.46**	**7.19**	**7.00**	**6.84**	**6.71**	**6.62**	**6.15**	**5.85**	**5.75**	**5.65**
8	5.32	4.46	4.07	3.84	3.69	3.58	3.50	3.44	3.39	3.34	3.15	3.03	2.98	2.93
	11.26	**8.65**	**7.59**	**7.01**	**6.63**	**6.37**	**6.19**	**6.03**	**5.91**	**5.82**	**5.36**	**5.06**	**4.96**	**4.86**
9	5.12	4.26	3.86	3.63	3.48	3.37	3.29	3.23	3.18	3.13	2.93	2.80	2.76	2.71
	10.56	**8.02**	**6.99**	**6.42**	**6.06**	**5.80**	**5.62**	**5.47**	**5.35**	**5.26**	**4.80**	**4.51**	**4.41**	**4.31**
10	4.96	4.10	3.71	3.48	3.33	3.22	3.14	3.07	3.02	2.97	2.77	2.64	2.59	2.54
	10.04	**7.56**	**6.55**	**5.99**	**5.64**	**5.39**	**5.21**	**5.06**	**4.95**	**4.85**	**4.41**	**4.12**	**4.01**	**3.91**
11	4.84	3.98	3.59	3.36	3.20	3.09	3.01	2.95	2.90	2.86	2.65	2.50	2.45	2.40
	9.56	**7.20**	**6.22**	**5.67**	**5.32**	**5.07**	**4.88**	**4.74**	**4.63**	**4.54**	**4.10**	**3.80**	**3.70**	**3.60**
12	4.75	3.88	3.49	3.26	3.11	3.00	2.92	2.85	2.80	2.76	2.54	2.40	2.35	2.30
	9.33	**6.93**	**5.95**	**5.41**	**5.06**	**4.82**	**4.65**	**4.50**	**4.39**	**4.30**	**3.86**	**3.56**	**3.46**	**3.36**
13	4.67	3.80	3.41	3.18	3.02	2.92	2.84	2.77	2.72	2.67	2.46	2.32	2.26	2.21
	9.07	**6.70**	**5.74**	**5.20**	**4.86**	**4.62**	**4.44**	**4.30**	**4.19**	**4.10**	**3.67**	**3.37**	**3.27**	**3.16**
14	4.60	3.74	3.34	3.11	2.96	2.85	2.77	2.70	2.65	2.60	2.39	2.24	2.19	2.13
	8.86	**6.51**	**5.56**	**5.03**	**4.69**	**4.46**	**4.28**	**4.14**	**4.03**	**3.94**	**3.51**	**3.21**	**3.11**	**3.00**

* The F-ratio is statistically significant when it exceeds or equals the values above. The .05 level is shown in light type; the .01 level in bold type.

(continued)

NEL

Critical Values of *F*

(continued)

Degrees of Freedom in Denominator	Degrees of Freedom in Numerator													
	1	2	3	4	5	6	7	8	9	10	20	50	100	∞
15	4.54	3.68	3.29	3.06	2.90	2.79	2.70	2.64	2.59	2.55	2.33	2.18	2.12	2.07
	8.68	6.36	5.42	4.89	4.56	4.32	4.14	4.00	3.89	3.80	3.36	3.07	2.97	2.87
16	4.49	3.63	3.24	3.01	2.85	2.74	2.66	2.59	2.54	2.49	2.28	2.13	2.07	2.01
	8.53	6.23	5.29	4.77	4.44	4.20	4.03	3.89	3.78	3.69	3.25	2.96	2.86	2.75
17	4.45	3.59	3.20	2.96	2.81	2.70	2.62	2.55	2.50	2.45	2.23	2.08	2.02	1.96
	8.40	6.11	5.18	4.67	4.34	4.10	3.93	3.79	3.68	3.59	3.16	2.86	2.76	2.65
18	4.41	3.55	3.16	2.93	2.77	2.66	2.58	2.51	2.46	2.41	2.19	2.04	1.98	1.92
	8.28	6.01	5.09	4.58	4.25	4.01	3.85	3.71	3.60	3.51	3.07	2.78	2.68	2.57
19	4.38	3.52	3.13	2.90	2.74	2.63	2.55	2.48	2.43	2.38	2.15	2.00	1.94	1.88
	8.18	5.93	5.01	4.50	4.17	3.94	3.77	3.63	3.52	3.43	3.00	2.70	2.60	2.49
20	4.35	3.49	3.10	2.87	2.71	2.60	2.52	2.45	2.40	2.35	2.12	1.96	1.90	1.84
	8.10	5.85	4.94	4.43	4.10	3.87	3.71	3.56	3.45	3.37	2.94	2.63	2.53	2.42
25	4.24	3.38	2.99	2.76	2.60	2.49	2.41	2.34	2.28	2.24	2.00	1.84	1.77	1.71
	7.77	5.57	4.68	4.18	3.86	3.63	3.46	3.32	3.21	3.13	2.70	2.40	2.29	2.17
30	4.17	3.32	2.92	2.69	2.53	2.42	2.34	2.27	2.21	2.16	1.93	1.76	1.69	1.62
	7.56	5.39	4.51	4.02	3.70	3.47	3.30	3.17	3.06	2.98	2.55	2.24	2.13	2.01
40	4.08	3.23	2.84	2.61	2.45	2.34	2.25	2.18	2.12	2.07	1.84	1.66	1.59	1.51
	7.31	5.18	4.31	3.83	3.51	3.29	3.12	2.99	2.88	2.80	2.37	2.05	1.94	1.81
50	4.03	3.18	2.79	2.56	2.40	2.29	2.20	2.13	2.07	2.02	1.78	1.60	1.52	1.44
	7.17	5.06	4.20	3.72	3.41	3.18	3.02	2.88	2.78	2.70	2.26	1.94	1.82	1.68
100	3.94	3.09	2.70	2.46	2.30	2.19	2.10	2.03	1.97	1.92	1.68	1.48	1.39	1.28
	6.90	4.82	3.98	3.51	3.20	2.99	2.82	2.69	2.59	2.51	2.06	1.73	1.59	1.43
200	3.89	3.04	2.65	2.41	2.26	2.14	2.05	1.98	1.92	1.87	1.62	1.42	1.32	1.19
	6.76	4.71	3.88	3.41	3.11	2.90	2.73	2.60	2.50	2.41	1.97	1.62	1.48	1.28
∞	3.84	3.00	2.60	2.37	2.21	2.10	2.01	1.94	1.88	1.83	1.57	1.35	1.24	1.00
	6.64	4.61	3.78	3.32	3.02	2.80	2.64	2.51	2.41	2.32	1.87	1.52	1.36	1.00

Source: B. Sommer and R. Sommer (1991), *A Practical Guide to Behavioral Research: Tools and Techniques,* 4th edition (New York: Oxford University Press). Copyright © 1997 by Oxford University Press. Used by permission of Oxford University Press, Inc.

ONE DAY AT A TIME:
Single-Parent Mothers in Academe[1]

Patricia Ratel

Abstract. This study offers an exploratory investigation into the lives of single-parent women who return to school in an effort to break the cycle of poverty in which they are caught. In-depth open-ended interviews were conducted with a purposively chosen sample of nine women who were attending university while acting as sole parent for one or more children. Results revealed that this additional status interacted with other elements of their lives in multiplicative fashion, creating an overwhelming burden for the women that manifested itself in physical and emotional deterioration notwithstanding the variety of adaptive strategies they employed. The women felt bureaucratic systems seemed designed to produce failure instead of success. Policy implications of their experiences are discussed.

INTRODUCTION

Single parenthood is becoming increasingly pervasive in Canada. Statistics Canada (1984) reports that the number of lone-parent families increased by 10% in the preceding decade. Although some of these families are headed by males, the vast majority (82.6%) are headed by females. Indeed, as a demographic category, "single mothers" comprise 11.3% of the total population, and every indicator suggests this will continue. Until recently, very little was known or understood regarding the dynamics of their particular niche, but recent studies have enhanced our knowledge in a variety of areas.

Statistically speaking, the majority of single mothers in Canada live in poverty. Twenty per cent of all single mothers earn less than $5,000 per year, while 37% earn less than $15,000 per year, and these women have the lowest income growth rate

in the country (Statistics Canada, 1984, p. 5). Norton and Glick (1986) compared single and two parent families on a variety of social and economic variables, and were led to conclude that:

> By most objective measures. the vast majority of these families hold a disadvantageous position in society relative to other family groups. They are characterized by a high rate of poverty, a high percentage of minority representation, relatively low education, and a high rate of mobility. In short, they generally have little equity or stature in society and constitute a group with unusually pressing social and economic needs. (p. 16)

Other researchers have examined the economic pressures associated with single motherhood and have demonstrated that a number of factors, unique to today's economic environment, play a

1. *Note from Palys:* This article originally appeared in *Starting from Where You Are* (1989), a compendium of student research edited by Ted Palys and produced with financial assistance from Simon Fraser University and the School of Criminology. Ms. Ratel, a single-parent mother at the time, completed the research and write-up in a single semester while taking a research methods course from Palys. The dissemination of this article to a new generation of students is done with her permission.

distinct role in perpetuating the poverty of these women. In most instances it is the woman who is least able to support the family, and yet, in eight out of ten cases it is the woman who assumes this responsibility. Inflation, high unemployment, job discrimination, lack of prior job experience, rising costs of adequate childcare, and inconsistent or non-existent child support all contribute to the feminization of poverty[2] (Grief, 1986).

In many instances, single mothers are maintained solely by the state, and their existence is meager at best.[3] In other cases women seek employment and some degree of self-sufficiency. However, Pett and Vaughn-Cole (1986) suggest that most single mothers acquire low status positions because of socialization processes and are fearful of taking the risks associated with pursuit of an education, career opportunities, or non-traditional jobs that would prove more lucrative. The researchers highlight this as one of their most troubling findings as it implies a *cul-de-sac* of serious and continued economic deprivation. They argue for changes in both public policy and public attitudes to facilitate the development of educational training programs and the provision of adequate financial support and childcare systems for the economically insecure and depressed single mother (p. 110).

Sanik and Maudlin (1986) have analyzed the role of work in the lives of single mothers—and particularly the impact of combined job and home life responsibilities—by comparing singles to marrieds, and parents to non-parents. They found that single mothers were particularly at risk for multiple role strain and reduced levels of emotional and physical well-being:

> It comes as no surprise that employed single mothers have the least amount of time to spend on household tasks, child care, personal care, and volunteer work ... In order to meet the demands of the family it is the single employed mother alone who sacrifices time in personal care activities including rest and sleep. (p. 56)

Burden (1986) examined the same issue and found identical results. She also found that despite the psychological and emotional strain experienced by these women, they nonetheless exhibited high levels of job satisfaction and did not incur higher rates of absenteeism. She suggests that an understanding of the varying time demands placed on women because of their marital status and employment could be of benefit to employers, and that such information should be utilized to improve the work environment for these employees.

Other researchers have focused on a variety of psychological and human challenges that face single-parent families. For example, Hill (1986) examined structural differences between intact, widowed, and single-parent families, and noted that single-parent families lack the personnel to fill all the normally expected positions of a family. Therefore, extra burdens are placed on the remaining family members who must compensate with increased effort to accomplish tasks such as physical maintenance, social control, and tension management (p. 28).

Wells Gladow and Ray (1986) found that positive adjustment to single parenthood was directly associated with the amount of social support received. Specifically, the authors found that friends and family contribute significantly to the emotional and physical well-being of single mothers. The 'network support' of friends eases emotional distress created by feelings of loneliness and isolation. They found this form of support to be of greater importance than the pursuit of love relationships, which the researchers suggest are over-emphasized in our culture, and can be detrimental to the adjustment process. Family support usually

---

2. This term has been applied primarily to the economic plight of women in today's society. It also has been employed to elucidate the circumstances that contribute to the poverty of specific groups of women, notably single mothers.

3. For example, a woman living in British Columbia with one child currently receives $640 per month from welfare. This amount is reduced by $50 after three months, to provide the women with incentive to seek employment.

takes the forms of financial aid, assistance with housing, childcare and other tangible problems. The researchers conclude that a single parent with both forms of support will be better able to make the necessary emotional and physical adjustments associated with this life transition.

Hanson (1986) undertook a multivariate analysis of factors associated with well-being among single mothers. Broad social support networks and communication skills were significantly correlated with stress management. The researcher noted particularly the inter-relatedness of physical and mental health, and that good health in the parent was associated with good health in the child. Hanson states,

> While single parent families experience many problems they are not necessarily less able to manage them than other family configurations. Single parent families can be healthy environments in which to live. (p. 131)

Not surprisingly, many researchers have focused on the effects of single parenting on the children. Heatherington, Cox, and Cox (1979), Kelly and Wallerstein (1980), and Blecham (1980) all have examined the emotional and behavioral problems associated with family dis-equilibrium following marital separation, and concluded that although these adjustments can be traumatic, they do not produce permanent disabilities for the children. Furthermore, the adjustments of children are closely associated with the adjustments of the mother. The pertinent factors associated with healthy readjustment include the general emotional availability of the parent, the ongoing level of family conflict, the ability of the parent to be warm and affectionate, the parent's personal support systems, financial stress, and the presence of additional stresses.

Finally, Duvall (1986) examined the impact of single-parent families on children to determine if these children "grew up a little faster" than other children. The findings indicated that this was the case to a certain extent, although the children did not have any more chores than the comparison group. However, more than half the children were "latch key kids" and it was felt that, because of this, the mothers were reluctant to allocate further responsibilities because of the intimate and confidante relationships that emanate from such circumstances. In this regard the children did "grow up a little faster."

Although the research in this area offers insight to the phenomenon of single parenthood, an investigation of the unique experiences of single mothers attending university has apparently not been undertaken. The present research represented an attempt to remedy this shortcoming. More specifically, the purpose of this study was to undertake an exploratory examination of the single mother experience in the academic context, by investigating a sample of women's lives in terms of their financial situations, their physical and emotional well-being, their social support systems, their academic experience, and the effects of their circumstances upon their children.

METHODOLOGY

The Women

As the research undertaken was exploratory in nature, a purposive sampling technique was utilized. This proved to be advantageous for several reasons. First, I was able to interview women whom I knew and, as a relationship of trust had been previously established, the participants were willing to grant me access to their lives. As I share their status, I believe they felt comfortable discussing their situations with me. Knowing that I had similar experiences gave the women confidence in my ability to report on the phenomenon and encouraged open disclosure.

The second reason a purposive sampling method was chosen was to ensure some variation within such a small sample. The ages of the women ranged from twenty-four to forty-one. Three of the women had one child, two were rearing three children, and the remainder had two children. One of the women had just started her first semester at university, while another woman had been in attendance for six years; the other women had been pursuing their education between two and four years. Furthermore, the women represented a variety of faculties, including business, education, psychology, criminology, anthropology, and fine arts. The experience of single motherhood also varied. One woman had been separated only a year; another had been on her own for twelve years.

A total of nine women were approached and agreed to be interviewed. One interview was deleted from the analysis as the process was treated lightly and the resulting responses were flippant and dubious at best. Another respondent was lost because of concerns with confidentiality and the possible repercussions of involvement in the study. The analysis below focuses on the remaining seven participants.

The Interviews

Interviews were conducted within the women's homes, and each lasted between three and four hours. The interviews proved to be an emotionally turbulent process for the women. It is difficult to encapsulate, in a few brief lines, the underlying essence of the interviews except to state, without reservation, that the women who approached the exercise seriously were forthright and honest in their responses.

The women discussed personal and intimate aspects of their lives. Since some of the women spoke of involvement in criminal and deviant behavior, confidentiality was a significant concern. The women were fully informed of the nature of the research, who would have access to it, and how the information would be used. Anonymity was guaranteed by ensuring that there would be no means of identification incorporated in the paper. In some instances excerpts were deleted from the report to protect the participants from any possible reprisals.

The research took the form of open-ended interviews. The women were informed of the general area of inquiry and presented with the specific topic areas for discussion. Following an introductory explanation and the gathering of demographic details, the women were free to discuss the issues as they saw fit. Notes were taken virtually verbatim and interjections were made only when it was necessary to elicit more details or to ensure a thorough understanding of the comments. This method was adopted in an attempt to ensure that my influence on the reporting was minimal. I was aware that I held particular opinions and speculations that emanated from my own experiences, and felt it imperative to maintain a receptive but neutral stance while conducting the interviews.

FINDINGS

Financial Circumstances

The women in this sample had returned to school for similar reasons. All had left poor and, in some cases, abusive relationships, and realized that they had to take sole responsibility for rearing their children. Every woman but one had some past experience with the welfare system and found it to be oppressive, degrading, and stigmatizing. Receiving social assistance placed the women in a state of complete dependence and subjected them to elements of social control they found intolerable. The assistance they received from the state maintained their families at a subsistence level, but effectively denied them any opportunity to improve their standard of living.

The women shared a common employment history of low paying, menial jobs which did not provide them with the financial means to maintain their families comfortably. Collectively, they felt unfulfilled and frustrated with their employment status; all, however, sensed their own potential, and sought some means of realizing it. For example, as Linda[4] stated:

---

4. All names are pseudonyms, in order to preserve confidentiality.

When I left my husband I had to go on welfare, but the state makes you so completely dependent. They make assumptions about your moral character and start dictating how you should live. I rebelled; I said "I don't want your fucking help," and I went to work on the fish boats with my son. During the off season I was collecting UIC and I decided that if I was ever going to have a chance to make it I'd better go back to school. So I packed up my son and moved and registered at SFU. Well, no sooner was I here than I got cut off UIC because I was unavailable for work. It doesn't make any sense because I could have stayed where I was and collected all winter. So, I was really broke and I got a part-time job, then the bastards denied me my daycare subsidies because my income, combined with my loan, which they consider to be income but which is actually a debt, put me just over the top financially. I appealed to the district supervisor and was told to quit my job. The district supervisor then told me that if my child wasn't in daycare he would have him apprehended. They just don't seem to understand, you're in a no win situation.

Each woman chose to discuss her financial situation first as this permeated every aspect of their lives. All of the women live below the poverty line and all have incurred large debts to pursue their education. Many of the women have already borrowed more than $30,000, are still attending university, and thus are accumulating further debt. The money they receive from student loans is not enough to support their families, providing them with just enough to pay for tuition, housing, and food. The women have to work to provide their children with the necessities of school supplies, adequate clothing, dental checkups and the luxuries of extra-curricular activities, birthday parties, and Christmas presents. Ironically, the need for employment extends the length of time they have to attend the university, which means incurring even greater debt.

Employment has other ramifications that warrant discussion. The women are struggling to alter

the dependent and destitute nature of their lives yet, as soon as the women start earning extra income, they can be denied some of the benefits available to them when they are in a completely indigent state. Their income is to be included in their loan applications, thereby possibly reducing the amount they will be given the following semester; this serves to perpetuate the necessity of maintaining employment. They can be denied reduced medical premiums and daycare subsidies, effectively negating any extra income they might be earning. The women find themselves in an economic Catch-22 and feel that their efforts are being thwarted by policies that are internally inconsistent and illogical.

In some instances their economic situation created a degree of frustration and desperation that motivated the women to certain acts of criminal behavior. Most of the women have left income undeclared; some have committed fraud and theft; one turned to selling illicit drugs to make ends meet; and others have maintained relationships with men for financial benefit. For example, Brenda stated,

My debt load is well over $32,000. To make ends meet I've had to collect welfare illegally while I've been at school. I've worked under the table and collected UIC and I'm terrified Big Brother is going to charge me with fraud. I'm always lying to the state to get by … The system's fucked; you try your best to get ahead and you have to fight every step of the way. The ironic thing is that I'm no better off than if I was on welfare and I take more risks. The only difference is that the stigma isn't there. It's OK to be a starving student, but you still starve. The really offensive thing is that the system will support you if you want to take a six-week secretarial course, but not if you want a career and some options in your life. There's no social support in the system. Last summer, I was so broke, I seriously considered hooking. I was so desperate for money, I was stealing food, toilet paper … and I've developed an amazing capacity for manipulating the phone company, the landlord, the loans department ... It's a total con; after a while you begin to believe what you're saying. You feminize your poverty by saying yes I'm poor; it's a scam, or it's survival. You tap into your poverty and it stares you back in the face. So you tell yourself that you're not really an East End welfare mom; you're a student but it's a false consciousness. You cling to your goal, but at the same time you're aware that there may not be anything out there for you when you're finished. I go downtown and look at the prostitutes and I don't see other women; I see myself and hope that I can stay out of it for another year.

Physical and Emotional Stress

Initially an attempt was made to differentiate between the emotional and physical stresses experienced by the women in this study. This proved to be an impossibility as I quickly discovered that the physical and emotional burdens associated with the women's status were inextricably intertwined and served to exacerbate each other.

All the women interviewed stated emphatically that they were physically exhausted. The multifaceted nature of their lives, the adoption of three separate and distinct roles (i.e., wage earner, student, and mother) created demands on their time and energy that were difficult to manage. Inevitably, the women sacrificed their own well-being to meet these demands. Collectively, they reported that they are in poor physical health and pointed to lack of sleep, lack of exercise, and inadequate diet as the key contributing factors. The women contend with some anxiety because of their financial situations, but also must face the pressures associated with the academic environment, as well as meeting the challenge of raising their children alone. There is a distinct cyclical element to this situation in which the inability to cope with the physical demands manifests itself in an inability to deal with the emotional stresses. This in turn takes a toll on their physical well-being. As Karen stated:

I was on anti-depressants for the first year I was in school. I came very close to having a nervous breakdown, twice actually. I have a prescription for Valium but I'm trying not to rely on the drugs any more. I live on coffee and cigarettes; I'm always exhausted. After I deal with the kids at night, cook and clean, read bedtime stories, you know ... I have to work until two or three in the morning because it's the only time I have to study. I get up at 5:30 in the morning so I can have a half an hour to myself before the kids get up and I start all over again. Occasionally, I force myself to back off and get some sleep. As soon as the semester starts, I'm counting down the weeks hoping I can make it through to the break. People tell me I don't deal with the stress appropriately, that I should get some exercise and get some more sleep. I know they're right but I have to laugh. Who's got the time? They just don't have a clue what I'm dealing with here.

The women readily admit that they do not cope with the stress well. In most cases they articulated an underlying feeling of panic and a realization that they were barely managing the demands placed upon them. In fact, it appears that any additional stress becomes overwhelming. In one case, a woman became pregnant and suffered an emotional collapse. In another instance, a woman took leave from the university because her ex-husband was attempting to take her children from her. A third woman found herself unable to carry on when her mother became seriously ill. Some of the women have experienced mental and physical breakdowns, and episodes of depression are not uncommon. A majority of the women have resorted at one time or another to various forms of substance use and abuse, including dependencies on alcohol, tranquilizers, cocaine, and marijuana, to temporarily alleviate their stress. Brenda stated:

I'm exhausted. I sleep four or maybe six hours a night, I'm totally unhealthy after two years of school ... I have no energy. Your whole life, every aspect—emotional, physical, spiritual, and social—

is ignored to get through. You tap into them occasionally to prevent yourself from going insane. Every minute of your day is scheduled. I keep telling myself that I have to get the damn degree; when I get it I can be a whole person again. I've had complete emotional and physical breakdowns ... You think you develop coping strategies, you think you're dealing with your stress, but you're just masking it because on a deep hurting emotional level ... you're not coping with it at all.

The Children

In each case the women's children represented one of the primary motivations for pursuing an education. Every woman hoped to offer her children a better lifestyle. This goal incorporates more than financial or material gain; the women also seek a sense of security and a variety of options and opportunities for their children. They cope with their circumstances largely "for" their children; and yet, their circumstances generate a degree of emotional and physical neglect that produces feelings of anxiety, guilt, and remorse.

In reviewing the financial difficulties experienced by the women, it became apparent that the children had to do without most of the luxuries afforded other children. In some instances, it was the necessities that were omitted and this has compelled some women to take drastic measures.

The demands placed on the women often detracted from their parenting skills. Most of the women stated they did not have the time or energy to manage their children effectively, and that this resulted in a degree of emotional neglect. In two cases, this neglect had manifested itself in behavioral problems. For example, one child is a chronic bed wetter at the age of eight. Another woman reported that her children are completely undisciplined and difficult to control.

Another factor that directly affects the majority of children in this study is the lack of quality childcare. It has been previously noted that daycare is not readily affordable, and unavailable to the women for this reason. Most of the women cannot afford to hire babysitters in place of daycare, and those who have taken these steps have had negative experiences. One woman was robbed by a sitter. Another discovered that her sitter was being sexually promiscuous in front of her children. A third woman discovered that her son was being psychologically abused by her sitter.[5] The ramifications of these situations were that more than half of the children in this study were "latch key kids" who must care for themselves when their mothers are absent because of classes or work. The women collectively assert that their children are forced to "grow up fast." The children have to assume domestic responsibilities and there is a demand for maturity and self-sufficiency placed upon them that is largely unavoidable. As Susan described,

> I look at my kids and I have enormous guilt. Some time ago I discovered that they were being sexually abused by their babysitter. I came very close to having a nervous breakdown. I had to withdraw from school. My husband wanted to take my kids away from me. It was the hardest thing I've ever dealt with. They're OK now but I'm scared for them. I worry about them all the time. Even if I had the time and money or the opportunity to go out socially, I wouldn't because I will not leave them with a babysitter again. They're latchkey kids. Sometimes they spend up to four hours a day by themselves. They have to cook their own dinner and look out for themselves. They've had to grow up very fast, but somehow they're OK. I think my kids are extraordinary. They're so supportive of what I'm doing, But the guilt bears pretty heavily on me.

Despite the apparent hardships, the women are generally optimistic that the experiences of their children will be beneficial in the long run. They maintain that their children are learning valuable

---

5.   The sitter kept threatening to cut off the boy's penis if he misbehaved.

lessons and are becoming strong and independent individuals. Many of the women assert that the experiences of their children are broadening their social consciousness and this may serve to better society for the next generation. One woman suggested, however, that this is a process of rationalizing pernicious situations and that the women have to believe this to carry on.

Social Support

The previous discussions have outlined, albeit implicitly, some of the factors that affect the women's social support systems. In many instances, the breakdown of the family resulted in some loss of previously established support networks. The rigorous conditions of their current situations results in further losses. The women state that they do not possess the resources—the time, the energy, or the financial means—to actively pursue companionship, and this further restricts their social outlets. The university setting fills the void to a certain degree as new acquaintances are made, but these relationships necessarily involve sporadic contact and do not provide substantial support for the women. There is an informal support network among single mothers at the university, but since all experience the same constraints and pressures, the support network is rendered weak and unstable. The women commonly experience a sense of solitude in their lives. And while their social support systems are deficient, their feelings of loneliness and isolation stem more directly from a lack of intimate personal relationships.

The women perceive the socialization processes of both men and women as playing a significant role in their common experiences with intimate relationships. Women are socialized to be nurturing and take an active, giving role in maintaining a relationship. The challenges they currently face demand a denial of this role, and the women report that men seem unable or reluctant to adjust to the complex and exacting nature of their lives. The women are unwilling to forsake their education, their goals, and/or their children

to accommodate such a relationship, and view such sacrifices as a prerequisite for entering into an intimate relationship. The women assert that men, in general, are only superficially supportive of their endeavors, and that the negation of socially prescribed roles contributes to this phenomenon.

Some of the women accept that they will be alone until they have completed the tasks at hand. Others adopt a stance that permits some intimacy as long as it does not interfere with their lives. They acknowledge, in both instances, that their physical and emotional needs are neglected, and that this creates additional stress as they attempt to suppress their sensuality. Despite this, the women consider this area of their lives as one that can be readily sacrificed. Indeed, they state that it must be sacrificed if they are going to accomplish their goals. Paradoxically, this serves to further limit their social support networks, increase their feelings of isolation and loneliness, and minimize opportunities for reprieve from the stresses they encounter. Once again, the women state they are in a no-win situation. As Karen noted:

> Relationships are difficult. I have no time for them. Most of my old friends have drifted away. I have new friends at school and socialize a little but even those relationships are hard to maintain. Men come third after my education and my kids. If I have a relationship it has to be scheduled. I have very little patience; if it disrupts my work or my kids, I get angry. And if they can't cope with the situation they can get lost. It doesn't work, you know it can't with everything else you're juggling. Intellectually, you can rationalize the situation but emotionally, the loneliness just eats away at you.

Lastly, the women commented extensively on the overall lack of support in contemporary society. Regardless of the fact that single mothers are an ever-increasing presence they are still regarded with a degree of contempt, and looked upon as failures. There is a stigma attached to the status of single mother that exists despite any efforts the women are making to improve themselves and their lives. Several women mentioned that although there are many women rearing children alone, they are considered as somehow deserving of their predicaments. In contrast, the few men that raise families by themselves are considered heroic and are often offered various forms of social support. While it is scandalous for a woman to leave her children, little is made of the men who abandon their families. Society simply expects women to assume responsibility for their children; and yet, even when they accept this responsibility fully, little support is offered by the state or society as a whole.

Academics

Scholastically, the women in the sample reported doing well; most achieve above-average grades. The women feel they must work harder and more efficiently to perform well because of the constraints and pressures associated with their status. The women put forth the argument that their circumstances impede their academic performance and, given more conducive lifestyles, they could improve their academic standing significantly. This may be a legitimate speculation, but it is important to note that the circumstances that hinder their capabilities also serve to compel the women to work as hard as they do. The women are highly motivated to succeed for two reasons. First, they view their education as the means by which they will alter their life chances. Second, it appears that the more they invest in this pursuit, and the more they sacrifice to achieve their goals, the more determined they are to succeed. If the women were not motivated to this extent, if their lives were utopian, it is conceivable that they might not perform as well as they do. As Susan indicated:

I really think that single mothers are extraordinary women. Not just because they deal with all

of this, but ... I think, perhaps, they are more intelligent or have greater capabilities than the majority of students ... I have much less time to do my work than other students and yet my grades are better than most of them. I manage to maintain a 3.5 GPA with about one fifth of the time allotted to other students ... I try never to use my situation to gain advantage either. I don't want to be thought of as a struggling single mother. I don't want exceptions made for me. I want to be taken seriously as an academic, and stand or fall on my own merit. So, for the most part, I never raise the issue. I take a great deal of pride in what I'm doing; it's part of my persona. People ask me, "How do you manage it all?" I don't quite honestly know. The bottom line is I love what I'm doing, I really do.

It must be recounted that these women also seek to realize their own potential. The pursuit of personal fulfillment was one of the key motivations for returning to school in most cases. The frustrations expressed with regards to their academic experience are indicative of this factor, over and above the difficulties stemming from their single parent status. For example, the women frequently take correspondence courses to permit them time to work and care for their children. Often, courses in which they are interested are offered only at night, and they are unable to attend. Similarly, there are many university-sponsored events and activities in which the women cannot participate because of their familial responsibilities. The women spoke of having to cut corners academically, and felt depressed and angry because they had to make these concessions with their education.[6] Although these frustrations arose because of their status, they were aired because the women did not feel that they were deriving full benefit from the university environment. Their academic pursuits are

---

6. The women reported that they never seem to have the time to thoroughly learn some material, thoroughly research a topic, or write several drafts until a paper is satisfactorily composed, and so forth. Their academic semester could be described as a period of crisis management more so than a period of quality education.

intrinsically valued. The women enjoy the pursuit and acquisition of knowledge and often feel cheated in the academic arena. As Linda asserted,

> I think that the university experience is probably very different for students without my responsibilities. It is supposed to be the best time of your life ... Well, it's the *hardest* time of my life, but I love it, and I have to do this for my own sake and for my children.

DISCUSSION AND CONCLUSIONS

The structural characteristics of Canadian society are changing rapidly, and the family unit has seen many transformations in the last twenty years. Nonetheless the traditional nuclear family still predominates, although any imaginable configuration can be found in contemporary society. One of the prevalent trends altering the face of Canadian families in the last two decades is the growing pervasiveness of the single parent. The majority of single-parent households are headed by women and, although we know something of them in the aggregate from statistical surveys, very little research has been done that shows the human face of this group. The purpose of this research was to do so by exploring the circumstances of a small and yet diverse sample of single mothers attending university, and examining some of the factors that shape their experiences.

It is apparent that the women contend with a variety of problems that are unique to their status. The women live in or near poverty, accrue large debts to pursue their goals, and suffer debilitating physical and emotional stress as they attempt to maintain three separate and distinct life roles. They have a limited amount of social support, and their children are subjected to a number of pressures, including some dereliction. Their education is of paramount importance as their overriding goal is to better their life chances and remove themselves from the experiences common to most single mothers.

The literature revealed that the majority of single mothers are struggling financially. Those who adopt dual roles by entering the work force are subjected to elevated levels of stress. It was acknowledged that the well-being of single mothers is correlated to the amount of social support they receive. Furthermore, a distinct relationship was found between their physical and mental well-being. Generally, the children experience some temporary emotional and behavioral problems while adjusting to the breakup of the family, and the demands placed upon their mothers served to enhance the need for emotional independence.

Although there are a number of obvious similarities between single mothers generally and those in the academic setting, the pursuit of an education clearly aggravates the pressures and problems normally experienced by single mothers. The endeavors undertaken create a situation in which each factor plays upon and exacerbates the rest. This experiential dynamic is unique to the women in this study, and its comprehension necessary for a thorough understanding of the phenomenon in question. Figure 1 depicts the interaction between the five variables examined in this study and demonstrates the complexity created with the adoption of this status. The cross-impacts make more transparent that adding a single element—attending university, in this case—adds not just a single element or impact to one's life, but a whole new set of pressures that affect and are affected by every other element of one's life.

The research unearthed a number of structural elements that contribute directly to the problems encountered by these women: a lack of financial support, a lack of affordable childcare, and provincial policies that are antagonistic to their endeavors. The most pertinent example is the absence of maintenance in the majority of cases. Only two women in this study received financial assistance from their estranged partners, and in both cases the support was minimal and sporadic. This situation exists despite the fact that these men have a legal responsibility to support their children; despite existing legislation, little enforcement takes place.

Figure 1

Illustration of the complex web of interrelationships among the factors examined in this study.

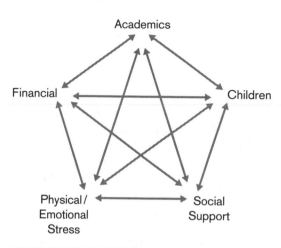

As Lou so aptly stated, "It's as if they want you to fail, as if they'd like to see you end up back on welfare!" Indeed, some women would argue that an insidious patriarchal conspiracy is at work. I find this contention to be excessive, although the general status of women in our society is not an irrelevant consideration. In the last two decades women have made some progress in altering their position in society, but substantive equality has not been realized. Motherhood is not a prestigious occupation; women who bear children are not generally honored and held in high esteem. Women with dependent children are a low-status and relatively powerless group and therefore, the ambivalence of legislators and policy makers is not unduly surprising. One cannot help but wonder how different the situation might be if it were reversed. Current indicators suggest that the trend of lone parenting will continue, and the plight of single mothers must be addressed. It is hoped that the current study will serve to enlighten readers and promote some understanding in this regard.

REFERENCES

Blecham, T.J. (1981). Are children with one-parent families at risk? *Journal of Marriage and the Family, 44,* 179–195.

Burden, D. (1986). Single parents and the work setting: The impact of multiple job and home life responsibilities. *Family Relations, 35,* 37–44.

Duvall, E. (1986). The impact of divorce and maternal employment on pre-adolescent children. *Family Relations, 35,* 153–160.

Grief, G. (1986). Mothers without custody and child support. *Family Relations, 35,* 87–95.

Hanson, S. (1986). Healthy single parent families. *Family Relations, 35,* 125–133.

Hill, R. (1986). Life cycle stages for types of single parent: Of family development theory. *Family Relations, 35,* 19–30.

Heatherington, E., Cox, M., and Cox, R. (1979). Family interaction and the social, economic, emotional, and cognitive development of children following divorce. *Journal of Social Issues, 35,* 26–49.

Kelly, J., and Wallerstein, G. (1980). Brief interviews with children in divorced families. *Journal of Orthopsychiatry, 47,* 23–39.

Norton, A., and Glick, P. (1986). One-parent families: A social and economic profile. *Family Relations, 35,* 26–49.

Pett, M., and Vaughn-Cole, B. (1986). The impact of income issues and social status on post-divorce adjustments of custodial parents. *Family Relations, 35,* 103–113.

Sanick, M., and Maudlin, T. (1986). Single versus two-parent families: A comparison of mother's time. *Family Relations, 35,* 53–56.

Statistics Canada. (1984). *Canada's Lone Parents.* Ottawa: Ministry of Supply and Services.

Wells Gladow, N., and Ray, M. (1986). The impact of support systems on the well-being of low-income single parents. *Family Relations, 35,* 114–124.

GLOSSARY

Accretion measures: measures that reflect some sort of addition to or building up of products or materials because of our physical presence or activity—documents we produce, products we manufacture, arts and crafts we create, graffiti we write, and so on. Contrasts with **erosion measures.**

Aggregated data: data from more than one case that have been combined for analysis. For example, suppose the students in your class each receive a score on the final exam. If we combine ("aggregate") all those scores, we can investigate their distribution, for example, their mean, variability, and so on. If we have other aggregated data on the same people (e.g., how many hours they spent studying or how much emphasis they place on grades), we can look for patterns in the relationships among these bits of information.

Analytic control: one of the two general approaches to research that attempts to make inferences about "causes." Contrasts with **manipulative control,** in which the researcher creates or actively intervenes in a situation to create conditions (e.g., as in the classic experiment) and to move people around (e.g., through the creation of control groups and *experimental groups* and through the random assignment of participants to conditions) so that clarity of inference is given the highest priority. In *analytic control,* the researcher takes an existing situation and, through his or her analytical powers alone, tries to "make sense" of the causal patterns that exist.

Analytic induction: a process of theory formulation characteristic of inductive approaches. The researcher begins by making observations and formulating a tentative explanation for those observations. Next, the researcher examines the adequacy of that explanation (does it account for all the data?) and revises the explanation until it successfully accounts for all observed data. Particular attention is paid to negative cases (observations that are inconsistent with the tentative explanatory scheme), since these will suggest revisions. Once an explanatory scheme has been devised that's consistent with all the data gathered to date, the researcher gathers more data to see whether they, too, are consistent with the explanation. If not, the process continues.

Anomalies: things that aren't supposed to happen, if indeed a theory is true. For example, early astronomers, who believed that the earth was the centre of the universe, were faced with the anomaly that Mars does not follow a circular or elliptical path around us, but occasionally "wanders" back and forth across the heavens. Recognition of this anomaly was a boon to theory development in astronomy; Copernicus eventually argued for the correctness of *his* theory (that we travel around the sun) because it accounted very simply for what only appeared to be Mars's irregular path, explaining why the illusion occurred.

Anonymize: the process of taking research data and deleting all names and other identifying information that could be used to identify the source of the data.

Assumption of pretest equivalence: the logic of the experiment is, "If two groups are equal to begin with (at the pretest) and treated identically in all respects but one, that one being the presence or absence of the independent (or treatment) variable, then any differences between the groups that is observed at the end of the experiment must be due to the one element on which they differed, that is, the independent variable." Note the phrase "if the two groups are equal to begin with ..."; this is the *assumption of pretest equivalence* (that is, that the groups are equal at the pretest). Violation of this assumption comes from selection biases, which threaten **internal validity.**

Bonferroni technique: a technique that involves splitting the adopted probability required for significance across the entire range of comparisons to be made. For example, if you're adopting a significance level of $p < .05$ and plan to undertake 10 separate t-tests (or chi-squares or Pearson correlations), the Bonferroni procedure involves spreading the .05 (known as the *experiment-wise error rate*) across the 10 comparisons, with the result that a $.05/10 = .005$ significance level would have to be achieved on any given comparison before you'd be prepared to consider it "reliable."

"Bottom-up" approaches: See **inductive approaches.**

Bounding: a way of dealing with the telescoping that often occurs when survey participants are asked to recall events, such as in a victimization survey. Bounding involves offering a signpost to assist in accurate recall. For example, instead of saying "in the last six months," you might cite a more memorable event, for example, "since Christmas."

Case study analysis: analysis of a single case (see also **idiographic analysis**).

Catalytic validity: the extent to which research empowers people by enhancing "self-understanding"

and facilitating social transformation. A work with no catalytic validity just sits on the shelf and collects dust once it is complete; one with high catalytic validity enhances people's understanding of themselves and the world, providing insights into how both they and the world might be transformed, should they wish to do so.

Category system: a type of coding scheme that involves using a set of mutually exclusive and exhaustive categories to code any given behaviour we observe. For example, to use a category system to code for violent content in a film, we'd typically begin by breaking the film into units (on, say, a minute-by-minute or a scene-by-scene basis) and code whether the behaviour in each minute or scene is predominantly violent, nonviolent, or whatever. Category systems give a better indication of the *temporal flow* of criterion acts during the observational period than do **sign systems.**

Ceteris paribus: a Latin phrase meaning "all else being equal." This phrase—often explicitly and always implicitly—underlies theoretical statements; that is, variables X and Y are related to each other, *ceteris paribus*. It's also the cornerstone of the experimentalist methods discussed in Chapters 9 and 10 and, to some extent, in Chapter 11. The true experiment embodies the *ceteris paribus* assumption by testing the effects of certain variables on other variables under conditions in which, overall, all other variables are equalized.

Comparison group: see **control group.**

Compensatory equalization of treatments: one of several possible threats to internal validity that can emerge in field settings when the treatment or program being evaluated involves goods and/or services considered desirable and where there is a large disparity between groups. Seeing the disparity, administrators, those charged with implementing the treatment, or some of the recipients may reroute some goods or provide access to services among some or all members of the disadvantaged group in an effort to alleviate the disparity. This practice makes the groups less distinct than they would otherwise have been, leading to an erroneous finding of "no difference."

Compensatory rivalry: one of several possible threats to internal validity that can emerge in field settings. If it's known that an evaluation is in progress, one may see compensatory rivalry by the respondents who are receiving the less desirable treatment(s). Knowing that one is in the disadvantaged group may spur a competitive spirit to overcome adversity and perform well. This is particularly likely to be the case in situations where the group already perceives itself as a group (e.g., work teams, crews, classes) and has a lot to lose if a difference is revealed.

Complete observer: one end of the traditional observational continuum. In this role, the researcher identifies himself or herself to the participants as a researcher who's engaged in observational research, either by conducting a study in his or her own setting (e.g., a laboratory or clinic) or by gaining access to another setting (e.g., an organization or a group) after seeking and obtaining permission from someone appropriate. Once in the setting, the complete observer typically does his or her best to remain relatively inconspicuous, doing nothing other than observe with the full knowledge of all who are present that that's why the researcher is there.

Complete participant: one end of the traditional observational continuum. In this role, the observer doesn't reveal himself or herself as a researcher; from the perspective of those being observed, the researcher *is* a participant. There are two ways this might occur: (1) *post hoc* observation, where a former participant writes his or her account of a setting or event well after the fact, and (2) surreptitious observation, where the researcher observes people without their knowing that they're being observed for the purpose of research. Contrasts with **complete observer** (the other extreme of the role continuum).

Concurrent validity: a type of validity that involves correlating responses on our measure to some other criterion. Suppose our measure of "romantic love" involves asking two people the question "Are you in love?" We must show that responses to that question are tied to some other independent measure of "love." For example, Zick Rubin's (1973) research on this topic shows that people who say they're "in love" tend to gaze into each other's eyes more often and for longer periods than do couples who do not say they're in love. If we take those measures at approximately the same time, we're engaging in concurrent validation. "Concurrent" means "at the same time"; temporal closeness between the two measures defines concurrent validation. Contrasts with **predictive validity.**

Constitutive definition: see **nominal definition.**

Constructionism: the view that we actively construct reality on the basis of our understandings, which are largely, though not completely, culturally shared. It thus becomes important to understand people's and society's constructions of things, because those constructions will have implications for how we study and make sense of the world. For example, men and women have been "constructed" as active and passive, respectively, for many years. This construction has even spread to our understandings of sexual intercourse and conception. We once envisioned active spermatozoa, released when the man ejaculates, swimming to the woman's ovum, which passively awaits fertilization. As our conceptions of women have changed in recent years, so, too, has our conception of conception. Now researchers bring a more egalitarian perspective to their understanding of the fertilization process: although the spermatozoa are still characterized as swimming to the ovum, the ovum is now considered to play a more active role in "send[ing] out messages to the sperm, participating actively in the process, until sperm and egg find each other and merge" (Flint 1995: D8).

Control group (comparison group): a group that is treated identically to the experimental group in *all* respects *except* that it does not receive the independent variable. Its purpose is to control for rival plausible explanations.

Convergent validity: the degree to which your measure is related to other measures to which it is supposed to be related. For example, a measure of how "in love" people are *should* be related to other measures of affection, intimacy, and commitment. If we show that our measure is related to those other indicators, we've demonstrated convergent validity.

Correlation matrix: a table that shows all possible intercorrelations among a set of variables.

Critical realism: Critical realism, or the *critical realist perspective,* can be seen as a midway resolution that acknowledges some truth in both realist and social constructionist perspectives. Like the constructionists, critical realists acknowledge that "reality" is indeed constructed and negotiated, but they also assert that reality is not *completely* negotiable, that is, all explanations are not equally viable. In other words, we *can* be "wrong." But, if we can be "wrong," there must be a reality out there that exists independent of our opinions of it.

Cross-sectional research: See under **longitudinal research.**

Deductive approaches: research perspectives characterized by the belief that researchers should begin with theory, from which they then deduce hypotheses, which they then test by gathering data. If the data support the hypothesis, the theory that gave rise to that hypothesis has gained some support, and further tests of the theory (through further hypothesizing and data gathering) are formulated. If the data do not support the hypothesis, the theory's adequacy is questioned, suggesting that the theory should be either rejected or revised. Also known as the hypothetico-deductive method, and sometimes as *"top-down" approaches.* Contrasts with **inductive approaches.**

Deductive method. See **hypothetico-deductive method.**

Definitional operationism: a play on the term "operational definition" that refers to a type of mono-operationism in which researchers engage in the tautology of operationally defining their variables of interest by definition. For example, a researcher may develop a measure of stupidity but, instead of showing that the measure possesses convergent and divergent validity with respect to other measures, may simply state that the measure is its own definition; that is, what we mean by stupidity is whatever our test measures. Needless to say, that's stupid.

Dependent variable: in research, the variable we measure in order to assess whether the independent variable exerts any effects. It gains its name because a person's status on the variable (e.g., his or her score) *depends* on whatever effects the independent variable has. Also sometimes known as the *outcome* variable.

Descriptive statistics: statistics that are used to summarize sample data. The major ones included in Chapter 12 are statistics that describe central tendency (the mean, the median, and the mode) and variability (the mean and the standard deviation).

Dichotomy: any division into two parts; an especially popular and appropriate term with respect to classification. A sample might be dichotomized into males and females or into an experimental and a control group. But dichotomies can also be less concrete; qualitative and quantitative approaches to science, for example, represent a dichotomy of research perspectives.

Diffusion (or imitation) of treatment: one of several possible threats to internal validity in field evaluations, where it's not unusual to be faced with intact groups that *cannot* be isolated from one another. Instead of having two (or more) comparison groups that are clearly distinct on the independent variable being considered, we may find that the boundaries between the groups are or become somewhat blurred. For example, if the groups are differentiated by their access to varying sets of information, any communication between groups about the nature of this information will make each group a little more like the other(s). This diffusion of treatment will act to minimize the groups' separation and heighten their similarity. The independent variable, in other words, doesn't have a real opportunity to "work."

Divergent validity: involves showing that your measure is not related to other measures to which it's not supposed to be related. For example, a measure of how "in love" people are *should not* be related to independent and different concepts like respect or tolerance (since each of these can exist without love being present). If we show that our measure is independent of (i.e., not correlated with) measures of those other indicators, we've demonstrated divergent validity.

Ecological fallacy: a term whose root is the word "ecology," which in turn refers to any self-sustaining and independent niche. What is true in one ecology may not necessarily be generalizable to another. Thus, if we generate an understanding in one ecology, then making the immediate assumption that we can generalize to another ecology is fallacious. For example, a general finding that people who are conservative tend also to be the most prejudicial doesn't mean that you, as a conservative, are necessarily prejudiced.

Ecological validity: a type of external validity that addresses issues of representativeness and generalizability in a slightly different way. Brunswik (1955) first used this term, which refers to the representativeness of the treatments and measures you use in relation to the particular milieu to which you wish to generalize.

Epistemic relationship: how well your nominal definition and your operational definition demonstrate goodness of fit; that is, how well your operational definition "gets at" or "assesses" what your nominal definition says you're interested in.

Erosion measures: measures that reflect some sort of wearing away or removal of products or materials because of our physical presence or activity. The wear on a jacket, worn pathways, and missing objects can all provide the basis for using *erosion measures*. Contrasts with **accretion measures.**

External validity: the *generalizability* of results beyond the specifics of the study, particularly to other people, situations, and times.

Funnelling: a technique used in questionnaires and interviews when open-ended and closed or structured questions on the same issue are mixed together. Funnelling involves starting with more general questions and gradually becoming more and more specific.

Grounded theory: a term made famous by Glaser and Strauss (1967) that describes theory that's *grounded* in observation. Although most consistent with an inductive approach, the term is not *in*consistent with deductive research: one may wish to test one's grounded theory deductively after it has been formulated.

Heterogeneity: the degree of diversity in a sample, a population, or a universe. In a maximally heterogeneous sample, all units sampled differ from one another with respect to the variable of interest. Contrasts with **homogeneity.**

Heuristic: can be used as either an adjective (e.g., a heuristic metaphor) or a noun (e.g., a decision-making heuristic). To say that something is heuristic is to say that it's helpful in getting closer to a solution or an explanation. Principles can be described as heuristic, as can theories, models, working hypotheses, and/or ideal types. For example, let's say that you're on the side of an unfamiliar hill in dense fog and are trying to get to the top. Because of the dense fog, you're worried that you will spend all your time walking in circles. A heuristic strategy in this case would be to employ the principle "make every step higher than the one before." Even though this strategy will not necessarily give you the speediest or most direct route to the top, if each step you take is a step up, eventually you will get to the top. Similarly, theories or models can be heuristic in social science because, even if they do not themselves offer a "correct" or "complete" explanation of a phenomenon of interest, they may nonetheless help you get closer to finding one.

History: in experimental research, one of many threats to internal validity. In this sense, the term refers to any specific events that occur during the course of the research in addition to the independent variable. To the extent that such other variables exist, they threaten internal validity because those other variables end up being rival plausible explanations for any changes we observe. History is effectively controlled by including a control group, which is a group that's treated identically in all respects to the experimental group (and hence subject to all the same historical factors), except for administration/receipt of the independent variable.

Homogeneity: the degree of sameness in a sample, a population, or a universe. In a completely homogeneous sample, all units sampled are the same with respect to the variables of interest. Contrasts with **heterogeneity.**

Hypothesis: an unambiguous statement about the results that you expect to occur in a situation if the theory that guides your work is true. Hypotheses are generally associated with deductive inquiry,

which believes that "good research" should begin with theory and should be directed toward testing theory. Stating your hypothesis before beginning your research is a bit like placing your bets ahead of time, so that you can't come back later and say, "Oh yes, I knew that was going to happen." If you knew, you should have said so.

Hypothetico-deductive method: the long name given to the process of deduction in social science research. The prefix "hypothetico" points to the role that the *a priori* (before-the-fact) specification of hypotheses plays in this brand of inquiry. Contrasts with **inductive approaches.**

Idiographic analysis: analysis of the relationships among variables within an individual case. For example, if you kept track of the levels of stress you feel and of your general mood each day, we could engage in idiographic analysis of the relationship between stress and mood for you. Contrasts with **nomothetic analysis.**

Imitation of treatment: see **diffusion of treatment.**

Independent variable: in research, the variable whose effects we wish to identify or assess. Also sometimes known as the *treatment* variable or the *causal* variable. Contrasts with **dependent variable.**

Inductive approaches: research perspectives characterized by the belief that research should begin with observation, since it is only on that basis that grounded theory will emerge. Thus, researchers observe, induce empirical generalizations based on their observations, and then, through analytic induction, attempt to develop a full-blown theory that adequately reflects the observed reality. Sometimes known as *"bottom-up" approaches;* contrasts with **deductive** (or "top-down") **approaches.**

Inductive fallacy: the assumption that patterns or trends that have held up until now will continue.

Although many argue that past behaviour is the best predictor of future performance (and, indeed, much of science is based on that assumption), there's no philosophically compelling reason to believe that that is necessarily the case.

Inferential statistics: statistics that are used to facilitate drawing conclusions about data—conclusions concerning the extent to which variables are associated and whether differences exist among groups—on the basis of population estimates derived from sample data. The techniques included in Chapter 12 are the *t*-test, the chi-square, and Pearson's product–moment correlation coefficient.

Informed consent: an ethical principle that suggests you should not do things to people unless they say it's alright to do so and only when their consent is given on the basis of knowing all aspects of the situation and the possible outcomes that might affect their willingness to participate. Consent cannot be considered binding unless it's given on an *informed* basis.

Instrumentation: one of many possible threats to the internal validity of research, in this instance arising from changes in the way data are collected or organized during the course of a study. For example, if we change the way a certain statistic is gathered, using the "old" way when collecting the pretest data and the "new" way when collecting the posttest data, we don't know whether any differences we observe between pretest and posttest are due to the independent variable or simply to the change in the way we gathered the data. Instrumentation effects also occur when data changes over time because coders or raters become more practised or fatigued or because equipment wears down.

Internal validity: the extent to which differences observed in an experimental study can be *unambiguously* attributed to the experimental treatment itself, rather than to other factors. In other words, to what extent can you be certain that the differences we observe are caused by the independent variable per se, rather than by rival plausible explanations?

Internet: a computer network through which millions of computers around the world may be linked. The Net (as it is also known) was originally conceived by the U.S. military as a way to deal with possible world war or nuclear attack. The idea was to link computers in a way that an enemy or disaster could not knock out; the system's security was safeguarded by having no centre to the network, so that the system as a whole would be impervious to destruction or sabotage. Since its inception, the Internet has grown exponentially, and that explosion shows no sign of stopping.

Interpretive: See **phenomenologism.**

Inter-rater reliability: the degree to which two or more people, using the same coding scheme and observing the same people, produce essentially the same results. Inter-rater agreement must normally be higher than 80 percent in order to be considered acceptable. Compare **test–retest reliability.**

Interrupted time-series designs: a type of *time-series design*, that is, a design that involves compiling data series that show a dependent measure over time (e.g., monthly, yearly, or whatever time period is meaningful and of interest). The "interruption" of interest is the independent variable. The benefit of looking at time-series data (rather than simply looking at singular before/after statistics) is that it helps to put any pre–post changes that are observed in context, so that one can see the overall trend that existed in the data when the independent variable came into effect. It is particularly useful for identifying threats due to regression toward the mean and for showing the maturation of the trend line.

Intranet: refers to privately constructed and maintained computer networks that can be accessed only by authorized persons within the company, organization or institution. Often connected to the

Internet, security is maintained by the use of fire-walls. Because of their universality of access within the organization, intranets can be used by authorized researchers to gain access to the entire population of the organization, or representative or targeted samples thereof.

Iterative processes: looped processes that feed back on themselves, so that some sort of change occurs with each passing cycle. Each cycle is known as an *iteration.*

Jackknifing: a technique used when you have a very large number of cases (e.g., ten times as many cases as you have variables) and want to assess the replicability or reliability of your results. There are several ways to perform this procedure, but the simplest is to randomly split your sample of cases into *two* samples, do the analyses you want to do separately in the two samples, and then focus only on those results that emerge as statistically significant in *both* data sets.

Legitimation: a term used in Chapter 2 to refer to how researchers justify their data and their interpretation of those data as authoritative. For qualitative researchers, this notion is intricately linked to **representation** and deals with essentially the same issues. But while representation focuses on the procedures we include in the study to ensure that the voices of participants are heard, legitimation refers to our justification of those procedures and our authority to speak for or with our research participants, in our thesis, journal article, or book.

Longitudinal research: one of two categories into which research projects fall: *cross-sectional* or *longitudinal.* A cross-sectional study, like a snapshot, provides a glimpse of a sample of people at one point in time. Longitudinal research, in contrast, looks at the same group over time.

Manipulation checks: a common element in experimental designs that involve manipulated independent variables. Because the question being

addressed is a validity question, the issue is whether you have indeed created the variable you thought you were creating and/or whether you are assessing the effect of the variable you think you are assessing.

Manipulative control: the active and intentional manipulation of the setting by the researcher in order to maximize clarity of inference by controlling rival plausible explanations. Manipulative control is epitomized by the laboratory experiment, where the experimenter exerts control over every aspect of the setting. Contrasts with **analytic control.**

Matching: a method of intentionally *creating* pretest equivalence. Contrasts with random assignment, which allows you to *assume* pretest equivalence. To use matching, we begin by identifying pairs of individuals who are matched (i.e., as similar as possible) on some variable (e.g., pretest scores), and then randomly assign one person from each pair to the experimental group and the other to the control group. In this way, we're guaranteed groups that are constituted equally with respect to that matching variable.

Maturation: in experimental research, one of many possible threats to internal validity. Defined as processes within the research participants that change as a function of time per se (not specific to particular events), such as growing older, more tired, getting hungrier, and so on. In other words, sometimes changes happen merely because of biological processes that happen over time, and we must be careful to recognize those processes and their effects when we're assessing the effects of other independent variables.

Memory fade: the tendency for events to be forgotten. In the context of victimization surveys, this term refers to victimizations that are not recalled even though they occurred during the designated time period under study.

Metaphysics: speculation about the nature of truth and being that goes beyond directly observable truths and into the realm of speculation and abstraction. Positivists, for example, would eschew metaphysics.

Modus operandi method: a concept advanced by Scriven (1976) to explain the kind of case study analysis that many people (physicians, mechanics, historians, coroners, etc.) do—and do well—all the time. The modus operandi method begins with the creation of a "causal checklist," that is, all those elements that go into producing a certain phenomenon. To explain the phenomenon's presence or absence, we look to that list. If only one element is present (or missing), that element is the cause of the phenomenon's presence or absence. In the event that *more than one* plausible factor emerges, Scriven (1976) suggests that we look for a modus operandi (MO) to help identify the actual cause, just as a detective might identify a criminal by the characteristic manner in which a crime is executed.

Mono-operationism and **mono-method bias:** two potential problems that can be produced when researchers become overly reliant on, respectively, a particular *measure* of a construct or a particular *way* of measuring it. *Mono-operationism* (sometimes called *mono-operation bias*) refers to the problem that develops when we use only one operational definition of a variable (e.g., if we use only IQ tests to measure intelligence, never trying to measure it any other way). *Mono-method bias* refers to reliance on only one method (e.g., self-report interviews) instead of investigating a phenomenon in a number of different ways (e.g., also incorporating observational and/or archival research). See also **definitional operationism.**

"Monte Carlo" computer simulation: a technique that's used to address what occurs when certain assumptions that are required by probability theory are violated. Much of probability theory, on which most social science statistics are based, is based on "long-run" expectations, expectations about what would be true if there were an infinite number of trials. One great advantage of computers

derives from the fact that they'll do the same thing over and over again—and do so incredibly quickly—until you tell them to stop. And although you cannot have them process any information an *infinite* number of times (since, by definition, the processing would never end), you can nonetheless instruct a computer to process a set of instructions a *very large* number of times, where "very large" is so large a number that the observed outcomes will closely approximate what you would find if you were to repeat the instructions an infinite number of times. Monte Carlo simulations have been used in this way to evaluate such questions as (a) whether you'd get incorrect results if you violated the assumptions of the *t*-test and found that the dependent variable is not normally distributed in the population; or (b) whether you'd be misled if you accidentally subjected ordinal data to a *t*-test.

Mortality: a situation in which some individuals drop out of the research before it's completed. Single-session, short-term laboratory experimentation virtually precludes mortality as a problem. But in the field, where time-series data and a succession of follow-ups are more likely, the mortality problem increases in relevance. Some individuals who are recorded as participants at the beginning of the study do not return to receive the dependent measure at follow-up; for example, they drop out of therapy, choose to resign from the group, move to another jurisdiction, are released on parole, join another club, get lost, or die. The problem is one of *selection bias*, since the people or units that "survive" to the posttest are no longer the same group that was measured at the pretest. Mortality threatens internal validity and may also limit external validity.

Negative cases or **negative case analysis:** a crucial part of analytic induction, in which researchers follow iteration after iteration of trying different explanations to see how well those explanations allow them to "make sense" of their data. Negative cases are those instances of the phenomenon that don't "fit" the developing explanation, suggesting that the explanation is not yet complete. Although ignoring negative cases can make one look good, at least temporarily, the qualitative researcher engaged in analytic induction will go out of his or her way to locate them, since they're a most informative source for how an explanation can be improved.

Neopositivism: See **postpositivism.**

Nominal definition: a statement of what a concept means to the researcher; much like a dictionary definition. Expressing nominal definitions for the key concepts or variables involved in your research allows other researchers to consider whether they would agree with your definition of the term. See also **epistemic relationship.**

Nomothetic analysis: the analysis of the relationships between variables across many cases. For example, we could ask many people to tell us how stressed they feel today and to describe their mood. If we analyzed the data from all these cases in order to examine the relationship between stress and mood, we'd be engaging in nomothetic analysis. Contrasts with **idiographic analysis.**

Non-probabilistic sampling: a set of sampling techniques in which the probability of selecting each sampling unit is unknown or unknowable. These techniques are optimal when a sampling frame is unavailable, when creative means must be used to locate "closet" samples, and/or when the research objectives would be best fulfilled by a strategically chosen sample. Contrasts with **probabilistic sampling.**

Observer-as-participant: see under **participant-as-observer.**

Occam's razor: a principle stating that if two theories are essentially equivalent in explanatory power, the simpler of the two should prevail.

Operational definition: the way we actually define the variables of interest within the confines of the research project. Suppose you're interested in

looking at romantic love. How will you determine whether any two people in your research are actually "in love"? You might decide to ask them, "Are you two in love?" If they say "yes," you will consider them "in love." Their response to the question "Are you in love?" has become the operational definition of the concept of "love" in your research. Contrasts with **nominal definition.**

Othering: Both the physical and the natural sciences have a long tradition of making a distinction between the detached researcher and the object of his or her investigations. For positivists, being "objective" involved remaining detached from the "other" and imposing the viewpoint and value judgments of science. Since "our" standards were "obviously" the "correct" ones, then "our" standards clearly comprised the most appropriate measuring stick to use in assessing and describing "reality." It was *our* job to describe *them*. But several problems arise from that approach, particularly when *they* are a marginalized and misunderstood group, and our description of them imposes our understandings, meanings, and standards in a manner that denies the understandings of, and thereby does an injustice to, the researched group. This process is referred to as othering.

Outcome variable: see **dependent variable.**

Overidentification: a term used by positivists to mean a researcher's taking on the values and perspectives of the group being studied, so that he or she cannot maintain the detached, analytical stance required, according to positivists, for effectively studying the world. Positivists believe that getting too "involved" with the people we study will destroy our objectivity.

Panel studies: a type of longitudinal research in which you identify a particular group (or panel) of people and return to those very same people again and again over time. This contrasts with a *trend study,* for example, where you'd return to the same population each time but take a new sample each time.

Participant-as-observer and **observer-as-partici-pant:** the two roles that occupy the middle of the traditional observational continuum. Both involve some participatory and observational aspects; they differ only in which role is emphasized. For the most part, both manifest an effort to reap the advantages of the two roles: their participatory aspects help minimize reactivity, while their observational aspects attempt to minimize ethical difficulties.

Periodicity: a phenomenon produced by the cyclical nature of some lists. Periodicity causes a problem in systematic sampling with random start when the list's cyclical nature becomes confounded with the sampling ratio or interval.

Phenomenologism: an approach to understanding whose adherents assert that we must "get inside people's heads" to understand how they perceive and interpret the world. According to theorists such as Weber, phenomenological understanding is a virtual prerequisite for achieving **Verstehen**.

Polemical: an adjective formed from the root "pole," as in "polar opposites." Originally used in a religious context to describe those whose views were antithetical to religious teachings. Now used more broadly to refer to any disputatious argument that strongly opposes accepted beliefs. The term typically has pejorative connotations, implying that the other person's position is so outlandish that it couldn't possibly be true and hence must be offering it purely for the sake of being argumentative.

Population: an aggregation of all sampling elements, that is, the total of all the sampling units that meet the criterion (or criteria) for inclusion in a study. The sampling frame, if available, defines the population.

Positivism: a school of thought marked by a *realist* perspective, an emphasis on quantitative precision, the belief that effective research requires avoiding overidentification, and a search for general truths unearthed through the gathering and analysis of aggregated data. Chapter 1 focuses on "orthodox" or classic positivism, which developed in the 19th and early 20th centuries. For the mellower positivism that has surfaced since then, see **postpositivism.**

Postmodernism: a perspective that begins with the premise that no method, theory, discourse, or genre has the right to proclaim itself *the* royal road to truth. Every method, theory, and so on is considered both equally deserving of the claim and equally suspect. This stance obviously poses a considerable challenge to the development of knowledge, since it's difficult to envision how one can decide what is "true" in the absence of universal criteria by which to evaluate truth-claims.

Postpositivism: a theoretical tradition that reflects classic positivism but differs in two ways. First, it is less rigidly realist, acknowledging that we may *not* be able to know things with certainty: knowledge may end up being *probabilistic* rather than certain. Second, postpositivists show considerably less hostility toward metaphysical concepts like attitudes and beliefs and now believe that verbal reports can include valid and reliable data.

Power–knowledge: a term first used by Michel Foucault, who argued that power and knowledge can't be separated and are inherently linked. Those who have social power can direct the course of knowledge, deciding which topics and social groups will be exposed to scrutiny and surveillance. And those who have knowledge about certain topics and social groups have power over them. More subtly, power–knowledge implies that we cannot fully appreciate any bit of knowledge unless we understand the power relations that underlie its production, nor can we fully appreciate power until we understand how it is manifested in the "facts" we "know" to be true.

Practice effects: see **testing.**

Predictive validity: a type of validity that involves assessing the extent to which your measure does in fact predict whatever it's supposed to predict. For example, if you develop tests like the LSAT (Law School Admission Test) or GRE (Graduate Records Exam), which are supposed to predict success in law school and graduate school, respectively, then demonstrating the tests' predictive validity would require you to show that scores on the test do indeed relate to later success in law school or graduate school, respectively. See also **concurrent validity.**

Pretest sensitization: see t**esting.**

Probabilistic sampling: a group of sampling techniques that meet two criteria: the probability of sampling a given individual is known (or at least is theoretically knowable), and each sampling element in the population has an equal probability of being selected. Contrasts with **non-probabilistic sampling.**

Pseudonym: A fictitious name used in order to conceal the real source of an interview or other research data.

Qualitative approaches: research methods characterized by an inductive perspective, a belief that theory should be grounded in the day-to-day realities of the people being studied, and a preference for applying phenomenology to the attempt to understand the many "truths" of reality. Such approaches tend to be constructionist. Qualitative researchers tend to be cautious about numbers, believing that the requirements of quantification distance us even further from phenomenological understanding we should embrace.

Quantitative approaches: research methods that emphasize numerical precision; a detached, aloof stance on the researcher's part (i.e., the avoidance of overidentification); and, often, a hypothetico-deductive approach.

Quasi-experimentation: an approach to research in which the logic underlying the traditional laboratory experiment is adapted for use in a field setting (e.g., evaluation research), where, unlike in the lab, the researcher does not have complete control over all aspects of the situation. Control over rival plausible explanations is achieved through **analytic control** rather than **manipulative control.**

Random assignment: a very powerful research procedure that directly addresses the assumption of pretest equivalence: the crucial experimental assumption that your experimental and control groups are equal in all respects *before* the imposition or administration of your independent variable. Given that you have a group of people ready to participate in your research, random assignment is achieved by letting "chance" be the *sole* determinant of which group (i.e., experimental or control) any given person is a member of. Random assignment, coupled with adequate group sizes (i.e., at least 30 per group), allows you to assume, with a reasonable degree of confidence, that the two (or more) groups, on average, are fairly equal on all pre-experimental variables.

Random error: refers to errors that have no systematic biasing effect on a study's results but merely reflect the vagaries of chance variation: the "noise" in measurement or sampling that occurs because of chance circumstances, events, coincidences, and errors.

Random sampling: a type of probabilistic sampling that meets two criteria: (1) nothing but chance governs the selection process, and (2) every sampling element has an equal probability of being selected. If those criteria are met, the resulting sample will be representative of the population included in the sampling frame, within the limits of sampling error.

Rate data: data that are expressed as a frequency per some unit of population, for example, birth rates, crime rates, death rates, unemployment rates, and infant mortality rates. For example, Vancouver's murder rate is currently about 6 per 100 000 per year. Specifying rates rather than raw numbers allows researchers to compare rates in a single location over time or to compare two or more locations despite differences in their population size.

Reactivity: the degree to which (if at all) the researcher's presence causes research participants to react by changing from their "usual" or "normal" behaviour patterns because they know they're being observed.

Realism: the idea that a reality exists out there independently of what and how we think about it. Contrasts with **constructionism** and idealism.

Realist perspective: see **realism.**

Regression toward the mean: see **statistical regression.**

Regulation of research ethics: refers to the way that bureaucratic entities (e.g., university research ethics boards, granting councils, disciplinary associations, and other professional bodies) that have the power to approve/impede research on ethical grounds actually implement ethics principles.

Reliability: the degree to which repeated observation of a phenomenon—the same phenomenon at different times, or the same instance of the phenomenon by two different observers—yields similar results. Underlying this concept are scientific beliefs about the importance of stability and repeatability in the generation of understanding. Two types of reliability are **inter-rater reliability** and **test–retest reliability.**

Replication: the efforts of one researcher to repeat the procedures another researcher has followed in order to ensure that the other researcher's findings are reliable.

Representation: a term used in Chapter 2 to refer to how we represent the voices of our research participants in our research design. For Denzin and Lincoln (1994), the concept involves two main issues: *means* (i.e., how will we give them a voice in the research?) and *authority* (i.e., how will we ensure that we have the authority to do so?). These issues pertain to all phases of the research process, including designing the study, gathering and interpreting the data, and writing the final report. For qualitative researchers, representation is an integral prerequisite to **legitimation.**

Representativeness: a term used to describe how well a sample represents the population from which it's drawn (see Chapter 6). A sample is considered representative when the distribution of characteristics in the sample mirrors the distribution of those characteristics in the population. The priority attached to achieving formal representativeness is influenced by your research objectives.

Research ethics: most directly, principles that guide our interactions with research participants to ensure that their rights and interests are best protected. More broadly, questions of research ethics concern every aspect of the research process, for example, moral issues that arise regarding the research questions we pose (or not) and how we pose them, who and what we look at (or not), and so on.

Resentful demoralization: one of several possible threats to internal validity that can emerge in field settings. Given the same situation as is described under **compensatory rivalry**—it's known that an evaluation is in progress—participants may demonstrate the opposite response to the discrepancy among groups. With compensatory rivalry, the disadvantaged group rises to the challenge. With resentful demoralization, members of that group perceive the result as adverse and inevitable; they therefore may not even try to compete, and may even intentionally reduce their performance. In this instance, the researcher may *overestimate* the actual potency of the treatment being evaluated.

Response rate: for a questionnaire or an interview, the number of people who actually agree to be questioned, divided by the total number you approached (i.e., those who accepted *and* those who refused), multiplied by 100 (to produce a percentage). For example, if you approach 50 people, and 20 of them agree to take part, your response rate is (20/50) ? 100 = 40 percent.

Response sets: the response tendencies that people sometimes exhibit independent of the content of the items in a questionnaire, an interview, or an attitude scale. For example, some people will tend to agree with your assertions unless they have some compelling reason to disagree, while others will disagree with your assertions unless they have some compelling reason to agree. The challenge in questionnaire and attitude-scale design is to ensure that these different response tendencies are controlled, so that data will reflect differences in people's reactions to the content of the items, not just differences in response set.

Rival plausible explanations: alternative factors that might also have accounted for the results you observe. Threats to internal validity, for example, are all rival plausible explanations. Sound research design aims to minimize these.

Sampling error: the degree to which the distribution of characteristics in a sample deviates from the distribution of those characteristics in the population from which the sample was drawn. Estimates of the sampling error can be computed only when random sampling has been done. The two types of sampling error are **systematic error** and **random error.**

Sampling frame: a complete list of all the sampling elements of the population we wish to study. For example, if we want to sample voters in an upcoming election, the voters' lists represent a sampling frame of all eligible voters who have been enumerated. The availability of a sampling frame can influence a researcher's choice of sampling techniques.

Sampling ratio: a way of expressing what proportion of a population is actually sampled. For example, if the population numbers 1000 people and if you sample 200 of them, your sampling ratio is 200:1000 (i.e., 200 out of 1000), or 1:5 (i.e., 1 in 5).

Selection: one of many possible threats to the internal validity of research, particularly experimental research, because it violates the fundamental premise of pretest equivalence, that is, the assumption that all experimental and control groups are equal before the experiment begins, so that any differences we observe after administering the independent variable must have arisen during the course of the study. See also **assumption of pretest equivalence.**

Selective deposit: a term referring to the fact that some people, groups, and processes have a higher likelihood than others of having their views, lives, and so on made a part of the historical record. Historians can study history based only on what's in the record; thus, our understanding of history is influenced by the factors that influence selective deposit into that record.

Selective survival: a term that reminds us that among those things that are initially put into the historical record (via the already biased process of selective deposit), some have a better chance of surviving the ravages of time than others. For example, stone materials have a better chance of survival than clay or paper materials.

Serendipity: discoveries that happen purely by accident, as when a prospector strikes oil while searching for gold. The searcher (whether prospector or researcher) must be sufficiently knowledgeable and aware to realize what he or she has found. Many people in history have been perturbed to discover later that a serendipitous discovery had been staring them right in the face but that they'd been too unaware to recognize it at the time.

Sign system: a type of coding scheme in which an observer defines what is of interest to him or her (e.g., instances of violence, prosocial behaviour, or a moral dilemma) and then waits and watches, noting each time one of the predetermined criterion behaviours occurs. Sign systems give a better indication of *how many* prosocial acts are witnessed than **category systems.**

Social facts: life's "big" realities (e.g., the legal and economic system), which wield significant influences on people and are beyond people's control in any direct sense. They are important to positivists because such social realities are believed to exert their effects no matter what we think about them.

Statistical regression (regression toward the mean): in experimental research, one of many possible threats to internal validity. Unlike testing, where *real* change occurs between pretest and posttest (e.g., because of practice, sensitization to issues, or greater motivation), statistical regression involves changes that are more apparent than real. Statistical regression refers to the propensity of extreme scorers on the first testing to score closer to the mean (average) of the group on the second testing. This phenomenon arises because of the random error that is present in any measurement and occurs because chance events are unlikely ever to stack up to precisely the same degree on two successive occasions.

Systematic error: one of two types of sampling error. Systematic error occurs when aspects of your sampling procedure act in a consistent, systematic way, to make some sampling elements more likely to be chosen for participation than others. For example, Chapter 4 describes a 1992 call-in survey in which an American TV program's viewers expressed their opinions about a presidential speech. To participate, respondents had to, among other things, own a Touch-Tone phone, be interested in and able to understand a TV show dealing with political analysis, and be motivated enough to

take the time to express their opinion. These factors created a systematically biased sample: wealthier people, more educated people, and people who wanted to complain were more likely to be represented in that sample than poorer people (who might be unable to afford a Touch-Tone phone), less educated people (who might be less able to follow the political analysis), and apathetic, uncertain, or contented people (who might have less motivation to call). Contrasts with **random error.**

Telescoping: the propensity of survey respondents to bring events that were *outside* the sample period into it. This problem can be reduced by **bounding.** Contrasts with **memory fade.**

Testing: in experimental research, one of many possible threats to internal validity. Testing refers to the effects of taking a test on scores in the second testing. Such effects can operate in several different ways. The first, *pretest sensitization,* involves the fact that taking a test can sensitize you to issues in a way that you wouldn't have been aware of otherwise. It threatens internal validity because, if we observe that your attitudes have changed, we can't be sure whether the change was produced by the independent variable or by the greater sensitization to issues induced by the pretest. Another way in which testing can threaten internal validity is through *practice effects.* If we were trying to assess your abilities, for example, it would be difficult to know in the posttest situation whether you had improved purely because of the practice the pretest gave you or because of the independent variable we had imposed upon you.

Test–retest reliability: the degree to which a measure shows reliability (i.e., consistency) by producing similar results when a test is administered on two successive occasions; that is, where the same group of people are tested and retested. If the test (or scale or other type of measure) is reliable, the two sets of scores should correlate highly: people who score high (or low) on one occasion should also score high (or low) on the second occasion. Compare **inter-rater reliability.**

Theory: a set of concepts and a description of how they're interrelated that, taken together, purport to explain a given phenomenon or set of phenomena. The word "theory" is also sometimes used more broadly to refer simply to abstractions; thus, when I look at your behaviour and call you studious, we are making the jump from the concrete (your observable behaviour, i.e., the number of hours per week you spend studying) to the theoretical (the concept of studiousness).

Time-series designs: see under **interrupted time-series designs.**

"Top-down" approaches: See **deductive approaches.**

Treatment variable: see **independent variable.**

True experiment: the creation of conditions in which the effects of one or more independent variables are assessed while all other variables (those *not* being assessed) are held equal overall. True experiments typically involve **manipulative control** (see also Chapter 9).

Universe: in the context of sampling, a *theoretical* aggregation of all possible sampling elements. Contrasts with **population.**

Validity: a term that refers, in the most general sense, to whether research measures what the researcher thinks is being measured. This text discusses many kinds of validity, including predictive validity, internal validity, external validity, and ecological validity. All relate to whether you are indeed accomplishing what you think you are.

Variable: stated most simply, anything that varies. For example, in your methods class, "sex" is prob-ably a variable, since the students in your class (unless you go to a sex-specific university or college) probably include both males and females. Variables contrast with *constants,* which are things that do *not* vary.

Verstehen: a German word, first used in the social sciences by Max Weber, that refers to a profound understanding evidenced by the ability to appreciate a person's behaviour in terms of the interpretive (i.e., phenomenological) meaning he or she attaches to it.

Volunteer bias: the result of the fact that people who volunteer to participate in research are often different in a number of ways from those who don't. Thus, if we select a random (and hence representative) sample of some population, but not everyone participates (as is usually the case), we cannot simply generalize the results from the sample who participated to the broader population unless we have some understanding of how, if at all, those who participated are different from those who didn't. Generally speaking, the smaller the response rate, the larger the volunteer bias.

Wigmore test: see **Wigmore criteria.**

Wigmore criteria: A set of four criteria used by Canadian and U.S. courts to evaluate whether communications in a certain relationship (e.g., researcher–participant, doctor–patient, priest–penitent) should be considered "privileged" and exempt from the normal requirement to testify in a court of law. The criteria require that (1) there be a shared expectation of confidentiality by those in the relationship; (2) confidentiality be essential to the relationship; (3) the relation be an important and socially valued one; and (4) the damage that would be done the relationship by disclosure be greater than the damage to the case at hand by nondisclosure.

REFERENCES

Abramson, P. R., & Hayashi, H. (1984). Pornography in Japan: Cross-cultural and theoretical considerations. In N.M. Malamuth & E. Donnerstein (Eds.), *Pornography and sexual aggression* (pp. 173–185). New York: Academic Press.

ACNielsen. 2004. ACNielsen study finds lower income and older households are closing the gap in PC ownership. [Press release]. Retrieved June 23, 2004, from http://www2.acnielsen.com/news/20040623_ca.shtml.

Adair, J. G. (1973). *The human subject*. Boston: Little, Brown.

Adler, P. A., & Adler, P. (1994). Observational techniques. In N. K. Denzin, & Y.S. Lincoln (Eds.), *Handbook of qualitative research* (pp. 377–392). Thousand Oaks, CA: Sage.

Adler, P. A., and Adler, P. (2002). Do university lawyers and the police define research values? In W. C. van den Hoonaard (Ed.), *Walking the tightrope: Ethical issues for qualitative researchers* (pp. 34–42). Toronto: University of Toronto Press.

Alfred, R. (1976). The church of Satan. In C. Glock & R. Bellah (Eds.), *The new religious consciousness* (pp. 180–202). Berkeley, CA: University of California Press.

Altemeyer, R. A. (1970). Adverbs and intervals: A study of "Likert scales." *Proceedings of the 78th annual convention of the American Psychological Association, 5,* 397–98.

Altemeyer, R. A. (1981). *Right-wing authoritarianism*. Winnipeg: University of Manitoba Press.

American Anthropological Association. (1971). *Statement on ethics: Principles of professional responsibility.* (Adopted by the Council of the AAA May 1971). An amended (1986) copy retrieved August 20, 2002, from http://www.aaanet.org/stmts/ethstmnt.htm

American Anthropological Association. (1986). *Statements on ethics: Principles of professional responsibility).* Retrieved August 20, 2002, from http://www.aaanet.org/stmts/ethstmnt.htm

American Anthropological Association. (1995). *Commission to Review the AAA Statements on Ethics Final Report.* [Statement submitted to the AAA Executive Board on September 16, 1995]. Retrieved April 30, 2002, from http://www.aaanet.org/committees/ethics/ethrpt.htm

American Anthropological Association. (1996). *Final report of the commission to review the AAA statements on ethics.* Retrieved August 20, 2002, from http://www.aaanet.org/committees/ethics/ethrpt.htm

American Political Science Association. (1997). *Guide to professional ethics in political science.* Retrieved August 20, 2002, from http://www.apsanet.org/pubs/ethics.cfm

American Political Science Association. (1998). *A guide to professional ethics in political science* (2nd ed.). Washington, DC: Author. Retrieved May 21, 2006, from http://www.apsanet.org/imgtest/ethicsguideweb.pdf

American Psychological Association. (1973). *Ethical principles in the conduct of research with human participants.* Washington, DC: Author.

American Psychological Association. (1992). Ethical principles of psychologists and code of conduct. *American Psychologist, 47* (12), 1597–1611. Retrieved August 21, 2002, from http://www.apa.org/ethics/code.html

American Psychological Association. (1994). *Publication manual of the American Psychological Association* (4th ed.). Washington, DC: Author.

American Psychological Association. (2002). *Ethical principles of psychologists and code of conduct.* Washington, DC: Author. Retrieved May 22, 2006, from http://www.apa.org/ethics/code2002.html.

American Society of Criminology. (2001). Draft *Code of ethics.*

American Sociological Association. (1968). Toward a code of ethics for sociologists. *American Sociologist, 3,* 316–18.

American Sociological Association. (1984). *Code of ethics*. Washington, DC: Author.

American Sociological Association. (1997). *Code of ethics*. Retrieved August 20, 2002, from http://www.asanet.org/members/ecoderev.html

Anderson, K., & Jack, D. C. (1991). Learning to listen: Interview techniques and analyses. In S. B. Gluck & D. Patai (Eds.), *Women's words: The feminist practice of oral history* (pp. 11–26). New York: Routledge.

Andrews, F. M., & Withey, S. B. (1976). *Social indicators of well-being: Americans' perceptions of life quality.* New York: Plenum.

Argyris, C. (1975). Dangers in applying results from experimental social psychology. *American Psychologist, 30*, 469–485.

Aronson, E., & Carlsmith, J. M. (1968). Experimentation in social psychology. In G. Lindsey & E. Aronson (Eds.), *The handbook of social psychology,* Vol. II (2nd ed., pp. 1–79). Reading, MA: Addison-Wesley.

Aronson, E., & Mills, J. (1959). The effect of severity of initiation on liking for a group. *Journal of Abnormal and Social Psychology, 59*, 157–158.

Asch, S. E. (1958). Effects of group pressure upon modification and distortion of judgements. In E E. Maccoby, T. M. Newcomb, & E. L. Hartly (Eds.), *Readings in social psychology* (3rd ed.). New York: Holt, Rinehart and Winston.

Atchison, C. (1996). Turning the trick: The development and partial implementation of a multi-dimensional research instrument designed for clients of sex sellers. BA (hons.) thesis, Simon Fraser University.

Atchison, C. (1998). Men who buy sex: A preliminary description based on the results from a survey of the Internet-using population. M.A. thesis,. Simon Fraser University.

Atchison, C. (1999). Navigating the virtual minefield: Using the Internet as a medium for conducting primary social research. In D. Currie, D. Hay, & B. MacLean (Eds.), *Exploring the social world: Social research in action.* Vancouver: Collective Press.

Atchison, C., Lowman, J., & Fraser, L. (1998). Men who buy sex: Preliminary findings of an exploratory study. In J. Elias, V. L. Bullough, & V. Elias (Eds.), *Prostitution: On whores, hustlers, and johns.* California: Prometheus Press.

Atkinson, P., & Hammersley, M. (1994). Ethnography and participant observation. In N. K. Denzin & Y. S. Lincoln (Eds.), *Handbook of qualitative research* (pp. 248–261). Thousand Oaks, CA: Sage.

Atkinson, T. (1977). *Is satisfaction a good measure of the perceived quality of life?* Paper presented at the annual meeting of the American Statistical Association.

Atlantic Sugar v. *United States.* (1980). 85 Cust. Ct. 128.

Babbie, E. (1989). *The practice of social research* (5th ed.). Belmont, CA: Wadsworth.

Bales, R. F. (1970). *Personality and interpersonal behavior.* New York: Holt, Rinehart and Winston.

Barber, B., & Fox, R. C. (1958). The case of the floppy-eared rabbits: An instance of serendipity gained and serendipity lost. *American Journal of Sociology, 54*, 128–136.

Barker, R., Dembo, T., & Lewin, K. (1943). Frustration and aggression. In R. Barker, J. Kounin, & H. Wright (Eds.), *Child behavior and child development* (pp. 441–458). New York: McGraw-Hill.

Barnes, J. A. (1977). *The ethics of inquiry in social science.* London: Oxford University Press.

Barrett, L and Barrett, D. J.. (2001). An introduction to computerized experience sampling in psychology. *Social Science Computer Review, 19*(2), 175–185.

Barry, D. (2001). Assessing culture via the Internet: Methods and techniques for psychological research. *Cyberpsychology and Behavior,* 4(1), 17–21.

Basi, R. (1999). WWW response rates to socio-demographic items. *Journal of the Market Research Society, 41*(4), 397.

Bauman, S, Airey, J., & Atak, H. (1998). "Effective use of web-based technology: Using the Internet for data collection and communication applications. *Internet Survey Research White Paper.*

Baumrind, D. (1964). Some thoughts on ethics of research: After reading Milgram's "Behavioral study of obedience." *American Psychologist, 19*, 421–423.

Becker, H. S. (1958). Problems of inference and proof in participant observation. *American Sociological Review, 23*, 652–660.

Becker, H. S. (1963). *Outsiders: Studies in the sociology of deviance.* New York: Free Press.

Becker, H. S. (1964). Against the code of ethics. *American Sociological Review, 29*, 409–410.

Becker, H. S. (1970). Problems of inference and proof in participant observation. In H.S. Becker, *Sociological work.* Chicago: Aldine.

Becker, H. S. (1979). Do photographs tell the truth? In T. D. Cook & C. S. Reichardt (Eds.), *Qualitative and quantitative methods in evaluation research* (pp. 99–117). Beverly Hills, CA: Sage.

Becker, H. S. (1986). *Writing for sociologists.* Chicago: University of Chicago Press.

Becker, H. S. (1993). How I learned what a 'crock' was. *Journal of Contemporary Ethnography, 22,* 28–35. Retrieved May 8, 2006, from http://home. earthlink.net/~hsbecker/crocks.html

Becker, H. S. (1996). The epistemology of qualitative research. In R. Jessor, A. Colby, & R. Schweder (Eds.), *Ethnography and human development: Context and meaning in social inquiry* (pp. 53–71). Chicago: University of Chicago Press. Available online at www.soc.ucsb.edu/faculty/hbecker/qa.html

Becker, H. S. (1998). *Trucks of trade: How to think about your research while you're doing it.* Chicago: University of Chicago Press.

Becker, H. S., Geer, B., Hughes, E. C., & Strauss, A. L. (1961). *Boys in white: Student culture in medical school.* Chicago: University of Chicago Press.

Benmayor, R. (1991). Testimony, action research, and empowerment: Puerto Rican women and popular education. In S. B. Gluck & D. Patai (Eds.), *Women's words: The feminist practice of oral history* (pp. 159–174). New York: Routledge.

Berg, B. L. (1989). *Qualitative research methods for the social sciences.* Boston: Allyn & Bacon.

Berg, B. L. (2001). *Qualitative research methods for the social sciences* (4th ed.). Boston: Allyn & Bacon.

Bcrg, B. L. (2007). *Qualitative research methods for the social sciences* (6th ed.). Boston: Pearson.

Berger, T. (1992). *A long and terrible shadow: White values, native rights in the Americas, 1492–1992.* Vancouver: Douglas & McIntyre.

Best, S., Krueger, B., & Smith, C. H. A. (2001). An assessment of the generalizability of Internet surveys." *Social Science Computer Review, 19*(2), 131–145.

Bhaskar, R. (1986). *Scientific realism and human emancipation.* Bristol, U.K.: Verso (New Left Books).

Bimber, B. (2000). The gender gap on the Internet. *Social Science Quarterly, 81,* 868–876.

Binik, Y. M., Mah, K. & Kiesler, S. (1999). Ethical issues in conducting research on the Internet. *Journal of Sex Research, 36*(1), 82–90.

Birnbaum, M, & Wakcher, S. V. (2002). Web-based experiments controlled by Javascript: An example from probability learning. *Behavior Research Methods, Instruments, and Computers, 34,* 189–199.

Black, D. J. (1970). Production of crime rates. *American Sociological Review, 35,* 733–748.

Black, D. J., & Reiss, A. (1970). Police control of juveniles. *American Sociological Review, 35,* 63–77.

Black, M & Ponirakis, A. (2000). Computer-administered interviews with children about maltreatment: methodological, developmental, and ethical issues. *Journal of Interpersonal Violence, 15,* 682–695.

Blomley, N., & Davis, S. (1998). Russel Ogden decision review. Report to President Jack Blaney of Simon Fraser University. Retrieved March 4, 2002, from http://www.sfu.ca/~palys/ogden.htm

Blumer, H. (1969). *Symbolic interactionism: Perspective and method.* Englewood Cliffs, NJ: Prentice-Hall.

Bogardus, E. (1925). Measuring social distance. *Journal of Applied Sociology, 9,* 299–308.

Bonta, J., & Gendreau, P. (1990). Reexamining the cruel and unusual punishment of prison life. *Law and Human Behaviour, 14,* 347–372.

Borland, K. (1991). "That's not what I said": Interpretive conflict in oral narrative research. In S. B. Gluck & D. Patai (Eds.), *Women's words: The feminist practice of oral history* (pp. 63–76). New York: Routledge.

Boruch, R. F., & Cecil, J. S. (1979). *Assuring the confidentiality of research data.* Philadelphia: University of Pennsylvania Press.

Bosnjak, M. &. Tuten, T. L. (2001). Classifying response behaviors in web-based surveys. *Journal of Computer Mediated Communication, 6*(3).

Boyd, N. (1991). *High society: Legal and illegal drugs in Canada.* Toronto: Key Porter Books.

Bradley, N. (1999). Sampling for Internet surveys. An examination of respondent selection for Internet research." *Journal of the Market Research Society, 41,* 387–395.

Brajuha, M., & Hallowell, L. (1986). Legal intrusion and the politics of fieldwork. *Urban Life, 14,* 454–478.

Brandt, L. L. (1975). Scientific psychology: What for? *Canadian Psychological Review, 16,* 23–34.

Brantingham, P. J. (1991). Patterns in Canadian crime. In M. A. Jackson & C. T. Griffiths (Eds.), *Canadian criminology: Perspectives on crime and criminality* (pp. 371–402). Toronto: Harcourt Brace Jovanovich.

Brantingham, P. J., & Brantingham, P. L. (1984). *Patterns in crime.* New York: Macmillan.

Brock, D. R., & Kinsman, G. (1986). Patriarchal relations ignored: An analysis and critique of the Badgley report on sexual offenses against children and youths. In J. Lowman, M. A. Jackson, T. S.

Palys, & S. Gavigan (Eds.), *Regulating sex: An anthology of commentaries on the findings and recommendations of the Badgley and Fraser reports* (pp. 107–126). Burnaby, BC: School of Criminology, Simon Fraser University.

Bronfenbrenner, U. (1977). Toward an experimental ecology of human development. *American Psychologist, 32,* 513–531.

Bronskill, J., & Blanchfield, M. (1998, September 20). Canadian convicts used as test subjects in experiments. *Vancouver Sun,* p. 41.

Bruner, J. (1986). *Actual minds, possible worlds.* Cambridge, MA: Harvard University Press.

Brunswik, E. (1955). Representative design and probabilistic theory in a functional psychology. *Psychological Review, 62,* 193–217.

Buchanan, T. (2000). Potential of the Internet for personality research." In M. H. Birnbaum (Ed.), *Psychological experiments on the Internet* (pp. 121–140). San Diego, CA: Academic Press.

Buchanan, T., & Smith, J. L. (1999). Using the Internet for psychological research: Personality testing on the World Wide Web. *British Journal of Psychology, 90*(1), 125–145.

Burchell, G., Gordon, C., & Miller, P. (Eds.). (1991). *The Foucault effect: Studies in governmentality.* Chicago: University of Chicago Press.

Byrne, D., & Kelley, K. (1989). Basing legislative action on research data: Prejudice, prudence, and empirical limitations. In D. Zillmann & J. Bryant (Eds.), *Pornography: Research advances and policy considerations* (pp. 363–385). Hillsdale, NJ: Erlbaum.

Campbell, D. T. (1950). The indirect assessment of social attitudes. *Psychological Bulletin, 47,* 15–38.

Campbell, D. T. (1957). Factors relevant to the validity of experiments in social settings. *Psychological Bulletin, 54,* 297–312.

Campbell, D. T. (1963). Social attitudes and other acquired behavioural dispositions. In S. Koch (Ed.), *Psychology: A study of a science* (Vol. 6, pp. 94–172). New York: McGraw-Hill.

Campbell, D. T. (1969a). Definitional versus multiple operationism. *Et al., 2*(1), 14–17.

Campbell, D. T. (1969b). Reforms as experiments. *American Psychologist, 24,* 409–429.

Campbell, D. T. (1975). Degrees of freedom and the case study. *Comparative Political Studies, 8,* 178–193.

Campbell, D. T. (1978). Qualitative knowing in action research. In M. Brenner, P. Marsh, & M. Brenner (Eds.), *The social contexts of methods* (pp. 184–209). London: Breem Helm.

Campbell, D. T. (1979). "Degrees of freedom" and the case study. In T. D. Cook & C. S. Reichardt (Eds.), *Qualitative and quantitative methods in evaluation research* (pp. 49–67). Beverly Hills, CA: Sage.

Campbell, D., Campbell, C., and Maglio, P. P. (1999). Facilitating navigation in information spaces: Road-signs on the World Wide Web. *International Journal of Human-Computer Studies* 50: 309-327.

Campbell, D. T., & Fiske, D. W. (1959). Convergent and discriminant validation by the multitrait-multimethod matrix. *Psychological Bulletin, 56,* 81–105.

Campbell, D. T., & Ross, L. H. (1968). The Connecticut crackdown on speeding: Time-series data in quasi-experimental analysis. *Law and Society, 3,* 33–53.

Campbell, D. T., & Stanley, J. C. (1963). *Experimental and quasi-experimental designs for research.* Chicago: Rand McNally.

Campbell, M. (1994, March 10). Too many immigrants, many say: Federal survey shows relatively less compassion, less tolerance. *Globe and Mail,* pp. A1, A5.

Canadian Association of University Teachers. (2004). Response to *From Granting Council to Knowledge Council: Consultation Framework on SSHRC Transformation.* Retrieved June 11, 2006, from http://www.caut.ca/en/publications/briefs/sshrcsubmission.pdf

Canadian Institutes of Health Research (CIHR), Natural Sciences and Engineering Research Council of Canada (NSERC), Social Sciences and Humanities Research Council of Canada (SSHRC), *Tri-Council Policy Statement: Ethical Conduct for Research Involving Humans.* (1998, with 2000, 2002 and 2005 amendments). Retrieved May 9, 2006, from http://www.pre.ethics.gc.ca/english/policystatement/policystatement.cfm

Canadian Psychological Association. (1991). *Canadian code of ethics for psychologists.* Ottawa: Author.

Canadian Psychological Association. (2000). Canadian code of ethics for psychologists (3rd ed.). Ottawa: Author. Retrieved May 22, 2006, from http://www.cpa.ca/cpasite/userfiles/Documents/Canadian%20Code%20of%20Ethics%20for%20Psycho.pdf

Canadian Sociology and Anthropology Association. (1994). *Statement of professional ethics.* Retrieved

February 25, 2002, from http://artsciccwin.con-cordia.ca/socanth/csaa/englcode.htm#protect

Cantril, H. (1965). *The pattern of human concerns*. New Brunswick, NJ: Rutgers University Press.

Caporaso, J. A. (1973). Quasi-experimental approaches to social science: Perspectives and problems. In J. A. Caporaso & L. L. Roos, Jr. (Eds.), *Quasi-experimental approaches: Testing theory and evaluating policy*. Chicago: Northwestern University Press.

Carlson, R. (1975). Personality. In M. R. Rosenzweig & L. W. Porter (Eds.), *Annual Review of Psychology, 26*, 393–414.

Cassidy, F. (Ed.). (1992). *Aboriginal title in British Columbia: Delgamuukw v the Queen*. Lantzville, BC: Oolichan Books.

CAUT critical of proposed SSHRC transformation. (2004, September). *CAUT Bulletin*. Retrieved June 11, 2006, from http://www.caut.ca/en/bulletin/issues/2004_sep/default.asp

Cecil, J. S., & Wetherington, G. T. (Eds.). (1996). Court-ordered disclosure of academic research: A clash of values of science and law. *Law and Contemporary Problems* (special issue), *59* (3).

Cellard, André. *Histoire de la Folie au Québec de 1600 à 1850*. Montréal: Boréal, 1991.

Chen, S., Effler, J. R., & De La Roche, A. L. (2001). Research article using Internet services to generate a research sampling frame. *Nursing and Health Sciences, 3*, 15–18.

Cho, H., & Larose, R. (1999). Privacy issues in Internet surveys. *Social Science Computer Review, 17*, 421–434.

Christians, C. (2000). Ethics and politics in qualitative research. In N. K. Denzin and Y. S. Lincoln (Eds). *Handbook of Qualitative Research* (2nd ed., pp. 133–155). Thousand Oaks, CA: Sage.

Chunn, D. E. & Menzies, R. (1998). "Out of mind, out of law: The regulation of 'criminally insane' women inside British Columbia's public mental hospitals, 1888–1973. *Canadian Journal of Women and the Law, 10*, 1–32

Churchill, W. (1994). *Indians are us? Culture and genocide in Native North America*. Toronto: Between the Lines.

Cicourel, A. V. (1964). *Method and measurement in sociology*. New York: Free Press.

Clayman, B. (1997, October 30). The law of the land. *Simon Fraser News*, p. 5.

Clifford, J. (1986). Introduction: Partial truths. In J. Clifford & G. E. Marcus (Eds.), *Writing culture: The poetics and politics of ethnography* (pp. 1–26). Berkeley, CA: University of California Press.

Clifford J., & Marcus, G. E. (Eds.). (1986). *Writing culture: The poetics and politics of ethnography*. Berkeley, CA: University of California Press.

Clinton, W. (1997, May 16). Remarks by the President in apology for study done in Tuskegee. The White House: Office of the Press Secretary. Retrieved March 28, 2002, from http://clinton4.nara.gov/textonly/New/Remarks/Fri/19970516-898.html

Collins, A. (1988). *The sleep room*. Toronto: Lester & Orpen Dennys.

Collins, P. H. (1991). Learning from the outsider within: The sociological significance of black feminist thought. In M. M. Fonow & J. A. Cook (Eds.), *Beyond methodology: Feminist scholarship as lived research* (pp. 35–59). Bloomington, IN: Indiana University Press.

Computer Industry Almanac. (2006). Worldwide Internet users top 1 billion in 2005. Retrieved September 14, 2006, from http://www.c-i-a.com/pr0106.htm

Cook, T. D., & Campbell, D. T. (1979). *Quasi-experimentation*. Boston: Houghton Mifflin.

Cooleya, P. C., Rogers, S. M., Turner, C. F., Al-Tayyibb, A. A. Willis, G., & Ganapathia L. (2001). Using touch screen audio-CASI to obtain data on sensitive topics. *Computers in Human Behavior, 17*, 285–293.

Coomber, R. (1997). Using the Internet for survey research. *Sociological Research Online, 2*(2). http://www.socresonline.org.uk/socresonline/2/2/2.htm

Corkrey, R., & Parkinson, L. (2002). A comparison of four computer-based telephone interviewing methods: Getting answers to sensitive questions. *Behavior Research Methods, Instruments, and Computers, 34*, 354–363.

Couper, M. (2000). Usability evaluation of computer-assisted survey instruments. Social *Science Computer Review, 18*, 384–396.

Cousins, M., & Hussain, A. (1984). *Michel Foucault*. London: Macmillan.

Cowles, M., & Davis, C. (1982). On the origins of the .05 level of statistical significance. *American Psychologist, 37*, 553–558.

Crabb, B. B. (1996). Judicially compelled disclosure of researchers' data: A judge's view. *Law and Contemporary Problems, 59*, 9–34.

Crawford, S., Couper, M. P., Lamias, M. J. (2001). Web surveys: Perceptions of burden. *Social Science Computer Review, 19*, 146–162.

Cressey, D. R. (1953). *Other people's money: A study in the social psychology of embezzlement*. New York: Free Press.

Culhane, D. (1998). *The pleasure of the Crown: Anthropology, law and First Nations*. Burnaby, BC: Talon Books.

Currey, M. M. (1993). *On the border: An exploratory study of Canadian customs inspector decision-making*. Unpublished master's thesis, Simon Fraser University.

Dahlen, M. (2002). "Learning the web: Internet user experience and response to web marketing in Sweden. *Journal of Interactive Advertising, 3*(1).

Daisley, B. (1994, December 28). Clear evidence needed to invoke Wigmore rules. *The Lawyer's Weekly*.

Darwin, C. (1859). *On the origin of species*. London: John Murray.

Davies, M. J. (1989) The patients' world: British Columbia's mental health facilities, 1910–1935. M.A. thesis. University of Waterloo.

Davis, M. (1971). That's interesting! Towards a phenomenology of sociology and a sociology of phenomenology. *Philosophy of the Social Sciences, 1,* 309–344.

Davis, S. (1990). Men as success objects and women as sex objects: A study of personal advertisements. *Sex Roles: A Journal of Research, 23,* 43–50.

Dawes, R. M. (1972). *Fundamentals of attitude measurement*. New York: Wiley.

Denzin, N. K. (1978). The logic of naturalistic inquiry. In N. K. Denzin (Ed.), *Sociological methods: A sourcebook*. New York: McGraw-Hill.

Denzin, N. K. (1989). *The research act: A theoretical introduction to sociological methods* (3rd ed.). Englewood Cliffs, NJ: Prentice-Hall.

Denzin, N. K., & Lincoln, Y. S. (1994). Introduction: Entering the field of qualitative research. In N. K. Denzin & Y. S. Lincoln (Eds.), *Handbook of qualitative research* (pp. 1–18). Thousand Oaks, CA: Sage.

Denzin, N. K., and Lincoln, Y. S. (2000). Introduction: The Discipline and Practice of Qualitative Research. In N. K. Denzin and Y. S. Lincoln (Eds.) *Handbook of Qualitative Research* (2nd ed., pp.1–29). Thousand Oaks, CA: Sage.

Deutsch, M. (1973). *The resolution of conflict: Constructive and destructive processes*. New Haven, CT: Yale University Press.

Deutsch, M., & Collins, M. E. (1951). *Interracial housing: A psychological evaluation of a social experiment*. Minneapolis, MN: University of Minnesota Press.

Dimaggio, P., Hargittai, E., Neuman, W. R., & Robinson, J. P. (2001). Social implications of the Internet. *Annual Review of Sociology, 27,* 307–336.

Dion, K. (Summer, 1998). A valediction. *Psynopsis: Canada's psychology newspaper*. Retrieved August 30, 2002, from http://www.cpa.ca/Psynopsis/dion.html

Ditton, J. (1979). *Contrology: Beyond criminology*. London: Macmillan Press.

Donnerstein, E., & Berkowitz, L. (1981). Victim reactions in aggressive erotic films as a factor in violence against women. *Journal of Personality and Social Psychology, 41,* 710–724.

Dougle, A. C. (1980). *The adventures of Sherlock Holmes*. London: Pan Books. (Originally published 1892.)

Dougle, A. C. (1987). The adventure of Silver Blaze. In A. C. Doyle, *The original illustrated Sherlock Holmes* (pp. 185–200). Secaucus, NJ: Castle Books. (Originally published 1892.)

Dow Chemical Co. v. Allen. 672 F.2d 1262, 1274-77 (7th Cir. 1982).

Dowbiggin, I. (1997). *Keeping America sane: Psychiatry and eugenics in the United States and Canada, 1880–1940*. Ithaca NY: Cornell University Press.

Dryburgh, H. (2002). Changing our ways: Why and how Canadians use the Internet. Statistics Canada. Available at http://www.statcan.ca/english/research/56F0006XIE/56F0006XIE.pdf

Duneier, M. (1999). *Sidewalk*. New York: Farrar, Straus & Giroux.

Durkheim, E. (1951). *Suicide: A study in sociology*. (Trans. J. Spaulding and G. Simpson). New York: Free Press.

Durkheim, E. (1968). Social facts. In M. Brodbeck (Ed.), *Readings in the philosophy of the social sciences* (pp. 245–254). New York: Macmillan. (Reprinted from E. Durkheim, 1938, *The rules of sociological method*, New York: Free Press.)

Dutton, D. G., Boyanowsky, E. O., Palys, T. S., & Heywood, R. (1982). *Community Policing: Preliminary results from a national study of the RCMP*. Research report prepared for the Research Division of the Solicitor General Canada.

Eichstaedt, J. (2001). An inaccurate-timing filter for reaction time measurement by Java applets implementing Internet-based experiments. *Behavior, Research Methods, Instruments and Computers, 33*(2), 179–186.

Einstein, A. (1940). Considerations concerning the fundaments of theoretical physics. *Science, 91,* 487–492.

Elms, A. C. (1975). The crisis of confidence in social psychology. *American Psychologist, 30,* 967–976.

Emerson, D. (2005). *RPP 2006–2006: Social Sciences and Humanities Research Council of Canada* (Minister of Industry's Report to Treasury Board). Retrieved June 12, 2006, from http://www.tbs-sct.gc.ca/est-pre/20052006/SSHRC-CRSHC/SSHRC-CRSHCr56-PR_e.asp?printable=True

Epstein, J., & Klinkenberg, W. D. (2001). From Eliza to Internet: A brief history of computerized assessment. *Computers in Human Behavior, 17,* 295–314.

Epstein, J, Klinkenberg, W. D., Wiley, D..& Mckinley, L. (2001). Insuring sample equivalence across Internet and paper-and-pencil assessments. *Computers in Human Behavior, 17,* 339–346.

Eribon, D. (1991). *Michel Foucault.* Cambridge, MA: Harvard University Press.

Etter-Lewis, G. (1991). Black women's life stories: Reclaiming self in narrative texts. In S. B. Gluck & D. Patai (Eds.), *Women's words: The feminist practice of oral history* (pp. 43–58). New York: Routledge.

Evans, D, Garcia, D. J., Garcia, D. M., & Baron, R. S. (2003). In the privacy of their own homes: Using the Internet to assess racial bias. *Personality and Social Psychology Bulletin, 29,* 273–284.

Eysenck, H. J. (1953). *The structure of human personality.* New York: Wiley.

Faith, K. (1993). *Unruly women: The politics of confinement and resistance.* Vancouver: Press Gang.

Faulconer, J. E., & Williams, R. N. (1985). Temporality in human action: An alternative to positivism and historicism. *American Psychologist, 40,* 1179–1188.

Festinger, L. (1953). Laboratory experiments. In L. Festinger & D. Katz (Eds.), *Research methods in the behavioral sciences* (pp. 136–172). New York: Holt, Rinehart and Winston.

Festinger, L. (1957). *A theory of cognitive dissonance.* Evanston, IL: Row, Peterson.

Festinger, L., & Katz, D. (Eds.). (1953). *Research methods in the behavioral sciences.* New York: Holt, Rinehart and Winston.

Festinger, L., Riecken, H. W., & Schachter, S. (1956). *When prophecy fails.* Minneapolis, MN: University of Minnesota Press.

Filstead, W. J. (1979). Qualitative methods: A needed perspective in evaluation research. In T. D. Cook & C. S. Reichardt (Eds.), *Qualitative and quantitative methods in evaluation research* (pp. 33–48). Beverly Hills, CA: Sage.

Fine, M. (1994). Working the hyphens: Reinventing self and other in qualitative research. In N. K. Denzin & Y. S. Lincoln (Eds.), *Handbook of qualitative research* (pp. 70–82). Thousand Oaks, CA: Sage.

Finney, S. (2001). Real-time data collection in Linux: A case study. *Behavior Research Methods, Instruments and Computers, 33,* 167–173.

Fishbein, M. (Ed.). (1967). *Readings in attitude theory and measurement.* New York: Wiley.

Fishbein, M., & Azjen, I. (1975). *Belief, attitude, intention, and behavior: An introduction to theory and research.* Reading, MA: Addison-Wesley.

Fisher, R. A. (1925). *Statistical methods for research workers.* Edinburgh: Oliver & Boyd.

Fisher, W. A. (1986). The emperor has no clothes: On the Badgley and Fraser Committees' rejection of social science research on pornography. In J. Lowman, M. A. Jackson, T. S. Palys, & S. Gavigan (Eds.), *Regulating sex: An anthology of commentaries on the findings and recommendations of the Badgley and Fraser Reports* (pp. 159–176). Burnaby, BC: School of Criminology, Simon Fraser University.

Fisher, W. A., & Grenier, G. (1994). Violent pornography, antiwoman thoughts, and antiwoman acts: In search of reliable effects. *The Journal of Sex Research, 31,* 23–38.

Flint, A. (1995, June 3). The scientists and the radicals square off. *Globe and Mail,* p. D9.

Fonow, M. M., & Cook, J. A. (Eds.). (1991). *Beyond methodology: Feminist scholarship as lived research.* Bloomington, IN: Indiana University Press.

Fontana, A., & Frey, J. H. (1994). Interviewing: The art of science. In N. K. Denzin & Y. S. Lincoln (Eds.), *Handbook of qualitative research* (pp. 361–376). Thousand Oaks, CA: Sage.

Foucault, M. (1970). *The order of things.* London: Tavistock.

Foucault, M. (1972). *The archeology of knowledge.* New York: Pantheon Books.

Fox, J., Murray, C., & Warm, A. (2003). Conducting research using web-based questionnaires: Practical, methodological and ethical considerations. *Social Research Methodology, 6,* 167–180.

Friedson, E. (1964). Against the code of ethics. *American Sociological Review, 29,* 410.

Fricker, R., & Rand, M. S. (2002). Advantages and disadvantages of Internet research surveys: Evidence from the literature." *Field Methods, 14,* 347–367

Gendreau, P., & Bonta, J. (1991). Boats against the current: A rebuttal. *Law and Human Behaviour, 15,* 563–565.

Gerard, H. B., & Mathewson, G. D. (1966). The effects of severity of initiation on liking for a group: A replication. *Journal of Experimental Social Psychology, 2,* 278–287.

Gergen, K. J. (1985). The social constructionist movement in modern psychology. *American Psychologist, 40,* 266–275.

Giddens, A. (1979). *Central problems in social theory: Action, structure and contradictions in social analysis.* London: Macmillan.

Gisday Wa & Delgam Uukw. (1992). *The spirit in the land: Statements of the Gitksan and Wet'suwet'en hereditary chiefs in the Supreme Court of British Columbia, 1987–1990.* Gabriola Island, BC: Reflections Press.

Glaser, B., & Strauss, A. L. (1967). *The discovery of grounded theory: Strategies for qualitative research.* Chicago: Aldine.

Gluck, S. B. (1984). What's so special about women: Women's oral history. In D. Dunaway & W. K. Baum (Eds.), *Oral history: An interdisciplinary anthology* (pp. 221–237). Nashville, TN: American Association for State and Local History.

Gluck, S. B. (1991). Advocacy oral history: Palestinian women in resistance. In S. B. Gluck & D. Patai (Eds.), *Women's words: The feminist practice of oral history* (pp. 205–220). New York: Routledge.

Gluck, S. B., & Patai, D. (Eds.). (1991). *Women's words: The feminist practice of oral history.* New York: Routledge.

Goffman, E. (1961). *Asylums.* Garden City, NY: Doubleday Anchor.

Gold, R. L. (1958). Roles in sociological field investigation. *Social Forces, 36,* 217–223.

Gorden, R. L. (1980). *Interviewing: Strategy, techniques and tactics* (3rd ed.). Homewood, IL: Dorsey Press.

Gordon, C. (Ed.). (1980). Power/Knowledge: Selected interviews and other writings (1972–1977) by Michel Foucault. New York: Pantheon.

Gosling, S, Vazire, S., Srivastava, John, O. P. (2004). Should we trust web-based studies? A comparative analysis of six preconceptions about Internet questionnaires. *American Psychologist, 59*(2), 93–104.

Gould, S. J. (1978). Morton's ranking of races by cranial capacity. *Science, 200,* 503–509.

Gould, S. J. (1981). The mismeasure of man. New York: Norton.

Government of Canada. (2005). New chair for the interagency advisory panel on research ethics. [Press release]. Retrieved May 24, 2006, from http://www.pre.ethics.gc.ca/english/newsandevents/whatsnew/claymanannouncements.cfm

Gravlee, C. (2002). Mobile computer-assisted personal interviewing with handheld computers: The Entryware System 3.0. *Field Methods, 14,* 322–336.

Gray, G., & Guppy, N. (1994). Successful surveys: Research methods and practice. Toronto: Thomson Nelson.

Greene, P. (2001). Review article: Handheld computers as tools for writing and managing field data. *Field Methods, 13,* 181–197.

Greschner, D. (1992). Aboriginal women, the constitution and criminal justice. *University of British Columbia Law Review* (special edition), 338–359.

Gutting, G. (1989). *Michel Foucault's archaeology of scientific reason.* Cambridge, U.K.: Cambridge University Press.

Hagan, F. E. (1989). *Research methods in criminal justice and criminology* (2nd ed.). New York: Macmillan.

Haggerty, K. D. (2004). Ethics creep: Governing social science research in the name of ethics. *Qualitative Sociology, 27,* 391–414.

Hale, S. (1991). Feminist method, process, and self-criticism: Interviewing Sudanese women. In S. B. Gluck & D. Patai (Eds.), *Women's words: The feminist practice of oral history* (pp. 121–136). New York: Routledge.

Hamburger, P. (2005). The new censorship: Institutional review boards. *Supreme Court Review, October 2004 Term,* 271–354.

Hamilton, D. (1994). Traditions, preferences, and postures in applied qualitative research. In N. K. Denzin & Y. S. Lincoln (Eds.), *Handbook of qualitative research* (pp. 60–69). Thousand Oaks, CA: Sage.

Hammersley, M., & Atkinson, P. (1983). *Ethnography: Principles in practice.* London: Tavistock.

Hampton, K., & Wellman, B. (1999). Netville online and offline: Observing and surveying a wired suburb. *The American Behavioral Scientist, 43,* 475–493.

Haney, C., Banks, W. C., & Zimbardo, P. G. (1973). Interpersonal dynamics in a simulated prison. *International Journal of Criminology and Penology, 1,* 69–97.

Henry, S. (1987). The construction and deconstruction of social control: Thoughts on the discursive production of state law and private justice. In J. Lowman, R. J. Menzies, & T. S. Palys (Eds.), *Transcarceration: Essays in the sociology of social control* (pp. 89–108). Aldershot, U.K.: Gower.

Hessler, R., Downing, J. Beltz, C., Pelliccio, A., Powell, M., & Vale, W. (2003). Qualitative research on adolescent risk using e-mail: A methodological assessment. *Qualitative Sociology, 26,* 111–124.

Hewson, C. M., Laurent, D., & Vogel, C. M. (1996). Proper methodologies for psychological and sociological studies conducted via the Internet. *Behavior Research Methods, Instruments, and Computers, 28,* 186–191.

Hoffman, J. E. (1980). Problems of access in the study of social elites and boards of directors. In W. B. Shaffir, R. A. Stebbins, & A. Turowetz (Eds.), *Fieldwork experience: Qualitative approaches to social research* (pp. 45–56). New York: St. Martin's Press.

hooks, b. (1989). *Talking back: Thinking feminist, thinking black.* Boston: South End.

Horn, M. (1999). *Academic freedom in Canada: A history.* Toronto: University of Toronto Press.

Horowitz, I. (1967). *The rise and fall of Project Camelot: Studies in the relationship between social science and practical politics.* Cambridge, MA: MIT Press.

Horowitz, R. (1983). *Honor and the American dream.* New Brunswick, NJ: Rutgers University Press.

Horswill, M., & Coster, M. E. (2001). User-controlled photographic animations, photograph-based questions, and questionnaires: Three Internet-based instruments for measuring drivers' risk-taking behavior. *Behavior Research Methods, Instruments, and Computers, 33,* 46–58.

House, E. R. (1976). Justice in evaluation. In G.V. Glass (Ed.), *Evaluation Studies Review Annual* (Vol.1, pp. 75–100). Beverly Hills, CA: Sage.

Huberman, A. M., & Miles, M. B. (1994). Data management and analysis methods. In N. K. Denzin & Y. S. Lincoln (Eds.), *Handbook of qualitative research* (pp. 428–444). Thousand Oaks, CA: Sage.

Huff, D. (1954). *How to lie with statistics.* NY: Norton (reissued in 1982 and 1993).

Humphreys, L. (1970). *Tearoom trade: Impersonal sex in public places.* Chicago: Aldine.

Inquest of Unknown Female. (1994, October 20). Oral reasons for judgement of the Honourable L.W. Campbell, 91-240-0838, Burnaby, BC.

In re Grand Jury Proceedings: James Richard Scarce. 5 F.3d 397 (9th Cir. 09/17/1993).

In re Michael A. Cusumano and David B. Yoffie [United States of America v. Microsoft Corporation], No. 98-2133, United States Court of Appeals for the First Circuit]. (1998). Retrieved August 20, 2002, from http://www.law.emory.edu/1circuit/dec98/98-2133.01a.html

Institute for Survey Research. (1982). Questions and answers: The responses to a survey can depend greatly on how questions are asked. *Institute for Survey Research Newsletter,* Spring/Summer, 1–3.

Irwin, J. (1970). *The felon.* Englewood Cliffs, NJ: Prentice-Hall.

Irwin, J. (1980). *Prisons in turmoil.* Boston: Little, Brown.

Irwin, J. (1985). *The Jail: Managing the Underclass in American Society.* Berkeley: University of California Press.

Israel, J., & Tajfel, H. (Eds.). (1972). *The context of social psychology: A critical assessment.* London: Academic Press.

Israel , M. (2004a) Ethics and the governance of criminological research in Australia. Report for the New South Wales Bureau of Crime Statistics and Research. http://www.lawlink.nsw.gov.au/bocsar1.nsf/files/r55.pdf/$file/r55.pdf

Israel, M. (2004b). Strictly confidential? Integrity and the disclosure of criminological and socio–legal research. *British Journal of Criminology, 44,* 715–740.

Jackson, A., & DeCormier, R. (1999). E-mail survey response rates: Targeting increases response. *Marketing Intelligence and Planning, 17*(3), 135–140.

Jackson, M. (1992). In search of the pathways to justice: Alternative dispute resolution in Aboriginal communities. *University of British Columbia Law Review* (special edition. Aboriginal Justice), 147–238.

Jackson, M., & MacCrimmon, M. (1999). Research confidentiality and academic privilege: A legal opinion. Submission prepared for the Simon Fraser University Ethics Policy Review Task Force. Retrieved August 21, 2002, from http://www.sfu.ca/~palys/JackMacOpinion.pdf

Jaffee v. Redmond (95-266). 518 U.S. 1 (1996).

Jennings, F. (1975). *The invasion of America: Indians, colonialism, and the cant of conquest.* Chapel Hill, NC: University of North Carolina Press.

Judd, C. M., Smith, E. R., & Kidder, L. H. (1991). *Research methods in social relations* (6th ed.). Fort Worth, TX: Holt, Rinehart and Winston.

Junker, B. H. (1960). *Field work: An introduction to the social sciences.* Chicago: University of Chicago Press.

Kahneman, D., Slovic, P., & Tversky, A. (1982). *Judgement under uncertainty: Heuristics and biases.* Cambridge: Cambridge University Press.

Karr, L. (2000). New horizons in cross-national experimentation. *Current Research in Social Psychology, 5*(13), 190–205.

Katz, D., & Braly, K. (1933). Racial stereotypes of one hundred college students. *Journal of Abnormal and Social Psychology, 28,* 280–290.

Katz, J, Rice, R. E., & Aspden, P. (2001). The Internet, 1995–2000: Access, civic involvement, and social interaction. *American Behavioral Scientist, 45,* 405–423.

Kaye, B., & Johnson, T. J. (1999). Research methodology: Taming the cyber frontier: Techniques for Improving online surveys. *Social Science Computer Review, 17,* 323–337.

Kelly, G. A. (1955). *The psychology of personal constructs* (2 vols.). New York: Norton.

Kelm, M-E. (1992). "The only place likely to do her any good": The admission of women to British Columbia's Provincial Hospital for the Insane. *BC Studies. 66,* 66–89.

Kelman, J. C. (1967). Human use of human subjects: The problem of deception in social psychological experiments. *Psychological Bulletin, 67,* 1–11.

Kerlinger, F. N. (1973). *Foundations of behavioral research* (2nd ed.). New York: Holt, Rinehart and Winston.

Kidder, L. H. (1981a). Qualitative research and quasi-experimental frameworks. In M. B. Brewer & B. E. Collins (Eds.), *Scientific inquiry and the social sciences: A volume in honor of Donald T. Campbell* (pp. 226–256). San Francisco: Jossey-Bass.

Kidder, L. H. (1981b). *Research methods in social relations* (4th ed.). New York: Holt, Rinehart and Winston.

Kidder, L. H., & Campbell, D. T. (1970). The indirect testing of social attitudes. In G. F. Summers (Ed.), *Attitude measurement* (pp. 333–385). Chicago: Rand McNally.

Kidder, L. H., & Fine, M. (1987). Qualitative and quantitative methods: When stories converge. In M. M. Mark & R. L. Shotland (Eds.), *Multiple methods in program evaluation* (pp. 57–75). San Francisco: Jossey-Bass.

Kiesler, S., & Sproull, L. S. (1986). Response effects in the electronic survey. *Public Opinion Quarterly, 50,* 402–413.

Kincheloe, J. L., & McLaren, P. L. (1994). Rethinking critical theory and qualitative research. In N. K. Denzin & Y. S. Lincoln (Eds.), *Handbook of qualitative research* (pp. 138–157). Thousand Oaks, CA: Sage.

Kirk, R. E. (1968). *Experimental design: Procedures for the behavioral sciences.* Belmont, CA: Brooks/Cole.

Kitchin, H. (2002). The Tri-Council on Cyberspace: Insights, oversights, and extrapolations. In W. C. van den Hoonaard, (Ed.), *Walking the tightrope: Ethical issues for qualitative researchers* (pp.160–174). Toronto: University of Toronto Press.

Kline, M. (1994). The colour of law: Ideological representations of first nations in legal discourse. *Social and Legal Studies, 3,* 451–476.

Knox, R. E., & Inkster, J. A. (1968). Postdecision dissonance at post time. *Journal of Personality and Social Psychology, 8,* 319–323.

Koch, S. (Ed.). (1959). *Psychology: A study of a science* (6 vols.). New York: McGraw-Hill.

Koch, N., & Emrey, J. A. (2001). The Internet and opinion measurement: Surveying marginalized populations. *Social Science Quarterly, 82*(1), 131–138.

Krantz, J. H., & Dalal, R. (2000). Validity of web-based psychological research. In M. H. Birnbaum (Ed.), *Psychological experiments on the Internet* (pp. 35–60). San Diego: Academic Press.

Krech, D., Crutchfield, R., & Ballachey, E. (1962). *Individual in society.* New York: McGraw-Hill.

Kuhn, T. S. (1970). The structure of scientific revolutions (2nd ed.). Chicago: University of Chicago Press.

Kvale, S. (1988). The 1000-page question. *Phenomenology and Pedagogy, 6*(2), 90–106.

Labovitz, S., & Hagedorn, R. (1981). *Introduction to social research* (3rd ed.). New York: McGraw-Hill.

Lakoff, G. (1987). *Women, fire, and dangerous things: What categories reveal about the mind.* Chicago: University of Chicago Press.

LaPiere, R. T. (1934). Attitudes versus actions. *Social Forces, 13,* 230–237.

Latham, G. (1999). Goal attainment. *Psynopsis.* Retrieved April 2, 2002, from http://www.cpa.ca/Psynopsis/Latham1-99.html

Lather, P. (1991). *Getting smart: Feminist research and pedagogy with/in the postmodern.* New York: Routledge.

Latour, B. (1987). *Science in action.* Cambridge, MA: Harvard University Press.

Lewontin, R. C. (1991). *Biology as ideology: The doctrine of DNA.* Concord, ON: Anansi Press.

Liazos, A. (1972). The poverty of the sociology of deviance: Nuts, sluts, and preverts. *Social Problems, 20,* 103–121.

Likert, R. (1932). A technique for the measurement of attitudes. *Archives of Psychology, 140,* 44–53.

Lindesmith, A. (1952). Comment on W. S. Robinson's The logical structure of analytic induction. *American Sociological Review, 17,* 492–493.

Liu, M, Papathanasiou, E., & Hao, Y-W. (2001). Exploring the use of multimedia examination formats in undergraduate teaching: Results from the fielding testing. *Computers in Human Behavior, 17,* 225–248.

Little Bear, L. (1994). What's Einstein got to do with it? In R. Gosse, J. Y. Henderson, & R. Carter (Eds.), *Continuing Poundmaker and Riel's quest: Presentations made at a conference on Aboriginal peoples and justice.* Saskatoon, SK: Purich Publishing.

Lofland, J. (1971). *Analyzing social settings: A guide to qualitative observation and analysis.* Belmont, CA: Wadsworth.

Lofland, J., & Lejeune, R. A. (1960). Initial interaction of newcomers in Alcoholics Anonymous. *Social Problems, 8,* 102–111.

Lofland, J., & Lofland, L. H. (1984). *Analyzing social settings: A guide to qualitative observation and analysis* (2nd ed.). Belmont, CA: Wadsworth.

Lofland, J., & Lofland, L. H. (1995). *Analyzing social settings: A guide to qualitative observation and analysis* (3rd ed.). Belmont, CA: Wadsworth.

Lofland, J., Snow, D., Anderson, L., & Lofland, L. H. (2006) *Analyzing social settings: A guide to qualitative observation and analysis* (4th ed.). Belmont, CA: Wadsworth.

Lofland, L. H. (1973). *A world of strangers. Order and action in urban public space.* New York: Basic Books.

Lombroso, C. (1911). *Crime: Its causes and remedies.* Boston: Little, Brown.

Lord, F. M. (1953). On the statistical treatment of football numbers. *American Psychologist, 8,* 750–751.

Lowman, J. (1983). *The geography of crime and social control.* Doctoral dissertation, Department of Geography, University of British Columbia, Vancouver, BC.

Lowman, J. (1984). *Vancouver field study of prostitution.* Working paper on Pornography and Prostitution (Report #8). Ottawa, ON: Department of Justice.

Lowman, J. (1989). *Street prostitution: Assessing the impact of the law (Vancouver).* Ottawa, ON: Ministry of Supply and Services.

Lowman, J., & Fraser, L. (1995). *Violence against persons who prostitute: The experience in British Columbia.* Research report prepared for Department of Justice, Canada.

Lowman, J., & Palys, T. S. (1991). Interpreting criminal justice system records of crime. In M. A. Jackson & C. T. Griffiths (Eds.), *Canadian criminology: Perspectives on crime and criminality* (pp. 349–369). Toronto: Harcourt Brace Jovanovich.

Lowman, J., & Palys, T. S. (1998). *The history of limited confidentiality at SFU.* Report on ethics issues prepared for the SFU Research Ethics Policy Revision Task Force. Retrieved March 11, 2002, from http://www.sfu.ca/~palys/History.pdf

Lowman, J., & Palys, T. S. (2000). Ethics and institutional conflict of interest: The research confidentiality controversy at Simon Fraser University. *Sociological Practice: A Journal of Clinical and Applied Sociology, 2,* 245–255.

Lowman, J., & Palys, T. S. (2001a). The ethics and law of confidentiality in criminological research. *International Journal of Criminal Justice, 11,* 1–33.

Lowman, J., & Palys, T.S. (2001b). Limited confidentiality, academic freedom, and matters of conscience: Where does CPA stand? *Canadian Journal of Criminology, 43,* 497–508.

Lowman, J., Atchison, C., & Fraser, L. (1997). *Sexuality in the 1990's: Survey results. [Men who buy sex, phase 2: Internet and British Columbia survey methodology and preliminary results from the Internet survey.]* Retrieved April 26, 2002, from http://users.uniserve.com/%7Elowman/ICSS/icss.htm

Lowman, J., Menzies, R. J., & Palys, T. S. (1987). *Transcarceration: Essays in the sociology of social control.* Aldershot, U.K.: Gower.

M.(A.) v. Ryan (1997). 1 S.C.R. 157.

MacElroy, B. (1999). Comparing seven forms of on-line surveying. *Quirk's Marketing Research Review.* Retrieved January 22, 2002, from http://www. Quirks.com/articles/article_print.asp?arg_articleid=510

MacInnes, W. J, & Taylor, T. L. (2001). Millisecond timing on PCs and Macs. *Behavior Research Methods, Instruments, and Computers, 33*(2), 174–178.

Malhotra, N., & Peterson. M. (2001). Marketing research in the new millennium: Emerging issues and trends. *Marketing Intelligence and Planning, 19*(4): 216–235.

Malamuth, N. M. (1978). *Erotica, aggression and perceived appropriateness.* Paper presented at the 86th annual convention of the American Psychological

Association, Toronto, ON. (Cited in Malamuth 1984.)

Malamuth, N. M. (1984). Aggression against women. In N. M. Malamuth & E. Donnerstein (Eds.), *Pornography and sexual aggression* (pp. 173–185). New York: Academic Press.

Malamuth, N. M. (1989). Sexually violent media, thought patterns, and antisocial behavior. In G. Comstock (Ed.), *Public communication and behaviour* (Vol. 2, pp. 159–204). New York: Academic Press.

Malamuth, N. M., & Donnerstein, E. (Eds.). (1984). *Pornography and sexual aggression.* New York: Academic Press.

Malinowski, B. (1922). *Argonauts of the western Pacific.* London: Routledge & Kegan Paul.

Malinowski, B. (1967). *A diary in the strict sense of the term.* New York: Harcourt Brace Jovanovich.

Manicas, P. T., & Secord, P. F. (1983). Implications for psychology of the new philosophy of science. *American Psychologist, 38,* 399–413.

Manning, P. K. (1991). Analytic induction. In K. Plummer (Ed.), *Symbolic interactionism: Contemporary issues* (Vol. 2, pp. 401–30). Brookfield, VT: Edward Elgar. (Reprinted from R. Smith & P. K. Manning [Eds.], 1982, *Qualitative methods.* Cambridge, MA: Ballinger.)

Marquart, J. W. (2001). Doing research in prison: The Strengths and weaknesses of full participation as a guard. In J. M. Miller & R. Tewksbury (Eds.), *Extreme methods: Innovative approaches to social science research* (pp. 35–47). Needham Heights, MA: Allyn & Bacon.

McDonald, M. (1998). The Tri-Council policy statement on ethical conduct for research involving humans. *Canadian Bioethics Society Newsletter, 3* (3). Retrieved August 20, 2002, from http://www.bioethics.ca/english/newsletter/3.3/#mcdonald

McDonald, M. (2001). *The governance of health research involving human subjects.* Ottawa: Law Commission of Canada. Retrieved August 20, 2002, from http://www.lcc.gc.ca/en/themes/gr/hrish/macdonald/macdonald.pdf

McDonald, M. (Ed.). (2001). *The governance of health research.* Ottawa: Law Commission of Canada.

McGhee, J. W. (1985). *Introductory statistics.* Los Angeles: West Publishing.

McGinn, M., & Palys, T. S. (2005). *Participants' perspectives on research ethics issues: A research proposal.* Unpublished proposal prepared to seek funding from the Social Sciences and Humanities Research Council and the Research Ethics Boards at Brock University and Simon Fraser University.

McGuire, W. J. (1973). The yin and yang of progress in social psychology: Seven koan. *Journal of Personality and Social Psychology, 26,* 446–456.

McKinlay, A., & Potter, J. (1987). Model discourse: Interpretive repertoires in scientists' conference talk. *Social Studies of Science, 17,* 443–463.

McReynolds, P. (1975). Historical antecedents of personality assessment. In P. McReynolds (Ed.), *Advances in psychological assessment* (Vol. 3, pp. 477–532). San Francisco: Jossey-Bass.

Mead, M. (1960). *Coming of age in Samoa: A psychological study of primitive youth for Western civilization.* New York: Mentor. (Originally published 1928.)

Medical Research Council (MRC), Natural Sciences and Engineering Research Council (NSERC), and Social Sciences and Humanities Research Council (SSHRC). (1998). *Tri-Council policy statement: Ethical conduct for research involving humans.* (Ottawa: Department of Supply and Services.) Retrieved August 20, 2002, from http://www.sshrc.ca/english/programinfo/policies/Index.htm

Menaud, L. (1996). The limits of academic freedom. In L. Menaud (Ed.), *The future of academic freedom* (pp. 3–20). Chicago: University of Chicago Press.

Menzies, R. (1999). "I do not care for a lunatic's role": Modes of regulation and resistance inside the Colquitz Mental Home, British Columbia, 1919–33. *Canadian Bulletin of Medical History 16,* 181–213.

Menzies, R., & Chunn D. E. (1999). The gender politics of criminal insanity: "Order-in-Council" women in British Columbia, 1888–1950." *Histoire Sociale/Social History, 31,* 241–279.

Menzies, R., & Palys, T. (1999). *Race, ethnicity, and psychiatric regulation in British Columbia, 1875–1950.* Unpublished grant proposal prepared for the Hannah Institute for the History of Medicine Grant-in-aid program. Burnaby, BC: School of Criminology, Simon Fraser University.

Menzies, R. J. (1985). *Doing violence: Psychiatric discretion and the prediction of dangerousness.* Doctoral dissertation, Department of Sociology, University of Toronto, ON.

Menzies, R. J. (1989). *Survival of the sanest: Order and disorder in a pre-trial psychiatric clinic.* Toronto: University of Toronto Press.

Menzies, R.J., and Palys, T. S. (2006). Turbulent spirits: Aboriginal patients in the British Columbia psychiatric system, 1879–1950. In J. E. Moran (Ed.), *Mental health and Canadian society: Historical perspectives* (pp.149–175). Montreal: McGill–Queen's University Press.

Menzies, R. J., Webster, C. D., & Sepejak, D. S. (1985). Hitting the forensic sound barrier: Predictions of dangerousness in a pretrial psychiatric clinic. In C. D. Webster, M. H. Ben-Aron, & S. J. Hucker (Eds.), *Dangerousness: Probability and prediction, psychiatry and public policy* (pp. 115–144). New York: Cambridge University Press.

Menzies, R. (1998). Governing mentalities: The deportation of "insane" and "feebleminded" immigrants out of British Columbia from Confederation to World War II. *Canadian Journal of Law and Society, 13*(2), 135–173.

Merton, R. K. (1973). *The sociology of science.* Chicago: University of Illinois Press.

Merton, R. K., & Kendall, P. L. (1946). The focussed interview. *American Journal of Sociology, 51,* 541–557.

Merton, R. K., Fiske, M., & Kendall, P. L. (1956). *The focussed interview.* Glencoe, IL: Free Press.

Milgram, S. (1963). Behavioral study of obedience. *Journal of Abnormal and Social Psychology, 67,* 371–378.

Milgram, S. (1974). *Obedience to authority: An experimental view.* New York: Harper & Row.

Mill, J. S. (1956). *On liberty.* Indianapolis, IN: Bobbs-Merrill. (Originally published 1859.)

Mill, J. S. (1965). *A system of logic.* London: Longman's, Green. (Reprint of 8th edition, originally published 1881; 1st edition published 1843.)

Miller, J. M., & Tewksbury, R. (Eds.). (2001). *Extreme methods: Innovative approaches to social science research.* Needham Heights, MA: Allyn & Bacon.

Mills, A. (1994). *Eagle down is our law: Witsuwit'en law, feasts, and land claims.* Vancouver: University of British Columbia Press.

Mills, C. W. (1959). *The sociological imagination.* New York: Oxford University Press.

Miner, H. (1956). Body ritual among the Nacirema. *American Anthropologist, 58,* pp. 503–507.

Minister, K. (1991). A feminist frame for the oral history interview. In S. B. Gluck & D. Patai (Eds.), *Women's words: The feminist practice of oral history* (pp. 27–42). New York: Routledge.

Mitchell, A. (1994a, July 13). Study debunks immigration myths: Harder working, better educated than Canadian-born, Statscan says. *Globe and Mail,* pp. A1, A2.

Mitchell, A. (1994b, December 31). Views on crime distorted, study says: Random incidents called chief factor. *Globe and Mail,* pp. A1, A4.

Mitchinson, W. (1991). *The nature of their bodies: Women and their doctors in Victorian Canada.* Toronto: University of Toronto Press.

Mixon, D. (1972). Instead of deception. *Journal for the Theory of Social Behaviour, 2,* 145–177.

Mockridge, N. (1968). *The scrawl of the wild: What people write on walls—and why.* Cleveland, OH: World Publishing.

Monette, D. R., Sullivan, T. J., & DeJong, C. R. (1994). *Applied social research: Tool for the human services.* Fort Worth, TX: Harcourt Brace.

Monture-Okanee, P. A. (1993). Reclaiming justice: Aboriginal women and justice initiatives in the 1990s. In Royal Commission on Aboriginal Peoples (Eds.), *Aboriginal peoples and the justice system* (pp. 105–132). Ottawa, ON: Canada Communication Group Publishing.

Monture-Okanee, P. A., & Turpel, M. E. (1992). Aboriginal peoples and Canadian criminal law: Rethinking justice. *University of British Columbia Law Review* (Special Edition: Aboriginal Justice), 239–279.

Mook, D. G. (1983). In defence of external invalidity. *American Psychologist, 38,* 379–387.

Morgan, D. L. (1986). Personal relationships as an interface between social networks and social cognitions. *Journal of Social and Personal Relationships, 3,* 403–422.

Morgan, D. L. (1988). *Focus groups as qualitative research.* Newbury Park, CA: Sage.

Morgan, D. L., & Spanish, M.T. (1984). Focus groups: A new tool for qualitative research. *Qualitative Sociology, 7,* 253–270.

Morgan, D. L., & Spanish, M. T. (1985). Social interaction and the cognitive organization of health-relevant behavior. *Sociology of Health and Illness, 7,* 401–422.

Morgan, G. (1983a). Knowledge, uncertainty and choice. In G. Morgan (Ed.), *Beyond method: Strategies for social research* (pp. 11–18). Beverly Hills, CA: Sage.

Morgan, G. (1983b). Research as engagement: A personal view. In G. Morgan (Ed.), *Beyond method:*

Strategies for social research (pp. 383–391). Beverly Hills, CA: Sage.

Morgan, R. (1980). Theory and practice: Pornography and rape. In L. Lederer (Ed.), *Take back the night: Women on pornography.* New York: William Morrow.

Morse, J. M. (1994). Designing funded qualitative research. In N. K. Denzin & Y. S. Lincoln (Eds.), *Handbook of qualitative research* (pp. 220–235). Thousand Oaks, CA: Sage.

Mueller, J. (2003). *The origins of the riotous elephant barricade (REB).* Paper presented at meeting of the Society for Academic Freedom and Scholarship, University of Western Ontario; London, Ontario.

Mueller, J. (2006). Best practices: What perspective, what evidence? *Journal of Social Distress and the Homeless, 15.* Retrieved May 24, 2006, from http://mueller.educ.ucalgary.ca/DV3-JM.pdf

Napoleon, V. (2005). *Delgamuukw*: A legal straight-jacket for oral histories? *Canadian Journal of Law and Society, 20,* 123–155.

National Institutes of Health. (2002). Certificates of Confidentiality Information Kiosk. Retrieved April 8, 2002, from http://grants.nih.gov/grants/policy/coc/index.htm

National Association of Criminal Justice Planners/ National Criminal Justice Information and Statistics Service. (1979). *Criminal victimization in the United States, 1977.* Washington, DC: Author.

Native kids "used for experiments." (2000, April 26). *Vancouver Sun,* p. A12.

Newburger, E. (2001). Home computers and Internet use in the United States: August 2000. *Current Population Reports.* U.S. Department of Commerce, Economics and Statistics Administration. U.S. Census Bureau.

Norusis, M. J. (1993). *SPSS® for Windows™: Base system user's guide, Release 6.0.* Chicago: SPSS Inc.

O'Neil, R. M. (1996). A researcher's privilege: Does any hope remain? *Law and Contemporary Problems, 59,* 35–50.

O'Neil, K., & Penrod, S. D. (2001). Methodological variables in web-based research that may affect results: Sample type, monetary incentives, and personal information. *Behavior Research Methods, Instruments, and Computers, 33,* 226–233.

Oakley, A. (1981). Interviewing women: A contradiction in terms. In H. Roberts (Ed.), *Doing feminist research* (pp. 30–61). London: Routledge and Kegan Paul.

Ogden, R. (1994). Euthanasia and assisted suicide in persons with acquired immunodeficiency syndrome (AIDS) or human immunodeficiency virus (HIV). Unpublished master's thesis, Simon Fraser University.

Olesen, V. (1994). Feminisms and models of qualitative research. In N. K. Denzin & Y. S. Lincoln (Eds.), *Handbook of qualitative research* (pp. 158–174). Thousand Oaks, CA: Sage.

Olson, K., & Shopes, L. (1991). Crossing boundaries, building bridges: Doing oral history among working-class men and women. In S. B. Gluck & D. Patai (Eds.), *Women's words: The feminist practice of oral history* (pp. 189–204). New York: Routledge.

Osgood, C. E., Suci, G. J., & Tannenbaum, P. H. (1957). *The measurement of meaning.* Urbana, IL: University of Illinois.

Oskamp, S. (1977). *Attitudes and opinions.* Englewood Cliffs, NJ: Prentice-Hall.

Ozer, M. (1999). The use of Internet-based groupware in new product forecasting. *Journal of the Market Research Society, 41,* 425–437.

Palys, T. S. (1971). *The appeal of the illicit.* Paper presented to the annual meetings of the Manitoba Psychological Society, Winnipeg, MN.

Palys, T. S. (1976). An assessment of legal and cultural stigma regarding unskilled workers. *Canadian Journal of Criminology and Corrections, 18,* 247–257.

Palys, T. S. (1977). *Simulation methods and social psychology: Pain, contrition, and the beginning of wisdom.* Unpublished manuscript, Department of Psychology, Carleton University, Ottawa, ON.

Palys, T. S. (1978). Simulation methods and social psychology. *Journal for the theory of social behavior, 8,* 343–368.

Palys, T. S. (1979). *Personal project systems and perceived life satisfaction.* Doctoral dissertation, Department of Psychology, Carleton University, Ottawa, ON.

Palys, T. S. (1982). *Beyond the black box: A study in judicial decision-making.* Research Report prepared for the Solicitor General of Canada Research Division, Ottawa, ON.

Palys, T. S. (1984). *A content analysis of sexually explicit videos in British Columbia.* Working Paper on Pornography and Prostitution (Report No. 15). Ottawa, ON: Department of Justice.

Palys, T. S. (1986). Testing the common wisdom: The social content of video pornography. *Canadian Psychology, 27,* 22–35.

Palys, T. S. (1988, April). The profs and profits picture. *Canadian Business,* pp. 157–158.

Palys, T. S. (1989). Addressing the "third criterion" in experimentalist research: Towards a balance of manipulative and analytic control. In I. Benbasat (Ed.), *The information systems research challenge: Experimental research methods.* Boston, MA: Harvard Business School. (Vol. 2 of the Harvard Business School Research Colloquium Series, J. I. Cash, Jr., & J. F. Nunamaker, Jr. [Eds.].)

Palys, T. S. (1993). Constructing organizations: Methods of research, methods of change. Paper presented at the Séminaire de doctorat en management at Université Laval, Quebec City, PQ. (Available online at www.sfu.ca/~palys/.)

Palys, T. S. (2003). *Research decisions: Qualitative and quantitative perspectives* (3rd ed.). Toronto: Thomson Nelson Canada.

Palys, T. S. (1994). Statement of Dr. Ted S. Palys: Comments on the statement by Dr. Neil Malamuth. Report prepared for Arvay Findlay, solicitors for Little Sister's Book and Art Emponum, for the case of *Little Sister's v. The Queen.* Retrieved April 29, 2002, from http://www .sfu.ca/~palys/court.htm

Palys, T. S. (1996a). *The ethics of ethics: Comments regarding the Tri-Council Working Group's March 1996 draft Code of Conduct for Research Involving Humans.* Personal submission to the Secretariat of the Tri-Council (SSHRC, NSERC, MRC) Working Group on Ethics. (Available online at www.sfu .ca/~palys/codecomm.htm, last checked 4 March 2002.)

Palys, T. S. (1996b). Histories of convenience: Understanding twentieth century Aboriginal film images in context. Paper presented at an international conference regarding Aboriginal peoples and film entitled "Screening culture: Constructing image and identity," York, U.K. (Available online at www.sfu.ca/~palys/).

Palys, T. S., Boyanowsky, E. O., & Dutton, D. G. (1983). *A behavioural evaluation of the Vancouver Police Department's mobile radio data system.* Research report prepared for the Behavioural Research Group, Department of Communications, Government of Canada, Ottawa, ON.

Palys, T. S., Boyanowsky, E. O., & Dutton, D. G. (1984). Mobile data access terminals and their implications for policing. *Journal of Social Issues, 40*(3), 113–127.

Palys, T. S., & Little, B. R. (1983). Perceived life satisfaction and the organization of personal project systems. *Journal of Personality and Social Psychology, 44,* 1221–1230.

Palys, T. S., & Lowman, J. (1984). *Methodological meta-issues in pornography research: Ecological representativeness and contextual integrity.* Paper presented at the annual meetings of the Canadian Psychological Association, Ottawa, ON.

Palys, T. S., & Lowman, J. (2000). Ethical and legal strategies for protecting confidential research information. *Canadian Journal of Law and Society, 15*(1), 39–80.

Palys, T. S., & Lowman, J. (2001). Social research with eyes wide shut: The limited confidentiality dilemma. *Canadian Journal of Criminology, 43,* 255–267.

Palys, T. S., & Lowman, J. (2002). Anticipating law: Research methods, ethics and the common law of privilege. *Sociological Methodology, 32,* 1–17.

Palys, T.S., and Lowman, J. (2006). Protecting Research Confidentiality: Towards a Research-Participant Shield Law. *Canadian Journal of Law and Society,* 21, No. 1, 163–185.

Palys, T. S., & Williams, D. W. (1983). *Attitudes regarding capital punishment: On the assessment of false dichotomies.* Paper presented at the annual meetings of the Canadian Psychological Association, Winnipeg, MN.

Palys, T. S., Olver, J. O., & Banks, L. K. (1983). *Social definitions of pornography.* Paper presented to the annual meetings of the Canadian Psychological Association, Winnipeg, MN.

Park, R. E. (1952). *The collected papers of Robert Ezra Park.* (Vol. 2, *Human communities: The city and human ecology.*) Glencoe, IL: Free Press.

Parsons, T. (1959). Some problems confronting sociology as a profession. *American Sociological Review, 24,* 547–559.

Patai, D. (1991). US academics and Third World women: Is ethical research possible? In S. B. Gluck & D. Patai (Eds.), *Women's words: The feminist practice of oral history* (pp. 137–154). New York: Routledge.

Pearce, M. (2002). Challenging the system: Rethinking ethics review of social research in Britain's National Health Service. In W. C. van den Hoonaard (Ed), *Walking the tightrope: Ethical issues for qualitative researchers* (pp. 43–58). Toronto: University of Toronto Press.

Pedhazur, E. J. (1982). *Multiple regression in behavioral research: Explanation and prediction* (2nd ed.). New York: Holt, Rinehart and Winston.

Peiris, D. R., Gregor, P., & Alm, N. (2000). The effects of simulating human conversational style in a computer-based interview. *Interacting With Computers, 12,* 635–650.

Pepinsky, H. (1987). Justice as information sharing. In J. Lowman, R. J. Menzies, & T. S. Palys (Eds.), *Transcarceration: Essays in the sociology of social control* (pp. 76–88). Aldershot, U.K.: Gower.

Petersen, A. M. (1994). *Waltzing with an elephant: First Nations women's experience in creating a shelter for women in crisis.* Unpublished master's thesis, Simon Fraser University, Burnaby, BC.

Pettit, F. (2002). A comparison of World-Wide Web and paper-and-pencil personality questionnaires. *Behavior Research Methods, Instruments, and Computers, 34,* 50–54.

Phone has become best friend to us talkative Canadians. (1989, August 12). *Vancouver Sun,* p. F6.

Popper, K. R. (1959). *The logic of scientific discovery.* New York: Basic Books.

Punch, M. (1994). Politics and ethics in qualitative research. In N. K. Denzin & Y. S. Lincoln (Eds.), *Handbook of qualitative research* (pp. 83–97). Thousand Oaks, CA: Sage.

R. v. Gruenke. 3 S.C.R. 263 (1991).

Ranchhod, A., & Zhou, F. (2001). Comparing respondents of e-mail and mail surveys: Understanding the implications of technology. *Marketing Intelligence and Planning, 19*(4): 254–262.

Ratel, P. (1989). One day at a time: Single parent mothers in academe. In T. S. Palys (Ed.), *Starting from where you are* (pp. 111–125). Burnaby, BC: School of Criminology, Simon Fraser University.

Rawls, J. (1971). *A theory of justice.* Cambridge, MA: Harvard University Press.

Refvik, K. *History of the Brandon Mental Health Centre 1891–1991.* Altona, MA: Friesen, 1991.

Reinharz, S. (1992). *Feminist methods in social research.* New York: Oxford University Press.

Reynolds, P. D. (1982). *Ethics and social science research.* Englewood Cliffs, NJ: Prentice-Hall.

Richards of Rockford Inc. v. Pacific Gas and Electric Co. 71 F.R.D. 388 (N.D. Cal, 1976).

Richards, T. J., & Richards, L. (1994). Using computers in qualitative research. In N. K. Denzin & Y. S. Lincoln (Eds.), *Handbook of qualitative research* (pp. 445–462). Thousand Oaks, CA: Sage.

Richardson, L. (1994). Writing: A method of inquiry. In N. K. Denzin & Y. S. Lincoln (Eds.), *Handbook of qualitative research* (pp. 516–529). Thousand Oaks, CA: Sage.

Riecken, H. W. (1969). The unidentified interviewer. In G. J. McCall & J. L. Simmons (Eds.), *Issues in participant observation* (pp. 39–43). Reading, MA: Addison-Wesley.

Rigakos, G. (1994). The politics of protection: Battered women, protective court orders, and the police in Delta. Unpublished master's thesis, School of Criminology, Simon Fraser University, Burnaby, BC.

Rigakos, G. (1995). Constructing the symbolic complainant: Police subculture and the non-enforcement of protection orders for battered women. *Violence and Victims, 10*(3), 127–147.

Ring, K. (1967). Experimental social psychology: Some sober questions about some frivolous values. *Journal of Experimental Social Psychology, 3,* 113–123.

Roberts, J. V., & Jackson, M. (1991). Boats against the current: A note on the effects of imprisonment. *Law and Human Behaviour, 15*(5), 557–562.

Romero, M. (1992). *Maid in the U.S.A.* New York: Routledge.

Rosaldo, R. (1989). *Culture and truth: The remaking of social analysis.* Boston: Beacon Books.

Rosenblatt, P. C. (1981). Ethnographic case studies. In M. B. Brewer & B. E. Collins (Eds.), *Scientific inquiry and the social sciences: A volume in honor of Donald T. Campbell* (pp. 226–256). San Francisco: Jossey-Bass.

Rosenthal, R., & Rosnow, R. L. (1984). *Essentials of behavioral research: Methods and data analysis.* New York: McGraw-Hill.

Ross, M., Daneback, K., Mansson, S-A. Tikkanen, R., & Cooper, A. (2003). Characteristics of men and women who complete or exit from an on-line internet sexuality questionnaire: A study of instrument dropout biases. *Journal of Sex Research, 40,* 396–403.

Roth, J. A. (1969). A codification of current prejudices. *American Sociologist, 4,* 159.

Rubenstein, S.M. (1995). *Surveying public opinion.* Belmont, NY: Wadsworth.

Rubin, Z. (1973). *Liking and loving.* New York: Holt, Rinehart and Winston.

Rubington, E., & Weinberg, M. S. (Eds.). (1968). *Deviance: The interactionist perspective.* New York: Macmillan.

Ruhleder, K. (2000). The virtual ethnographer: Fieldwork in distributed electronic environments. *Field Methods, 12*(1), 3–17.

Russel Ogden v. *Simon Fraser University.* [1998] B.C.J. No. 2288. Burnaby Registry No. 26780. British Columbia Provincial Court (Small Claims Division), Burnaby, British Columbia, Steinberg Prov. Ct. J. June 10, 1998.

Salamon, E. (1984). *The kept woman: Mistresses in the '80s.* London: Orbis.

Salazar, C. (1991). A Third World woman's text: Between the politics of criticism and cultural politics. In S. B. Gluck & D. Patai (Eds.), *Women's words: The feminist practice of oral history* (pp. 93–106). New York: Routledge.

Scarce, R. (1994). (No) trial (but) tribulations: When courts and ethnography conflict. *Journal of Contemporary Ethnography, 23,* 123–149.

Scarce, R. (1999). Good faith, bad ethics: When scholars go the distance and scholarly associations do not. *Law and Social Inquiry, 24,* 977–986.

Schachter, S. (1959). *The psychology of affiliation.* Stanford, CA: Stanford University Press.

Schaefer, D., & Dillman, D. A. (1998). Development of a standard e-mail methodology: Results of an experiment. *Public Opinion Quarterly, 62,* 378–397.

Schatzman, L., & Strauss, A. L. (1973). *Field research: Strategies for a natural sociology.* Englewood Cliffs, NJ: Prentice-Hall.

Schmidt, W. C. (1997). World Wide Web survey research: Benefits, potential problems, and solutions. *Behaviour Research Methods, Instruments, and Computers, 29,* 274–279.

Schmidt, W. C. (2001). Presentation accuracy of Web animation methods. *Behavior Research Methods, Instruments, and Computers, 33,* 187–200

Schmidt, W. C. (2002). A server-side program for delivering experiments with animations. *Behavior Research Methods, Instruments, and Computers, 34,* 208–217.

Schuler, E. A. (1967). Report of the Committee on Professional Ethics. *American Sociologist, 2,* 242–244.

Schultz, D. P. (1969). The human subject in psychological research. *Psychological Bulletin, 72,* 214–228.

Schuman, H., & Presser, S. (1981). *Questions and answers in attitude surveys: Experiments on question form, wording and context.* New York: Academic Press.

Schutz, A. (1970). Interpretive sociology. In H. R. Wagner (Ed.), *Alfred Schutz: On phenomenology and social relations* (pp. 265–293). Chicago: University of Chicago Press.

Schwandt, T. A. (1994). Constructivist, interpretivist approaches to human inquiry. In N. K. Denzin & Y. S. Lincoln (Eds.), *Handbook of qualitative research* (pp. 118–137). Thousand Oaks, CA: Sage.

Schwartz, H., & Jacobs, J. (1979). *Qualitative sociology: A method to the madness.* New York: The Free Press.

Scriven, M. (1976). Maximizing the power of causal investigations: The modus operandi method. In G. V. Glass (Ed.), *Evaluation Studies Review Annual* (Vol. I, pp. 101–118). Beverly Hills, CA: Sage.

Seidman, D., & Couzens, M. (1974). Getting the crime rate down: Political pressure and crime reporting. *Law and Society Review, 8,* 457–493.

Selltiz, C., Wrightsman, L. S., & Cook, S. W. (1976). *Research methods in social relations* (3rd ed.). New York: Holt, Rinehart and Winston.

Shadish, W. R., Cook, T. D. and Campbell, D. T. (2001). *Experimental and quasi-experimental designs for generalized causal inference.* NY: Houghton Mifflin.

Shea, C. (2000). Don't talk to the humans: The crackdown on social science research. *Linguafranca, 10* (6), 1–17.

Sherif, M. (1935). A study of some social factors in perception. *Archives of Psychology, 27*(187), 1–60.

Sherif, M., Harvey, O. J., White, B. J., Hood, W. E., & Sherif, C. W. (1961). *Intergroup conflict and cooperation: The Robber's Cave experiment.* Norman, OK: University of Oklahoma Book Exchange.

Sheehan, K. B., & Hoy, M. G. (1999). Using e-mail to survey Internet users in the United States: Methodology and assessment. *Journal of Computer Mediated Communication, 4*(3). [On-line]. http://www.ascusc.org/jcmc/vol4/issue3/sheehan.html

Shortt, S. E. D. (1986). *Victorian lunacy: Richard M. Bucke and the practice of late nineteenth-century psychiatry*. Cambridge: Cambridge University Press.

Silverman, D. (1985). *Qualitative methodology and sociology*. Brookfield, VT: Gower.

Sinclair, C., Poizner, S., Gilmour-Barrett, K., & Randall, D. (1987). The development of a code of ethics for Canadian psychologists. *Canadian Psychology, 28*, 1–8.

Sioui, G. E. (1992). *For an Amerindian autohistory: An essay on the foundations of a social ethic*. Montreal: McGill–Queen's University Press.

Skinner, B. F. (1953). *Science and human behavior*. New York: Macmillan.

Skogan, W. G. (1975). Measurement problems in official and survey crime rates. *Journal of Criminal Justice, 3*, 17–32.

Smith v. Jones [1999] 1 S.C.R. 455.

Smith, C. B. (1997). Casting the Net: Surveying an Internet population. *Journal of Computer Mediated Communication, 3*(1). Retrieved September 6, 2006, at http://jcmc.indiana.edu/vol3/issue1/smith.html

Smith, L. T. (1999). *Decolonizing methodologies: Research and indigenous peoples*. London: Zed Books.

Smith, R., & Manning, P. K. (1982). *Qualitative methods*. Cambridge, MA: Ballinger.

Social Sciences and Humanities Research Council of Canada (SSHRC). (1990). *SSHRC grants: Guide for applicants*. Ottawa, ON: Author.

Social Sciences and Humanities Research Council of Canada. (2004). *From granting council to knowledge council: Renewing the social sciences and humanities*. Ottawa: SSHRC. Retrieved June 6, 2006, from http://www.sshrc.ca/web/whatsnew/initiatives/transformation/consultation_framework_e.pdf

Social Sciences and Humanities Research Ethics Special Working Committee (SSHWC). (2004). *Giving voice to the spectrum: Report of the Social Sciences and Humanities Research Ethics Special Working Committee*. Report prepared for the federal Interagency Advisory Panel on Research Ethics. Retrieved June 6, 2006, from http://www.pre.ethics.gc.ca/english/workgroups/sshwc/SSHWCVoiceReportJune2004.pdf

Social Sciences and Humanities Research Ethics Special Working Committee. (2006). *Reconsidering Privacy and Confidentiality in the TCPS: A Discussion Paper*. Retrieved May 12, 2006, from http://www.pre.ethics.gc.ca/english/workgroups/sshwc/consultation.cfm

Special Committee on Pornography and Prostitution (Fraser Committee). (1985). *Pornography and prostitution in Canada* (2 vols.). Ottawa, ON: Ministry of Supply and Services Canada.

Starr, L. (1984). Oral history. In D. Dunaway & W. K. Baum (Eds.), *Oral history: An interdisciplinary anthology* (pp. 3–26). Nashville, TN: American Association for State and Local History.

Steinem, G. (1980). Erotica and pornography: A clear and present difference. In L. Lederer (Ed.), *Take back the night: Women on pornography*. New York: William Morrow.

Stevens, S. S. (1951). Mathematics, measurement, and psychophysics. In S. S. Stevens (Ed.,) *Handbook of experimental psychology* (pp. 1–49). New York: Wiley.

Stinchcombe, A. (1968). *Constructing social theories*. New York: Harcourt Brace Jovanovich.

Strauss, A., and Corbin, J. (Eds.) (1997) *Grounded theory in practice*. Thousand Oaks, CA: Sage.

Strauss, A. L. (1987). *Qualitative analysis for social scientists*. New York: Cambridge University Press.

Stricker, L. J. (1967). The true deceiver. *Psychological Bulletin, 68*, 13–20.

Strickland, L. H., Aboud, F. E., & Gergen, K. J. (Eds.). (1976). *Social psychology in transition*. New York: Plenum.

Strunk, W., Jr. (1999). *The elements of style*. NY: Bartleby. (Originally published 1918). Retrieved May 28, 2002, from www.bartleby.com/141

Subgroup on Procedural Issues for the TCPS (ProGroup). (2005). *Refinements to the Proportionate Approach to Research Ethics Review in the* Tri-Council Policy Statement: Ethical Conduct for Research Involving Humans (TCPS). Retrieved June 10, 2006, from http://pre.ethics.gc.ca/english/workgroups/progroup/Consultation.cfm

Sudman, S., & Bradburn, N. M. (1982). *Asking questions*. San Francisco: Jossey-Bass.

Sweet, C. (2001). Designing and conducting virtual focus groups. *Qualitative Market Research: An International Journal, 4*, 130–135.

Tajfel, H. (1972). Experiments in a vacuum. In J. Israel & H. Tajfel (Eds.), *The context of social psychology* (pp. 69–119). London: Academic Press.

Talarico, S. M. (Ed.). (1980). *Criminal justice research.* Atlanta, GA: Anderson.

Tashakkori, A., & Teddlie, C. (Eds.). (2003). *Handbook on mixed methods in the behavioral and social sciences.* Thousand Oaks, CA: Sage.

Terkel, S. (1975). *Working.* New York: Avon.

Terry, W. (1984). *Bloods: An oral history of the Vietnam War by black veterans.* New York: Random House.

Thomas, W. I. (1928). *The child in America: Behavior problems and programs.* New York: Knopf.

Toby, J. (1986). Going native in criminology. *The Criminologist, 11* (May/June), 2.

Traynor, M. (1996). Countering the excessive subpoena for scholarly research. *Law and Contemporary Problems, 59,* 119–148.

Trigger, B. G. (1988). The historians' Indian: Native Americans in Canadian historical writing from Charlevoix to the present. In R. Fisher & K. Coates (Eds.), *Out of the background: Readings on Canadian Native history* (pp. 19–44). Toronto, ON: Copp Clark Pitman.

Truell, A., Bartlett, J. E., & Alexander, M. W. (2002). Response rate, speed, and completeness: A comparison of Internet-based and mail surveys. *Behavior Research Methods, Instruments, and Computers, 34,* 46–49.

Tse, A. (1999). Conducting electronic focus group discussions among Chinese respondents. *Journal of the Market Research Society, 41,* 407–415.

United Nations. (2004). *Information and communications technology (ICT): Vital statistics.* Retrieved September 7, 2004, from http://cyberschoolbus.un.org/Cyberschoolbus/Briefing/Technology/Index.htm

United States Commission on Obscenity and Pornography. (1970). *The report of the commission on obscenity and pornography.* New York: Bantam Books.

Upton, L. F. S. (1988). The extermination of the Beothuks of Newfoundland. In R. Fisher & K. Coates (Eds.), *Out of the background: Readings on Canadian Native history* (pp. 45–65). Toronto: Copp Clark Pitman.

van den Hoonaard, W.C. (2002). *Walking the Tightrope: Ethical Issues for Qualitative Researchers.* Toronto: University of Toronto Press.

Vancouver Island native Indians demand return of blood. (2000, September 25). *Globe and Mail,* p. A4.

Vidich, A. J., & Lyman, S. M. (1994). Qualitative methods: Their history in sociology and anthropology. In N. K. Denzin & Y. S. Lincoln (Eds.), *Handbook of qualitative research* (pp. 23–59). Thousand Oaks, CA: Sage.

Wagner, D. G. (1984). *The growth of sociological theories.* Beverly Hills, CA: Sage.

Wallace, W. (1971). *The logic of science in sociology.* Chicago: Aldine-Atherton.

Warwick, D. P., & Lininger, C. A. (1975). *The sample survey: Theory and practice.* New York: McGraw-Hill.

Watson, J. B. (1913). Psychology as the behaviorist views it. *Psychological Review, 20,* 158–177.

Webb, E. T., Campbell, D. T., Schwartz, R. D., & Sechrest, L. (1966). *Unobtrusive measures: Non-reactive research in the social sciences.* Skokie, IL: Rand McNally.

Webb, E. T., Campbell, D. T., Schwartz, R. D., Sechrest, L., & Grove, J. B. (1981). *Non-reactive measures in the social sciences* (2nd ed.). Boston: Houghton Mifflin.

Weber, M. (1968a). Objectivity in social science. In M. Brodbeck (Ed.), *Readings in the philosophy of the social sciences* (pp. 85–97). New York: Macmillan. (Reprinted from M. Weber, 1949, *The methodology of the social sciences,* New York: The Free Press.)

Weber, M. (1968b). The interpretive understanding of social action. In M. Brodbeck (Ed.), *Readings in the philosophy of the social sciences* (pp. 19–33). New York: Macmillan. (Reprinted from M. Weber, 1947, *The theory of social and economic organization,* New York: Oxford University Press.)

Weber, T. (2004). Poorer people closing PC gap. Retrieved June 24, 2004, from https://secure.globeadvisor.com/servlet/articlenews/story/rtgam/20040623/wcompute0623#

Weick, K. E. (1968). Systematic observational methods. In E. Aronson & G. Lindzey (Eds.), *The handbook of social psychology* (Vol. 2). Reading, MA: Addison-Wesley.

Weiss, C. H. (1987). Where politics and evaluation research meet. In D. J. Palumbo (Ed.), *The politics of program evaluation* (pp. 47–70). Newbury Park, CA: Sage.

Weiss, C. H. (1975). Evaluation research in the political context. In E. L. Streuning and M. Guttentag (Eds.) *Handbook of evaluation research* (Vol. 1, pp. 13–26). Beverly Hills, CA: Sage.

Whyte, W. F. (1943). *Street corner society: The social structure of an Italian slum.* Chicago: University of Chicago Press.

Wiggins, E. C., & McKenna, J. A. (1996). Researchers' reactions to compelled disclosure of scientific information. In J. S. Cecil & G. T. Wetherington (Eds.), Court-ordered disclosure of academic research: A clash of values of science and law. *Law and Contemporary Problems* (special issue), *59*(3), 67–94.

Wigmore, J.H. (1905). *A treatise on the system of evidence in trials at common law, including the statutes and judicial decisions of all jurisdictions of the United States, England, and Canada.* Boston: Little, Brown.

Wilson, W. C. (1973). The emergence of a social issue and the beginning of psychological study. *Journal of Social Issues, 29*(3), 7–18.

Wolcott, H. F. (1992). *Writing up qualitative research.* Newbury Park, CA: Sage.

Wolfe, C., & Reyna, V. F. (2002). Using Netcloak to develop server-side Web-based experiments without writing CGI programs. *Behavior Research Methods, Instruments, and Computers, 34,* 204–207.

Wolf, E. R. (1982). *Europe and the people without history.* Berkeley, CA: University of California Press.

Woong Yun, W., & Trumbo, C. W. (2000). Comparative response to a survey executed by post, e-mail, and web form. *Journal of Computer Mediated Communication, 6*(1).

Wright, R. (1992). *Stolen continents: The "New World" through Indian eyes since 1492.* Toronto: Penguin.

Yeager, M. (2004). *Getting the usual treatment: Censorship and the marginalization of convict criminology.* Paper presented at the annual meetings of the American Society of Criminology held in Nashville, TN; 18 November 2004.

Yerkes, R. M., & Dodson, J. D. (1908). The relation of strength of stimulus to rapidity of habit-formation. *Journal of Comparative Neurology and Psychology, 18,* 459–482.

Zimbardo, P. (1972). The Pathology of Imprisonment. *Society, 9,* 4–6.

Zimbardo, P. G., Ebbesen, E. B., & Maslach, C. (1977). *Influencing attitudes and changing behavior* (2nd ed.). Reading, MA: Addison-Wesley.

Zimmerman, M. K. (1977). *Passage through abortion: The personal and social reality of women's experiences.* New York: Praeger

Zinger, I. (1999). *The psychological effects of 60 days in administrative segregation.* Doctoral dissertation: Department of Psychology, Carleton University.

Zinger, I., Wichmann, C., & Andrews, D. A. (2001). The effects of administrative segregation. *Canadian Journal of Criminology, 43,* 47–83.

COPYRIGHT ACKNOWLEDGMENTS

Grateful acknowledgment is made to the copyright holders who granted permission to use previously published material. Where it was possible to provide acknowledgment in the chapters, this was done; where it was not possible, provision is made on this page, which constitutes an extension of the copyright page.

Block quotation, page 25 ("Foucault [makes] explicit the view ..."), from Ted Palys, "Constructing Organizations: Methods of Research, Methods of Change," a paper presented in 1993 at the Séminaire de doctorat en management, Université Laval, Quebec City, QC. Used with permission.

Block quotations on pages 378, ("Statistically speaking, the majority ..."), 381 ("The second reason ..."), 382 ("The research took the form ..."), 383–384 ("All the women interviewed ..."), 384–385 ("The women all relied heavily ..."), 386–387 ("The structural characteristics ..."), 387 ("The literature revealed ..."), 387 ("Although there are a number ..."), and 388 ("The research unearthed ..."); Figure 13.1 (Illustration of the Complex Web of Interrelationships among the Factors Examined in This Study); and Appendix F (One Day at a Time: Single-Parent Mothers in Academe) are all from Patricia Ratel, "One Day at a Time: Single Parent Mothers in Academe," a paper in T. S. Palys, ed., *Starting from Where You Are* (Burnaby, BC: School of Criminology, Simon Fraser University, 1989). Reprinted with permission from Patricia Ratel.

INDEX